T0215869

Lecture Notes in Computer Science   11724

Commenced Publication in 1973
Founding and Former Series Editors:
Gerhard Goos, Juris Hartmanis, and Jan van Leeuwen

Formal Methods

Subline of Lectures Notes in Computer Science

More information about this series at http://www.springer.com/series/7407

Peter Csaba Ölveczky · Gwen Salaün (Eds.)

Software Engineering and Formal Methods

17th International Conference, SEFM 2019
Oslo, Norway, September 18–20, 2019
Proceedings

 Springer

Editors
Peter Csaba Ölveczky
University of Oslo
Oslo, Norway

Gwen Salaün
University of Grenoble Alpes
Montbonnot, France

ISSN 0302-9743   ISSN 1611-3349   (electronic)
Lecture Notes in Computer Science
ISBN 978-3-030-30445-4   ISBN 978-3-030-30446-1   (eBook)
https://doi.org/10.1007/978-3-030-30446-1

LNCS Sublibrary: SL1 – Theoretical Computer Science and General Issues

This Springer imprint is published by the registered company Springer Nature Switzerland AG
The registered company address is: Gewerbestrasse 11, 6330 Cham, Switzerland

Preface

This volume contains the proceedings of the 17th International Conference on Software Engineering and Formal Methods (SEFM 2019), which was held during September 18–20, 2019, in Oslo, Norway.

The conference aims to bring together leading researchers and practitioners from academia, industry, and government to advance the state of the art in formal methods, to facilitate their uptake in the software industry, and to encourage their integration within practical software engineering methods and tools.

SEFM 2019 received 89 full paper submissions. Each paper received at least three reviews. Based on the reviews and extensive discussions, the program committee decided to accept 27 papers. This volume contains the revised versions of those 27 papers, which cover a wide variety of topics, including testing, formal verification, program analysis, runtime verification, malware and attack detection, and software development and evolution. The papers address a wide range of systems, such as cyber-physical systems, UAVs, autonomous robots, and feature-oriented and operating systems.

The conference also featured invited talks by Wil van der Aalst (RWTH Aachen University), David Basin (ETH Zürich), and Koushik Sen (University of California, Berkeley). Abstracts of two of these invited talks, and a full paper accompanying the invited talk by van der Aalst, are included in this volume.

Many colleagues and friends contributed to SEFM 2019. We thank Wil van der Aalst, David Basin, and Koushik Sen for accepting our invitations to give invited talks, and the authors who submitted their work to SEFM 2019. We are grateful to the members of the program committee and the external reviewers for providing timely and insightful reviews, as well as for their involvement in the post-reviewing discussions. We would also like to thank the members of the organizing committee, in particular its hard-working co-chair Martin Steffen, for all their work in organizing SEFM 2019, the SEFM steering committee chair Antonio Cerone for useful assistance, the workshop chairs (Javier Camara and Martin Steffen) for supervising the organization of the SEFM 2019 workshops, Lina Marsso for her excellent job attracting submissions, and Ajay Krishna for maintaining the conference web pages.

We appreciated very much the convenience of the EasyChair system for handling the submission and review processes, and for preparing these proceedings. Finally, we gratefully acknowledge financial support from The Research Council of Norway.

September 2019

Peter Csaba Ölveczky
Gwen Salaün

Organization

Program Chairs

Peter Csaba Ölveczky   University of Oslo, Norway
Gwen Salaün   University of Grenoble Alpes, France

Steering Committee

Radu Calinescu   University of York, UK
Antonio Cerone (Chair)   Nazarbayev University, Kazakhstan
Rocco De Nicola   IMT School for Advanced Studies Lucca, Italy
Einar Broch Johnsen   University of Oslo, Norway
Peter Csaba Ölveczky   University of Oslo, Norway
Gwen Salaün   University of Grenoble Alpes, France
Ina Schaefer   Technical University of Braunschweig, Germany
Marjan Sirjani   Mälardalen University, Sweden

Program Committee

Erika Ábrahám   RWTH Aachen University, Germany
Cyrille Artho   KTH Royal Institute of Technology, Sweden
Kyungmin Bae   Pohang University of Science and Technology, South Korea
Olivier Barais   University of Rennes, France
Luis Barbosa   University of Minho, Portugal
Dirk Beyer   Ludwig-Maximilian University Munich, Germany
Roberto Bruni   University of Pisa, Italy
Ana Cavalcanti   University of York, UK
Alessandro Cimatti   FBK, Italy
Robert Clarisó   Open University of Catalonia, Spain
Rocco De Nicola   IMT School for Advanced Studies Lucca, Italy
John Derrick   University of Sheffield, UK
José Luiz Fiadeiro   Royal Holloway, University of London, UK
Osman Hasan   National University of Sciences and Technology, Pakistan
Klaus Havelund   Jet Propulsion Laboratory, USA
Reiko Heckel   University of Leicester, UK
Marieke Huisman   University of Twente, The Netherlands
Alexander Knapp   Augsburg University, Germany
Nikolai Kosmatov   CEA LIST, France
Frédéric Mallet   University of Nice Sophia Antipolis, France
Tiziana Margaria   Lero, Ireland

Hernán Melgratti	University of Buenos Aires, Argentina
Madhavan Mukund	Chennai Mathematical Institute, India
Peter Csaba Ölveczky	University of Oslo, Norway
Marc Pantel	IRIT, INPT, University of Toulouse, France
Anna Philippou	University of Cyprus, Cyprus
Grigore Rosu	University of Illinois, USA
Gwen Salaün	University of Grenoble Alpes, France
Augusto Sampaio	Federal University of Pernambuco, Brazil
César Sánchez	IMDEA Software Institute, Spain
Ina Schaefer	Technical University of Braunschweig, Germany
Gerardo Schneider	University of Gothenburg, Sweden
Graeme Smith	The University of Queensland, Australia
Jun Sun	Singapore University of Technology and Design, Singapore
Maurice H. ter Beek	ISTI-CNR, Italy
Antonio Vallecillo	University of Málaga, Spain
Dániel Varró	Budapest University of Technology and Economics, Hungary and McGill University, Canada
Heike Wehrheim	University of Paderborn, Germany
Franz Wotawa	University of Graz, Austria

External Reviewers

Yehia Abd	Karlheinz Friedberger
Michael Abir	Letterio Galletta
Waqar Ahmad	Luca Geatti
Alif Akbar Pranata	Alberto Griggio
Pedro Antonino	Rebecca Haehn
Sebastien Bardin	Patrick Healy
Flavia Barros	Omar Inverso
Sarah Beecham	Shaista Jabeen
Chiara Bodei	Cyrille Jegourel
Johann Bourcier	Seema Jehan
Marco Bozzano	Richard Johansson
Antonio Bucchiarone	Sebastiaan Joosten
Márton Búr	Georgia Kapitsaki
Nathalie Cauchi	Alexander Knüppel
Gabriele Costa	Jürgen König
Ferruccio Damiani	Ajay Krishna
Luca Di Stefano	Dimitrios Kouzapas
Gidon Ernst	Sophie Lathouwers
Alessandro Fantechi	Jean-Christophe Léchenet
Alessio Ferrari	Thomas Lemberger
Michael Foster	Yun Lin
Leo Freitas	Sascha Lity

Piergiuseppe Mallozzi
Carlos Matos
Ilaria Matteucci
Marcel Vinicius Medeiros Oliveira
Vince Molnár
Carlo Montangero
Raul Monti
Alexandre Mota
Vadim Mutilin
Sidney C. Nogueira
Dan O'Keeffe
Wytse Oortwijn
Felix Pauck
Karen Petrie
Marinella Petrocchi
Pablo Picazo-Sanchez
Virgile Prevosto
Adnan Rashid

Virgile Robles
Marco Roveri
Tobias Runge
Stefan Schupp
Alexander Schlie
Oszkár Semeráth
Umair Siddique
Arnab Sharma
Ling Shi
Martin Spiessl
Ketil Stølen
Ivan Stojic
Ibrahim Tariq-Javed
Manuel Toews
Stefano Tonetta
Evangelia Vanezi
Philipp Wendler

Abstracts of Invited Talks

Security Protocols: Model Checking Standards

David Basin

Department of Computer Science, ETH Zurich, Switzerland

The design of security protocols is typically approached as an art, rather than a science, and often with disastrous consequences. But this need not be so! I have been working for ca. 20 years on foundations, methods, and tools, both for developing protocols that are correct by construction [9, 10] and for the post-hoc verification of existing designs [1–4, 8]. In this talk I will introduce my work in this area and describe my experience analyzing, improving, and contributing to different industry standards, both existing and upcoming [5–7].

References

1. Basin, D.: Lazy infinite-state analysis of security protocols. In: Secure Networking—CQRE [Secure] 1999. LNCS, vol.1740, pp. 30–42. Springer-Verlag, Düsseldorf, November 1999
2. Basin, D., Cremers, C., Dreier, J., Sasse, R.: Symbolically analyzing security protocols using tamarin. SIGLOG News 4(4), 19–30 (2017). https://doi.org/10.1145/3157831.3157835
3. Basin, D., Cremers, C., Meadows, C.: Model checking security protocols. In: Clarke, E., Henzinger, T., Veith, H., Bloem, R. (eds.) Handbook of Model Checking, pp. 727–762. Springer, Cham (2018). https://doi.org/10.1007/978-3-319-10575-8_22
4. Basin, D., Mödersheim, S., Viganò, L.: OFMC: a symbolic model checker for security protocols. Int. J. Inf. Secur. 4(3), 181–208 (2005). Published online December 2004
5. Basin, D., Cremers, C., Meier, S.: Provably repairing the ISO/IEC 9798 standard for entity authentication. J. Comput. Secur. 21(6), 817–846 (2013)
6. Basin, D., Cremers, C.J.F., Miyazaki, K., Radomirovic, S., Watanabe, D.: Improving the security of cryptographic protocol standards. IEEE Secur. Privac. 13(3), 24–31 (2015). https://doi.org/10.1109/MSP.2013.162
7. Basin, D., Dreier, J., Hirschi, L., Radomirovic, S., Sasse, R., Stettler, V.: Formal analysis of 5G authentication. In: Proceedings of the 2018 ACM Conference on Computer and Communications Security (CCS), pp. 1383–1396 (2018)
8. Schmidt, B., Meier, S., Cremers, C., Basin, D.: Automated analysis of Diffie-Hellman protocols and advanced security properties. In: Proceedings of the 25th IEEE Computer Security Foundations Symposium (CSF), pp. 78–94 (2012)
9. Sprenger, C., Basin, D.: Refining key establishment. In: Proceedings of the 25th IEEE Computer Security Foundations Symposium (CSF), pp. 230–246 (2012)
10. Sprenger, C., Basin, D.: Refining security protocols. J. Comput. Secur. 26(1), 71–120 (2018). https://doi.org/10.3233/JCS-16814

Automated Test Generation: A Journey from Symbolic Execution to Smart Fuzzing and Beyond

Koushik Sen

EECS Department, UC Berkeley, CA, USA
ksen@cs.berkeley.edu

Abstract. In the last two decades, automation has had a significant impact on software testing and analysis. Automated testing techniques, such as symbolic execution, concolic testing, and feedback-directed fuzzing, have found numerous critical faults, security vulnerabilities, and performance bottlenecks in mature and well-tested software systems. The key strength of automated techniques is their ability to quickly search state spaces by performing repetitive and expensive computational tasks at a rate far beyond the human attention span and computation speed. In this talk, I will give a brief overview of our past and recent research contributions in automated test generation using symbolic execution, program analysis, constraint solving, and fuzzing. I will also describe a new technique, called constraint-directed fuzzing, where given a pre-condition on a program as a logical formula, we can efficiently generate millions of test inputs satisfying the pre-condition.

Contents

Program Analysis

Relating Models and Implementations

Runtime Verification

Security

Verification

Invited Paper

Object-Centric Process Mining: Dealing with Divergence and Convergence in Event Data

Wil M. P. van der Aalst[1,2]([✉]) [iD]

[1] Process and Data Science (PADS), RWTH Aachen University,
Aachen, Germany
wvdaalst@pads.rwth-aachen.de
[2] Fraunhofer Institute for Applied Information Technology,
Sankt Augustin, Germany

Abstract. Process mining techniques use event data to answer a variety of process-related questions. Process discovery, conformance checking, model enhancement, and operational support are used to improve performance and compliance. Process mining starts from recorded events that are characterized by a case identifier, an activity name, a timestamp, and optional attributes like resource or costs. In many applications, there are multiple candidate identifiers leading to different views on the same process. Moreover, one event may be related to different cases (convergence) and, for a given case, there may be multiple instances of the same activity within a case (divergence). To create a traditional process model, the event data need to be "flattened". There are typically multiple choices possible, leading to different views that are disconnected. Therefore, one quickly loses the overview and event data need to be exacted multiple times (for the different views). Different approaches have been proposed to tackle the problem. This paper discusses the gap between real event data and the event logs required by traditional process mining techniques. The main purpose is to create awareness and to provide ways to characterize event data. A specific logging format is proposed where events can be related to objects of different types. Moreover, basic notations and a baseline discovery approach are presented to facilitate discussion and understanding.

Keywords: Process mining · Process discovery · Divergence · Convergence · Artifact-centric modeling

1 Introduction

Operational processes are often characterized by the 80/20 rule, also known as the Pareto principle. Often, 80% of the observed process executions (cases) can be described by less than 20% of the observed process variants. This implies that the remaining 20% of the observed process executions account for 80% of the observed process variants. Therefore, it is often relatively easy to create a precise

P. C. Ölveczky and G. Salaün (Eds.): SEFM 2019, LNCS 11724, pp. 3–25, 2019.
https://doi.org/10.1007/978-3-030-30446-1_1

and simple process model describing 80% of the cases. However, to add the remaining 20% of the cases, discovery techniques create models that are either complex and overfitting or severely underfitting. Standard processes such as the *Purchase-to-Pay (P2P)* and *Order-to-Cash (O2C)* seem simple at first: Just a handful of activities executed in a well-defined order. Although the majority of P2P and O2C process instances can be described by a simple process model, the number of process variants may be enormous. There may be thousands of ways to execute the P2P and O2C process due to exceptions, rework, deviations, and errors. In some organizations, one can observe close to one million different ways to perform the O2C process in a single year. Unfortunately, often the 20% least frequent behavior may cause most of the compliance and performance problems. This is called *organizational friction*. *Process mining* aims to identify and remove such organizational friction.

The author started to develop the first process mining techniques in the late 1990-ties [2]. Input for process mining is an *event log*. An event log 'views' a process from a particular angle. Each event in the log refers to (1) a particular process *instance* (called *case*), (2) an *activity*, and (3) a *timestamp*. There may be additional event attributes referring to resources, people, costs, etc., but these are optional. Events logs are related to process models (discovered or hand-made). Process models can be expressed using different formalisms ranging from *Directly-Follows Graphs* (DFGs) and *accepting automata* to *Petri nets*, *BPMN diagrams*, and *UML activity diagrams*. Typically, four types of process mining are identified:

- *Process discovery*: Learning process models from event data. A discovery technique takes an event log and produces a process model without using additional information [2]. An example is the well-known Alpha-algorithm [12], which takes an event log as input and produces a Petri net explaining the behavior recorded in the log. Most of the commercial process mining tools first discover DFGs before conducting further analysis.
- *Conformance checking*: Detecting and diagnosing both differences and commonalities between an event log and a process model [15]. Conformance checking can be used to check if reality, as recorded in the log, conforms to the model and vice versa [2]. The process model used as input may be descriptive or normative. Moreover, the process model may have been made by hand or learned using process discovery.
- *Process reengineering*: Improving or extending the model based on event data. Like for conformance checking, both an event log and a process model are used as input. However, now, the goal is not to diagnose differences. The goal is to change the process model. For example, it is possible to repair the model to better reflect reality. It is also possible to enrich an existing process model with additional perspectives. For example, replay techniques can be used to show bottlenecks or resource usage. Process reengineering yields updated models. These models can be used to improve the actual processes.
- *Operational support*: Directly influencing the process by providing warnings, predictions, or recommendations [2]. Conformance checking can be done "on-the-fly" allowing people to act the moment processes deviate. Based on the

model and event data related to running process instances, one can predict the remaining flow time, the likelihood of meeting the legal deadline, the associated costs, the probability that a case will be rejected, etc. The process is not improved by changing the model, but by directly providing data-driven support in the form of warnings, predictions, and/or recommendations.

Process mining aims to provide *actionable* results, e.g., automated alerts, interventions, reconfigurations, policy changes, and redesign. The uptake of process mining is industry is accelerating in recent years. Currently, there are more than 30 commercial offerings of process mining software (e.g., Celonis, Disco, ProcessGold, myInvenio, PAFnow, Minit, QPR, Mehrwerk, Puzzledata, Lana-Labs, StereoLogic, Everflow, TimelinePI, Signavio, and Logpickr).

In this paper, we challenge the following two commonly used assumptions:

- There is a *single* case notion.
- Each event refers to *precisely one* case.

We assume that there are multiple case notions (called object types) and that an event may refer to any number of objects corresponding to different object types. This idea is not new (see Sect. 2) and was already elaborated in [2]. However, existing process mining tools and techniques still assume that there is a single case notion and precisely one case per event.

When extracting an event log from some information system (e.g., the thousands of tables of SAP), the resulting log may suffer from *convergence* (one event is related to multiple cases) and *divergence* (independent, repeated executions of a group of activities within a single case). This may lead to the replication of events and thus misleading results (e.g., duplicated events are counted twice). It may also lead to loops in process models which are not really loops (but concurrency at the sub-instance level). These problems are partly unavoidable. However, it is good to be aware of these phenomena and to demand process mining tools supporting *object-centric process mining*.

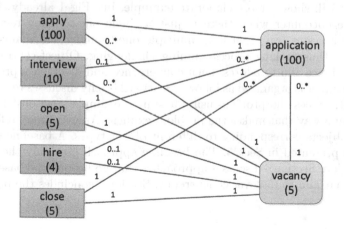

Fig. 1. A simple example explaining convergence and divergence problems. There are five activities (left-hand side) and two possible case notions (right-hand side).

To explain convergence and divergence, consider the example shown in Fig. 1. In a hiring process, we deal with two types of objects: *application* and *vacancy* (see right-hand side). Moreover, assume that there are five different activities: *apply* (new application for an open vacancy), *interview* (interview with an applicant for an open vacancy), *open* (create a vacancy after which people can apply), *hire* (hire an applicant for a specific vacancy), and *close* (close the vacancy). These activities are shown on the left-hand side of Fig. 1. The figure also shows cardinality constraints that need to hold at the end.

There are two possible case notions when applying traditional process mining approaches: *application* or *vacancy*. Assume that we have 100 applications and 5 vacancies. Each application refers to precisely one vacancy. Ten applications resulted in an interview and four persons were hired. Figure 1 shows the frequencies of activities and object types.

Suppose that we want to use *application* as a case notion and want to include the opening and closing of the corresponding position in the process model. This means that, when applying traditional process mining approaches, we need 100 *open* and *close* events rather than just five. This is called *convergence*. One *open* or *close* event is related to multiple cases. The problem is that events are replicated and process mining results are no longer showing to the actual number of events.

Suppose that we want to use *vacancy* as a case notion and want to include the applications and interviews of the corresponding applicants in the process model. This means that within a single case there many be many *apply* and *interview* events. Of course each *interview* event is preceded by precisely one *apply* event. However, because we cannot distinguish between the different applicants within a case, we see seemingly random interleavings of the two activities. However, there is a clear precedence at the level of individual applications (an interview never precedes an application). This is called *divergence*. Ordering information at the sub-instance level is lost, thus leading to loops in the process model that do not really exist in the real process.

Later we will show a more elaborate example, but Fig. 1 already shows the problems we encounter when there is just a single one-to-many relationship. In real-life processes, we often have multiple one-to-many and many-to-many relationships, thus making process mining challenging. Object-centric process mining techniques aim to address such convergence and divergence problems.

The remainder is organized as follows. Section 2 briefly discusses related work. Section 3 introduces the problem using a simple example. Section 4 formalizes event data in a way that makes the problem explicit: An event may refer to any number of objects corresponding to different object types. A baseline discovery approach is presented in Sect. 5. The baseline approach uses only the directly-follows relation. Section 6 discusses approaches that go beyond the baseline approach and that aim to discover concurrency. Section 7 concludes the paper.

2 Related Work on Object-Centric Process Mining

For a basic introduction to *process mining*, we refer to [2]. Chapter 5 of the process mining book focuses on the input side of process mining. Specifically, Sect. 5.5 discusses the need to "flatten" event data to produce traditional process models.

Traditional process models ranging from *workflow nets* [1,8] and *process trees* [24] to *Business Process Modeling Notation (BPMN) models* [31] and *Event-driven Process Chains (EPCs)* [34] assume a single case notion. This means that cases are considered in isolation. This is consistent with the standard notion of event logs where events refer to an activity, a timestamp, and precisely one case identifier [2].

The problem that many processes cannot be captured using a single case notion was identified early on. IBM's *FlowMark* system already supported the so-called "bundle" concept to handle cases composed of subcases [22]. This is related to the *multiple instance patterns*, i.e., a category of *workflow patterns* identified around the turn of the century [9]. One of the first process modeling notations trying to address the problem were the so-called *proclets* [6,7]. Proclets are lightweight interacting workflow processes. By promoting interactions to first-class citizens, it is possible to model complex workflows in a more natural manner using proclets.

This was followed by other approaches such as the *artifact-centric modeling notations* [14,16,27,30]. See [19] for an up-to-date overview of the challenges that arise when instances of processes may interact with each other in a one-to-many or many-to-many fashion.

Most of the work done on interacting processes with converging and diverging instances has focused on developing novel modeling notations and supporting the implementation of such processes. Only a few approaches focused on the problem in a process mining context. This is surprising since one quickly encounters the problem when applying process mining to ERP systems from SAP, Oracle, Microsoft, and other vendors of enterprise software.

In [17] techniques are described to extract "non-flat" event data from source systems and prepare these for traditional process mining. The *eXtensible Event Stream* (XES) format [23] is the current standard which requires a case notion to correlate events. XES is the official IEEE standard for storing events, supported by many process mining vendors. Next to the standard IEEE XES format [23], new storage formats such as *eXtensible Object-Centric* (XOC) [25] have been proposed to deal with object-centric data (e.g., database tables) having one-to-many and many-to-many relations. The XOC format does not require a case notion to avoid flattening multi-dimensional data. An XOC log can precisely store the evolution of the database along with corresponding events. An obvious drawback is that XOC logs tend to be very large.

The approaches described in [20,21,28] focus on interacting processes where each process uses its own case identifiers. In [28] interacting artifacts are discovered from ERP systems. In [20] traditional conformance checking was adapted to check compliance for interacting artifacts.

One of the main challenges is that artifact models tend to become complex and difficult to understand. In an attempt to tackle this problem, Van Eck et al. use a simpler setting with multiple perspectives, each modeled by a simple transition system [18,35]. These are also called *artifact-centric process models* but are simpler than the models used in [14,16,20,21,27,28,30]. The state of a case is decomposed onto one state per perspective, thus simplifying the overall model. Relations between sub-states are viewed as correlations rather than hard causality constraints. Concurrency only exists between the different perspectives and not within an individual perspective. In a recent extension, each perspective can be instantiated multiple times, i.e., many-to-many relations between artifact types can be visualized [35].

The above techniques have the drawback that the overall process is not visualized in a single diagram, but shown as a collection of interconnected diagrams using different (sub-)case notions. The so-called *Object-Centric Behavioral Constraint* (OCBC) models address this problem and also incorporate the data perspective in a single diagram [5,10,13,26]. OCBC models extend data models with a behavioral perspective. Data models can easily deal with many-to-many and one-to-many relationships. This is exploited to create process models that can also model complex interactions between different types of instances. Classical multiple-instance problems are circumvented by using the data model for event correlation. Activities are related to the data perspective and have ordering constraints inspired by declarative languages like *Declare* [11]. Instead of LTL-based constraints, simpler cardinality constraints are used. Several discovery techniques have been developed for OCBC models [26]. It is also possible to check conformance and project performance information on such models. OCBC models are appealing because they faithfully describe the relationship between behavior and data and are able to capture all information in a single integrated diagram. However, OCBC models tend to be too complex and the corresponding discovery and conformance checking techniques are not very scalable.

The complexity and scalability problems of OCBC models led to the development of the so-called *Multiple Viewpoint (MVP) models*, earlier named StarStar models [4]. MVP models are learned from data stored in relational databases. Based on the relations and timestamps in a traditional database, first, a so-called E2O graph is built that relates events and objects. Based on the E2O graph, an E2E multigraph is learned that relates events through objects. Finally, an A2A multigraph is learned to relate activities. The A2A graph shows relations between activities and each relation is based on one of the object classes used as input. This is a very promising approach because it is simple and scalable. Although this paper does not present a concrete discovery approach, the ideas are consistent with the MVP models and discovery techniques developed by Berti and van der Aalst [4].

Although commercial vendors have recognized the problems related to convergence and divergence of event data, there is no real support for concepts comparable to artifact-centric models, Object-Centric Behavioral Constraint (OCBC) models, and Multiple Viewpoint (MVP) models. Yet, there are a few initial attempts by some vendors. An example is *Celonis*, which supports the use of a secondary case identifier to avoid "Spaghetti-like" models where concurrency between sub-instances is translated into loops. The directly-follows graphs in Celonis do not consider interactions between sub-instances, thus producing simpler models. Another example is the multi-level discovery technique supported by *myInvenio*. The resulting models can be seen as simplified MVP models where different activities may correspond to different case notions (but one case notion per activity). The problem of this approach is that in reality the same event may refer to multiple case notions and choosing one is often misleading, especially since it influences the frequencies shown in the diagram.

In spite of the recent progress in process mining, problems related to multiple interacting process instances have not been solved adequately. One of the problems is the lack of standardized event data that goes beyond the "flattened" event data found in XES. Hence, process mining competitions tend to focus on classical event logs. This paper aims to shift the focus towards object-centric process mining.

3   The Problem

Event data can be found in any domain, e.g., logistics, manufacturing, finance, healthcare, customer relationship management, e-learning, and e-government. The events found in these domains typically refer to activities executed by resources at particular times and for a particular case (i.e., process instances). Process mining techniques are able to exploit such data. In this paper, we focus on process discovery. However, conformance checking, performance analysis, decision mining, organizational mining, predictions, and recommendations are also valuable forms of process mining that can benefit from the insights provided by this paper.

In a traditional event log, each event refers to a case (process instance), activity, a timestamp, and any number of additional attributes (e.g., cost, resources, etc.). The timestamp is used to order events. Since each event refers to precisely one case, each case can be represented by a *sequence of activities* (i.e., a *trace*). An example trace is $\langle a, d, d, d, e \rangle$, i.e., activity a followed by three activities d, followed by activity e. Different cases may have the same trace. Hence, an event log is a multiset of traces.[1] For example $L = [\langle a, b, c, e \rangle^{40}, \langle a, c, b, e \rangle^{30}, \langle a, d, e \rangle^{20},$ $\langle a, d, d, e \rangle^5, \langle a, d, d, d, e \rangle^3, \langle a, d, d, d, d, e \rangle^2]$ is an event log describing the traces of 100 cases. Traditional process mining techniques use such event data.

Figure 2 shows different process mining results obtained using *ProM* for an event log extracted from SAP. *ProM* provides a range of discovery techniques able to show the underlying process. Discovered process models may also show

---

[1] Multisets are represented using square brackets, e.g., $M = [x^2, y^3, z]$ has six elements. Unlike sets the same element can appear multiple times: $M(x) = 2$, $M(y) = 3$, and $M(z) = 1$. $[f(x) \mid x \in X]$ creates a multiset, i.e., if multiple elements x map onto the same value $f(x)$, these are counted multiple times.

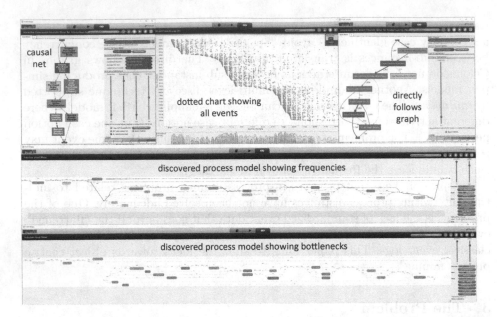

Fig. 2. Various screenshots of *ProM* showing discovered process models that can be used to address performance and compliance problems.

frequencies and bottlenecks. Moreover, it is possible to perform root-cause analysis for compliance and performance problems and one can drill-down to individual cases and events. In Fig. 2, we used a specific case notion allowing us to apply conventional process mining techniques working on "flattened" event logs.

The assumption that there is just one case notion and that each event refers to precisely one case is problematic in real-life processes. To illustrate this, consider the simplified order handling process from an online shop like Amazon, Alibaba, Bol, Otto, or Walmart. We are interested in the process that starts with a customer ordering products and ends with the actual delivery of all items. Figure 3 shows the activities (left-hand side) and object types (right-hand side). The four main object types are *order*, *item*, *package*, and *route*. Each order consists of one or more order lines, called items. A customer can first place an order with two items followed by an order consisting of three items. Depending on availability, items ordered for one customer are wrapped into packages. Note that one package may contain items from multiple orders. Moreover, items from a single order may be split over multiple packages. Packages are loaded into a truck that drives a route to deliver the packages in a particular order. Customers may not be home resulting in a failed delivery. The undelivered packages are stored and part of a later route. Hence, a route may involve multiple packages and the same package can be part of multiple routes.

The right-hand side of Fig. 3 shows the cardinalities of the relations between the four object types. Each item is part of one order and one package. How-

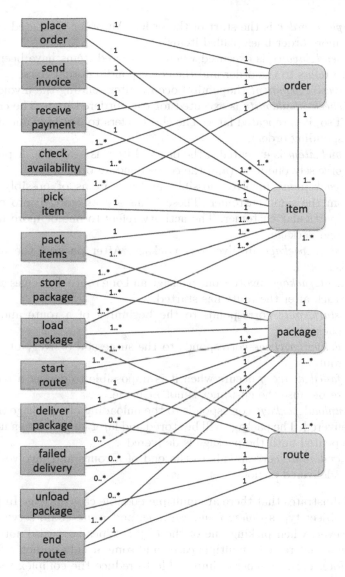

Fig. 3. Overview of the relationship between activities (left) and object types (right).

ever, orders and packages may contain multiple items. There is a many-to-many relation between packages and routes. Moreover, implicitly there is also a many-to-many relation between orders and packages.

The right-hand side of Fig. 3 shows the different activities. Most of the names are self-explanatory. The cardinality constraints between activities and object types help to understand the semantics of the activities.

- Activity *place_order* is the start of the order. An order is created consisting of one or more order lines (called items).
- Activity *send_invoice* is executed when all ordered items have been packed. An invoice refers to the order and the corresponding order lines.
- Activity *receive_payment* (hopefully) occurs after sending the invoice.
- Activity *check_availability* is executed for each ordered item. The check may fail and, if so, it is repeated later. The check refers to precisely one item (and the corresponding order).
- Activity *pick_item* is executed if the ordered item is available. A pick action refers to precisely one item (and the corresponding order).
- Activity *pack_items* involves possibly multiple items of possibly multiple orders from the same customer. These items are assembled into one package for a particular customer. The activity refers to one or more items and precisely one package.
- Activity *store_package* involves one package. After packing the items, the package is stored.
- Activity *load_package* involves one package and one route. Packages are loaded into the truck after the route has started.
- Activity *start_route* corresponds to the beginning of a route and involves multiple packages.
- Activity *deliver_package* corresponds to the successful delivery of a package on some route.
- Activity *failed_delivery* occurs when it is impossible to deliver a package on some route because the customer is not at home.
- Activity *unload_package* corresponds to the unloading of a package that could not be delivered. The package will be stored and later loaded onto a new route. This is repeated until the package is delivered.
- Activity *end_route* corresponds to the end of a route and involves multiple packages (delivered or not).

Figure 3 illustrates that there are multiple possible case notions. In principle, each of the object types *order*, *item*, *package*, and *route* could serve as a case notion. However, when picking one of the object types as a case notion, there may be events that refer to multiple cases and some events do not refer to any case. Therefore, it is, in general, impossible to reduce the complex reality to a classical event log.

Table 1 shows a fragment of an example instance of the problem. Each event is described by an event identifier, an activity name, a timestamp, the objects involved, and other optional attributes (here customer and costs). Let us focus on the columns showing which objects are involved. o_1, o_2, etc. are objects of type *order*, i_1, i_2, etc. are objects of type *item*, p_1, p_2, etc. are objects of type *package*, and r_1, r_2, etc. are objects of type *route*.

Following an object in a column, one can clearly see in which events (and related activities) the object is involved. For example, order o_1 is involved in events 9911 (activity *place_order*), 9912 (activity *check_availability*), 9914

Table 1. A fragment of some event log: Each line corresponds to an event.

Event identifier	Activity name	Timestamp	Objects involved				Attribute values	
			Order	Item	Package	Route	Customer	Costs
...	...	...	...	...	...	...	...	...
9911	place_order	20-7-2019:08.15	$\{o_1\}$	$\{i_1, i_2\}$	$\emptyset$	$\emptyset$	Apple	3500€
9912	check_availability	20-7-2019:09.35	$\{o_1\}$	$\{i_1\}$	$\emptyset$	$\emptyset$		
9913	place_order	20-7-2019:09.38	$\{o_2\}$	$\{i_3, i_4, i_5\}$	$\emptyset$	$\emptyset$	Google	4129€
9914	check_availability	20-7-2019:10.20	$\{o_1\}$	$\{i_2\}$	$\emptyset$	$\emptyset$		
9915	pick_item	20-7-2019:11.05	$\{o_1\}$	$\{i_1\}$	$\emptyset$	$\emptyset$		
9916	check_availability	20-7-2019:11.19	$\{o_2\}$	$\{i_3\}$	$\emptyset$	$\emptyset$		
9917	pick_item	20-7-2019:11.55	$\{o_2\}$	$\{i_3\}$	$\emptyset$	$\emptyset$		
9918	check_availability	20-7-2019:13.15	$\{o_2\}$	$\{i_4\}$	$\emptyset$	$\emptyset$		
9919	pick_item	20-7-2019:14.25	$\{o_2\}$	$\{i_4\}$	$\emptyset$	$\emptyset$		
9920	check_availability	20-7-2019:15.25	$\{o_2\}$	$\{i_5\}$	$\emptyset$	$\emptyset$		
9921	check_availability	20-7-2019:16.34	$\{o_1\}$	$\{i_2\}$	$\emptyset$	$\emptyset$		
9922	pick_item	20-7-2019:16.38	$\{o_1\}$	$\{i_2\}$	$\emptyset$	$\emptyset$		
9923	pack_items	20-7-2019:16.44	$\emptyset$	$\{i_1, i_2, i_3\}$	$\{p_1\}$	$\emptyset$		
9924	store_package	20-7-2019:16.55	$\emptyset$	$\{i_1, i_2, i_3\}$	$\{p_1\}$	$\emptyset$		
9925	start_route	20-7-2019:16.56	$\emptyset$	$\emptyset$	$\{p_1\}$	$\{r_1\}$		
9926	load_package	21-7-2019:08.00	$\emptyset$	$\{i_1, i_2, i_3\}$	$\{p_1\}$	$\{r_1\}$		
9927	send_invoice	21-7-2019:08.17	$\{o_1\}$	$\{i_1, i_2\}$	$\emptyset$	$\emptyset$		
9928	place_order	21-7-2019:08.25	$\{o_3\}$	$\{i_6\}$	$\emptyset$	$\emptyset$	Microsoft	1894€
9929	failed_delivery	21-7-2019:08.33	$\emptyset$	$\emptyset$	$\{p_1\}$	$\{r_1\}$		
9930	unload_package	21-7-2019:08.56	$\emptyset$	$\emptyset$	$\{p_1\}$	$\{r_1\}$		
9931	end_route	21-7-2019:09.15	$\emptyset$	$\emptyset$	$\{p_1\}$	$\{r_1\}$		
9932	check_availability	21-7-2019:10.25	$\{o_3\}$	$\{i_6\}$	$\emptyset$	$\emptyset$		
9933	receive_payment	21-7-2019:11.55	$\{o_1\}$	$\{i_1, i_2\}$	$\emptyset$	$\emptyset$		
9934	check_availability	22-7-2019:08.10	$\{o_2\}$	$\{i_5\}$	$\emptyset$	$\emptyset$		
9935	pick_item	22-7-2019:08.44	$\{o_2\}$	$\{i_5\}$	$\emptyset$	$\emptyset$		
9936	send_invoice	22-7-2019:08.55	$\{o_2\}$	$\{i_3, i_4, i_5\}$	$\emptyset$	$\emptyset$		
9937	receive_payment	22-7-2019:09.15	$\{o_2\}$	$\{i_3, i_4, i_5\}$	$\emptyset$	$\emptyset$		
9938	check_availability	22-7-2019:10.35	$\{o_3\}$	$\{i_6\}$	$\emptyset$	$\emptyset$		
9939	pick_item	22-7-2019:11.23	$\{o_3\}$	$\{i_6\}$	$\emptyset$	$\emptyset$		
9941	pack_items	23-7-2019:09.11	$\emptyset$	$\{i_4, i_5, i_6\}$	$\{p_2\}$	$\emptyset$		
9942	send_invoice	22-7-2019:11.45	$\{o_3\}$	$\{i_6\}$	$\emptyset$	$\emptyset$		
9943	store_package	23-7-2019:09.19	$\emptyset$	$\{i_4, i_5, i_6\}$	$\{p_2\}$	$\emptyset$		
9944	start_route	23-7-2019:09.28	$\emptyset$	$\emptyset$	$\{p_1, p_2\}$	$\{r_2\}$		
9945	load_package	23-7-2019:10.05	$\emptyset$	$\{i_1, i_2, i_3\}$	$\{p_1\}$	$\{r_2\}$		
9946	load_package	23-7-2019:10.09	$\emptyset$	$\{i_4, i_5, i_6\}$	$\{p_2\}$	$\{r_2\}$		
9947	deliver_package	23-7-2019:11.25	$\emptyset$	$\emptyset$	$\{p_2\}$	$\{r_2\}$		
9948	deliver_package	24-7-2019:09.37	$\emptyset$	$\emptyset$	$\{p_1\}$	$\{r_2\}$		
9949	end_route	24-7-2019:09.48	$\emptyset$	$\emptyset$	$\{p_1, p_2\}$	$\{r_2\}$		
9950	receive_payment	24-7-2019:09.55	$\{o_3\}$	$\{i_6\}$	$\emptyset$	$\emptyset$		
...	...	...	...	...	...	...	...	...

(another *check_availability*), 9915 (activity *pick_item*), etc. Route r_1 is involved in events 9925 (activity *start_route*), 9926 (activity *load_package*), 9929 (activity *failed_delivery*), etc.

To cast Table 1 into a traditional event log (e.g., in XES format), we would need to have precisely one case identifier per event. This is impossible without duplicating events (convergence problem) or ordering unrelated events (divergence problem). Moreover, the example shows that a traditional event log is merely a view on the more complex reality depicted in Table 1.

4 Defining Event Data

As illustrated by the example in the previous section, we *cannot* assume that there is a *single* case notion and that each event refers to *precisely one* case. Therefore, we provide a more realistic event log notion where multiple case notions (called object types) may coexist and where an event may refer to any number of objects corresponding to different object types. To do this, we start by defining some universes.

Definition 1 (Universes). *We define the following universes to be used throughout the paper:*

- $\mathbb{U}_{ei}$ *is the universe of event identifiers,*
- $\mathbb{U}_{act}$ *is the universe of activity names,*
- $\mathbb{U}_{time}$ *is the universe of timestamps,*
- $\mathbb{U}_{ot}$ *is the universe of object types (also called classes),*
- $\mathbb{U}_{oi}$ *is the universe of object identifiers (also called entities),*
- $type \in \mathbb{U}_{oi} \to \mathbb{U}_{ot}$ *assigns precisely one type to each object identifier,*
- $\mathbb{U}_{omap} = \{omap \in \mathbb{U}_{ot} \to \mathcal{P}(\mathbb{U}_{oi}) \mid \forall_{ot \in \mathbb{U}_{ot}} \forall_{oi \in omap(ot)} type(oi) = ot\}$ *is the universe of all object mappings indicating which object identifiers are included per type,*[2]
- $\mathbb{U}_{att}$ *is the universe of attribute names,*
- $\mathbb{U}_{val}$ *is the universe of attribute values,*
- $\mathbb{U}_{vmap} = \mathbb{U}_{att} \nrightarrow \mathbb{U}_{val}$ *is the universe of value assignments,*[3] *and*
- $\mathbb{U}_{event} = \mathbb{U}_{ei} \times \mathbb{U}_{act} \times \mathbb{U}_{time} \times \mathbb{U}_{omap} \times \mathbb{U}_{vmap}$ *is the universe of events.*

$e = (ei, act, time, omap, vmap) \in \mathbb{U}_{event}$ is an event with identifier ei, corresponding to the execution of activity act at time $time$, referring to the objects specified in $omap$, and having attribute values specified by $vmap$. Each row in Table 1 defines such an event.

Definition 2 (Event Projection). *Given* $e = (ei, act, time, omap, vmap) \in \mathbb{U}_{event}$, $\pi_{ei}(e) = ei$, $\pi_{act}(e) = act$, $\pi_{time}(e) = time$, $\pi_{omap}(e) = omap$, *and* $\pi_{vmap}(e) = vmap$.

---

[2] $\mathcal{P}(\mathbb{U}_{oi})$ is the powerset of the universe of object identifiers, i.e., objects types are mapped onto sets of object identifiers.

[3] $\mathbb{U}_{att} \nrightarrow \mathbb{U}_{val}$ is the set of all partial functions mapping a subset of attribute names onto the corresponding values.

Let e_{9911} be the first event depicted in Table 1. $\pi_{ei}(e_{9911}) = 9911$, $\pi_{act}(e_{9911}) = place\_order$, $\pi_{time}(e_{9911}) = 20\text{-}7\text{-}2019\text{:}08.15$, $\pi_{omap}(e_{9911}) = omap_{9911}$, and $\pi_{vmap}(e_{9911}) = vmap_{9911}$ such that $omap_{9911}(order) = \{o_1\}$, $omap_{9911}(item) = \{i_1, i_2\}$, $omap_{9911}(package) = \emptyset$, $omap_{9911}(route) = \emptyset$, $vmap_{9911}(customer) = Apple$ and $vmap_{9911}(costs) = 3500€$.

An event log is a collection of *partially ordered events*. Event identifiers are unique, i.e., two events cannot have the same event identifier.

Definition 3 (Event Log). $(E, \preceq_E)$ *is an event log with* $E \subseteq \mathbb{U}_{event}$ *and* $\preceq_E \subseteq E \times E$ *such that:*

- $\preceq_E$ *defines a partial order (reflexive, antisymmetric, and transitive),*
- $\forall_{e_1, e_2 \in E} \ \pi_{ei}(e_1) = \pi_{ei}(e_2) \Rightarrow e_1 = e_2$, *and*
- $\forall_{e_1, e_2 \in E} \ e_1 \preceq_E e_2 \Rightarrow \pi_{time}(e_1) \leq \pi_{time}(e_2)$.

Table 1 shows an example of an event log. Note that the values in the first column need to be unique and time is non-decreasing. Although Table 1 is totally ordered, we can also consider partially ordered events logs. There are two main reasons to use partially ordered event logs:

- When the timestamps are coarse-grained, we may not know the actual order. For example, event logs may only show the day and not the precise time. In such cases, we do not want to order the events taking place on the same day.
- We may exploit information about causality. When two causally unrelated events occur, we may deliberately not use the order in which they occurred. This makes it easy to create better process models that also capture concurrency without seeing all possible interleavings.

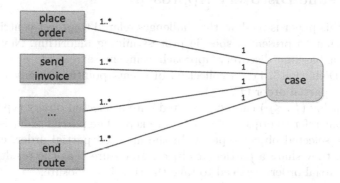

Fig. 4. Classical event log where each event refers to precisely one case identifier.

We advocate using event logs that follow Definition 3 rather than flattened, totally ordered event logs using a single case notion. Note that conventional event logs are a special case of Definition 3 as illustrated by the following definition.

Definition 4 (Classical Event Log). *An event log $(E, \preceq_E)$ is a classical event log if and only if $\preceq_E$ is a total order and there exists an $ot \in \mathbb{U}_{ot}$ such that for any $e \in E$: $|\pi_{omap}(e)(ot)| = 1$ and for all $ot' \in \mathbb{U}_{ot} \setminus \{ot\}$: $\pi_{omap}(e)(ot') = \emptyset$.*

By comparing Figs. 3 and 4 one can clearly see that in most cases it does not make any sense to try and straightjacket event data into a conventional event log. This only makes sense for selected views on the event data.

In Table 1, *check_availability* events refer to an item and an order. One could argue that the reference to the order is redundant, after a *place_order* event the items are linked to the order and do not need to be repeated. Similarly, *store_package* events refer to the items in the corresponding package, but one could argue that after the *pack_items* event, these are known and the relation does not need to be repeated in later events related to the package. Compare Fig. 5 to Fig. 3. Both show the relation between the activities (left-hand side) and object types (right-hand side). However, Fig. 5 aims to remove some of the redundancy (i.e., not include information that can be derived from other events). Table 2 shows the event log where fewer objects are associated with events (based on Fig. 5).

The choice between Tables 1 and 2 depends on the intended process scope. For example, are *check_availability* and *pick_item* part of the lifecycle of an order? Are *store_package*, *load_package*, *send_invoice*, and *receive_payment* part of the lifecycle of an item? Are *start_route* and *end_route* part of the lifecycle of a package? These are important scoping choices that influence the models generated using process mining techniques.

In Table 2, *load_package*, *deliver_package*, *failed_delivery*, and *unload_package* events still refer to both a package and a route. This is due to the fact that the same package may be part of multiple routes.

5   A Baseline Discovery Approach

The goal of this paper is to show the challenges related to object-centric process mining, and not to present a specific process mining algorithm. Nevertheless, we describe a baseline discovery approach using more realistic event data as specified in Definition 3, i.e., a collection of events pointing to any number of objects and a partial order $(E, \preceq_E)$.

Any event log $(E, \preceq_E)$ can be projected onto a selected object type ot. Just the events that refer to objects of type ot are kept. The partial order is updated based on the selected object type ot. In the updated partial order, events are related when they share a particular object. To ensure that the resulting order is indeed a partial order, we need to take the transitive closure.

Definition 5 (Object Type Projection). *Let $(E, \preceq_E)$ be an event log and $ot \in \mathbb{U}_{ot}$ an object type. $(E^{ot}, \preceq_E^{ot})$ is the event log projected onto object type ot where $E^{ot} = \{e \in E \mid \pi_{omap}(e)(ot) \neq \emptyset\}$ and $\preceq_E^{ot} = \{(e_1, e_2) \in E^{ot} \times E^{ot} \mid e_1 \preceq_E e_2 \wedge \pi_{omap}(e_1)(ot) \cap \pi_{omap}(e_2)(ot) \neq \emptyset\}^*$.*[4]

---

[4] R^* is the transitive closure of relation R. Hence, $\preceq_E^{ot}$ is a partial order (reflexive, antisymmetric, and transitive).

Table 2. A modified version of the event log in Table 1. Still, each line corresponds to an event, but events refer to a minimal amount of object types. Also, the additional attributes are not shown.

Event identifier	Activity name	Timestamp	Order	Item	Package	Route
. . .	. . .	. . .	. . .	. . .	. . .	. . .
9911	place_order	20-7-2019:08.15	$\{o_1\}$	$\{i_1, i_2\}$	$\emptyset$	$\emptyset$
9912	check_availability	20-7-2019:09.35	$\emptyset$	$\{i_1\}$	$\emptyset$	$\emptyset$
9913	place_order	20-7-2019:09.38	$\{o_2\}$	$\{i_3, i_4, i_5\}$	$\emptyset$	$\emptyset$
9914	check_availability	20-7-2019:10.20	$\emptyset$	$\{i_2\}$	$\emptyset$	$\emptyset$
9915	pick_item	20-7-2019:11.05	$\emptyset$	$\{i_1\}$	$\emptyset$	$\emptyset$
9916	check_availability	20-7-2019:11.19	$\emptyset$	$\{i_3\}$	$\emptyset$	$\emptyset$
9917	pick_item	20-7-2019:11.55	$\emptyset$	$\{i_3\}$	$\emptyset$	$\emptyset$
9918	check_availability	20-7-2019:13.15	$\emptyset$	$\{i_4\}$	$\emptyset$	$\emptyset$
9919	pick_item	20-7-2019:14.25	$\emptyset$	$\{i_4\}$	$\emptyset$	$\emptyset$
9920	check_availability	20-7-2019:15.25	$\emptyset$	$\{i_5\}$	$\emptyset$	$\emptyset$
9921	check_availability	20-7-2019:16.34	$\emptyset$	$\{i_2\}$	$\emptyset$	$\emptyset$
9922	pick_item	20-7-2019:16.38	$\emptyset$	$\{i_2\}$	$\emptyset$	$\emptyset$
9923	pack_items	20-7-2019:16.44	$\emptyset$	$\{i_1, i_2, i_3\}$	$\{p_1\}$	$\emptyset$
9924	store_package	20-7-2019:16.55	$\emptyset$	$\emptyset$	$\{p_1\}$	$\emptyset$
9925	start_route	20-7-2019:16.56	$\emptyset$	$\emptyset$	$\emptyset$	$\{r_1\}$
9926	load_package	21-7-2019:08.00	$\emptyset$	$\emptyset$	$\{p_1\}$	$\{r_1\}$
9927	send_invoice	21-7-2019:08.17	$\{o_1\}$	$\emptyset$	$\emptyset$	$\emptyset$
9928	place_order	21-7-2019:08.25	$\{o_3\}$	$\{i_6\}$	$\emptyset$	$\emptyset$
9929	failed_delivery	21-7-2019:08.33	$\emptyset$	$\emptyset$	$\{p_1\}$	$\{r_1\}$
9930	unload_package	21-7-2019:08.56	$\emptyset$	$\emptyset$	$\{p_1\}$	$\{r_1\}$
9931	end_route	21-7-2019:09.15	$\emptyset$	$\emptyset$	$\emptyset$	$\{r_1\}$
9932	check_availability	21-7-2019:10.25	$\emptyset$	$\{i_6\}$	$\emptyset$	$\emptyset$
9933	receive_payment	21-7-2019:11.55	$\{o_1\}$	$\emptyset$	$\emptyset$	$\emptyset$
9934	check_availability	22-7-2019:08.19	$\emptyset$	$\{i_5\}$	$\emptyset$	$\emptyset$
9935	pick_item	22-7-2019:08.44	$\emptyset$	$\{i_5\}$	$\emptyset$	$\emptyset$
9936	send_invoice	22-7-2019:08.55	$\{o_2\}$	$\emptyset$	$\emptyset$	$\emptyset$
9937	receive_payment	22-7-2019:09.15	$\{o_2\}$	$\emptyset$	$\emptyset$	$\emptyset$
9938	check_availability	22-7-2019:10.35	$\emptyset$	$\{i_6\}$	$\emptyset$	$\emptyset$
9939	pick_item	22-7-2019:11.23	$\emptyset$	$\{i_6\}$	$\emptyset$	$\emptyset$
9941	pack_items	23-7-2019:09.11	$\emptyset$	$\{i_4, i_5, i_6\}$	$\{p_2\}$	$\emptyset$
9942	send_invoice	22-7-2019:11.45	$\{o_3\}$	$\emptyset$	$\emptyset$	$\emptyset$
9943	store_package	23-7-2019:09.19	$\emptyset$	$\emptyset$	$\{p_2\}$	$\emptyset$
9944	start_route	23-7-2019:09.28	$\emptyset$	$\emptyset$	$\emptyset$	$\{r_2\}$
9945	load_package	23-7-2019:10.05	$\emptyset$	$\emptyset$	$\{p_1\}$	$\{r_2\}$
9946	load_package	23-7-2019:10.09	$\emptyset$	$\emptyset$	$\{p_2\}$	$\{r_2\}$
9947	deliver_package	23-7-2019:11.25	$\emptyset$	$\emptyset$	$\{p_2\}$	$\{r_2\}$
9948	deliver_package	24-7-2019:09.37	$\emptyset$	$\emptyset$	$\{p_1\}$	$\{r_2\}$
9949	end_route	24-7-2019:09.48	$\emptyset$	$\emptyset$	$\emptyset$	$\{r_2\}$
9950	receive_payment	24-7-2019:09.55	$\{o_3\}$	$\emptyset$	$\emptyset$	$\emptyset$
. . .	. . .	. . .	. . .	. . .	. . .	. . .

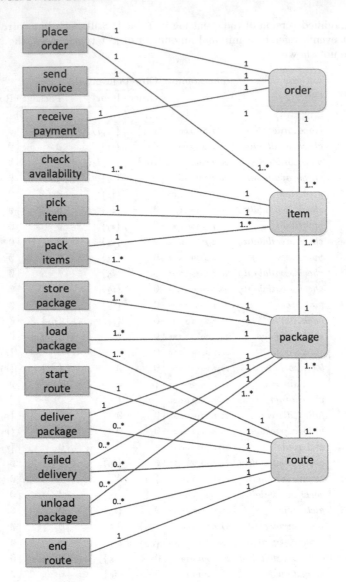

Fig. 5. Relating activities (left-hand side) to object types (right-hand side) while minimizing redundancy compared to Fig. 3.

It is easy to verify that $\preceq_E^{ot}$ is indeed reflexive, antisymmetric, and transitive. Also note that if there are three events $e_1 \preceq_E e_2 \preceq_E e_3$ with $\pi_{omap}(e_1)(ot) = \{o_1\}$, $\pi_{omap}(e_2)(ot) = \{o_1, o_2\}$, and $\pi_{omap}(e_3)(ot) = \{o_2\}$, then $e_1 \preceq_E^{ot} e_3$ although $\pi_{omap}(e_1)(ot) \cap \pi_{omap}(e_3)(ot) = \emptyset$.

Projections can be generalized to multiple object types. For $OT \subseteq \mathbb{U}_{ot}$: $E^{OT} = \{e \in E \mid \exists_{ot \in OT} \; \pi_{omap}(e)(ot) \neq \emptyset\}$ and $\preceq_{E}^{OT} = \{(e_1, e_2) \in E^{OT} \times E^{OT} \mid e_1 \preceq_E e_2 \land \exists_{ot \in OT} \; \pi_{omap}(e_1)(ot) \cap \pi_{omap}(e_2)(ot) \neq \emptyset\}^*$.

We would like to discover Directly-Follows Graphs (DFGs) based on the projections specified in Definition 5. To do this, we use the well-known covering relation to capture the direct causal relations between events. The covering relation is the equivalent of the transitive reduction of a finite directed acyclic graph, but applied to relations rather than graphs.

Definition 6 (Covering Relation). *Let $\preceq$ be a partial order (reflexive, antisymmetric, and transitive). $\prec = \{(x, y) \in \preceq \mid x \neq y\}$. $\lessdot$ is the covering relation of $\preceq$, i.e., $\lessdot = \{(x, y) \in \prec \mid \nexists_z \; x \prec z \prec y\}$.*

We can construct the covering relation for any partially ordered set of events. It is known that the covering relation is unique. The graphical representation of the partial order based on the covering relation is also known as the Hasse diagram. $\lessdot_E$ and $\lessdot_E^{ot}$ refer to the covering relations of $\preceq_E$ and $\preceq_E^{ot}$ respectively.

Using the covering relation $\lessdot_E^{ot}$ for an event log $(E, \preceq_E)$ projected onto an object type ot, we can construct a variant of the Directly-Follows Graph (DFG). However, there are two differences with a normal DFG: we consider partial orders and focus on the projection.

Definition 7 (Directly-Follows Graph). *Let $(E, \preceq_E)$ be an event log and $ot \in \mathbb{U}_{ot}$ an object type. (A^{ot}, R^{ot}) with $A^{ot} = [\pi_{act}(e) \mid e \in E^{ot}]$ and $R^{ot} = [(\pi_{act}(e_1), \pi_{act}(e_2)) \mid (e_1, e_2) \in \lessdot_E^{ot}]$ is the Directly-Follows Graph (DFG) for object type ot.*

The resulting DFG (A^{ot}, R^{ot}) has a multiset of activity nodes A^{ot} and a multiset of arcs R^{ot}. Both are multisets, because we would like to keep track of frequencies. Given some activity a, $A^{ot}(a)$ is the number of a events that refer to an object of type ot. Given a pair of activities (a_1, a_2), $R^{ot}(a_1, a_2)$ is the number times an a_1 event was causally followed by an a_2 event where both events shared an object of type ot.

Figure 6 shows an example DFG (without multiplicities) for each object type using the event log illustrated by Table 1. Note that we also indicate the initial and final activities (shown using the incoming arcs and outgoing arcs). This can be achieved by adding a dummy start and end activity to each object type. The dummy start corresponds to the creation of the object. The dummy end activity corresponds to its completion. These dummy activities are not shown in Fig. 6, but the corresponding arcs are.

As mentioned before, the scoping of object identifiers greatly influences the process models that are returned. To illustrate this, consider the reduced event log shown in Table 2 again. Figure 7 shows the DFGs (again without multiplicities) for each object type using this reduced event log. As before, we indicate start and end activities.

The different DFGs can be simply merged into a *labeled multigraph* where the arcs correspond to specific object types. The arcs are now labeled with object

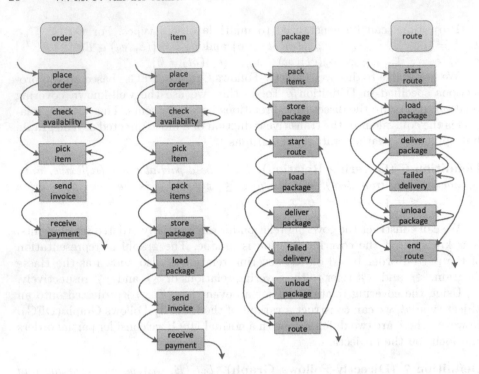

Fig. 6. DFGs per object type learned from Table 1. Not all arcs are included and also note that Table 1 is just an excerpt of the larger event log.

types. For example, (a_1, ot, a_2) is the arc connecting activities a_1 and a_2 via objects of type ot. Two arcs may connect the same pair of activities. As before, we use multisets to represent cardinalities, i.e., $R(a_1, ot, a_2)$ is the frequency of the arc connecting activities a_1 and a_2 via objects of type ot.

Definition 8 (Overall Directly-Follows Multigraph). *Let* $(E, \preceq_E)$ *be an event log.* (A, R) *with* $A = [\pi_{act}(e) \mid \exists_{ot \in \mathbb{U}_{ot}} e \in E^{ot}]$ *and* $R = [(\pi_{act}(e_1), ot, \pi_{act}(e_2)) \mid \exists_{ot \in \mathbb{U}_{ot}} (e_1, e_2) \in \,<_E^{ot}]$ *is the Overall Directly-Follows Multigraph (ODFM).*

In general, the Overall Directly-Follows Multigraph (ODFM) will often be too complicated to understand easily. Nevertheless, it is valuable to see the whole event log with multiple case notions in a single diagram. To simplify the multigraph, it is possible to consider any subset of object types $OT \subseteq \mathbb{U}_{ot}$.

Definition 9 (Selected Directly-Follows Multigraph). *Let* $(E, \preceq_E)$ *be an event log and* $OT \subseteq \mathbb{U}_{ot}$ *a set of object types.* (A^{OT}, R^{OT}) *with* $A^{OT} = [\pi_{act}(e) \mid \exists_{ot \in OT} e \in E^{ot}]$ *and* $R^{OT} = [(\pi_{act}(e_1), ot, \pi_{act}(e_2)) \mid \exists_{ot \in OT} (e_1, e_2) \in \,<_E^{ot}]$ *is the Selected Directly-Follows Multigraph (SDFM).*

The Selected Directly-Follows Multigraph (SDFM) selects two or more object types to create a particular view on the event data. As an example, we can take

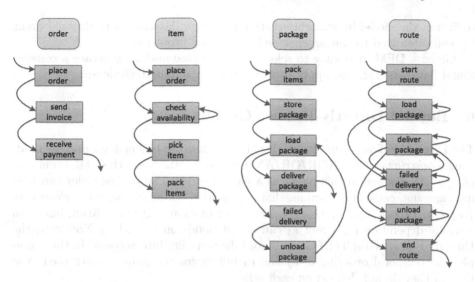

Fig. 7. DFGs per object type learned from Table 2.

$OT = \{order, item, package\}$ as shown in Fig. 8. The object types included are *order*, *item*, and *package*, i.e., only *route* is excluded to provide the view. The arcs are colored based on the corresponding object types. For clarity, also the names have been added. Again we do not show multiplicities on nodes and arcs. Also note that the start and end activities are indicated.

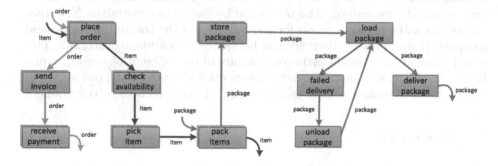

Fig. 8. Directly-Follows Multigraph (DFM) learned from Table 2 for the object types *order*, *item*, and *package*.

An ODFM is a special case of SDFM, i.e., $OT = \mathbb{U}_{ot}$. Therefore, we will use the term Directly-Follows Multigraph (DFM) to refer to both.

The DFM shown in Fig. 8 illustrates that it is possible to deal with non-flattened event data. The diagram shows the relationships between different activities that are connected through various types of objects. DFMs are not as easy to interpret as traditional DFGs using a single case notion. However, trying to flatten the model by straightjacketing the event data into a traditional event log will often lead to convergence and divergence problems.

Given a DFM, it is easy to select a desired case notion, generate a conventional flat event log, and apply standard process mining techniques.

6   Beyond Directly-Follows Graphs

The Directly-Follows Multigraph (DFM) does not use higher-level process modeling constructs (e.g., XOR/OR/AND-splits/joins). Note that an event log $(E, \preceq_E)$, as defined in this paper, is a partial order. The partial order can take into account causality. Assume that $\preceq_E$ is the reflexive transitive closure of $\{(e_1, e_2), (e_1, e_3), (e_2, e_4), (e_3, e_4)\}$. The order of e_2 and e_3 is not fixed, but both causally depend on e_1. Event e_4 causally depends on e_2 and e_3. Normally, the Directly Follows Graph (DFG) does not take causality into account. In the example, the temporal ordering of e_2 and e_3 influences the graph constructed even though they do not depend on each other.

Although the partial order can take into account causality, the resulting DFM does not explicitly show concurrency. However, traditional process mining approaches can be used starting from event data projected onto a specific object type. Recall that the DFG for object type ot, i.e., (A^{ot}, R^{ot}), is based on a projected event log. We can use the same approach in conjunction with existing process discovery techniques. Two examples are the Petri-net-based place discovery technique presented in [3] and the *Declare*-based discovery techniques presented in [29,32,33]. In [3] monotonicity results are used to exploit finding places that are constraining behavior to the behavior seen. In [29,32,33] LTL-based declarative constraints are learned. Also places can be viewed as constraints. Note that a Petri net without places allows for any behavior of the transitions (activities) included. Hence, process discovery can be viewed as learning constraints. This view is compatible with the orthogonal nature of the different object types in a DFM. Therefore, it is not difficult to enhance DFMs such as the one shown in Fig. 8 with more sophisticated constraints (e.g., places or LTL-based constraints).

7   Conclusion

This paper focused on the limitations of process mining techniques that assume a single case notion and just one case per event. Yet, existing approaches assume "flattened event data" (e.g., stored using XES or a CSV file with one column for the case identifier). Real-life processes are often more complex, not allowing for these simplifying assumptions. Flattened event data only provide one of many possible views, leading to convergence and divergence problems.

To address the problem, we proposed a more faithful event log notion $(E, \preceq_E)$ where events can refer to any number of objects and these may be of different object types. Hence, events can depend on each other in different ways. Moreover, we assume partially ordered events. For example, events may refer to mixtures of orders, items, packages, and delivery routes. The Directly-Follows Multigraph (DFM) can be used to get a more holistic view on the process.

The paper is also a "call for action". First of all, it is important to extract more realistic event logs. Currently, techniques developed in research and the tools provided by vendors assume "flat" event data (e.g., in XES format), because it is the information widely available (in public data sets and the data sets used in competitions). However, the data stored in information systems are not flat. Availability of more realistic event data will positively influence research and tools. Second, novel techniques are needed. The DFM is just a starting point for more sophisticated object-centric process mining techniques. However, it is vital to keep things simple and avoid the complexity associated with artifact-centric approaches. Whereas the focus in this paper is on process discovery, the insights also apply to other forms of process mining such as conformance checking, bottleneck analysis, and operational support (e.g., prediction).

Acknowledgments. We thank the Alexander von Humboldt (AvH) Stiftung for supporting our research.

References

1. van der Aalst, W.M.P.: The application of Petri Nets to workflow management. J. Circ. Syst. Comput. 8(1), 21–66 (1998)
2. van der Aalst, W.M.P.: Process Mining: Data Science in Action. Springer, Heidelberg (2016). https://doi.org/10.1007/978-3-662-49851-4
3. van der Aalst, W.M.P.: Discovering the "Glue" connecting activities - exploiting monotonicity to learn places faster. In: de Boer, F., Bonsangue, M., Rutten, J. (eds.) It's All About Coordination. Lecture Notes in Computer Science, pp. 1–20. Springer-Verlag, Berlin (2018)
4. Berti, A., van der Aalst, W.M.P.: StarStar models: using events at database level for process analysis. In: Ceravolo, P., Gomez Lopez, M.T., van Keulen, M. (eds.) International Symposium on Data-driven Process Discovery and Analysis (SIM-PDA 2018), volume 2270 of CEUR Workshop Proceedings, pp. 60–64. CEUR-WS.org (2018)
5. van der Aalst, Artale, A., Montali, M., Tritini, S.: Object-centric behavioral constraints: integrating data and declarative process modelling. In: Proceedings of the 30th International Workshop on Description Logics (DL 2017), volume 1879 of CEUR Workshop Proceedings. CEUR-WS.org (2017)
6. van der Aalst, W.M.P., Barthelmess, P., Ellis, C.A., Wainer, J.: Workflow modeling using proclets. In: Scheuermann, P., Etzion, O. (eds.) CoopIS 2000. LNCS, vol. 1901, pp. 198–209. Springer, Heidelberg (2000). https://doi.org/10.1007/10722620_20
7. van der Aalst, W.M.P., Barthelmess, P., Ellis, C.A., Wainer, J.: Proclets: a framework for lightweight interacting workflow processes. Int. J. Coop. Inf. Syst. 10(4), 443–482 (2001)
8. van der Aalst, W.M.P., et al.: Soundness of workflow nets: classification, decidability, and analysis. Form. Asp. Comput. 23(3), 333–363 (2011)
9. van der Aalst, W.M.P., ter Hofstede, A.H.M., Kiepuszewski, B., Barros, A.P.: Workflow patterns. Distrib. Parallel Databases 14(1), 5–51 (2003)

10. van der Aalst, W.M.P., Li, G., Montali, M.: Object-Centric Behavioral Constraints. CoRR, abs/1703.05740 (2017)
11. van der Aalst, W.M.P., Pesic, M., Schonenberg, H.: Declarative workflows: balancing between flexibility and support. Comput. Sci.-Res. Dev. **23**(2), 99–113 (2009)
12. van der Aalst, W.M.P., Weijters, A.J.M.M., Maruster, L.: Workflow mining: discovering process models from event logs. IEEE Trans. Knowl. Data Eng. **16**(9), 1128–1142 (2004)
13. Artale, A., Calvanese, D., Montali, M., van der Aalst, W.M.P.: Enriching data models with behavioral constraints. In: Borgo, S. (ed.) Ontology Makes Sense (Essays in honor of Nicola Guarino), pp. 257–277. IOS Press (2019)
14. Bhattacharya, K., Gerede, C., Hull, R., Liu, R., Su, J.: Towards formal analysis of artifact-centric business process models. In: Alonso, G., Dadam, P., Rosemann, M. (eds.) BPM 2007. LNCS, vol. 4714, pp. 288–304. Springer, Heidelberg (2007). https://doi.org/10.1007/978-3-540-75183-0_21
15. Carmona, J., van Dongen, B., Solti, A., Weidlich, M.: Conformance Checking: Relating Processes and Models. Springer, Heidelberg (2018). https://doi.org/10.1007/978-3-319-99414-7
16. Cohn, D., Hull, R.: Business artifacts: a data-centric approach to modeling business operations and processes. IEEE Data Eng. Bull. **32**(3), 3–9 (2009)
17. González López de Murillas, E., Reijers, H.A., van der Aalst, W.M.P.: Connecting databases with process mining: a meta model and toolset. In: Schmidt, R., Guédria, W., Bider, I., Guerreiro, S. (eds.) BPMDS/EMMSAD -2016. LNBIP, vol. 248, pp. 231–249. Springer, Cham (2016). https://doi.org/10.1007/978-3-319-39429-9_15
18. van Eck, M.L., Sidorova, N., van der Aalst, W.M.P.: Guided interaction exploration in artifact-centric process models. In: IEEE Conference on Business Informatics (CBI 2017), pp. 109–118. IEEE Computer Society (2017)
19. Fahland, D.: Describing behavior of processes with many-to-many interactions. In: Donatelli, S., Haar, S. (eds.) PETRI NETS 2019. LNCS, vol. 11522, pp. 3–24. Springer, Cham (2019). https://doi.org/10.1007/978-3-030-21571-2_1
20. Fahland, D., de Leoni, M., van Dongen, B.F., van der Aalst, W.M.P.: Behavioral conformance of artifact-centric process models. In: Abramowicz, W. (ed.) BIS 2011. LNBIP, vol. 87, pp. 37–49. Springer, Heidelberg (2011). https://doi.org/10.1007/978-3-642-21863-7_4
21. Fahland, D., De Leoni, M., van Dongen, B., van der Aalst, W.M.P.: Many-to-many: some observations on interactions in artifact choreographies. In: Eichhorn, D., Koschmider, A., Zhang, H. (eds.) Proceedings of the 3rd Central-European Workshop on Services and Their Composition (ZEUS 2011), CEUR Workshop Proceedings, pp. 9–15. CEUR-WS.org (2011)
22. IBM. IBM MQSeries Workflow - Getting Started With Buildtime. IBM Deutschland Entwicklung GmbH, Boeblingen, Germany (1999)
23. IEEE Task Force on Process Mining. XES Standard Definition (2013). http://www.xes-standard.org/
24. Leemans, S.J.J., Fahland, D., van der Aalst, W.M.P.: Discovering block-structured process models from event logs: a constructive approach. In: Colom, J.M., Desel, J. (eds.) Applications and Theory of Petri Nets 2013. Lecture Notes in Computer Science, vol. 7927, pp. 311–329. Springer-Verlag, Berlin (2013)
25. Li, G., de Murillas, E.G.L., de Carvalho, R.M., van der Aalst, W.M.P.: Extracting object-centric event logs to support process mining on databases. In: Mendling, J., Mouratidis, H. (eds.) CAiSE 2018. LNBIP, vol. 317, pp. 182–199. Springer, Cham (2018). https://doi.org/10.1007/978-3-319-92901-9_16

26. Li, G., de Carvalho, R.M., van der Aalst, W.M.P.: Automatic discovery of object-centric behavioral constraint models. In: Abramowicz, W. (ed.) BIS 2017. LNBIP, vol. 288, pp. 43–58. Springer, Cham (2017). https://doi.org/10.1007/978-3-319-59336-4_4

27. Lohmann, N.: Compliance by design for artifact-centric business processes. In: Rinderle-Ma, S., Toumani, F., Wolf, K. (eds.) BPM 2011. LNCS, vol. 6896, pp. 99–115. Springer, Heidelberg (2011). https://doi.org/10.1007/978-3-642-23059-2_11

28. Lu, X., Nagelkerke, M., van de Wiel, D., Fahland, D.: Discovering interacting artifacts from ERP systems. IEEE Trans. Serv. Comput. 8(6), 861–873 (2015)

29. Maggi, F.M., Bose, R.P.J.C., van der Aalst, W.M.P.: Efficient discovery of understandable declarative process models from event logs. In: Ralyté, J., Franch, X., Brinkkemper, S., Wrycza, S. (eds.) CAiSE 2012. LNCS, vol. 7328, pp. 270–285. Springer, Heidelberg (2012). https://doi.org/10.1007/978-3-642-31095-9_18

30. Nigam, A., Caswell, N.S.: Business artifacts: an approach to operational specification. IBM Syst. J. 42(3), 428–445 (2003)

31. OMG. Business Process Model and Notation (BPMN). Object Management Group, formal/2011-01-03 (2011)

32. Rovani, M., Maggi, F.M., de Leoni, M., van der Aalst, W.M.P.: Declarative process mining in healthcare. Expert Syst. Appl. 42(23), 9236–9251 (2015)

33. Bose, R.P.J.C., Maggi, F.M., van der Aalst, W.M.P.: Enhancing declare maps based on event correlations. In: Daniel, F., Wang, J., Weber, B. (eds.) BPM 2013. LNCS, vol. 8094, pp. 97–112. Springer, Heidelberg (2013). https://doi.org/10.1007/978-3-642-40176-3_9

34. Scheer, A.W.: Business Process Engineering: Reference Models for Industrial Enterprises. Springer, Heidelberg (1994). https://doi.org/10.1007/978-3-642-79142-0

35. van Eck, M.L., Sidorova, N., van der Aalst, W.M.P.: Multi-instance mining: discovering synchronisation in artifact-centric processes. In: Daniel, F., Sheng, Q.Z., Motahari, H. (eds.) BPM 2018. LNBIP, vol. 342, pp. 18–30. Springer, Cham (2019). https://doi.org/10.1007/978-3-030-11641-5_2

Cooperative Asynchronous Systems

Relating Session Types and Behavioural Contracts: The Asynchronous Case

Mario Bravetti[✉] and Gianluigi Zavattaro

Department of Computer Science and Engineering & Focus Team, Inria,
University of Bologna, Bologna, Italy
bravetti@cs.unibo.it

Abstract. We discuss the relationship between session types and behavioural contracts under the assumption that processes communicate asynchronously. We show the existence of a fully abstract interpretation of session types into a fragment of contracts, that maps session subtyping into binary compliance-preserving contract refinement. In this way, the recent undecidability result for asynchronous session subtyping can be used to obtain an original undecidability result for asynchronous contract refinement.

1 Introduction

Session types are used to specify the structure of communication between the endpoints of a distributed system or the processes of a concurrent program. In recent years, session types have been integrated into several mainstream programming languages (see, e.g., [1,18,21,26–29]) where they specify the pattern of interactions that each endpoint must follow, i.e., a communication protocol. In this way, once the expected communication protocol at an endpoint has been expressed in terms of a session type, the behavioural correctness of a program at that endpoint can be checked by exploiting syntax-based type checking techniques. The overall correctness of the system is guaranteed when the session types of the interacting endpoints satisfy some deadlock/termination related (see, e.g., [13,16]) compatibility notion. For instance, in case of binary communication, i.e., interaction between two endpoints, *session duality* rules out communication errors like, e.g., deadlocks: by session duality we mean that each send (resp. receive) action in the session type of one endpoint, is matched by a corresponding receive (resp. send) action of the session type at the opposite endpoint. Namely, we have that two endpoints following respectively session types T and $\overline{T}$ ($\overline{T}$ is the dual of T) will communicate correctly.

Duality is a rather restrictive notion of compatibility since it forces endpoints to follow specular protocols. In many cases, endpoints correctly interact even if their corresponding session types are not dual. A typical example is when an endpoint is in receiving state and has the ability to accept more messages than

Research partly supported by the H2020-MSCA-RISE project ID 778233 "Behavioural Application Program Interfaces (BEHAPI)".

© Springer Nature Switzerland AG 2019
P. C. Ölveczky and G. Salaün (Eds.): SEFM 2019, LNCS 11724, pp. 29–47, 2019.
https://doi.org/10.1007/978-3-030-30446-1_2

those that could be emitted by the opposite endpoint. These cases are dealt with by considering *session subtyping*: an endpoint with session type T_1 can always be safely replaced by another endpoint with session type T_2, whenever T_2 is a subtype of T_1 (here denoted by $T_2 \leq T_1$). In this way, besides being safe to combine an endpoint with type T_1 with a specular one with type $\overline{T_1}$, it is also safe to combine any such T_2 with $\overline{T_1}$. The typical notion of subtyping for session types is the one by Gay and Hole [17] defined by considering synchronous communication: *synchronous session subtyping* only allows for a subtype to have fewer internal choices (sends), and more external choices (receives), than its supertype. *Asynchronous session subtyping* has been more recently investigated [6,8,15,24,25]: it is more permissive because it widens the synchronous subtyping relation by allowing the subtype to *anticipate* send actions, under the assumption that the subsequent communication protocol is not influenced by the anticipation. Anticipation is admitted because, in the presence of message queues, the effect of anticipating a send is simply that of enqueueing earlier, in the communication channel, the corresponding message. As an example, a session type $\oplus\{l : \&\{l' : \mathbf{end}\}\}$ with a send action on l followed by a receive action on l', is an asynchronous subtype of $\&\{l' : \oplus\{l : \mathbf{end}\}\}$ that performs the same actions, but in reverse order. This admits the safe combination of two endpoints with session types $\oplus\{l : \&\{l' : \mathbf{end}\}\}$ and $\oplus\{l' : \&\{l : \mathbf{end}\}\}$, respectively, because each program has a type which is an asynchronous subtype of the dual type of the partner. Intuitively, the combination is safe in that the initially sent messages are first enqueued in the communication channels, and then consumed.

Behavioural contracts [9–11,14,19] (contracts, for short) represent an alternative way for describing the communication behaviour of processes. While session types are defined to be checked against concurrent programs written in some specific programming language, contracts can be considered a language independent approach strongly inspired by automata-based communication models. Contracts follow the tradition of Communicating Finite State Machines (CFSMs) [4], which describe the possible send/receive actions in terms of a labeled-transition system: each transition corresponds with a possible communication action and alternative transitions represent choices that can involve both sends and receives (so called *mixed-choices*, which are usually disregarded in session types). A system is then modeled as the parallel composition of the contracts of its constituting processes. Also in the context of contracts, safe process replacement has been investigated by introducing the notion of *contract refinement*: if a contract C_1 is part of a correct system, then correctness is preserved when C_1 is replaced by one of its subcontracts C_2 (written $C_2 \preceq C_1$ in this paper). Obviously, different notions of contract refinement can be defined, based on possible alternative notions of system correctness. For instance, for binary client/service interaction where correctness is interpreted as the successful completion of the client protocol, the *server pre-order* (see e.g. [3]) has been defined as a refinement of server contracts that preserves client satisfaction. On the other hand, if we move to multi-party systems, and we consider a notion of correctness, called *compliance*, that requires the successful completion of all the partners, an alternative compliance preserving *subcontract relation* [10] is obtained.

Given that both session types and behavioural contracts have been developed for formal reasoning on communication-centered systems, and given that session subtyping and contract refinement have been respectively defined to characterize the notion of safe replacement, it is common understanding that there exists a strong correspondence between these session subtyping and contract refinement. Such a correspondence has been formally investigated for synchronous communication by Bernardi and Hennessy [3]: there exists a natural interpretation of session types into a fragment of contracts where mixed-choice is disallowed, called *session contracts*, such that synchronous subtyping is mapped into a notion of refinement that preserves client satisfaction (but can be applied to both clients and servers; and not only to servers as the server pre-order mentioned above).

The correspondence between session subtyping and contract refinement under asynchronous communication is still an open problem. In this paper we solve such a problem by identifying the fragment of asynchronously communicating contracts for which refinement corresponds to asynchronous session subtyping: besides disallowing mixed-choices as for the synchronous case, we consider a specific form of communication (i.e., FIFO channels for each pair of processes as in the communication model of CFSMs) and restrict to binary systems (i.e., systems composed of two contracts only).

In all, this paper contribution encompasses: (i) a new theory of asynchronous behavioural contracts that coincide with CFSMs and includes the notions of contract compliance (correct, i.e. deadlock free, system of CFSMs) and contract refinement (preservation of compliance under any test); and (ii) a precise discussion about the notion of *refinement*, showing under which conditions it coincides with asynchronous session subtyping, which is known to be undecidable [7].

More precisely, concerning (ii), we show asynchronous subtyping over session types to be encodable into refinement over binary and non mixed-choice asynchronous behavioral contracts (CFSMs). This means that, for contracts of this kind, refined contracts can anticipate outputs w.r.t. the original contract as it happens in the context of session subtyping. Moreover we show that it is crucial, for such a correspondence to hold, that, when establishing refinement between two binary and non mixed-choice asynchronous behavioral contracts, *only tests that are actually binary* (a single interacting contract) *and non mixed-choice are considered*: if we also consider tests that are either multiparty (mutliple interacting contracts) or mixed-choice, in general, a binary and non mixed-choice contract C' that anticipates output w.r.t. a binary and non mixed-choice contract C is not a subcontract of it. This observation has deep implications on decidability properties in the context of general asynchronous behavioral contracts (CFSMs): while *compliance*, i.e. (non) reachability of deadlocking global CFSM states over asynchronous behavioral contracts (CFSMs) is known to be undecidable [4], an obvious argument showing undecidability cannot be found for the refinement relation: such a relation can be put in direct correspondence with asynchronous session subtyping *only for the restricted binary and non mixed-choice setting (including also tests)*. Therefore, since in general an asynchronous behavioral contract (CFSMs) C' that anticipates output w.r.t. a contract C is

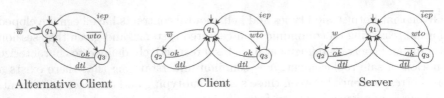

Fig. 1. Fragment of a UDP server serving Write/WriteTo requests, with specular client and alternative client that records replies only after WriteTo requests.

not a subcontract of it, decidability of refinement over general asynchronous behavioral contracts (CFSMs) remains, quite unexpectedly, an open problem.

Structure of the Paper. In Sect. 2 we define our model of asynchronous behavioural contracts inspired by CFSMs [4]; we define syntax, semantics, correct contract composition, and the notion of contract refinement. In Sect. 3 we recall session types, focusing on the notion of asynchronous session subtyping [7,25]. In Sect. 4 we present a fragment of behavioural contracts and we prove that there exists a natural encoding of session types into this fragment of contracts which maps asynchronous session subtyping into contract refinement. Finally, in Sect. 5 we report some concluding remarks.

2 Behavioural Contracts

In this section we present behavioural contracts (simply contracts for short), in the form of a process algebra (see, e.g. [2,22,23]) based formalization of Communicating Finite State Machines (CFSMs) [4]. CFSMs are used to represent FIFO systems, composed by automata performing send and receive actions having the effect of introducing/retrieving messages to/from FIFO channel. One channel is considered for each pair of sender/receiver automata.

As an example, we can consider a client/service interaction (inspired by the UDP communication protocol) depicted in Fig. 1. Communication protocols are denoted by means of automata with transitions representing communication actions: overlined labels denote send actions, while non-overlined labels denote receive actions. The server is always available to serve both Write (w for short) and WriteTo (wto) requests. In the first case, the server replies with OK (ok) or DataTooLarge (dtl), depending on the success of the request or its failure due to an exceeding size of the message. On the other hand, in case of WriteTo, the server has a third possible reply, InvalidEndPoint (iep), in case of wrongly specified destination. We consider two possible clients: a client following a specular protocol, and an alternative client that (given the connectionless nature of UDP) does not synchronize the reception of the server replies with the corresponding requests, but records them asynchronously after WriteTo requests only.

We now present contracts, that can be seen as a syntax for CFSMs. Differently from the examples of communicating automata reported in Fig. 1, the send

Table 1. Semantic rules for contracts.

$$\frac{j \in I}{\sum_{i \in I} \alpha_i.C_i \xrightarrow{\alpha_j} C_j} \qquad \frac{C\{recX.C/X\} \xrightarrow{\lambda} C'}{recX.C \xrightarrow{\lambda} C'}$$

(resp. receive) actions will be decorated with a location identifying the expected receiver (resp. sender) contract. This was not considered in the example because, in case of two interacting partners, the sender and receiver of the communication actions can be left implicit.

Definition 1 (Behavioural Contracts). *We consider three denumerable sets: the set $\mathcal{N}$ of message names ranged over by a, b, $\cdots$, the location names Loc, ranged over by l, l', $\cdots$, and the contract variables Var ranged over by X, Y, $\cdots$. The syntax of contracts is defined by the following grammar:*

$$C ::= 1 \quad | \quad \sum_{i \in I} \alpha_i.C_i \quad | \quad X \quad | \quad recX.C \qquad\qquad \alpha ::= a_l \quad | \quad \overline{a}_l$$

where the set of index I is assumed to be non-empty, and $recX.\_$ is a binder for the process variable X denoting recursive definition of processes: in $recX.C$ a (free) occurrence of X inside C represents a jump going back to the beginning of C. We assume that in a contract C all process variables are bound and all recursive definitions are guarded, i.e. in $recX.C$ all occurrences of X are included in the scope of a prefix operator $\sum_{i \in I} \alpha_i.C_i$. Following CFSMs, we assume contracts to be deterministic, i.e., in $\sum_{i \in I} \alpha_i.C_i$, we have $\alpha_i = \alpha_j$ iff $i = j$. In the following we will omit trailing ".1" when writing contracts.

We use α to range over the actions: $\overline{a}_l$ is a send action, with message a, towards the location l; a_l is the receive of a sent from the location l. The contract $\sum_{i \in I} \alpha_i.C_i$ (also denoted with $\alpha_1.C_1 + \alpha_2.C_2 + \cdots + \alpha_n.C_n$ when $I = \{1, 2, \ldots, n\}$) performs any of the actions α_i and activates the continuation C_i. In case there is only one action, we use the simplified notation $\alpha.C$, where α is such a unique action, and C is its continuation. The contract 1 denotes a final successful state.

The operational semantics of contracts C is defined in terms of a transition system labeled over $\{a_l, \overline{a}_l, \mid a \in \mathcal{N}, l \in Loc\}$, ranged over by λ, λ', $\ldots$, obtained by the rules in Table 1. We use $C\{\_/\_\}$ to denote syntactic replacement. The first rule states that contract $\sum_{i \in I} \alpha_i.C_i$ can perform any of the actions α_i and then activate the corresponding continuation C_i. The second rule is the standard one for recursion unfolding (replacing any occurrence of X with the operator $recX.C$ binding it, so to represent the backward jump described above).

The semantics of a contract C yields a *finite-state* labeled transition system,[1] whose states are the contracts reachable from C. It is interesting to observe that such a transition system can be interpreted as a communicating automaton of a CFSM, with transitions $\overline{a}_l$ (resp. a_l) denoting send (resp. receive) actions.

---

[1] As for basic CCS [22] finite-stateness is an obvious consequence of the fact that the process algebra does not include static operators, like parallel or restriction.

The final contract **1** coincides with states of communicating automata that have no outgoing transitions. Moreover, we have that each communicating automaton can be expressed as a contract; this is possible by adopting standard techniques [22] to translate finite labeled transition systems into recursively defined process algebraic terms. Hence we can conclude that our contracts coincide with the communicating automata as defined for CFSMs.

Example 1. As an example of contracts used to denote communicating automata, the alternative client and the server in Fig. 1 respectively correspond to the following contracts:[2]

$$Client = recX.(\overline{w}.X + \overline{wto}.(ok.X + dtl.X + iep.X))$$
$$Server = recX.(w.(\overline{ok}.X + \overline{dtl}.X) + wto.(\overline{ok}.X + \overline{dtl}.X + \overline{iep}.X))$$

Notice that we have not explicitly indicated the locations associated to the send and receive actions; in fact interaction is binary and the sender and receiver of each communication is obviously the partner location, and we leave it implicit.

We now move to the formalization of contract systems. A contract system is the parallel composition of contracts, each one located at a given location, that communicate by means of FIFO channels. More precisely, we use $[C, \mathcal{Q}]_l$ to denote a contract C located at location l with an input queue $\mathcal{Q}$. The queue contains messages denoted with $a_{l'}$, where l' is the location of the sender of such message a. This queue should be considered as the union of many input channels, one for each sender; in fact the FIFO order of reception is guaranteed only among messages coming from the same sender, while two messages coming from different senders can be consumed in any order, independently from the order of introduction in the queue $\mathcal{Q}$. This coincides with the communication model considered in CFSMs.

Definition 2 (FIFO Contract Systems). *The syntax of FIFO contract systems is defined by the following grammar:*

$$P ::= [C, \mathcal{Q}]_l \quad | \quad P \| P \qquad\qquad \mathcal{Q} ::= \epsilon \quad | \quad a_l :: \mathcal{Q}$$

We assume that every FIFO contract system P is such that: (i) all locations are different (i.e. every subterm $[C, \mathcal{Q}]_l$ occurs in P with a different location l), (ii) all actions refer to locations present in the system (i.e., for every a_l or $\overline{a}_l$ occurring in P, there exists a subterm $[C, \mathcal{Q}]_l$ of P), (iii) receive and send actions executed by a contract consider a location different from the location of that contract (i.e. every action a_l or $\overline{a}_l$ does not occur inside a subterm $[C, \mathcal{Q}]_l$ of P), and (iv) messages in a queue comes from a location different from the location of the queue (i.e. every message a_l does not occur inside the queue $\mathcal{Q}$ of a subterm $[C, \mathcal{Q}]_l$ of P).

---

[2] The correspondence is as follows: the labeled transition systems of the indicated contracts and the corresponding automata in Fig. 1 are isomorphic.

Table 2. Asynchronous system semantics (symmetric rules for $\|$ omitted).

$$\frac{C \xrightarrow{\overline{a}_{l'}} C'}{[C,\mathcal{Q}]_l \xrightarrow{\overline{a}_{l,l'}} [C',\mathcal{Q}]_l} \qquad [C,\mathcal{Q}]_{l'} \xrightarrow{a_{l,l'}} [C,\mathcal{Q}::a_l]_{l'} \qquad \frac{P \xrightarrow{\overline{a}_{l,l'}} P' \quad Q \xrightarrow{a_{l,l'}} Q'}{P\|Q \xrightarrow{\tau} P'\|Q'}$$

$$\frac{C \xrightarrow{a_l} C' \quad l \notin \mathcal{Q}}{[C,\mathcal{Q}::a_l::\mathcal{Q}']_{l'} \xrightarrow{\tau} [C',\mathcal{Q}::\mathcal{Q}']_{l'}} \qquad \frac{P \xrightarrow{\lambda} P'}{P\|Q \xrightarrow{\lambda} P'\|Q}$$

Terms $\mathcal{Q}$ denote message queues: they are sequences of messages $a_{l_1}^1 :: a_{l_2}^2 :: \ldots :: a_{l_n}^n :: \epsilon$,[3] where "$\epsilon$" denotes the empty message queue. Trailing ϵ are usually left implicit (hence the above queue is denoted with $a_{l_1}^1 :: a_{l_2}^2 :: \ldots :: a_{l_n}^n$). We overload :: to denote also queue concatenation, i.e., given $\mathcal{Q} = a_{l_1}^1 :: a_{l_2}^2 :: \ldots :: a_{l_n}^n$ and $\mathcal{Q}' = b_{l'_1}^1 :: b_{l'_2}^2 :: \ldots :: b_{l'_m}^m$, then $\mathcal{Q}::\mathcal{Q}' = a_{l_1}^1 :: a_{l_2}^2 :: \ldots :: a_{l_n}^n :: b_{l'_1}^1 :: b_{l'_2}^2 :: \ldots :: b_{l'_m}^m$. In the following, we will use the notation $l \notin \mathcal{Q}$ to state that if $a_{l'}$ is in $\mathcal{Q}$ then $l \neq l'$, moreover we will use the shorthand $[C]$ to stand for $[C,\epsilon]$.

The operational semantics of FIFO contract systems is defined in terms of a transition system labeled over $\{a_{l,l'}, \overline{a}_{l,l'}, \tau \mid l, l' \in Loc, a \in \mathcal{N}\}$, also in this case ranged over by $\lambda, \lambda', \ldots$, obtained by the rules in Table 2 (plus the symmetric version for the first two rules of parallel composition). The first rule indicates that a send action $\overline{a}_{l'}$ executed by a contract located at location l, becomes an action $\overline{a}_{l,l'}$: the two locations l and l' denote the sender and receiver locations, respectively. The second rule states that, at the receiver location l', it is always possible to execute a complementary action $a_{l,l'}$ (that can synchronize with $\overline{a}_{l,l'}$) whose effect is to enqueue, in the local queue, a_l: notice that only the sender location l remains associated to message a. The third rule is the synchronization rule between the two complementary labels $\overline{a}_{l,l'}$ and $a_{l,l'}$. The fourth rule is for message consumption: a contract can remove a message a_l from its queue, only if a_l is not preceded by messages sent from the same location l. This guarantees that messages from the same location are consumed in FIFO order. The last rule is the usual local rule used to extend to the entire system actions performed by a part of it.

In the following, we call computation step a τ-labeled transition $P \xrightarrow{\tau} P'$; a computation, on the other hand, is a (possibly empty) sequence of τ-labeled transitions $P \xrightarrow{\tau}^* P'$, in this case starting from the system P and leading to P'. To simplify the notation, we omit the τ labels, i.e., we use $P \longrightarrow P'$ for computation steps, and $P \longrightarrow^* P'$ for computations.

We now move to the definition of *correct* composition of contracts. We take inspiration from the notion of *compliance* among contracts as defined, e.g., by Bernardi and Hennessy [3]. Informally, we say that a contract system is correct if all its reachable states (via any computation) are such that: the system has successfully completed or it is able to perform computation steps (i.e. τ transi-

---

[3] As usual, we consider :: right associative.

tions) and after each step it moves to a system which is, in turn, correct. In other terms, a system is correct if all of its maximal sequences of τ labeled transitions either lead to a successfully completed system or are infinite (do not terminate). The notion of *successful completion* for a system is formalized by a predicate $P\sqrt{}$ defined as follows:

$$([C_1, \mathcal{Q}_1] \| \ldots \| [C_n, \mathcal{Q}_n]) \sqrt{} \ \ \textit{iff} \ \ \forall i \in \{1, \ldots, n\}. \ C_i = recX_1 \ldots recX_{m_i}.\mathbf{1} \wedge \mathcal{Q}_i = \epsilon$$

Notice that the predicate checks whether all input queues are empty and all contracts coincide with the terminated contract $\mathbf{1}$ (possibly guarded by some recursive definition).

We are now ready to define our notion of correct contract composition.

Definition 3 (Correct Contract Composition – Compliance). *A system P is a correct contract composition according to compliance, denoted $P\downarrow$, if for every P' such that $P \longrightarrow^* P'$, then either P' is a successfully completed system, i.e. $P'\sqrt{}$, or there exists an additional computation step $P' \longrightarrow P''$.*

Example 2. As an example of correct system we can consider $[Client]_c \| [Server]_s$ where $Client$ is the contract defined in Example 1 above for the alternative client in Fig. 1 in which all actions are decorated with s, while $Server$ is the contract for the server in which all actions are decorated with c. In this system successful completion cannot be reached, but the system never stucks, i.e., every system reachable via a computation always has an additional computation step.

Notice that the above $Client/Server$ system is a correct contract composition even if the considered $Client$ does not behave specularly w.r.t. the server. When we replace a contract with another one by preserving system correctness, we say that we refine the initial contract. As an example, consider the correct system $[b_{l'}.\overline{a}_{l'}]_l \| [\overline{b}_l.a_l]_{l'}$ composed of two specular contracts. We can replace the contract $b_{l'}.\overline{a}_{l'}$ with $\overline{a}_{l'}.b_{l'}$ by preserving system correctness (i.e. $[\overline{a}_{l'}.b_{l'}]_l \| [\overline{b}_l.a_l]_{l'}$ is still correct). The latter differs from the former in that it anticipates the send action $\overline{a}_{l'}$ w.r.t. the receive action $b_{l'}$. This transformation is usually called *output anticipation* (see e.g. [25]). Intuitively, output anticipation is possible because, under asynchronous communication, its effect is simply that of anticipating the introduction of a message in the partner queue. In the context of asynchronous session types, for instance, output anticipation is admitted by the notion of session subtyping [15,25] that, as we will discuss in the following sections, is the counterpart of contract refinement in the context of session types.

We now formally define contract refinement and we observe that, differently from session types, output anticipation is not admitted as a general contract refinement mechanism.

Definition 4 (Contract Refinement). *A contract C' is a refinement of a contract C, denoted $C' \preceq C$, if and only if, for all FIFO contract systems $([C]_l \| P)$ we have that: if $([C]_l \| P)\downarrow$ then $([C']_l \| P)\downarrow$.*

In the following, whenever $C' \preceq C$ we will also say that C' is a subcontract of C (or equivalently that C is a supercontract of C').

The above definition contains a universal quantification on all possible contract systems P and locations l, hence it cannot be directly used to algorithmically check contract refinement. To the best of our knowledge, there exists no general algorithmic characterization (or proof of undecidability) for such a relation. Nevertheless, we can use the definition on some examples.

For instance, consider the two contracts $C = b_{l'}.\bar{a}_{l'}$ and $C' = \bar{a}_{l'}.b_{l'}$ discussed above. We have seen that C' is a safe replacement of C in the specific context $[\,]_l \| [\bar{b}_l.a_l]_{l'}$. But we have that $C' \not\preceq C$ because there exists a discriminating context $[\,]_l \| [\bar{b}_l.a_l + a_l]_{l'}$. In fact, when combined with C', the contract in l' can take the alternative branch a_l, leading to an incorrect system where the contract at l blocks waiting for a never incoming message $b_{l'}$.

The above example shows that output anticipation, admitted in the context of asynchronous session types, is not a correct refinement mechanism for contracts. The remainder of the paper is dedicated to the definition of a fragment of contracts in which it is correct to admit output anticipation, but we first recall session types and asynchronous subtyping.

3   Asynchronous Session Types

In this section we recall session types, in particular we discuss binary session types for asynchronous communication. In fact, for this specific class of session types, subtyping admits output anticipation.

We start with the formal syntax of binary session types, adopting a simplified notation (used, e.g., in [7,8]) without dedicated constructs for sending an output/receiving an input. We instead represent outputs and inputs directly inside choices. More precisely, we consider output selection $\oplus\{l_i : T_i\}_{i \in I}$, expressing an internal choice among outputs, and input branching $\&\{l_i : T_i\}_{i \in I}$, expressing an external choice among inputs. Each possible choice is labeled by a label l_i, taken from a global set of labels L, followed by a session continuation T_i. Labels in a branching/selection are assumed to be pairwise distinct.

Definition 5 (Session Types). *Given a set of labels L, ranged over by l, the syntax of binary session types is given by the following grammar:*

$$T \ \&::= \quad \oplus\{l_i : T_i\}_{i \in I} \quad | \quad \&\{l_i : T_i\}_{i \in I} \quad | \quad \mu t.T \quad | \quad \mathbf{t} \quad | \quad \mathbf{end}$$

In the sequel, we leave implicit the index set $i \in I$ in input branchings and output selections when it is already clear from the denotation of the types. Note also that we abstract from the type of the message that could be sent over the channel, since this is orthogonal to our results in this paper. Types $\mu t.T$ and $\mathbf{t}$ denote standard tail recursion for recursive types. We assume recursion to be guarded: in $\mu t.T$, the recursion variable $\mathbf{t}$ occurs within the scope of an output or an input type. In the following, we will consider closed terms only, i.e., types with all recursion variables $\mathbf{t}$ occurring under the scope of a corresponding definition $\mu t.T$. Type $\mathbf{end}$ denotes the type of a closed session, i.e., a session that can no longer be used.

For session types, we define the usual notion of duality: given a session type T, its dual $\overline{T}$ is defined as: $\overline{\oplus\{l_i : T_i\}_{i \in I}} = \&\{l_i : \overline{T_i}\}_{i \in I}$, $\overline{\&\{l_i : T_i\}_{i \in I}} = \oplus\{l_i : \overline{T_i}\}_{i \in I}$, $\overline{\mathbf{end}} = \mathbf{end}$, $\overline{\mathbf{t}} = \mathbf{t}$, and $\overline{\mu\mathbf{t}.T} = \mu\mathbf{t}.\overline{T}$.

We now move to the session subtyping relation, under the assumption that communication is asynchronous. The subtyping relation was initially defined by Gay and Hole [17] for synchronous communication; we adopt a similar co-inductive definition but, to be more consistent with the contract theory that we will discuss in the next sections, we follow a slightly different approach, being process-oriented instead of channel-based oriented.[4] Moreover, following [25], we consider a generalized version of unfolding that allows us to unfold recursions $\mu\mathbf{t}.T$ as many times as needed.

Definition 6 (n-unfolding).

$$\mathsf{unfold}^0(T) = T \qquad \mathsf{unfold}^1(\oplus\{l_i : T_i\}_{i \in I}) = \oplus\{l_i : \mathsf{unfold}^1(T_i)\}_{i \in I}$$
$$\mathsf{unfold}^1(\mu\mathbf{t}.T) = T\{\mu\mathbf{t}.T/\mathbf{t}\} \qquad \mathsf{unfold}^1(\&\{l_i : T_i\}_{i \in I}) = \&\{l_i : \mathsf{unfold}^1(T_i)\}_{i \in I}$$
$$\mathsf{unfold}^1(\mathbf{end}) = \mathbf{end} \qquad \mathsf{unfold}^n(T) = \mathsf{unfold}^1(\mathsf{unfold}^{n-1}(T))$$

Another auxiliary notation that we will use is that of input context which is useful to identify sequences of initial input branchings; this is useful because, as we will discuss in the following, in the definition of asynchronous session subtyping it is important to identify those output selections that are guarded by input branchings.

Definition 7 (Input Context). *An input context $\mathcal{A}$ is a session type with multiple holes defined by the syntax:*

$$\mathcal{A} ::= \quad [\,]^n \quad | \quad \&\{l_i : \mathcal{A}_i\}_{i \in I}$$

The holes $[\,]^n$, with $n \in \mathbb{N}^+$, of an input context $\mathcal{A}$ are assumed to be consistently enumerated, i.e. there exists $m \geq 1$ such that $\mathcal{A}$ includes one and only one $[\,]^n$ for each $n \leq m$. Given types $T_1, \ldots, T_m$, we use $\mathcal{A}[T_k]^{k \in \{1,\ldots,m\}}$ to denote the type obtained by filling each hole k in $\mathcal{A}$ with the corresponding term T_k.

As an example of how input contexts are used, consider the session type $\&\{l_1 : \oplus\{l : \mathbf{end}\}, l_2 : \oplus\{l : \mathbf{end}\}\}$. It can be decomposed as the input context $\&\{l_1 : [\,]^1, l_2 : [\,]^2\}$ with two holes that can be both filled with $\oplus\{l : \mathbf{end}\}$.

We are now ready to recall the *asynchronous* subtyping $\leq$ introduced by Mostrous et al. [24] following the simplified formulation in [7].

Definition 8 (Asynchronous Subtyping, $\leq$). *$\mathcal{R}$ is an asynchronous subtyping relation whenever $(T, S) \in \mathcal{R}$ implies that:*

1. *if $T = \mathbf{end}$ then $\exists n \geq 0$ such that $\mathsf{unfold}^n(S) = \mathbf{end}$;*
2. *if $T = \oplus\{l_i : T_i\}_{i \in I}$ then $\exists n \geq 0, \mathcal{A}$ such that*

---

[4] Differently from our definitions, in the channel-based approach of Gay and Hole [17] subtyping is covariant on branchings and contra-variant on selections.

$\quad$ – $\text{unfold}^n(S) = \mathcal{A}[\oplus\{l_j : S_{kj}\}_{j \in J_k}]^{k \in \{1,\ldots,m\}}$,

$\quad$ – $\forall k \in \{1, \ldots, m\}. I \subseteq J_k$ and

$\quad$ – $\forall i \in I, (T_i, \mathcal{A}[S_{ki}]^{k \in \{1,\ldots,m\}}) \in \mathcal{R}$;

3. if $T = \&\{l_i : T_i\}_{i \in I}$ then $\exists n \geq 0$ such that $\text{unfold}^n(S) = \&\{l_j : S_j\}_{j \in J}$, $J \subseteq I$ and $\forall j \in J. (T_j, S_j) \in \mathcal{R}$;

4. if $T = \mu t.T'$ then $(T'\{T/t\}, S) \in \mathcal{R}$.

T is an asynchronous subtype of S, written $T \leq S$, if there is an asynchronous subtyping relation $\mathcal{R}$ such that $(T, S) \in \mathcal{R}$.

$\quad$ Intuitively, the above co-inductive definition says that it is possibile to play a simulation game between a subtype T and its supertype S as follows: if T is the **end** type, then also S is ended; if T starts with an output selection, then S can reply by outputting at least all the labels in the selection (output covariance), and the simulation game continues; if T starts with an input branching, then S can reply by inputting at most some of the labels in the branching (input contravariance), and the simulation game continues. The unique non trivial case is the case of output selection; in fact, in this case the supertype could reply with output selections that are guarded by input branchings. As an example of application of this rule, consider the session type $T = \oplus\{l : \&\{l_1 : \textbf{end}, l_2 : \textbf{end}\}\}$. We have that T is a subtype of $S = \&\{l_1 : \oplus\{l : \textbf{end}\}, l_2 : \oplus\{l : \textbf{end}\}\}$, previously introduced. In fact, we have that the following relation

$$\{ (T, S) , (\&\{l_1 : \textbf{end}, l_2 : \textbf{end}\}, \&\{l_1 : \textbf{end}, l_2 : \textbf{end}\}) , (\textbf{end}, \textbf{end}) \}$$

is an asynchronous subtyping relation. Rule 2. of the definition is applied on the first pair (T, S). The first item of the rule is used to decompose S (as discussed above) as the input context $\&\{l_1 : [\,]^1, l_2 : [\,]^2\}$ with two holes both filled with $\oplus\{l : \textbf{end}\}$. The second item trivially holds because the output selection at the beginning of T has only one label l, as also the output selections filling the holes in the decomposition of S. Finally, the third item holds because of the pair $(\&\{l_1 : \textbf{end}, l_2 : \textbf{end}\}, \&\{l_1 : \textbf{end}, l_2 : \textbf{end}\})$ present in the relation. The first element of the pair is obtained by consuming the output selection at the beginning of T, while the second element by consuming the initial output selection of the terms filling the holes of the considered input context.

$\quad$ The rationale behind asynchronous session subtyping is that under asynchronous communication it is unobservable whether an output is anticipated before an input or not. In fact, anticipating an output simply introduces in advance the corresponding message in the communication queue. For this reason, rule 2. of the asynchronous subtyping definition admits the supertype to have inputs in front of the outputs used in the simulation game.

$\quad$ As a further example, consider the types $T = \mu t.\&\{l : \oplus\{l : t\}\}$ and $S = \mu t.\&\{l : \&\{l : \oplus\{l : t\}\}\}$. We have $T \leq S$ by considering an infinite subtyping relation including pairs (T', S'), with S' being $\&\{l : S\}$, $\&\{l : \&\{l : S\}\}$, $\&\{l : \&\{l : \&\{l : S\}\}\}$, $\ldots$; that is, the effect of each output anticipation is that a new input $\&\{l : \_\}$ is accumulated in the initial part of the r.h.s. It is worth to observe that every accumulated input $\&\{l : \_\}$ is eventually consumed in the simulation game, but the accumulated inputs grows unboundedly.

There are, on the contrary, cases in which the accumulated input is not consumed, as in the infinite simulation game between $T = \mu t. \oplus \{l : t\}$ and $S = \mu t.\&\{l : \oplus\{l : t\}\}$, in which only output selections are present in the subtype, and an instance of the input branching in the supertype is accumulated in each step of the simulation game.

Example 3. As a less trivial example, we can express as session types the two client protocols depicted in Fig. 1:

$$SpecularClient = \mu t. \oplus \{w.\&\{ok.t + dtl.t\}, wto.\&\{ok.t + dtl.t + iep.t\}\}$$
$$RefinedClient = \mu t. \oplus \{w.t, wto.\&\{ok.t + dtl.t + iep.t\}\}$$

We have that $RefinedClient \leq SpecularClient$ because the subtyping simulation game can go on forever: when $RefinedClient$ selects the output w a input branching is accumulated in front of the r.h.s. type ($SpecularClient$ and its derived types), while if wto is selected there is no new input accumulation as a (contravariant) input branching follows such a selected output.

A final observation is concerned with specific limit cases of application of rule *2.*; as discussed above, such a rule assume the possibility to decompose the candidate supertype into an initial input context, with holes filled by types starting with output selections. We notice that there exist session types that cannot be decomposed in such a way. Consider, for instance, the session type $S = \mu t.\&\{l_1 : t, l_2 : \oplus\{l : t\}\}$. This session type cannot be decomposed as an input context with holes filled by output branchings because, for every n, $\mathsf{unfold}^n(S)$ will contain a sequence of input branchings (labeled with l_1) that terminate in a term starting with the recursive definition $\mu t.\_$. Our opinion is that the definition of asynchronous subtyping does not manage properly these limit cases. For instance, the above session type S could be reasonably considered a supertype of $\mu t. \oplus \{l : \&\{l_1 : t, l_2 : t\}\}$, that simply anticipates the output selection with label l. Such a type has runs with more output selections, because S has a loop of the recursive definition that does not include the output selection; but this is not problematic because such outputs could be simply stored in the message queue. Nevertheless, we have that such a session type is not a subtype of S due to the above observation about the inapplicability of rule *2.*

For this reason, in the following, we will restrict to session types that do not contain infinite sequences of receive actions. Formally, given a session type S and a subterm $\mu t.T$ of S, we assume that all free occurrences of t occur in T inside an output selection $\oplus\{\_\}$.

We conclude this section by observing that asynchronous session subtyping was considered decidable (see [25]), but recently Bravetti, Carbone and Zavattaro proved that it is undecidable [7].[5]

---

[5] Lange and Yoshida [20] independently proved that a slight variant of asynchronous subtyping, called orphan-message-free subtyping was undecidable.

4   Mapping Session Types into Behavioural Contracts

In the previous sections we have defined a notion of refinement for contracts and we have seen that output anticipation is not admitted as a general refinement mechanism. Then we have recalled session types where, on the contrary, output anticipation is admitted by asynchronous session subtyping. In this section we show that it is possible to define a fragment of contracts for which refinement turns out to coincide with asynchronous session subtyping. More precisely, the natural encoding of session types into contracts maps asynchronous session subtyping into refinement, in the sense that two types are in subtyping relation if and only if the corresponding contracts are in refinement relation.

The first restriction that we discuss is about mixed-choice, i.e., the possibility to perform from the same state both send and receive actions. This is clearly not possible in session types having either output selections or input branchings. But removing mixed-choice from contracts is not sufficient to admit output anticipation. For instance, the system $[b_{l_2}.\overline{c}_{l_2}, \epsilon]_{l_1} \parallel [(a_{l_3}.\overline{b}_{l_1}.c_{l_1}) + c_{l_1}, \epsilon]_{l_2} \parallel [\overline{a}_{l_2}, \epsilon]_{l_3}$ is correct; but if we replace the contract at location l_1 with $\overline{c}_{l_2}.b_{l_2}$, that simply anticipates an output, we obtain $[\overline{c}_{l_2}.b_{l_2}, \epsilon]_{l_1} \parallel [(a_{l_3}.\overline{b}_{l_1}.c_{l_1}) + c_{l_1}, \epsilon]_{l_2} \parallel [\overline{a}_{l_2}, \epsilon]_{l_3}$ which is no longer correct in that the alternative branch c_{l_1} can be taken by the contract in l_2, thus reaching a system in which the contract at l_1 will wait indefinitely for b_{l_2}.

For this reason we need an additional restriction on choices: besides imposing that all the branchings should be guarded by either send or receive actions, we impose all such actions to address the same location l. This is obtained by means of a final restriction about the number of locations: we will consider systems with only two locations, as our objective is to obtain a refinement which is fully abstract w.r.t. subtyping as defined in Sect. 3, where we considered binary session types (i.e. types for sessions between two endpoints). Given that there are only two locations, each contract can receive only from the location of the partner; hence all receives in a choice address the same location. In general, we will omit the locations associated to send and receive actions: in fact, as already discussed also in Example 1, these can be left implicit because when there are only two locations all actions in one location consider the other location.

A final restriction follows from having restricted our analysis to session types in which there are no infinite sequences of input branchings (see the discussion, at the end of the previous section, about the inapplicability in these cases of rule 2. of Definition def:subtyping). We consider a similar restriction for contracts, by imposing that it is not possible to have infinite sequences of receive actions.

We are now ready to formally define the restricted syntax of contracts considered in this section; it coincides with *session contracts* as defined in [3] plus the restriction on contracts that do not contain infinite sequences of receive actions.

Definition 9 (Session contracts). *Session contracts are behavioural contracts obtained by considering the following restricted syntax:*

$$C \ ::= 1 \ \mid \ \sum_{i \in I} a^i.C_i \ \mid \ \sum_{i \in I} \overline{a^i}.C_i \ \mid \ X \ \mid \ recX.C$$

where given a session contract recX.C, we have that all free occurrences of X occur in C inside a subterm $\sum_{i \in I} \overline{a^i}.C_i$. Notice that we omit the locations l *associated to the send and receive actions (which is present in the contract syntax as defined in Definition 1). This simplification is justified because we will consider systems with only two locations, and we implicitly assume all actions of the contract in one location to be decorated with the other location.*

In the remainder of this section we will restrict our investigation to FIFO contract systems with only two locations and by considering only session contracts. We will omit the location names also in the denotation of such binary contract systems. Namely, we will use $[C, \mathcal{Q}] \| [C', \mathcal{Q}']$ to denote binary contract systems, thus omitting the names of the two locations as any pair of distinct locations l and l' could be considered.

In the restricted setting of binary session contracts, we can redefine the notion of refinement as follows.

Definition 10 (Binary Session Contract Refinement). *A session contract C' is a binary session contract refinement of a session contract C, denoted with $C' \preceq_s C$, if and only if, for all session contract D, if $([C] \| [D]) \downarrow$ then $([C'] \| [D]) \downarrow$.*

We now define a natural interpretation of session types as session contract; we will subsequently show that this encoding maps asynchronous subtyping into session contract refinement.

Definition 11. *Let T be a session type. We inductively define a function $[\![T]\!]$ from session types to session contracts as follows:*

- $[\![T = \oplus\{l_i : T_i\}_{i \in I}]\!] = \sum_{i \in I} \overline{l_i}.[\![T_i]\!]; \quad [\![T = \&\{l_i : T_i\}_{i \in I}]\!] = \sum_{i \in I} l_i.[\![T_i]\!];$
- $[\![\mu t.T]\!] = rec\,t.[\![T]\!]; \quad [\![t]\!] = t; \quad [\![end]\!] = 1.$

We now move to our main result, i.e., the proof that given two session types T and S we have that $T \leq S$ if and only if $[\![T]\!] \preceq_s [\![S]\!]$. This result has two main consequences. On the one hand, as a positive consequence, we can use the characterization of session subtyping in Definition 8 to prove also session contract refinement. For instance, if we consider the two session subtypes *RefinedClient* and *SpecularClient* of Example 3, we can conclude that

$$recX.(\overline{w}.X + \overline{wto}.(ok.X + dtl.X + iep.X)) \preceq_s$$
$$recX.(\overline{w}.(ok.X + dtl.X) + \overline{wto}.(ok.X + dtl.X + iep.X))$$

because, these two contracts are the encodings of the two above session types according to $[\![\,]\!]$ (notice that these two contracts coincide with the two clients represented in Fig. 1). On the other hand, as a negative consequence, we have that session contract refinement $\preceq_s$ is in general undecidable, because asynchronous subtyping $\leq$ is also undecidable as recalled in Sect. 3.

The first result is about soundness of the mapping of asynchronous session subtyping into session contract refinement, i.e., given two session types T and S, if $T \leq S$ then $[\![T]\!] \preceq_s [\![S]\!]$. In the proof of this result we exploit an intermediary result that simply formalizes the rationale behind asynchronous session subtyping that we have commented after Definition 8: given a correct session contract system, if we anticipate an output w.r.t. a preceding input context, the obtained system is still correct.

Proposition 1. *Consider the two following session contract systems*
$P_1 = [[\mathcal{A}[S_k]^{k \in \{1,\dots,m\}}], \mathcal{Q}] \| [D, \mathcal{Q}' :: l]$ *and*
$P_2 = [[\mathcal{A}[\oplus\{l.S_k\}]^{k \in \{1,\dots,m\}}], \mathcal{Q}] \| [D, \mathcal{Q}']$. *If* $P_2 \downarrow$ *then also* $P_1 \downarrow$.

Soundness is formalized by the following Theorem.

Theorem 1. *Given two session types T and S, if $T \leq S$ then $[[T]] \preceq_s [[S]]$.*

Proof. (Sketch) This theorem is proved by showing that the following relation

$$\mathcal{S} = \{ \ (\ [[S]], \mathcal{Q}] \| [D, \mathcal{Q}'] \ , \ [[T]], \mathcal{Q}] \| [D, \mathcal{Q}'] \ ) \ | \ T \leq S \ \}$$

is such that if $(P_1, P_2) \in \mathcal{S}$ and $P_1 \downarrow$, then also $P_2 \downarrow$.

To prove this result it is sufficient to consider all possible computation steps $[[T]], \mathcal{Q}] \| [D, \mathcal{Q}'] \longrightarrow P_2'$ and show that there exists P_1' such that $P_1' \downarrow$ and $(P_1', P_2') \in \mathcal{S}$. For all possible computation steps but one the proof of the above result is easy because, thanks to the subtyping simulation game, the existence of P_1' is guaranteed by a corresponding computation step $P_1 \longrightarrow P_1'$. The unique non trivial case is for send actions executed by the contract $[[T]]$. In this case the existence of P_1' is guaranteed by Proposition 1 applied to $[[S]], \mathcal{Q}]$: in fact, $[[S]]$ can have the corresponding output after some initial inputs, and P_1' is obtained by removing the output selections from $[[S]]$ and introducing the selected label directly in the partner's queue. This term P_1' is such that $P_1 \downarrow$ thanks to Proposition 1.

Given the above relation $\mathcal{S}$, as a consequence of its properties we have that if $T \leq S$ then $[[T]]$ is always a safe replacement for $[[S]]$, in every context, hence $[[T]] \preceq_s [[S]]$.   □

A second theorem states completeness, i.e., given two session types T and S, if $[[T]] \preceq_s [[S]]$ then $T \leq S$. Actually, we prove the contrapositive statement.

Theorem 2. *Given two session types T and S, if $T \not\leq S$ then $[[T]] \not\preceq_s [[S]]$.*

Proof. (Sketch) The proof of this theorem is based on the identification of a context that discriminates, in case $T \not\leq S$, the two contracts $[[T]]$ and $[[S]]$. Such a context exists under the assumption that $T \not\leq S$. The context is obtained by considering the encoding of the dual of S, i.e., the specular session type $\overline{S}$. In fact, we have that $[[S]] \| [[\overline{S}]] \downarrow$ because the two contracts follow specular protocols, while $[[T]] \| [[\overline{S}]] \downarrow$ does not hold. This last result follows from $T \not\leq S$; we consider a run of the subtyping simulation game between T and S that fails (such a run exists because $T \not\leq S$). If the computation corresponding to this run is executed by $[[T]] \| [[\overline{S}]]$, we have that a stuck system is reached, hence $[[T]] \| [[\overline{S}]] \downarrow$ does not hold.   □

As a direct corollary of the two previous Theorems we have the following full abstraction result.

Corollary 1. *Given two session types T and S, $T \leq S$ if and only if $[[T]] \preceq_s [[S]]$.*

We conclude by discussing the "fragility" of this full-abstraction result; small variations in the contract language, or in the notion of compliance, break such a result. For instance, consider a communication model (similar to actor-based communication) in which each location has only one input FIFO channel, instead of many (one for each potential sender as for CFSMs). In this model, input actions can be expressed simply with a instead of a_l, indicating that a is expected to be consumed from the unique local input queue. Under this variant output anticipation is no longer admitted. Consider, e.g., $[a.\bar{b}_{l_2}]_{l_1} \, \| [c.\bar{a}_{l_1}.b]_{l_2} \, \| \, [\bar{c}_{l_2}]_{l_3}$, which is a correct system. If we replace the contract at location l_1 with $\bar{b}_{l_2}.a$, that simply anticipates an output, we obtain $[\bar{b}_{l_2}.a]_{l_1} \, \| [c.\bar{a}_{l_1}.b]_{l_2} \, \| \, [\bar{c}_{l_2}]_{l_3}$, which is no longer correct, because in case message b (sent from l_1) is enqueued at l_2 before message c (sent from l_3), the entire system is stuck.

Consider another communication model in which there are many input queues, but instead of naming them implicitly with the sender location, we consider explicit channel names like in CCS [22] or π-calculus [5,23]. In this case, a send actions can be written $\bar{a}_{l,\pi}$, indicating that the message a should be inserted in the input queue π at location l. A receive action can be written a_π, indicating that the message a is expected to be consumed from the input queue π. Also in this model output anticipation is not admitted. In fact, we can rephrase the above counter-example as follows: $[a_{\pi_1}.\bar{b}_{l_2,\pi_2}]_{l_1} \, \| [c_{\pi_2}.\bar{a}_{l_1,\pi_1}.b_{\pi_2}]_{l_2} \, \| \, [\bar{c}_{l_2,\pi_2}]_{l_3}$.

Another interesting observation is concerned with the notion of compliance. In other papers about asynchronous behavioural contracts [12], compliance is more restrictive, in that it requires that, under fair exit from loops, the computation eventually successfully terminates. Consider, for instance, the binary system $[recX.(\bar{a}+\bar{b}.X)] \, \| \, [recX.(a+b.X)]$. It satisfies the condition above because, if we consider only fair computations, the send action $\bar{a}$ will be eventually executed thus guaranteeing successful termination. In this case, output covariance, admitted by synchronous session subtyping, is not correct. If we consider the contract $recX.(\bar{b}.X)$ having less output branches (hence following the output covariance principle), and we use it as a replacement for the first contract above, we obtain the system $[recX.(\bar{b}.X)] \, \| \, [recX.(a+b.X)]$ that does not satisfy the above definition of compliance because it cannot reach successful termination.

5   Related Work and Conclusion

In this paper we introduced a behavioural contract theory based on a definition of *compliance* (correctness of composition of a set of interacting contracts) and *refinement* (preservation of compliance under any test, i.e. set of interacting contracts): the two basic notions on which behavioural contract theories are usually based [10,11,14,19]. In particular, the definitions of behavioural contracts and compliance considered in this paper have been devised so to formally represent Communicating Finite State Machines (CFSMs) [4], i.e. systems composed by automata performing send and receive actions (the interacting contracts) that communicate by means of FIFO channels. Behavioural contracts with asynchronous communication have been previously considered, see e.g. [12]; however, to the best of our knowledge, this is the first paper defining contracts that formally represent CFSMs. Concerning [12], where at each location an independent FIFO queue of received messages is considered for each channel name "a" (enqueuing only messages of type "a" coming from any location "l_1", "l_2",...), here, instead, we consider contracts that represent CFSMs, i.e. such that, at each location, an independent FIFO queue of received messages is considered for each sender location "l" (enqueuing only messages coming from "l" and having any type "a" , "b", ...). Moreover, while in this paper we make use of a notion of compliance that corresponds to absence of deadlocking global CFSM states [4] (globally the system of interacting contracts either reaches successful completion or loops forever), in [12] a totally different definition of compliance is considered, which requires global looping behaviours to be eventually terminated under a fairness assumption.

Concerning previous work on (variants of) CFSMs, our approach has some commonalities with [20]. In [20] a restricted version of CFSMs is considered w.r.t. [4], by constraining them to be binary (a system is always composed of two CFSMs only) and not to use mixed choice (i.e. choices involving both inputs and outputs). A specific notion of compliance is considered which, besides absence of deadlocking global CFSM states [4] (i.e. compliance as in this paper) also requires each sent message to be eventually received. Thanks to a mapping from the CFSMs of [20] to session types, compliance of a CFSM A with a CFSM B is shown to correspond to subtyping, as defined in [15], between the mapped session type $T(A)$ and the dual of the mapped session type $T(B)$, i.e. $\overline{T(B)}$. With respect to the subtyping definition used in this paper, [15] adds a requirement that corresponds to the eventual reception of sent messages considered in the definition of compliance by [20]: the whole approach of [20] is critically based on the dual closeness property, i.e. $T' \leq T \Leftrightarrow \overline{T} \leq \overline{T'}$, enjoyed (only) by such a variant of subtyping. Notice that, while [20] makes use of a notion of compliance, it does not consider, as in this paper, a notion of refinement defined in terms of compliance preserving testing (as usual in behavioural contract theories where communicating entities have a syntax).

Concerning previous work on session types, our approach has some commonalities with the above mentioned [15]. The above discussed subtyping variant considered in [15] is shown to correspond to substitutability, in the context of concurrent programs written in a variant of the π-calculus, of a piece of code with session type T with a piece of code with session type T', while preserving error-freedom. A specific error-freedom notion is formalized for such a language, that corresponds to absence of communication error (similar to our notion of compliance) plus the guaranteed eventual reception of all emitted messages (an orphan-message-free property that we do not consider). While the program (context) in which the piece of code is substituted can be seen as corresponding to a test in contract refinement, the subtyping characterization in [15] is based on a specific programming language, while in this paper we consider as tests a generic, language independent, set of CFSMs and we discuss the conditions on tests under which we can characterize asynchronous session subtyping.

In this paper we, thus, discussed the notion of *refinement* over asynchronous behavioural contracts that formalize CFSMs, showing precisely under which conditions it coincides with asynchronous session subtyping, which is known to be undecidable. Under different conditions, e.g., not restricting to binary and non mixed-choice contracts only, alternative notions of refinements are obtained on which the already known undecidability results are not directly applicable. This opens a new problem, concerned with the identification of possibly decidable refinement notions for contracts/CFSMs.

References

1. Ancona, D., et al.: Behavioral types in programming languages. Found. Trends Program. Lang. **3**(2–3), 95–230 (2016)
2. Baeten, J.C.M., Bravetti, M.: A ground-complete axiomatisation of finite-state processes in a generic process algebra. Math. Struct. Comput. Sci. **18**(6), 1057–1089 (2008)
3. Bernardi, G.T., Hennessy, M.: Modelling session types using contracts. Math. Struct. Comput. Sci. **26**(3), 510–560 (2016)
4. Brand, D., Zafiropulo, P.: On communicating finite-state machines. J. ACM **30**(2), 323–342 (1983)
5. Bravetti, M.: Reduction semantics in Markovian process algebra. J. Log. Algebr. Meth. Program. **96**, 41–64 (2018)
6. Bravetti, M., Carbone, M., Lange, J., Yoshida, N., Zavattaro, G.: A sound algorithm for asynchronous session subtyping. In: Proceedings of 30th International Conference on Concurrency Theory, CONCUR 2019, Leibniz International Proceedings in Informatics. Schloss Dagstuhl (2019, to appear)
7. Bravetti, M., Carbone, M., Zavattaro, G.: Undecidability of asynchronous session subtyping. Inf. Comput. **256**, 300–320 (2017)
8. Bravetti, M., Carbone, M., Zavattaro, G.: On the boundary between decidability and undecidability of asynchronous session subtyping. Theor. Comput. Sci. **722**, 19–51 (2018)
9. Bravetti, M., Lanese, I., Zavattaro, G.: Contract-driven implementation of choreographies. In: Kaklamanis, C., Nielson, F. (eds.) TGC 2008. LNCS, vol. 5474, pp. 1–18. Springer, Heidelberg (2009). https://doi.org/10.1007/978-3-642-00945-7_1
10. Bravetti, M., Zavattaro, G.: Contract based multi-party service composition. In: Arbab, F., Sirjani, M. (eds.) FSEN 2007. LNCS, vol. 4767, pp. 207–222. Springer, Heidelberg (2007). https://doi.org/10.1007/978-3-540-75698-9_14
11. Bravetti, M., Zavattaro, G.: Towards a unifying theory for choreography conformance and contract compliance. In: Lumpe, M., Vanderperren, W. (eds.) SC 2007. LNCS, vol. 4829, pp. 34–50. Springer, Heidelberg (2007). https://doi.org/10.1007/978-3-540-77351-1_4
12. Bravetti, M., Zavattaro, G.: Contract compliance and choreography conformance in the presence of message queues. In: Bruni, R., Wolf, K. (eds.) WS-FM 2008. LNCS, vol. 5387, pp. 37–54. Springer, Heidelberg (2009). https://doi.org/10.1007/978-3-642-01364-5_3
13. Bravetti, M., Zavattaro, G.: On the expressive power of process interruption and compensation. Math. Struct. Comput. Sci. **19**(3), 565–599 (2009)

14. Castagna, G., Gesbert, N., Padovani, L.: A theory of contracts for web services. In: Proceedings of the 35th ACM SIGPLAN-SIGACT Symposium on Principles of Programming Languages, POPL 2008, pp. 261–272. ACM (2008)
15. Chen, T., Dezani-Ciancaglini, M., Scalas, A., Yoshida, N.: On the preciseness of subtyping in session types. Log. Methods Comput. Sci. **13**(2) (2017)
16. de Boer, F.S., Bravetti, M., Lee, M.D., Zavattaro, G.: A petri net based modeling of active objects and futures. Fundam. Inform. **159**(3), 197–256 (2018)
17. Gay, S.J., Hole, M.: Subtyping for session types in the pi calculus. Acta Inf. **42**(2–3), 191–225 (2005)
18. Hu, R., Yoshida, N.: Hybrid session verification through endpoint API generation. In: Stevens, P., Wąsowski, A. (eds.) FASE 2016. LNCS, vol. 9633, pp. 401–418. Springer, Heidelberg (2016). https://doi.org/10.1007/978-3-662-49665-7_24
19. Laneve, C., Padovani, L.: The *Must* preorder revisited. In: Caires, L., Vasconcelos, V.T. (eds.) CONCUR 2007. LNCS, vol. 4703, pp. 212–225. Springer, Heidelberg (2007). https://doi.org/10.1007/978-3-540-74407-8_15
20. Lange, J., Yoshida, N.: On the undecidability of asynchronous session subtyping. In: Esparza, J., Murawski, A.S. (eds.) FoSSaCS 2017. LNCS, vol. 10203, pp. 441–457. Springer, Heidelberg (2017). https://doi.org/10.1007/978-3-662-54458-7_26
21. Lindley, S., Morris, J.G.: Embedding session types in Haskell. Haskell **2016**, 133–145 (2016)
22. Milner, R.: Communication and Concurrency. Prentice Hall, Upper Saddle River (1989)
23. Milner, R., Parrow, J., Walker, D.: A calculus of mobile processes I/II. Inf. Comput. **100**(1), 1–40 (1992)
24. Mostrous, D., Yoshida, N.: Session typing and asynchronous subtyping for the higher-order π-calculus. Inf. Comput. **241**, 227–263 (2015)
25. Mostrous, D., Yoshida, N., Honda, K.: Global principal typing in partially commutative asynchronous sessions. In: Castagna, G. (ed.) ESOP 2009. LNCS, vol. 5502, pp. 316–332. Springer, Heidelberg (2009). https://doi.org/10.1007/978-3-642-00590-9_23
26. Neykova, R., Hu, R., Yoshida, N., Abdeljallal, F.: A session type provider: compile-time API generation for distributed protocols with interaction refinements in F♯. In: CC 2018. ACM (2018)
27. Orchard, D.A., Yoshida, N.: Effects as sessions, sessions as effects. POPL **2016**, 568–581 (2016)
28. Padovani, L.: A simple library implementation of binary sessions. J. Funct. Program. **27**, e4 (2017)
29. Scalas, A., Yoshida, N.: Lightweight session programming in scala. In: ECOOP 2016, pp. 21:1–21:28 (2016)

Asynchronous Cooperative Contracts
for Cooperative Scheduling

Eduard Kamburjan[1]([✉]), Crystal Chang Din[2], Reiner Hähnle[1],
and Einar Broch Johnsen[2]

[1] Department of Computer Science, Technische Universität Darmstadt,
Darmstadt, Germany
{kamburjan,haehnle}@cs.tu-darmstadt.de
[2] Department of Informatics, University of Oslo, Oslo, Norway
{crystald,einarj}@ifi.uio.no

Abstract. Formal specification of multi-threaded programs is notoriously hard, because thread execution may be preempted at any point. In contrast, abstract concurrency models such as actors seriously restrict concurrency to obtain race-free programs. Languages with *cooperative scheduling* occupy a middle ground between these extremes by explicit scheduling points. They have been used to model complex, industrial concurrent systems. This paper introduces *cooperative contracts*, a contract-based specification approach for asynchronous method calls in presence of cooperative scheduling. It permits to specify complex concurrent behavior succinctly and intuitively. We design a compositional program logic to verify cooperative contracts and discuss how global analyses can be soundly integrated into the program logic.

1 Introduction

Formal verification of complex software requires decomposition of the verification task to combat state explosion. The *design-by-contract* [41] approach associates with each method a declarative contract capturing its behavior. Contracts allow the behavior of method calls to be *approximated* by static properties. Contracts work very well for sequential programs [4], but writing contracts becomes much harder for languages such as Java or C that exhibit a low-level form of concurrency: contracts become bulky, hard to write, and even harder to understand [10]. The main culprit is *preemption*, leading to myriads of interleavings that cause complex data races which are hard to contain and to characterize.

In contrast, methods in actor-based, distributed programming [7] are executed atomically and concurrency only occurs among actors with disjoint heaps. In this setting behavior can be completely specified at the level of interfaces, typically in terms of behavioral invariants jointly maintained by an object's methods [16,19]. However, this restricted concurrency forces systems to be modeled and specified at a high level of abstraction, essentially as protocols. It precludes the modeling of concurrent behavior that is close to real programs, such as waiting for results computed asynchronously on the same processor and heap.

P. C. Ölveczky and G. Salaün (Eds.): SEFM 2019, LNCS 11724, pp. 48–66, 2019.
https://doi.org/10.1007/978-3-030-30446-1_3

Active object languages [15] occupy a middle ground between preemption and full distribution, based on an actor-like model of concurrency [3] and *futures* to handle return values from asynchronous calls (e.g., [9,13,16,21,24,40,45]). ABS [33] is an active-object language which supports *cooperative scheduling* between asynchronously called methods. With cooperative scheduling, tasks may explicitly and voluntarily suspend their execution, such that a required result may be provided by another task. This way, method activations on the same processor and heap *cooperate* to achieve a common goal. This is realized using a guarded command construct **await** f?, where f is a reference to a future. The effect of this construct is that the current task suspends itself and only resumes once the value of f is available. Although only one task can execute at any time, several tasks may depend on the same condition, which may cause internal non-determinism.

The aim of this paper is to generalize method contracts from the sequential to the active object setting with asynchronous method calls, futures and cooperative scheduling. This generalization raises the following challenges:

1. **Call Time Gap.** There is a delay between the asynchronous invocation of a method and the activation of the associated process. During this delay, the called object ("callee") may execute other processes. To enter the callee's contract the precondition must hold. But even when that precondition holds at invocation time, it does not necessarily hold at activation time.
2. **Strong Encapsulation.** Each object has exclusive access to its fields. Since the caller object cannot access the fields of the callee, it cannot ensure the validity of a contract precondition that depends on the callee's fields.
3. **Interleaving.** In cooperative scheduling, processes interleave at explicitly declared scheduling points. At these points, it is necessary to know which functional properties will hold when a process is scheduled and which properties must be guaranteed when a process is suspended.
4. **Return Time Gap.** Active objects use futures to decouple method calls from local control flow. Since futures can be passed around, an object reading a future f knows in general neither to which method f corresponds nor the postcondition that held when the result value was computed.

The main contributions of this paper are (i) a formal *specification*-by-contract technique for methods in a *concurrency context* with asynchronous calls, futures, and cooperative scheduling; and (ii) a contract-based, compositional *verification* system for functional properties of asynchronous methods that addresses the above challenges. We call our generalized contracts *cooperative contracts*, because they cooperate through propagation of conditions according to the specified concurrency context. Their concrete syntax is an extension of the popular formal specification language JML [39]. We demonstrate by example that the proposed contracts allow complex concurrent behavior to be specified in a succinct and intelligible manner. Proofs can be found in our accompanying report [38].

2   Method Contracts for Asynchronous Method Calls

We introduce the main concepts of active object (AO) languages and present the methodology of our analysis framework in an example-driven way. AO languages model loosely coupled parallel entities that communicate by means of asynchronous method calls and futures (i.e., mailboxes). They are closely tied to the OO programming paradigm and its programming abstractions. We go through an example implemented in the ABS language [2,33], an AO modeling language with cooperative scheduling which has been used to model complex, industrial concurrent systems [5].

Running Example. We consider a distributed computation of *moving averages*, a common task in data analysis that renders long-term trends clearer in smoothened data. Given data points $x_1, \ldots, x_n$, many forms of moving average $\mathsf{avg}(x_1, \ldots, x_n)$ can be expressed by a function cmp that takes the average of the first $n - 1$ data points, the last data point and a parameter α:

$$\mathsf{avg}(x_1, \ldots, x_n) = \mathrm{cmp}(\mathsf{avg}(x_1, \ldots, x_{n-1}), x_n, \alpha)$$

For example, an exponential moving average demands that α is between 0 and 1 and is expressed as $\mathsf{avg}(x_1, \ldots, x_n) = \alpha * x_n + (1 - \alpha) * \mathsf{avg}(x_1, \ldots, x_{n-1})$.

Figure 1 shows the central class Smoothing. Each Smoothing instance holds a Computation instance comp in c, where the actual computation happens and cmp is encapsulated as a method. A Smoothing instance is called with smooth, passes the data piecewise to c and collects the return values in the list of intermediate results inter. During this time, it stays responsive: getCounter lets one inquire how many data points are processed already. Decoupling list processing and value computation increases usability: one Smoothing instance may be reused with different Computation instances. There are several useful properties one would like to specify for smooth: (i) c has been assigned before it is called and is not changed during its execution, (ii) no two executions of smooth overlap during suspension and (iii) the returned result is a smoothened version of the input.

We explain some specification elements. *Atomic segments* of statements between suspension points are assigned unique names, labeled by the *annotation* [atom:"string"] at an await statement. The named scope "string" is the code segment from the end of the previous atomic segment up to the annotation. The first atomic segment starts at the beginning of a method body, the final atomic segment extends to the end of a method body and is labeled with the method name. There are sync labels at future reads, which are used to identify the statement. We use a ghost field [31] lock to model whether an invocation of smooth is running or not. A ghost field is not part of the specified code. It is read and assigned in specification annotations which are only used by the verification system.

```
 1 interface ISmoothing                    19 List<Rat> smooth(List<Rat> input, Rat a) {
 2     extends IPositive {                  20 //@ lock = True;
 3 Unit setup(Computation comp);            21 counter = 1;
 4 Int getCounter();                        22 List<Rat> work = tail(input);
 5 List<Rat>                                23 List<Rat> inter = list[input[0]];
 6     smooth(List<Rat> input, Rat a);      24 while (work != Nil) {
 7 }                                        25   Fut<Rat> f = c!cmp(last(inter), work[0], a);
 8 class Smoothing                          26   counter = counter + 1;
 9     implements ISmoothing {              27   [atom: "awSmt"] await f?;
10 Computation c = null;                    28   [sync: "sync"] Rat res = f.get;
11 Int counter = 1;                         29   inter = concat(inter, list[res]);
12 //@ ghost Bool lock = False;             30   work = tail(work);
13 Unit setup(Computation comp) {           31 }
14     c = comp;                            32 //@ lock = False;
15 }                                        33 counter = 1;
16 Int getCounter() {                       34 return inter;
17     return counter;                      35 }
18 }                                        36 }
```

Fig. 1. ABS code of the controller part of the distributed moving average

2.1 Specifying State in an Asynchronous Setting

During the delay between a method call and the start of its execution, method parameters stay invariant, but the heap may change. This motivates breaking up the precondition of asynchronous method contracts into one part for parameters and a separate part for the heap. The *parameter precondition* is guaranteed by the *caller* who knows the appropriate synchronization pattern. It is part of the callee's interface declaration and exposed to clients. (Without parameters, the parameter precondition is true.) The *callee* guarantees the *heap precondition*. It is declared in the class implementing the interface and not exposed to clients.

Example 1. The parameters of method smooth must fulfill the precondition that the passed data and parameter are valid. The heap precondition expresses that a Computation instance is stored in c.

```
interface ISmoothing { ...
/*@ requires 1 > a > 0 && len(input) > 0 @
*/
List<Rat> smooth(List<Rat> input, Rat a); }
```

```
class Smoothing { ...
/*@ requires !lock && c != null @*/
List<Rat> smooth( ... ) { ... } }
```

To handle inheritance we follow [4] and implement behavioral subtyping. If ISmoothing extended another interface IPositive, the specification of that interface is *refined* and must be implied by all ISmoothing instances:

```
interface IPositive{ ...
/*@ requires \forall Int i; 0 <= i < len(input) ; input[i] > 0 @*/
List<Rat> smooth(List<Rat> input, Rat a); }
interface  ISmoothing extends IPositive { ... } // inherits parameter precondition
```

A caller must fulfill the called method's parameter precondition, but the most recently completed process inside the callee's object establishes the heap precondition. To express this a method is specified to run in a *concurrency context*, in addition to the memory context of its heap precondition. The concurrency context appears in a contract as two *context sets*: sets with atomic segment names:

- *Succeeds:* Each atomic segment in the context set *succeeds* must guarantee the heap precondition when it terminates and at least one of them must run before the specified method starts execution.
- *Overlaps:* Each atomic segment in the context set *overlaps* must preserve the heap precondition. Between the termination of the last atomic segment from *succeeds* and the start of the execution of the specified atomic segment, only atomic segments from *overlaps* are allowed to run.

Context sets are part of the interface specification and exposed in the interface. Classes may extend context sets by adding private methods and atomic segment names. Observe that context sets represent *global information* unavailable when a method is analyzed in isolation. If context sets are not specified in the code, they default to the set of *all* atomic segments, whence the heap precondition degenerates into a class invariant and must be guaranteed by each process at each suspension point [18]. Method implementation contracts need to know their expected context, but the global protocol at the object level can be specified and exposed in a separate coordination language, such as session types [30]. This enforces a separation of concerns in specifications: method contracts are local and specify a single method and its context; the coordination language specifies a global view on the whole protocol. Of course, local method contracts and global protocols expressed with session types [36,37] must be proven consistent. Context sets can also be verified by static analysis once the whole program is available (see Sect. 2.3).

Example 2. The heap precondition of `smooth` is established by `setup` or by the termination of the previous `smooth` process. Between two sessions (and between `setup` and the start of the first session) only `getCount` may run. Recall that the method name labels the final atomic segment of the method body.

Postconditions (*ensures*) use two JML-constructs: \result refers to the return value and \last evaluates its argument in the state at the *start* of the method. We specify that the method returns a strictly positive list of equal length to the input, which is bounded by the input list. Furthermore, the object is not locked. For readability, irrelevant parts of the contracts are omitted.

```
interface ISmoothing { ...
/*@ succeeds {setup, smooth};
      overlaps {getCounter};  @*/
List<Rat> smooth(List<Rat> input, Rat a); }
class Smoothing { ...
/*@ ensures !lock && len(\result) == len(input) &&
            \forall Int i; 0 <= i < len(\result);
               \result[i] > 0 && min(input) <= \result[i] <= max(input); @*/
List<Rat> smooth(List<Rat> input, Rat a) { ... } }
```

The specified concurrency context is used to *enrich* the existing method contracts: the heap precondition of a method specified with context sets is implicitly *propagated* to the postcondition of all atomic segments in *succeeds*, and to pre- *and* postconditions of all atomic segments in *overlaps*.

Example 3. We continue Example 2. After propagation, the specifications of setup, smooth and getCounter are as follows. The origin of the propagated formula is indicated in comments.

```
/*@ ensures <as before> && !lock && c != null // succeeds smooth @*/
List<Rat> smooth(List<Rat> input, Rat a) { ... }
/*@ ensures !lock && c != null // succeeds smooth @*/
Unit setup(Computation comp) { ... }
/*@ ensures \last(!lock && c != null) -> !lock && c != null // overlaps smooth @*/
Int getCounter() { ... }
```

In case of inheritance, the context sets of the extended interface are implicitly included in those of the extending class or interface. A class may extend context sets with private methods not visible to the outside. It is the obligation of that class to ensure that private methods do not disrupt correct call sequences from the outside. From an analysis point of view, private methods are no different than public ones.

2.2 Specifying Interleavings

An **await** statement introduces a scheduling point where process execution may be suspended and possibly interleaved with the execution of other processes. From a local perspective, the **await** statement can be seen as a *suspension point* where information about the heap memory is lost. This can be addressed by similar reasoning as for heap preconditions: What is guaranteed at the release of control, what can be assumed upon reactivation, and who has the obligation to guarantee the heap property. Hence, each suspension point is annotated by a *suspension contract* containing the same elements as a method contract: An *ensures* clause for the condition that holds upon suspension, a *requires* clause for the condition which holds upon reactivation, a *succeeds* context set for the atomic segments which must have run before reactivation and an *overlaps* context set for atomic segments whose execution may interleave. (As method names label the final atomic segments, all such atomic segments contain a **return** statement. A name may refer to multiple atomic segments in case of, for example, loops.)

Example 4. We specify the behavior of the suspension point at the **await** statement with label "awSmt" (below left): At the continuation, the object is still locked and the Computation instance c must be present. During suspension, only the method getCounter is allowed to run. By adding the method itself to the succeeds set, we ensure that the suspension has to establish its own suspension assumption. The specification after *propagation* is shown below right. (The propagation from context sets into pre- and postconditions of suspension contracts is analogous to the procedure for method contracts.)

```
/*@ requires lock && c != null;
    ensures True;
    succeeds {awSmt};
    overlaps {getCounter}; @*/
[atom: "awSmt"] await f?;
```

```
/*@ requires lock && c != null;
    ensures lock && c != null;
    succeeds {awSmt};
    overlaps {getCounter}; @*/
[atom: "awSmt"] await f?;
```

The postcondition of `getCounter` is now as follows and encodes a case distinction.

```
/*@ ensures \last(!lock && c != null) -> !lock && c != null // overlaps smooth
       && \last( lock && c != null) ->  lock && c != null // overlaps awSmt @*/
Int getCounter() { ... }
```

2.3   Composition

The specification above is modular in the following sense: To prove that a method adheres to the pre- and postcondition of its own contract and respects the pre- and postcondition of called methods, only requires to analyze its own class. To verify that a system respects all context sets, however, requires global information, because the call order is not established by a single process in a single object. This separation of concerns between functional and non-functional specification allows to decompose verification into two phases that allow reuse of contracts. In the first phase, deductive verification [17] is used to *locally* show that single methods implement their pre- and postconditions correctly. In the second phase, a *global* light-weight, fully automatic dependency analysis is used to approximate call sequences. In consequence, if a method is changed with only local effects it is sufficient to re-prove its contract and re-run the dependency analysis. The proofs of the other method contracts remain unchanged.

The dependency analysis of context sets is detailed in the technical report [38]; we only give an example for rejected and accepted call sequences here.

Example 5. Consider the three code fragments interacting with a `Smoothing` instance s given below. The left fragment fails to verify the context sets specified above: although called last, method `smooth` can be executed first due to reordering, failing its *succeeds* clause. The middle fragment also fails: The first `smooth` needs not terminate before the next `smooth` activation starts. They may interleave and violate the `overlaps` set of the suspension. The right fragment verifies. We use **await** `o!m();` as a shorthand for **Fut<T>** `f = o!m();` **await** `f?;`.

```
s!setup(c);            await s!setup(c);       await s!setup(c);
s!smooth(1,0.5);       s!smooth(1,0.5);        await s!smooth(1,0.5);
s!smooth(m,0.4);       s!smooth(m,0.4);        s!smooth(m,0.4);
```

The client accessing a future might not be its creator, so properties of method parameters and class fields in the postcondition of the method associated to the future should be hidden. The postcondition in the implementation of a method may contain properties of fields, parameters and results upon termination. We abstract that postcondition into a postcondition for the corresponding method at the interface level, which only reads the result at the client side. In analogy to the split of precondition, we name the two types of postcondition *interface postcondition* and *class postcondition*, respectively. Only if the call context is known, the class postcondition may be used in addition to the interface postcondition.

$$\text{Prgm} ::= \overline{I}\ \overline{C}\ \textbf{main}\{s\} \qquad I ::= \textbf{interface}\ I\ \{\overline{S}\} \qquad C ::= \textbf{class}\ C(\overline{T\ x})\ \{\overline{M}\ \overline{T\ x = e}\}$$
$$M ::= S\{\overline{s}; \textbf{return}\ e\} \qquad S ::= T\ m(\overline{T\ x}) \qquad \textit{rhs} ::= e!m(\overline{e})\ |\ e\ |\ \textbf{new}\ C(\overline{e})$$
$$s ::= [\textbf{sync}: \text{``string''}]\, x = e.\textbf{get}\ |\ x = \textit{rhs}\ |\ [\textbf{atom}: \text{``string''}]\ \textbf{await}\ g$$
$$|\ \textbf{if}\ (e)\ \{\overline{s}\}\ \textbf{else}\ \{\overline{s}\}\ |\ \textbf{while}\ (e)\ \{\overline{s}\}\ |\ \textbf{skip} \qquad g ::= e\ |\ e?\qquad x = v\ |\ \textbf{this.f}$$

Fig. 2. Syntax of the Async language.

3 An Active Object Language

Syntax. Consider a simple active object language Async, based on ABS [33]; the syntax is shown in Fig. 2. We explain the language features related to communication and synchronization, other features are standard. Objects communicate with each other by asynchronous method calls, written $e!m(\overline{e})$, with an associated future. The value of a future f can be accessed by a statement $x = f.\textbf{get}$ once it is resolved, i.e. when the process associated with f has terminated. Futures can be shared between objects. Field access between different objects is indirect through method calls, amounting to strong encapsulation. Cooperative scheduling is realized in Async as follows: at most one process is active on an object at any time and all scheduling points are *explicit* in the code using **await** statements. The execution between these points is sequential and cannot be preempted.

Objects in Async are active. We assume that all programs are well-typed, that their main block only contains statements of the form $v = \textbf{new}\ C(\overline{e})$, and that each class has a `run()` method which is automatically activated when an instance of the class is generated. Compared to ABS, Async features optional annotations for atomic segments as discussed in Sect. 2. A *synchronize* annotation **sync** associates a label with each assignment which has a **get** right-hand side. We assume all names to be unique in a program.

Observable Behavior. A distributed system can be specified by the externally observable behavior of its parts, and the behavior of each component by the possible communication histories over its observable events [18,29]. Theoretically this is justified because fully abstract semantics of object-oriented languages are based on communication histories [32]. We strive for *compositional* communication histories of asynchronously communicating systems and use separate events for method invocation, reaction upon a method call, resolving a future, fetching the value of a future, suspending a process, reactivating a process, and for object creation. Note that each of these events is witnessed by *exactly one object*, namely the generating object; different objects do not share events.

Definition 1 (Events).

$$\text{ev} ::= \textsf{invEv}(X, X', f, \textsf{m}, \overline{\textsf{e}})\ |\ \textsf{invREv}(X, X', f, \textsf{m}, \overline{\textsf{e}})\ |\ \textsf{newEv}(X, X', \overline{\textsf{e}})\ |\ \textsf{noEv}$$
$$|\ \textsf{suspEv}(X, f, \textsf{m}, i)\ |\ \textsf{reacEv}(X, f, \textsf{m}, i)\ |\ \textsf{futEv}(X, f, \textsf{m}, \textsf{e})\ |\ \textsf{futREv}(X, f, \textsf{e}, i)$$

An invocation event invEv and an invocation reaction event invREv record the caller X, callee X′, generated future f, invoked method m, and method parameters $\bar{e}$ of a method call and its activation, respectively. A termination event futEv records the callee X, the future f, the executed method m, and the method result e when the method terminates and resolves its associated future. A future reaction event futREv records the current object X, the accessed future f, the value e stored in the future, and the label i of the associated **get** statement. A suspension event suspEv records the current object X, the current future f and method name m associated to the process being suspended, and the name i of the **await** statement that caused the suspension. Reactivation events reacEv are dual to suspension events, where the future f belongs to the process being reactivated. A new event newEv records the current object X, the created object X′ and the object initialization parameters $\bar{e}$ for object creation. The event noEv is a marker for transitions without communication.

Operational Semantics. The operational semantics of Async is given by a transition relation $\to_{ev}$ between configurations, where ev is the event generated by the transition step. We first define configurations and their transition system, before defining terminating runs and traces over this relation. A configuration C contains processes, futures, objects and messages:

$$C ::= \mathbf{prc}(X, f, \mathtt{m}(\mathtt{s}), \sigma) \mid \mathbf{fut}(f, e) \mid \mathbf{ob}(X, f, \rho) \mid \mathbf{msg}(X, X', f, \mathtt{m}, \bar{e}) \mid C\,C$$

In the runtime syntax, a process $\mathbf{prc}(X, f, \mathtt{m}(\mathtt{s}), \sigma)$ contains the current object X, the future f that will contain its execution result, the executed method m, statements s in that method, and a local state σ. A future $\mathbf{fut}(f, e)$ contains the future's identity f and the value e stored by the future. An object $\mathbf{ob}(X, f, \rho)$ contains the object identity X, the future f associated with the currently executing process, and the heap ρ of the object. Let $\bot$ denote that no process is currently executing at X. A message $\mathbf{msg}(X, X', f, \mathtt{m}, \bar{e})$ contains the caller object identity X, the callee object identity X′, the future identity f, the invoked method m, and the method parameters $\bar{e}$.

A selection of the transition rules is given in Fig. 3. Function $[\![e]\!]_{\sigma,\rho}$ evaluates an expression e in the context of a local state σ and an object heap ρ. Rule **async** expresses that the caller of an asynchronous call generates a future with a fresh identifier f' for the result and a method invocation message. An invocation event is generated to record the asynchronous call. Rule **start** represents the start of a method execution, in which an invocation reaction event is generated. The message is removed from the configuration and a new process to handle the call in created. Function M returns the body of a method, and $\widehat{M}$ returns the initial local state of a method by evaluating its parameters. Observe that a process can only start when its associated object is idle. Rule **return** resolves future f with the return value from the method activation. A termination event is generated. Rule **get** models future access. Provided that the accessed future is resolved (i.e., the future occurs in the configuration), its value can be fetched and a future reaction event generated. In this rule x is a local variable and is modified

$$(\text{async}) \frac{f' \text{ is fresh in } \mathsf{C}}{\mathbf{prc}(\mathsf{X}, f, \mathtt{m}(x = \mathtt{e!m'}(\overline{e'}); \mathtt{s}), \sigma) \; \mathbf{ob}(\mathsf{X}, f, \rho) \; \mathsf{C} \to_{\mathsf{invEv}(\mathsf{X}, [\![e]\!]_{\sigma,\rho}, f', \mathtt{m'}, [\![\overline{e'}]\!]_{\sigma,\rho})}}{\mathbf{prc}(\mathsf{X}, f, \mathtt{m}(\mathtt{s}), \sigma[x := f']) \; \mathbf{msg}(\mathsf{X}, [\![e]\!]_{\sigma,\rho}, f', \mathtt{m'}, [\![\overline{e'}]\!]_{\sigma,\rho}) \; \mathbf{ob}(\mathsf{X}, f, \rho) \; \mathsf{C}}$$

$$(\text{start}) \frac{\mathbf{msg}(\mathsf{X'}, \mathsf{X}, f, \mathtt{m}, \overline{e}) \; \mathbf{ob}(\mathsf{X}, \bot, \rho) \; \mathsf{C} \to_{\mathsf{invREv}(\mathsf{X'}, \mathsf{X}, f, \mathtt{m}, \overline{e})}}{\mathbf{prc}(\mathsf{X}, f, \mathtt{m}(M(\mathtt{m})), \widehat{M}(\mathtt{m}, \overline{e})) \; \mathbf{ob}(\mathsf{X}, f, \rho) \; \mathsf{C}}$$

$$(\text{return}) \frac{\mathbf{prc}(\mathsf{X}, f, \mathtt{m}(\mathbf{return}\ e), \sigma) \; \mathbf{ob}(\mathsf{X}, f, \rho) \; \mathsf{C} \to_{\mathsf{futEv}(\mathsf{X}, f, \mathtt{m}, e)}}{\mathbf{fut}(f, [\![e]\!]_{\sigma,\rho}) \; \mathbf{ob}(\mathsf{X}, \bot, \rho) \; \mathsf{C}}$$

$$(\text{get}) \frac{\mathbf{prc}(\mathsf{X}, f, \mathtt{m}([\mathbf{sync}:\ \text{``}i\text{''}]x = e.\mathbf{get}; \mathtt{s}), \sigma) \; \mathbf{ob}(\mathsf{X}, f, \rho) \; \mathbf{fut}([\![e]\!]_{\sigma,\rho}, e') \; \mathsf{C}}{\to_{\mathsf{futREv}(\mathsf{X}, [\![e]\!]_{\sigma,\rho}, e', i)} \mathbf{prc}(\mathsf{X}, f, \mathtt{m}(\mathtt{s}), \sigma[x := e']) \; \mathbf{ob}(\mathsf{X}, f, \rho) \; \mathbf{fut}([\![e]\!]_{\sigma,\rho}, e') \; \mathsf{C}}$$

Fig. 3. Selected operational semantics rules for Async. Further rules are in [38].

to e'. If the future is not resolved, the rule is not applicable and execution in object X is blocked.

Definition 2 (Big-Step Semantics). *Let* Prgm *be an* Async *program with initial configuration* C_1. *A run from* C_1 *to* C_n *is a finite sequence of transitions*

$$\mathsf{C}_1 \to_{\mathsf{ev}_1} \mathsf{C}_2 \to_{\mathsf{ev}_2} \cdots \to_{\mathsf{ev}_{n-1}} \mathsf{C}_n.$$

The trace *of the run is the finite sequence* $(\mathsf{ev}_1, \mathsf{C}_1), \ldots, (\mathsf{ev}_{n-1}, \mathsf{C}_{n-1}), (\mathsf{noEv}, \mathsf{C}_n)$ *of pairs of events and configurations. Program* Prgm *generates a trace* tr *if there is a run to some configuration with* tr *as the trace, such that the final configuration is terminated, i.e., has no process* **prc**.

4 Formalizing Method Contracts

To reason about logical constraints, we use *deductive verification* over *dynamic logic* (DL) [27]. It can be thought of as the language of Hoare triples, syntactically closed under logical operators and first-order quantifiers; we base our account on [4]. Assertions about program behavior are expressed in DL by integrating programs and formulas into a single language. The big step semantics of statements s is captured by the *modality* [s]post, which is true provided that the formula post holds in any terminating state of s, expressing partial correctness. The reserved program variable *heap* models the heap by mapping field names to their value [4,44]. The variable *heapOld* holds the heap the most recent time the current method was scheduled. DL features symbolic state updates on formulas of the form $\{v := t\}\varphi$, meaning that v has the value of t in φ.

We formalize method contracts in terms of constraints imposed on runs and configurations. Their semantics is given as first-order constraints over traces, with two additional primitives: the term $\mathsf{ev}^{tr}[i]$ is the i-th event in trace tr and the formula $C^{tr}[i] \models \varphi$ expresses that the i-th configuration in tr is a model for the modality-free DL formula φ. To distinguish DL from first-order logic over traces, we use the term *formula* and variables $\varphi, \psi, \chi, \ldots$ for DL and the term *constraint* and variables $\alpha, \beta, \ldots$ for first-order logic over traces.

Definition 3 (Method Contract). *Let* B *be the set of names for all atomic segments and methods in a given program. A contract for a method* C.m *has the following components:*

Context clauses. *1. A heap precondition φ_m over field symbols for* C; *2. a parameter precondition ψ_m over formal parameters of* C.m; *3. a class postcondition χ_m over formal parameters of* C.m, *field symbols for* C, *and the reserved program variable* \result; *4. an interface postcondition ζ_m only over the reserved program variable* \result. *All context clauses may also contain constants and function symbols for fixed theories, such as arithmetic.*

Context sets. *The sets* $\mathsf{succeeds}_m, \mathsf{overlaps}_m \subseteq$ B.

Suspension contracts. *For each suspension point j in* m, *a suspension contract containing 1. a suspension assumption φ_j with the same restrictions as the heap precondition; 2. a suspension assertion χ_j with the same restrictions; 3. context sets* $\mathsf{succeeds}_j, \mathsf{overlaps}_j \subseteq$ B.

Each run method has the contract $\varphi_{\mathsf{run}} = \psi_{\mathsf{run}} = \mathbf{True}$ and $\mathsf{succeeds}_{\mathsf{run}} = \emptyset$. Methods without a specification have the default contract $\varphi_m = \psi_m = \chi_m = \zeta_m = \mathbf{True}$ and $\mathsf{succeeds}_m = \mathsf{overlaps}_m = $ B. As its default contract, the main block can only create objects. A method's entry and exit points are implicit suspension points: the precondition then becomes the suspension assumption of the first atomic segment, and the postcondition becomes the suspension assertion of the last atomic segment. A suspension point may end in several atomic segments.

Contracts as Constraints. Let $\mathcal{M}_m$ be the method contract for m. The semantics of $\mathcal{M}_m$ consists of three constraints over traces (formalized in Definitions 4 and 5 below): (i) $\mathsf{assert}(\mathcal{M}_m, tr)$ expresses that the postcondition and all suspension assertions hold in tr; (ii) $\mathsf{assume}(\mathcal{M}_m, tr)$ that the precondition and all suspension assumptions hold in tr; (iii) $\mathsf{context}(\mathcal{M}_m, tr)$ that context sets describe the behavior of the object in tr. If the method name is clear from the context, we write $\mathcal{M}$ instead of $\mathcal{M}_m$. In the constraints, all unbound symbols are implicitly universally quantified, such as f, e, X, etc.

Definition 4 (Semantics of Context Clauses). *Let $\mathcal{M}_m$ be a method contract, tr a trace, and* $\mathsf{susp}(m)$ *the set of suspension points in* m:

$$\mathsf{assert}(\mathcal{M}_m, tr) = \forall i \in \mathbb{N}.\ \mathsf{ev}^{tr}[i] \doteq \mathsf{futEv}(X, f, m, e) \to C^{tr}[i] \models \chi_m \wedge \zeta_m$$
$$\wedge\ \forall j \in \mathsf{susp}(m).\ \forall i \in \mathbb{N}.\ \mathsf{ev}^{tr}[i] \doteq \mathsf{suspEv}(X, f, m, j) \to C^{tr}[i] \models \chi_j$$
$$\mathsf{assume}(\mathcal{M}_m, tr) = \forall i \in \mathbb{N}.\ \mathsf{ev}^{tr}[i] \doteq \mathsf{invREv}(X', X, f, m, \bar{e}) \to C^{tr}[i] \models \varphi_m \wedge \psi_m$$
$$\wedge\ \forall j \in \mathsf{susp}(m).\ \forall i \in \mathbb{N}.\ \mathsf{ev}^{tr}[i] \doteq \mathsf{reacEv}(X, f, m, j) \to C^{tr}[i] \models \varphi_j$$

The third constraint context models context sets and is defined for both method and suspension contracts. In contrast to context clauses, it constrains the order of events belonging to different processes. The constraint $\mathsf{context}(\mathcal{S}_n, tr)$ formalizes the context sets of a suspension contract $\mathcal{S}_n$ for suspension point n: Before a reactivation event at position i in tr, there is a terminating event at a position $k < i$ on the same object from the *succeeds* set, such that all terminating events on the object at positions k' with $k < k' < i$ are from the *overlaps* set.

Definition 5 (Semantics of Context Sets). *Let $\mathcal{S}_n$ be a suspension contract, tr a trace, and $\mathsf{termEvent}(i)$ the terminating event of i, where i may be either a method name or the name of a suspension point. The predicate $\mathsf{isClose}(\mathsf{ev}^{tr}[i])$ holds if $\mathsf{ev}^{tr}[i]$ is a suspension or future event. The semantics of context sets of a suspension contract $\mathcal{S}_n$ is defined by the following constraint $\mathsf{context}(\mathcal{S}_n, tr)$:*

$$\forall i, i' \in \mathbb{N}. \ \left(\mathsf{ev}^{tr}[i] \doteq \mathsf{reacEv}(\mathsf{X}, f, \mathtt{m}, n) \wedge \mathsf{ev}^{tr}[i'] \doteq \mathsf{suspEv}(\mathsf{X}, f, \mathtt{m}, n)\right) \rightarrow$$

$$\exists k \in \mathbb{N}. \ i' < k < i \wedge \Big(\bigvee_{j' \in \mathsf{succeeds}_n} \mathsf{ev}^{tr}[k] \doteq \mathsf{termEvent}(j') \ \wedge$$

$$\forall k' \in \mathbb{N}. \ k < k' < i \wedge \mathsf{isClose}(\mathsf{ev}^{tr}[k']) \rightarrow \Big(\bigvee_{j' \in \mathsf{overlaps}_n} \mathsf{ev}^{tr}[k'] \doteq \mathsf{termEvent}(j') \Big)\Big)$$

The predicate $\mathsf{context}(\mathcal{M}_\mathtt{m}, tr)$ for method contracts is defined similarly, but includes an extra conjunction of the $\mathsf{context}(\mathcal{S}_n, tr)$ constraints for all $\mathcal{S}_n$ in $\mathcal{M}_\mathtt{m}$.

Context sets describe behavior required from other methods, so method contracts are not independent of each other. Each referenced method or method in a context set must have a contract which proves the precondition (or suspension assumption). Recall that method names are names for the last atomic segment, φ_i is the heap precondition/suspension assumption of atomic segment i and χ_i is its postcondition/suspension assertion. The following definition formalizes the intuition we gave about the interplay of context sets, i.e. that the atomic segments in the succeeds set establish a precondition/suspension assumption and the atomic segments in overlaps preserve a precondition/suspension assumption.

Definition 6 (Coherence). *Let $\mathsf{CNF}(\varphi)$ be the conjunctive normal form of φ, such that all function and relation symbols also adhere to some theory specific normal form. Let M be a set of method contracts. M is coherent if for each method and suspension contract $\mathcal{S}_i$ in M, the following holds:*

- *The assertion χ_j of each atomic segment j in $\mathsf{succeeds}_i$ guarantees assumption φ_i: Each conjunct of $\mathsf{CNF}(\varphi_i)$ is a conjunct of $\mathsf{CNF}(\chi_j)$*
- *Each atomic segment j in $\mathsf{overlaps}_i$ preserves suspension assumption φ_i: suspension assertion χ_j has the form $\chi_j' \wedge \left((\{heap := heapOld\}\varphi_i) \rightarrow \varphi_i\right)$.*

A program is coherent if the set of all its method contracts is coherent.

This notion of coherence is easy to enforce and to check syntactically.

Lemma 1 (Sound Propagation). *Given a non-coherent set of method contracts M, a coherent set $\widehat{M}$ can be generated from M, such that for every contract $\mathcal{M} \in M$ there is a $\widehat{\mathcal{M}} \in \widehat{M}$ with identical context sets and*

$$\forall tr. \left(\mathsf{assert}(\widehat{\mathcal{M}}, tr) \to \mathsf{assert}(\mathcal{M}, tr)\right) \wedge \left(\mathsf{assume}(\widehat{\mathcal{M}}, tr) \leftrightarrow \mathsf{assume}(\mathcal{M}, tr)\right)$$

The requirement for $\widehat{M}$ ensures that the new, coherent contracts extend the old contracts. In the border case where all context sets contain all blocks, all heap preconditions and suspension assumptions become invariants.

5   Verification

Method contracts appear in comments before their interface and class declaration, following JML [39]. Our specifications use DL formulas directly, extended with a \last operator referring to the evaluation of a formula in the state where the current method was last scheduled, i.e. the most recent reactivation/method start. Restrictions on the occurrence of fields and parameters are as above.

Definition 7. *Let* str *range over strings, φ over DL formulas. The clauses used for specification are defined as follows:*

Spec ::= /*@ Require Ensure Runs @*/ $\psi ::= \varphi \mid \backslash last(\varphi)$
Require ::= *requires* ψ;   Ensure ::= *ensures* ψ;   Runs ::= *succeeds* $\overline{\mathtt{str}}$; *overlaps* $\overline{\mathtt{str}}$;

We do not consider loop invariants here which are standard. For ghost fields and ghost assignments, we follow JML [39].

As described above, our program logic for deductive verification is a dynamic logic based on the work of Din et al. [18]. The verification of context sets is *not* part of the program logic: our soundness theorem requires that the context sets are adhered to, in addition to proving the DL proof obligations. Context sets, however, can be verified with light-weight causality-based approaches, such as May-Happen-in-Parallel analysis [6]. Separating the DL proof obligation from the causal structure allows us to give a relatively simple proof system and reuse existing techniques to verify the context sets.

The DL calculus rewrites a formula [s;r]post with a leading statement s into the formula [r]post with suitable first-order constraints. Repeated rule application yields symbolic execution of the program in the modality. *Updates* (see Sect. 4) accumulate during symbolic execution to capture state changes; e.g., [v = e; r]post is rewritten to {v := e}[r]post, expressing that v has the value of e during the symbolic execution of r. When a program s has been completely executed, the modality is empty and the accumulated updates are applied to the postcondition post, resulting in a pure first-order formula that represents the weakest precondition of s and post. We use a sequent calculus to prove validity of DL formulas [4,17]. In sequent notation pre $\to$ [s]post is written as Γ, pre $\implies$ [s]post, Δ, where Γ and Δ are (possibly empty) sets of side formulas. A formal proof is a tree of proof rule applications leading from axioms to a formula (a theorem). The formal semantics is described in [38].

$$(\text{local}) \quad \frac{\Longrightarrow \{U\}\{\mathtt{v} := \mathtt{e}\}[\mathtt{s}]\chi}{\Longrightarrow \{U\}[\mathtt{v} = \mathtt{e};\mathtt{s}]\chi} \qquad (\text{field}) \quad \frac{\Longrightarrow \{U\}\{heap := store(heap, \mathtt{f}, \mathtt{e})\}[\mathtt{s}]\chi}{\Longrightarrow \{U\}[\mathtt{this.f} = \mathtt{e};\mathtt{s}]\chi}$$

$$(\text{async}) \quad \frac{\begin{array}{c} \Longrightarrow \{U\}\psi_{\mathtt{m}}(\bar{\mathtt{e}}) \\ fresh(\mathtt{f}, \mathfrak{t}) \Longrightarrow \{U\}\{\mathtt{v}:=\mathtt{f}\}\{\mathfrak{t} := \mathfrak{t} \cdot invEv(\mathtt{this}, \mathtt{o}, \mathtt{f}, \mathtt{m}, \bar{\mathtt{e}})\}[\mathtt{s}]\chi \end{array}}{\Longrightarrow \{U\}[\mathtt{v} = \mathtt{o!m}(\bar{\mathtt{e}});\mathtt{s}]\chi}$$

$$(\text{get-m}) \quad \frac{\begin{array}{c} fresh(\mathtt{r}, \mathfrak{t}), \{U\} (\exists\, \mathtt{Int}\; \mathtt{j};\; invocOn(\mathfrak{t}[j], \mathtt{f}, \mathtt{m}) \rightarrow \zeta_{\mathtt{m}}(\mathtt{r})) \Longrightarrow \\ \{U\}\{\mathtt{v}:=\mathtt{r}\}\{\mathfrak{t} := \mathfrak{t} \cdot futREv(\mathtt{this}, \mathtt{f}, \mathtt{r}, i)\}[\mathtt{s}]\chi \end{array}}{\Longrightarrow \{U\}[[\mathtt{sync}:\; \texttt{"i"}]\; \mathtt{v} = \mathtt{f.get};\mathtt{s}]\chi}$$

$$(\text{await}) \quad \frac{\begin{array}{c} \Longrightarrow \{U\}\{\mathfrak{t} := \mathfrak{t} \cdot suspEv(\mathtt{this}, \mathfrak{f}, \mathtt{m}, i)\}\chi_i \\ fresh(t, \mathfrak{t}) \Longrightarrow \{U\}\{\mathfrak{t} := \mathfrak{t} \cdot suspEv(\mathtt{this}, \mathfrak{f}, \mathtt{m}, i)\}\{heapOld := heap\} \\ \{heap := heap_A\}\{\mathfrak{t} := \mathfrak{t} \cdot t \cdot reacEv(\mathtt{this}, \mathfrak{f}, \mathtt{m}, i)\}(\varphi_i \rightarrow [\mathtt{s}]\chi) \end{array}}{\Longrightarrow \{U\}[[\mathtt{atom}:\; \texttt{"i"}]\; \mathbf{await}\; \mathtt{f?};\mathtt{s}]\chi}$$

Fig. 4. Selected DL proof rules.

We formulate DL proof obligations for the correctness of method contracts, given a method m with body s and contract $\mathcal{M}_{\mathtt{m}}$ as in Definition 3, as follows:

$$\varphi_{\mathtt{m}}, \psi_{\mathtt{m}}, \mathsf{wellFormed}(trace) \Longrightarrow \{heapOld := heap\} \qquad (\text{PO})$$
$$\{\mathfrak{t} := trace\}\{\mathtt{this} := o\}\{\mathfrak{f} := f\}\{\mathtt{m} := \mathtt{m}\}[\mathtt{s}]\widetilde{\chi_{\mathtt{m}}}$$

The heap and parameter preconditions $\varphi_{\mathtt{m}}$ and $\psi_{\mathtt{m}}$ of $\mathcal{M}_{\mathtt{m}}$ are assumed when execution starts, likewise it is assumed that the trace of the object up to now is well-formed. The class postcondition $\widetilde{\chi_{\mathtt{m}}}$ is modified, because \last is part of the specification language, but not of the logic: Any heap access in the argument of \last is replaced by $heapOld$. Reserved variables $\mathfrak{t}$, this, $\mathfrak{f}$, and m record the current trace, object, future, and method, respectively, during symbolic execution.

The above proof obligation must be proved for each method of a program using schematic proof rules as shown in Fig. 4. There is one rule for each kind of Async statement. We omit the standard rules for sequential statements. To improve readability, we leave out the sequent contexts Γ, Δ and assume that all formulas are evaluated relative to a current update U representing all symbolic updates of local variables, the heap, as well as $\mathfrak{t}$, this, $\mathfrak{f}$, m up to this point. These updates are extended in the premisses of some rules.

Rule **local** captures updates of local variables by side-effect free expressions. Rule **field** captures updates of class fields by side-effect free expressions. It is nearly identical to **local**, except the heap is updated with the *store* function. This function follows the usual definition from the theory of arrays to model heaps in dynamic logics [44]. Rule **async** for assignments with an asynchronous method call has two premisses. The first establishes the parameter precondition $\psi_{\mathtt{m}}$ of $\mathcal{M}_{\mathtt{m}}$. The second creates a fresh future f relative to the current trace $\mathfrak{t}$ to hold the result of the call. In the succedent an invocation event recording the call is generated and symbolic execution continues uninterrupted. We stress that the called method is syntactically known.

For each method m we define a rule **get**-m. It creates a fresh constant r representing the value stored in future f. Per se, nothing about this value is known. However, the term in the antecedent of the premise expresses that *if* it is possible to show that the future stored in f stems from a call on m, then the postcondition of m can be assumed to show r. The predicate $\mathsf{invocOn}(\mathsf{ev}, f, \mathsf{m})$ holds if the event ev is an invocation reaction event with future f on method m.

Rule **await** handles process suspension. The first premise proves the postcondition χ_i of the suspension contract $\mathcal{S}_i$ in the current trace, extended by a suspension event. When resuming execution we can only use the suspension assumption φ_i of $\mathcal{S}_i$; the remaining heap must be reset by an "anonymizing update' $heap_A$ [4,44], which is a fresh function symbol. Also a reaction event is generated. In both events f is not the future in the **await** statement, but the currently computed future that is suspended and reactivated.

Theorem 1 (Soundness of Compositional Reasoning). *Let $\widehat{M}$ be the coherent set generated from the method contracts M of a program* Prgm. *If*

(i) $\mathsf{context}(\mathcal{M}_\mathsf{m}, tr)$ *holds for all methods and generated traces, and*
(ii) for each $\mathcal{M}_\mathsf{m} \in \widehat{M}$, *the proof obligation (PO) for* m *holds,*

then the following holds for all terminating traces tr *of* Prgm:

$$\bigwedge_{\mathcal{M}_\mathsf{m} \in \widehat{M}} \left(\mathsf{assert}(\mathcal{M}_\mathsf{m}, tr) \wedge \mathsf{assume}(\mathcal{M}_\mathsf{m}, tr) \right)$$

6   Related Work and Conclusion

Related Work. Wait conditions were introduced as program statements (not in method contracts) in the pioneering work of Brinch-Hansen [25,26] and Hoare [28]. SCOOP [8] explores preconditions as wait/when conditions. Previous approaches to AO verification [16,18] consider only object invariants that must be preserved by every atomic segment of every method. As discussed, this is a special case of our system. Actor services [43] are compositional event patterns for modular reasoning about asynchronous message passing for actors. They are formulated for pure actors and do not address futures or cooperative scheduling. Method preconditions are restricted to input values, the heap is specified by an object invariant. A rely-guarantee proof system [1,34] implemented on top of Frama-C by Gavran et al. [22] demonstrated modular proofs of partial correctness for asynchronous C programs restricted to using the Libevent library.

Contracts for channel-based communication are partly supported by session types [11,30]. These have been adapted to the AO concurrency model [37], including assertions on heap memory [36], but they require composition to be explicit in the specification. Stateful session types for active objects [36] contain a propagation step (cf. Sect. 2.1): Postconditions are propagated to preconditions of methods that are specified to run subsequently. In contrast, the propagation in the current paper goes in the opposite direction, where a contract specifies what a method *relies* on and one propagates to the method that is obliged to prove it. Session types, with their global system view, specify an *obligation* for a method and propagate to the methods that can rely on it.

Compositional specification of concurrency models outside rely-guarantee was mainly proposed based on separation logic [12,42]. Closest to our line of research are shared regions [20] which relate predicates over the heap that must be stable, i.e. invariant, when accessed. Even though approaches to specify regions precisely have been developed [14,20], their combination with interaction modes beyond heap access (such as asynchronous calls and futures) is not well explored. It is worth noting that AO do not require the concept of regions in the logic, because strong encapsulation and cooperative scheduling ensure that two threads never run in parallel on the same heap. The central goal of separation *logic*—separation of heaps—is a design feature of the AO *concurrency model*.

Conclusion. This paper generalizes rely-guarantee reasoning with method contracts from sequential OO programs to active objects with asynchronous method calls and cooperative scheduling. The main challenges are: the delay between the invocation and the actual start of a method, strong object encapsulation, and interleaving of atomic segments via cooperative scheduling. To deal with these issues, preconditions of contracts are separated into a caller specification (parameter precondition) and a callee specification (heap precondition); likewise, into an interface postcondition and a class postcondition. The heap precondition and the class postcondition can be stronger than a class invariant, because they do not need to be respected by all methods of a class. Instead, context sets specify those methods that establish or preserve the heap precondition. The context sets are justified separately via a global analysis of possible call sequences. This separation of concerns enables class-modular verification. Preconditions need not contain global information, rather, this is automatically propagated within a class with the help of external global analyses.

Future Work. In this paper, we did not consider all features present in synchronous method contracts, such as termination witnesses [23], and it is unclear how these can be used in an asynchronous setting due to interleaving. Other contract extensions, such as exceptional behavior [4], are largely orthogonal to concurrency and could be easily added. Furthermore, we plan to explore recursion: In this case, specifications working with program-point identifiers, i.e. at the statement-level, are not precise enough, because they cannot distinguish between multiple processes of the same method.

Beyond implementation and addition of features from synchronous method contracts, we plan to connect cooperative contracts with our work on session types [36] with the aim to integrate local and global specifications by formulating them in the framework of Behavioral Program Logic [35]. We also expect such a formalization to enable runtime verification.

Acknowledgments. This work is supported by the SIRIUS Centre for Scalable Data Access and the FormbaR project, part of AG Signalling/DB RailLab in the Innovation Alliance of Deutsche Bahn AG and TU Darmstadt.

References

1. Abadi, M., Lamport, L.: Conjoining specifications. ACM Trans. Program. Lang. Syst. **17**(3), 507–534 (1995)
2. ABS Development Team. The ABS Language Specification, January 2018. http://docs.abs-models.org/
3. Agha, G., Hewitt, C.: Actors: a conceptual foundation for concurrent object-oriented programming. In: Research Directions in Object-Oriented Programming, pp. 49–74. MIT Press (1987)
4. Ahrendt, W., Beckert, B., Bubel, R., Hähnle, R., Schmitt, P.H., Ulbrich, M. (eds.): Deductive Software Verification - The KeY Book - From Theory to Practice. LNCS, vol. 10001. Springer, Heidelberg (2016). https://doi.org/10.1007/978-3-319-49812-6
5. Albert, E., et al.: Formal modeling of resource management for cloud architectures: an industrial case study using real-time ABS. J. Serv.-Oriented Comput. Appl. **8**(4), 323–339 (2014)
6. Albert, E., Flores-Montoya, A., Genaim, S., Martin-Martin, E.: May-happen-in-parallel analysis for actor-based concurrency. ACM Trans. Comput. Log. **17**(2), 11:1–11:39 (2016)
7. Armstrong, J.: Programming Erlang: Software for a Concurrent World. Pragmatic Bookshelf Series, Pragmatic Bookshelf (2007)
8. Arslan, V., Eugster, P., Nienaltowski, P., Vaucouleur, S.: SCOOP - concurrency made easy. In: Dependable Systems: Software, Computing, Networks, Research Results of the DICS Program, pp. 82–102 (2006)
9. Baker, H.G., Hewitt, C.E.: The incremental garbage collection of processes. In: Proceeding of the Symposium on Artificial Intelligence Programming Languages, Number 12 in SIGPLAN Notices, p. 11, August 1977
10. Baumann, C., Beckert, B., Blasum, H., Bormer, T.: Lessons learned from micro-kernel verification - specification is the new bottleneck. In: Cassez, F., Huuck, R., Klein, G., Schlich, B. (eds.) Proceedings of the 7th Conference on Systems Software Verification, volume 102 of EPTCS, pp. 18–32 (2012)
11. Bocchi, L., Lange, J., Tuosto, E.: Three algorithms and a methodology for amending contracts for choreographies. Sci. Ann. Comp. Sci. **22**(1), 61–104 (2012)
12. Brookes, S., O'Hearn, P.W.: Concurrent separation logic. ACM SIGLOG News **3**(3), 47–65 (2016)
13. Caromel, D., Henrio, L., Serpette, B. Asynchronous and deterministic objects. In: Proceedings of the 31st ACM Symposium on Principles of Programming Languages (POPL 2004), pp. 123–134. ACM Press (2004)
14. da Rocha Pinto, P., Dinsdale-Young, T., Gardner, P.: TaDA: a logic for time and data abstraction. In: Jones, R. (ed.) ECOOP 2014. LNCS, vol. 8586, pp. 207–231. Springer, Heidelberg (2014). https://doi.org/10.1007/978-3-662-44202-9_9

15. de Boer, F., et al.: A survey of active object languages. ACM Comput. Surv. **50**(5), 76:1–76:39 (2017)
16. de Boer, F.S., Clarke, D., Johnsen, E.B.: A complete guide to the future. In: De Nicola, R. (ed.) ESOP 2007. LNCS, vol. 4421, pp. 316–330. Springer, Heidelberg (2007). https://doi.org/10.1007/978-3-540-71316-6_22
17. Din, C.C., Bubel, R., Hähnle, R.: KeY-ABS: a deductive verification tool for the concurrent modelling language ABS. In: Felty, A.P., Middeldorp, A. (eds.) CADE 2015. LNCS (LNAI), vol. 9195, pp. 517–526. Springer, Cham (2015). https://doi.org/10.1007/978-3-319-21401-6_35
18. Din, C.C., Owe, O.: Compositional reasoning about active objects with shared futures. Form. Asp. Comput. **27**(3), 551–572 (2015)
19. Din, C.C., Tapia Tarifa, S.L., Hähnle, R., Johnsen, E.B.: History-based specification and verification of scalable concurrent and distributed systems. In: Butler, M., Conchon, S., Zaïdi, F. (eds.) ICFEM 2015. LNCS, vol. 9407, pp. 217–233. Springer, Cham (2015). https://doi.org/10.1007/978-3-319-25423-4_14
20. Dinsdale-Young, T., da Rocha Pinto, P., Gardner, P.: A perspective on specifying and verifying concurrent modules. J. Log. Algebr. Methods Program. **98**, 1–25 (2018)
21. Flanagan, C., Felleisen, M.: The semantics of future and an application. J. Funct. Program. **9**(1), 1–31 (1999)
22. Gavran, I., Niksic, F., Kanade, A., Majumdar, R., Vafeiadis, V.: Rely/guarantee reasoning for asynchronous programs. In: Aceto, L., de Frutos Escrig, D. (eds.) 26th International Conference on Concurrency Theory (CONCUR 2015), volume 42 of Leibniz International Proceedings in Informatics (LIPIcs), pp. 483–496. Schloss Dagstuhl-Leibniz-Zentrum fuer Informatik (2015)
23. Grahl, D., Bubel, R., Mostowski, W., Schmitt, P.H., Ulbrich, M., Weiß, B.: Modular specification and verification. Deductive Software Verification – The KeY Book. LNCS, vol. 10001, pp. 289–351. Springer, Cham (2016). https://doi.org/10.1007/978-3-319-49812-6_9
24. Halstead Jr., R.H.: MULTILISP: a language for concurrent symbolic computation. ACM Trans. Program. Lang. Syst. **7**(4), 501–538 (1985)
25. Hansen, P.B.: Structured multiprogramming. Commun. ACM **15**(7), 574–578 (1972)
26. Hansen, P.B.: Operating System Principles. Prentice-Hall Inc., Upper Saddle River (1973)
27. Harel, D., Kozen, D., Tiuryn, J.: Dynamic logic. SIGACT News **32**(1), 66–69 (2001)
28. Hoare, C.A.R.: Towards a theory of parallel programming. In: Operating System Techniques, pp. 61–71 (1972)
29. Hoare, C.A.R.: Communicating Sequential Processes. Prentice-Hall Inc., Upper Saddle River (1985)
30. Honda, K., Yoshida, N., Carbone, M.: Multiparty asynchronous session types. In: Proceedings of the 35th ACM SIGPLAN-SIGACT Symposium on Principles of Programming Languages, POPL 2008, pp. 273–284 (2008)
31. Huisman, M., Ahrendt, W., Grahl, D., Hentschel, M.: Formal specification with the Java modeling language. Deductive Software Verification – The KeY Book. LNCS, vol. 10001, pp. 193–241. Springer, Cham (2016). https://doi.org/10.1007/978-3-319-49812-6_7
32. Jeffrey, A., Rathke, J.: Java JR: fully abstract trace semantics for a core Java language. In: Sagiv, M. (ed.) ESOP 2005. LNCS, vol. 3444, pp. 423–438. Springer, Heidelberg (2005). https://doi.org/10.1007/978-3-540-31987-0_29

33. Johnsen, E.B., Hähnle, R., Schäfer, J., Schlatte, R., Steffen, M.: ABS: a core language for abstract behavioral specification. In: Aichernig, B.K., de Boer, F.S., Bonsangue, M.M. (eds.) FMCO 2010. LNCS, vol. 6957, pp. 142–164. Springer, Heidelberg (2011). https://doi.org/10.1007/978-3-642-25271-6_8
34. Jones, C.B.: Tentative steps toward a development method for interfering programs. ACM Trans. Program. Lang. Syst. **5**(4), 596–619 (1983)
35. Kamburjan, E.: Behavioral program logic. To appear in the proceedings of TABLEAUX 2019, technical report. https://arxiv.org/abs/1904.13338
36. Kamburjan, E., Chen, T.-C.: Stateful behavioral types for active objects. In: Furia, C.A., Winter, K. (eds.) IFM 2018. LNCS, vol. 11023, pp. 214–235. Springer, Cham (2018). https://doi.org/10.1007/978-3-319-98938-9_13
37. Kamburjan, E., Din, C.C., Chen, T.-C.: Session-based compositional analysis for actor-based languages using futures. In: Ogata, K., Lawford, M., Liu, S. (eds.) ICFEM 2016. LNCS, vol. 10009, pp. 296–312. Springer, Cham (2016). https://doi.org/10.1007/978-3-319-47846-3_19
38. Kamburjan, E., Din, C.C., Hähnle, R., Johnsen, E.B.: Asynchronous cooperative contracts for cooperative scheduling. Technical report, TU Darmstadt (2019). http://formbar.raillab.de/en/techreportcontract/
39. Leavens, G.T., et al.: JML Reference Manual, May 2013. Draft revision 2344
40. Liskov, B.H., Shrira, L.: Promises: linguistic support for efficient asynchronous procedure calls in distributed systems. In: Wise, D.S. (ed.) Proceedings of the SIGPLAN Conference on Programming Language Design and Implementation (PLDI 1988), pp. 260–267. ACM Press, June 1988
41. Meyer, B.: Applying "design by contract". IEEE Comput. **25**(10), 40–51 (1992)
42. O'Hearn, P., Reynolds, J., Yang, H.: Local reasoning about programs that alter data structures. In: Fribourg, L. (ed.) CSL 2001. LNCS, vol. 2142, pp. 1–19. Springer, Heidelberg (2001). https://doi.org/10.1007/3-540-44802-0_1
43. Summers, A.J., Müller, P.: Actor services. In: Thiemann, P. (ed.) ESOP 2016. LNCS, vol. 9632, pp. 699–726. Springer, Heidelberg (2016). https://doi.org/10.1007/978-3-662-49498-1_27
44. Weiß, B.: Deductive verification of object-oriented software: dynamic frames, dynamic logic and predicate abstraction. Ph.D. thesis, Karlsruhe Institute of Technology (2011)
45. Yonezawa, A., Briot, J.-P., Shibayama, E.: Object-oriented concurrent programming in ABCL/1. In: Conference on Object-Oriented Programming Systems, Languages and Applications (OOPSLA 1986). Sigplan Notices, vol. 21, no. 11, pp. 258–268, November 1986

Cyber-Physical Systems

Automatic Failure Explanation in CPS Models

Ezio Bartocci[1], Niveditha Manjunath[1,2(✉)], Leonardo Mariani[3],
Cristinel Mateis[2], and Dejan Ničković[2]

[1] Vienna University of Technology, Vienna, Austria
[2] AIT Austrian Institute of Technology, Vienna, Austria
niveditha.manjunath@ait.ac.al
[3] University of Milano-Bicocca, Milan, Italy

Abstract. Debugging Cyber-Physical System (CPS) models can be extremely complex. Indeed, only detection of a failure is insufficient to know how to correct a faulty model. Faults can propagate in time and in space producing observable misbehaviours in locations completely different from the location of the fault. Understanding the reason of an observed failure is typically a challenging and laborious task left to the experience and domain knowledge of the designers.

In this paper, we propose CPSDebug, a novel approach that combines testing, specification mining, and failure analysis, to automatically explain failures in Simulink/Stateflow models. We evaluate CPSDebug on two case studies, involving two use scenarios and several classes of faults, demonstrating the potential value of our approach.

1 Introduction

Cyber-Physical Systems (CPS) combine computational and physical entities that interact with sophisticated and unpredictable environments via sensors and actuators. To cost-efficiently study their behavior, engineers typically apply model-based development methodologies, which combine modeling and simulation activities with prototyping. The successful development of CPS is thus strongly dependent on the quality and correctness of their models.

CPS models can be extremely complex: they may include hundreds of variables, signals, look-up tables and components, combining continuous and discrete dynamics. Verification and testing activities are thus of critical importance to early detect problems in the models [2,5,7,16,17], before they propagate to the actual CPS. Discovering faults is however only a part of the problem. Due to their complexity, debugging CPS models by identifying the causes of failures can be as challenging as identifying problems themselves [15].

CPS functionalities are often modelled using the MathWorks™ Simulink environment where *falsification-based testing* can be used to find bugs in Simulink/Stateflow models [2,22,25]. This approach is based on quantifying (by monitoring [4]) how much a simulated trace of CPS behavior is close to violate a requirement expressed in a formal specification language, such as Signal

© Springer Nature Switzerland AG 2019
P. C. Ölveczky and G. Salaün (Eds.): SEFM 2019, LNCS 11724, pp. 69–86, 2019.
https://doi.org/10.1007/978-3-030-30446-1_4

Temporal Logic (STL) [20]. This measure enables a systematic exploration of the input space searching for the first input sequence responsible for a violation. However, this method does not provide any suitable information about which components should be inspected to resolve the violation. Trace diagnostics [10] identifies (small) segments of the observable model behavior that are sufficient to imply the violation of the formula, thus providing a failure explanation at the input/output model interface level. However, this is a black-box technique that does not attempt to delve into the model and explain the failure in terms of its internal signals and components.

In this paper, we advance the knowledge in failure analysis of CPS models by presenting CPSDebug, a debugging technique that combines testing, specification mining, and failure analysis to identify the causes of failures. CPSDebug first exercises the CPS model under analysis by running the available test cases, while discriminating passing and failing executions using requirements formalized as a set of STL formulas. While running the test cases, CPSDebug records information about the internal behavior of the CPS model, In particular, it collects the values of all internal system variables at every timestamp. The values collected from passing test cases are used to infer properties about the variables and components involved in the computations. These properties capture the correct behavior of the system.

CPSDebug checks the mined properties against the traces collected from failed test cases to discover the internal variables, and its corresponding components, that are responsible for the violation of the requirements. Finally, failure evidence is analyzed using trace diagnostics [10] and clustering [12] to produce a time-ordered sequence of snapshots that show where the anomalous variables values originated and how they propagated within the system.

CPSDebug thus overcomes the limitation of state of the art approaches that do not guide engineers in the analysis, but only indicate the inputs or code locations that might be responsible for the failure. The sequence of snapshots returned by CPSDebug provides a step by step illustration of the failure with explicit indication of the faulty behaviors. We evaluated CPSDebug against three classes of faults and two actual CPS models. Results suggest that CPSDebug can effectively and efficiently assist developers in their debugging tasks. The feedback that we collected from industry engineers further confirmed that the output produced by CPSDebug can be indeed valuable to ease failure analysis and debugging of CPS models.

The rest of the paper is organized as follows. We provide background information in Sect. 2 and we describe the case study in Sect. 3. In Sect. 4 we present our approach for failure explanation while in Sect. 5 we provide the empirical evaluation. We discuss the related work in Sect. 6 and we draw our conclusions in Sect. 7.

2   Background

2.1   Signals and Signal Temporal Logic

We define $S = \{s_1, \ldots, s_n\}$ to be a set of signal variables. A *signal* or *trace* w is a function $\mathbb{T} \to \mathbb{R}^n$, where $\mathbb{T}$ is the time domain in the form of $[0, d] \subset \mathbb{R}$. We can also see a multi-dimensional signal w as a vector of real-valued uni-dimensional signals $w_i : \mathbb{T} \to \mathbb{R}$ associated with variables s_i for $i = 1, \ldots, n$. We assume that every signal w_i is piecewise-linear. Given two signals $u : \mathbb{T} \to \mathbb{R}^l$ and $v : \mathbb{T} \to \mathbb{R}^m$, we define their parallel composition $u \| v : \mathbb{T} \to \mathbb{R}^{l+m}$ in the expected way. Given a signal $w : \mathbb{T} \to \mathbb{R}^n$ defined over the set of variables S and a subset of variables $R \subseteq S$, we denote by w_R the projection of w to R, where $w_R = \|_{s_i \in R} w_i$.

Let Θ be a set of terms of the form $f(R)$ where $R \subseteq S$ are subsets of variables and $f : \mathbb{R}^{|R|} \to \mathbb{R}$ are interpreted functions. The syntax of STL with both *future* and *past* operators is defined by the grammar:

$$\varphi :: = \top \mid f(R) > 0 \mid \neg\varphi \mid \varphi_1 \vee \varphi_2 \mid \varphi_1 \, \mathcal{U}_I \, \varphi_2 \mid \varphi_1 \, \mathcal{S}_I \, \varphi_2 \, ,$$

where $f(R)$ are terms in Θ and I are real intervals with bounds in $\mathbb{Q}_{\geq 0} \cup \{\infty\}$. As customary, we use the shorthands $\Diamond_I \varphi \equiv \top \mathcal{U}_I \varphi$ for *eventually*, $\Box_I \varphi \equiv \neg \Diamond_I \neg\varphi$ for *always*, $\Diamond_I \varphi \equiv \top \mathcal{S}_I \varphi$ for *once*, $\boxminus_I \varphi \equiv \neg \Diamond_I \neg\varphi$ for *historically*, $\uparrow \varphi \equiv \varphi \wedge \top \mathcal{S} \neg\varphi$ for *rising edge* and $\uparrow \varphi \equiv \neg\varphi \wedge \top \mathcal{S} \varphi$ for *falling edge*[1]. We interpret STL with its classical semantics defined in [19].

2.2   Daikon

Daikon is a template-based property inference tool that, starting from a set of variables and a set of observations, can infer a set of properties that are likely to hold for the input variables [9]. More formally, given a set of variables $V = V_1, \ldots, V_n$ defined over the domains $D_1, \ldots D_n$, an observation for these variables is a tuple $\bar{v} = (v_1, \ldots, v_n)$, with $v_i \in D_i$.

Given a set of variables V and multiple observations $\bar{v}_1 \ldots \bar{v}_m$ for these same variables, Daikon is a function $D(V, \bar{v}_1 \ldots \bar{v}_m)$ that returns a set of properties $\{p_1, \ldots p_k\}$, such that $\bar{v}_i \models p_j \forall i, j$, that is, all the observations satisfy the inferred properties. For example, considering two variables x and y and considering the observations $(1, 3)$, $(2, 2)$, $(4, 0)$ for the tuple (x, y), Daikon can infer properties such as $x > 0$, $x + y = 4$, and $y \geq 0$.

The inference of the properties is driven by a set of template operators that Daikon instantiates over the input variables and checks against the input data. Since template-based inference can generate redundant and implied properties, Daikon automatically detects them and reports the relevant properties only. Finally, to guarantee that the inferred properties are relevant, Daikon computes the probability that the inferred property holds by chance for all the properties. Only properties that are statistically significant with a probability higher than 0.99 are assumed to be reliable and are reported in the output.

---

[1] We omit the timing modality I when $I = [0, \infty)$.

In our approach, we use Daikon to automatically generate properties that capture the behavior of the individual components and individual signals in the model under analysis. These properties can be used to precisely detect misbehaviours and their propagation.

3 Case Study

We now introduce a case study that we use as a running example to illustrate our approach step by step. We consider the Aircraft Elevator Control System (AECS) introduced in [11] to illustrate model-based development of a Fault Detection, Isolation and Recovery (FDIR) application for a redundant actuator control system.

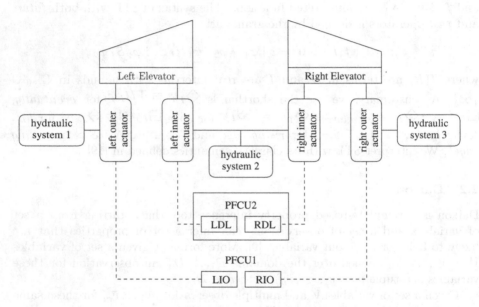

Fig. 1. Aircraft elevator control system [11].

Figure 1 shows the architecture of an aircraft elevator control system with redundancy, with one elevator on the left and one on the right side. Each elevator is equipped with two hydraulic actuators. Both actuators can position the elevator, but only one shall be active at any point in time. There are three different hydraulic systems that drive the four actuators. The left (LIO) and right (RIO) outer actuators are controlled by a Primary Flight Control Unit (PFCU1) with a sophisticated input/output control law. If a failure occurs, a less sophisticated Direct-Link (DL/PFCU2) control law with reduced functionality takes over to handle the left (LDL) and right (RDL) inner actuators. The system uses state machines to coordinate the redundancy and assure its continual fail-operational activity.

This model has one input variable, the input Pilot Command, and two output variables, the position of left and right actuators, as measured by the sensors.

This is a complex model that could be extremely hard to analyze in case of failure. In fact, the model has 426 signals, from which 361 are internal variables that are instrumented (279 real-valued, 62 Boolean and 20 enumerated - state machine - variables) and any of them, or even a combination of them, might be responsible for an observed failure.

The model comes with a failure injection mechanism, which allows to dynamically insert failures that represent hardware/ageing problems into different components of the system during its simulation. This mechanism allows insertion of (1) low pressure failures for each of the three hydraulic systems, and (2) failures of sensor position components in each of the four actuators. Due to the use of redundancy in the design of the control system, a single failure is not sufficient to alter its intended behavior. In some cases even two failures are not sufficient to produce faulty behaviors. For instance, the control system is able to correctly function when both a left and a right sensor position components simultaneously fail. This challenges the understanding of failures because there are multiple causes that must be identified to explain a single failure.

To present our approach we consider the analysis of a system failure caused by the activation of two failures: the sensor measuring Left Outer Actuator Position failing at time 2 and the sensor measuring Left Inner Actuator Position failing at time 4. To collect evidence of how the system behaves, we executed the Simulink model with 150 test cases with different pilot commands and collected the input-output behavior both with and without the failures.

When the system behaves correctly, the intended position of the aircraft required by the pilot must be achieved within a predetermined time limit and with a certain accuracy. This can be captured with several requirements. One of them says that whenever Pilot Command cmd goes above a threshold m, the actuator position measured by the sensor must stabilize (become at most n units away from the command signal) within $T + t$ time units. This requirement is formalized in STL with the following specification:

$$\varphi \equiv \Box(\uparrow (cmd \geq m) \rightarrow \Diamond_{[0,T]} \Box_{[0,t]}(|cmd - pos| \leq n)). \tag{1}$$

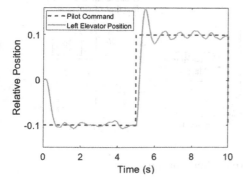
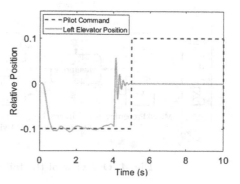

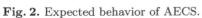

Fig. 2. Expected behavior of AECS.   **Fig. 3.** Failure of the AECS.

Figures 2 and 3 shows the correct and faulty behavior of the system. The control system clearly stops following the reference signal after 4 seconds. The failure observed on the input/output interface of the model does not give any indication within the model on the reason leading to the property violation. In the next section, we present how our failure explanation technique can address this case producing a valuable output for engineers.

4   Failure Explanation

In this section we describe how CPSDebug works with help of the case study introduced in Sect. 3. Figure 4 illustrates the main steps of the workflow. Briefly, the workflow starts from a target CPS model and a test suite with some passing and failing test cases, and produces a failure explanation for each failing test case. The workflow consists of three sequential phases:

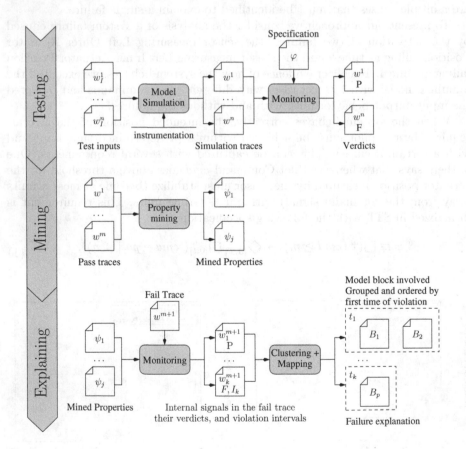

Fig. 4. Overview of the failure explanation procedure.

(i) *Testing*, which simulates the instrumented CPS model with the available test cases to collect information about its behavior, both for passing and failing executions,

(ii) *Mining*, which mines properties from the traces produced by passing test cases; intuitively these properties capture the expected behavior of the model,

(iii) *Explaining*, which uses mined properties to analyze the traces produced by failures and generate failure explanations, including information about the root events responsible for the failure and their propagation.

4.1 Testing

CPSDebug starts by instrumenting the CPS model. This is an important pre-processing step that is done before testing the model and that allows to log the internal signals in the model. Model *instrumentation* is inductively defined on the hierarchical structure of the Simulink/Stateflow model and is performed in a bottom-up fashion. For every signal variable having the real, Boolean or enumeration type, CPSDebug assigns a unique name to it and makes the simulation engine to log its values. Similarly, CPSDebug instruments look-up tables and state machines. Each look-up table is associated with a dedicated variable which is used to produce a simulation trace that reports the unique cell index that is exercised by the input at every point in time. CPSDebug also instruments state-machines by associating two dedicated variables per state-machine, one reporting the transitions taken and one reporting the locations visited during the simulation. We denote by V the set of all instrumented model variables.

The first step of the testing phase, namely *Model Simulation*, runs the available *test cases* $\{w_I^k | 1 \leq k \leq n\}$ against the *instrumented* version of the simulation model under analysis. The number of available test cases may vary case by case, for instance in our case study the test suite included $n = 150$ tests.

The result of the model simulation consists of one simulation trace w^k for each test case w_I^k. The trace w^k stores the sequence of (simulation time, value) pairs w_v^k for every instrumented variable $v \in V$ collected during simulation.

To determine the nature of each trace, we transform the informal model *specification*, which is typically provided in form of free text, into an STL formula φ that can be automatically evaluated by a *monitor*. In fact, CPSDebug checks every trace w^k against the STL formula φ, $1 \leq k \leq n$ and labels the trace with a *pass verdict* if w^k satisfies φ, or a *fail verdict* otherwise. In our case study, the STL formula 1 in Sect. 3 labeled 149 traces as passing and 1 trace as failing.

4.2 Mining

In the mining phase, CPSDebug selects the traces labeled with a pass verdict and exploits them for *property mining*.

Prior to the property inference, CPSDebug performs several intermediate steps that facilitate the mining task. First, CPSDebug reduces the set of variables V to its subset $\hat{V}$ of *significant* variables by using cross-correlation. Intuitively, the presence of two highly correlated variables implies that one variable adds little information on top of the other one, and thus the analysis may actually focus on one variable only. The approach initializes $\hat{V} = V$ and then checks the cross-correlation coefficient between all the logged variables computed on the data obtained from the pass traces. The cross-correlation coefficient $P(v_1, v_2)$ between two variables v_1 and v_2 is computed with the Pearson method, i.e. $P(v_1, v_2) = \frac{cov(v_1, v_2)}{\sigma_{v_1}\sigma_{v_2}}$ which is defined in terms of the *covariance* of v_1 and v_2 and their standard deviations. Whenever the cross-correlation coefficient between two variables is higher than 0.99, that is $P(v_1, v_2) > 0.99$, CPSDebug removes one of the two variables (and its associated traces) from further analysis, that is, $\hat{V} = \hat{V} \setminus v_1$. In our case study, $|V| = 361$ and $|\hat{V}| = 121$, resulting in a reduction of 240 variables.

In the next step, CPSDebug associates each variable $v \in \hat{V}$ to (1) its domain D and (2) its parent Simulink-block B. We denote by $V_{D,B} \subseteq \hat{V}$ the set $\{v_1, \ldots, v_n\}$ of variables with the domain D associated with block B. CPSDebug collects all observations $\overline{v}_1 \ldots \overline{v}_n$ from all samples in all traces associated with variables in $V_{D,B}$ and uses the Daikon function $D(V_{D,B}, \overline{v}_1 \ldots \overline{v}_n)$ to infer a set of properties $\{p_1, \ldots, p_k\}$ related to the block B and the domain D. Running property mining per model block and model domain allows to avoid (1) combinatorial explosion of learned properties and (2) learning properties between incompatible domains.

Finally, CPSDebug collects all the learned properties from all the blocks and the domains, and translates them to an STL specification, where each Daikon property p is transformed to an STL assertion of type $\square\, p$.

In our case study, Daikon returned 96 behavioral properties involving 121 variables, hence CPSDebug generated an STL property ψ with 96 temporal assertions, i.e., $\psi = [\psi_1 \psi_2 \ldots \psi_{96}]$. Equations 2 and 3 shows two examples of behavioral properties inferred from our case study by Daikon and translated to STL. Variables *mode*, *LI_pos_fail* and *LO_pos_fail* denote internal signals Mode, Left Inner Position Failure and Left Outer Position Failure from the aircraft position control Simulink model. The first property states that the Mode signal is always in the state 2 (Passive) or 3 (Standby), while the second property states that the Left Inner Position Failure is encoded the same than the Left Outer Position Failure.

$$\varphi_1 \equiv \square(mode \in \{2, 3\}) \tag{2}$$

$$\varphi_2 \equiv \square(LI\_pos\_fail == LO\_pos\_fail) \tag{3}$$

4.3   Explaining

This phase analyzes a trace w collected from a failing execution and produces a failure explanation. The *Monitoring* step analyzes the trace against the mined properties and returns the signals that violate the properties and the time intervals in which the properties are violated. CPSDebug subsequently labels with F

(*fail*) the internal signals involved in the violated properties and with P (*pass*) the remaining signals from the trace. To each fail-annotated signal, CPSDebug also assigns the violation time intervals of the corresponding violated properties returned by the monitoring tool.

In our case study, the analysis of the left inner and the left outer sensor failure resulted in the violation of 17 mined properties involving 19 internal signals.

For each internal signal there can be several fail-annotated signal instances, each one with a different violation time interval. CPSDebug selects the instance that occurs first in time, ignoring all other instances. This is because, to reach the root cause of a failure, CPSDebug has to focus on the events that cause observable misbehaviours first.

Table 1 summarizes the set of property-violating signals, the block they belong to, and the instant of time the signal has first violated a property for our case study. We can observe that the 17 signals participating in the violation of at least one mined property belong to only 5 different Simulink blocks. In addition, we can see that all the violations naturally cluster around two time instants – 2 s and 4 s. This suggests that CPSDebug can effectively *isolate in space and time* a limited number of events likely responsible for the failure.

Table 1. Internal signals that violate at least one learned invariant and Simulink blocks to which they belong. The column $\tau(s)$ denotes the first time that each signal participates in an invariant violation.

Index	Signal name	Block	$\tau(s)$
s_{252}	LI_pos_fail:1→Switch:2	Meas. Left In. Act. Pos.	1.99
s_{253}	Outlier/failure:1→Switch:1	Meas. Left In. Act. Pos.	1.99
s_{254}	Measured Position3:1→Mux:3	Meas. Left In. Act. Pos.	1.99
s_{255}	Measured Position2:1→Mux:2	Meas. Left In. Act. Pos.	1.99
s_{256}	Measured Position1:1→Mux:1	Meas. Left In. Act. Pos.	1.99
s_{55}	BusSelector:2→Mux1:2	Controller	2.03
s_{328}	In2:1→Mux1:2	L_pos_failures	2.03
s_{329}	In1:1→Mux1:1	L_pos_failures	2.03
s_{332}	Right Outer Pos. Mon.:2→R_pos_failures:1	Actuator Positions	2.03
s_{333}	Right Inner Pos. Mon.:2→R_pos_failures:2	Actuator Positions	2.03
s_{334}	Left Outer Pos. Mon.:2→L_pos_failures:1	Actuator Positions	2.03
s_{335}	Right Inner Pos. Mon.:3→Goto3:1	Actuator Positions	2.03
s_{338}	Left Outer Pos. Mon.:3→Goto:1	Actuator Positions	2.03
s_{341}	Left Inner Pos. Mon.:2→L_pos_failures:2	Actuator Positions	2.03
s_{272}	LO_pos_fail:1→Switch:2	Meas. Left Out. Act. Pos.	3.99
s_{273}	Outlier/failure:1→Switch:1	Meas. Left Out. Act. Pos.	3.99
s_{275}	Measured Position1:1→Mux:1	Meas. Left Out. Act. Pos.	3.99
s_{276}	Measured Position2:1→Mux:2	Meas. Left Out. Act. Pos.	3.99
s_{277}	Measured Position3:1→Mux:3	Meas. Left Out. Act. Pos.	4.00

The *Clustering & Mapping* step then (1) clusters the resulting fail-annotated signal instances by their violation time intervals and (2) maps them to the corresponding model blocks, i.e., to the model blocks that have some of the fail-annotated signal instances as internal signals.

Finally, CPSDebug generates failure explanations that capture how the fault originated and propagated in space and time. In particular, the failure explanation is a sequence of snapshots of the system, one for each cluster of property violations. Each snapshot reports (1) the mean time as approximative time when the violations represented in the cluster occurred, (2) the model blocks $\{B_1, ..., B_p\}$ that originate the violations reported in the cluster, (3) the properties violated by the cluster, representing the reason why the cluster of anomalies exist, and (4) the internal signals that participate to the violations of the properties associated with the cluster. Intuitively a snapshot represents a new relevant state of the system, and the sequence shows how the execution progresses from the violation of set of properties to the final violation of the specification. The engineer is supposed to exploit the sequence of snapshots to understand the failure, and the first snapshot to localize the root cause of the problem. Figure 5 shows the first snapshot of the failure explanation that CPSDebug generated for the case study. We can see that the explanation of the failure at time 2 involves the Sensors block, and propagates to Signal conditioning and failures and Controller

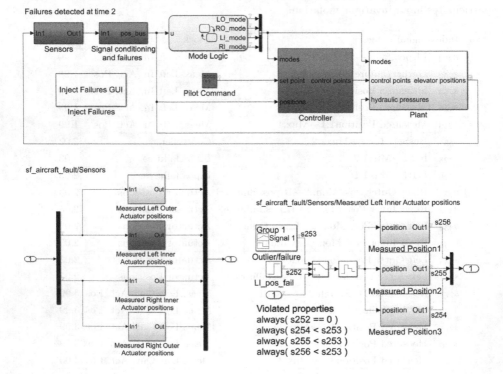

Fig. 5. Failure explanation as a sequence of snapshots - part of the first snapshot.

blocks. By opening the Sensors block, we can immediately see that something is wrong with the sensor that measures the left inner position of the actuator. Going one level below, we can see that the signal s_{252} produced by *LI_pos_fail* is suspicious – indeed the fault was injected exactly in that block at time 2. It is not a surprise that the malfunctioning of the sensor measuring the left inner position of the actuator affects the Signal conditioning and failures block (the block that detects if there is a sensor that fails) and the Controller block. However, at time 2 the failure in one sensor does not affect yet the correctness of the overall system, hence the STL specification is not yet violated. The second snapshot (not shown here) generated by CPSDebug reveals that the sensor measuring the left outer position of the actuator fails at time 4. The redundancy mechanism is not able to cope with multiple sensor faults, hence anomalies manifest in the observable behavior. From this sequence of snapshots, the engineer can conclude that the problem is in the failure of the two sensors - one measuring the left inner and the other measuring the left outer position of the actuator that stop functioning at times 2 and 4, respectively.

5   Empirical Evaluation

We empirically evaluated our approach against three classes of faults: *multiple hardware faults in fault-tolerant systems*, which is the case of multiple components that incrementally fail in a system designed to tolerate multiple malfunctioning units; *incorrect look-up tables*, which is the case of look-up tables containing incorrect values; and *erroneous guard conditions*, which is the case of imprecise conditions in the transitions that determine the state-based behavior of the system. Note that these classes of faults are highly heterogenous. In fact, their analysis requires a technique flexible enough to deal with multiple failure causes, but also with the internal structure of complex data structures and finally with state-based models.

We consider two different systems to introduce faults belonging to these three classes. We use the fault-tolerant aircraft elevator control system [11] presented in Sect. 3 to study the capability of our approach to identify failures caused by multiple overlapping faults. In particular, we study cases obtained by (1) injecting a low pressure fault into two out of three hydraulic components (fault $h_1 h_2$), and (2) inserting a fault in the left inner and left outer sensor position components (fault *lilo*).

We use the automatic transmission control system [13] to study the other classes of faults. Automatic transmission control system is composed of 51 variables, includes 4 look-up tables of size between 4 and 110 and two finite state machines running in parallel with 3 and 4 states, respectively, as well as 6 transitions each. We used the 7 STL specifications defined in [13] to reveal failures in this system. We studied cases obtained by (1) modifying a transition guard in the StateFlow chart (fault *guard*), and (2) altering an entry in the look-up table Engine (fault *eng_lt*).

To study these faults, we considered two use scenarios. For the aircraft elevator control system, we executed 150 test cases in which we systematically changed the amplitude and the frequency of the pilot command steps. These tests were executed on a non-faulty model. We then executed an additional test on the model to which we dynamically injected $h_1 h_2$ and *lilo* faults. For the automatic transmission control system, we executed 100 tests in which we systematically changed the step input of the throttle by varying the amplitude, the offset and the absolute time of the step. All the tests were executed on a faulty model. In both cases, we divided the failed tests from the passing tests. CPSDebug used the data collected from the passing tests to infer models necessary for the analysis of the failed tests.

We evaluated the output produced by our approach considering four main aspects: Scope Reduction, Cause Detection, Quality of the Analysis, and Computation Time. Scope Reduction measures how well our approach narrows down the number of elements to be inspected to a small number of anomalous signals that require the attention of the engineer, in comparison to the set of variables involved in the failed execution. Cause detection indicates if the first cluster of anomalous values reported by our approach includes any property violation caused by the signal that is directly affected by the fault. Intuitively, it would be highly desirable that the first cluster of anomalies reported by our technique includes violations caused by the root cause of the failure. For instance, if a fault directly affects the values of the signal Right Inner Pos., we expect these values to cause a violation of a property about this same signal. We qualitatively discuss the set of violated properties reported for the various faults and explain why they offer a comprehensive view about the problem that caused the failure. Finally, we analyze the computation time of CPSDebug and its components and compare it to the simulation time of the model.

To further confirm the effectiveness of our approach, we contacted 3 engineers from (1) an automotive OEM with over 300.000 employees ($E1$), (2) a major modeling and simulation tool vendor with more than 3.000 employees ($E2$), and (3) an SME that develops tools for verification and testing of CPS models ($E3$). We asked them to evaluate the outcomes of our tool for a selection of faults (it was infeasible to ask them to inspect all the results we collected). In particular, we sent them the faulty program, an explanation of both the program and the fault, and the output generated by our tool, and we asked them to answer the following questions:

Q1 How helpful is the output to understand the cause(s) of the failure? (Very useful/Somewhat useful/Useless/Misleading)

Q2 Would you consider experimenting our tool with your projects? (Yes/May be/No)

Q3 Considering the sets of violations that have been reported, is there anything that should be removed from the output? (open question)

Q4 Is there anything more you would like to see in the output produced by our tool? (open question)

In the following, we report the results that we obtained for each of the analyzed aspects.

5.1 Scope Reduction, Cause Detection and Qualitative Analysis

Table 2 shows the degree of reduction achieved for the analyzed faults. Column *system* indicates the faulty application used in the evaluation. Column *# vars* indicates the size of the model in terms of the number of its variables. Column *fault* indicates the specific fault analyzed. Column *# ψ* gives the number of learned invariants. Column *# suspicious vars (reduction)* indicates the number of variables involved in the violated properties and the reduction achieved. Column *fault detected* indicates whether the explanation included a variable associated with the output of the block in which the fault was injected.

Table 2. Scope reduction and cause detection.

system	# vars	fault	# ψ	# suspicious vars	fault detected
Aircraft	426	*lilo*	96	17(96%)	✓
		h_1h_2	96	44(90%)	✓
Transmission	51	*guard*	41	1(98%)	
		eng_lt	39	4(92%)	✓

We can see from Table 2 that CPSDebug successfully detected the exact origin of the fault in 3 out of 4 cases. In the case of the aircraft elevator control system, CPSDebug clearly identifies the problem with the respective sensors (fault *lilo*) and hydraulic components (fault h_1h_2). Overall, the scope reduction ranged from 90% to 98% of the model signals, allowing engineers to focus on a small subset of the suspicious signals. Note that a strong scope reduction is useful also when CPSDebug is not effective with a fault, since engineers could quickly conclude that the fault is not in the (few) recommended locations without wasting their time (such as for the *guard* fault).

In the case of the automatic transmission control, CPSDebug associates the misbehavior of the model with the Engine look-up table and points to its right entry. The scope reduction in this case is 90%. On the other hand, CPSDebug misses the exact origin of the *guard* fault and fails to point to the altered transition. This happens because the faulty guard alters only the *timing* but not the *qualitative* behavior of the state machine. Since Daikon is able to learn only invariant properties, CPSDebug is not able to discriminate between passing and failing tests in that case. Nevertheless, CPSDebug does associate the entire state machine to the anomalous behavior, since the observable signal that violates the STL specification is generated by the state machine.

5.2 Computation Time

Table 3 summarizes computation time of CPSDebug applied to the two case studies. We can make two main conclusions from these experimental results: (1) the overall computation time of CPSDebug-specific activities is comparable to the overall simulation time and (2) property mining dominates by far the computation of the explanation. We finally report in the last row the translation of the Simulink simulation traces recorded in the Common Separated Values (csv) format to the specific input format that is used by Daikon. In our prototype implementation of CPSDebug, we use an inefficient format translation that results in excessive time. We believe that investing an additional effort can result in improving the translation time by several orders of magnitude.

Table 3. CPSDebug computation time.

	Aircraft	Transmission
# tests	150	100
# samples per test	1001	751
	Time (s)	
Simulation	654	35
Instrumentation	1	0.7
Mining	501	52
Monitoring properties	0.7	0.6
Analysis	1.5	1.6
File format translation	2063	150

5.3 Evaluation by Professional Engineers

We analyze in this section the feedback provided by engineers $E1$–$E3$ to the questions $Q1$–$Q4$.

Q1 $E1$ found CPSDebug potentially very useful. $E2$ and $E3$ found CPSDebug somewhat useful.

Q2 All engineers said that they would experiment with CPSDebug.

Q3 None of the engineers found anything that should be removed from the tool outcome.

Q4 $E2$ and $E3$ wished to see better visual highlighting of suspicious signals. $E2$ wished to see the actual trace for each suspicious signal. $E2$ and $E3$ wished a clearer presentation of cause-effect relations.

Apart from the direct responses to $Q1 - 4$, we received other useful information. All engineers shared appreciation for the visual presentation of outcomes, and especially the marking of suspicious Simulink blocks in red. $E1$ highlighted that real production models typically do not only contain Simulink and State-Flow blocks, but also SimEvent and SimScape blocks, Bus Objects, Model Reference, Variant Subsystems, etc., which may limit the applicability of the current prototype implementation.

Overall, engineers confirmed that CPSDebug can be a useful technology. At the same time, they offered valuable feedback to improve it, especially the presentation of the output produced by the tool.

6   Related Work

The analysis of software failures has been addressed with two main classes of related approaches: fault localization and failure explanation techniques.

Fault localization techniques aim at identifying the location of the faults that caused one or more observed failures (an extensive survey can be found in [27]). A popular example is *spectrum-based fault-localization* (SBFL) [1], an efficient statistical technique that, by measuring the code coverage in the failed and successful tests, can rank the program components (e.g., the statements) that are most likely responsible for a fault.

SBFL has been recently employed to localize faults in Simulink/Stateflow CPS models [5,7,16–18], showing similar accuracy as in the application to software systems [18]. The explanatory power of this approach is however limited, because it generates neither information that can help the engineers understanding if a selected code location is really faulty nor information about how a fault propagated across components resulting on an actual failure. Furthermore, SBFL is agnostic to the nature of the oracle requiring to know only whether the system passes or not a specific test case. This prevents the exploitation of any additional information concerning why and when the oracle decides that the test is not conformed with respect to the desired behavior. In Bartocci et al. [5] the authors try to overcome this limitation by assuming that the oracle is a monitor generated from an STL specification. This approach allows the use of the trace diagnostic method proposed in Ferrère et al. [10] to obtain more information (e.g., the time interval when the cause of violation first occurs) about the failed tests improving the fault-localization. Although this additional knowledge can improve the confidence on the localization, still little is known about the root cause of the problem and its impact on the runtime behavior of the CPS model.

CPSDebug complements and improves SBFL techniques generating information that helps engineers identifying the cause of failures, understanding how faults resulted in chains of anomalous events that eventually led to the observed failures, and producing a corpus of information well-suited to support engineers in their debugging tasks, as confirmed by the subjects who responded to our questionnaire.

Failure explanation techniques analyze software failures in the attempt of producing information about failures and their causes. For instance, a few approaches combined mining and dynamic analysis in the context of component-based and object-oriented applications to reveal [24] and explain failures [3,6,21]. These approaches are not however straightforwardly applicable to CPS models, since they exploit the discrete nature of component-based and object-oriented applications that is radically different from the data-flow oriented nature of CPS models, which include mixed-analog signals, hybrid (continuous and discrete) components, and a complex dynamics.

CPSDebug originally addresses failure explanation in the context of CPS models. The closest work to CPSDebug is probably Hynger [14,23], which exploits invariant generation to detect specification mismatches, that is, a mismatch between an actual and an inferred specification, in Simulink models. Specification mismatches can indicate the presence of problems in the models. Differently from Hynger, CPSDebug does not compare specifications but exploits inferred properties to identify anomalous behaviors in observed failures. Moreover, CPSDebug exploits correlation and clustering techniques to maintain the output compact, and to generate a sequence of snapshots that helps comprehensively defining the story of the failure. Our results show that this output can be the basis for cost-effective debugging.

A related body of research consists of approaches for anomaly detection of Cyber-Physical Systems [8,26]. However, anomaly detection approaches aim at detecting misbehaviours, rather than analyzing failures and detecting their root causes as CPSDebug does.

7 Future Work and Conclusions

We have presented CPSDebug, an automatic approach for explaining failures in Simulink models. Our approach combines testing, specification mining and failure analysis to provide a concise explanation consisting of time-ordered sequence of model snapshots that show the variable exhibiting anomalous behavior and their propagation in the model. We evaluated the effectiveness CPSDebug on two models, involving two use scenarios and several classes of faults.

We believe that this paper opens several research directions. In this work, we only considered mining of invariant specifications. However, we have observed that invariant properties are not sufficient to explain timing issues, hence we plan to experiment in future work with mining of *real-time temporal* specifications. In particular, we will study the trade-off between the finer characterization of the model that temporal specification mining can provide and its computational cost. We also plan to study systematic ways to explain failures in presence of heterogeneous components. In this paper, we consider the setting in which we have multiple passing tests, but we only use a single fail test to explain the failure. We will study whether the presence of multiple failing tests can be used to improve the explanations. In this work, we have performed manual fault injection and our focus was on studying the effectiveness of CPSDebug on providing meaningful failure explanations for different use scenarios and classes of faults. We plan in the future to develop automatic fault injection and perform systematic experiments for evaluating how often CPSDebug is able to find the root cause.

Acknowledgments. This report was partially supported by the Productive 4.0 project (ECSEL 737459). The ECSEL Joint Undertaking receives support from the European Union's Horizon 2020 research and innovation programme and Austria, Denmark, Germany, Finland, Czech Republic, Italy, Spain, Portugal, Poland, Ireland, Belgium, France, Netherlands, United Kingdom, Slovakia, Norway.

References

1. Abreu, R., Zoeteweij, P., van Gemund, A.J.C.: On the accuracy of spectrum-based fault localization. In: Testing: Academic and Industrial Conference Practice and Research Techniques, pp. 89–98. IEEE (2007)
2. Annpureddy, Y., Liu, C., Fainekos, G., Sankaranarayanan, S.: S-TaLiRo: a tool for temporal logic falsification for hybrid systems. In: Abdulla, P.A., Leino, K.R.M. (eds.) TACAS 2011. LNCS, vol. 6605, pp. 254–257. Springer, Heidelberg (2011). https://doi.org/10.1007/978-3-642-19835-9_21
3. Babenko, A., Mariani, L., Pastore, F.: AVA: automated interpretation of dynamically detected anomalies. In: proceedings of the International Symposium on Software Testing and Analysis (ISSTA) (2009)
4. Bartocci, E., et al.: Specification-based monitoring of cyber-physical systems: a survey on theory, tools and applications. In: Bartocci, E., Falcone, Y. (eds.) Lectures on Runtime Verification. LNCS, vol. 10457, pp. 135–175. Springer, Cham (2018). https://doi.org/10.1007/978-3-319-75632-5_5
5. Bartocci, E., Ferrère, T., Manjunath, N., Nickovic, D.: Localizing faults in Simulink/Stateflow models with STL. In: Proceedings of HSCC 2018: The 21st International Conference on Hybrid Systems: Computation and Control, pp. 197–206. ACM (2018)
6. Befrouei, M.T., Wang, C., Weissenbacher, G.: Abstraction and mining of traces to explain concurrency bugs. Form. Methods Syst. Des. **49**(1–2), 1–32 (2016)
7. Deshmukh, J.V., Jin, X., Majumdar, R., Prabhu, V.S.: Parameter optimization in control software using statistical fault localization techniques. In: Proceedings of ICCPS 2018: the 9th ACM/IEEE International Conference on Cyber-Physical Systems, pp. 220–231. IEEE Computer Society/ACM (2018)
8. Ding, M., Chen, H., Sharma, A., Yoshihira, K., Jiang, G.: A data analytic engine towards self-management of cyber-physical systems. In: Proceedings of the International Conference on Distributed Computing Workshop. IEEE Computer Society (2013)
9. Ernst, M., et al.: The daikon system for dynamic detection of likely invariants. Sci. Comput. Program. **69**(1–3), 35–45 (2007)
10. Ferrère, T., Maler, O., Ničković, D.: Trace diagnostics using temporal implicants. In: Finkbeiner, B., Pu, G., Zhang, L. (eds.) ATVA 2015. LNCS, vol. 9364, pp. 241–258. Springer, Cham (2015). https://doi.org/10.1007/978-3-319-24953-7_20
11. Ghidella, J., Mosterman, P.: Requirements-based testing in aircraft control design. In: AIAA Modeling and Simulation Technologies Conference and Exhibit, p. 5886 (2005)
12. Hastie, T., Tibshirani, R., Friedman, J.H.: The Elements of Statistical Learning: Data Mining, Inference, and Prediction. Springer Series in Statistics, 2nd edn. Springer, Heidelberg (2009)
13. Hoxha, B., Abbas, H., Fainekos, G.E.: Benchmarks for temporal logic requirements for automotive systems. In: International Workshop on Applied veRification for Continuous and Hybrid Systems, volume 34 of EPiC Series in Computing, pp. 25–30. EasyChair (2015)
14. Johnson, T.T., Bak, S., Drager, S.: Cyber-physical specification mismatch identification with dynamic analysis. In: Proceedings of ICCPS 2015: The ACM/IEEE Sixth International Conference on Cyber-Physical Systems, pp. 208–217. ACM (2015)

15. Lee, E.A.: Cyber physical systems: design challenges. In: Proceedings of ISORC 2008: The 11th IEEE International Symposium on Object-Oriented Real-Time Distributed Computing, pp. 363–369. IEEE Computer Society (2008)
16. Liu, B., Nejati, S., Briand, L.C.: Improving fault localization for Simulink models using search-based testing and prediction models. In: International Conference on Software Analysis, Evolution and Reengineering, pp. 359–370. IEEE Computer Society (2017)
17. Liu, B., Lucia, Nejati, S., Briand, L.C., Bruckmann, T.: Localizing multiple faults in Simulink models. In: International Conference on Software Analysis, Evolution, and Reengineering, pp. 146–156. IEEE Computer Society (2016)
18. Liu, B., Lucia, Nejati, S., Briand, L.C., Bruckmann, T.: Simulink fault localization: an iterative statistical debugging approach. Softw. Test. Verif. Reliab. **26**(6), 431–459 (2016)
19. Maler, O., Nickovic, D.: Monitoring properties of analog and mixed-signal circuits. STTT **15**(3), 247–268 (2013)
20. Maler, O., Nickovic, D.: Monitoring temporal properties of continuous signals. In: Lakhnech, Y., Yovine, S. (eds.) FORMATS/FTRTFT -2004. LNCS, vol. 3253, pp. 152–166. Springer, Heidelberg (2004). https://doi.org/10.1007/978-3-540-30206-3_12
21. Mariani, L., Pastore, F., Pezzè, M.: Dynamic analysis for diagnosing integration faults. IEEE Trans. Softw. Eng. (TSE) **37**(4), 486–508 (2011)
22. Nghiem, T., Sankaranarayanan, S., Fainekos, G.E., Ivancic, F., Gupta, A., Pappas, G.J.: Monte-Carlo techniques for falsification of temporal properties of non-linear hybrid systems. In: International Conference on Hybrid Systems: Computation and Control, pp. 211–220 (2010)
23. Nguyen, L.V., Hoque, K.A., Bak, S., Drager, S., Johnson, T.T.: Cyber-physical specification mismatches. TCPS **2**(4), 23:1–23:26 (2018)
24. Pastore, F., et al.: Verification-aided regression testing. In: International Symposium on Software Testing and Analysis, ISSTA 2014, San Jose, CA, USA - 21–26 July 2014, pp. 37–48 (2014)
25. Sankaranarayanan S., Fainekos, G.E.: Falsification of temporal properties of hybrid systems using the cross-entropy method. In: International Conference on Hybrid Systems: Computation and Control, pp. 125–134. ACM (2012)
26. Sharma, A.B., Chen, H., Ding, M., Yoshihira, K., Jiang, G.: Fault detection and localization in distributed systems using invariant relationships. In: Proceedings of DSN 2013: The 2013 43rd Annual IEEE/IFIP International Conference on Dependable Systems and Networks, pp. 1–8. IEEE Computer Society (2013)
27. Wong, W.E., Gao, R., Li, Y., Abreu, R., Wotawa, F.: A survey on software fault localization. IEEE Trans. Software Eng. **42**(8), 707–740 (2016)

Evolution of Formal Model-Based Assurance Cases for Autonomous Robots

Mario Gleirscher[✉], Simon Foster, and Yakoub Nemouchi

Department of Computer Science, University of York, York, UK
{mario.gleirscher,simon.foster,yakoub.nemouchi}@york.ac.uk
http://www.cs.york.ac.uk

Abstract. An assurance case should carry sufficient evidence for a compelling argument that a system fulfils its guarantees under specific environmental assumptions. Assurance cases are often subject of maintenance, evolution, and reuse. In this paper, we demonstrate how evidence of an assurance case can be formalised, and how an assurance case can be refined using this formalisation to increase argument confidence and to react to changing operational needs. Moreover, we propose two argument patterns for construction and extension and we implement these patterns using the generic proof assistant Isabelle. We illustrate our approach for an autonomous mobile ground robot. Finally, we relate our approach to international standards (e.g. DO-178C, ISO 26262) recommending the delivery and maintenance of assurance cases.

Keywords: Assurance case · Formal verification · Refinement ·
Autonomous robot · Integrated formal methods ·
Model-based engineering

1 Introduction

Autonomous robots in complex multi-participant environments can engage in risky events (e.g. because of faults or partial state knowledge) possibly leading to accidents. To reduce the opportunities for all participants to engage in such events or their consequences, one wishes to observe only specific machine behaviours. *Assurance Cases* (ACs) [20] are structured arguments, supported by evidence, intended to demonstrate that such machines fulfil their *assurance guarantees* [22], subject to certain *assumptions* about their environment [18,32]. Among the wide variety of assurance objectives, we will focus on *safety* in the rest of this paper, with a careful eye on *liveness*.

Compelling ACs require models to describe the behaviour of the real-world artefacts subjected to the assurance claims, and to provide evidence for these, contingent on validation. In particular, formal methods (FMs) can be applied to

M. Gleirscher—Supported by the German Research Foundation (DFG grant no. 381212925).

© Springer Nature Switzerland AG 2019
P. C. Ölveczky and G. Salaün (Eds.): SEFM 2019, LNCS 11724, pp. 87–104, 2019.
https://doi.org/10.1007/978-3-030-30446-1_5

the rigorous analysis of a system's state space, and to the computer-assisted verification of requirements. However, verification and validation can, in reality, fail to deliver safe systems, for example, due to an inadequate model that abstracts from essential detail. Such shortcomings can be difficult to identify in advance, and consequently, models and assurance cases have to *evolve* [2, 7]. Particularly, one might want to modify or *extend* an existing AC, for example, weaken its assumptions, make its model more precise, or strengthen its guarantees. Several such steps might be required to arrive at an acceptable confidence level.

In their study of assurance practice, Nair et al. [27] report that *evidence completeness and change impact* is managed mostly manually using traceability matrices. These authors observe a lack of tool support for change management and that evidence structuring is done mostly textually rather than with model-based ACs. Importantly, their study raises the question of *how evolution and change impact is identified, assessed, and managed at the level of ACs?*

Contributions. We consider *formal model-based assurance cases* (FMACs) to construct assurance arguments in a rigorous and step-wise manner. We define an FMAC as an AC *module* that conveys formal verification results with respect to a model and certain environmental assumptions. Our motivation is the assurance of physical systems such as autonomous mobile robots, and so we chose to support models and requirements in differential dynamic logic ($d\mathcal{L}$) [33].

We underpin our approach by AC *patterns* for the incremental construction of increasingly richer models, guarantees, and proofs that these models fulfil the guarantees. We provide two patterns, one for AC *construction* and one for AC *extension*, particularly, for increasing confidence in an AC by making the formalisation successively more precise. Both patterns provide guidance to how successive engineering steps can preserve assurance results from previous steps. We implement these patterns in Isabelle/SACM [28] and show how they can be instantiated and how assurance claims can be linked to verification results.

We complement recent approaches to robot verification (e.g. [26]) by a *data refinement* [40] for $d\mathcal{L}$ that is lifted to the level of AC construction and evolution. For a mobile ground robot, we illustrate two refinement steps from a maximally abstract model to one describing safe path planning and emergency braking. We indicate how one can derive safety guarantees from hazard analysis yet avoiding too conservative solutions by adding liveness guarantees. We demonstrate our proofs in Isabelle/HOL [29] by formalising the robot model in an implementation of $d\mathcal{L}$ in Isabelle/UTP [10,11].

Related Work. Bate and Kelly [2] discuss the notion of AC modules, interfaces, and their composition into an AC architecture via claim matching and *assumption/guarantee* (A/G)-style reasoning (e.g. weakening of assumptions). Following their discussion of AC change with a focus on traceability and change impact analysis, we focus on AC extension for the verified evolution of AC modules.

Prokhorova et al. [34] propose the construction of formal model-based safety cases based on a classification of safety requirements using Event-B. The authors discuss argument patterns for all classes of requirements. The patterns integrate proof and model-checking evidence[1] and cover refinement steps. Complementing their Event-B application, our approach supports hybrid system modelling. We cover their requirements classification, except for temporal and timing properties requiring binary modalities. We focus on step safety and liveness, and path safety. To support argument maintenance and scalability, we separate system modelling and proof derivation from argumentation, keeping model and proof details separate from the argument structure. This separation is facilitated in our Isabelle-based implementation by using $d\mathcal{L}$ for system modelling and verification and the FMAC concept for assurance argumentation.

Oliveira et al. [30] propose hierarchical modular safety cases to reuse common product-line features in general safety arguments and to decompose and refine the general argument into feature-specific argument modules. While the authors cover hazard analysis (viz. model-based failure analysis) and product-line modelling, our notion of AC extension based on data refinement can be useful for the verified derivation of a product-specific AC from the product-line AC.

For adaptive systems, Calinescu et al. [4] elaborate on the idea of through-life argument maintenance [7,31], focusing on the maintenance of a parametric AC whose parameters are subject of optimisation during the operation of a system. We complement their approach by a notion of data refinement to accommodate fundamental structural changes frequently desired for argument evolution.

Overview. The remainder of this article is structured as follows: We introduce the concepts in Sect. 2, explain our contributions in Sect. 3, evaluate our approach with a robot example in Sect. 4, discuss implications on formal robot verification and certification practice in Sect. 5, and conclude in Sect. 6.

2   Background and Formal Preliminaries

We introduce assurance cases from a practical viewpoint and provide the preliminaries on system specification and verification.

2.1   Assurance Cases

An AC is a compelling[2] argument, supported by evidence, that a system in a specific context fulfils (or refuses to fulfil) guarantees of interest, for example, freedom of hazards (*safety*), sustained correct service (*reliability*), freedom of unauthorised access (*security*), or productivity (*performance*). Intuitively, an AC is a hierarchical structure, with *claims* that are broken down into subclaims using argumentation *strategies*, and referencing an appropriate *context*, such as system element descriptions and environmental assumptions. An AC is deemed to be "finished" when all leaf claims are supported by adequate *evidence*, though there is always the possibility of evolution.

---

[1] From the Rodin tool and from LTL and timed CTL checkers.
[2] Usually structured, balanced, and exhibiting many further argumentation qualities.

We consider ACs as formalised in the *Structured Assurance Case Metamodel* (SACM), an OMG standard.[3] Wei et al. [39] summarise the work around SACM and demonstrate how established frameworks like the Goal Structuring Notation (GSN) [19] and *Claims Arguments Evidence* (CAE)[4] can be represented using SACM. SACM thus connects users of these techniques with rigorous model-based AC construction. SACM can be characterised by three principal concepts:

1. **arguments**, that present the claims and inferential links between them;
2. **artifacts**, evidence to support leaf claims, and the relations between them. Examples include outputs of hazard analysis, actors, test reports, system data sheets, formal models, and verification results. An AC whose evidence is based on results obtained from analysis of system models, such as formal verification, is called a *model-based assurance case* [16,39];
3. **terminology**, to support controlled languages for expressing claims, that are otherwise specified using free-form natural language. Often, these are used to refer to model elements in model-based ACs;

In AC *modules*, certain top-level claims and artefacts can be made public by an A/G-style AC *interface*. Several modules can then be composed to produce the overall AC. Claims can be *supported* by an argument within the module or *assumed* to hold of the *context*. In the latter case, corresponding external arguments have to be imported from other AC modules. This can be achieved by A/G reasoning, as is present in the design-by-contract paradigm [25]. Additionally, AC modules adhere to the standardised SACM package concept.

AC modules often need to evolve, for example, because of updates of the system design or the hazard list. Such evolutions should be conservative, in that existing claims should remain supported, assumptions should remain satisfiable, and terminology should stay consistent. This need motivates our notion of AC *extension*, the key contribution of this paper, fostering step-wise development and evolution of ACs. For this, we further develop Isabelle/SACM, our implementation of SACM as an interactive DSL for AC construction in the proof assistant Isabelle. Isabelle/SACM extends the document model Isabelle/DOF [3] to accommodate AC concepts and to provide well-formedness checking for ACs. Isabelle/SACM allows us to describe ACs with claims and evidence obtained from various formal methods. Details on Isabelle/SACM are explained in [28].

2.2 Isabelle/UTP and Differential Dynamic Logic

The evidence for an FMAC is obtained by formal verification using an implementation of d$\mathcal{L}$ [33] in our verification framework, Isabelle/UTP [10,11]. d$\mathcal{L}$ specialises Dynamic Logic by combining a modelling notation for hybrid systems, called *hybrid programs*, with a formal property language for reasoning about such programs. In a hybrid program, we can use operators like sequential composition, assignment, branches and iteration, and an operator for specifying

---

[3] See https://www.omg.org/spec/SACM/2.0/.
[4] See https://claimsargumentsevidence.org.

systems of ordinary differential equations (ODEs). It can therefore be used to represent hybrid systems that combine continuous evolution and discrete control. The property language extends predicate calculus with two modalities: $[P]\phi$, which specifies that ϕ holds in every state reachable from P; and $\langle P \rangle \phi$, which specifies that there is at least one state reachable from P satisfying ϕ.

Isabelle/UTP implements Hoare and He's *Unifying Theories of Programming* (UTP) [17], a framework for development of semantic models for programming and modelling languages based on heterogeneous paradigms using an alphabetised relational calculus. Isabelle/UTP develops this idea by allowing UTP semantic models to be adapted into verification tools, such as Hoare calculus deductive reasoning. Then, we can harness the array of automated proof techniques in Isabelle/HOL [29], such as integrated automated theorem provers, to discharge resulting verification conditions. We apply this approach to develop the d$\mathcal{L}$ hybrid program model, and the associated proof calculus as a set of derived theorems. Moreover, we have developed a tactic, **wp-tac**, which calculates $[P]\phi$ and $\langle P \rangle \phi$ conditions using Isabelle's simplifier and thus automates proof.

3 Formal Model-Based Assurance Cases

In this section, we develop FMACs, that is ACs that contain a formal model from which evidence for the top-level claims is derived. The informal structure of an FMAC is provided through Isabelle/SACM. We formalise claims using the modalities from d$\mathcal{L}$, which allows us to formulate LTL-style guarantees of the form $p \Rightarrow \circ q$, $p \Rightarrow \Diamond q$, and $p \Rightarrow \Box q$. This integration of dynamic and temporal logic supports the objective underlying many ACs, that is, to integrate evidence from different provenance. We develop a formal notion of FMAC *extension*, which employs both A/G reasoning and *data refinement* [40], which allows us to elaborate models in a style similar to Event-B refinement [34].

3.1 Assurance Case Construction

In this section, we introduce a generalised model of d$\mathcal{L}$-style hybrid programs, use these to define the notion of a Cyber-Physical Machine (CPM), and then define FMACs, which assure properties of a CPM using formal verification.

Hybrid programs are defined with respect to an alphabet, $\mathcal{A}$, of typed state variable declarations $(x : t)$, whose names are drawn from the set $\mathcal{V}$. $\mathcal{A}$ induces a state space Σ, and hybrid programs are modelled as potentially heterogeneous alphabetised relations over state spaces, that is, subsets of $\Sigma_1 \times \Sigma_2$. We give the following syntax for such relations.

Definition 1 (Generalised Hybrid Programs).

$$\mathcal{P} ::= \mathcal{P} \, ; \mathcal{P} \mid \mathcal{P} \sqcap \mathcal{P} \mid \mathcal{P}^* \mid ?\mathcal{E} \mid \langle \mathcal{S} \rangle \mid \mathcal{V} := * \mid \{\mathcal{S} \mid \mathcal{E}\}$$
$$\mathcal{S} ::= \mathbf{id} \mid \mathbf{nil} \mid \mathcal{S}(\mathcal{V} \mapsto \mathcal{E})$$

Here, $\mathcal{E}$ gives syntax for expressions over $\mathcal{A}$. Hybrid programs, $\mathcal{P}$, are composed using sequential composition $(P \, ; \, Q)$, nondeterministic choice $(P \sqcap Q)$, Kleene star (P^*), conditional tests $(?b)$, assignments $(\langle \sigma \rangle)$, nondeterministic assignments $(x := *)$, and ODEs $(\{\sigma \mid b\})$. Each of these operators is semantically denoted as a relational predicate (for details see [10,11]). As usual in UTP [17], relations are partially ordered by refinement $(P \sqsubseteq Q)$, which corresponds to universally closed reverse implication. Most of the operators follow the d$\mathcal{L}$ hybrid program notation, the exceptions being assignments and ODEs, whose generalisations help support data refinement.

Generalised assignment, $\langle \sigma \rangle$, uses a *substitution*, σ: a potentially heterogeneous total function between state spaces, $\Sigma_1 \to \Sigma_2$. The basic substitution $id : \Sigma \to \Sigma$ maps every variable to its present value. Then, $\langle id \rangle$ is the ineffectual program (**skip**). Moreover, $nil : \Sigma_1 \to \Sigma_2$ is a heterogeneous substitution that assigns arbitrary values to every variable, ignoring the initial state.

An existing substitution can be *updated* with a maplet $x \mapsto e$, assuming x and e have the same type. We then use the notation $[x_1 \mapsto e_1, \cdots, x_n \mapsto e_n]$ to denote $id(x_1 \mapsto e_1, \cdots, x_n \mapsto e_n)$, that is, the substitution that assigns n expressions to n variables, whilst leaving all other variables in the alphabet unchanged. Then, the usual singleton assignment $x := e$ can be represented as $\langle [x \mapsto e] \rangle$. Similarly, the notation $(\!| x_1 \mapsto e_1, \cdots |\!)$ constructs a heterogeneous substitution where x_1 and e_1 are from different state spaces. Moreover, substitutions can be applied to expressions using $\sigma \dagger e$, which substitutes all variables in e with those specified in σ. ODEs, $\{\sigma \mid b\}$, are modelled similarly but here σ represents the mapping of variables to their derivatives, and b is a boundary condition, as in d$\mathcal{L}$.

In our model of hybrid programs, we define the modalities $\langle P \rangle \phi$ and $[P] \phi$ from d$\mathcal{L}$ using the corresponding UTP definitions for weakest precondition (**wp**) and weakest liberal precondition (**wlp**) [17], respectively:

Definition 2 (Modalities). $\langle P \rangle \phi \triangleq (\exists \, v' \bullet P \, ; \, ?\phi) \quad [P] \phi \triangleq \neg \langle P \rangle (\neg \phi)$ 🜚

Here, v' refers to the final value of the state. Thus, $\langle P \rangle \phi$ is the relational preimage of P under ϕ, and $[P] \phi$ is its dual defined by conjugation. From these definitions the usual laws of d$\mathcal{L}$ can be proved as theorems. We use hybrid programs to represent CPMs, whose form is inspired by Parnas' four-variable model [32]:

Definition 3. *A CPM is a tuple* $\mathcal{M} = (\mathcal{A}, \mathcal{I}, Inv, \mathcal{T})$ *where* 🜚

- $\mathcal{A}$ *is an alphabet formalising the state space, which is divided into disjoint regions for controlled (**ctrl**), monitored (**mon**), and internal variables (**st**);*
- $\mathcal{I} \subseteq \mathcal{A}$ *is an initialiser that assigns initial values to state variables;*
- $Inv \subseteq \mathcal{A}$ *is an invariant predicate over **st** and **ctrl**;*
- $\mathcal{T} \subseteq \mathcal{A} \times \mathcal{A}$ *is the machine's transition relation.*

To reduce dependencies on the environment, we chose to not allow Inv to use monitored variables. The transition relation specifies the steps the machine can take, and is formulated using hybrid programs of the form

$$\mathcal{T} = (?g_1 \, ; \, P_1 \sqcap ?g_2 \, ; \, P_2 \sqcap \cdots \sqcap ?g_n \, ; \, P_n)$$

which corresponds to a set of non-deterministic guarded commands ($g_i \rightarrow$ P_i). Then, a CPM behaves like a cyclic executive that reads monitored variables (**mon**), executes the transition relation ($\mathcal{T}$), and writes controlled variables (**ctrl**), in the style of Parnas [32]. We impose the following validity constraints on CPMs:

Definition 4. *A CPM is valid if the following conditions hold:*

1. $\mathcal{I} \cap Inv \neq \emptyset$ — *there is a valid initial state satisfying the invariant;*
2. $Inv \Rightarrow [\mathcal{T}]\,Inv$ — *the invariant is maintained by all transitions;*
3. $Inv \Rightarrow \langle\mathcal{T}\rangle\,true$ — *if the invariant holds, there is an enabled transition;*
4. $\forall r \bullet \langle\mathcal{T}\rangle r \Rightarrow (\exists(\textbf{ctrl},\textbf{st}) \bullet r)$ — *only controlled and state variables are changed by the body; any predicate r, refering to **mon** only, is invariant.*

The conditions together ensure the machine is well-formed, maintains the invariant, and is free of deadlock. We can now use CPMs to define FMACs:

Definition 5. *An FMAC is a tuple $AC = (\mathcal{M}, As, Gr)$ with*

- *a valid cyber-physical machine ($\mathcal{M}$) describing the system behaviours;*
- *a set of environmental assumptions (As), specified as predicates on **mon**;*
- *a set of guarantees (Gr), specified as predicates on **mon**, **ctrl**, **st**.*

The assumption As constrains the environment with a predicate on the monitored variables. The guarantee predicates are LTL formulas corresponding to a subset of $d\mathcal{L}$ formulae, namely:

- $p \Rightarrow \circ q$: if p holds currently, then q holds in the next state;
- $p \Rightarrow \Box q$: if p holds, then q holds in all subsequent states;
- $p \Rightarrow \Diamond q$: if p holds, then q holds in at least one subsequent state.

Below, Gr^s denotes a set of *(s)afety* predicates of the kind $p \Rightarrow \circ q$ and $p \Rightarrow \Box q$, and Gr^l a set of *(l)iveness* predicates ($p \Rightarrow \Diamond q$). In Sect. 4, we use this convention to identify corresponding predicates. Next, we define a satisfaction relation $\mathcal{M} \models \phi$ (spoken: "the machine $\mathcal{M}$ satisfies the formula ϕ").

Definition 6 (Satisfaction Relation).

$$\mathcal{M} \models (p \Rightarrow \circ q) \triangleq (As \wedge Inv \wedge p \Rightarrow [\mathcal{T}]\,q)$$
$$\mathcal{M} \models (p \Rightarrow \Box q) \triangleq (\exists I \bullet (I \Rightarrow [\mathcal{T}]\,I) \wedge (As \wedge Inv \wedge p \Rightarrow I) \wedge (As \wedge Inv \wedge I \Rightarrow q))$$
$$\mathcal{M} \models (p \Rightarrow \Diamond q) \triangleq (As \wedge Inv \wedge p \Rightarrow \langle\mathcal{T}^*\rangle q)$$

$\mathcal{M}$ satisfies $p \Rightarrow \circ q$ when **wlp** of $\mathcal{T}$ under q—i.e., the set of states from which $\mathcal{T}$ leads to a state satisfying q or is undefined—is implied by p. Similarly, $\mathcal{M}$ satisfies $p \Rightarrow \Diamond q$ when **wp** of $\mathcal{T}^*$ under q is implied by p. For universal properties, our definition requires an invariant. $\mathcal{M}$ satisfies $p \Rightarrow \Box q$ if there is an expression I such that (1) I is an invariant of $\mathcal{T}$; (2) I is implied by $As \wedge Inv \wedge p$; and (3) I, conjoined with As and Inv, implies q. From this definition, we obtain a property similar to the other definitions as a theorem:

Theorem 1 (*-Global). *If $M \models (p \Rightarrow \Box q)$ then $As \wedge Inv \wedge p \Rightarrow [\mathcal{T}^*]\, q$.*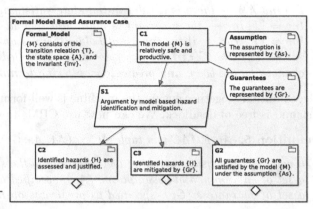

Finally, we define a notion of validity for FMACs themselves:

Definition 7 (Validity). *FMAC is valid if $\mathcal{M}$ is a valid CPM, and all guarantees are satisfied, that is, $\forall\, g \in Gr \bullet \mathcal{M} \models g$.*

With a formal definition of FMACs in Isabelle, we can now show how this information is presented in an AC module. A GSN diagram visualising the SACM pattern for an FMAC is shown in Fig. 1. This pattern refers to the CPM model (Definition 3), with its state space, invariant, and transition relation. The AC module has a top-level claim of relative safety

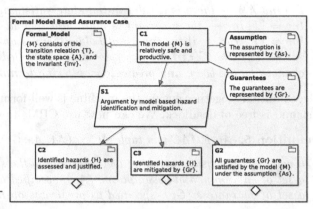

Fig. 1. FMAC pattern

with respect to the model, $\mathcal{M}$. It requires a set of hazards, an assumption, and a set of guarantees that mitigate the hazards. The main claims, $C1$–$C4$, are made public (indicated by the folder icon), so they can be used as components in another AC. As indicated by the diamonds, the reasoning for hazard mitigation and guarantee satisfaction is left to be developed as part of the instantiation of the pattern.

3.2   Assurance Case Extension

FMAC extension allows us to extend an existing AC by refining the CPM model, weakening the assumptions, and adding new guarantees. In this way, the guarantees of the original FMAC can be carried over from the old to the new AC. For this, we define a notion of machine refinement.

Definition 8. *A machine refinement is a triple $(\mathcal{M}_a, \mathcal{M}_c, \rho)$, for retrieve function $\rho\colon \Sigma_c \to \Sigma_a$, such that the following conditions hold:*

1. $Inv_c \Rightarrow (\rho \dagger Inv_a)$ — *the abstract invariant is strengthened by the concrete invariant;*
2. $(?Inv_c \mathbin{;} \langle\rho\rangle \mathbin{;} \mathcal{T}_a) \sqsubseteq (?Inv_c \mathbin{;} \mathcal{T}_c \mathbin{;} \langle\rho\rangle)$ —*when the concrete invariant holds initially, each transition in the abstract machine can be matched by a transition in the concrete machine (simulation [40]).*

We write $\mathcal{M}_a \sqsubseteq_\rho^s \mathcal{M}_c$ when $(\mathcal{M}_a, \mathcal{M}_c, \rho)$ is a machine refinement.

Typically, ρ shows how the variables of $\mathcal{A}_a$ are defined in terms of the variables of $\mathcal{A}_c$, with the following form:

$$\rho \triangleq (\!|x_1 \mapsto e_1(y_1, \cdots, y_n), x_2 \mapsto e_2(y_1, \cdots, y_n), \cdots |\!),\ \text{for } x_i \in \mathcal{A}_a \text{ and } y_i \in \mathcal{A}_c$$

Each abstract variable is mapped to an expression e_i in terms of the concrete variables. Definition 8 encodes a backwards functional refinement [40] between $\mathcal{M}_a$ and $\mathcal{M}_c$. We require that (1) Inv_a is strengthened by Inv_c, when the retrieve function ρ is applied; and (2) $\mathcal{T}_a$ is simulated by $\mathcal{T}_c$ modulo ρ, which is expressed using a refinement statement of the usual form [40].

From Definition 8, we prove the following theorem about safety invariants:

Theorem 2. *If $\mathcal{M}_a \sqsubseteq_\rho^s \mathcal{M}_c$ and $(Inv_a \wedge \phi) \Rightarrow [\mathcal{T}_a]\,\phi$, that is ϕ is an invariant of $\mathcal{M}_a$, then it follows that $(Inv_c \wedge \rho \dagger \phi) \Rightarrow [\mathcal{T}_c]\,(\rho \dagger \phi)$, where $\rho \dagger \phi$ is the retrieve function ρ applied as a substitution to ϕ.* ☣

This theorem shows that any invariant of the abstract CPM is also an invariant of the concrete CPM, modulo ρ. Consequently, we now have a method for adapting safety guarantees from an abstract to a concrete assurance case via data refinement. We now use this to define the extension operator for FMACs.

Definition 9. *Given AC_a and AC_c according to Definition 5, then we define $AC_a \oplus_\rho AC_c \triangleq (\mathcal{M}_c, As_c, Gr_c \cup \{r \uparrow_\rho \mid r \in Gr_a^s\})$ where* ☣

$$(p \Rightarrow \circ q) \uparrow_\rho \triangleq ((\rho \dagger p) \Rightarrow \circ(\rho \dagger q)) \qquad (p \Rightarrow \Box q) \uparrow_\rho \triangleq ((\rho \dagger p) \Rightarrow \Box(\rho \dagger q))$$

In an AC extension, every abstract safety guarantee is lifted to a concrete guarantee through the retrieve function. By applying ρ as a substitution, we compute the meaning of each of the safety guarantees in the refined state space. We do not map $\Diamond q$ guarantees, as these are not in general preserved by refinement. Refinements allow one to restrict behaviours to specific trace subsets. Traces establishing liveness guarantees might get excluded while meeting invariants and safety guarantees. Here, we leave liveness guarantees to be translated manually from Gr_a to Gr_c. Finally, we demonstrate when an AC extension is valid:

Theorem 3. *$AC_a \oplus_\rho AC_c$ is a valid FMAC provided that:* ☣

1. *$\mathcal{M}_a$ and $\mathcal{M}_c$ are both valid CPMs;*
2. *AC_a is a valid FMAC;*
3. *$\mathcal{M}_a \sqsubseteq_\rho^s \mathcal{M}_c$—machine refinement holds;*
4. *$(\rho \dagger As_a) \Rightarrow As_c$—the assumption is weakened modulo ρ;*
5. *$\forall g \in Gr_c \bullet \mathcal{M}_c \models g$—all additional guarantees are satisfied.*

This theorem shows that the existing safety guarantees can be verified with respect to the refined model. Essentially, Definition 7 is met because (1) any invariant can be transferred from abstract to concrete (Theorem 2); and (2) satisfaction of $\Box q$ properties requires an explicit invariant (Definition 6).

Figure 2 summarises the formal relationships between the artefacts of the extension argument. We then claim that AC_c extends AC_a modulo ρ. The following steps are carried through in Isabelle/UTP for each extension of AC_a:

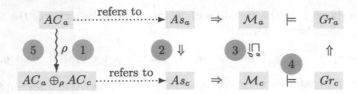

Fig. 2. Artefacts and satisfaction relationships of an extension step

1. We define the retrieve function ρ.
2. We prove that the concrete assumptions weaken the abstract assumptions translated using ρ, that is, $As_c \Leftarrow (\rho \dagger As_a)$.
3. By establishing the refinement $\mathcal{M}_a \sqsubseteq_\rho^s \mathcal{M}_c$, we ensure that $\mathcal{M}_c$ preserves all safety guarantees in Gr_a modulo ρ.
4. We establish the satisfaction relationship $Gr_c \models \mathcal{M}_c$ to verify all safety and liveness guarantees introduced by the extension AC_c.[5]
5. By help of ρ, the steps 2 to 4 establish the *extension* $AC_a \oplus_\rho AC_c$ representing the extended assurance case AC_c.

Figure 3 summarises the extension argument pattern. The FMAC extension readjusts or increases *confidence* over AC_a by following three principles:

1. Regarding the existing assumptions and guarantees, and modulo ρ, the claims **C5** and **C8** establish *consistency* of AC_c with the previous AC_a and thus help to *preserve* argument confidence.
2. Based on **RET_FUN**, claim **C6** aims at *increased precision*, that is, any strict data refinement of the existing alphabet, the guarantees (i.e., existing hazards), and the transition relation increases argument confidence.
3. The claims **C6** and **C7** aim at *completion*, that is, any strict extension of the set of hazards and, potentially, guarantees, while *not* strengthening the assumptions, increases argument confidence.

We implemented the FMAC patterns in Isabelle/SACM, particularly, their argument structure and the linking of claims with artefacts in Isabelle/UTP (Sect. 2.1). Unlike GSN, SACM allows us to structure contextual elements, e.g. one can express inferential links between **Formal_Model** (Fig. 1) and its components As, Gr, and Inv.

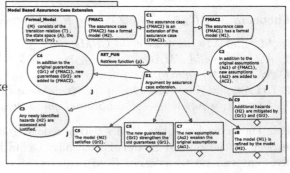

Fig. 3. GSN version of the FMAC extension pattern

---

[5] The steps 3 and 4 imply that the concrete safety guarantees strengthen the abstract safety guarantees, that is, $Gr_c^s \Rightarrow (\rho \dagger Gr_a^s)$.

Table 1. Overview of the guarantees for the initial assurance case and its extensions

AC	Guar.	Informal description
AC_0	Gr_0^s	The robot shall not cause harm to anything
	Gr_0^l	The robot shall be able to perform movements
AC_1	Gr_1^s	(a) While the robot traverses a location, no other objects occupy this location. (b) The robot only traverses locations that are not occupied by other objects
	Gr_1^l	If there are free locations other than the robot's current location, the robot immediately leaves its current location and moves to another free location
AC_2	$Gr_{2.1}^s$	The route planned to an intermediate location does not overlap with the detected occupancy of the workspace by other (fixed and moving) objects
	$Gr_{2.2}^s$	If overlaps are detected while moving the robot intervenes by rerouting and/or by braking
	Gr_2^l	The robot eventually reaches its goal (a prespecified location) given that it is reachable via a finite sequence of routes/path segments.

This way, SACM exceeds GSN's expressiveness. Our implementation in Isabelle/SACM is described in more detail in [13].

4   Application to Mobile Ground Robot

Mobile ground robots are required to achieve a variety of tasks by moving through a workspace while manipulating and transferring objects. Such robots are used for transport in warehouses or hospitals, for cleaning in buildings, for manufacturing in factories. In this paper, we focus on safety and liveness of the *movement* part in such tasks. Hence, our FMAC will argue about safe steps of movement, route planning with obstacle avoidance, and emergency braking.

We now instantiate the FMAC patterns from Sect. 3 to get three successively more detailed assurance cases of such a robot, called AC_0, AC_1, and AC_2. Table 1 summarises the guarantees for the corresponding evolution steps.

4.1 AC_0: Initial Assurance Case

In $\mathcal{M}_0$, we only consider the propositional variable *harm* which is true if any harm to any asset has occurred *because* of the robot's behaviour.

$$\mathcal{I}_0 \triangleq [harm \mapsto \mathbf{false}]$$
$$Inv_0 \triangleq Gr_0 \triangleq \neg harm$$
$$\mathcal{T}_0 \triangleq Move \triangleq ?\mathbf{true} \, \mathring{,} \, \mathbf{skip}$$

Because we do not have any elements in the model to express bad things, *Move* has to cover only and exactly the safe movements the robot can make in order to fulfil Gr_0. If *harm* is **true** then it is not because of *Move*. Hence, it must have been **true** before but this contradicts our assumption. Although the latter technically provides an argument for safety, clearly, this argument is not anywhere near a compelling or meaningful one. Thus, we have to increase confidence.

4.2 AC_1: First Extension

Given *LOCATION* as the non-empty set of locations, $p\colon LOCATION$ denotes the current position of the robot, and $aim\colon LOCATION$ the current choice of the next location to move to. The operation *Move* now gets the atomic assignment $p := aim$. Furthermore, in $\mathcal{M}_1$, we include a state function $occ\colon LOCATION \Rightarrow bool$ which is **true** for all locations occupied by objects other than the robot, **false** otherwise. For a weak notion of liveness with respect to *Move*, the robot is required to choose *aim* such that it keeps moving as long as *occ* is **false** for some location in *LOCATION*. In $\mathcal{M}_1$, the choice of *aim* is implemented by a type-safe and constrained non-deterministic assignment. The following listing summarises the FMAC consisting of the model $\mathcal{M}_1$ and the assurance case AC_1:

$$\mathcal{I}_1 \triangleq \textbf{id}$$
$$Inv_1 \triangleq \neg occ(p)$$
$$\mathcal{T}_1 \triangleq Move \triangleq aim := * \,\mathring{,}\, ?aim \in freeLocs \wedge aim \neq p \wedge \neg occ(aim) \,\mathring{,}\, p := aim$$
$$As_1 \triangleq \neg occ(p) \wedge freeLocs \neq \varnothing$$
$$Gr_1 \triangleq ?(p = aim) \,\mathring{,}\, \neg occ(aim)$$
$$\rho_1 \triangleq (\!|harm \mapsto occ(p)|\!)$$

We assume that while the robot performs a *Move* to location *aim*, the environment will not occupy *aim*. Regarding the confidence of AC_1, this assumption is realistic if locations are close enough to each other and the maximum speed of other objects is low enough. With As_1, we assume that *occ* changes (i.e., other objects can be randomly (re)located in *LOCATION*) beyond that restriction only after a *Move* of the robot is completed.[6] Also, Gr_1 encodes the assumption that whenever the robot has reached *aim* in this state, no other object can have reached *aim* in the same state. Hence, a location is deemed occupied if a moving object is expected to touch this location during the current *Move* of the robot. A more detailed model for AC_1 is given in ([13], Sects. 4 and 5).

Now, to argue that AC_1 is an extension of AC_0 as explained in Sect. 3.2, we first prove that As_0 is weakened by As_1 modulo ρ and show that the existing safety guarantees are preserved by establishing the refinement $\mathcal{M}_0 \sqsubseteq^s_\rho \mathcal{M}_1$. Finally, we show by establishing Definition 7 in Isabelle that AC_1 is valid.

Regarding the confidence of AC_1, the introduced location model, the conditional *Move*, and the occupancy-based safety guarantee illustrate how we slightly but correctly increased the precision of our argument for the claim that *the robot*

---

[6] In the CPM model, environmental changes are encoded by $mon := *$, see [13].

is safe. The extension from AC_0 to AC_1 is an instance of the pattern in Fig. 3. A complete pattern instance for this step is provided in ([13], Fig. 6).

4.3 AC_2: Second Extension

For $\mathcal{M}_2$, we refine the data model of $\mathcal{M}_1$, where each location is reachable from everywhere, by a relation $Connection \subseteq LOCATION \times LOCATION$. Our model also contains a notion of distance between locations and allows to mark a specific location as the *goal*. Based on $Connection$, we extend $\mathcal{A}_2$ by a variable $trj: LOCATION$ *list* to manage routes and $oldDist$ to measure the progress towards the final *goal*. The following list summarises the model $\mathcal{M}_2$ and the corresponding extension AC_2:

$$
\begin{aligned}
\mathcal{I}_2 &\triangleq [trj \mapsto [\,], occ \mapsto occ] \\
Inv_2 &\triangleq \neg occ(p) \\
\mathcal{T}_2 &\triangleq Plan \sqcap MicroMove \sqcap EmgBrake \\
As_2 &\triangleq minBrakingPrefix(trj) \in clearPaths \\
Gr_{2.1}^s &\triangleq hazardousMove \Rightarrow \neg occ(p) \\
Gr_2^l &\triangleq clearPaths \neq \varnothing \wedge p \neq goal \wedge (\neg hazardousMicroMove) \\
&\quad \Rightarrow oldDist > dist(p, goal) \\
\rho_2 &\triangleq (\!| occ(p) \mapsto minBrakingPrefix(trj) \notin clearPaths, occ(aim) \mapsto occ(aim) |\!)
\end{aligned}
$$

Safety in $\mathcal{M}_2$ relies on the assumption As_2 that any update of occ by the environment will not lead to an occupancy of any prefix of the planned route trj shorter than the minimum braking distance, that is, $minBrakingPrefix(trj) \notin clearPaths$. Based on As_2, $Gr_{2.1}^s$ guarantees safe emergency braking, that is, not actively hitting any (moving) objects beyond minimum braking distance. This corresponds to the notion of *passive safety* in [26].

For liveness in $\mathcal{M}_2$, we use a conjunct $p \neq goal$ in the precondition for Gr_2^l that specifies the termination of the robot's goal seeking activity. The postcondition of Gr_2^l states that after each $MicroMove$, the robot should strictly get closer to the goal. Gr_2^l is required for the desired liveness property of $\mathcal{M}_2$. However, only if $clearPath = \varnothing$ cannot occur infinitely often, Gr_2^l implies termination.

The proof that AC_2 actually extends AC_1 works in a way similar to the extension proof for AC_1, now based on ρ_2. For $\mathcal{M}_2$, we use further parameters and definitions. These as well as the definitions of the three operations $Plan$, $MicroMove$, and $EmgBrake$ are provided in the model in ([13], Sect. 6).

5 Discussion

Here, we put our FMAC patterns into the context of formal robot verification, robotic engineering practice, and practically relevant standards. We also relate our contribution to model validation arguments.

Formal Robot Verification. Early work by Rahimi et al. [35] models a robot controller as a set of actions specified by pre/post conditions derived from hazard analysis. The authors use real-time logic to verify whether action implementations in software comply with these conditions. Beyond their work, our robot example demonstrates proof automation, refinement verification, and integration of proof evidence into a maintainable AC for certification.

Based on a CSP-inspired process algebra with the operational semantics of message-synchronous port automata, Lyons et al. [24] propose a plant model composed of environment, machine, and controller. Their controller model corresponds to our Kleene-starred CPM transition relation (cf. Theorem 1). The authors verify an elaborate plant model against *performance* (i.e., a generalisation of safety and liveness) guarantees by proving observational equivalence with reducing the embedded SAT problem to a filtering problem on Bayesian networks. Our approach based on Isabelle/UTP facilitates more generic abstraction and proof assistance based on relations and d$\mathcal{L}$.

Mitsch et al. [26] model robots in d$\mathcal{L}$ and verify successively refined notions of safety and liveness. These include *static safety* (i.e., no collision with static obstacles), *passive safety* (i.e., no active collision), *passive friendly safety* (i.e., safe braking circle does not intersect with other moving objects' safe braking circle), and *passive orientation safety* (i.e., braking cone does not intersect with other moving objects' braking cones). While our robot model is less detailed, we formalise the transition between increasingly precise notions of safety by data refinement, assumption weakening, and guarantee strengthening. Beyond [24] and [26], we demonstrate how robot validity and refinement proofs can be evolved within a standardised AC framework.

Though [26] does not explicitly invoke refinement in their stepwise development, refinement in d$\mathcal{L}$ was previously investigated by Loos and Platzer [23]. They extend d$\mathcal{L}$ with a refinement operator $\alpha \leq \beta$, that specifies that a hybrid program α is more deterministic than a program β. If a safety guarantee, $\theta \Rightarrow [\beta]\phi$, can be proved for β, then the guarantee can automatically be derived for the refinement α (Theorem 2). Their notion of refinement permits local reasoning, such that subcomponents of a program need only demonstrate refinement under the condition they are reachable. Our refinement notion is global; however it is possible to derive their localised refinement relation in our setting. Effectively, our work can be seen as an extension of [23] with data refinement, which we believe can support stepwise development in the style of [26].

For a multi-robotic system, Desai et al. [8] verify safety and liveness properties of a trajectory coordination protocol based on a verified state-machine abstraction of almost-synchronously clocked plan execution units and asynchronous analysis and planning units. They apply SMT and A*-search for safe plan generation and model-checking of the coordination protocol. While their assumptions for modelling multi-robot coordination differ strongly from the assumptions applied in our single robot example, we can see the opportunity to enhance their fixed-model approach with data refinement to integrate multi-robot verification evidence into an extensible FMAC.

Industrial Standards and Verification Practices. Cooper et al. [6] demonstrate how formal methods (e.g. Z [38]) can be effectively practiced for security certification according to the Common Criteria standard [5]. However, back then, proof automation in AC construction was less researched and developed. Inspired by such examples, it is reasonable to aim for a transfer of our approach to the robotics and other safety-critical domains where FMs and ACs are highly recommended. For example, in the context of RTCA DO-178C, the FM supplement DO-333 [36] recommends the creation of "formal analysis cases" providing evidence for a variety of claims (e.g. Clauses FM 6.3.1-6.3.4), particularly, the satisfaction of high- and low-level safety guarantees. The automotive standard ISO 26262 (e.g. Part 2, Clause 6.4.5.4) recommends a safety case for each system component with a safety goal and that these safety cases are subject of configuration and change management, thus, maintenance and evolution. Overall, these standards provide many opportunities for FMACs and Isabelle/SACM.

Adequacy and Completeness of the Formalisation. For controller design and synthesis, control engineers perform *model validation experiments* to assess how well a model of the process, they want to control, complies with the real world [37]. Likewise, the formal model associated with an FMAC (extension) has to be accompanied by an argument (potentially based on experiments using simulation and test [9]) that this model *faithfully abstracts from and predicts* [21] the implemented controller (i.e., the potentially distributed embedded system) and the surrounding plant. Isabelle/SACM allows us to enhance arguments accordingly. However, a further discussion of model validity arguments is out of scope.

Safety guarantees result from accident experience, domain expertise, and *hazard analysis* [22]. Regarding continuous hazard analysis, the pattern in Fig. 3 accommodates changes of the hazard list and the corresponding guarantees as assumed claims (**C3,C4**) and the corresponding hazard mitigation as an undeveloped claim (**C9**). The step from hazard analysis to the derivation of new guarantees and model improvements is discussed in more detail in [12].

6   Conclusions

Assurance cases have to evolve to readjust or increase confidence [7]. Hence, we propose a framework for *formal model-based assurance case* construction and extension. Our framework is based on Isabelle/UTP whose semantic foundations allow one to express the system model for the construction of the assurance case in various but precisely linked formalisms, for example, relations and d$\mathcal{L}$. This linking, paramount to the engineering of many critical systems [14], enables the step-wise refinement of the system model including data refinement and the simultaneous extension of an existing assurance case, resulting in an evolved assurance case readjusting or increasing the level of confidence of the argument. In [15], we discuss how model-based engineering can accommodate the way how innovation typically drives the evolution of requirements and designs. Extensible FMACs further develop this idea towards continuous model-based assurance.

Beyond the State of the Art. We propose the application of verification principles as recommended by, for example, DO-178C to mobile robot controllers. Our approach fosters *scalability* in two directions: first, via AC modules (i.e., A/G-style reasoning) devoted to specific assurance aspects, second, via compositional reasoning in Isabelle/UTP to isolate and reason about parts of large robot models. Regarding the former, we support *arguments at scale* by separation of the detailed proof structure in Isabelle/UTP from the overarching argument and evidence structure using Isabelle/SACM. This separation keeps the argument lean while maintaining traceability to all proof and model details.

Next Steps. The use of A/G-style specification for FMACs paired with invariants as constraints on the controlled and internal state variables improves the preservation of properties of FMAC compositions. To deal with more complex FMACs, we want to simplify composition and refinement at the level of FMACs by providing a new operator, $AC_a \sqsubseteq_\rho^{arg} AC_c$. We also want to improve the *modifiability* of an existing FMAC, particularly, support the deletion or substitution of guarantees on updates from hazard analysis. Furthermore, we want to enhance the handling of liveness guarantees across an extension step via $\oplus_\rho$.

Inspired by [1,34], we want to investigate the benefits of a further integration of Isabelle/Isar with the argument structure in Isabelle/SACM. Particularly, Basir [1] discusses how natural deduction program proofs (e.g. using Hoare logic) can formally underpin an argument and how interactive theorem proving can aid in checking the soundness of this argument.

Acknowledgements. This work is partly supported by the EPSRC projects CyPhyAssure[7], grant reference EP/S001190/1, and RoboCalc, grant reference EP/M025756/1.

References

1. Basir, N.: Safety cases for the formal verification of automatically generated code. Ph.D. thesis, University of Southampton (2010)
2. Bate, I., Kelly, T.: Architectural considerations in the certification of modular systems. Reliab. Eng. Syst. Saf. **81**(3), 303–324 (2003). https://doi.org/10.1016/S0951-8320(03)00094-2
3. Brucker, A.D., Ait-Sadoune, I., Crisafulli, P., Wolff, B.: Using the isabelle ontology framework. In: Rabe, F., Farmer, W.M., Passmore, G.O., Youssef, A. (eds.) CICM 2018. LNCS (LNAI), vol. 11006, pp. 23–38. Springer, Cham (2018). https://doi.org/10.1007/978-3-319-96812-4_3
4. Calinescu, R., Weyns, D., Gerasimou, S., Iftikhar, M.U., Habli, I., Kelly, T.: Engineering trustworthy self-adaptive software with dynamic assurance cases. IEEE Trans. Softw. Eng. **44**(11), 1039–1069 (2018). https://doi.org/10.1109/tse.2017.2738640
5. Common Criteria Consortium: Common criteria for information technology security evaluation - part 1: Introduction and general model, Technical report, CCMB-2017-04-001 (2017). https://www.commoncriteriaportal.org

---

[7] CyPhyAssure Project: https://www.cs.york.ac.uk/circus/CyPhyAssure/.

6. Cooper, D., et al.: Tokeneer ID Station: Formal Specification, Technical report, Praxis High Integrity Systems, August 2008. https://www.adacore.com/tokeneer
7. Denney, E., Pai, G., Habli, I.: Dynamic safety cases for through-life safety assurance. In: 2015 IEEE/ACM 37th IEEE International Conference on Software Engineering. IEEE, May 2015. https://doi.org/10.1109/icse.2015.199
8. Desai, A., Saha, I., Yang, J., Qadeer, S., Seshia, S.A.: DRONA: a framework for safe distributed mobile robotics. In: Proceedings of the 8th International Conference on Cyber-Physical Systems - ICCPS 2017. ACM Press (2017). https://doi.org/10.1145/3055004.3055022
9. Edwards, S., Lavagno, L., Lee, E.A., Sangiovanni-Vincentelli, A.: Design of embedded systems: formal models, validation, and synthesis. Proc. IEEE **85**(3), 366–90 (1997). https://doi.org/10.1109/5.558710
10. Foster, S., Baxter, J., Cavalcanti, A., Woodcock, J., Zeyda, F.: Unifying semantic foundations for automated verification tools in Isabelle/UTP. Submitted to Science of Computer Programming, March 2019. https://arxiv.org/abs/1905.05500
11. Foster, S., Zeyda, F., Nemouchi, Y., Ribeiro, P., Wolff, B.: Isabelle/UTP: mechanised theory engineering for unifying theories of programming. Arch. Formal Proofs (2019). https://www.isa-afp.org/entries/UTP.html
12. Gleirscher, M., Carlan, C.: Arguing from hazard analysis in safety cases: a modular argument pattern. In: 18th International Symposium High Assurance Systems Engineering (HASE), January 2017. https://doi.org/10.1109/hase.2017.15
13. Gleirscher, M., Foster, S., Nemouchi, Y.: Evolution of formal model based assurance cases for autonomous robots. University of York (2019). Supplemental material. https://doi.org/10.5281/zenodo.3344489
14. Gleirscher, M., Foster, S., Woodcock, J.: New opportunities for integrated formal methods. ACM Comput. Surv. (2019, inpress). ISSN. 0360-0300. https://arxiv.org/abs/1812.10103
15. Gleirscher, M., Vogelsang, A., Fuhrmann, S.: A model-based approach to innovation management of automotive control systems. In: 8th International Workshop on Software Product Management (IWSPM). IEEE digital library (2014). https://doi.org/10.1109/IWSPM.2014.6891062
16. Hawkins, R., Habli, I., Kolovos, D., Paige, R., Kelly, T.: Weaving and assurance case from design: a model-based approach. In: Proceedings of the 16th International Symposium on High Assurance Systems Engineering. IEEE (2015)
17. Hoare, C.A.R., He, J.: Unifying Theories of Programming. Prentice-Hall, Upper Saddle River (1998)
18. Jackson, M.A.: Problem Frames: Analysing and Structuring Software Development Problems. Addison-Wesley, Boston (2001)
19. Kelly, T.: Arguing Safety - A Systematic Approach to Safety Case Management, Ph.D. thesis, University of York (1998)
20. Kelly, T.P., McDermid, J.A.: Safety case construction and reuse using patterns. In: Daniel, P. (ed.) Safe Comp 97, pp. 55–69. Springer, London (1997). https://doi.org/10.1007/978-1-4471-0997-6_5
21. Lee, E.A., Sirjani, M.: What good are models? In: Bae, K., Ölveczky, P.C. (eds.) FACS 2018. LNCS, vol. 11222, pp. 3–31. Springer, Cham (2018). https://doi.org/10.1007/978-3-030-02146-7_1
22. Leveson, N.G.: Engineering a Safer World: Systems Thinking Applied to Safety. MIT Press, Cambridge (2012). https://doi.org/10.7551/mitpress/8179.001.0001. Engineering Systems
23. Loos, S.M., Platzer, A.: Differential refinement logic. In: Proceeding of the 31st International Symposium on Logic in Computer Science (LICS). ACM, July 2016

24. Lyons, D.M., Arkin, R.C., Jiang, S., Liu, T.M., Nirmal, P.: Performance verification for behavior-based robot missions. IEEE Trans. Robot. **31**(3), 619–636 (2015). https://doi.org/10.1109/tro.2015.2418592
25. Meyer, B.: Applying "design by contract". IEEE Comput. **25**(10), 40–51 (1992)
26. Mitsch, S., Ghorbal, K., Vogelbacher, D., Platzer, A.: Formal verification of obstacle avoidance and navigation of ground robots, CoRR (2016). http://arxiv.org/abs/1605.00604
27. Nair, S., de la Vara, J.L., Sabetzadeh, M., Falessi, D.: Evidence management for compliance of critical systems with safety standards: a survey on the state of practice. Inf. Softw. Technol. **60**, 1–15 (2015). https://doi.org/10.1016/j.infsof.2014.12.002
28. Nemouchi, Y., Foster, S., Gleirscher, M., Kelly, T.: Mechanised assurance cases with integrated formal methods in Isabelle. In: Submitted to iFM 2019 (2019). https://arxiv.org/abs/1905.06192
29. Nipkow, T., Wenzel, M., Paulson, L.C. (eds.): Isabelle/HOL. LNCS, vol. 2283. Springer, Heidelberg (2002). https://doi.org/10.1007/3-540-45949-9
30. de Oliveira, A.L., Braga, R.T., Masiero, P.C., Papadopoulos, Y., Habli, I., Kelly, T.: Supporting the automated generation of modular product line safety cases. Adv. Intell. Syst. Comput. **365**, 319–330 (2015). https://doi.org/10.1007/978-3-319-19216-1_30
31. Palin, R., Habli, I.: Assurance of automotive safety – a safety case approach. In: Schoitsch, E. (ed.) SAFECOMP 2010. LNCS, vol. 6351, pp. 82–96. Springer, Heidelberg (2010). https://doi.org/10.1007/978-3-642-15651-9_7
32. Parnas, D.L., Madley, J.: Function documents for computer systems. Sci. Comput. Program. **25**, 41–61 (1995)
33. Platzer, A.: Differential dynamic logic for hybrid systems. J. Autom. Reasoning **41**, 143–189 (2008)
34. Prokhorova, Y., Laibinis, L., Troubitsyna, E.: Facilitating construction of safety cases from formal models in event-B. Inf. Softw. Technol. **60**, 51–76 (2015). https://doi.org/10.1016/j.infsof.2015.01.001
35. Rahimi, M., Xiadong, X.: A framework for software safety verification of industrial robot operations. Comput. Ind. Eng. **20**(2), 279–287 (1991). https://doi.org/10.1016/0360-8352(91)90032-2
36. RTCA: DO-333: Formal Methods Supplement to DO-178C and DO-278A (2012)
37. Smith, R.S., Doyle, J.C.: Model validation: a connection between robust control and identification. IEEE Trans. Autom. Control **37**(7), 942–952 (1992). https://doi.org/10.1109/9.148346
38. Spivey, J.: The Z Notation: A Reference Manual. Prentice Hall, Upper Saddle River (1992)
39. Wei, R., Kelly, T., Dai, X., Zhao, S., Hawkins, R.: Model based system assurance using the structured assurance case metamodel. J. Softw. Syst. **154**, 211–233 (2019)
40. Woodcock, J., Davies, J.: Using Z: Specification, Refinement, and Proof. Prentice Hall, Upper Saddle River (1996)

Towards Integrating Formal Verification of Autonomous Robots with Battery Prognostics and Health Management

Xingyu Zhao[1]([⊠]), Matt Osborne[1], Jenny Lantair[1], Valentin Robu[1], David Flynn[1], Xiaowei Huang[2], Michael Fisher[2], Fabio Papacchini[2], and Angelo Ferrando[2]

[1] School of Engineering and Physical Sciences, Heriot-Watt University, Edinburgh EH14 4AS, UK
{xingyu.zhao,mho1,jl153,v.robu,d.flynn}@hw.ac.uk
[2] Department of Computer Science, University of Liverpool, Liverpool L69 3BX, UK
{xiaowei.huang,mfisher,fabio.papacchini,angelo.ferrando}@liverpool.ac.uk

Abstract. The battery is a key component of autonomous robots. Its performance limits the robot's safety and reliability. Unlike liquid-fuel, a battery, as a chemical device, exhibits complicated features, including (i) capacity fade over successive recharges and (ii) increasing discharge rate as the state of charge (SOC) goes down for a given power demand. Existing formal verification studies of autonomous robots, when considering energy constraints, formalise the energy component in a generic manner such that the battery features are overlooked. In this paper, we model an unmanned aerial vehicle (UAV) inspection mission on a wind farm and via probabilistic model checking in PRISM show (i) how the battery features may affect the verification results significantly in practical cases; and (ii) how the battery features, together with dynamic environments and battery safety strategies, jointly affect the verification results. Potential solutions to explicitly integrate battery prognostics and health management (PHM) with formal verification of autonomous robots are also discussed to motivate future work.

Keywords: Formal verification · Probabilistic model checking · PRISM · Autonomous systems · Unmanned aerial vehicle · Battery PHM

Supported by the UK EPSRC through the Offshore Robotics for Certification of Assets (ORCA) [EP/R026173/1], Robotics and Artificial Intelligence for Nuclear (RAIN) [EP/R026084] and Science of Sensor System Software (S4) [EP/N007565].

P. C. Ölveczky and G. Salaün (Eds.): SEFM 2019, LNCS 11724, pp. 105–124, 2019.
https://doi.org/10.1007/978-3-030-30446-1_6

1   Introduction

Autonomous robots, such as unmanned aerial vehicles (UAV) (commonly termed drones[1]), unmanned underwater vehicles (UUV), self-driving cars and legged-robots, obtain increasingly widespread applications in many domains [14]. Extreme environments – a term used by UK EPSRC[2] to denote environments that are remote and hazardous for humans – are the most promising domains in which autonomous robots can be deployed to carry out a task, such as exploration, inspection of oil/gas equipment on the seabed, maintenance of offshore wind turbines, and monitoring of nuclear plants in high radiation conditions [26].

However, autonomy poses a great challenge to the assurance of safety and reliability of robots, whose failures may cause both a detriment to human health and well-being and huge financial losses. Thus, there are increasing demands on regulation of autonomous robots to build public trust in their use, whilst the development, verification and certification of autonomous robots is inherently difficult due to the sheer complexity of the system design and inevitable uncertainties in their operation [6,8,9,34]. For instance, [21] shows the infeasibility of demonstrating the safety of self-driving cars from road testing alone, and both [23] and [21] argue the need for alternative verification methods to supplement testing. Formal techniques, e.g. model checking and theorem proving, offer a substantial opportunity in this direction [12]. Indeed, formal methods for autonomous robots have received great attention [6,28], both in controller synthesis, see e.g. [12,30], and in verifying safety and reliability when the control policy is given, see e.g. [11,18,42].

The battery as the power source of autonomous robots plays a key role in real-life missions [41]. However to the best of our knowledge, most existing formal verification studies of autonomous robots, when considering energy constraints, formalise the energy component in a generic and simplified manner such that some battery features are overlooked:

- **Capacity fading:** Over successive recharges, unlike a liquid-fuelled system whose tank volume normally remains unchanged, the charge storage capacity of a battery will diminish over time.
- **Increasing discharge rate:** In one discharge cycle, since the voltage drops as the battery is being discharged, for a constant power output (a product of the voltage and the current), the current increases meaning an increased discharge rate occurs. This is different to a liquid-fuelled system in which a constant power output typically means a constant rate of fuel consumption.

Thus, usual assumptions, like (i) a fixed battery capacity regardless the number of recharges and (ii) constant energy consumption for a given action regardless the stage in a discharge cycle, become potentially problematic.

On the other hand, the battery prognostics and health management (PHM) community has been developing techniques to accurately forecast the battery

---

[1] We have used the word "drone" interchangeably with the abbreviation UAV as a less formal naming convention throughout the paper.

[2] https://epsrc.ukri.org/files/funding/calls/2017/raihubs.

behaviour in both a life-cycle and a discharge-cycle. We believe such battery PHM results should be integrated into formal studies (either controller synthesis or verification) of robots to refine the analysis. To take a step forward in this direction, in this paper, our main work is as follows:

- We formalise a UAV inspection mission on an offshore wind farm, in which the mission scenario and choice of model parameters are based on a real industry survey project. The UAV takes a sequence of actions and follows a fixed inspection route on a 6×6 wind farm. It autonomously decides when to return to the base for recharges based on the health/states of the battery. Uncertainties come from the dynamic environment which causes different levels of power demand.
- We explicitly consider the two battery features in our modelling and show (i) how different battery safety strategies, dynamic environments (i.e. different levels of power demand) and the battery chemical features jointly affect the formal verification results; and (ii) the verification results could be either dangerously optimistic or too pessimistic in practical cases, without the modelling of the battery features.
- We discuss important future work on explicitly integrating battery PHM with formal verification, given the trend that advanced PHM algorithms are mostly based on real-time readings from sensors deployed on the battery.

The organisation of the paper is as follows. In the next section, we present preliminaries on probabilistic model checking and battery PHM. The running example is described in Sect. 3. We show our probabilistic model and verification results in Sects. 4 and 5, respectively. Section 6 summarises the related work. Future work and contributions are concluded in Sect. 7.

2 Background

2.1 Probabilistic Model Checking

Probabilistic model checking (PMC) [25] has been successfully used to analyse quantitative properties of systems across a variety of application domains, including robotics [28]. This involves the construction of a probabilistic model, commonly using Discrete Time Markov Chain (DTMC), Continuous Time Markov Chain (CTMC) or Markov Decision Process (MDP), that formally represent the behaviour of a system over time. The properties of interest are usually specified with e.g., Linear Temporal Logic (LTL) or Probabilistic Computational Tree Logic (PCTL), and then systematic exploration and analysis is performed to check if a claimed property holds. In this paper, we adopt DTMC and PCTL whose definitions are as follows.

Definition 1. A DTMC is a tuple $(S, s_1, \mathbf{P}, L)$, where:

- S is a (finite) set of states; and $s_1 \in S$ is an initial state;
- $\mathbf{P} : S \times S \rightarrow [0,1]$ is a probabilistic transition matrix such that $\sum_{s' \in S} \mathbf{P}(s, s') = 1$ for all $s \in S$;

- $L : S \rightarrow 2^{AP}$ is a labelling function assigning to each state a set of atomic propositions from a set AP.

Definition 2. AP is a set of atomic propositions and $ap \in AP, p \in [0,1], t \in \mathbb{N}$ and $\bowtie \in \{<, \leq, >, \geq\}$. The syntax of PCTL is defined by *state formulae* Φ and *path formulae* Ψ.

$$\Phi ::= true \mid ap \mid \Phi \wedge \Phi \mid \neg \Phi \mid \mathcal{P}_{\bowtie p}(\Psi)$$

$$\Psi ::= X \Phi \mid \Phi U^{\leq t} \Phi \mid \Phi U \Phi$$

where the temporal operator X is called "next", $U^{\leq t}$ is called "bounded until" and U is called "until". Also, $F \Phi$ is normally defined as $true\, U \Phi$ which is called "eventually". State formulae Φ is evaluated to be either true or false in each state. Satisfaction relations for a state s are defined:

$$s \models true \quad , \quad s \models ap \quad \text{iff} \quad ap \in L(s)$$
$$s \models \neg \Phi \quad \text{iff} \quad s \not\models \Phi$$
$$s \models \Phi_1 \wedge \Phi_2 \quad \text{iff} \quad s \models \Phi_1 \text{ and } s \models \Phi_2$$
$$s \models \mathcal{P}_{\bowtie p}(\Psi) \quad \text{iff} \quad Pr(s \models \Psi) \bowtie p$$

$Pr(s \models \Psi) \bowtie p$ is the probability of the set of paths starting in s and satisfying Ψ. Given a path ψ, if denote its i-th state as $\psi[i]$ and $\psi[0]$ is the initial state. Then the satisfaction relation for a path formula for a path ψ is defined as:

$$\psi \models X \Phi \quad \text{iff} \quad \psi[1] \models \Phi$$
$$\psi \models \Phi_1 U^{\leq t} \Phi_2 \quad \text{iff} \quad \exists 0 \leq j \leq t$$
$$(\psi[j] \models \Phi_2 \wedge (\forall 0 \leq k < j\; \psi[k] \models \Phi_1))$$

It is worthwhile mentioning that both DTMC and PCTL can be augmented with rewards/costs [7], which can be used to model, e.g. the energy consumption of robots in a mission. Indeed, this is the typical way used in existing studies, and differs from our modelling of battery in this study.

After formalising the system and its requirements in DTMC and PCTL, respectively, the verification focus shifts to the checking of *reachability* in a DTMC. In other words, PCTL expresses the constraints that must be satisfied, concerning the probability of, starting from the initial state, reaching some states labelled as, e.g. unsafe, success, etc. Automated tools have been developed to solve the reachability problem. We use PRISM [24] which employs a symbolic model checking algorithm to calculate the probability that a path formulae is satisfied. More often, it is of interest to know the actual probability that a path formula is satisfied, rather than just whether or not the probability meets a required bound. So the PCTL definition can be extended to allow *numerical queries* by the form $\mathcal{P}_{=?}(\Psi)$ [25].

In general, a PRISM module contains a number of local variables which constitute the state of the module. The transition behaviour of the states in a module is described by a set of commands which take the form of:

$$[Action]\, Guard \rightarrow Prob_1 : Update_1 + ... + Prob_n : Update_n;$$

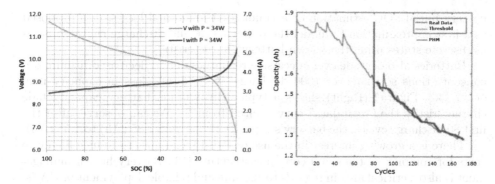

Fig. 1. (Left) The non-linear dynamics of voltage and current vs SOC for a constant power demand from [38]. (Right) Cited from [1], the "real data" curve showing a Lithium-ion battery capacity fade and its PHM predictions (thick green line). (Color figure online)

As described by the PRISM manual[3], the guard is a predicate over all the variables (including those belonging to other modules. Thus, together with the action labels, it allows modules to synchronise). Each update describes a transition which the module can make if the guard is true. A transition is specified by giving the new values of the variables in the module, possibly as a function of other variables. Each update is also assigned a probability (in our DTMC case) which will be assigned to the corresponding transition.

2.2 Battery Modelling and PHM

Electric batteries exhibit non-linear charge and discharge characteristics due to a number of factors. The voltage varies with the state of charge (SOC) because of changing chemical properties within the cell, such as increasing electrolyte resistance, non-linear diffusion dynamics and Warburg inductance [15]. Figure 1-(Left), derived from the experimental test in [38], shows such non-linear results of voltage and current vs SOC profile for a constant power demand.

A constant power demand means that an increase in current is drawn as the voltage falls with SOC. For our study, we are interested in a UAV with a battery capacity of around 11Ah and nominal voltage of 22 V. The energy supply is 180Wh from a lithium polymer battery. For a 22 V battery the voltage at full charge is ~25V and will drop to ~20V at a safe threshold of 30% SOC.

The easiest way to measure a change in SOC is by integrating the current discharge over time from a known initial SOC, called Coulomb counting [17]:

$$SOC(k+1) = SOC(k) - \frac{I(k) \times \Delta t}{Q_{max}} \tag{1}$$

where Q_{max} is the maximum SOC, $I(k)$ is the time dependent current, $SOC(k)$ is the SOC percentage at the discrete time step k, Δt is the time step interval. Although this simplification does not take into consideration inaccuracies in the

---

[3] https://www.prismmodelchecker.org/manual/.

battery initial SOC estimation or account for the internal losses, it is proposed as a first approximation to model the power usage and discharge characteristics as discrete states using the known battery characteristics.

Batteries also degrade over successive recharges due to decreased lithium-ion concentrations so that over 1000 discharge cycles a 20% loss in capacity may occur [36]. Figure 1-(Right) shows a typical lithium-ion battery capacity fade characteristics the ("real data" curve), cited from [1]. We can observe, after the first 80 discharge cycles, the battery's capacity drops from 1.85 (Ah) to 1.55 (Ah).

There is a growing interest in the use of PHM techniques to reduce life-cycle costs for complex systems and core infrastructure [13]. Battery health management is also a critical area in regards to the safe and reliable deployment of UAVs. Numerous studies into battery PHM techniques have been carried out, e.g. the use of Neural Nets [10], Unscented Kalman Filters [17,19], Unscented Transform [4], Hardy Space H_∞ Observers [41] and Physics Based models [16]. Although we are assuming a hypothetical/generic battery PHM method in this paper to provide parameters in our latter modelling, it is envisaged that advanced PHM techniques can be integrated in our future verification framework.

3   The Running Example

As UAV technology improves, energy companies are looking to adopt the technology to reduce maintenance and operating costs. The *resident drone* idea is to station a UAV at locations where aerial surveys are conducted repeatedly. The advantages of such resident drone inspection system are the possibility of increased availability for data collection (e.g. to feed in techniques reviewed in [37]), reduced manual labour, improved safety and more cost effective maintenance strategies. We model a typical application of such system in this paper, based on a survey utilising commercial technologies.

A simplified wind farm drone inspection mission as a 6×6 grid of turbines with a UAV located at the centre is considered. Wind turbines are typically

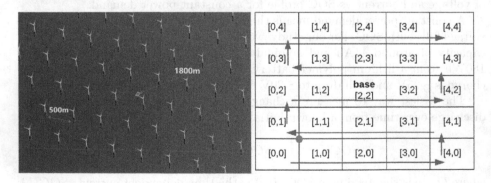

Fig. 2. (Left) A fully autonomous UAV inspection mission in a 6×6 wind farm. (Right) The fixed controller of a UAV inspection mission on the wind farm. Intersections and cell spaces represent wind turbines and transportation channels respectively. (Color figure online)

distributed between 5 and 12 turbine blade diameters apart, so a square distribution of turbines is modelled, each 500 m apart, as shown in Fig. 2-(Left).

The drone mission requires the drone take-off and land at the base station, fly a distance determined by the number of grid spaces to a turbine, carry out an inspection and return to the base or continue the mission with a single battery charge. For this mission a drone transit velocity of ∼10 m/s is assumed. An inspection is expected to take 15 min and the take-off and landing time is estimated less than 1 min. The battery recharge time is around 1.5 h.

4   The Modelling in PRISM

Our formal model of the running example presented in Sect. 3 is a product (via parallel composition in PRISM) of four modules – *Drone*, *Grid*, *Environment* and *Battery*. Depending upon the model parameters used, a typical instance of our model has roughly 100,000 states and 170,000 transitions. In what follows, we introduce the modules separately and describe key assumptions, constants, and variables used in each module. Given the page limits, we only show some typical PRISM commands in the modules and omit some sophisticated synchronisation and parallel composition among modules. The complete sources code in the PRISM language can be found in our repository[4].

4.1   The *Drone* Module

The *Drone* module is essentially a finite state machine describing the behaviour of the UAV during the inspection mission, as shown in Fig. 3. The UAV begins the mission in a fully charged state (S0) at the base. Once the UAV successfully takes off (S1), it may either directly land due to violation of the *battery safety strategy* (see Sect. 4.4), or fly to the target cell (S2) and then carry out an inspection of the wind turbine (S3). Depending upon the battery safety strategy and the battery SOC left after the inspection, the UAV will either fly back to the base for recharging (S4), stay in the same cell if there are more than one wind turbines to be inspected, or fly to the next target cell (S2) if all wind turbines of the current cell have been inspected. Once landed at the base (S5), the UAV will declare success of the mission if all wind turbines on the wind farm have been inspected, or recharge and continue the above work-flow otherwise.

The dotted lines in Fig. 3 represent events where the battery SOC falls to 0, leading to an out-of-battery state (S6). Note, the transition from S0 to S6 means that the fully charged capacity is not sufficient to do the next inspection at the target cell and thus the UAV declares the mission failed without further actions.

It is worthwhile to mention that, realistically, there should be some probability of failure for each action, e.g. 10^{-4} for landing. However, since we are only interested in the particular failure mode of out-of-battery here, we simplify our model by setting the failure probability of each action to 0. Thus, the only source of uncertainty we consider is from the dynamic environment which causes different levels of power demand for each action. We will discuss this in Sect. 4.3.

---

[4] https://x-y-zhao.github.io/files/VeriBatterySEFM19.prism.

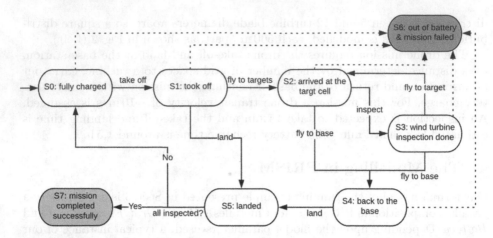

Fig. 3. A finite state machine of the UAV behaviour modelled by the *Drone* module.

4.2 The *Grid* Module

We formalise the wind farm as a 5×5 grid as shown in Fig. 2-(Right) in which the intersections represent wind turbines and the cell spaces (labelled by coordinates $[x,y]$) represent transport channels. In this study, we assume a given control policy (CP) of the UAV as follows:

- CP1: The UAV will follow the snake shaped route, as shown by the red arrows in Fig. 2-(Right), to carry out the inspection in each cell.
- CP2: Depending upon the coordinates of the cell, there can be 1, 2 or 4 *appointed* wind turbines to be inspected within a cell. For instance, at cell [0,0], the wind turbine located at the left-bottom corner is the only appointed one; both the two bottom corners at cell [2,0] need to be inspected; and for cell [2,2], all 4 wind turbines around it should be inspected. Indeed, it would be unwise (i.e. requiring more energy) to fly to cell [0,0] to inspect the green dotted wind turbine in Fig. 2-(Right), rather than fly with the shortest route to cell [1,1].
- CP3: Depending upon the battery safety strategy and the remaining SOC, the UAV may suspend the mission and return to the base for recharging. It will resume the mission at the cell where the mission was suspended.

A part of the PRISM commands in this module are shown in Fig. 4. Note, the transitions probabilities are simplified to 1.

4.3 The *Environment* Module

We explicitly consider the environmental dynamics due to its primary impact on the battery's power demand. For simplicity, only one major factor – wind speed – was considered when developing the *Environment* module. We formalise two

```
module Grid
  cpos_x : [0..4] init base_x;// the current position
  cpos_y : [0..4] init base_y;// the current position
  tpos_x : [0..4] init 0;// the target position
  tpos_y : [0..4] init 0;// the target position
  //if the target cell has been visited before: 0 -- no.  1 -- yes.
  is_tar_visited : [0..1] init 0;
  n_uc_wt :[0 ..4 ] init 1;// number of unchecked wind turbines in a given cell
  ...

  // in the cell [0,0], there is only one bottom-left corner needs to be inspected
  [ins] (s=2)&(cpos_x=0)&(cpos_y=0)&(n_uc_wt=1)
        -> (tpos_x'=cpos_x+1)&(tpos_y'=cpos_y)&(n_uc_wt'=0)&(is_tar_visited'=0);
  ...

  // in the cell [2,0], the bottom-left and bottom-right corners need to be inspected
  [ins] (s=2)&(cpos_x=2)&(cpos_y=0)&(n_uc_wt=2) -> (n_uc_wt'=1);
  [ins] (s=2)&(cpos_x=2)&(cpos_y=0)&(n_uc_wt=1)
        -> (tpos_x'=cpos_x+1)&(tpos_y'=cpos_y)&(n_uc_wt'=0)&(is_tar_visited'=0);
  ...

  //after the inspection, fly to next cell, excluding the case of the last cell [4,4].
  [flytt] (s=3) & ((cpos_x!=tpos_x) | (cpos_y!=tpos_y)) &!((cpos_x=4)&(cpos_y=4))
        -> (cpos_x'=tpos_x) & (cpos_y'=tpos_y)&(n_uc_wt'=n_wt_to_ins)&(is_tar_visited'=1)
  ...
endmodule
```

Fig. 4. Some PRISM commands of the *Grid* module.

levels of wind speed, and use a parameter p_wsp_c to capture the dynamics of the wind. Environmental assumptions (EA) are listed below:

- EA1: The UAV will only attempt to take off in a low wind speed condition.
- EA2: The change of wind speed (either from low to high or the other way around) occurs, with a probability of p_wsp_c, before each action is taken in the *Drone* module.

```
module Environment
  wsp : [1..2] init 1;// 1 -- low wind speed. 2-- high wind speed.

  [] wsp=1 -> (1-p_wsp_c) : (wsp'=1) + p_wsp_c : (wsp'=2);
  [] wsp=2 -> (1-p_wsp_c) : (wsp'=2) + p_wsp_c : (wsp'=1);
endmodule
```

Fig. 5. The PRISM commands of the *Environment* module.

From EA2, we know that the higher the p_wsp_c is, the more dynamic the environment, and it is this assumption that introduces uncertainty in the energy consumption for a given action. The PRISM commands are shown in Fig. 5.

4.4   The *Battery* Module

Figure 6 shows two abstracted state machines of the *Battery* module which run in parallel to describe the battery behaviour. The battery features of capacity fading (over successive recharges) and increasing discharge rate (in a single discharge cycle) are captured by battery assumptions (BA) as follows:

- BA1: After each recharge, the battery's fully charged capacity (i.e. c_full in Fig. 6) cannot be recovered to the new battery's capacity. Rather, it decreases with a rate which can be obtained from battery PHM experiments, e.g. as observed from the results in [1], for the first 100-ish discharge cycles, at each recharge, the capacity will fade at an average rate of 0.2%.
- BA2: For a given wind speed, the UAV is working at a constant power demand for all actions. Since we considered 2 levels of wind speed in the *Environment* module, there are 2 levels of constant power demand as well.
- BA3: In one discharge cycle, the battery's voltage is essentially a non-linear function of its SOC. We use a step-wise function to approximate the non-linear function – high voltage V_2 (SOC > 0.75), medium voltage V_1 (0.75 $\geq$ SOC $\geq$ 0.25) and low voltage V_0 (SOC < 0.25).

In line with the BA2 and BA3, we use the following Eq. (2) to estimate the battery consumption (Ah) for an action j (denoted as c_act in Fig. 6) under different levels of voltage V_i and a power demand level k:

$$C_j = \frac{E_{spec} \cdot t_j}{V_i \cdot T_k} \tag{2}$$

where E_{spec} is the specified battery energy, T_k is the total running time under a constant power level k, V_i is the level of voltage, and t_j is the estimated execution time of action j.

For instance, a typical UAV battery with a specified energy of 180 Wh ($E_{spec} = 180$) can fly 30 min at the normal level of workload ($T_k = 0.5$ and k represents the normal level of power demand). The specified normal working voltage is 22 V ($V_1 = 22$) (with a maximum level of 25 V, $V_2 = 25$, and minimum level of 20 V, $V_0 = 20$). The average time for inspecting a wind turbine is 15 min (if action j represents the inspection, then $t_j = 0.25$). Via Eq. (2) and those estimated parameters above, we obtain the last row in Table 1 (results are rounded to one decimal place). Similarly for the battery consumption of each action at the high power demand level (high wind speed environment), the values can be calculated in the same way but are not shown in this paper.

Table 1. Battery consumption (Ah) of actions under different levels of voltage in low wind speed environment (i.e. the normal level of power demand).

	Low voltage	Medium voltage	High voltage
Take-off/land	0.3	0.2	0.1
Transport per cell	0.5	0.4	0.3
Inspection per wind turbine	4.5	4.0	3.6

So far, in our modelling, instead of assuming a fixed battery consumption for each action, we have 6 possibilities of the battery consumption after an action (3 voltage levels × 2 power demand levels).

Engineers are aware of the higher risks associated from operating with a lower SOC battery, thus there are requirements on the battery PHM to provide warnings when the SOC falls below a certain threshold [35] (and to recommend that the mission be discontinued), e.g. a typical 30% threshold is adopted by NASA in [19]. In line with that battery safety strategy (BS), we also define a parameter $safe\_t$ as a safety threshold:

– BS1: before each of the actions, take-off, fly-to-target and inspect, the UAV will check if the SOC will fall below $safe\_t$ after a sequence of actions to perform an intended inspection. If there is sufficient SOC, then take the action, otherwise return for recharging.

An instance of BS1 is that, before flying to the target cell, the UAV will predict the remaining SOC (based on the current battery health/state and wind conditions) *after* flying to the target and performing one inspection. If there is no safe battery life remained (i.e. SOC< $safe\_t$) after the intended inspection, the UAV will go back for recharging. Some typical PRISM commands of this module and associated formulas are shown in Fig. 7.

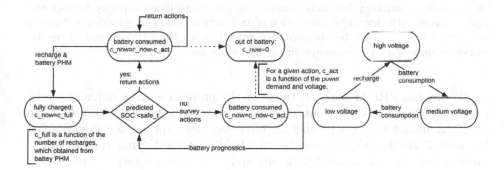

Fig. 6. Abstracted state machines of the *Battery* module.

5 Results

The main properties of interest and their corresponding PCTL formulas are:

– The probability of mission success[5]: $P_{=?}[\ F\ (s = 7)]$;
– The expected mission time: $R\{\text{"mt"}\}_{=?}[\ F\ (s = 7)|(s = 6)]$;
– The expected number of recharges: $R\{\text{"rc"}\}_{=?}[\ F\ (s = 7)|(s = 6)]$.

---

[5] Since we focus on the particular failure mode of out-off-battery in our model, rigorously this should be the probability of seeing no out-off-battery failures in a mission.

```
module Battery
   v : [0..2] init 2;
   // 2 - high terminal voltage , 100%-75% SoC
   // 1 - medium terminal voltage , 75%-25% SoC
   // 0 - low terminal voltage , 25%-0% SoC
   c_now:[0..c_full] init c_full;//The capacity of the battery now.
   n_charge: [0..max_charge_num] init 0;//number of recharges

   // according to the SoC to determine v
   [TO] ((c_now-c_tol)/c_full_vary>0.75)& ((c_now-c_tol-c_ftt-c_ins)/c_full_vary>=safe_t)
        -> (c_now'=c_now-c_tol)&(v'=2);
   ...
   [TO] ((c_now-c_tol)/c_full_vary<0.25) & ((c_now-c_tol-c_ftt-c_ins)/c_full_vary>=safe_t)
        -> (c_now'=c_now-c_tol)&(v'=0);
   //don't have enough battery to do a single inspection
   [lack_batt] (s=0)&((c_now-c_tol-c_ftt-c_ins)/c_full_vary<safe_t)-> true;
   //recharge
   [recharge] n_charge < max_charge_num-> (c_now'=c_full_vary)&(v'=2)&(n_charge'=n_charge+1)
   ...
endmodule
...
// the capacity cost of flying to target asuming, per cell
// v-low takes 0.5Ah, v-medium takes 0.4Ah ,v-high takes 0.3Ah.
formula c_ftt = dis_ct* (v=2 ? (3*wsp): (v=1 ? (4*wsp) : (5*wsp)));
// to calculate the distance from the current position to the target position
formula dis_ct=(max(cpos_x,tpos_x)-min(cpos_x,tpos_x))+(max(cpos_y,tpos_y)-min(cpos_y,tpos_y))
...
```

Fig. 7. Some PRISM commands of the *Battery* module and global formulas. Note, the key variables *c_full_vary* (the fully-charged capacity considering capacity fading) and *c_ftt*, *c_ins* etc. (the battery consumption of each action, which are generically denoted as *c_act* in Fig. 6) should be obtained dynamically from the PHM system in reality, whilst we make simplified assumptions in the source codes.

We use the PRISM tool [24] to check the properties given different model parameters in later subsections. Indeed, we may only be concerned with the expected mission time (or number of recharges) *given* the mission is successful. However, PRISM can only solve the "reachability reward" properties when the target set of states is reached with probability 1, thus our target state here is $(s = 7)|(s = 6)$. In our later numerical examples, we only show the expected mission time when the probability of the mission failing is very small so that its contribution to the average mission time is negligible. Note, this limitation of PRISM has been studied in [29].

5.1 Effects of Battery Safety Strategies and Dynamic Environments

For a typical new battery with 11Ah capacity, we highlight the verification results of four representative cases, as shown in Table 2, by setting the above mentioned model parameters (cf. BS1 and EA2) as:

- #1, the common case and baseline: $safe\_t = 0.3$, $p\_wsp\_c = 0.1$.
- #2, a risky battery strategy: $safe\_t = 0.25$, $p\_wsp\_c = 0.1$
- #3, a more dynamic environment: $safe\_t = 0.3$, $p\_wsp\_c = 0.3$.

– #4, a risky battery strategy in a more dynamic environment: $safe\_t = 0.25$, $p\_wsp\_c = 0.3$.

Table 2. Verification results of some typical cases with a new battery capacity of 11Ah.

	No. of states	No. of transitions	Prob. mission success	Exp. mission time	Exp. no. of recharges
#1	108,688	163,076	1	4700.20	42.65
#2	117,765	177,278	0.91	3885.95	34.59
#3	108,688	163,076	1	7482.86	72.16
#4	117,765	177,278	0.89	5621.66	53.07

The example of #1 represents the common case that serves as a baseline in Table 2. Case #2 represents the use of a relatively risky strategy by reducing the battery safety threshold from 0.3 to 0.25. Indeed, in Table 2, we see a decreased probability of mission success (from 1 to 0.91), whilst the expected mission time and number of recharges also significantly reduce, which is the benefit of taking more risk. Comparing case #3 and #1, given a fairly safe battery strategy (i.e. $safe\_t = 0.3$), a more dynamic environment will significantly increase the mission time and number of recharges. Because the more dynamic the environment is, the more often the UAV decides to go back for recharges for battery safety reasons. Note, the probability of mission success remains (i.e. 1), since the battery strategy is conservative enough to guarantee a safe trip back to base in all possible circumstances. On the contrary, if we adopt a risky battery strategy in a more dynamic environment (#4), then not only the expected mission time increases but also the probability of mission success decreases (cf. #4 and #2), because there are cases that the UAV does not reserve enough battery to fly back to base due to a sudden change of environments.

5.2 Comparison of Models, Disregarding the Battery Features

Most existing verification studies of autonomous robots, when considering energy constraints, formalise the energy component in a generic/simplified manner such that battery features are overlooked. In this section, we illustrate the difference between a simplified battery model and our relatively advanced model, considering the battery chemical features.

Figure 8 shows the probability of mission success, via different models, as a function of the new battery's capacity (Ah). The solid curve labelled as "advanced" represents our proposed model considering the battery features (BA1 and BA3). The other curves represent the basic models without considering battery features, e.g. the "basic_high" curve is the case when there is no capacity fading and the battery always works at a high level of voltage.

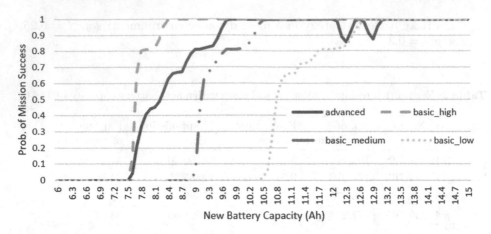

Fig. 8. Probability of mission success, via different model assumptions on batteries, as a function of the new battery capacity.

In Fig. 8, we can observe that, for a given model, there is a required minimum new battery capacity to have non-zero probability to succeed. Indeed, the capacity should be at least enough for the inspection of the first wind turbine and a safe trip back. Since the battery consumption of each action is higher (and highest) when assuming that the battery is always working at a medium (and low) voltage level, such a required minimum capacity increases. Similarly, to guarantee a successful mission, "basic_high" requires that the relatively smallest new battery capacity (around 8.4Ah) due to its obviously optimistic assumptions, i.e. no capacity fading and always working at a high voltage level.

Note, although the "advanced" model is bounded by "basic_high" and "basic_medium", it is still dangerous to use such simplified bounds to do approximation, due to the observed "dip" on the "advanced" curve in the range of 12 Ah–13 Ah. That dip of probability of mission success happens because, when the new battery's capacity increases (but is still not big enough), the UAV may decide to take more risk to perform more actions in one trip (i.e. one discharge cycle), after which there might not be enough SOC left for a safe trip back in some edge cases (e.g. a degraded battery working at a low voltage in a high wind speed environment). To eliminate this phenomenon, the simplest way is to raise the battery safety threshold, which is confirmed by our extra experiments.

An example path of a failed mission is presented in Fig. 9, in which the new battery's capacity is 12.8Ah (thus within the "dip" range in Fig. 8). After 22 recharges at step #148, the UAV flies to the target cell [0,4] and the wind speed changes to high ($wsp = 2$). At step #150, the predicted SOC after the intended inspection is higher than the safety threshold of 0.3. So instead of returning to the base, the UAV continues the inspection in high-speed wind. Although after managing to return to base, the drone fails to land in a high wind speed and at the lower voltage level. Also, if we naively ignore the capacity fading and/or assuming the battery never works at a low voltage, then the UAV would land safely in this example. That's why we don't observe the "dips" on the curves of the basic models in Fig. 8.

Step		Drone	Grid				Environment		Battery	
Action	#	s	cpos_x	cpos_y	tpos_x	tpos_y	wsp	v	c_now	n_charge
[land]	147	5	2	2	0	4	2	2	121	21
[recharge]	148	0	2	2	0	4	1	2	122	22
[TO]	149	1	2	2	0	4	1	2	121	22
[flytt]	150	2	0	4	0	4	2	2	109	22
[ins]	151	3	0	4	1	4	2	1	37	22
[rettb]	152	4	2	2	1	4	2	0	5	22
[lack_batt]	153	6	2	2	1	4	2	0	5	22

Fig. 9. A fragment of a failed mission path generated by the PRISM simulator, which is an example of the "dip" in Fig. 8 with the new battery's capacity as 12.8 Ah. Note, only key variables of the 4 modules are configured to be viewed here.

Figure 10 shows the expected mission time (upper graph curves) from the specified battery models and the differences (lower curves) between them. We observe that, in the practical range of the new battery's capacity (i.e. <13 Ah, base on our survey), the basic models could give either too optimistic (500 min less) or over pessimistic (1500 min more) results. Such a variance of 1 to 3 working days will mislead wind farm maintenance activities and thus cause significant economic loss. Not surprisingly, as the new battery capacity tends to infinity (i.e. the battery is no longer a bottle neck of the given mission), the verification results of all models tends to the same value (as do the results in Fig. 8).

6   Related Work

How autonomous robots should be verified is a new challenging question [6,9], and it has received great attention in recent years, e.g. [11,30,33,42]. When considering energy constraints, the energy consumption is usually formalised in a linear way that being generic for both liquid-fuel and batteries. For instance, in the analysis of robot swarms [22,27] the authors assume constant energy cost at each time step and a fixed capacity when obtaining energy from "food". Again, in the modelling of UAV missions [12,18], a fixed battery capacity and constant battery consumption over time is assumed. In [11], energy consumption of UUV sensors is modelled as a reward/cost for each state, which exhibits a linear behaviour over time. Indeed, such generic and simplified assumptions do not necessarily mean that they are unrealistic, whilst we believe more rigorous discussions and studies should be carried out prior to their adoption.

The study in [3] highlights the difference between real and ideal batteries, with a case study on controlling an energy-constrained robot. But it focuses on another battery feature – "recovery effect" (e.g. a smart phone might shutdown due to an out-of-battery failure, but then become live again after an idle period).

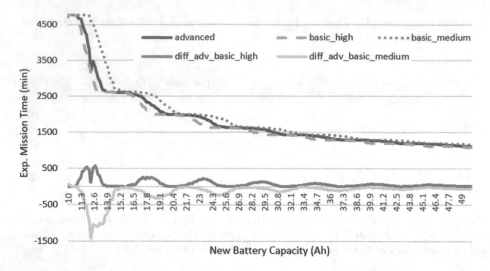

Fig. 10. The upper graph curves show the expected mission time, for the specified battery model, as a function of the new battery capacity. The lower graph curves show the differences of the expected mission times from the specified models.

Beyond the scope of robotics systems, battery behaviour does draw attention for verification. For instance, in [39], the battery of a satellite is described by the Kinetic Battery Model which is formalised as a timed automata to precisely model the discharge behaviour. However they leave out the capacity fading feature as future work. Similarly in [20], the Kinetic Battery Model is used for analysing wireless sensor protocols. For smartphones, [5] uses runtime verification to check whether the actual battery consumption is within the expected limits that are derived from battery consumption profiles for smartphone apps.

7   Discussions, Conclusions and Future Work

In this paper, we formalise a UAV inspection mission of an offshore wind farm, and then do probabilistic model checking in PRISM to show (i) how the battery's non-linear features significantly affect the verification results in most practical cases; and (ii) how battery safety strategies, dynamic environments and battery features jointly affect the verification results.

Most existing formal verification studies of robots make simplified linear assumptions on energy consumption, which is indeed preferable in the case that the capacity is far beyond the total battery cost of the whole mission (i.e. when there is no recharges and the battery's working voltage is fairly stable due to a considerable SOC margin remaining at the end of the mission). In contrast, our work shows how such a simplification can significantly affect the verification results in the case that there are multiple recharges in the autonomous mission. Thus, we believe our work highlights this risk and calls for more rigorous discussions prior to any battery assumptions made in future formal verification of robots, especially when recharges are expected in the mission scenarios.

Moreover, we believe that battery PHM techniques should be explicitly integrated into the formal verification of robots. Although in this paper we use a hypothetical/generic battery PHM technique to provide the parameters used in the *Battery* module, it is clear how PHM can aid the rigorous modelling of battery for formal verification. For now, both the battery PHM experiments and formal verification are assumed to be carried out in the lab, i.e. prior to the mission. To improve the accuracy, an appealing idea is to integrate both at runtime, since there is a trend of doing online battery PHM based on real-time readings from the sensors deployed on the battery, e.g. [2,40]. Whilst there will be a scalability issue if running both online battery PHM and formal verification algorithms at runtime. A compromised solution, in our example, is to invoke the formal verification and PHM during the recharging at the base (where substantial computing resources can be used) with newly collected log-data from recent flights. Thus the verification result will be updated with the up-to-date data. We plan to implement this solution in our future work.

Apart from highlighting the need of integrating battery PHM techniques, this work only serves as a first approximation[6] of the verification of the residential drone inspection mission. More rigorous verification/planning of the mission is needed in future, e.g. by gradually refining the fundamental PRISM model based on observations from various sources of data [31,32].

In summary, our main contributions are:

- We formalise a UAV inspection mission on a wind farm based on a real industry survey project, which can be reused and extended as an exemplar for future research of similar UAV missions.
- We do a sequence of what-if calculations, via probabilistic model checking, to show (i) the importance of considering non-linear battery features in formal verification of autonomous robots; and (ii) how such battery features, together with the dynamic environments and battery safety strategy, jointly affect the verification results.
- We discuss the need of explicitly integrating battery PHM techniques into formal verification of robots, and propose a potential solution which forms important future work.

References

1. Andoni, M., Tang, W., Robu, V., Flynn, D.: Data analysis of battery storage systems. CIRED - Open Access Proc. J. **2017**(1), 96–99 (2017)
2. Barré, A., Suard, F., Gérard, M., Riu, D.: A real-time data-driven method for battery health prognostics in electric vehicle use. In: Proceedings of the 2nd European Conference of the Prognostics and Health Management Society, pp. 1–8 (2014)

---

[6] It is a first approximation in the sense of, e.g. the simplification of two levels of wind speed and the round estimations of battery consumption in Table 1.

3. Boker, U., Henzinger, T.A., Radhakrishna, A.: Battery transition systems. In: Proceedings of the 41st ACM SIGPLAN-SIGACT Symposium on Principles of Programming Languages, POPL 2014, San Diego, California, USA, pp. 595–606. ACM (2014)

4. Daigle, M., Goebel, K.: Improving computational efficiency of prediction in model-based prognostics using the unscented transform. In: Annual Conference of the Prognostics and Health Management Society (2010)

5. Espada, A.R., del Mar Gallardo, M., Salmerón, A., Merino, P.: Runtime verification of expected energy consumption in smartphones. In: Fischer, B., Geldenhuys, J. (eds.) SPIN 2015. LNCS, vol. 9232, pp. 132–149. Springer, Cham (2015). https://doi.org/10.1007/978-3-319-23404-5_10

6. Farrell, M., Luckcuck, M., Fisher, M.: Robotics and integrated formal methods: necessity meets opportunity. In: Furia, C.A., Winter, K. (eds.) IFM 2018. LNCS, vol. 11023, pp. 161–171. Springer, Cham (2018). https://doi.org/10.1007/978-3-319-98938-9_10

7. Filieri, A., Tamburrelli, G.: Probabilistic verification at runtime for self-adaptive systems. In: Cámara, J., de Lemos, R., Ghezzi, C., Lopes, A. (eds.) Assurances for Self-Adaptive Systems. LNCS, vol. 7740, pp. 30–59. Springer, Heidelberg (2013). https://doi.org/10.1007/978-3-642-36249-1_2

8. Fisher, M., et al.: Verifiable self-certifying autonomous systems. In: 2018 IEEE International Symposium on Software Reliability Engineering Workshops (ISSREW), pp. 341–348 (2018)

9. Fisher, M., Dennis, L., Webster, M.: Verifying autonomous systems. Commun. ACM **56**(9), 84–93 (2013)

10. Gao, D., Huang, M., Xie, J.: A novel indirect health indicator extraction based on charging data for lithium-ion batteries remaining useful life prognostics. SAE Int. J. Altern. Powertrains **6**(2), 183–193 (2017)

11. Gerasimou, S., Calinescu, R., Banks, A.: Efficient runtime quantitative verification using caching, lookahead, and nearlyoptimal reconfiguration. In: Proceedings of the 9th International Symposium on Software Engineering for Adaptive and Self-Managing Systems, SEAMS 2014, pp. 115–124. ACM, New York (2014)

12. Giaquinta, R., Hoffmann, R., Ireland, M., Miller, A., Norman, G.: Strategy synthesis for autonomous agents using PRISM. In: Dutle, A., Muñoz, C., Narkawicz, A. (eds.) NFM 2018. LNCS, vol. 10811, pp. 220–236. Springer, Cham (2018). https://doi.org/10.1007/978-3-319-77935-5_16

13. Goebel, K., Celaya, J., Sankararaman, S., Roychoudhury, I., Daigle, M., Saxena, A.: Prognostics: The Science of Making Predictions. 1st edn. CreateSpace Independent Publishing Platform (2017)

14. Guiochet, J., Machin, M., Waeselynck, H.: Safety-critical advanced robots: a survey. Robot. Auton. Syst. **94**, 43–52 (2017)

15. Hariharan, K.S.: Mathematical Modeling of Lithium Batteries From Electrochemical Models to State Estimator Algorithms. Green Energy and Technology. Springer, New York (2018). https://doi.org/10.1007/978-3-319-03527-7

16. He, W., Pecht, M., Flynn, D., Dinmohammadi, F.: A physics-based electrochemical model for lithium-ion battery state-of-charge estimation solved by an optimised projection-based method and moving-window filtering. Energies **11**(8), 2120 (2018)

17. He, W., Williard, N., Chen, C., Pecht, M.: State of charge estimation for electric vehicle batteries using unscented Kalman filtering. Microelectron. Reliab. **53**(6), 840–847 (2013)

18. Hoffmann, R., Ireland, M., Miller, A., Norman, G., Veres, S.: Autonomous agent behaviour modelled in PRISM – a case study. In: Bošnački, D., Wijs, A. (eds.) SPIN 2016. LNCS, vol. 9641, pp. 104–110. Springer, Cham (2016). https://doi.org/10.1007/978-3-319-32582-8_7

19. Hogge, E.F., et al.: Verification of prognostic algorithms to predict remaining flying time for electric unmanned vehicles. Int. J. Prognostics Health Manag. 9(1), 1–15 (2018)

20. Ivanov, D., Larsen, K.G., Schupp, S., Srba, J.: Analytical solution for long battery lifetime prediction in nonadaptive systems. In: McIver, A., Horvath, A. (eds.) QEST 2018. LNCS, vol. 11024, pp. 173–189. Springer, Cham (2018). https://doi.org/10.1007/978-3-319-99154-2_11

21. Kalra, N., Paddock, S.M.: Driving to safety: how many miles of driving would it take to demonstrate autonomous vehicle reliability? Transp. Res. Part A: Policy Pract. 94, 182–193 (2016)

22. Konur, S., Dixon, C., Fisher, M.: Analysing robot swarm behaviour via probabilistic model checking. Robot. Auton. Syst. 60(2), 199–213 (2012)

23. Koopman, P., Wagner, M.: Autonomous vehicle safety: an interdisciplinary challenge. IEEE Intell. Transp. Syst. Mag. 9(1), 90–96 (2017)

24. Kwiatkowska, M., Norman, G., Parker, D.: PRISM 4.0: verification of probabilistic real-time systems. In: Gopalakrishnan, G., Qadeer, S. (eds.) CAV 2011. LNCS, vol. 6806, pp. 585–591. Springer, Heidelberg (2011). https://doi.org/10.1007/978-3-642-22110-1_47

25. Kwiatkowska, M., Norman, G., Parker, D.: Probabilistic model checking: advances and applications. In: Drechsler, R. (ed.) Formal System Verification, pp. 73–121. Springer, Cham (2018). https://doi.org/10.1007/978-3-319-57685-5_3

26. Lane, D., Bisset, D., Buckingham, R., Pegman, G., Prescott, T.: New foresight review on robotics and autonomous systems. Technical report, No. 2016.1, Lloyd's Register Foundation, London, U.K. (2016)

27. Liu, W., Winfield, A.: Modeling and optimization of adaptive foraging in swarm robotic systems. Int. J. Robot. Res. 29(14), 1743–1760 (2010)

28. Luckcuck, M., Farrell, M., Dennis, L., Dixon, C., Fisher, M.: Formal specification and verification of autonomous robotic systems: a survey. arXiv preprint arXiv:1807.00048 (2018)

29. Märcker, S., Baier, C., Klein, J., Klüppelholz, S.: Computing conditional probabilities: implementation and evaluation. In: Cimatti, A., Sirjani, M. (eds.) SEFM 2017. LNCS, vol. 10469, pp. 349–366. Springer, Cham (2017). https://doi.org/10.1007/978-3-319-66197-1_22

30. Norman, G., Parker, D., Zou, X.: Verification and control of partially observable probabilistic systems. Real-Time Syst. 53(3), 354–402 (2017)

31. Paterson, C.A., Calinescu, R.: Observation-enhanced QoS analysis of component-based systems. IEEE Trans. Softw. Eng. (2019). https://doi.org/10.1109/TSE.2018.2864159. (Early Access)

32. Paterson, C., Calinescu, R., Wang, D., Manandhar, S.: Using unstructured data to improve the continuous planning of critical processes involving humans. In: 14th International Symposium on Software Engineering for Adaptive and Self-Managing Systems (2019)

33. Pathak, S., Pulina, L., Tacchella, A.: Verification and repair of control policies for safe reinforcement learning. Appl. Intell. 48(4), 886–908 (2018)

34. Robu, V., Flynn, D., Lane, D.: Train robots to self-certify as safe. Nature 553(7688), 281 (2018)

35. Saxena, A., Roychoudhury, I., Celaya, J., Saha, B., Saha, S., Goebel, K.: Requirements flowdown for prognostics and health management. In: Infotech@Aerospace. American Institute of Aeronautics and Astronautics (2012)
36. Spotnitz, R.: Simulation of capacity fade in lithium-ion batteries. J. Power Sources **113**(1), 72–80 (2003)
37. Stetco, A., et al.: Machine learning methods for wind turbine condition monitoring: a review. Renew. Energy **133**, 620–635 (2019)
38. Traub, L.W.: Calculation of constant power lithium battery discharge curves. Batteries **2**(2), 17 (2016)
39. Wognsen, E.R., Hansen, R.R., Larsen, K.G.: Battery-aware scheduling of mixed criticality systems. In: Margaria, T., Steffen, B. (eds.) ISoLA 2014. LNCS, vol. 8803, pp. 208–222. Springer, Heidelberg (2014). https://doi.org/10.1007/978-3-662-45231-8_15
40. Zhang, C., Allafi, W., Dinh, Q., Ascencio, P., Marco, J.: Online estimation of battery equivalent circuit model parameters and state of charge using decoupled least squares technique. Energy **142**, 678–688 (2018)
41. Zhang, F., Liu, G., Fang, L., Wang, H.: Estimation of battery state of charge with H_∞ observer: applied to a robot for inspecting power transmission lines. IEEE Trans. Ind. Electron. **59**(2), 1086–1095 (2012)
42. Zhao, X., Robu, V., Flynn, D., Dinmohammadi, F., Fisher, M., Webster, M.: Probabilistic model checking of robots deployed in extreme environments. In: The 33rd AAAI Conference on Artificial Intelligence, Honolulu, Hawaii, USA (2019, in Press)

Feature-Oriented and Versioned Systems

SAT Encodings of the At-Most-k Constraint
A Case Study on Configuring University Courses

Paul Maximilian Bittner[(⊠)] [iD], Thomas Thüm [iD], and Ina Schaefer

TU Braunschweig, Brunswick, Germany
{p.bittner,t.thuem,i.schaefer}@tu-braunschweig.de

Abstract. At universities, some fields of study offer multiple branches to graduate in. These branches are defined by mandatory and optional courses. Configuring a branch manually can be a difficult task, especially if some courses have already been attended. Hence, a tool providing guidance on choosing courses is desired. Feature models enable modelling such behaviour, as they are designed to define valid configurations from a set of features. Unfortunately, the branches contain constraints instructing to choose at least k out of n courses in essence. Encoding some of these constraints naïvely in propositional calculus is practically infeasible. We develop a new encoding by combining existing approaches. Furthermore, we report on our experience of encoding the constraints of the computer science master at TU Braunschweig and discuss the impact for research on configurability.

1 Introduction

Universities offer various fields of study to graduate in. In our rapidly growing economics and academia, the need for custom variants or even hybrid areas of study arises. Usually, this would lead to the introduction of a new field of study. However, if the changes are only slight or partial, allowing the graduation in different sub-branches within the same field saves bureaucratic effort and thereby time and money. Such branches are usually bound to two constraints in selection of courses. First, some courses are mandatory for graduating in the desired branch. Second, courses from a given list for at least a certain amount of credit points have to be attended. These *compulsory elective* courses and the amount of required credit points often vary for each branch. For example, the TU Braunschweig offers various branches of study in their masters degree program for computer science.[1] That allows not only studying computer science, but also putting emphasis on individual branches like visual computing, networked systems, or robotics.

Usually, informal specifications of the branches tend to be ambiguous and inconsistent, as noticed at TU Braunschweig. Furthermore, students often

---

[1] https://www.tu-braunschweig.de/informatik-msc/struktur/studienrichtungen.

© Springer Nature Switzerland AG 2019
P. C. Ölveczky and G. Salaün (Eds.): SEFM 2019, LNCS 11724, pp. 127–144, 2019.
https://doi.org/10.1007/978-3-030-30446-1_7

enquire whether they still have the opportunity to graduate in a certain branch after they already completed a number of possibly unrelated courses. A configuration tool for these branches to automate this process and specify the branches precisely is desired.

Feature models are designed to describe relations between individual features (e.g., the courses), such that only specific subsets of features can be chosen [1]. Thereby, they separate configuration logic from the configuration process itself. In contrast to ad-hoc programming and using SMT solvers, we can profit from reusing existing research and tooling on configuration and decision propagation when using feature models [4,14,16–18,20]. For example, guidance for feature selection and explanations for automatic decisions are available [11]. Hence, a configurator comes for free if we can model the branches as a feature model.

As feature models are translated to a boolean formula for analysis, constraints are expressed in propositional calculus [3]. Unfortunately, the *compulsory elective* constraints become a bottleneck. These essentially break down to the $atmost_k$ constraint describing that at most k out of n variables can be set to *true*. This constraint grows exponentially in n when encoded naïvely in propositional calculus. For example, we obtained a formula of about 1 GB text for the branch of Automotive Informatics. Formulas this huge are intractable for common SAT solvers and cannot even be generated in Conjunctive Normal Form (CNF) in a reasonable time even though required by SAT solvers.

Albeit the $atmost_k$ constraint can be encoded to first-order logic naturally, using SMT solvers requires upgrading existing tools and research on boolean feature models. These not only provide configurators with decision propagation already, but are also able to inform the user when and why features are (de-) selected automatically due to model constraints. Thus, course selection would be fully transparent in the resulting tool. Such configurators do not yet exist for first-order logic.

Our research question is: Can we express branches of study as boolean feature models? Therefore we split the problem into multiple steps:

- We developed a new encoding for the $atmost_k$ constraint to minimise formula size by combining existing state-of-the-art encodings [8,12,19]. This is not only useful for feature models but SAT queries in general.
- To describe branches of study we created a Domain Specific Language (DSL) and a compiler, translating the DSL artefacts to a feature model including the constraints.
- We propose a method for generating propositional formulas requiring a sum of weighted variables to be reached. We show its usability for resolving different amounts of credit points.
- We compare performance of different encodings by generating constraints for the branches of study at TU Braunschweig.

In order to test and evaluate our encoding, we implemented each reviewed encoding, our DSL, and our compiler in an open-source project. Our final Branch of study Tool (BroT) and all data are publicly available online at GitHub.[2]

---

[2] https://github.com/PaulAtTUBS/BroT.

Encoding	atmost$_1$($\{A, B, C\}$)
Binomial	$(\neg B \vee \neg C) \wedge (\neg A \vee \neg C) \wedge (\neg A \vee \neg B)$
Binary	$(T_0 \vee \neg A) \wedge (\neg T_0 \vee \neg B_0) \wedge (\neg T_0 \vee \neg B_1)$ $(T_1 \vee \neg B) \wedge (\neg T_1 \vee B_0) \wedge (\neg T_1 \vee \neg B_1)$ $(T_2 \vee \neg C) \wedge (\neg T_2 \vee \neg B_0) \wedge (\neg T_2 \vee B_1)$
Sequential Counter	$(\neg A \vee R_0) \wedge (\neg B \vee R_1)$ $\neg R_0 \vee R_1$ $(\neg B \vee \neg R_0) \wedge (\neg C \vee \neg R_1)$
Commander	$A \vee B \vee \neg c_0$ $(\neg B \vee c_0) \wedge (\neg A \vee c_0) \wedge (\neg A \vee \neg B)$ $C \vee \neg c_1$ $\neg C \vee c_1$ $\neg c_0 \vee \neg c_1$

Fig. 1. With each encoding atmost$_1$($\{A, B, C\}$) is generated. For readability, formulas are split upon multiple rows and are concatenated with $\wedge$. For the same reason, some generated variable indices are shortened.

2   Encoding At-Most-k Constraints

In this section, we elaborate on the atmost$_k$ constraint and how it can be expressed in propositional calculus and introduce our novel *selective* encoding for it. Albeit, the atmost$_k$ constraint is essential for describing *compulsory elective* constraints, choosing at most k out of n elements, where $k, n \in \mathbb{N}, 0 < k < n$, is a common problem. Translated to propositional calculus, the atmost$_k$ constraint requires not more than k variables from a given set V to be true:

$$\bigwedge_{\substack{X \subseteq V, \\ |X| = k+1}} \bigvee_{x \in X} \neg x \tag{1}$$

As this encoding creates $\binom{|V|}{k+1}$ clauses, it is called the *binomial* encoding [8]. Unfortunately, in this representation, formula size grows too fast to be suitable for most use cases. Thus, we further review the encodings *binary* [9,10], *commander* [8,12], and *sequential counter* [19]. Each of them introduces new variables summarizing some information about the original variables' values. Figure 1 exemplifies these encodings for atmost$_1$($\{A, B, C\}$). The *binary* encoding introduces k Bit-Strings of length $\lceil \log_2(n) \rceil$ identifying exactly one variable each. It does not generate a CNF per default as required by SAT solvers. Hence, we use a variation of the *binary* encoding presented by Frisch and Giannaros [8], creating a CNF directly. The *sequential counter* encoding uses n unary registers of size k to count the number of true variables sequentially. An overflow is disallowed because then more than k variables would to be true. The *commander* encoding recursively groups the variables and assigns k commander variables to each group. These contain information whether no or some of the variables in their corresponding group are true. We refer interested readers for details on those encodings to the paper by Frisch and Giannaros [8].

To minimise the resulting formula size, we develop a meta-encoding, called *selective* encoding, which chooses the most efficient of the reviewed encodings considering formula size:

$$\text{selective}(n, k) = \begin{cases} \text{binomial} & k_{binom}(n) \leq k, \\ \text{binary} & k_{split}(n) < k < k_{binom}(n), \\ \text{seq. counter} & \text{otherwise.} \end{cases} \tag{2}$$

As *selective* encoding is motivated by our evaluation results we present its construction as well as the bounds k_{binom} and k_{split} and the reason for the *commander* encoding not being used in Sect. 4.2.

Our use cases mostly rely on the related atleast_k and exactly_k constraints as illustrated later. We express atleast_k by reducing it to atmost_k. If at least k variables have to be true, not more than the remaining number of variables can be false:

$$\text{atleast}_k(S) = \text{atmost}_{n-k}(\{\neg s \mid s \in S\}) \tag{3}$$

By combining atleast_k and atmost_k, we obtain an expression for choosing exactly k variables:

$$\text{exactly}_k(S) = \text{atleast}_k(S) \wedge \text{atmost}_k(S) \tag{4}$$

We encode exactly_k by using our new encoding for atleast_k and atmost_k respectively.

3   Modelling Configuration of University Courses as Feature Models

In this section, we describe our pipeline for branch configuration. First, we formally define the concept of branches of study to give an unequivocal reference as informal specifications usually tend to be ambiguous. Therefore we refer to the four terms *field, branch, subject,* and *category*. A whole area of study at a university like physics, biology and computer science is referred to as a *field* of study. *Branches* of study are subtypes of a field of study and are more fine-grained. Students can specialise in a branch fitting their individual interests. Working units granting credit points like lectures, labs and theses are referred to as *subjects*. *Categories* group subjects belonging to a common department. Second, we present our DSL allowing users to create and edit fields of study including branches. Third, as we are interested in the possibility of expressing branches of study as boolean feature models, we present our compiler, translating artefacts of our DSL to a feature model. Thereby, special attention is given to differing amounts of credit points.

Compulsory subjects (35 credit points)
 Seminar IT-Security (5 credit points)
 Master's Thesis (30 credit points)

Compulsory elective subjects (35 credit points)
 Category System Security
  Advanced IT-Security (5 credit points)
  Machine Learning for IT-Security (5 credit points)
  Lab on IT-Security (5 credit points)
  Lab on Intelligent System Security (5 credit points)
  Project Thesis (15 credit points)
 Category Connected and Mobile Systems
  Management of Information Security (5 credit points)
 Category Distributed Systems
  Operating Systems Security (5 credit points)

Fig. 2. Example for specification of *IT-Security* branch at TU Braunschweig (translated from German).

3.1 Formalizing Branches of Study

Branches of study are subtypes of a field of study. They are a concept for dealing with the need for more customised fields of study at universities due to growing complexity of economy and science. Instead of constructing new fields of study, branches can be introduced to existing fields if they are similar enough. For our case study, we look at the branches of study at TU Braunschweig, but nevertheless, the concept of branches is analogous for other universities and institutions. Credit points granted at this university are ECTS-points (European Credit Transfer System points).

 Graduating in a branch is optional, but not more than one can be chosen. To complete a branch its constraints for choosing courses have to be fulfilled. These consist of a *compulsory* and one or more *compulsory elective* constraints, containing a set of subjects each:

- *Compulsory* subjects have to be attended.
- *Compulsory elective* subjects have to be attended, such that a certain amount of credit points is reached.

As an example, the specification of the IT-Security branch at TU Braunschweig is given in Fig. 2. Next to its mandatory seminar and master's thesis, subjects from a given *compulsory elective* pool have to be attended, such that at least 35 credit points are reached. The project thesis is listed optional here, but is actually mandatory because the sum of all other subjects does not reach the required 35 credit points. Our tool BroT will detect this issue and automatically select the project thesis when this branch is picked.

```
Field "Computer Science"
  Category "Master Thesis" [1, 1] {
    "Master Thesis IT-Security" 30 CP
    "Master Thesis Computer Graphics" 30 CP
    ...
  }
  Category "Subjects" {
    Category "IT-Security" {
      "Advanced IT-Security" 5 CP
      "Lab on IT-Security" 5 CP
      ...
    }
    ...
  }
  ...
  Branch "IT-Security"
  Compulsory
      "Master Thesis IT-Security"
      "Seminar IT-Security"
  CompulsoryElective 35 CP
      "Advanced IT-Security"
      "Machine Learning for IT-Security"
      "Lab on IT-Security"
      "Lab on Intelligent System Security"
      "Project Thesis IT-Security"
      "Management of Information Security"
      "Operating Systems Security"
```

Fig. 3. Excerpt of DSL artifact specifying the *IT-Security* branch described in Fig. 2. Subjects referenced by a branch have to be specified with their corresponding credit points.

3.2   A DSL to Describe Fields and Branches of Study

Creating a feature model for a field of study directly is practically infeasible. The branches constraints would have to be written by hand in propositional calculus, but due to their extent and complexity, this task is highly error-prone and time-consuming. Hence, we provide a DSL from which the branches can be translated to a feature model.

Our DSL allows specifying fields, branches and subjects of study (e.g. courses, theses) with their corresponding amount of credit points granted on completion. Branches are described by a set of constraints. A constraint is a subset of subjects and is either *compulsory* or *compulsory elective*. Furthermore, subjects can be grouped. For example, all possible master's theses are grouped in category *Master Thesis*. That allows for specifying cardinalities $[a, b] \subset \mathbb{Z}, 0 \leq a$, describing how many subjects have to be attended at least and at most. For example, the *Master Thesis* in Fig. 3, having cardinality $[1, 1]$, has to be written exactly

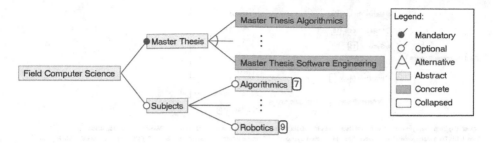

Fig. 4. Example of a feature model describing a simplified version of the field of study computer science at TU Braunschweig. Dots denote that some features are omitted for readability. The modules `Algorithmics` and `Robotics` contain 7 and 9 courses respectively. These are collapsed for readability, too.

once. A value of -1 for b denotes an arbitrary amount, otherwise b has to be greater or equal to a. The default value for cardinalities is $[0, -1]$.

Typically, branches are described by one *compulsory* and one *compulsory elective* constraint, but the official specifications may contain additional side conditions. For example, in *Visual Computing*, auxiliary to the *compulsory* constraint, selecting one of three pre-defined courses is mandatory. The other two courses will then be added to the pool of subjects of the *compulsory elective* constraint. We resolve this issue by introducing a new *compulsory elective* constraint and adjusting the required credit points of the original one.

3.3   Compilation of Our DSL to a Feature Model

As feature models come with dedicated and well investigated analysis tools [4, 11, 16, 18, 20], these can be reused as is for configuring branches of study when encoding the branches as a proper feature model.

Originally introduced to manage configurations of software product lines, feature models are far more general. They define individual features in a tree hierarchy. In Fig. 4, a simplified model describing the field of study *Computer Science* (without the branches) is given. Features can only be selected if their parent feature is selected. Optionally, features can be cumulated in *alternative* or *or* groups. For example, the children of `Master Thesis` in Fig. 4 are in an *alternative* group, as only one master's thesis can be written. Additionally, the `Master Thesis` feature is marked mandatory because it has to be selected. An *or* group requires at least one of its children to be selected. The `Subjects` are grouped by their categories and collapsed in this example. Features can be marked abstract, indicating that they do not have a concrete implementation and are used for modelling purposes only. Auxiliary to parent relationships, each feature can be part of additional arbitrary constraints. These have to be given in propositional calculus, as shown in Fig. 5.

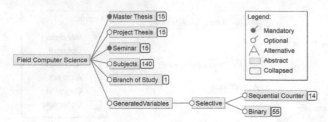

"Branch Big Data Management" → "Relational Data Bases II" ∧ "Data Warehousing & Data Mining Techniques" ∧ "Master Thesis Information Systems"
"Branch Big Data Management" → ¬"Project Thesis Information Systems" ∧ ("Seminar Informationssysteme" ∨ S0_R_0_0) ∧ ("Digital Libraries" ∨ S0_R_1_0) ∧ ...

Fig. 5. The feature model generated for branch *Big Data Management*: Numbers behind collapsed features indicate their number of children. The feature `GeneratedVariables` is artificial and groups all variables that were generated for atmost$_k$ constraints by the respective encoding.

Subjects and Categories. Each subject and branch is translated to a feature. For traceability, features are grouped as children of abstract features if their corresponding subjects are grouped. Specific cardinalities of categories can directly be translated to the feature model hierarchy. The feature of a category with cardinality $[c_{min}, c_{max}]$ is mandatory if $c_{min} > 0$, i.e., at least one subject has to be selected. Otherwise, it is optional. Furthermore, the group type can be derived as follows:

- *alternative* if $c_{max} = 1$, i.e., at most one child can be selected,
- *or*   if $c_{min} \geq 1$, i.e., at least one child has to be selected.

Moreover, the branches' constraints are translated to propositional calculus, such that they can be added to the feature model. It is important that these constraints are only valid if their corresponding branch is chosen (i.e., feature is selected). We achieve this by means of an implication.

Figure 5 exemplarily shows the feature model of the branch *Big Data Management* compiled from its corresponding DSL artefact. If the feature `Branch Big Data Management` is selected, the two constraints at the bottom will ensure that the right subjects have to be chosen for the configuration to be valid. The first constraint describes the *compulsory* subjects according to Eq. 5. The second constraint describing *compulsory elective* subjects according to Eq. 10 is too long to be shown here entirely. It was computed with our *selective* encoding. Thereby, the *sequential counter* encoding was used to encode atleast$_6(\{1, ..., 8\})$ and produced $14 = (8 - 1)(8 - 6) = (n - 1)k$ variables. 55 variables were generated by the *binary* encoding for atleast$_3(\{1, ..., 8\})$.

Compulsory and Compulsory Elective Constraints. In the following, we show how our compiler translates constraints consisting of a set of subjects S_B for a given branch B.

In *compulsory* constraints all subjects are mandatory, meaning that they have to be attended if their corresponding branch is chosen:

$$B \implies \bigwedge_{s \in S_B} s \tag{5}$$

Compulsory elective constraints are defined by the amount of credit points p to achieve at least by selecting a subset of its subjects S_B.

$$B \implies \text{atleast}_k(S_B), \tag{6}$$

Assuming that each subject in S_B grants an equal amount c of credit points, we can determine the number k of required subjects via $k = \lceil p / c \rceil$. For example, if all subjects grant 5 credit points and a *compulsory elective* constraint requires at least 35 credit points (like in Fig. 2), at least $7 = 35$ CP/5 CP subjects have to be chosen. Occasionally, some subjects grant a different amount of credit points, wherefore Eq. 6 is insufficient. In these cases a more advanced approach is necessary, which we discuss in the next section.

3.4   Resolving Differing Credit Points

If all subjects grant equally high credit points, all variables have equal weight. Hence, the actual value of credit points must only be considered to obtain the total number of subjects to choose at least. However, many branches' *compulsory elective* subjects differ in their credit points.

We solve this problem by recursively splitting our set of subjects S in two sets H (high) and L (low). All subjects granting the most credit points are put into H, the rest goes to L. Accordingly, all subjects in H grant an equal amount of credit points. By choosing an exact amount of subjects from H, the remaining credit points can be obtained. These remaining credit points can then be chosen from subjects in L. If all subjects in L grant an equal amount of credit points we can use Eq. 6, otherwise we recursively split L again.

Formally, we define $cp(s) \in \mathbb{N}$ as the amount of credit points a subject s grants. If all subjects in a set of subjects S grant the same amount c of credit points, we define $cp(S) = c$. To split S, we introduce the former set H as a function

$$H(S) = \{x \in S \mid \forall s \in S : cp(x) \geq cp(s)\}, \tag{7}$$

which returns all subjects with the highest amount of credit points. For given subjects S and credit points c, our resulting *compulsory elective* constraint CEC is constructed as follows:

$$\text{CEC}(S, c) = \begin{cases} \text{true} & c \leq 0 \\ \text{false} & c > \sum_{s \in S} cp(s) \\ \text{atleast}_{\lceil c / cp(S) \rceil}(S) & H(S) = S \wedge 0 < c \leq \sum_{s \in S} cp(s) \\ \text{split}(S, c) & \text{otherwise} \end{cases} \tag{8}$$

If the amount of credit points is smaller or equal to zero, enough of them are already reached. If the amount of credit points to achieve c is greater than the credit points all subjects grant together, we never can choose enough subjects. If all subjects grant an equal amount of credit points, the previous solution from Eq. 6 can be used. Finally, we formalise our approach of splitting S into two sets and choosing a definite amount from the higher credit subjects:

$$\text{split}(S, c) = \bigvee_{k=0}^{|\mathrm{H}(S)|} \text{exactly}_k(\mathrm{H}(S)) \wedge \mathrm{CEC}(S \backslash \mathrm{H}(S), c - k * cp(\mathrm{H}(S))) \quad (9)$$

The recursive call to CEC is done on the remaining subjects $S \backslash \mathrm{H}(S)$ and remaining credits $k * cp(\mathrm{H}(S))$. Hence, the problem is simplified to a smaller instance of itself with one amount of credit points removed from the set of subjects. By combining Eqs. 6 and 8, we obtain the final constraint for a given branch B with *compulsory elective* subjects S_B and credit points c_B:

$$B \implies \mathrm{CEC}(S_B, c_B) \quad (10)$$

As a post-processing step, some of the clauses generated by the split function can be omitted in the first place if they are not satisfiable considering the feature model. This commonly occurs if all subjects in $\mathrm{H}(S)$ are in the same category with an upper bound $c_{max} > 0$ where one can never choose more subjects than c_{max}. Thus, $\text{exactly}_k(\mathrm{H}(S))$ can never be true for $k > c_{max}$.

Finally, we can generate feature models representing any fields of study, including branches and subjects with arbitrary credit points. Our upcoming evaluation focuses on their applicability for configuring the modelled branches. Furthermore, we derive our *selective* encoding for the atmost$_k$ constraint by measuring the other encodings performance. We evaluate it by generating the *compulsory elective* constraints for all branches according to Eq. 10.

4   Evaluation

We evaluate the four considered encodings *binomial*, *binary*, *sequential counter*, and *commander*, in terms of produced literals and generated variables. Additionally, we report our experiences when implementing, testing and applying these encodings. We introduce our new encoding, called *selective* encoding, that combines the other encodings to choose the most efficient one considering formula size. By generating the *compulsory elective* constraints for each branch with each encoding, we can evaluate the performance of our new *selective* encoding.

4.1   Tool Support for Implementation

For the opportunity to reuse dedicated libraries and frameworks, we implemented our tool BroT in Java. The FeatureIDE library [13] allows expressing formulas

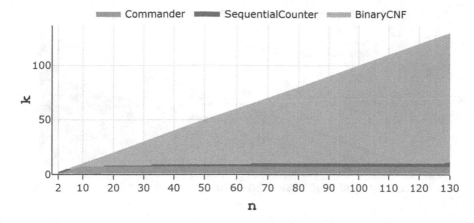

Fig. 6. Encodings producing the lowest number of variables when encoding atmost$_k(n)$. The *binomial* encoding is not considered because it does not introduce any new variables.

of propositional calculus as well as describing feature models. Additionally, the FeatureIDE plugin [17] for the Eclipse IDE [21] contains graphical editors for feature models and their configurations. We created our DSL with the plugin EMFText[3], which integrates well into the other tools.

4.2   At-Most-k Encoding Performance Comparison

First, we evaluate the atmost$_k$ encodings in terms of generated variables. Here, the *binomial* encoding is not considered because it always produces the lowest amount of variables, namely none. Second, we investigate formula size by counting the number of literals to be independent of clause size. Thereby, we develop our new *selective* encoding, as it is motivated by these results.

To detect the most efficient encoding, we encoded atmost$_k(n)$ for each $2 \leq n \leq 130, 1 \leq k < n$ with each encoding. Many instances with $n > 26$ became too big for the *binomial* and *commander* encoding, resulting in a memory overflow. In these cases, we assessed them to produce infinitely many variables and literals.

Remarkably, for both criteria, the results split into three connected areas. Hence, stack plots identifying the encoding producing the lowest amount of variables and literals for each k and n are shown in Figs. 6 and 7 respectively. Our plots are available as scatter and stack plots as interactive HTML versions bundled with our code to allow investigating the exact values.[4]

---

[3] https://github.com/DevBoost/EMFText.
[4] https://github.com/PaulAtTUBS/BroT/tree/master/Evaluation/Encodings.

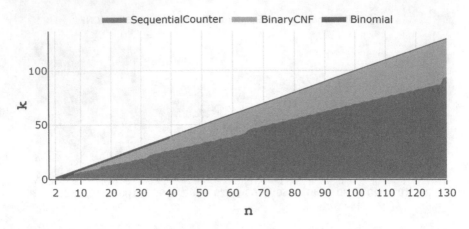

Fig. 7. Encodings producing the lowest number of literals when encoding atmost$_k(n)$. These results serve as the basis for our *selective* encoding.

Number of Generated Variables. As shown in Fig. 6, the *binary* encoding performs best in most cases. For each $k > 7$, it introduces the lowest amount of variables in the investigated data range of $1 < n \leq 130$. The *commander* encoding is best for small k. It groups the variables and assigns new commander variables to each group. Thereby, it depends heavily on the size of its groups. We discovered, that an optimal group size can only be chosen for the very rare case of $k(k + 2) < n$. We hypothesise this to be the reason for the *commander* encoding producing the lowest amount of variables only for small k. As the *commander* encoding is recursive, it could be further optimised by not using the *binomial* encoding at end of recursion, but a more sophisticated one like *binary*, *sequential counter*, or even our *selective* encoding, introduced in the next section. In some rare cases, the *sequential counter* encoding generates the lowest number of variables, especially for small k.

Formula Size. In this section, we quantitatively assess encoding performance in terms of the number of generated literals. Motivated by these results, we develop our new *selective* encoding by combining the evaluated methods. If two encodings produced the same number of literals, we chose the encoding with fewer total variables.

The *commander* encoding never generated the smallest formula. We hypothesise the usage of the *binomial* encoding at the end of recursion to be the reason. As expected, the *binomial* encoding produces the smallest formula for very small $n < 6$, close to the suggested bound of $n < 7$ by Frisch and Giannaros [8]. Advanced encodings do not decompose to smaller formulas in those cases because the overhead of introducing new variables is too big. Furthermore, *binomial* is the most efficient encoding for $k = n - 1$, where it decomposes to a simple disjunction. Surprisingly, this naïve encoding produces the lowest number of literals for $k = n - 2, n < 40$, too. To describe the cases, where the *binomial* encoding performs best, we introduce a function giving the lowest k for which it produces the smallest formula:

$$k_{binom}(n) = \begin{cases} 1 & n < 6, \\ n - 2 & 6 \leq n < 40, \\ n - 1 & \text{otherwise.} \end{cases} \tag{11}$$

The remaining input pairs (k, n) are shared between the *binary* and *sequential counter* encoding. The split between their areas consists of almost linear segments separated by little jumps, which are located at powers of two. When n exceeds a power of two, the binary encoding needs another bit, i.e. another variable. We hypothesise this to be the reason for the *sequential counter* encoding producing less literals than the *binary* encoding at these jumps. To describe the split, we consider the number of literals each encoding produces. For given n, the split is located at k for which both encodings produce the same amount of literals. Thereby, we derive a formula describing exactly the highest k for which the *sequential counter* encoding still produces less literals than the *binary* encoding.

$$k_{split}(n) = \left\lfloor \frac{b + \sqrt{b^2 - 4a}}{2a} \right\rfloor, \text{ with}$$

$$a = 1 + 2\lceil log_2(n) \rceil$$

$$b = 2(\lceil log_2(n) \rceil(n + 1) - 2n + 5) \tag{12}$$

Finally, we can define our *selective* encoding by choosing the encoding producing the smallest formula in Eq. 2.

4.3   Branches Evaluation

We test our *selective* encoding by comparing its performance when generating feature models for each branch of study at TU Braunschweig with the reviewed encodings. The size of a feature model file in XML turned out to be a good initial indication of a model being usable by our configurator, i.e., can be loaded and handled in feasible time spans. We consider formula size and the total number of variables for all *compulsory elective* constraints at once. The results are shown in Fig. 8. We do not consider the *commander* encoding here because it never produced the lowest amount of literals, as outlined in Sect. 4.2.

Indeed, our *selective* encoding always produces the lowest amount of literals as highlighted in Fig. 9. Thereby, it is able to reduce the amount of literals by up to 20% compared to the respective best of the reviewed encodings. Although we developed it to optimise formula size, it also generates the lowest number of variables in seven out of nine cases as visible in Fig. 10 (without considering the *binomial* encoding). For the branch *Hardware-/Software-System Design* it even nearly halves the amount of variables. In the remaining two branches *Industrial Data Science* and *Networked Systems*, it is also competitive, as it produces only 0.5% and 10% more variables respectively. If we compose all branches

Branch of Study	Binomial			Binary			Seq. Counter			Selective					
	kB	#var.	#lit.	kB	#var.	#lit.	kB	#var.	#lit.	kB	#var.	#lit.	Δ#kB%	Δ#var.%	Δ#lit.%
Automotive Informatics	82,682	32	895,347	1,414	1,159	6,541	1,694	2,107	10,135	1,295	1,007	**6,287**	8.42	13.11	3.88
Big Data Management	46	9	338	52	64	256	45	58	237	46	58	**221**	-2.22	0	6.75
H.-/S.-System Design	10,228	36	126,738	728	788	3,834	795	1,135	5,363	538	455	**3,074**	26.10	42.26	19.82
IT-Security	21	7	61	26	23	77	21	17	**50**	21	17	**50**	0	0	0
Industrial Data Science	2,223	22	28,052	170	202	1,018	153	246	1,095	145	203	**930**	5.23	-0.50	8.64
Medical Informatics	3,115	15	31,609	316	313	1,732	254	351	1,630	264	308	**1,513**	-3.94	1.60	7.18
Networked Systems	6,220	27	87,375	201	246	1,241	203	343	1,542	184	270	**1,227**	8.46	-9.76	1.13
Robotics	557	17	6,845	193	212	**977**	239	339	1,570	193	212	**977**	0	0	0
Visual Computing	108	14	1,205	98	124	547	84	131	560	88	124	**524**	-4.76	0	4.20
All Branches (Sum)	105,200	179	1,177,570	3,198	3,131	16,223	3,488	4,727	22,182	2,774	2,654	14,803	13.6	15.2	8.6

Fig. 8. For each branch of study at TU Braunschweig we encoded all its *compulsory elective* constraints with each encoding to compare their performance in terms of model file size, number of total variables, and literals. The minimal number of literals per row is highlighted. The last three columns show the improvement of our encoding in percent compared to the best of the single encodings. The *binomial* encoding is not considered for $\Delta\#$var.%.

as necessary for the complete field of study model, *binary* performs best from the reviewed encodings in each category. *Selective* encoding further reduces file size, number of variables, and number of literals by 13.6%, 15.2%, and 8.6%, respectively.

We developed our *selective* encoding in favour of formula size. Nevertheless, the solving time is an important metric for efficiency of formula generation [15, p. 413]. We found branch models loaded to our configuration tool BroT to be configurable without any lags. However, the loading times for the models exceed several minutes for most of the branches. This time span is mainly caused by the configuration initialisation. As it is branch specific and only necessary a single time, it could be pre-computed and stored on disk. Thus, BroT could enable instantaneous branch loading and configuration. Unfortunately, we were not able to load the branches *Automotive Informatics*, *Hardware-/Software-System Design*, and *Medical Informatics* yet as the configuration generation took too much time. We suspect our resolving of different credit points (Eq. 8) to impair performance immensely because the expression it generates is not in CNF.

4.4 Threats to Validity

In this section we reflect on our experiment design for evaluation of *selective* encoding in Sect. 4.3. We compare its performance with the reviewed encodings by generating the constraints for each branch of study at TU Braunschweig. Although, this is a very special use case, it emerges from a real-world problem for which a solution was even enquired at TU Braunschweig. At other universities or institutions this problem may arise analogously. Furthermore, each branch demands 5 to 45 atmost$_k$ formulas with $k \in [0, 19] \subset \mathbb{N}$ and $n \in [1, 20] \subset \mathbb{N}$ as specified at the universities website and in our DSL files delivered with our tool.

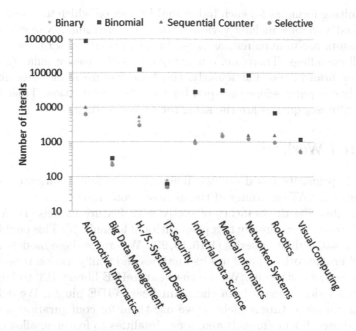

Fig. 9. Number of literals in *compulsory elective* constraints generated by each encoding per branch.

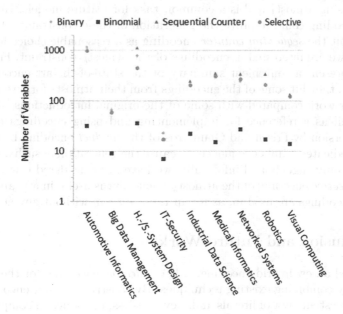

Fig. 10. Number of total variables in *compulsory elective* constraints generated by each encoding per branch.

The resulting formulas for each individual branch on which we count number of literals and variables include various atmost$_k$ constraints. Nevertheless, our usability results are unimpaired, as these branch specific descriptions are constant for all encodings. Therefore, our *compulsory elective* formulas (see Eq. 8) are fixed per branch, too. Particularly, the base feature model describing the field of study computer science is equal for the whole evaluation. Thus, for each branch the atmost$_k$ queries are the same for each encoding.

5 Related Work

This work is primarily based on two fields, namely feature-oriented software development and SAT encodings of the atmost$_k$ constraint.

First, we describe the branches of study with feature models [1]. A feature model can be converted directly to a propositional formula [3]. This enables analysis based on satisfiability queries [4,16,18,20]. We create these models with the FeatureIDE Framework [17] and use its analysis and configuration tools for testing and evaluating our results. We use the FeatureIDE library [13] to implement the encodings independently from the main FeatureIDE plugin. We detected a new application for feature models, as we use them for configuration of courses. Cardinality-based feature models assign cardinalities to features, allowing them to occur multiple times [6,7]. Our new *selective* encoding can be used to express the bounds of group cardinalities and, thus, cardinality-based feature models could profit from our encoding. Formulating alternative groups is the special case of choosing atmost$_1$ and is a common task for feature models. Hence, our *selective* encoding could improve the generation of these constraints. Here, our results exhibit the *sequential counter* encoding as a reasonable choice for $n > 5$.

Second, we are interested in encodings of the atmost$_k$ constraint. Frisch and Giannaros present a convenient summary of the state-of-the-art encodings [8]. Additionally, they lift some of the encodings from their atmost$_1$ form to atmost$_k$. We use their work compared with some of the original introductions [12,19] for further detail as a reference for implementing and using encodings correctly. The lifted version by Frisch and Giannaros of the *product* encoding by Chen [5] requires a dedicated number sequence. Because the generation of such a sequence is described only vaguely and informally, we have not considered this encoding. Our new *selective* encoding of the atmost$_k$ constraint is useful in any application the other encodings are used in, as it can replace them without any adaptions.

6 Conclusion and Future Work

We presented a new hybrid encoding, called *selective* encoding, for the atmost$_k$ constraint by combining existing techniques. By construction, our encoding produces the lowest amount of literals and, nevertheless, introduces a comparatively low amount of new variables.

We used *selective* encoding successfully for generating feature models that can be used for configuring branches of study. We showed that choosing a suitable encoding for the atmost$_k$ constraint makes a difference of up to 20% in terms of literals for our branch study. Furthermore, our tool BroT using our DSL as input can be useful for universities and institutions facing similar problems. Our approach for resolving different amounts of credit points can be generalised to domains, where each element is weighted. Hence, it can be useful in any task where a sum of weights has to be reached by choosing arbitrary elements.

To improve our *selective* encoding and results on *compulsory elective* constraint generation, further encodings like *parallel sequential counter* by Sinz [19] or *totalizer* by Bailleux and Boufkhad [2] could be investigated, too. Especially the second one is of interest, as it can handle atmost and atleast constraints simultaneously, which could optimise our frequent exactly constraints in Eq. 9 when dealing with different amounts of credit points. Additionally, our *selective* encoding could be tested on handling alternative groups in feature models as these require the special case of atmost$_1$. Furthermore, the question why the encodings count for generated literals and variables split into distinct connected areas that allowed deriving our encoding, is still open.

Acknowledgements. We thank Moritz Kappel, Chico Sundermann, Timo Günther, Marc Kassubeck, Jan-Philipp Tauscher, and Moritz Mühlhausen for reviewing our paper in the earlier stages. Additional thanks go to the SEFM reviewers for giving very detailed and constructive remarks.

References

1. Apel, S., Batory, D., Kästner, C., Saake, G.: Feature-Oriented Software Product Lines (2013)
2. Bailleux, O., Boufkhad, Y.: Efficient CNF encoding of boolean cardinality constraints. In: Rossi, F. (ed.) CP 2003. LNCS, vol. 2833, pp. 108–122. Springer, Heidelberg (2003). https://doi.org/10.1007/978-3-540-45193-8_8
3. Batory, D.: Feature models, grammars, and propositional formulas. In: Obbink, H., Pohl, K. (eds.) SPLC 2005. LNCS, vol. 3714, pp. 7–20. Springer, Heidelberg (2005). https://doi.org/10.1007/11554844_3
4. Benavides, D., Segura, S., Ruiz-Cortés, A.: Automated analysis of feature models 20 years later: a literature review. Inf. Syst. **35**(6), 615–708 (2010)
5. Chen, J.: A new SAT encoding of the at-most-one constraint. In: Proceedings of the Constraint Modelling and Reformulation (2010)
6. Czarnecki, K., Helsen, S., Eisenecker, U.: Formalizing cardinality-based feature models and their specialization. Softw. Process: Improv. Pract. **10**, 7–29 (2005)
7. Czarnecki, K., Kim, C.H.P.: Cardinality-based feature modeling and constraints: a progress report, pp. 16–20 (2005)
8. Frisch, A.M., Giannaros, P.A.: SAT encodings of the at-most-k constraint. some old, some new, some fast, some slow. In: Proceedings of the Ninth International Workshop of Constraint Modelling and Reformulation (2010)
9. Frisch, A.M., Peugniez, T.J.: Solving non-boolean satisfiability problems with stochastic local search. In: IJCAI, vol. 2001, pp. 282–290 (2001)
10. Frisch, A.M., Peugniez, T.J., Doggett, A.J., Nightingale, P.W.: Solving non-boolean satisfiability problems with stochastic local search: a comparison of encodings. J. Autom. Reason. **35**(1–3), 143–179 (2005). https://doi.org/10.1007/s10817-005-9011-0

11. Günther, T.: Explaining satisfiability queries for software product lines. Master's thesis, Braunschweig (2017). https://doi.org/10.24355/dbbs.084-201711171100. https://publikationsserver.tu-braunschweig.de/receive/dbbs_mods_00065308
12. Klieber, W., Kwon, G.: Efficient CNF encoding for selecting 1 from n objects. In: Proceedings of the International Workshop on Constraints in Formal Verification (2007)
13. Krieter, S., et al.: FeatureIDE: empowering third-party developers, pp. 42–45 (2017). https://doi.org/10.1145/3109729.3109751
14. Krieter, S., Thüm, T., Schulze, S., Schröter, R., Saake, G.: Propagating configuration decisions with modal implication graphs, pp. 898–909, May 2018. https://doi.org/10.1145/3180155.3180159
15. Kučera, P., Savický, P., Vorel, V.: A lower bound on CNF encodings of the at-most-one constraint. In: Gaspers, S., Walsh, T. (eds.) SAT 2017. LNCS, vol. 10491, pp. 412–428. Springer, Cham (2017). https://doi.org/10.1007/978-3-319-66263-3_26
16. Mannion, M.: Using first-order logic for product line model validation, pp. 176–187 (2002)
17. Meinicke, J., Thüm, T., Schröter, R., Benduhn, F., Leich, T., Saake, G.: Mastering Software Variability with FeatureIDE. Springer, Cham (2017). https://doi.org/10.1007/978-3-319-61443-4
18. Mendonça, M.: Efficient reasoning techniques for large scale feature models. Ph.D. thesis, University of Waterloo, Canada (2009)
19. Sinz, C.: Towards an optimal CNF encoding of boolean cardinality constraints. In: van Beek, P. (ed.) CP 2005. LNCS, vol. 3709, pp. 827–831. Springer, Heidelberg (2005). https://doi.org/10.1007/11564751_73
20. Thüm, T., Apel, S., Kästner, C., Schaefer, I., Saake, G.: Analysis strategies for software product lines: a classification and survey, pp. 57–58, Gesellschaft für Informatik (GI), Bonn, Germany, March 2015
21. Wiegand, J., et al.: Eclipse: a platform for integrating development tools. IBM Syst. J. **43**(2), 371–383 (2004)

Software Evolution with a Typeful Version Control System

Luís Carvalho$^{(\boxtimes)}$ and João Costa Seco$^{(\boxtimes)}$

Faculdade de Ciências e Tecnologia, Universidade NOVA de Lisboa, NOVA-LINCS,
Lisbon, Portugal
la.carvalho@campus.fct.unl.pt, joao.seco@fct.unl.pt

Abstract. Agile software development comprises small evolution steps that require discipline and planning to maintain the soundness between all the components of a system. Software product lines pose similar challenges when the soundness between different branches of a product is at stake. Such challenges are usually tackled by engineering methods that focus on the development process, and not on the subject of attention, the code. The risk of code inconsistency between versions has been mostly supported by analysis of the history of releases and by evaluating feature interferences.

In this paper, we propose a language-based approach to provide a certifying version control system that enables the explicit specification of the evolution steps of a software artifact throughout its life-cycle, and ensures the sane sharing of code between versions. Our model is suitable to be integrated into a smart development environment to help manage the whole code base of an application. This enables the static verification of program evolution steps, based on the correctness of state transformations between related versions, and for the stable coexistence of multiple versions at run-time. We instantiate our formal developments in a core language that extends Featherweight Java and implements the verification as a type system.

1 Introduction

Agile development methods advocate for controlled and incremental steps in the construction and evolution of a system, and that all software life-cycle activities are also of similar evolutive kind. Common activities include bug fixing, implementing user-requested features, porting code to new hardware, updating business requirements, and many other tasks that essentially represent steps in the life-cycle of a software system. With faster release cycles it is much more difficult to cope with the discipline necessary to constantly adapt the existing code to interact with new and updated code. Managing the evolution of software systems is always a difficult task, in particular to maintain multiple versions of a software product [18]. Evolution entails complexity in all cases, unless some energy is spent to explicitly reduce it [13]. Version control systems (e.g. git, svn, mercurial) are becoming a fundamental piece of software product lines, and

© Springer Nature Switzerland AG 2019
P. C. Ölveczky and G. Salaün (Eds.): SEFM 2019, LNCS 11724, pp. 145–161, 2019.
https://doi.org/10.1007/978-3-030-30446-1_8

exist precisely to aid in the fast evolution of a system. However, while very good at managing changes to *information*, VCS give no semantic meaning to each delta (*diff*), allowing for inconsistent code to be committed. As a result, VCS are often coupled with continuous delivery pipelines (e.g. Jenkins pipelines) that make sure each deployment is consistent (by running code linters, unit tests, regression tests, etc.). This adds another layer of complexity (*DevOps*), where the developer now has to reason about how to manage the changes (git branching workflows) and how the multiple versions of the software interact with each other (CD pipelines), which can entail additional security risks [3, 4].

Contributions. We propose a language-based approach to providing a certifying version control system that tackles the aforementioned problems. We propose the use of a centralized model to store the whole code base of a project into a single application representation, very much inspired in application models of low-code platforms like OutSystems[1] or Mendix[2], and we believe that a smart IDE can also perform the same kind of management for text based versioned code bases. Our model allows the definition of a version graph, the incremental definition of programming elements, and the tagging of each program element definition (in our model, the fields, methods, and class constructors) with a version identifier to mark the snapshot where it was last edited. Versions are marked with different modes that capture the different flavors of software evolution, such as unforeseen hot fixes, planned upgrades or code refactoring, among others. We instantiate our abstract model in an object-oriented core functional language, VFJ (Versioned Featherweight Java), extending Featherweigth Java [9] as a model for a full fledged source code version control system.

A VFJ program is a syntactic entity that represents multiple versions of a program simultaneously. A fragment of a class declaration on a program with versions **init** and **date** defining state variables would be represented by

```
version init
version date upgrades init
class Song extends Object {
  @init string title; @init int year;
  @date string title; @date Date date;
  ...
```

The header defines the relationship between both versions, and each field is tagged with the version to which it belongs. The same kind of version annotation is used for class constructors and methods.

As in any source code version control system, each version in VFJ represents a branch or a commit in a repository and provides deltas to the parent version. Single versions correspond to an unparented branch, *upgrade* versions correspond to branching from an existing branch (Fig. 1a), and *replacement* versions correspond to commits rooted in an existing version of the system, that force a rebase for all versions branching off of the replaced version (Fig. 1b). In

---

[1] www.outsystems.com.
[2] www.mendix.com.

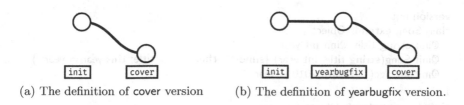

(a) The definition of cover version   (b) The definition of yearbugfix version.

Fig. 1. Branching graphs

this way, it is possible to define a new version of a VFJ program by extending an existing version, and adding just the necessary code deltas to achieve the version's objective. Our model guarantees compile-time safety of code reuse from previous snapshots, as well as forward and backward compatibility with other snapshots, through type-safe state transformation functions (lenses).

Crucially, we introduce a version expression of the form @date(e) that executes expression e in the context of version date, using all the definitions from that version and switching to version init whenever necessary. We also introduce the notion of version lenses, which are mappings between the object's state in one version to its state in another. We present a static and dynamic semantics for our language (VFJ) to serve as reference to what should be the specification of a compiling/rewriting algorithm that always produces the up-to-date code for a given version of a product. This mechanism is suited to be implemented in language-based tools that support the plain evolution of a single product, or as support for a software product line that maintains different live versions of the same set of components.

In summary, our main contributions are:

– An abstract representation for versioned programming elements declarations,
– A versioning model that captures the essential steps on evolution of software, capturing both planned (upgrades) and unforeseen changess (replacements),
– A typing discipline for changes in programs that preserves soundness,
– An operational semantics that ensures the safe coexistence and execution of multiple versions of programs, and
– A specification for a compilation algorithm that creates a sound snapshot of a version from a versioned repository.

2   The Journey of a Class

We now present a sequence of steps in the development of an application that illustrates how the static and dynamic semantics of VFJ support the sound evolution of a program. VFJ is an extension of the core language Featherweight Java [9] with constructions for the versioning of classes, its fields, constructors, and methods, and the versioned execution of language expressions. In this example we edit the underlying model of the code, including versioning meta-information which could, in principle, be automatically introduced by a smart,

```
version init
class Song extends Object {
  @init string title; @init int year;
  @init Song(string title, int year) {super(); this.title = title; this.year = year; }
  @init int age() {return 2019 − year; }
}
class Server extends Object {
  @init SongList songs;
  @init Server(SongList songs) {super(); this.songs = songs; }
  @init Song get(string title) {this.songs.get(title); }
  @init Server put(string title, int year) {
    return new Server(this.songs.put(new Song(title, year)));
  }
}
class Client extends Object {
  @init Server server;
  @init Client(Server server) {super(); this.server = server; }
  @init string info(string title) {return title+" <>" +this.server.get(title).age();}
}
```

Fig. 2. Initial stage of the Server classes

version-aware, IDE. Consider classes Server, Song, and Client of a music metadata application.

Step 0 - introduction of a simple metadata server. The listing in Fig. 2 defines class Server to represent a music metadata server, class Song to represent the songs stored in the server, and class Client to represent a music client that connects to an object of class Server and displays metadata in some screen. We assume an existing class SongList. The initial snapshot of the application is depicted by the code in a version with tag init. In version init, a song is defined by fields title and year. The class constructor is declared as expected, initializing the fields, and we define method age to compute the age of a song. All declarations are annotated with a version label. The init version of class Server is concerned with the operations over a list of songs, and class Client is defined to access the server and interact with objects of class Song. Again, note that annotations do not have to be explicitly written by the developer and may be managed by the IDE, automatically incorporated into the source code or the abstract representation of a DSL of a low-code platform.

These classes can then be used in the context of version init, by means of a version context expression of the form @v(e), which executes expression e in the context of version v. For instance, expression

```
@init( new Client(
  new Server().put("Yellow Submarine", 1966).put("Let It Be", 1970)).info("Let It Be"
    ));
```

```
version init
version yearbugfix replaces init
class Song extends Object {

  ...

  @yearbugfix int age() { return (new Date()).year() − this.year; }

  ...
```

Fig. 3. Version yearbugfix of the Song class

creates a server, adds songs to its list of songs and yields a server object in version init that is then used by a client object to retrieve and display a given song's information.

A more careful observation of method age in class Song identifies a potential bug in the code of the version init. It should compute its result using the current year instead of assuming the literal value of 2019. In our journey, we need to issue a fix for this error.

Step 1 - fixing a bug. To fix the bug we create a new version of class Song modifying only method age. In order to have an immediate effect on existing code, we declare a new version (yearbugfix) declared to replace the init version. This is depicted in the header of Fig. 3, where we declare the versions and their relations. We then add a new declaration of method age in version yearbugfix. Hereafter we assume that there is a class Date with a method to retrieve the year.

The new method definition is added with @yearbugfix version tag and all other definitions of the codebase are kept in place. The bug is fixed in version yearbugfix. The expression that is part of the client code in the context of version init, @init (new Song("Let It Be", 1970, 0).age()), now executes the code in version yearbugfix and returns the correct result for all years. The nature of replacement versions dictates that changes are automatically propagated without the need to change old client code. We simply introduce the deltas from version init, which in this case corresponds to re-implementing method age, and the compiler can then produce, by slicing, the snapshot containing the correct code for version init.

Step 2 - supporting new hardware. In this step we introduce support for a new kind of client that can also display a song's cover artwork. To add support for this we need to change both the Song class, which now has to store a cover art in its fields, and the Server class, which now has to download the cover art and store it when uploading a new song. For the sake of the argument we assume an existing class Image that represents pictures and a class Images that allows the download of cover arts. Showing and downloading images may be impossible to old hardware, and some servers and clients can still use code in the init version.

Consider the code in Fig. 4. Note that all the previous code is part of the snapshots, but elided in the figure, as all the deltas of a git repository are kept in the internal structure of its holding directory. Version cover declares a constructor and redefines the representation type of the class (its fields). This is a key feature

```
version init
version yearbugfix replaces init
version cover upgrades init
class Song extends Object {
  @cover int year; @cover string title; @cover Image cover;
  @init Song(string title, int year) {
    ...
    this@cover(title, year, new Image("placeholder.jpg"));
  }
  @cover Song(string title, int year, Image cover) {
    super();
    this.title = title; this.year = year; this.cover = cover;
    this@init(title, year);
  }
  @cover Image cover() {return this.cover; }
  ...
}
class Server extends Object {
  ...
  @cover Server put(string title, int year) {
    return new Server(this.songs.put(new Song(title,year,Images.download(title))));
  }
}
class Client extends Object {
  ...
  @cover Image cover(string title) {
    return this.server.get(title).getCover().render();
  }
}
```

Fig. 4. Second version of the Server classes

of our language: it defines what we call a *base version* in relation to class Song. Since we want to keep existing song's fields in version cover, we must re-declare them all (again, this can be aided by the IDE). Version cover adds a new field that stores the artwork, and changes the constructor accordingly. Version cover also adds a method to retrieve said picture.

To avoid rewriting existing code, we define a mapping between version cover and version init, with the declaration this@init(title, year, plays); in the constructor of Fig. 4. We call this mechanism a lens, in this case from version cover to version init. Finally, in version cover of class Server we update method put that downloads the correct cover art for the song. By upgrading the song server we can now store cover art in a song with the expression:

@cover(new Server().put("Yellow Submarine", 1966).put("Let It Be", 1970));

A client supporting such feature can then display the artwork by

```
                              class Song extends Object {
                                ...
                                @date Date date; @date string title;
                                @init Song(string title, int year) {
                                  ...
version init                      this@date(title, new Date(0, 0, year));
version yearbugfix replaces init  }
version cover upgrades init      @date Song(string title, Date date) {
version date replaces yearbugfix   super();
                                  this.title = title; this.date = date;
                                  this@init(title, date.year());
                                }
                                ...
                                @date Date getDate() { return this.date(); }
                                ...
```

Fig. 5. Version date in class Song.

```
@cover(new Client(...).cover("Let It Be"))
```

and if a client that supports displaying artworks connects to a server that has not yet been upgraded, using the following code, the placeholder image is returned

```
@cover((new Client(@init(...))).cover("Let It Be"))
```

as defined by the lens between versions init and cover.

Step 3 - refactor to full dates. Consider a scenario, defined in Fig. 5, where we want to store a full date in all song objects instead of just the year component. To refactor class Song in such a way, we add field date of type Date, define a new constructor in version date, and modify the existing constructors to enable the transformation of objects from version init to version date when necessary. We add a lens from version date to version init to the constructor of version date. We add a method in version date of class Server to store a song with updated data.

```
class Server extends Object {
  ...
  @date Server put(string title, Date date)
  { return new Server(this.songs.put(new Song(title, date))); }
```

Finally, we also upgrade class Client with a new definition for method displayInfo,

```
class Client extends Object {
  ...
  @date Date info(string title) { return title+"<>"+this.server.get( title).getDate(); }
```

A server running in the init version can use the new definition of method put:

```
@init(new Server()
    .put("Yellow Submarine", 1966).put("Let It Be", 1970).put("Help!", 19, 7, 1965));
```

$$P ::= \overline{V}\,\overline{L}\,@v(e)$$
$$V ::= \text{version } v \mid \text{version } v \text{ upgrades } v' \mid \text{version } v \text{ replaces } v'$$
$$L ::= \text{class } C \text{ extends } D \,\{\ \overline{@v\ C\ f};\ \overline{K}\ \overline{M}\ \}$$
$$K ::= @v\ C(\overline{C\ f})\{\ \text{super}(\overline{f});\ \overline{\text{this}@v(\overline{e})};\ \overline{\text{this}.f = f};\ \}$$
$$M ::= @v\ C\ m(\overline{C\ x})\{\ \text{return } e;\ \}$$
$$e ::= x \mid e.f \mid e.m(\overline{e}) \mid \text{new } C(\overline{e}) \mid @v(e) \mid \text{this}$$

Fig. 6. Syntax for the VFJ language

A client running in the context of init version can display the correct information:

@init(**new** Client(...).info("Let It Be"); **new** Client(...).info("Help!"));

3   Versioned Featherweight Java

In this section we present the syntax and semantics (static and dynamic) of Versioned Featherweight Java (VFJ), a functional object language that is the formal vehicle to transmit our certified version control model.

Syntax. Figure 6 presents the language's syntax that is an extension of the syntax of the original FJ language [9]. A VFJ program comprises a list of version declarations ($\overline{V}$), a list of class declarations ($\overline{L}$), and a main expression ($@v(e)$) that is executed in the context of some version v and given the previous declarations. Recall that this is an abstract representation for a concrete syntax and that all the version labels can be inferred by the development environment. Version declarations define single, upgrade, or replacement versions. Again, this graph is intended to be built by the development environment according to the commit history. Classes (L) are defined as extending some other class (class Object is predefined), and comprise a set of versioned fields ($\overline{@v\ C\ f}$), constructors ($\overline{K}$), and method definitions ($\overline{M}$). Unlike in FJ, we allow multiple constructors, one per version. Constructors are defined in the context of a given version. They follow the rigid structure comprised by the call to the super class constructor (super($\overline{f}$)), the definition of lenses from version v to other versions (this@$v(\overline{e})$), and the initialization of the object fields (this.$f = f$). Declarations of methods ($\overline{M}$), also annotated with a version identifier, contain a set of parameters and a method body (an expression). Finally, the expression language (e) includes variables (x), object fields ($e.f$), method invocation ($e.m(\overline{e})$), object creation (new $C(\overline{e})$), and the this object reference. We extend the syntax of FJ expressions with a version context expression ($@v(e)$) that executes an expression e in the context of version v.

Static Semantics. We define a type system that ensures that a program comprising code from different versions, given a set of state transformations between versions and documenting the changes made on each step, is well-typed.

$$\frac{}{\vdash \varnothing \; OK} \; \text{(VT-Empty)} \qquad \frac{\vdash V \; OK \quad v \notin dom(V)}{\vdash V, v \; OK} \; \text{(VT-Single)}$$

$$\frac{\vdash V \; OK \quad v' \notin dom(V) \quad v \in dom(V)}{\vdash V, v' \; \text{upgrades} \; v \; OK} \; \text{(VT-Up)} \qquad \frac{\vdash V \; OK \quad v \in dom(V) \quad v' \notin dom(V) \quad w \; \text{replaces} \; v \notin V}{\vdash V, v' \; \text{replaces} \; v \; OK} \; \text{(VT-Rep)}$$

Fig. 7. Rules for a well-formed version table

$$\frac{}{\Gamma \vdash_v x : \Gamma(x)} \; \text{(T-Var)} \qquad \frac{\Gamma \vdash_v e_0 : C_0 \quad vfields(v, C_0) = \overline{C} \; \overline{f}}{\Gamma \vdash_v e_0.f_i : C_i} \; \text{(T-Field)}$$

$$\frac{\Gamma \vdash_v e_0 : C_0 \quad u = mversion(\overline{V}, v, C_0, m) \quad mtype(u, C_0, m) = \overline{D} \to C \quad \Gamma \vdash_v \overline{e} : \overline{C} \quad \overline{C} <: \overline{D}}{V, \Gamma \vdash_v e_0.m(\overline{e}) : C} \; \text{(T-Invk)}$$

$$\frac{vfields(v, C) = \overline{D} \; \overline{f} \quad \Gamma \vdash_v \overline{e} : \overline{C} \quad \overline{C} <: \overline{D}}{\Gamma \vdash_v \text{new} \; C(\overline{e}) : C} \; \text{(T-New)} \qquad \frac{\Gamma \vdash_{v'} e : C}{\Gamma \vdash_v @v'(e) : C} \; \text{(T-Version)}$$

Fig. 8. Typing rules for expressions

The first step to ensure that a versioned program is well typed, is to check that it operates on a sound version graph. We inductively define this well-formed relation, represented in a judgement of the form $\vdash V \; OK$, by the set of post rules of Fig. 7. The relation is based on an empty version table, that is trivially well-formed (VT-Empty). Adding a single version to the graph V produces a well-formed version graph if there are no repetition of version names (VT-Single). This condition is premise on the introduction of all other kinds of versions. An upgrade version can be added if it upgrades an existing version on the graph (VT-Up). A replacement version can be added if it replaces an existing version and there is no replacement version for that given version (VT-Rep). This will become an invariant condition in all the graph.

Given a well-formed version table, we type VFJ expressions in the context of some version using the standard judgement $\Gamma \vdash_v e : C$ and the rules of Fig. 8. Notice that in our calculus, the possible results for expressions are objects, and their types are classes. Rule (T-Var) matches the type of a variable with that of the environment association (Γ, which stores the usual association between variables and their values). Rule (T-Field) uses versioned lookup for fields, using the current version (v), to check the type of the field being selected. Rule (T-Invk) finds the method's type signature, using versioned lookup functions in the context of version v, then checks that arguments match the parameters types, and finally types the method call expression with the declared return type. Rule (T-New) checks that arguments to the constructor match the types of the fields as returned by the versioned lookup function. Finally, rule (T-Version)

$$\frac{}{\vdash \varnothing \ OK \ in \ C} \ (\text{T-}V_C\text{-EMPTY}) \qquad \frac{\vdash V \ OK \ in \ C}{\vdash V, v \ OK \ in \ C} \ (\text{T-}V_C\text{-SINGLE})$$

$$\frac{\vdash V \ OK \ in \ C \quad path(v, v', C) = p}{\vdash V \vdash up(v', v) \ OK \ in \ C \quad V \vdash keep(v', v) \ OK \ in \ C}{\vdash V, v' \ \text{replaces} \ v \ OK \ in \ C} \ (\text{T-}V_C\text{-REP})$$

$$\frac{\vdash V \ OK \ in \ C \quad V \vdash up(v', v) \ OK \ in \ C}{V \vdash overrides(v', v) \ OK \ in \ C}{\vdash V, v' \ \text{upgrades} \ v \ OK \ in \ C} \ (\text{T-}V_C\text{-UP})$$

Fig. 9. Well-formed version table for classes

$$\frac{\begin{array}{c}M_v = methods(\overline{V}, v, C) \\ M_{v'} = methods(\{\,v'\,\}, v', C) \quad M_v \subseteq M_{v'}\end{array}}{\vdash up(v', v) \ OK \ in \ C} \ (\text{UP}) \qquad \frac{path(v', v, C) = p}{\vdash up(v', v) \ OK \ in \ C} \ (\text{UP})$$

$$\frac{\begin{array}{c}M_v = methods(\overline{V}, v, C) \quad M_{v'} = methods(\{\,v'\,\}, v, C) \\ \forall_{m \in M_v \cap M_{v'}} : u = mversion(\overline{V}, v, C, m) \wedge mtype(u, C, m) = mtype(v', C, m)\end{array}}{\vdash keep(v', v) \ OK \ in \ C} \ (\text{KEEP})$$

$$\frac{\begin{array}{c}M_v = methods(\overline{V}, v, C) \quad M_{v'} = methods(\{\,v'\,\}, v', C) \\ \forall_{G \ m@u(\overline{Df})\{\,\dots\,\} \in M_v \setminus M_{v'}} : if \ C <: G \ then \ path(u, v', G) = p\end{array}}{\vdash overrides(v', v) \ OK \ in \ C} \ (\text{OVERRIDES})$$

Fig. 10. Well-formed version table for classes

defines that the version context expression $@v'(e)$ types the inner expression in the context of the explicitly noted version v'.

The typing of expressions is essential to establish if the whole class table is well-formed. We define the typing of class interfaces, segmented per version, in the judgement $\vdash V \ OK \ in \ C$ with the rules in Fig. 9. Rules (T-V_C-EMPTY) and (T-V_C-SINGLE) are trivial, and the remaining rules (T-V_C-REP) and (T-V_C-UP) discipline how methods can be overridden from one version to another. In both cases, the rules ensure any well-typed instance of class C in the context of v is also well typed in the context of v'. The intuition for these rules is that any method available at version v must be available at v' (either by a lens or by overriding it). Special attention is needed when inheriting methods that return objects of a subtype of C, as these need to be correctly translated to version v' (again, either by a lens or by overriding it). In the particular case of (T-V_C-REP), the type system also ensures any well-typed instance of class C in the context of v' is also well typed in the context of v, and as such any method overridden must have its type preserved.

$$\frac{class \ G \ extends \ H\{ \ ... \ \} \in \overline{L}}{\vdash \overline{F}, @v \ G \ f \ OK \ in \ C} \ \text{(T-Field)}$$

$$\frac{\overline{x}:\overline{C}, \ \text{this}:C \vdash_v e_0:C \qquad class \ C \ extends \ D\{ \ ... \ \} \in \overline{L}}{if \ u = mversion(\overline{V}, v, D, m) \ then \ \overline{C} \ \to C_0 = mtype(u, D, m)} \ \text{(T-Method)}$$
$$\overline{\frac{}{\vdash \overline{M}, @v \ C_0 \ m(\overline{C} \ \overline{x})\{ \ return \ e_0; \ \} \ OK \ in \ C}}$$

$$\frac{class \ C \ extends \ D\{ \ ... \ \} \in \overline{L} \quad vfields(v, D) = \overline{D} \ \overline{g}}{vfields(v, C) = \overline{D} \ \overline{g}, \overline{C} \ \overline{f} \quad vfields(v_l, C) = \overline{C_i} \ \overline{x_i}}$$
$$\frac{\overline{D} \ \overline{g}, \overline{C} \ \overline{f} \vdash_v \overline{e_i}:\overline{G_i} \quad \overline{G_i} <: \overline{C_i} \quad i = 1..n}{@v \ C \ (\overline{D} \ \overline{g}, \overline{C} \ \overline{f})\{ \ super(\overline{g}); \ \text{this}@v_l(\overline{e}); \ \text{this}.\overline{f} = \overline{f}; \ \} \ OK \ in \ C} \ \text{(T-Constr)}$$

$$\frac{\overline{F}, \overline{K}, \overline{M} \ OK \ in \ C}{class \ C \ extends \ D\{ \ \overline{F} \ \overline{K} \ \overline{M} \ \} \ OK} \ \text{(T-Class)} \qquad \frac{\vdash \overline{V} \ OK \quad \vdash \overline{V} \ OK \ in \ \overline{L}}{\vdash \overline{L} \ OK \quad \overline{L}, \overline{V} \vdash_v e:C} \ \text{(T-Prog)}$$
$$\overline{V}, \overline{L}, @v(e) \vdash P \ OK$$

Fig. 11. Typing rules for classes and programs

The typing of each class is described in a series of judgements defined by the rules shown in Fig. 11. A program comprises a version table, a set of classes, and a main expression running in the context of a given version. A program is well-typed if (1) the version table is well-formed, (2) the version table is well-formed for the given classes, and (3) the classes are well-typed (Fig. 11). Intuitively, a program being well-typed means it should be possible to execute it without errors, use code from different versions, and compile it to code for a single version that produces no runtime typing errors. We follow the standard FJ rules, but use versioned lookup functions for field, constructor, and method definitions.

To implement the versioned lookup functions we need some auxiliary notation, functions, and relations, in particular fields and methods lookup functions and the definitions of lenses. We define the relations $v' > v$ if v' upgrades $v \in \overline{V}$, and $v' \succ v$ if v' replaces $v \in \overline{V}$. We also define the transitive closure of these relations, $v' >^* v$ and $v' \succ^* v$. Given these relations, we may start defining some lookup functions that allow us to fetch the right type signature and the right implementation for a given method, a given field, in a given version context. The first one is to define the *base* version of a given version v, where its fields and constructor are defined. For a single version, this corresponds to itself. An upgrade or replacement version is base of itself if it defines a constructor. Otherwise, the base version corresponds to the base version of the version being extended.

$$base(v, C) \triangleq \begin{cases} v & if \ C@v(\overline{Cf})\{ \ ... \ \} \in C \\ base(v', C) & if \ v > v' \ or \ v \succ v' \end{cases}$$

In Sect. 2 we have $base(date, Song) = date$ and $base(date, Client) = init$. The identification of which is the version that establishes the types of the fields is crucial to type the method bodies of intermediate versions. The base version is used as reference for the versioned fields lookup function $vfields(v, C)$, which denotes the fields declared in class C, and its superclass D.

$$vfields(v, C) \triangleq \begin{cases} \varepsilon & \text{if } C = \mathsf{Object} \\ \overline{C\ f}, vfields(v, D) & \text{if } v' = base(v, C) \text{ and} \\ & class\ C\ extends\ D\{\overline{C\ f}@v'; \ldots\} \in \overline{L} \end{cases}$$

In the example of Sect. 2, we have $vfields(date, \mathsf{Client}) = Server\ server$, which corresponds to the field declared in version init of class Client. For an object to change from the context of some version v to the context of another version v', there must be a path (made of lenses) from v to v' in class C. An empty path (ε) means that the two versions share the same base. A path of the form (v, v') means there is a lens, declared in the base version of v, to the base version of v'. Paths may be composed in the form $(path(v, w, C), path(w, v', C))$, meaning there is a path from version v to some version w, to which there is a path to version v'. We define function $path(v, v', C)$ below to build such a path from version v to version v' in class C.

$$path(v, v', C) \triangleq \begin{cases} \varepsilon & \text{if } base(v, C) = base(v', C) \\ (v, v') & \text{if } C@w(\overline{x})\{\ \mathsf{this}@w'(\overline{e'}); \ldots\ \} \in C, \\ & base(v, C), w' = base(v', C) \\ path(v, w, C), path(w, v', C) & \text{if } v \notin path(w, v', C) \end{cases}$$

In Sect. 2 we have that $path(cover, date, \mathsf{Song}) = ((cover, init), (init, date))$, illustrating the composition of version paths. Whenever a path is defined between two versions v, v' in some class C, an object can cross from the version context of v to v' by having its state (value of object's fields, $\overline{e}$) transformed according to the mapping(s) defined in the lens(es). To do so, we define a lens by the function $\mathcal{L}_{C:v \to v'}(\overline{e})$ that produces such mapping(s). The particular case of the empty path (ε) means no transformation is applied, and the lens corresponds to the identity function ($\mathcal{L}_{C:v \to v'}(\overline{e}) = \overline{e}$). For a path of the form (v, v'), the lens defined from the base version of v to the base version of v' ($\overline{e'}$) is evaluated in the context of version v, by replacing the constructor arguments ($\overline{x}$) with the object's field values ($@v(e'\{\overline{e}/\overline{x}\})$). For composed paths the lens function is applied recursively for each intermediate step of the form (v, w).

$$\mathcal{L}_{C:v \to v'}(\overline{e}) \triangleq \begin{cases} \overline{e} & \text{if } path(v, v', C) = \epsilon \\ @v(e'\{\overline{e}/\overline{x}\}) & \text{if } path(v, v', C) = (v, v') \\ & , w = base(v, C), w' = base(v', C) \\ & , C@w(\overline{x})\{ \ldots \mathsf{this}@w'(\overline{e'})\ \} \in C \\ \mathcal{L}_{C:w \to v'}(\mathcal{L}_{C:v \to w}(\overline{e})) & \text{if } path(v, v', C) = (v, w), p \end{cases}$$

In the example of Sect. 2, we have the following composition of lenses

$$\mathcal{L}_{Song:date \to cover}((``Help!", 19, 7, 1965)) = (``Help", 1965, \mathsf{new}\ Image(``help.jpg"))$$

$$\frac{\overline{e'} = \mathcal{L}_{C:v \to v'}(\overline{e})}{@v(\text{new } C(\overline{e})) \xrightarrow{v'} \text{new } C(\overline{e'})} \text{ (R-Upgrade)} \qquad \frac{\textit{vfields}(v, C) = \overline{C}\,\overline{f}}{\text{new } C(\overline{e}).f_i \xrightarrow{v} e_i} \text{ (R-Field)}$$

$$\frac{u = \textit{mversion}(\overline{V}, v, C, m) \quad \textit{mbody}(u, C, m) = (\overline{x}.e_0)}{\text{new } C(\overline{e}).m(\overline{f}) \xrightarrow{v} @u(e_0\{^{@v(\overline{f})}/_{\overline{x}}\}\{^{@v(\text{new } C(\overline{e}))}/_{\text{this}}\})} \text{ (R-Invk)}$$

$$\frac{e_0 \xrightarrow{v} e_0'}{e_0.f \xrightarrow{v} e_0'.f} \text{ (RC-Field)} \qquad \frac{e_0 \xrightarrow{v} e_0'}{e_0.m(\overline{e}) \xrightarrow{v} e_0'.m(\overline{e})} \text{ (RC-Invk)} \qquad \frac{e \xrightarrow{v} e'}{@v(e) \xrightarrow{v'} @v(e')} \text{ (RC-Version)}$$

Fig. 12. Structural operational semantics rules

We follow the standard functions for method type and body lookup as defined in [9] ($\textit{mtype}(v, C, m)$ and $\textit{mbody}(v, C, m)$), with the exception that the annotated version in the method definition (v) is also given as argument.

$$\textit{mtype}(v, C, m) \triangleq \begin{cases} \overline{B} \to B & \text{if } M \in \overline{M} \\ \textit{mtype}(v, D, m) & \text{otherwise} \end{cases} \text{ with } \textit{class } C \textit{ extends } D\{\overline{C}\,\overline{f};$$

$$\textit{mbody}(v, C, m) \triangleq \begin{cases} \overline{x}.e & \text{if } M \in \overline{M} \\ \textit{mbody}(v, D, m) & \text{otherwise} \end{cases}$$

$\overline{K}; \overline{M}\} \in \overline{L}$ and $M = \text{B } m@v(\overline{B}\overline{x})\{\text{return e; }\}$.

We also define function $\textit{mversion}(\overline{V}, v, C, m)$ that yields the version, in a version graph $\overline{V}$, at which a method m is defined in class C in the context of a given version v. A method definition is first searched recursively across all versions v' such that $v' \succ^* v$, with the latest one being selected. If no such version defines the method m, then it is searched in version v. If it is neither defined in v nor in its replacements, then the method m must be inherited from some version v' such that (1) $v \succ^* v'$ xor (2) $v >^* v'$. In (1) the function is applied to version v', but with version v removed from $\overline{V}$, to prevent loops. Finally, in (2), the function is applied to version v', and proceeds as explained above.

$$\textit{mversion}(\overline{V}, v, C, m) \triangleq \begin{cases} w \text{ if } v' \succ v \in \overline{V} \wedge \textit{mversion}(\overline{V}, v', C, m) = w \\ v \text{ if } \textit{mtype}(v, m, C) = \overline{D} \to D \\ w \text{ if } v > v' \in \overline{V} \wedge \textit{mversion}(\overline{V}, v', C, m) = w \\ w \text{ if } v \succ v' \in \overline{V} \wedge \textit{mversion}(\overline{V} \setminus \{\,v\,\}, v', C, m) = w \end{cases}$$

In the example of Sect. 2 we have that $\textit{mversion}(\overline{V}, \textit{init}, \textit{Server}, \textit{put}) = \textit{date}$, illustrating the versioned lookup of method definitions. Now that we defined $\textit{mversion}(\overline{V}, v, C, m)$, we can produce the list of methods available in class C at version v by the function $\textit{methods}(\overline{V}, v, C)$. This chooses the methods $\overline{m}$ from class C whose annotated version corresponds to the lookup version of m from version v: $\textit{methods}(\overline{V}, v, C) \triangleq \{\, m@w \in M \mid w = \textit{mversion}(\overline{V}, v, C, m) \,\}$.

Dynamic Semantics. In this section we present the operational semantics for our language, in the form of the set of rules in Fig. 12 that define a reduction relation $e \xrightarrow{v} e'$ where an expression e evaluates to expression e' in the context of version v.

The semantic rules express exactly how evaluation happens in the context of a version and how the corresponding context switch operations work. This is expressed in rule (R-UPGRADE) where the transformation of an object from its representation in version v to version v' happens by the application of a lens, if it exists. Recall the definition of lenses before to check that inner expressions may themselves be still in the context of version v. Rules (R-FIELD) and (R-INVK) depend on the aforementioned versioned lookups for fields and methods. In the case of method invocation, special attention is needed to maintain the correct version context of method arguments and also the reference *this*. The remaining rules express the congruence of the reduction relation, in the context of a field selection, a method call, or the version context expression.

Type soundness, in the style of Wright and Felleisen [21], implies that the whole version graph can co-exist in a single program without introducing runtime type errors. We define the usual type preservation theorem and sketch its proof[3].

Theorem (Subject Reduction). If $\Gamma \vdash_v e : C$ and $e \xrightarrow{v} e'$ then $\Gamma \vdash_v e' : C'$ for some C' with $C' <: C$.

We prove this theorem by induction on the typing relation and case analysis on the last rule applied. The main challenge in the proof is to ensure that the version switching operations use the correct typing of the state being used at each time (the base version), checking that the version coercions are in the right places, and enforcing the necessary signature preservation conditions. A particularly sensible spot is to require all needed lenses to be well-formed and ensure that switching versions is well-typed. This completes the presentation of the language semantics, reference to algorithms processing a versioned code base.

4   Future Work

We consider the following regarding future work.

Program Slicing. Given the semantics presented in Sect. 3, we have designed a (rough-sketched) code slicing algorithm[4] that produces the snapshot of code for a specific version, by applying static state transformations whenever it is necessary to cross version contexts. This is suited for an automated continuous delivery setting targeting software for a specific version, producing a static binary with only the necessary code for that version. We illustrate this in Fig. 13, representing a slice of class Song for version date. Notice how the code for method age is inherited from version yearbugfix, and re-written with the state transformation specified in the lens this@init(...,**this**.date.year()).

Richer Version Graph. The constructors for the version graph allow the creation of single, upgrade, or replacement version. We intend on enriching this

---

[3] Proofs at http://ctp.di.fct.unl.pt/~jcs/papers/versions-extended.pdf.

[4] Available at https://bitbucket.org/liveprogrammingteam/vfj/.

```
class Song extends Object {
    string title; Date date;
    Song(string title, Date date) {this.title = title; this.date = date; }
    Date getDate() {return this.date();}
    int age() {return (new Date()).year() - this.date().year();}
}
```

Fig. 13. Code re-written for the date versions based on lenses and version graph

constructors and allow a single version to merge several versions. Coupled with a mechanism for solving conflicts locally, we believe this will allow the design of more complex work flows that closely resemble those adopted in the industry [19].

Imperative Paradigm. We plan to instantiate our model in the imperative paradigm and study the same transformations in a more general setting, and providing a pragmatic mechanism for a language like Java and a suitable development environment.

5   Related Work

The management of multi-version software focuses on the interaction, design, and maintenance of a corpus of versions of a single software product. We relate to the following approaches surrounding this topic. ***Update Programming.*** Erwig and Ren [6] introduce an extension to Haskell that supports update programming. A program is an abstract data type whose building blocks are language terms. They provide a mechanism to script changes in programs creating new terms and changing existing ones. Hazelnut [14] is a core calculus that builds on typed "holes" and a gradual type theory that features a type system for expressions with holes and a language of edit actions ensuring that every edit state has static meaning. This allows for progressive program construction, as well as giving semantic meaning to incomplete code.

Delta Oriented Programming. Schaefer et al. [16] introduce DOP, a programming language for designing SPL based on the concept of program deltas. The implementation of a SPL is divided into a core module, comprising a complete valid product, and a set of delta modules, changes to be applied to the core module to target other products/variations. The language further ensures all product variations are well typed.

Multi-Version Systems Analyses. The analysis of multi-version systems is usually a project management activity that tries to detect change patterns in the code, and assessing risks of interferences between development threads that may result in the introduction of vulnerabilities [11], code repetition [12] and maintenance hurdles [2,5,10,20], and the other difficulties in the management of multiple versions [7,8,17,22]. We maintain the history of programming versions, well-formed by construction, instead of defining semantics for partial programs [15]. Our approach acts preventively by detecting illegal evolution steps in the development history [2,5,10,20] and also complements update and delta oriented programming approaches [1,6,16] by recording a modification history and allowing (legal) branching in the code base.

6 Conclusions

In this work we have presented an abstract certifying version control model that enables the explicit specification of sound evolution steps in the development of a software artifact. We instantiate our abstract model in an object-oriented core calculus, extending Featherweigth Java [9] with version annotations in declarations of fields, constructors and methods. The model supports safe version switching so that each evolution step only requires the least amount of new declarations as possible, and that old code is still active and compatible with the new declarations, via implicit and explicit version switching operations. We rely on standard subject reduction results that imply that no execution runtime type errors occur, even in the presence of version switching operations.

Acknowledgements. This work is funded by NOVA LINCS UID/CEC/04516/2013, COST CA15123, FC&T Project CLAY - PTDC/EEI-CTP/4293/2014.

References

1. Amsden, E., Newton, R., Siek, J.: Editing functional programs without breaking them. In: IFL 2014 (2014)
2. Bennett, K.H., Rajlich, V.T.: Software maintenance and evolution: a roadmap. In: Proceedings of the Conference on the Future of Software Engineering (2000)
3. Cimpanu, C.: Over 100,000 GitHub repos have leaked API or cryptographic keys. https://www.zdnet.com/article/over-100000-github-repos-have-leaked-api-or-cryptographic-keys/
4. Cimpanu, C.: Security flaws in 100+ Jenkins plugins put enterprise networks at risk. https://www.zdnet.com/article/security-flaws-in-100-jenkins-plugins-put-enterprise-networks-at-risk/
5. Eick, S.G., Graves, T.L., Karr, A.F., Marron, J.S., Mockus, A.: Does code decay? assessing the evidence from change management data. IEEE Trans. Softw. Eng. **27**(1), 1–2 (2001)
6. Erwig, M., Ren, D.: A rule-based language for programming software updates. In: Proceedings of the 2002 ACM SIGPLAN Workshop on Rule-Based Programming - RULE 2002, Pittsburgh, Pennsylvania (2002)
7. Graves, T., Karr, A., Marron, J., Siy, H.: Predicting fault incidence using software change history. IEEE Trans. Softw. Eng. **26**(7), 653–661 (2000)
8. Hosek, P., Cadar, C.: Safe software updates via multi-version execution. In: 2013 35th International Conference on Software Engineering (ICSE), May 2013
9. Igarashi, A., Pierce, B.C., Wadler, P.: Featherweight Java: a minimal core calculus for Java and GJ. ACM Trans. Program. Lang. Syst. **23**(3), 396–450 (2001)
10. Izurieta, C., Bieman, J.M.: How software designs decay: a pilot study of pattern evolution. In: First International Symposium on Empirical Software Engineering and Measurement (ESEM 2007) (2007)

11. Kim, J., Malaiya, Y.K., Ray, I.: Vulnerability discovery in multi-version software systems. In: 10th IEEE High Assurance Systems Engineering Symposium (HASE 2007) (2007)
12. Kim, M., Notkin, D.: Program element matching for multi-version program analyses. In: Proceedings of the 2006 International Workshop on Mining Software Repositories - MSR 2006 (2006)
13. Lehman, M.M.: Laws of software evolution revisited. In: Montangero, C. (ed.) EWSPT 1996. LNCS, vol. 1149, pp. 108–124. Springer, Heidelberg (1996). https://doi.org/10.1007/BFb0017737
14. Omar, C., Voysey, I., Chugh, R., Hammer, M.A.: Live functional programming with typed holes. Proc. ACM Program. Lang. **3**, 14 (2019)
15. Omar, C., Voysey, I., Hilton, M., Aldrich, J., Hammer, M.A.: Hazelnut: a bidirectionally typed structure editor calculus. ACM SIGPLAN Not. **52**(1), 86–99 (2017)
16. Schaefer, I., Bettini, L., Bono, V., Damiani, F., Tanzarella, N.: Delta-oriented programming of software product lines. In: Bosch, J., Lee, J. (eds.) SPLC 2010. LNCS, vol. 6287, pp. 77–91. Springer, Heidelberg (2010). https://doi.org/10.1007/978-3-642-15579-6_6
17. Subramanian, S., Hicks, M., McKinley, K.S.: Dynamic software updates: a VM-centric approach. SIGPLAN Not. **44**(6), 1–12 (2009)
18. Swanson, E.B.: The dimensions of maintenance. In: Proceedings of the 2nd International Conference on Software Engineering (1976)
19. Driessen, V.: A successful Git branching model, January 2010. https://nvie.com/posts/a-successful-git-branching-model/
20. Wash, R., Rader, E., Vaniea, K., Rizor, M.: Out of the loop: how automated software updates cause unintended security consequences. In: 10th Symposium On Usable Privacy and Security ({SOUPS} 2014) (2014)
21. Wright, A.K., Felleisen, M.: A syntactic approach to type soundness. Inf. Comput. **115**(1), 38–94 (1994)
22. Zimmermann, T., Zeller, A., Weissgerber, P., Diehl, S.: Mining version histories to guide software changes. IEEE Trans. Softw. Eng. **31**(6), 429–445 (2005)

Compositional Feature-Oriented Systems

Clemens Dubslaff[✉]

Technische Universität Dresden, Dresden, Germany
clemens.dubslaff@tu-dresden.de

Abstract. Feature-oriented systems describe system variants through features as first-class abstractions of optional or incremental units of systems functionality. The choice how to treat modularity and composition in feature-oriented systems strongly influences their design and behavioral modeling. Popular paradigms for the composition of features are superimposition and parallel composition. We approach both in a unified formal way for programs in guarded command language by introducing *compositional feature-oriented systems (CFOSs)*. We show how both compositions relate to each other by providing transformations that preserve the behaviors of system variants. Family models of feature-oriented systems encapsulate all behaviors of system variants in a single model, prominently used in family-based analysis approaches. We introduce *family-ready* CFOSs that admit a family model and show by an annotative approach that every CFOS can be transformed into a family-ready one that has the same modularity and behaviors.

1 Introduction

Feature-oriented systems [29,18,2] excel in their concept of behavioral modularity [40,31] that is provided through features, i.e., first-class abstractions of an optional or incremental unit of functionality [40]. They are first and foremost used to model *software product lines (SPLs)* [16] where each software product corresponds to a combination of features. However, feature-oriented concepts have shown to be applicable in a wide range of areas, e.g., to model contexts [1] or heterogeneous (hardware) systems [22,21,5]. A central aspect within feature-oriented systems is the actual construction of a product from a given feature combination [30]. Annotative approaches, prominently applied in *featured transition systems (FTSs)* [14], incorporate all behaviors of any product in a single *family model* by annotating *feature guards* to behaviors. Behaviors are then effective in those products where the feature combination fulfills the feature guard. Family models are successful in the context of feature-oriented system analysis: a symbolic representation of the model in combination with a single

The author has been supported by the DFG through the Cluster of Excellence EXC 2050/1 (CeTI, project ID 390696704, as part of Germany's Excellence Strategy), the Collaborative Research Centers CRC 912 (HAEC) and TRR 248 (see https://perspicuous-computing.science, project ID 389792660), the Research Training Group RoSI (GRK 1907), Deutsche Telekom Stiftung, and the 5G Lab Germany.

© Springer Nature Switzerland AG 2019
P. C. Ölveczky and G. Salaün (Eds.): SEFM 2019, LNCS 11724, pp. 162–180, 2019.
https://doi.org/10.1007/978-3-030-30446-1_9

analysis run may avoid the exponential blowup in the number of features that arises when analyzing every product one-by-one [15,21]. Opposed to annotative approaches, compositional approaches model the behaviors of features separately through *feature modules* [31,21] that are composed towards a product. The de-facto standard composition operators for feature modules are *superimposition* [8,33] and *parallel composition* [36], both syntactically defined on the chosen behavioral formalism for feature modules. Superimposition describes how a base behavior is changed when composing a feature module, a concept also apparent in delta-oriented modeling [39]. This approach is mainly used in the software-engineering domain and formalized, e.g., for feature-oriented variants of JAVA [3,7] and C++ [4]. But also for low-level programming languages such as guarded command languages [20], superimposition approaches have been applied for the analysis of feature-oriented systems [37,13]. On the other hand, parallel composition focuses on the interaction between composed feature modules via shared actions. Paramount in formal methods, it is not surprising that parallel-composition approaches are mainly used when it comes to the verification and analysis of feature-oriented systems [25,14,22]. Verification tools mostly rely on an input language based on guarded commands, which lead to FPROMELA [12] and PROFEAT [9], feature-oriented extensions of the model-checker input languages of SPIN [27] and PRISM [34], respectively.

Although both composition operators are widely used for the design and analysis of feature-oriented systems and there are common foundations in the case of guarded command languages, yet there does not exist any framework that covers both composition operators. We introduce *compositional feature-oriented systems (CFOSs)* that follow the usual two-level approach for feature-oriented systems comprising a feature model and behavioral model, but with the focus on compositional specification. In particular, we consider feature modules given in a featured variant of guarded command language as behavioral model, composed towards products specified in the feature model through parallel composition or superimposition. Provided the concept of CFOSs, we mainly answer the following research questions in this paper:

(RQ1) Is there an automated annotative approach for CFOSs that admits a family model and maintains behaviors, modularity, and locality?

(RQ2) Are there automated translations between CFOSs on superimposition and parallel composition that maintain behaviors, modularity, and locality?

Here, maintaining modularity is understood as preserving the feature model and the assignment of feature modules to features, while maintaining locality [31] ensures that variables over which the feature modules are specified do not change. Answering **(RQ1)** positively would provide a unified annotative and compositional approach to specify feature-oriented systems. For this, we introduce *family-ready* CFOSs where composing all feature modules yields a family model for the whole feature-oriented system but still allows for the compositional construction of single products. We show that any CFOS can be turned into a family-ready CFOS of polynomial size, mainly following a *lifting* approach [38]. Family-ready CFOSs facilitate the specification of compositional *dynamic feature-oriented systems* [24,19,21], i.e., systems where feature combinations can change during runtime. Given a reconfiguration graph that describes the changes of feature combinations, the behavior of the dynamic (family-ready) CFOS is then provided by a simple product construction that resolves the feature guards in the composition of all features in the CFOS. The question **(RQ2)** addresses the relationship between superimposition and parallel composition and a positive answer would provide the foundations to use both formalisms interchangeably, e.g., analyzing feature-oriented systems specified with superimposition with tools that have an input language based on parallel composition or vice versa, generating programs based on superimposition out from verified CFOSs based on parallel composition. We show that any parallel-composition CFOS can be transferred into a superimposition CFOS that has exponential size and maintains behaviors, modularity, and locality. The converse is only possible not requiring locality and we present a transformation that turns any superimposition CFOSs into an exponentially-sized parallel-composition CFOS.

Further Related Work. In [23], a superimposition operator on interacting parallel processes (an extension of guarded command language) has been considered. While we consider superimposition on the same level as parallel composition, they developed a calculus where superimposition is applied on processes appearing in a fixed parallel composition.

Transformations akin to the one addressed in **(RQ1)** have been already addressed in the context of FTSs and their probabilistic counterparts. The lifted feature composition of [13] is a superimposition variant that incorporates case distinctions depending on possible feature combinations in the input language of NuSMV [11]. Their approach requires a modified composition other than the standard one in NuSMV and, applied to our guarded command language setting, would yield an exponential blowup while we present a polynomial translation. Also in [12] and [9], the lifting approach has been applied towards family models specified in FPROMELA and PROFEAT, respectively. However, their semantics might introduce stutter steps and thus is not family-ready. Concerning dynamic feature-oriented systems, [24] and [19] describe feature switches through reconfiguration patterns and rules, respectively, while we follow the concept of reconfiguration graphs also used in [21]. However, [21] inherently requires the feature-oriented system specified to be family-ready while this is usually not the case during the development: feature modules do not a priori include information about all other features of the feature-oriented system to maintain reusability within similar but different systems.

2   Theoretical Foundations

In this section we introduce our formal framework used throughout the paper. Although not yet been considered like this in the literature, it mainly relies on standard concepts [20,21,14]. We denote by $\wp(X)$ the power set of a set X. Given partial functions $f_i \colon X_i \rightharpoonup Y_i$ for $i \in \{1,2\}$ we define $f_1 \bowtie f_2 \colon X_1 \cup X_2 \rightharpoonup Y_1 \cup Y_2$ by $(f_1 \bowtie f_2)(x) = f_2(x)$ in case $f_2(x)$ is defined and $(f_1 \bowtie f_2)(x) = f_1(x)$ otherwise.

Interfaces. An *interface* $I = \langle Int, Ext \rangle$ with $Int \cap Ext = \varnothing$ characterizes *internal* and *external* elements through finite sets Int and Ext, respectively. If there is no chance of confusion we sometimes write I for the set $Int \cup Ext$. In case two interfaces $\langle X, X' \rangle$ and $\langle Y, Y' \rangle$ have disjoint internal elements, i.e., $X \cap Y = \varnothing$, they are *composable*. We define a composition operator $\oplus$ where $\langle X, X' \rangle \oplus \langle Y, Y' \rangle = \langle Z, Z' \backslash Z \rangle$ with $Z = X \cup Y$ and $Z' = X' \cup Y'$.

Arithmetic Expressions and Constraints. Let Var be a finite set of *variables*, on which we define *evaluations* as functions $\eta \colon Var \to \mathbb{Z}$. The set of evaluations over Var is denoted by $Eval(Var)$. Let z range over $\mathbb{Z}$ and v range over Var, then the set of *arithmetic expressions* $\mathbb{A}(Var)$ is defined by the grammar $a ::= z \mid v \mid (a + a) \mid (a \cdot a)$. Variable evaluations are extended to arithmetic expressions by $\eta(z) = z$, $\eta(a_1 + a_2) = \eta(a_1) + \eta(a_2)$, and $\eta(\alpha_1 \cdot \alpha_2) = \eta(a_1) \cdot \eta(a_2)$. $\mathbb{C}(Var)$ denotes the set of *constraints* over Var, i.e., terms of the form $(a \sim z)$ with $a \in \mathbb{A}(Var)$, $\sim \in \{>, \geq, =, \leq, <, \neq\}$, and $z \in \mathbb{Z}$. For a given evaluation $\eta \in Eval(Var)$ and constraint $(a \sim z) \in \mathbb{C}(Var)$, we write $\eta \models (a \sim z)$ iff $\eta(a) \sim z$. Note that with integer-valued variables we can mimic Boolean variables $x \in Var$ by identifying x with $(x \geq 1)$ and $\neg x$ with $(x = 0)$.

Boolean Expressions. For a countable nonempty set X, we define *Boolean expressions* $\mathbb{B}(X)$ by the grammar $\psi ::= \mathtt{tt} \mid x \mid \neg \psi \mid \psi \wedge \psi$ where $x \in X$. We might denote by $\mathtt{ff} = \neg \mathtt{tt}$ and use well-known Boolean connectives such as disjunction $\vee$, implication $\to$, etc. from which a Boolean expression can be easily obtained using standard syntactic transformations. The *satisfaction relation* for Boolean expressions $\models \subseteq \wp(X) \times \mathbb{B}(X)$ is defined in the usual way, i.e., for any $Y \subseteq X \colon Y \models x$ iff $x \in Y$, $Y \models \neg \psi$ iff $Y \not\models \psi$, and $Y \models \psi_1 \wedge \psi_2$ iff $Y \models \psi_1$ and $Y \models \psi_2$. For an evaluation $\eta \in Eval(Var)$ and $\psi \in \mathbb{B}(\mathbb{C}(Var))$, we write $\eta \models \psi$ iff $\{c \in \mathbb{C}(Var) : \eta \models c\} \models \psi$.

Transition Systems. A *transition system* is a tuple $T = (S, Act, T, \iota)$ where S is a finite set of states, Act a finite set of actions, $T \subseteq S \times Act \times S$ is a transition relation, and $\iota \in S$ is an initial state. We usually write $s \xrightarrow{\alpha} s'$ in case $(s, \alpha, s') \in T$. For transition systems $T_i = (S_i, Act_i, T_i, \iota_i)$ with $i \in \{1, 2\}$ we denote by $\underline{S_i}$ the set of *reachable* states in T_i, i.e., $\underline{S_i} \subseteq S_i$ is the smallest set for which $\iota_i \in \underline{S_i}$ and where for any $s \in \underline{S_i}$, $(s, \alpha, s') \in T_i$ we have $s' \in \underline{S_i}$. We call T_1 and T_2 *equivalent up to isomorphism*, denoted $T_1 \cong T_2$, if there is a bijection $\xi \colon \underline{S_1} \to \underline{S_2}$ such that $\xi(\iota_1) = \iota_2$ and $(s, \alpha, s') \in T_1$ iff $(\xi(s), \alpha, \xi(s')) \in T_2$.

2.1 Feature Models

Feature-oriented systems are usually specified by a *feature model* and a *featured behavioral model*. Given an abstract set of features F, a feature model $\mathcal{F}$ expresses variability in the system over valid combinations of features $\mathfrak{V}[\mathcal{F}] \subseteq \wp(F)$. The featured behavioral model describes the operational behaviors of features, i.e., their actual functionality.

Feature Diagrams. The de-facto standard feature model for static feature-oriented systems such as software product lines (SPL) is provided through *feature*

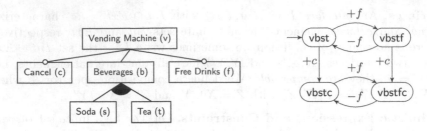

Fig. 1. Feature diagram (left) and reconfiguration graph (right) for a vending machine

diagrams [29]. They are tree-like hierarchical structures over nodes representing features. Figure 1 (left) depicts a feature diagram of a vending machine SPL [6,14] over features $F = \{v, b, s, t, f, c\}$. Feature v encapsulates the basic functionality of a vending machine, b has the functionality of providing drinks to the customer, either soda (feature s), or tea (feature t), or both. While usually drinks have to be paid, the optional feature f (indicated by the circle on top of the feature) adds the possibility to provide free drinks. When the second optional feature c is active, the customer can cancel any vending process, leading to a cash back. In our setting, it suffices to regard a feature diagram $\mathcal{D}$ as a compact representation of *valid feature combinations* $\mathfrak{V}[\mathcal{D}] \subseteq \wp(F)$. Within the vending machine SPL, there are 12 valid feature combinations.

Reconfiguration Graphs. *Dynamic feature-oriented systems* [24,26] allow to change feature combinations during system execution. A *reconfiguration graph* [19] (also called feature controller [21]) describes feature changes by a transition system $\mathcal{G} = \big(Loc \times \wp(F), Act, R, (\ell_0, I)\big)$ where Loc is a finite set of locations and $(\ell_0, I) \in Loc \times \wp(F)$ is an initial location with an initial feature combination. The set of valid feature combinations $\mathfrak{V}[\mathcal{G}]$ is the set of feature combinations reachable in $\mathcal{G}$. In Fig. 1 (right) a reconfiguration graph for a vending machine SPL is depicted, where we abbreviate a node $(\ell, \{f_1, \ldots, f_n\})$ over the single location ℓ by $f_1 \ldots f_n$. The basic variant serves both soda and tea, and can be step-wise upgraded with features c and f, providing the functionality for cancel and free drinks, respectively. While a cancel upgrade cannot be reverted, it is possible to switch back from free to paid drinks.

2.2   Featured Transition Systems

As behavioral model for feature-oriented systems, [15] introduced the concept of *featured transition systems (FTSs)*. FTSs are transition systems whose transitions are amended with *feature guards*, i.e., Boolean expressions over the set of features. Formally, an FTS is a tuple $\mathsf{Fts} = (S, F, Act, T, \iota)$ where S, F, and Act are finite sets of states, features, and actions, respectively, $T \subseteq S \times \mathbb{B}(F) \times Act \times S$ is a featured transition relation, and $\iota \in S$ is an initial state. Given a feature combination $X \subseteq F$, Fts induces a transition system $\mathsf{Fts}(X) = (S, Act, T_X, \iota)$ where $(s, \alpha, s') \in T_X$ iff $(s, f, \alpha, s') \in T$ and

Pv : ⟨{m = 0}, ∅⟩
[pay] tt & tt ↦ m' := m+1
[cancel] c & tt ↦ m' := 0
[select s] s∧¬f & m>0 ↦ m' := m−1
[select s] s∧f & tt ↦ ∅
[select t] t∧¬f & m>0 ↦ m' := m−1
[select t] t∧f & tt ↦ ∅

Ps : ⟨{ns = 100}, ∅⟩
[refill] tt & tt ↦ ns' := 100
[select s] tt & ns>0 ↦ ns' := ns−1

Pt : ⟨{nt = 20}, ∅⟩
[refill] tt & tt ↦ nt' := 20
[select t] tt & nt>0 ↦ nt' := nt−1

Pvst : ⟨{m = 0, ns = 100, nt = 20}, ∅⟩
[pay] tt & tt ↦ m' := m+1
[cancel] c & tt ↦ m' := 0
[refill] tt∧tt & tt∧tt ↦ ns' := 100, nt' := 20
[select s] s∧¬f & tt & m>0∧ns>0 ↦ m' := m−1, ns' := ns−1
[select s] s∧f∧tt & tt∧ns>0 ↦ ns' := ns−1
[select t] t∧¬f∧tt & m>0∧nt>0 ↦ m' := m−1, nt' := nt−1
[select t] t∧f∧tt & tt∧nt>0 ↦ nt' := nt−1

Fig. 2. Simple programs for the vending machine SPL

$X \models f$. An FTS usually encodes all behaviors of valid feature combinations in a feature-oriented system, i.e., it is a *family model*. Family models facilitate the description of operational behaviors w.r.t. dynamic feature models and can be used for a family-based analysis [21]. The transition-system semantics of Fts and a reconfiguration graph $\mathcal{G} = \left(Loc \times \wp(F), Act', R, (\ell_0, I)\right)$ is defined as $\mathsf{Fts} \bowtie \mathcal{G} = \left(S \times Loc \times \wp(F), Act \cup Act', T_\mathcal{G}, (\iota, \ell_0, I)\right)$ where $T_\mathcal{G}$ is the smallest transition relation that satisfy the rules

$$\frac{(s,f,\alpha,s') \in T \quad (\ell,X) \in Loc \times \wp(F) \quad X \models f \quad \alpha \notin Act'}{(s,\ell,X) \xrightarrow{\alpha} (s',\ell,X)} \qquad \frac{s \in S \quad ((\ell,X),\alpha,(\ell',X')) \in R \quad \alpha \notin Act}{(s,\ell,X) \xrightarrow{\alpha} (s,\ell',X')}$$

$$\frac{(s,f,\alpha,s') \in T \quad ((\ell,X),\alpha,(\ell',X')) \in R \quad X \models f \quad \alpha \in Act \cap Act'}{(s,\ell,X) \xrightarrow{\alpha} (s',\ell',X')}$$

2.3 Featured Programs

Towards a compositional specification of FTSs, we rely on programs in a featured variant of Dijkstra's *guarded command language* [20], following a similar approach as within featured program graphs [12]. Let $V = \langle IntV, ExtV \rangle$ be a *variable interface* over *internal variables* $IntV$ and *external variables* $ExtV$, and F and Act finite nonempty sets of features and actions, respectively. We define $Cmd(V, F, Act)$ to be the set of *commands* $\langle f, g, \alpha, u \rangle$ where $f \in \mathbb{B}(F)$ is a feature guard, $g \in \mathbb{B}(\mathbb{C}(V))$ is a *guard*, $\alpha \in Act$ an action, and $u \colon IntV \rightharpoonup \mathbb{A}(V)$ is a partial function called *update*. For better readability, we usually write "$[\alpha]\, f \,\&\, g \mapsto u$" for "$\langle f, g, \alpha, u \rangle$".

Then, a *program* is a tuple $\mathsf{Prog} = (V, F, Act, C, \nu)$ where $C \subseteq Cmd(V, F, Act)$ is a finite set of commands and $\nu \in Eval(IntV)$ is an initial evaluation of internal variables. We assume w.l.o.g. that for every action in Act there is a command, i.e., for all $\alpha \in Act$ there are f, g, and u such that $[\alpha]\, f \,\&\, g \mapsto u \in C$, and that for each variable there is at least one command containing this variable. On the left of Fig. 2 three programs Pv, Ps, and Pt are depicted, following the vending machine SPL example by implementing features v, s, and t, respectively. We indicated the initial variable evaluation in the variable interface and denoted updates (v, e) for some variable v and expression e by $v' := e$.

Following the concepts of delta-oriented formalisms [39], we define a *delta-program* as a pair (Prog, Δ) where Δ is a *modification* function

$$\Delta \colon Cmd\big(\langle ExtV, IntV \rangle, F, Act\big) \;\rightarrow\; \wp\big(Cmd(\langle V, \varnothing \rangle, F, Act)\big).$$

We require that only finitely many commands involved in modifications, i.e., when D_Δ denotes the set of commands $c \in Cmd(\langle ExtV, IntV \rangle, F, Act)$ where $\Delta(c) \neq \{c\}$, we require D_Δ and $\Delta(c)$ to be finite for each $c \in D_\Delta$. The size of Δ is then defined as $|\Delta| = |D_\Delta| + \sum_{c \in D_\Delta} |\Delta(c)|$. We usually specify modification functions by only providing the finitely many modifications. Modification functions are naturally extended to sets of commands $E \subseteq Cmd(\langle ExtV, IntV \rangle, F, Act)$ by $\Delta(E) = \bigcup_{c \in E} \Delta(c)$. The *size* $|(\mathsf{Prog}, \Delta)|$ of a delta-program (Prog, Δ) is the number of commands in C and in modifications of Δ, i.e., $|(\mathsf{Prog}, \Delta)| = |C| + |\Delta|$.

Compositions. Let $\mathsf{Prog}_i = (V_i, F_i, Act_i, C_i, \nu_i)$ for $i \in \{1, 2\}$ be programs with $IntV_1 \cap IntV_2 = \varnothing$ and set $V = V_1 \oplus V_2$, $F = F_1 \cup F_2$, $Act = Act_1 \cup Act_2$, and $\nu = \nu_1 \times \nu_2$. The *parallel composition* of Prog_1 and Prog_2 is defined as $\mathsf{Prog}_1 \| \mathsf{Prog}_2 = (V, F, Act, C, \nu)$ where C is the smallest set of commands satisfying the following rules:

$$(\text{int}_1) \frac{[\alpha]\, f_1 \,\&\, g_1 \mapsto u_1 \in C_1 \quad \alpha \notin Act_2}{[\alpha]\, f_1 \,\&\, g_1 \mapsto u_1 \in C} \qquad (\text{int}_2) \frac{[\alpha]\, f_2 \,\&\, g_2 \mapsto u_2 \in C_2 \quad \alpha \notin Act_1}{[\alpha]\, f_2 \,\&\, g_2 \mapsto u_2 \in C}$$

$$(\text{sync}) \frac{[\alpha]\, f_1 \,\&\, g_1 \mapsto u_1 \in C_1 \quad [\alpha]\, f_2 \,\&\, g_2 \mapsto u_2 \in C_2}{[\alpha]\, f_1 \wedge f_2 \,\&\, g_1 \wedge g_2 \mapsto u_1 \times u_2 \in C}$$

When $(\mathsf{Prog}_2, \Delta)$ is a delta-program with $\Delta(C_1) \subseteq Cmd(V, F, Act)$, the *superimposition* of Prog_1 *by* $(\mathsf{Prog}_2, \Delta)$ is defined as the program $\mathsf{Prog}_1 \bullet (\mathsf{Prog}_2, \Delta) = (V, F, Act, C_2 \cup \Delta(C_1), \nu)$. Intuitively, superimposition modifies the commands of Prog_1 according to Δ and adds the commands of Prog_2 to Prog_1. The result of a superimposition is a program, i.e., a delta-program with empty modifications. In this sense, superimposition also provides a composition on delta-programs by disregarding the modification sets of the first component and amending the empty modification set to the superimposition result.

Example 1. On the right of Fig. 2, the parallel composition $\mathsf{Pvst} = \mathsf{Pv} \| \mathsf{Ps} \| \mathsf{Pt}$ is listed. Note that parallel composition is purely syntactic and select actions synchronize through rule (sync). The same result could be obtained through superimposition, i.e., $\mathsf{Pvst} = \mathsf{Pv} \bullet (\mathsf{Ps}', \Delta_\mathsf{s}) \bullet (\mathsf{Pt}', \Delta_\mathsf{t})$ where Ps' is as Ps but without the *select s* command (i.e., only the *refill* command) and Pt' is as Pt but with an empty set of commands. Further,

$$\Delta_\mathsf{s} = \{(\, [\textit{select } s]\, \mathsf{s} \wedge \neg \mathsf{f} \,\&\, m>0 \mapsto m' := m-1,$$
$$\{\, [\textit{select } s]\, \mathsf{s} \wedge \neg \mathsf{f} \wedge \mathsf{tt} \,\&\, m>0 \wedge ns>0 \mapsto m' := m-1, ns' := ns-1\,\}),$$
$$(\, [\textit{select } s]\, \mathsf{s} \wedge \mathsf{f} \,\&\, \mathsf{tt} \mapsto \varnothing, \{\, [\textit{select } s]\, \mathsf{s} \wedge \mathsf{f} \wedge \mathsf{tt} \,\&\, \mathsf{tt} \wedge ns>0 \mapsto ns' := ns-1\,\})\}$$
$$\Delta_\mathsf{t} = \{(\, [\textit{select } t]\, \mathsf{t} \wedge \neg \mathsf{f} \,\&\, m>0 \mapsto m' := m-1,$$
$$\{\, [\textit{select } t]\, \mathsf{t} \wedge \neg \mathsf{f} \wedge \mathsf{tt} \,\&\, m>0 \wedge nt>0 \mapsto m' := m-1, nt' := nt-1\,\}),$$
$$(\, [\textit{select } t]\, \mathsf{t} \wedge \mathsf{f} \,\&\, \mathsf{tt} \mapsto \varnothing, \{\, [\textit{select } t]\, \mathsf{t} \wedge \mathsf{f} \wedge \mathsf{tt} \,\&\, \mathsf{tt} \wedge nt>0 \mapsto nt' := nt-1\,\})$$
$$(\, [\textit{refill}]\, \mathsf{tt} \,\&\, \mathsf{tt} \mapsto ns' := 100, \{\, [\textit{refill}]\, \mathsf{tt} \wedge \mathsf{tt} \,\&\, \mathsf{tt} \wedge \mathsf{tt} \mapsto ns' := 100, nt' := 20\,\})\}$$

Semantics. A program where no external variable appears in any command intuitively behaves as follows. Starting in the initial variable evaluation, the evaluations of the internal variables are changed according to the updates of one of the *enabled* commands, i.e., commands where its guard and feature guard are satisfied in the current variable evaluation and feature combination. Formally, the FTS semantics of a program $\mathsf{Prog} = (\langle IntV, ExtV \rangle, F, Act, C, \nu)$ with $C \subseteq Cmd(\langle IntV, \varnothing \rangle, F, Act)$ is defined as $\mathsf{Fts}[\mathsf{Prog}] = (Eval(IntV), F, Act, T, \nu)$ where $(\eta, f, \alpha, \eta') \in T$ iff there is some $[\alpha]\, f \,\&\, g \mapsto u \in C$ with $\eta \models g$ and $\eta' = \eta/u$. Here, $\eta/u \in Eval(IntV)$ formalizes the *effect* of an update u onto an evaluation η, i.e., $(\eta/u)(v) = \eta(u(v))$ for all $v \in IntV$ where $u(v)$ is defined and $(\eta/u)(v) = \eta(v)$ otherwise.

3 Compositional Feature-Oriented Systems

While an FTS is a monolithic behavioral model for feature-oriented systems, compositional approaches describe the behavior for each feature encapsulated in *feature modules* and how to combine feature modules towards a behavioral model for a specific feature combination.

Definition 1. *A compositional feature-oriented system (CFOS) is a tuple*

$$\mathsf{S} = (\, F,\, \mathcal{F},\, \mathfrak{M},\, \phi,\, \prec,\, \circ\,)$$

where F is a finite feature domain, $\mathcal{F}$ is a feature model over F, $\mathfrak{M}$ is a finite set of feature modules assigned to features through a function $\phi\colon F \to \mathfrak{M}$, $\prec\, \subseteq F \times F$ is a total order on F, and $\circ$ is a composition operation on feature modules.

In the following let S denote a CFOS as defined above and assume that for every feature $x \in F$ there is a valid feature combination $X \in \mathfrak{V}[\mathcal{F}]$ with $x \in X$. The *size* of S, denoted $|\mathsf{S}|$ is the sum of the sizes of the feature modules assigned to its features. For any nonempty feature combination $X \subseteq F$, we define the *product* $\mathsf{S}(X)$ recursively via

$$\mathsf{S}(\{x\}) = \phi(x) \qquad\qquad \text{for } x \in F$$
$$\mathsf{S}(X) = \mathsf{S}(X \backslash \{x\}) \circ \phi(x) \quad \text{for } x = \max_{\prec}(X)$$

where $\max_{\prec}(X)$ stands for the maximal feature in X with respect to $\prec$.

While in Definition 1 we defined CFOS in a generic fashion, in the following we focus on feature modules whose specification relies on programs and delta-programs (see Sect. 2.2).

Definition 2. *A CFOS $\mathsf{S} = (F, \mathcal{F}, \mathfrak{M}, \phi, \prec, \circ)$ is called*

- ∥-*CFOS when $\circ = \|$ and $\mathfrak{M}$ comprises pairwise composable programs, and*
- •-*CFOS when $\circ = \bullet$ and $\mathfrak{M}$ comprises pairwise composable delta-programs.*

Example 2. Following the vending machine SPL of Fig. 1, we define a $\|$-CFOS $S_v = (F_v, \mathcal{F}_v, \mathfrak{M}_v, \phi_v, \prec_v, \|)$ where $F_v = \{v, b, s, t, f, c\}$, $\mathcal{F}_v$ is one of the feature models of Fig. 1, $\mathfrak{M}_v = \{Pv, Ps, Pt, \epsilon\}$ as given in Fig. 2 and ϵ stands for an empty feature module, and $\phi_v(v) = Pv$, $\phi_v(s) = Ps$, $\phi_v(t) = Pt$, and $\phi_v(i) = \epsilon$ for $i \in \{b, f, c\}$, and $v \prec_v b \prec_v s \prec_v t \prec_v f \prec_v c$, Then, $S(\{v, b, s, t\}) = Pvst$ as specified in Fig. 2.

We close this section with some technical definitions concerning CFOSs that are used throughout the paper.

Definition 3. *For a fixed feature domain F and total order $\prec \subseteq F \times F$, we define the characteristic function $\chi\colon \wp(F) \to \mathbb{B}(F)$ for any $X \subseteq F$ by*

$$\chi(X) = (x_1 \wedge x_2 \wedge \ldots \wedge x_m) \wedge (y_1 \wedge y_2 \wedge \ldots \wedge y_n)$$

where $x_1 \cup x_2 \cup \ldots \cup x_m = X$, $y_1 \cup y_2 \cup \ldots \cup y_n = F \setminus X$, $x_1 \prec x_2 \prec \ldots \prec x_m$, and $y_1 \prec y_2 \prec \ldots \prec y_n$.

The characteristic function of a feature combination $X \subseteq F$ provides a uniquely defined Boolean expression that characterizes X, i.e., for all $Y \subseteq F$ we have $Y \models \chi(X)$ iff $X = Y$.

Definition 4. *Let $S_i = (F, \mathcal{F}_i, \mathfrak{M}_i, \phi_i, \prec_i, \circ_i)$ be some $\circ_i$-CFOS with $\circ_i \in \{\|, \bullet\}$ for $i \in \{1, 2\}$ and $\mathfrak{V}[\mathcal{F}_1] = \mathfrak{V}[\mathcal{F}_2]$. In case for all $X \in \mathfrak{V}[\mathcal{F}_1]$*

– $\mathsf{Fts}\big[S_1(X)\big](X) = \mathsf{Fts}\big[S_2(X)\big](X)$ *we call S_1 and S_2 product equivalent*
– $\mathsf{Fts}\big[S_1(X)\big](X) \cong \mathsf{Fts}\big[S_2(X)\big](X)$ *we call S_1 and S_2 behavioral equivalent*

Intuitively, product equivalence also requires the same variable names and evaluations on both products, while behavioral equivalence only focuses on isomorphic behaviors. Clearly, product equivalence implies behavioral equivalence. In this paper we focus on these rather strong notions of equivalence as they can be guaranteed as such in our transformations we present in the next sections. However, other notions of equivalences, e.g., following the concept of *bisimulation* [36], could be imagined in the context of *labeled FTSs*.

4   Family-Ready Systems

Family models for feature-oriented systems are appealing as they contain all behaviors of the system in a single model. Thus, they can help to avoid the construction of every product one-by-one, facilitate the specification of dynamic feature-oriented systems, enable a family-based analysis, and profit from concise symbolic representations exploiting shared behaviors between products. Towards a family model for some CFOS S, a naive annotative approach would be to amend each product $S(X)$ for valid feature combinations X with feature guards $\chi(X)$[1]

---

[1] Recall Definition 3 of $\chi(X)$, the characteristic Boolean expression of X.

and join these modified products to a single model. For CFOSs relying on programs as defined in Sect. 2.3, the family model would then be the program that comprises exactly those commands $[\alpha]\,\chi(X) \wedge f \& g \mapsto u$ for which there is a valid feature combination X and a command $[\alpha]\,f \& g \mapsto u$ in the product $S(X)$. This approach, however, leads to a monolithic model that discards all modularity and further requires to construct every product one-by-one beforehand.

In this section, we introduce the notion of *family-readiness*, capturing those CFOSs where the composition of all feature modules yields a family model for the feature-oriented system. Not all CFOSs are family-ready as feature modules only have to include information about their feature interactions with other required features and not their role within the whole feature-oriented system. This might be desired during system design, e.g., to ensure reusability of feature modules within other but similar CFOSs or simply for separating concerns. However, in later design steps, the benefits imposed by family-readiness prevail, e.g., when it comes to product deployment and analyzing all products of the CFOS. Furthermore, family-ready CFOSs unite the advantages from compositional and annotative approaches as issued in [30]. Addressing research question **(RQ1)** of the introduction, we provide automated translations of $\|$-CFOSs and $\bullet$-CFOSs into product equivalent family-ready $\|$-CFOSs and $\bullet$-CFOSs, respectively.

For the rest of this section, let us fix a $\circ$-CFOS $S = (F, \mathcal{F}, \mathfrak{M}, \phi, \prec, \circ)$ for $\circ \in \{\|, \bullet\}$. Note that for any feature combination $X \subseteq F$, and in particular $X = F$, $S(X)$ is defined as feature modules are pairwise composable. Furthermore, $S(X)$ does not contain any command referring to external variables, providing that its FTS semantics $\mathsf{Fts}[S(X)]$ is defined.

Definition 5. S *is family-ready if for all* $X \in \mathfrak{V}[\mathcal{F}]$

$$\mathsf{Fts}[S(F)](X) \;\cong\; \mathsf{Fts}[S(X)](X).$$

Stated in words, a CFOS is family-ready if the composition of any valid feature combination X admits the same behavior as composing all feature modules and then performing a projection to feature combination X.

Example 3. Returning to the $\|$-CFOS S_v for the vending machine SPL provided in Example 2, we show that not every CFOS is a priori family-ready. $S_v(F) =$ Pvst where Pvst is the program illustrated in Fig. 2 on the right. However, for the feature combination $X = \{v, b, t\}$, the transition system $\mathsf{Fts}[S_v(F)](X)$ contains behaviors refilling soda, represented by the command with action *refill* in Pvst, not present in the transition system $\mathsf{Fts}[S_v(X)](X)$.

The rest of this section is mainly devoted to the proof of the following theorem:

Theorem 1. *From any* $\circ$-*CFOS with* $\circ \in \{\|, \bullet\}$ *we can construct in polynomial time a product equivalent and family-ready* $\circ$-*CFOS.*

As the approach towards a family-ready system crucially depends on the composition operator and the corresponding feature module formalism, we sketch the proof for Theorem 1 separately for $\|$-CFOS and $\bullet$-CFOS. For both we propose

$Pv^{\|} : \langle\{m = 0\}, \varnothing\rangle$
[pay] $v\wedge tt \,\&\, tt \mapsto m' := m+1$
[cancel] $v\wedge c\,\&\, tt \mapsto m' := 0$
[select s] $v\wedge s\wedge\neg f\,\&\, m>0 \mapsto m' := m-1$
[select s] $v\wedge s\wedge f\,\&\, tt \mapsto \varnothing$
[select t] $v\wedge t\wedge\neg f\,\&\, m>0 \mapsto m' := m-1$
[select t] $v\wedge t\wedge f\,\&\, tt \mapsto \varnothing$
[pay] $\neg v\wedge ff\,\&\, tt \mapsto \varnothing$
[cancel] $\neg v\wedge ff\,\&\, tt \mapsto \varnothing$
[select s] $\neg v\wedge s\,\&\, tt \mapsto \varnothing$
[select t] $\neg v\wedge t\,\&\, tt \mapsto \varnothing$

$Ps^{\|} : \langle\{ns = 100\}, \varnothing\rangle$
[refill] $s\wedge tt\,\&\, tt \mapsto ns' := 100$
[select s] $s\wedge tt\,\&\, ns>0 \mapsto ns' := ns-1$
[refill] $\neg s\wedge tt\,\&\, tt \mapsto \varnothing$
[select s] $\neg s\wedge v\,\&\, tt \mapsto \varnothing$

$Pt^{\|} : \langle\{nt = 20\}, \varnothing\rangle$
[refill] $t\wedge tt\,\&\, tt \mapsto nt' := 20$
[select t] $t\wedge tt\,\&\, ns>0 \mapsto nt' := nt-1$
[refill] $\neg t\wedge s\,\&\, tt \mapsto \varnothing$
[select t] $\neg t\wedge v\,\&\, tt \mapsto \varnothing$

$C_s^{\bullet} :$
[refill] $s\wedge\neg t\wedge tt\,\&\, tt \mapsto ns' := 100$
$\Delta_s^{\bullet} :$
$\{(\,$ [select s] $\neg s\wedge s\wedge tt\,\&\, m>0 \mapsto m' := m-1,$
$\{$ [select s] $\neg s\wedge s\wedge tt\,\&\, m>0 \mapsto m' := m-1,$
[select s] $s\wedge s\wedge\neg f\wedge tt\,\&\, m>0\wedge ns>0 \mapsto$
$\qquad m' := m-1, ns' := ns-1\}),$
$(\,$ [select s] $\neg s\wedge s\wedge tt\,\&\, tt \mapsto \varnothing,$
$\{$ [select s] $\neg s\wedge s\wedge f\,\&\, tt \mapsto \varnothing,$
[select s] $s\wedge s\wedge f\wedge tt\,\&\, tt\wedge ns>0 \mapsto$
$\qquad ns' := ns-1\})\}$

Fig. 3. Family-ready transformed feature modules for the vending machine SPL

local transformations that enrich feature modules with information about feature combinations in such a way that the modular structure of the system is maintained and the transformed model is family-ready.

4.1 Parallel Composition

Let S be a $\|$-CFOS and define the $\|$-CFOS $S^{\|} = (F, \mathcal{F}, \mathfrak{M}^{\|}, \phi^{\|}, \prec, \|)$ through feature modules $\mathfrak{M}^{\|} = \{Prog^{\|} : Prog \in \mathfrak{M}\}$ where $\phi^{\|}(x) = (\phi(x))^{\|}$ for all $x \in F$. For any feature $x \in F$ we set $\phi(x) = (V_x, F_x, Act_x, C_x, \nu_x)$ and specify $(\phi(x))^{\|} = (V_x, F_x, Act_x, C_x^{\|}, \nu_x)$ by

$$C_x^{\|} \;=\; \{\; [\alpha]\, x\wedge f\,\&\, g \mapsto u \;:\; [\alpha]\, f\,\&\, g \mapsto u \;\in C_x \;\}\cup \qquad (1)$$

$$\bigcup_{\alpha\in Act_x} \{\; [\alpha]\, \neg x\wedge \bigvee_{y\in F(\alpha)\setminus\{x\}} y\,\&\, tt \mapsto \varnothing \;\} \qquad (2)$$

Here, $F(\alpha)$ denotes the set of features whose modules contain an action $\alpha \in Act_x$, i.e., $y \in F(\alpha)$ iff $\alpha \in Act_y$. Intuitively, our transformation towards $C_x^{\|}$ can be justified as follows. Adding a feature guard x to every command in feature module $\phi(x)$ ensures that the command is only enabled in case the feature is active (1). Commands in (2) guarantee that if feature x is not active but another feature that has a synchronizing action, the feature module $\phi(x)$ does not block the actions of other feature modules.

Example 4. Figure 3 on the left shows feature modules of the family-ready CFOS $S_v^{\|}$ that arises from the CFOS S_v for the vending machine SPL defined in Example 2. As no other feature module contains a command with action *pay*, the command [pay] $\neg v\wedge ff\,\&\, tt \mapsto \varnothing$ is introduced for $Pv^{\|}$ but never enabled[2]. The command [refill] $\neg s\wedge t\,\&\, tt \mapsto \varnothing$ ensures that the *refill* action is not blocked in the family model when feature s is inactive and t is active.

The transformation can be performed in polynomial time in $|S|$ as $F(\alpha)$ is computable in polynomial time and $|S^{\|}| \leq |Act|\cdot|F| + |S|$ where Act is the set of all actions in feature modules of S.

---

[2] Note that an empty disjunction always evaluates to ff.

4.2 Superimposition

Let S be a $\bullet$-CFOS and define the $\bullet$-CFOS $S^\bullet = (F, \mathcal{F}, \mathfrak{M}^\bullet, \phi^\bullet, \prec, \bullet)$ through feature modules $\mathfrak{M}^\bullet = \{\mathsf{Prog}^\bullet : \mathsf{Prog} \in \mathfrak{M}\}$ where $\phi^\bullet(x) = (\phi(x))^\bullet$ for all $x \in F$. Similar as within parallel composition, for any feature $x \in F$ we set $\phi(x) = (V_x, F_x, Act_x, C_x, \nu_x, \Delta_x)$ and specify $(\phi(x))^\bullet = (V_x, F_x, Act_x, C_x^\bullet, \nu_x, \Delta_x^\bullet)$. The naive solution to specify $C_x^\bullet$ and $\Delta_x^\bullet$ is to define for every command c appearing in C_x or Δ_x a feature guard $\sigma(c) \in \mathbb{B}(F)$ that stands for those valid feature combinations X where c appears in $S(X)$, i.e., for all $X \in \mathfrak{V}[\mathcal{F}]$ we have $X \models \sigma(c)$ iff c appears in $S(X)$. In this way, we encode those feature combinations explicitly in the feature guards where superimposed commands are effective:

$$C_x^\bullet = \{\ [\alpha]\,\sigma(c) \wedge f\,\&\,g \mapsto u \ : \ c = [\alpha]\,f\,\&\,g \mapsto u \in C_x\ \} \qquad (3)$$

$$\Delta_x^\bullet = \{\ (\,[\alpha]\,\sigma(c) \wedge f\,\&\,g \mapsto u, \{\,[\alpha]\,\sigma(c) \wedge f\,\&\,g \mapsto u\} \cup \qquad (4)$$

$$\{\,[\alpha]\,\sigma(\underline{c}) \wedge \underline{f}\,\&\,\underline{g} \mapsto \underline{u} : \underline{c} = [\underline{\alpha}]\,\underline{f}\,\&\,\underline{g} \mapsto \underline{u} \in \Delta_x(c)\}\,) : (5)$$

$$c = [\alpha]\,f\,\&\,g \mapsto u\ \}$$

The rule (3) generates commands also in products, rule (4) preserves the commands that would be modified by later composed feature modules, and modifications are included by (5), adapted with fresh feature guards that include $\sigma(\cdot)$.

Example 5. On the right of Fig. 3, the transformed feature module (Ps', Δ_s) of Example 1 is depicted. Here, $\sigma(\cdot)$ is always either s or $\neg$s.

The construction of $\sigma(c)$ for any command c can be achieved by stepwise composing feature modules and adjusting the combinations $\sigma(c)$. For this, not all products have to be explicitly constructed, avoiding an exponential blowup: a computed table for all commands appearing in any set of commands and modifications in the modules suffices, step-by-step adjusting the feature guards $\sigma(\cdot)$ until all feature modules have been processed. Note that $|S^\bullet| \leq 2 \cdot |S|$ as at most one command is added by (4) to each command modified, at most doubling the overall number of commands in S.

4.3 Dynamics and Family Models

Given a family-ready CFOS S, the product $S(F)$ is a family model of the feature-oriented system, enabling an operational semantics for dynamic feature-oriented systems: when $\mathcal{G}$ is a reconfiguration graph over F, used as feature model in S, then $\mathsf{Fts}[S(F)] \bowtie \mathcal{G}$ defines the transition-system semantics of S. However, this interpretation requires the construction of the FTS semantics of S, flattening the modular structure. Another approach also applied by the tool PROFEAT [9] is to interpret feature variables as standard internal variables of a reconfiguration module (describing the reconfiguration graph) and then turn every featured program into a standard program where feature guards are conjoint with the command guards. In this way, a (non-featured) compositional system arises that can be used, e.g., for verification purposes using standard methods. Note that this approach is applicable to both, superimposed and parallel composition CFOSs that are family-ready.

5   Between Composition Worlds

In this section we address research question **(RQ2)** posed in the introduction, i.e., whether the classes of $\|$-CFOSs and $\bullet$-CFOSs are expressively equivalent and whether there are automated transformations to turn a $\|$-CFOS into a product equivalent $\bullet$-CFOS and vice versa.

5.1   From Parallel Composition to Superimposition

Theorem 2. *For any $\|$-CFOS* S *over features* F *there is a* $\bullet$-*CFOS* S' *with* $|S'| \in \mathcal{O}(2^{|F|^2} \cdot |S|^{|F|+1})$ *that is product equivalent to* S.

Let us sketch the proof of Theorem 2 assuming we have given a $\|$-CFOS S $= (F, \mathcal{F}, \mathfrak{M}, \phi, \prec, \|)$. We define a $\bullet$-CFOS S' $= (F, \mathcal{F}, \mathfrak{M}', \phi', \prec, \bullet)$ such that S and S' are product equivalent. Intuitively, the synchronization between commands in different feature modules of S has to be explicitly encoded into the sets of modifications in feature modules of S'.

To this end, we consider δ-programs $\mathfrak{M}' = \{\mathsf{Prog}' : \mathsf{Prog} \in \mathfrak{M}\}$ where $\phi'(x) = (\phi(x))'$ for all $x \in F$. For any feature $x \in F$ we set $\phi(x) = (V_x, F_x, Act_x, C_x, \nu_x)$, $V_x = \langle IntV_x, ExtV_x \rangle$, and specify $(\phi(x))' = (V'_x, F_x, Act_x, C'_x, \nu_x, \Delta'_x)$. Let $\downarrow x = \{y \in F : y \prec x\}$ and recall that $F(\alpha) = \{y \in F : \alpha \in Act_y\}$. We define $V'_x = \langle IntV_x, ExtV \rangle$ with $ExtV = \bigcup_{y \in \downarrow x} V_y \setminus IntV_x$. For the definition of C'_x, let $B(x, \alpha) \in \mathbb{B}(F)$ be recursively defined by $B(x, \alpha) = \mathtt{ff}$ if $\downarrow x \cap F(\alpha) = \varnothing$ and $B(x, \alpha) = B(y, \alpha) \vee x$ for $y = \max_{\prec}(\downarrow x \cap F(\alpha))$.

$$C'_x = \{ \ [\alpha] \ \neg B(x,\alpha) \wedge f \& g \mapsto u \ : \ [\alpha] \ f \& g \mapsto u \in C_x \ \} \qquad (6)$$

The ratio behind the adapted feature guard in (6) is that modifications in δ-programs can only modify *existing* commands during a composition and hence, there have to be initial commands in "$\prec$-minimal" features. All commands of "$\prec$-greater" features that would synchronize in case of parallel composition then only modify already composed commands towards a synchronized command. Without the added feature guard $\neg B(x, \alpha)$ in (6), commands of single features could be executable even they would have synchronized with other features.

Following the composition order $\prec$ on features, we recursively define Δ'_x for each $x \in F$. In case $x = \min_{\prec}(F)$, we set $\Delta'_x = \varnothing$. Assume we have defined Δ'_y for all $y \prec x$ and define $\Gamma(X)$ for any $X \subseteq \downarrow x$ as the set of commands arising from superimposing the feature modules $(\phi(y))'$ for all $y \in X$ according to $\prec$. Formally, we set $\Gamma(\varnothing) = \varnothing$ and $\Gamma(X) = C'_y \cup \Delta'_y(\Gamma(X \setminus \{y\}))$ for $y = \max_{\prec}(X)$.

$$\Delta'_x = \bigcup_{X \subseteq \downarrow x} \{ \ (\ [\alpha] \ f \& g \mapsto u, \{ \ [\alpha] \ f \wedge \underline{f} \& g \wedge \underline{g} \mapsto u \times \underline{u} : \qquad (7)$$

$$[\alpha] \ \underline{f} \& \underline{g} \mapsto \underline{u} \in C_x \}) : [\alpha] \ f \& g \mapsto u \in \Gamma(X), \alpha \in Act_x \ \}$$

Intuitively, (7) makes the parallel composition of commands in $\phi(x)$ with commands in previously composed feature modules explicit. S' is constructible in exponential time in $|S|$ and we have $|S'| \leq |S|^{|F|+1}$. In fact, one cannot hope to construct a product equivalent •-CFOS that avoids an exponential blowup:

Proposition 1. *There is a sequence of* $\|$-*CFOS* S_n, $n \in \mathbb{N}$, *with* $|S_n| = 2 \cdot |S_{n-1}|$ *for which there is no* $k \in \mathbb{N}$ *where* S_k *has a product equivalent* •-*CFOS* S'_k *with* $|S'_k| < 2^{|S_k|-1}$.

We sketch the proof of the above proposition. For $F_n = \{x_1, \ldots, x_n\}$, consider the $\|$-CFOS $S_n = (F_n, \mathcal{F}_n, \{\mathcal{M}_1, \ldots, \mathcal{M}_n\}, \phi_n, \prec_n, \|)$ with $\mathfrak{V}[\mathcal{F}_n] = \wp(F_n)$, $\phi_n(x_i) = \mathcal{M}_i$ and $x_i \prec_n x_j$ for all $i < j \in \{1, \ldots, n\}$. For $i \in \{1, \ldots, n\}$ we define $\mathcal{M}_i - (V_i, \varnothing, \{\alpha\}, C_i, \nu_i)$ where $V_i = \langle \{v_i, w_i\}, V_{i-1} \rangle$ with $V_0 = \varnothing$,

$$C_i = \{ \, [\alpha] \, \text{tt} \, \& \, \text{tt} \mapsto \{(v_i, 1)\}, \, [\alpha] \, \text{tt} \, \& \, \text{tt} \mapsto \{(w_i, 1)\} \, \},$$

and $\nu_i = \{(v_i, 0), (w_i, 0)\}$. Then $|S_n| = 2 \cdot n$. Assume there is a $k \in \mathbb{N}$ such that there is a •-CFOS S'_k that is product equivalent to S_k with $|S'_k| < 2^{|S_k|-1}$. Then in particular $\text{Fts}\big[S_k(F_k)\big](F_k) = \text{Fts}\big[S'_k(F_k)\big](F_k)$ and hence, all 2^k combinations of updates of v_i and w_i to 1 have to be captured by modifications. As furthermore there are $2^k - 1$ nonempty feature combinations, we have at least $2^k \cdot (2^k - 1)$ required modifications in S'_k. Hence, $|S'_k| \geq 2^{2k} - 2^k \geq 2^{|S_k|-1}$, contradicting the assumption $|S'_k| < 2^{|S_k|-1}$.

The above proposition is closely related to the well-known fact that performing parallel compositions might yield programs that have exponential size in the number of components.

5.2   From Superimposition to Parallel Composition

While for every $\|$-CFOS there is a product equivalent •-CFOS, such a result for the converse direction cannot be expected.

Proposition 2. *There is a* •-*CFOS for which there is no product equivalent* $\|$-*CFOS.*

Proof. Consider the •-CFOS $S = (F, \mathcal{F}, \{\mathcal{M}_a, \mathcal{M}_b\}, \phi, \prec, •)$ where $F = \{a, b\}$, $\mathfrak{V}[\mathcal{F}] = \wp(F)$, $a \prec b$, and for $\tau \in F$ we have $\mathcal{M}_\tau = (V_\tau, F, \{\alpha\}, C_\tau, \nu_\tau, \Delta_\tau)$, $C_\tau = \{ \, [\alpha] \, \text{tt} \, \& \, \text{tt} \mapsto u_\tau \}$ with $u_\tau = \{(v_\tau, 1)\}$, $\nu_\tau = \{(v_\tau, 0)\}$, $\phi(\tau) = \mathcal{M}_\tau$, $V_a = \langle \{v_a\}, \varnothing \rangle$ and $V_b = \langle \{v_b\}, \{v_a\} \rangle$, and $\Delta_a = \varnothing$ and

$$\Delta_b = \{ \, (\underline{c} = [\alpha] \, \text{tt} \, \& \, \text{tt} \mapsto u_a, \{\underline{c} = [\alpha] \, \text{tt} \, \& \, \text{tt} \mapsto \underline{u}\}) \, \}$$

with $\underline{u} = \{(v_a, 2), (v_b, 2)\}$. Assume there is a $\|$-CFOS S' over feature modules $\mathcal{M}'_\tau$ for $\tau \in F$ that is product equivalent to S. Then, for any $\tau \in F$ variable v_τ has to be internal in $\mathcal{M}'_\tau = S'(\{\tau\})$ as $\text{Fts}[\mathcal{M}_\tau](\{\tau\}) = \text{Fts}[\mathcal{M}'_\tau](\{\tau\})$. Consequently, $\mathcal{M}'_a$ has to contain at least one α-command updating v_a to 1 not enabled when b is active and at least one α-command updating v_a to 2 when b is active. Similarly, $\mathcal{M}'_b$ has to contain at least one α-command updating v_b to 1 and at least one

α-command updating v_b to 2 when a is active. Following the definition of parallel composition yields that the α-commands synchronize towards $\mathsf{S}'(F)$, leading to at least one α-command that updates v_a to 2 *and* v_b to 1. This commands yields a behavior in $\mathsf{S}'(F)$ not apparent in $\mathsf{S}(F)$. Hence, $\mathsf{Fts}[\mathsf{S}(F)](F) \neq \mathsf{Fts}[\mathsf{S}'(F)](F)$ and thus there is no such a S' product equivalent to S.   □

However, by explicitly encoding the behaviors of some product of the •-CFOS in a single feature module with copies of variables and guarding them with the corresponding feature combination, we obtain a behavioral equivalent ‖-CFOS.

Theorem 3. *For any* •-*CFOS* S *over features* F *there is a* ‖-*CFOS* S' *with* $|\mathsf{S}'| \in \mathcal{O}(|\mathsf{S}| \cdot 2^{|F|})$ *that is behavioral equivalent to* S.

We sketch the construction on which the proof of Theorem 3 is based on. Let $\mathsf{S} = (F, \mathcal{F}, \mathfrak{M}, \phi, \prec, \bullet)$ be a •-CFOS and define a ‖-CFOS $\mathsf{S}' = (F, \mathcal{F}, \mathfrak{M}', \phi', \prec, \|)$ through feature modules $\mathfrak{M}' = \{\mathsf{Prog}' : \mathsf{Prog} \in \mathfrak{M}\}$ where $\phi'(x) = (\phi(x))'$ for all $x \in F$. For any valid feature combination $X \in \mathfrak{V}[\mathcal{F}]$, let $\mathsf{S}(X) = (V_X, F_X, Act_X, C_X, \nu_X)$ with $V_X = \langle IntV_X, ExtV_X \rangle$ and define for all $x \in F$ a feature module $(\phi(x))' = (\langle IntV'_x, \varnothing \rangle, F, Act'_x, C'_x, \nu'_x)$. Let furthermore $\mathfrak{V}_x \subseteq \mathfrak{V}[\mathcal{F}]$ denote the set of all valid feature combinations containing $x \in F$, i.e., $\mathfrak{V}_x = \{X \in \mathfrak{V}[\mathcal{F}] : x \in X\}$, $\mathfrak{V}_x^{\prec} \subseteq \mathfrak{V}_x$ denote the set of all valid feature combinations where $x \in F$ is maximal, i.e., $\mathfrak{V}_x^{\prec} = \{X \in \mathfrak{V}_x : x = \max_{\prec}(X)\}$. Then, $IntV'_x = \bigcup_{X \in \mathfrak{V}_x^{\prec}} \{v_x : v \in IntV_X\}$ comprises copies of internal variables in feature modules of S, $Act'_x = \bigcup_{X \in \mathfrak{V}_x} Act_X$, $\nu'_x = \bigcup_{X \in \mathfrak{V}_x^{\prec}} \{(v_x, z) : (v, z) \in \nu_X\}$, and

$$C'_x = \bigcup_{X \in \mathfrak{V}_x^{\prec}} \left\{ [\alpha]\, \chi(X) \wedge f \,\&\, [g]_x \mapsto [u]_x : [\alpha]\, f \,\&\, g \mapsto u \in C_X \right\} \cup \qquad (8)$$

$$\left\{ [\alpha]\, \bigvee_{Y \in \mathfrak{V}_x \setminus \mathfrak{V}_x^{\prec}, \alpha \in Act_Y} \chi(Y) \,\&\, \mathsf{tt} \mapsto \varnothing : \alpha \in Act'_x \right\} \qquad (9)$$

Here, $[g]_x$ and $[u]_x$ denote the guards and updates, respectively, where each variable v is syntactically replaced by v_x. Via (8) the behavior of $\mathsf{S}(X)$ is mimicked in the commands of the maximal feature in X, guarded by X (i.e., they are effective iff X is active). The second part (9) guarantees that features not maximal in a feature combination X do not block the behaviors encoded in its maximal feature, again guarded by X through $\chi(X)$. For any feature combination $X \in \mathfrak{V}[\mathcal{F}]$ the product $\mathsf{S}(X)$ has at most $|\mathsf{S}|$ commands, added to at most one feature module in S' by (8). The number of valid feature combinations is bounded by $2^{|F|}$ and for each of them, which leads to at most $|\mathsf{S}| \cdot 2^{|F|}$ commands in S' as a result of (8). Also the number of actions in any feature module is bounded by $|\mathsf{S}|$, leading to at most $|\mathsf{S}|$ commands for each feature module by (9). Consequently, $|\mathsf{S}'| \leq |\mathsf{S}| \cdot (2^{|F|} + |F|)$.

Remark on Locality and Dynamics. The transformation presented yields a family-ready CFOS S', but might violate *locality* [31], a central principle of feature-oriented systems that imposes commands and variables to be placed in those feature modules they belong to. Hence, S' is not suitable to be interpreted with a dynamic feature model as S' and $S^\bullet$ (see Sect. 4.2) might not be behavioral equivalent. Another approach towards a $\|$-CFOS that preserves locality could be to introduce multiple copies of actions splitting the updates across the feature modules. This could ensure that the feature modules are combined through synchronization with the same action. However, this requires to alter the meaning of actions and product equivalence to S is only obtained after projecting the copies of the actions to the original actions.

6 Concluding Remarks

We have presented compositional feature-oriented systems (CFOSs), a unified formalism for feature-oriented systems that are specified through feature modules in guarded command language, composed via superimposition or parallel composition. With providing transformations towards family-ready CFOSs, we connected annotative and compositional approaches for feature-oriented systems [30]. Our transformations between CFOSs with different kinds of composition operators connect feature-oriented software engineering (where superimposition is paramount) and the area of formal analysis of feature-oriented systems (mainly relying on parallel composition). As the concepts presented are quite generic in its nature, they could be applicable also to other kinds of feature-oriented programming paradigms than featured guarded command languages.

Extensions. For the sake of a clean presentation, we did not introduce the framework of CFOSs in full generality. However, many extensions can be imagined where the concepts take over immediately. Additional feature module granularity can be achieved by adopting delta-oriented concepts [39,19]. Given a set of components described through programs, each feature module could be described not by a single module but by composing multiple components. This enables the reuse of components in multiple feature modules and enables solutions for the optional feature problem [32]. Numeric features and multifeatures [17], can be included in a similar way as presented in [21], i.e., evaluating feature variables to non-negative integers and either treat them as attributes and cardinalities, respectively. When interpreted as cardinalities, also the product definition for CFOSs is affected, requiring to compose multiple instances of the feature. Furthermore, feature modules in CFOSs could also be probabilistic programs and delta-programs where updates in guarded commands are replaced by stochastic distributions over updates. As our transformations are completely specified on the syntactic level of guarded commands, our results would also take over to this probabilistic case. While we introduced superimposition by explicitly stating exact commands to be modified, also pattern-matching rules could be imagined that modify parts of a command after matching. Also this extension does not change much in the transformations, however one has to take care including sufficient feature-guard information into the superimposition patterns.

Further Work. An interesting direction that also motivated our work towards research question (**RQ2**) is the verification of programs from feature-oriented programming paradigms such as delta-oriented approaches with FEATHER-WEIGHT JAVA [28,7]. Using known translations from JAVA to guarded command language [35] and then applying our transformation from superimposition CFOSs to parallel CFOSs paves the way to use standard verification tools that rely on guarded command languages as input [11,27,34]. We plan to investigate more clever transformations than the one presented here that could avoid large parts of the explicit encoding of superimposition into single feature modules. Another direction for which we would also rely on results presented in this paper is to include superimposition concepts into our tool PROFEAT [10] to enable quantitative analysis of probabilistic superimposition CFOSs.

References

1. Acher, M., Collet, P., Fleurey, F., Lahire, P., Moisan, S., Rigault, J.-P.: Modeling context and dynamic adaptations with feature models. In: 4th International Workshop Models@run.time at Models 2009 (MRT 2009), p. 10 (2009)
2. Apel, S., Kästner, C.: An overview of feature-oriented software development. J. Object Technol. **8**, 49–84 (2009)
3. Apel, S., Kästner, C., Lengauer, C.: Feature featherweight Java: a calculus for feature-oriented programming and stepwise refinement. In: Proceedings of the 7th International Conference on Generative Programming and Component Engineering, GPCE 2008, pp. 101–112. ACM, New York (2008)
4. Apel, S., Leich, T., Rosenmüller, M., Saake, G.: FeatureC++: on the symbiosis of feature-oriented and aspect-oriented programming. In: Glück, R., Lowry, M. (eds.) GPCE 2005. LNCS, vol. 3676, pp. 125–140. Springer, Heidelberg (2005). https://doi.org/10.1007/11561347_10
5. Baier, C., Dubslaff, C.: From verification to synthesis under cost-utility constraints. ACM SIGLOG News **5**(4), 26–46 (2018)
6. Baier, C., Katoen, J.-P.: Principles of Model Checking. MIT Press, Cambridge (2008)
7. Bettini, L., Damiani, F., Schaefer, I.: Compositional type checking of delta-oriented software product lines. Acta Informatica **50**(2), 77–122 (2013)
8. Chandy, K.M., Misra, J.: A Foundation of Parallel Program Design. Addison-Wesley, Reading (1988)
9. Chrszon, P., Dubslaff, C., Klüppelholz, S., Baier, C.: Family-based modeling and analysis for probabilistic systems – featuring ProFeat. In: Stevens, P., Wąsowski, A. (eds.) FASE 2016. LNCS, vol. 9633, pp. 287–304. Springer, Heidelberg (2016). https://doi.org/10.1007/978-3-662-49665-7_17
10. Chrszon, P., Dubslaff, C., Klüppelholz, S., Baier, C.: Profeat: feature-oriented engineering for family-based probabilistic model checking. Formal Aspects Comput. **30**(1), 45–75 (2018)
11. Cimatti, A., et al.: NuSMV 2: an opensource tool for symbolic model checking. In: Brinksma, E., Larsen, K.G. (eds.) CAV 2002. LNCS, vol. 2404, pp. 359–364. Springer, Heidelberg (2002). https://doi.org/10.1007/3-540-45657-0_29
12. Classen, A., Cordy, M., Heymans, P., Legay, A., Schobbens, P.-Y.: Model checking software product lines with SNIP. Int. J. Softw. Tools Technol. Transf. **14**(5), 589–612 (2012)

13. Classen, A., Cordy, M., Heymans, P., Legay, A., Schobbens, P.-Y.: Formal semantics, modular specification, and symbolic verification of product-line behaviour. Sci. Comput. Program. **80**, 416–439 (2014)
14. Classen, A., Cordy, M., Schobbens, P.-Y., Heymans, P., Legay, A., Raskin, J.-F.: Featured transition systems: foundations for verifying variability-intensive systems and their application to LTL model checking. IEEE Trans. Softw. Eng. **39**(8), 1069–1089 (2013)
15. Classen, A., Heymans, P., Schobbens, P.-Y., Legay, A., Raskin, J.-F.: Model checking lots of systems: efficient verification of temporal properties in software product lines. In: Proceedings of ICSE 2010, pp. 335–344. ACM (2010)
16. Clements, P., Northrop, L.: Software Product Lines : Practices and Patterns. Addison-Wesley Professional, Boston (2001)
17. Cordy, M., Schobbens, P.-Y., Heymans, P., Legay, A.: Beyond Boolean product-line model checking: dealing with feature attributes and multi-features. In: Proceedings of the 2013 International Conference on Software Engineering, ICSE 2013, pp. 472–481. IEEE Press, Piscataway (2013)
18. Czarnecki, K., Eisenecker, U.W.: Generative Programming: Methods, Tools, and Applications. ACM Press/Addison-Wesley Publishing Co. (2000)
19. Damiani, F., Schaefer, I.: Dynamic delta-oriented programming. In: Proceedings of the 15th Software Product Line Conference (SPLC), vol. 2, pp. 34:1–34:8. ACM (2011)
20. Dijkstra, E.W.: A Discipline of Programming. Prentice-Hall, Upper Saddle River (1976)
21. Dubslaff, C., Baier, C., Klüppelholz, S.: Probabilistic model checking for feature-oriented systems. Trans. Aspect-Oriented Softw. Dev. **12**, 180–220 (2015)
22. Dubslaff, C., Klüppelholz, S., Baier, C.: Probabilistic model checking for energy analysis in software product lines. In: 13th International Conference on Modularity (MODULARITY), pp. 169–180. ACM (2014)
23. Francez, N., Forman, I.R.: Superimposition for interacting processes. In: Baeten, J.C.M., Klop, J.W. (eds.) CONCUR 1990. LNCS, vol. 458, pp. 230–245. Springer, Heidelberg (1990). https://doi.org/10.1007/BFb0039063
24. Gomaa, H., Hussein, M.: Dynamic software reconfiguration in software product families. In: van der Linden, F.J. (ed.) PFE 2003. LNCS, vol. 3014, pp. 435–444. Springer, Heidelberg (2004). https://doi.org/10.1007/978-3-540-24667-1_33
25. Gruler, A., Leucker, M., Scheidemann, K.: Modeling and model checking software product lines. In: Barthe, G., de Boer, F.S. (eds.) FMOODS 2008. LNCS, vol. 5051, pp. 113–131. Springer, Heidelberg (2008). https://doi.org/10.1007/978-3-540-68863-1_8
26. Hallsteinsen, S., Hinchey, M., Park, S., Schmid, K.: Dynamic software product lines. Computer **41**(4), 93–95 (2008)
27. Holzmann, G.J.: The SPIN Model Checker: Primer and Reference Manual, vol. 1003. Addison-Wesley, Reading (2004)
28. Igarashi, A., Pierce, B.C., Wadler, P.: Featherweight Java: a minimal core calculus for Java and GJ. ACM Trans. Program. Lang. Syst. **23**(3), 396–450 (2001)
29. Kang, K.C., Cohen, S.G., Hess, J.A., Novak, W.E., Peterson, A.S.: Feature-oriented domain analysis (FODA) feasibility study. Technical report, Carnegie-Mellon University Software Engineering Institute, November 1990
30. Kästner, C., Apel, S., Kuhlemann, M.: Granularity in software product lines. In: 2008 ACM/IEEE 30th International Conference on Software Engineering, pp. 311–320 (2008)

31. Kästner, C., Apel, S., Ostermann, K.: The road to feature modularity? In: Proceedings of the 15th International Software Product Line Conference, SPLC 2011, vol. 2, pp. 5:1–5:8. ACM, New York (2011)

32. Kästner, C., Apel, S., ur Rahman, S.S., Rosenmüller, M., Batory, D.S., Saake, G.: On the impact of the optional feature problem: analysis and case studies. In: 2009 Proceedings of 13th International Conference on Software Product Lines, SPLC 2009, San Francisco, California, USA, 24–28 August, pp. 181–190 (2009)

33. Katz, S.: A superimposition control construct for distributed systems. ACM Trans. Program. Lang. Syst. (TOPLAS) 15(2), 337–356 (1993)

34. Kwiatkowska, M., Norman, G., Parker, D.: PRISM 4.0: verification of probabilistic real-time systems. In: Gopalakrishnan, G., Qadeer, S. (eds.) CAV 2011. LNCS, vol. 6806, pp. 585–591. Springer, Heidelberg (2011). https://doi.org/10.1007/978-3-642-22110-1_47

35. Leino, K.R.M., Saxe, J.B., Stata, R.: Checking java programs via guarded commands. In: Leino, K.R.M., Saxe, J.B., Stata, R. (eds.) Workshop on Object-oriented Technology, pp. 110–111. Springer, Heidelberg (1999)

36. Milner, R.: Communication and Concurrency. PHI Series in Computer Science. Prentice Hall, Upper Saddle River (1989)

37. Plath, M., Ryan, M.: Feature integration using a feature construct. Sci. Comput. Program. 41(1), 53–84 (2001)

38. Post, H., Sinz, C.: Configuration lifting: verification meets software configuration. In: Proceedings of the 2008 23rd IEEE/ACM International Conference on Automated Software Engineering, ASE 2008, pp. 347–350. IEEE Computer Society, Washington, DC (2008)

39. Schaefer, I., Worret, A., Poetzsch-Heffter, A.: A model-based framework for automated product derivation. In: Proceedings of the 1st International Workshop on Model-driven Approaches in Software Product Line Engineering (MAPLE 2009), collocated with the 13th International Software Product Line Conference (SPLC 2009), San Francisco, USA, 24 August 2009 (2009)

40. Zave, P.: Feature-oriented description, formal methods, and DFC. In: Gilmore, S., Ryan, M. (eds.) Language Constructs for Describing Features, pp. 11–26. Springer, London (2001). https://doi.org/10.1007/978-1-4471-0287-8_2

Model-Based Testing

Multi-objective Search for Effective Testing of Cyber-Physical Systems

Hugo Araujo[1]([⊠]), Gustavo Carvalho[1], Mohammad Reza Mousavi[2], and Augusto Sampaio[1]

[1] Universidade Federal de Pernambuco, Recife, Brazil
{hlsa,ghpc,acas}@cin.ufpe.br
[2] University of Leicester, Leicester, UK
mm789@leicester.ac.uk

Abstract. We propose a multi-objective strategy for finding effective inputs for fault detection in Cyber Physical Systems (CPSs). The main goal is to provide input signals for a system in such a way that they maximise the distance between the system's output and an ideal target, thus leading the system towards a fault; this is based on Genetic Algorithm and Simulated Annealing heuristics. Additionally, we take into consideration the discrete locations (of hybrid system models) and a notion of input diversity to increase coverage. We implement our strategy and present an empirical analysis to estimate its effectiveness.

Keywords: Cyber-Physical Systems · Search based · Input selection

1 Introduction

Cyber-Physical Systems (CPSs) integrate computational systems into their physical environments; components for products such as automobiles and airplanes [32] are examples of modern CPSs. In order to model the continuous and discrete dynamics often present in CPSs, hybrid models have been extensively used [6]. A typical type of CPS is a system where sensors feed input signals to a digital controller (discrete component) attached to physical actuators (continuous component) and also outputs continuous signals.

Such systems are complex since their design is typically multidisciplinary. It is not uncommon for a system component to deal with aspects of different subject areas such as computer science, physics and control engineering [21]. The importance of safety and reliability in such complex and heterogeneous systems warrant the need for further research into their verification.

Model-Based Testing techniques (MBT) can play an important role in the verification of these systems by providing precise mathematical assurances [38]. Particularly, one can design a test strategy based on a mathematical relation that decides whether the System Under Test (SUT) behaves as expected, with respect to a given specification; this is also known as a conformance relation [23].

© Springer Nature Switzerland AG 2019
P. C. Ölveczky and G. Salaün (Eds.): SEFM 2019, LNCS 11724, pp. 183–202, 2019.
https://doi.org/10.1007/978-3-030-30446-1_10

However, finding effective inputs for detecting faults, i.e., witnesses for non-conformance, in a continuous system is not a straightforward task. Typically, one needs a search algorithm optimised for the continuous domain in order to select values to maximise the goal, e.g., a witness to a conformance relation violation.

In the present work, we adopt the (τ,ϵ)-conformance notion [1,2]. Briefly speaking, under the same input stimuli, that are given for both specification and implementation models, the difference in the output behaviour of both systems is analysed and a distance metric is used to verify if the output behaviours of the specification and the implementation models are close enough to each other. We propose a multi-objective search for selecting inputs that violate this relation.

Our first search objective is defined as the observed distance between the output of the model and the ideal output. By maximising the distance between the outputs (of the system under test model and those of the ideal target), we can steer the system towards a fault or, more precisely, towards a challenging situation that maximises the possibility of a non-conforming verdict during conformance testing.

As for the second objective, we make use of the control elements found in hybrid system models to achieve structural coverage. Particularly, we consider the locations in a Hybrid Automata [20] model as a measure for coverage.

Finally, we propose a diversity notion as our third objective. We adopt a distance-based diversity metric that computes the Euclidean distance of previously generated inputs to generate new diverse inputs. We also make use of change point analysis in our diversity computation, so that we generate inputs that cover different areas and behave in different shapes.

The contributions of this work can be summarised as follows. We propose a multi-objective search strategy for input selection that (i) maximises the distance between the system's output and its ideal target, (ii) makes use of the control elements found in hybrid system models to achieve structural coverage, and (iii) employs a diversity metric to generate additional tests covering different areas and shapes. Furthermore, another important contribution is (iv) the empirical evaluation of these objectives in producing effective and efficient tests. We contrast our results against related approaches using examples from the literature. The formulation of the first and third objective in our context is, to the best of our knowledge, novel. Additionally, their combined usage in multi-objective search-based heuristics, and the particular way we use them for increased fault detection, is novel as well.

Section 2 considers related work. Section 3 provides the necessary background. Section 4 presents our strategy for finding inputs. Section 5 presents a case study and the results of the experiment we have performed. Finally, Sect. 6 gives a summary of our results and presents the next steps in our research agenda.

2   Related Work

In the literature, we can find several strategies for input selection for both discrete and continuous systems separately. For instance, discrete systems can be covered using structural notions such as node, edge and path coverage [9]. As for continuous systems, generating test data can usually be seen as an optimisation problem, which can be solved using search techniques [39]. However, in the case of hybrid systems, which involve both discrete and continuous behaviour, only a few approaches have been proposed, and are discussed in the sequel.

One class of approaches is called property falsification, exemplified by tools such as Breach [16] and S-Taliro [10]. S-Taliro is a tool that offers an alternative solution for conformance testing of hybrid systems. Temporal verification is used to prove or falsify temporal logic properties of the system by searching for system behaviours that falsify the specification, i.e., counterexamples to Metric Temporal Logic (MTL) properties. Its conformance testing component uses the (τ, ϵ)-conformance notion [1,2], which is proposed by the same authors. As for input selection, it uses randomised testing based on stochastic optimisation techniques, such as Simulated Annealing [24], Genetic Algorithm [30], Ant Colony Optimisation [17] and Cross Entropy [37]. In our work, even though we offer fewer search-based techniques (Simulated Annealing and Genetic Algorithm), the modular structure of our solution allows for additional heuristics to be implemented. The main difference, however, is that our search is multi-objective; we consider 3 search objectives simultaneously: (i) maximising output distance from an ideal target, (ii) discrete coverage, and (iii) diversity.

A strategy that uses a notion of test diversity [28,29] for test suite generation and selection can be seen as complementary work. It uses a search algorithm, based on Hill-Climbing, that is guided to produce test outputs exhibiting a diverse set of signal features. Their approach outperforms Simulink Design Verifier (SLDV) and random test generation. Later, the same authors refined the strategy into one that considers output diversity (distance and feature based) as search criteria [27]. Unlike their strategy, we do not focus only on Simulink models nor only on outputs. We employ diversity in the input space as search criteria and consider a notion of distance from an ideal target for outputs. Moreover, we make use of change point analysis to achieve different shapes for the inputs.

As for coverage, a framework for conformance testing of hybrid systems has been proposed [14] to guide a test generation process. It focuses on state space coverage and how much of the reachable sets of the system are covered, using a notion called *star discrepancy*, which indicates how uniformly distributed are a set of testing points in the state space. As an extension [3], a coverage-based falsification strategy is presented. Instead of focusing on state coverage, a new strategy is developed based on input space coverage. The new strategy sub-divides the search space and takes random samples from these sub-regions, prioritising the ones with low robustness, where negative robustness indicates a property violation. We adopt a structural coverage as our main notion. However, the coverage of the input space is further emphasised by our diversity metric, which helps covering areas of the input space distant from the ones already covered.

3 Preliminaires

Cyber-Physical Systems [7] feature a tight integration of discrete and continuous dynamics; the semantics of CPSs can be suitably modelled as hybrid systems

[15]. Here, we use hybrid automata [8] to model CPSs since it is a well-established and solid formalism, with an intuitive semantics, besides having tools supporting different analyses [10,13,18,35].

We use hybrid automata to capture the desired behaviour at a higher-level of abstraction, to make the input generation feasible. Our approach imposes no constraints on the concrete design or implementation of CPSs. Moreover, the semantics of many formalisms can be expressed in terms of hybrid automata [5]; hence, our approach can be applied to such formalisms as well.

3.1   Analysis of Cyber-Physical Systems

We first consider a running example. Then we introduce a formal definition of hybrid automata, and finally we present a relation that captures a conformance notion of an implementation with respect to a specification.

Running Example - DC-DC Boost Converter. A DC-DC boost converter boosts the input voltage E to a higher output voltage. Figure 1 depicts the basic schematic of a boost converter. The system works by increasing and decreasing the inductor current. For that, the system has a switch that can be opened or closed. While the switch is closed, the current flows through the inductor generating a magnetic field. Once the switch is opened, the magnetic field is destroyed and the current must flow through the diode, transferring the accumulated energy into the capacitor. Since power must be conserved ($P = VI$), the decrease in the current means an increase in the voltage. This cycle is then repeated. Note that the control element of the boost converter transforms the otherwise continuous system into a hybrid one. For more details, see [21].

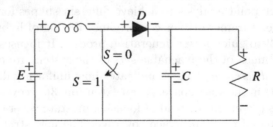

Fig. 1. DC-DC boost converter [21].

Hybrid Automata. Hybrid automata, defined below, can be seen as an extension of finite and timed automata. Guards, reset maps, invariants and specific dynamics for each location are added to these models, in order to allow the specification of continuous dynamics.

In the remainder of this paper, $\mathbb{N}$, $\mathbb{R}$, and $\mathbb{R}_+$ denote the set of non-negative integers, real numbers, and non-negative real-numbers, respectively. Consider a set of real-valued variables V. A valuation of V is a function of type $V \to \mathbb{R}$, which assigns a real number to each variable $v \in V$. The set of all valuations of V is denoted by $Val(V)$. Furthermore, the domain of a function f is denoted by $\mathrm{dom}(f)$.

Definition 1 (Hybrid Automata [20]). *A hybrid automaton is defined as a tuple (Loc, V, (l_0, v_0), $\to$, I, F), where*

- *Loc is the finite set of locations;*
- *$V = V_I \uplus V_O$ is the set of continuous variables, where V_I and V_O denote the disjoint sets of input and output variables, respectively;*
- *l_0 denotes the initial location and v_0 is an initial valuation of V;*
- *$\to \subseteq Loc \times \mathcal{B}(V) \times Reset(V) \times Loc$ is the set of jumps, where:*
  - *$\mathcal{B}(V) \subseteq Val(V)$ indicates the guards under which the jump may be performed, and*
  - *$Reset(V) = \bigcup_{V' \subseteq V} Val(V')$ is the set of value assignments to the variables in V after the jump;*
- *$I : Loc \to \mathcal{B}(V)$ determines the allowed valuation of variables in each location (called the invariant of the location); and*
- *$F : Loc \to \mathcal{B}\left(V \cup \dot{V}\right)$ describes some constraints on variables and their derivatives and specifies the allowed continuous behaviour in each location.*

Locations are discrete states where each one can be viewed as a purely continuous system. Furthermore, the continuous behaviour of the entire hybrid system is captured by the valuation of a set V of continuous variables. We assume that V is partitioned into disjoint sets of input variables, denoted by V_I, and output variables, denoted by V_O. A jump represents a change in the current operating location. To perform a jump, the transition guard has to hold. Moreover, a jump is an immediate action, which does not require time to pass. During a jump event, the valuation of the continuous variables can be reset. Each location also contains a set of differential equations to describe how the continuous variables evolve in that location.

Figure 2 shows the hybrid automaton of our running example. The four discrete states of the system are dependent on the switch (S) and diode (D) modes. The switch can be open or closed while the diode can be blocking or conducting. For instance, modes 1 and 3 represent the system state where the switch is open; in modes 2 and 4, the switch is closed. Analogously, the diode is conducting in modes 3 and 4 and blocking in modes 1 and 2. The inputs for the system are the switch S, the current I_{240} and the voltage V_{24}. The output parameters are the current I_{24} and the boosted output voltage V_{240}. Furthermore, Φ is the magnetic flux produced by the inductor, L is the inductance, q is the electric charge and C represents the capacitance.

Hybrid Conformance. As previously mentioned, the authors of [1,2] propose a conformance relation based on the output behaviour of a system specification and implementation models. This is formalised in a closeness relation (see Definition 2). This section is based on the theory presented in [2].

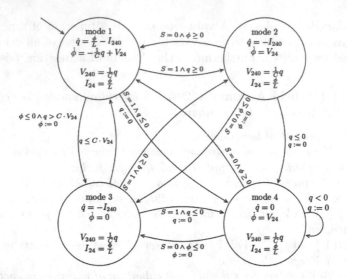

Fig. 2. Hybrid automaton of the DC-DC boost converter [4].

In practice, due to un-modelled physical occurrences such as noise and delays, the implementation behaviour often deviates in time and value with respect to the model [1]. The absence of margins of error can lead to undesired non-conforming verdicts due to intrinsic imprecision in measurement devices and calibration of the implementation and testing infrastructure. Hence, in the (τ, ϵ)-conformance relation, a maximum temporal error of τ and spatial error of ϵ are allowed between the output signals (of the implementation and specification).

In the following definition, a trajectory captures the dynamical evolution of the system, representing its valuation through time. The notion of trajectory abstracts away from discrete locations. A trajectory y is a mapping $y : E \to Val(V)$, where $Val(V)$ denotes the valuation of a set of variables V, and E represents a set of the Hybrid Time Domain, which is a subset of $\mathbb{R}_+ \times \mathbb{N}$. A Hybrid Time is a tuple (t, j) corresponding to the point t in time and the number j of jumps. The set of all trajectories for a hybrid automata $\mathcal{HA}$ is denoted by $\mathrm{Trajs}(\mathcal{HA})$.

Definition 2 ((τ, ϵ)-Closeness). *Consider a test duration $T \in \mathbb{R}_+$, a maximum number of jumps $J \in \mathbb{N}$, and $\tau, \epsilon > 0$; then two trajectories y_1 and y_2 are said to be (τ, ϵ)-close, denoted by $y_1 \approx_{(\tau, \epsilon)} y_2$, if 1 and 2 below hold.*

1. $\forall t : \mathbb{R}_+; \ i : \mathbb{N} \mid (t, i) \in dom(y_1) \wedge t \leq T \wedge i \leq J \bullet$
   $\exists s : \mathbb{R}_+; \ j : \mathbb{N} \mid (s, j) \in dom(y_2) \bullet$
   $\mid t - s \mid \leq \tau \wedge \parallel y_1(t, i) - y_2(s, j) \parallel \leq \epsilon.$

2. $\forall t : \mathbb{R}_+; \ i : \mathbb{N} \mid (t, i) \in dom(y_2) \wedge t \leq T \wedge i \leq J \bullet$
   $\exists s : \mathbb{R}_+; \ j : \mathbb{N} \mid (s, j) \in dom(y_1) \bullet$
   $\mid t - s \mid \leq \tau \wedge \parallel y_2(t, i) - y_1(s, j) \parallel \leq \epsilon.$

The notation $| \, e \, |$ stands for the absolute value of e, whilst $\| \, a - b \, \|$ stands for the (Euclidean) distance between a and b. A solution for a $\mathcal{HA}$ is a function $s : E \rightarrow Loc \times Val(V)$, which yields a location and a valuation given a Hybrid Time [2].

Definition 3 (Solution Pair). *Let u and y be two trajectories of types $E \rightarrow Val(V_I)$ and $E \rightarrow Val(V_O)$, respectively; (u, y) is a solution pair to a hybrid automaton $\mathcal{HA}$ if*

- *$dom(u) = dom(y)$, and*
- *$\exists \phi : E \rightarrow Val(V) \mid \phi \in Trajs(\mathcal{HA}) \bullet dom(\phi) = dom(u) \wedge u = \phi \downarrow V_I \wedge y = \phi \downarrow V_O$, where $y \downarrow V$ stands for the restriction of trajectory y to the set of variables V*

The notion of solution pair is necessary in order to abstract away from locations and distinguish between input and output trajectories. Two trajectories are considered a solution pair for a hybrid automata $\mathcal{HA}$, if there exists a trajectory for $\mathcal{HA}$ that captures the behaviour of both trajectories when it is restricted to input and output variables. We denote by $Sols(\mathcal{HA})$ the set of all Solution Pairs for $\mathcal{HA}$. Definition 4 formalises the (τ, ϵ)-conformance relation.

Definition 4 (Conformance Relation). *Consider two hybrid automata $\mathcal{HA}_1$ and $\mathcal{HA}_2$. Given a test duration $T \in \mathbb{R}_+$, a maximum number of jumps $J \in \mathbb{N}$, and $\tau, \epsilon > 0$, $\mathcal{HA}_2$ conforms to $\mathcal{HA}_1$, denoted by $\mathcal{HA}_2 \approx_{(\tau,\epsilon)} \mathcal{HA}_1$, if and only if*

$$\forall u : E \rightarrow Val(V_I); \ y_1 : E \rightarrow Val(V_O) \mid (u, y_1) \in Sols(\mathcal{HA}_1) \bullet$$
$$\exists y_2 : E \rightarrow Val(V_O) \mid (u, y_2) \in Sols(\mathcal{HA}_2) \bullet y_1 \approx_{(\tau,\epsilon)} y_2$$

In the above definition, T and J are implicitly used in the expression $y_1 \approx_{(\tau,\epsilon)} y_2$.

4 Finding Inputs via Search-Based Heuristics

In this section, we present our strategy for input selection: a modular and scalable process for finding inputs that are directed towards detecting non-conformance.

The main motivation behind our strategy is an efficient way to generate inputs that not only provide structural coverage and maximise diversity metrics but also maximise the possibility of finding faults. Particularly, we consider a notion called critical epsilon, which is related to the distance between two trajectories, e.g., ouput and reference signals. Our search is performed in such a way to maximise the critical epsilon, thus, also maximising the chances to detect non-conformance. We emphasise that this particular combination is novel in this domain and our experiments (see Sect. 5) show that it can lead to effective test cases.

4.1 Search Based Inputs and Critical Epsilon

Given two (reference and output) signals in the specification and a fixed τ, we denote by critical epsilon the smallest ϵ that makes the two signals (τ, ϵ)-close. We formally define it as follows.

Definition 5 (Critical Epsilon). *Consider two trajectories y_1 and y_2, a test duration $T \in \mathbb{R}_+$, a maximum number of jumps $J \in \mathbb{N}$, then, the critical epsilon for y_1, y_2 and a given $\tau > 0$ is*

$$ce(\tau, y_1, y_2) = min\{\epsilon : \mathbb{R}_+ \mid y_1 \approx_{(\tau,\epsilon)} y2 \bullet \epsilon\}$$

Thus, by fixing the temporal margins, it is possible to build a function that computes the critical epsilon. We use this function to select the input points that generate the highest critical epsilon (see Definition 6); such inputs steer the implementation towards the area in which it is more likely to show deviating behaviour and thus a non-conforming verdict.

Definition 6 (Highest Critical Epsilon). *Consider two hybrid automata $\mathcal{HA}_1$ and $\mathcal{HA}_2$, a set of inputs $U : E \to Val(V_I)$ and outputs $y_1^u, y_2^u : E \to Val(V_O) \mid (u, y_1) \in Sols(\mathcal{HA}_1) \wedge (u, y_2) \in Sols(\mathcal{HA}_2) \wedge u \in U$, then, the highest critical epsilon for U, $\mathcal{HA}_1$ and $\mathcal{HA}_2$ and a given $\tau > 0$ is:*

$$hce(\tau, U, \mathcal{HA}_1, \mathcal{HA}_2) = max\{u : U \bullet ce(\tau, y_1^u, y_2^u)\}$$

In summary, our strategy consists of searching for inputs that yield a greater spatial distance between the reference and the system output.

However, since continuous input spaces are infinite by definition, it is not feasible to consider every possible input. A search must be performed, which reduces test-case generation into a global optimisation problem.

For that, we have implemented two approaches: Simulated Annealing and Genetic Algorithms, which are well established probabilistic algorithms for computing global optima [19,30]. Given a function f, they attempt to heuristically approximate the global maxima or minima of f. However, their heuristic nature brings a certain degree of imprecision; this is mitigated by adjusting the parameters in such a way to find a compromise between accuracy and performance.

Figure 3a shows the core idea behind the input generation. In summary, given an input, whose time interval is $[0, t]$, we search for the input value at $(t+1)$ that better satisfies our search metrics, e.g., the highest critical epsilon. Note that the initial input value (where $t = 0$) must be given. This process is repeated until the end of the simulation.

Since the basic algorithm only searches for input values for one timestep at a time $(t+1, t+2, ...)$, it is possible that a choice that gives a lower critical epsilon at $(t + 1)$ (and therefore is not selected), might result in a non-conformance verdict in the future (e.g., at $t + 10$). This will not be detected by the algorithm

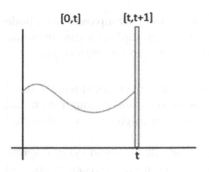
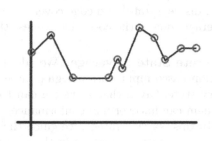

(a) Input generated by a search heuristic.

(b) Input generated and its change point analysis.

Fig. 3. Example of inputs.

and then the non-conformance will be missed. Thus, testing the system using multiple input trajectories should increase the odds of detecting faults, which led us to proposing notions of coverage and diversity to remedy this.

A drawback of this strategy is that it can yield unrealistic inputs. For instance, the variation rate of the resulting signal can be impractical. However, unrealistic inputs do not necessarily mean invalid inputs. The algorithm searches for inputs that fit the input domain. For instance, consider a turbine with a sensor that measures wind speed in the range of 0 to 100 m/s as input and that our algorithm finds a fault whenever the wind changes its speed from 0 to 100 m/s in 0.01 s. Although a fault was detected, such a high variance in wind speed might have never been recorded before and could be considered unrealistic. We consider this input unrealistic, but not strictly invalid.

These scenarios are then useful to further constrain the model. One solution we propose is for the developers to refine the model to disallow such inputs by defining preconditions (e.g., bounds of derivatives) on inputs.

4.2 Notions of Coverage

Test coverage can be used as an indicator for measuring test quality [22], and a positive relationship between test coverage and code reliability has been empirically established [26]. However, coverage has a cost associated with it, and achieving high degrees of coverage is not always feasible or necessary [31]. A contribution of this work is the integration of coverage criteria into our strategy. In this section, we show how we have implemented structural coverage criteria that are able to impose some control on the input selection algorithm, ensuring that the generated test cases cover particular elements of the hybrid automata.

We have considered three types of structural coverage: discrete state, edge and prime path coverage [9]. Discrete state guarantees that each discrete state in the model will be visited by our strategy. Edge coverage is achieved by triggering all transitions. Finally, path coverage is a stronger notion of coverage that aims to cover a particular set of transitions in the model and encompasses both node (i.e., discrete state) and edge coverage. In this work, we emphasize discrete state coverage, due to the cost effectiveness that we obtained in our experiments.

Discrete State Coverage. We adopt discrete state coverage, since a critical epsilon-based input does not guarantee that the system runs through each and every state. Given that a system can have issues in multiple states, visiting all of them can uncover non-conformance.

In this search strategy, we guide the system towards each and every discrete state (i.e., location) present in the specification. Once we move to an uncovered state, we switch the priority to finding the highest critical epsilon. This way we guarantee at least one test per location. The main idea is to generate inputs that will guide the system towards each discrete state as quickly as possible and, then, search for problems that might arise once the system is in those specific states.

In order to guide the system towards the desired discrete state, we require information on its boundaries and information on transitions obtained through the hybrid automaton specification provided by the user.

4.3 A Notion of Diversity

As an additional criterion for our search we consider a diversity metric. More precisely, we adopt a distance-based diversity metric that computes the Euclidean distance of previously generated inputs to generate a new diverse input. Diversity is employed alongside the critical epsilon search.

However, a pure Euclidean distance evaluation on all points could lead to inputs that have the same shape and simple spatial shift, such as two constant signals that are distant from each other. To avoid this, our diversity metric takes in consideration the change points in the input signals. A change point analysis [34] detects sampling points in a trajectory in which there is an abrupt change. Thus, to generate more interesting and effective inputs, we only employ the diversity criteria to the change points of the previously generated ones.

In order to properly employ diversity, one needs inputs generated beforehand, from which the new inputs can be diversified. Our strategy is as follows. In the first step, a core group of inputs are generated using the highest critical epsilon metric with discrete coverage. From this group, we execute the second step, where more tests are generated using a combination of diversity metric with critical epsilon. Consider the trajectory in Fig. 3b as an input generated in the first step (coverage + critical epsilon) and its change points, which are circled around. As the new input is being produced in the second step, the priority assigned to diversity and critical epsilon changes proportionally to the distance to a change point. The closer the new input gets to a change point, the more we increase the priority of the diversity metric and decrease the priority of critical epsilon, so that the new input will distance itself from regions covered by old inputs. Analogously, the further the new input gets from the change points, the more we decrease the priority of diversity and increase the priority of critical epsilon.

Lastly, employing diversity means that we can generate diverse inputs indefinitely. Hence, we have decided to let the user set a maximum number of inputs as stopping criteria; we plan to employ a more systematic approach in the future.

4.4   Mechanisation

Currently, our tool, HyConf, can read Simulink models and perform conformance testing using (τ, ϵ)-conformance notion based on user-defined parameters (τ and ϵ). Given a fixed τ, it can compute the critical epsilon for the user. For the input generation, the tool requires information about the discrete locations, which is not automatically inferred from the Simulink models. We plan to handle this transition automatically, using, for instance, an algorithm [5] for conversion between Simulink and hybrid automata.

The strategy requires two signals in the specification: a command (or reference) signal, denoting the ideal target of the system, and an output signal, denoting the current state of the system. The choice of these signals is domain specific and requires some knowledge of the specification.

Figure 4 shows the pseudo-code for our strategy. Given the set of locations in a hybrid automaton and the initial value for the input, the algorithm uses a search-based heuristic, e.g., Simulated Annealing, to find the next value for the input signal that results in either a change of locations or the highest critical epsilon. The output of this algorithm is a discretised input.

The algorithm works as follows. It first creates a core group of inputs generated based on critical epsilon and discrete coverage (lines 01 to 04). This group of inputs is typically small (the same number of locations in the HA) but very effective. Consider the running example depicted in Fig. 1, since there are 4 states, our strategy generates a core group of 4 input trajectories. Notice that, for the initial state, the algorithm only needs to prioritise critical epsilon. For the remaining states, the algorithm takes in consideration the possible values of the variables in order to enter the state and the path it can take. For instance, in order to cover the state *"mode 2"* from the initial state (*"mode 1"*), the switch must be connected ($S = 0$) and the algorithm searches for inputs where the electric charge is greater than zero ($q \geq 0$). Once these two criteria have been met, the algorithm detects it has entered the state *"mode 2"* and only focus on critical epsilon (lines 15 to 19 in Fig. 4).

After that, it uses a diversity metric coupled with critical epsilon to find inputs that are distant from the ones already generated (lines 05 to 08). As mentioned in Sect. 4.3, the diversity only considers the change points of past inputs (line 27). The weight of the critical epsilon metric is proportional to the distance to the change points while the weight of the diversity metric is inversely proportional (lines 31 and 32). Thus, as the new input point being created approaches the position of a change point, the search increases the priority of the diversity metric and lowers the priority of the critical epsilon. It is worth mentioning that the initial point in every input is always a change point, thus the initial point for the new inputs being created is always distant from the existent ones.

```
00  function main(){
01      foreach location in HA{
02          testcase = createInput(location, HA, initialInput);
03          testSuite.add(testcase);
04      }
05      for (i = 0;  i <= maxAdditionalInputs;  i + +) {
06          testcase = createDiverseInput(testSuite, initialInput);
07          testSuite.add(testcase);
08      }
09      return testSuite;
10  }
11
12
13  function createInput(location, HA, input){
14      for (i = 0;  i <= simulationEndTime;  i + +) {
15          if (system.currentLocation ≠ location) {
16              iteration = search(guideToLocation(location, HA), criticalEpsilon(), input);
17          }else{
18              iteration = search(criticalEpsilon(), input);
19          }
20          input.append(iteration);
21      }
22      return input;
23  }
24
25
26  function createDiverseInput(testSuite, initialInput){
27      changePoints = changePointAnalysis(testSuite);
28      for (i = 0;  i <= simulationEndTime;  i + +) {
29          foreach changePoint in changePoints{
30              d = euclideanDistance(input, changePoint);
31              changePriority(criticalWeight, d);
32              changePriority(diversityWeight, 1 / d);
33          }
34          iteration = search(diversity(), criticalEpsilon(), diversityWeight, criticalWeight);
35          input.append(iteration);
36      }
37      return input;
38  }
```

Fig. 4. Pseudo-code used in HyConf.

Being a multi-objective search [25] means that the objectives are meant to be fulfilled concurrently. Whenever the search heuristic uses *guideToLocation*() or *euclideanDistance*() as a metric, it also takes in consideration *criticalEpsilon*().

5   Empirical Analysis

In this section, we describe the experiments performed using the proposed strategy. Section 5.1 briefly describes the case study used in the experiment; Sect. 5.2 details the experimental plan along with its methodology and threats to validity; and Sect. 5.3 presents the results of the experiment.

5.1   Case Study

In addition to the running example, we use a case study based on an automotive pneumatic suspension system [33]. The system's goal is to increase driving comfort by adjusting the chassis level to compensate for road disturbances. This is achieved by a pneumatic suspension that connects the valves attached to each wheel to a compressor and an escape valve.

The system aims to keep the chassis level as close as possible to a defined set point in each of the four wheels. The decision to increase or decrease the chassis level is based on the tolerance intervals defined for each wheel. The full automaton of our version of this system and its behaviour slightly differs from the original one [33]. The original model contains some unsupported features by the tools we use, such as synchronised parallel components and non-deterministic differential equations. We have serialised the model (by computing the overall behaviour of the constituent hybrid automata), but kept the overall behaviour intact, except for the removal of non-determinism. We have changed the non deterministic assignments to input assignments and, thus, we added inputs that can take the same values within the original intervals and are now assigned directly to the corresponding variable derivative. The final model contains 4 locations with several differential equations each.

5.2   Experimental Plan

The main goal of this study is the evaluation of strategies for input generation to test Cyber-Physical Systems (CPS). Additionally, this experiment aims to verify whether the strategy we implemented in our tool, HyConf, is more effective and efficient in terms of performance compared with the alternatives found in the literature. Another motivation behind this study is the fact that there are few empirical and controlled experiments to evaluate the efficacy of MBT (Model-Based Testing) tools in regard to Cyber-Physical Systems. We compare our strategy against another tool called S-Taliro and also against random input generation, which can serve as a baseline measurement.

- **RQ1:** Can HyConf detect more faults than the alternatives?
- **RQ2:** Can HyConf detect faults faster than the alternatives?

We analyse the effectiveness of our strategies using mutation analysis. The mutation operators used in this experiment were chosen based on a study on mutation operators for Simulink models [11] and are shown in Table 1, along with the number of inserted faults for the Boost Converter (BC) and Suspension System (SS) models.

In the experiment, a higher priority was given to variable change and constant change due to the complexity in detecting this type of faults. In total, we inserted 82 and 105 faults in the boost converter and suspension system models.

The mutation score is used to determine the effectiveness of the strategies (RQ1). In this experiment, the strategy that kills more mutants is deemed more effective. In order to assert efficiency (RQ2), however, we collected the number of time steps it takes for the test suites to kill mutants, and then we compute the median. The strategy with lower median is considered the faster one.

Table 1. Mutation operators and number of faults.

Operator	BC	SS
Constant change	12	14
Variable change	13	18
Variable negation	6	9
Constant replacement	8	12
Statement change	9	13
Delay change	8	13
Relational operator replacement	10	10
Arithmetic operator replacement	10	10
Total for each model	82	105

Methodology. In order to answer our research questions, we define the metrics MS, which represents the Mutation Score, and Average Time of Faults Detected, ATFD, which is an extension of the APFD metric (Average Percentage of Faults Detected) [36]. The experiment is followed by a statistical analysis and a comparison of the yielded results.

The mutation score can be obtained by dividing the number of mutants killed by the total number of mutants created. In this work, we do not distinguish equivalent mutants, i.e., those mutants that conform to the specification. It is generally difficult to check whether the mutant is equivalent in a continuous domain and, thus, we assume that all mutants are not equivalent.

The ATFD metric tells us which test suite can detect mutants faster and is formally defined as follows.

Definition 7 (Average Time of Faults Detected). *Let T be a test suite containing n timesteps and let M be a set of m models with a single distinct mutant each. Let T' be an ordering of T. Let TS_i be the first time step in T' that detects the fault i. The ATFD for T' is:*

$$ATFD_{T'} = 1 - \frac{TS_1 + TS_2 + ... + TS_m}{nm} + \frac{1}{2n}$$

Similarly to APFD, ATFD can vary from 0 to 1 and a higher ATFD indicates a faster fault-detection rate. One can see the ATFD as an APFD where each time step is a distinct test case. However, if a test suite T cannot detect a fault i, then we assign to TS_i the max number of timesteps in that test suite (n). Here, timesteps can serve as time measurement, since to obtain the correct simulation time, one only needs to multiply the number of timesteps by the sampling rate.

In this experiment, each strategy creates inputs for 2 models. Due to the random nature of the search algorithms used in these tools and also to grant statistical significance, each strategy was executed 30 times for each model. The first model is the pneumatic suspension system and the second one is the boost converter (Fig. 2). Once the inputs were created, we performed mutation testing analysis in order to determine which strategy was more effective and accept or reject Hypothesis A (see below). Additionally, the time steps will be recorded during the execution of each strategy. These measurements were then used to assert Hypothesis B (see below).

The stopping criteria for our diversity notion in this experiment (variable *maxAdditionalInputs* in Fig. 4) is the generation of 20 inputs. For S-Taliro we have matched the same number of inputs. As for the random strategy, due to its much faster input generation capabilities, instead of limiting the number of inputs generated, we let it run for the same amount of time as the slowest approach. We believe this is a fair approach to all strategies.

Hypotheses. Hypotheses A and B aim to evaluate the research questions that have been explained previously. For this, null hypotheses are defined, which states that there is no difference between the strategies being analysed. This experiment aims to refute such hypotheses. Thus, alternative hypotheses are also defined, which have a complementary role to the null hypotheses, and can be accepted in case its counterpart hypotheses are rejected. We define 4 hypotheses: A0 and A1 (null and alternate, respectively), compares whether the mutation score (MS) obtained by using our strategy (HyConf) is less than or equal to the mutation score obtained by using the other strategies (OTH). Analogously, hypotheses B0 and B1 (null and alternate, respectively) consider ATFD.

$$H_{A0} : MS_{HyConf} \leq MS_{OTH} \qquad H_{A1} : MS_{HyConf} > MS_{OTH}$$
$$H_{B0} : ATFD_{HyConf} \leq ATFD_{OTH} \qquad H_{B1} \ ATFD_{HyConf} > ATFD_{OTH}$$

Threats to Validity. Here we list the threats to validity that apply to this experiment. As **Internal Validity**, the mutation operators used in this experiment were chosen based on a study on mutation operators for Simulink models [11]. The number of inserted faults is decided manually, based on the complexity of each system. Furthermore, there is no limit to the amount of inputs the random approach can generate and this can be a threat to fairness amongst strategies. Thus, we have decided to let this strategy run for the same time as the slowest approach. Concerning **External Validity**, this experiment only considers 2, relatively small, examples; we cannot generalise the outcome of this experiment for a general class of CPSs. Besides, since we introduced the faults ourselves, the mutants may also not represent real world faults. As **Construct Validity**, assessment of equivalent mutants for CPS was not performed. In this case, we assume that all mutants could have been detected. Moreover, the values for τ and ϵ have a direct impact on the results: sufficiently large values would have detected all mutants and small values would have detected none. The values we have chosen are based on prior experiments and domain knowledge.

Statistical Analysis. The purpose of this analysis is to verify whether one should reject or accept the null and alternative hypotheses. Here, we used the

RStudio, where the comparison was made between averages MS and ATFD computed using HyConf, S-Taliro and random input generation. Since our samples follow a normal distribution, the "t-test" statistical technique with a p-value < 0.05 and level of confidence of 95% is used to analyse our data.

5.3 Results

To answer the first research question, we ran the experiment 30 times for each pair (strategy × model) and analysed the mutation score (see Table 2). The experiment was carried out using a computer with Intel Core i5 processor, 8 GB of RAM and Windows 10 as operating system and the Matlab 2018b framework. The models shown in the table, BC and SS, are the ones presented earlier, i.e., Boost Converter (Sect. 3.1) and Suspension System (Sect. 5.1), respectively. Despite the slight input variations due to the randomness of the employed heuristics, the number of mutants detected by HyConf were the same for each run of the experiment, and similarly for S-Taliro; this was not the case for random testing. Each group of random inputs killed a different number of mutants; in this case, we show the median score. For our tool, we show the results of using different criteria combinations: highest critical epsilon (HCE), coverage and diversity. As can be observed, HyConf consistently detected more mutants when it employs all three combined.

Table 2. Experiment results.

	Mutation Score		ATFD	
	BC	SS	BC	SS
HyConf (SA): HCE + Coverage	63/82	81/105	0.325	0.312
HyConf (SA): HCE + Diversity	55/82	68/105	0.277	0.281
HyConf (SA): HCE + Coverage + Diversity	69/82	88/105	0.364	0.362
HyConf (GA): HCE + Coverage	64/82	85/105	0.342	0.339
HyConf (GA): HCE + Diversity	59/82	70/105	0.301	0.314
HyConf (GA): HCE + Coverage + Diversity	71/82	94/105	0.373	0.371
S-Taliro (SA)	60/82	76/105	0.311	0.293
S-Taliro (GA)	62/82	80/105	0.327	0.309
Random Inputs	43/82	61/105	0.228	0.222

Analogously, to answer the second question, we computed the amount of time steps necessary to detect each mutant. We used this information to calculate the ATFD values. The median values for the 30 execution are also shown in Table 2.

We should mention that each model was simulated for a maximum of 10 time units using a sampling rate of 0.01, which gives us 1000 time steps for each created input. Since we are not interested in prioritisation of the test suites, they had a randomised order in each execution.

Furthermore, Table 3 shows the statistical test results obtained from comparing the ATFD metric. Due to the lack of variation in the collected mutation score

Table 3. Test results (p-values)

	Boost Converter	Suspension
HyConf (SA) v. S-Taliro (SA)	$6.11 * 10^{-08}$	$3.98 * 10^{-14}$
HyConf (GA) v. S-Taliro (GA)	$6.86 * 10^{-08}$	$7.74 * 10^{-14}$
HyConf (GA) v. Random	$8.73 * 10^{-10}$	$5.21 * 10^{-15}$

(i.e, the HyConf and S-Taliro were constant), a t-test could not be performed to evaluate the MS metric; however, the results are clear.

The tests outcome indicate that HyConf performed better than the alternatives, and statistically, the results are significant. Thus, based on the data shown, we can reject the null hypotheses H_{A0} and H_{B0}, and accept their alternatives which tell us that our strategy can obtain a higher mutation score than the other tools and also a higher ATFD. Another conclusion is that even though Genetic Algorithm obtained a higher mutation score and ATFD compared to Simulated Annealing, it has a higher computation cost. This trade-off is left for the engineer to decide.

6   Conclusions and Future Work

In this work we have proposed a strategy for generating fault-oriented inputs for Cyber-Physical Systems. The idea behind these inputs is to maximise the distance between a system's output and its ideal target, thus, leading to fault.

In order to generate inputs for continuous systems, a search based approach is often necessary; in our case, we adopt simulated annealing and genetic algorithm. We look for inputs that lead to a potential conformance violation, particularly with respect to the (τ, ϵ)-conformance notion. Also, we make use of a discrete coverage notion to find inputs that can guide the system towards new locations and we also employ a diversity metric into our input selection strategy. By doing this, we aim to increase coverage and find faults that are more difficult to detect.

Moreover, we have conducted a controlled experiment to compare the strategy we propose with related alternatives. This was performed on two distinct systems: a boost converter and a pneumatic suspension system. Overall, our approach produced evidence of superior fault detection capabilities and efficiency.

As future work, we plan to further improve our input generation strategy. For instance, we are studying additional types of coverage that we can consider and which other types of parameters we can use to tune our multi-objective search. With our diversity metric, we can generate inputs indefinitely. Thus, we let the user define a maximum number but we plan to use a more systematic approach in the future. Additionally, some of the steps in this strategy can be mechanised further and fully integrated into our tool. Finally, we also plan to integrate our strategy with the NAT2TEST [12] framework, which would allow us to define a test strategy for CPS based on natural-language specifications.

References

1. Abbas, H., Hoxha, B., Fainekos, G.E., Deshmukh, J.V., Kapinski, J., Ueda, K.: Conformance testing as falsification for cyber-physical systems. In: Proceedings of the ACM/IEEE 5th International Conference on Cyber-Physical Systems (ICCPS 2014), p. 211. IEEE (2014)
2. Abbas, H.Y.: Test-based falsification and conformance testing for cyber-physical systems. Ph.D. thesis, Arizona State University (2015)
3. Adimoolam, A., Dang, T., Donzé, A., Kapinski, J., Jin, X.: Classification and coverage-based falsification for embedded control systems. In: Majumdar, R., Kunčak, V. (eds.) CAV 2017. LNCS, vol. 10426, pp. 483–503. Springer, Cham (2017). https://doi.org/10.1007/978-3-319-63387-9_24
4. Aerts, A.: Model-based design and testing of mechatronic systems: an industrial case study. Master's thesis, Eindhoven University of Technology, Eindhoven, Netherlands (2016)
5. Agrawal, A., Simon, G., Karsai, G.: Semantic translation of simulink/stateflow models to hybrid automata using graph transformations. Electron. Notes Theoret. Comput. Sci. **109**, 43–56 (2004)
6. Alur, R.: Principles of Cyber-Physical Systems. MIT Press, Cambridge (2015)
7. Alur, R., et al.: The algorithmic analysis of hybrid systems. Theor. Comput. Sci. **138**(1), 3–34 (1995)
8. Alur, R., Courcoubetis, C., Henzinger, T.A., Ho, P.-H.: Hybrid automata: an algorithmic approach to the specification and verification of hybrid systems. In: Grossman, R.L., Nerode, A., Ravn, A.P., Rischel, H. (eds.) HS 1991-1992. LNCS, vol. 736, pp. 209–229. Springer, Heidelberg (1993). https://doi.org/10.1007/3-540-57318-6_30
9. Ammann, P., Offutt, J.: Introduction to Software Testing. Cambridge University Press, Cambridge (2016)
10. Annpureddy, Y., Liu, C., Fainekos, G., Sankaranarayanan, S.: S-TaLiRo: a tool for temporal logic falsification for hybrid systems. In: Abdulla, P.A., Leino, K.R.M. (eds.) TACAS 2011. LNCS, vol. 6605, pp. 254–257. Springer, Heidelberg (2011). https://doi.org/10.1007/978-3-642-19835-9_21
11. Binh, N.T., et al.: Mutation operators for simulink models. In: 2012 Fourth International Conference on Knowledge and Systems Engineering (KSE), pp. 54–59. IEEE (2012)
12. Carvalho, G., Barros, F., Carvalho, A., Cavalcanti, A., Mota, A., Sampaio, A.: NAT2TEST tool: from natural language requirements to test cases based on CSP. In: Calinescu, R., Rumpe, B. (eds.) SEFM 2015. LNCS, vol. 9276, pp. 283–290. Springer, Cham (2015). https://doi.org/10.1007/978-3-319-22969-0_20
13. Chen, X., Ábrahám, E., Sankaranarayanan, S.: Flow*: an analyzer for non-linear hybrid systems. In: Sharygina, N., Veith, H. (eds.) CAV 2013. LNCS, vol. 8044, pp. 258–263. Springer, Heidelberg (2013). https://doi.org/10.1007/978-3-642-39799-8_18
14. Dang, T., Nahhal, T.: Coverage-guided test generation for continuous and hybrid systems. Formal Methods Syst. Des. **34**(2), 183–213 (2009)
15. De Schutter, B., Heemels, W., Lunze, J., Prieur, C., et al.: Survey of modeling, analysis, and control of hybrid systems. In: Handbook of Hybrid Systems Control-Theory, Tools, Applications, pp. 31–55 (2009)

16. Donzé, A.: Breach, a toolbox for verification and parameter synthesis of hybrid systems. In: Touili, T., Cook, B., Jackson, P. (eds.) CAV 2010. LNCS, vol. 6174, pp. 167–170. Springer, Heidelberg (2010). https://doi.org/10.1007/978-3-642-14295-6_17

17. Dorigo, M., Birattari, M.: Ant Colony Optimization. Springer, Heidelberg (2010)

18. Frehse, G., et al.: SpaceEx: scalable verification of hybrid systems. In: Gopalakrishnan, G., Qadeer, S. (eds.) CAV 2011. LNCS, vol. 6806, pp. 379–395. Springer, Heidelberg (2011). https://doi.org/10.1007/978-3-642-22110-1_30

19. Gelfand, S.B., Mitter, S.K.: Analysis of simulated annealing for optimization. In: 1985 24th IEEE Conference on Decision and Control, vol. 24, pp. 779–786. IEEE (1985)

20. Goebel, R., Sanfelice, R.G., Teel, A.R.: Hybrid dynamical systems. IEEE Control Syst. 29(2), 28–93 (2009)

21. Heemels, W., De Schutter, B.: Modeling and control of hybrid dynamical systems. TU Eindhoven, Lecture notes course 4K160 (2013)

22. Horgan, J.R., London, S., Lyu, M.R.: Achieving software quality with testing coverage measures. Computer 27(9), 60–69 (1994)

23. Khakpour, N., Mousavi, M.R.: Notions of conformance testing for cyber-physical systems: overview and roadmap (invited paper). In: Aceto, L., de Frutos Escrig, D. (eds.) 26th International Conference on Concurrency Theory (CONCUR 2015). Leibniz International Proceedings in Informatics (LIPIcs), vol. 42, pp. 18–40. Schloss Dagstuhl-Leibniz-Zentrum fuer Informatik, Dagstuhl, Germany (2015)

24. Kirkpatrick, S., Gelatt, C.D., Vecchi, M.P.: Optimization by simulated annealing. Science 220(4598), 671–680 (1983)

25. Konak, A., Coit, D.W., Smith, A.E.: Multi-objective optimization using genetic algorithms: a tutorial. Reliab. Eng. Syst. Saf. 91(9), 992–1007 (2006)

26. Malaiya, Y.K., Li, M.N., Bieman, J.M., Karcich, R., Skibbe, B., et al.: The relationship between test coverage and reliability. In: Proceedings of 1994 IEEE International Symposium on Software Reliability Engineering, pp. 186–195. IEEE (1994)

27. Matinnejad, R., Nejati, S., Briand, L., Bruckmann, T.: Test generation and test prioritization for simulink models with dynamic behavior. IEEE Trans. Softw. Eng. (2018)

28. Matinnejad, R., Nejati, S., Briand, L.C., Bruckmann, T.: Effective test suites for mixed discrete-continuous stateflow controllers. In: Proceedings of the 2015 10th Joint Meeting on Foundations of Software Engineering, pp. 84–95. ACM (2015)

29. Matinnejad, R., Nejati, S., Briand, L.C., Bruckmann, T.: Automated test suite generation for time-continuous simulink models. In: proceedings of the 38th International Conference on Software Engineering, pp. 595–606. ACM (2016)

30. Mitchell, M.: An Introduction to Genetic Algorithms. MIT Press, Cambridge (1998)

31. Mockus, A., Nagappan, N., Dinh-Trong, T.T.: Test coverage and post-verification defects: a multiple case study. In: 2009 3rd International Symposium on Empirical Software Engineering and Measurement, ESEM 2009, pp. 291–301. IEEE (2009)

32. Mosterman, P.J., Zander, J.: Cyber-physical systems challenges: a needs analysis for collaborating embedded software systems. Softw. Syst. Model. 15(1), 5–16 (2016)

33. Müller, O., Stauner, T.: Modelling and verification using linear hybrid automata-a case study. Math. Comput. Model. Dyn. Syst. 6(1), 71–89 (2000)

34. Picard, D.: Testing and estimating change-points in time series. Adv. Appl. Probab. 17(4), 841–867 (1985)

35. Platzer, A., Quesel, J.-D.: KeYmaera: a hybrid theorem prover for hybrid systems (system description). In: Armando, A., Baumgartner, P., Dowek, G. (eds.) IJCAR 2008. LNCS (LNAI), vol. 5195, pp. 171–178. Springer, Heidelberg (2008). https://doi.org/10.1007/978-3-540-71070-7_15

36. Rothermel, G., Untch, R.H., Chu, C., Harrold, M.J.: Test case prioritization: an empirical study. In: 1999 Proceedings of IEEE International Conference on Software Maintenance (ICSM 1999), pp. 179–188. IEEE (1999)

37. Rubinstein, R.Y., Kroese, D.P.: The Cross-entropy Method: A Unified Approach to Combinatorial Optimization. Monte-Carlo Simulation and Machine Learning. Springer, Heidelberg (2013)

38. Tretmans, J.: Model based testing with labelled transition systems. In: Hierons, R.M., Bowen, J.P., Harman, M. (eds.) Formal Methods and Testing. LNCS, vol. 4949, pp. 1–38. Springer, Heidelberg (2008). https://doi.org/10.1007/978-3-540-78917-8_1

39. Windisch, A., Al Moubayed, N.: Signal generation for search-based testing of continuous systems. In: 2009 International Conference on Software Testing, Verification and Validation Workshops, ICSTW 2009, pp. 121–130. IEEE (2009)

Mutation Testing with Hyperproperties

Andreas Fellner[1,2]([⊠]), Mitra Tabaei Befrouei[2], and Georg Weissenbacher[2]

[1] AIT Austrian Institute of Technology, Vienna, Austria
andreas.fellner@ait.ac.at
[2] TU Wien, Vienna, Austria

Abstract. We present a new method for model-based mutation-driven test case generation. Mutants are generated by making small syntactical modifications to the model or source code of the system under test. A test case kills a mutant if the behavior of the mutant deviates from the original system when running the test. In this work, we use hyperproperties—which allow to express relations between multiple executions—to formalize different notions of *killing* for both deterministic as well as non-deterministic models. The resulting hyperproperties are universal in the sense that they apply to arbitrary reactive models and mutants. Moreover, an off-the-shelf model checking tool for hyperproperties can be used to generate test cases. We evaluate our approach on a number of models expressed in two different modeling languages by generating tests using a state-of-the-art mutation testing tool.

1 Introduction

Mutations—small syntactic modifications of programs that mimic typical programming errors—are used to assess the quality of existing test suites. A test *kills* a mutated program (or *mutant*), obtained by applying a *mutation operator* to a program, if its outcome for the mutant deviates from the outcome for the unmodified program. The percentage of mutants killed by a given test suite serves as a metric for test quality. The approach is based on two assumptions: (a) the *competent programmer hypothesis* [11], which states that implementations are typically close-to-correct, and (b) the *coupling effect* [27], which states that a test suites ability to detect simple errors (and mutations) is indicative of its ability to detect complex errors.

In the context of model-based testing, mutations are also used to design tests. Model-based test case generation is the process of deriving tests from a reference model (which is assumed to be free of faults) in such a way that they reveal any non-conformance of the reference model and its mutants, i.e., kill the

The research was supported by ECSEL JU under the project H2020 737469 AutoDrive—Advancing failaware, fail-safe, and fail-operational electronic components, systems, and architectures for fully automated driving to make future mobility safer, affordable, and end-user acceptable, by the Vienna Science and Technology Fund (WWTF) through grant VRG11-005, and by the Austrian National Research Network S11403-N23 (RiSE).

P. C. Ölveczky and G. Salaün (Eds.): SEFM 2019, LNCS 11724, pp. 203–221, 2019.
https://doi.org/10.1007/978-3-030-30446-1_11

mutants. The tests detect potential errors (modeled by mutation operators) of implementations, treated as a black box in this setting, that conform to a mutant instead of the reference model. A test *strongly* kills a mutant if it triggers an observable difference in behavior [11], and *weakly* kills a mutant if the deviation is merely in a difference in traversed program states [22].

The aim of our work is to automatically construct tests that strongly kill mutants derived from a reference model. To this end, we present two main contributions:

(1) A formalization of mutation killing in terms of *hyperproperties* [14], a formalism to relate multiple execution traces of a program which has recently gained popularity due to its ability to express security properties such as non-interference and observational determinism. Notably, our formalization also takes into account potential non-determinism, which significantly complicates killing of mutants due to the unpredictability of the test outcome.

(2) An approach that enables the automated construction of tests by means of *model checking* the proposed hyperproperties on a model that aggregates the reference model and a mutant of it. To circumvent limitations of currently available model checking tools for hyperproperties, we present a transformation that enables the control of non-determinism via additional program inputs. We evaluate our approach using a state-of-the-art model checker on a number of models expressed in two different modeling languages.

Running Example. We illustrate the main concepts of our work in Fig. 1. Figure 1a shows the SMV [25] model of a beverage machine, which non-deterministically serves coff (coffee) or tea after input req (request), assuming that there is still enough wtr (water) in the tank. Water can be refilled with input fill. The symbol ε represents absence of input and output, respectively.

The code in Fig. 1a includes the variable mut (initialized non-deterministically in line 4), which enables the activation of a mutation in line 10. The mutant refills 1 unit of water only, whereas the original model fills 2 units.

Figure 1b states a hyperproperty over the inputs and outputs of the model formalizing that the mutant can be killed *definitely* (i.e., independently of non-deterministic choices). The execution shown in Fig. 1c is a witness for this claim: the test requests two drinks after filling the tank. For the mutant, the second request will necessarily fail, as indicated in Fig. 1d, which shows all possible output sequences for the given test.

Outline. Section 2 introduces our system model and HyperLTL. Section 3 explains the notions of *potential* and *definite* killing of mutants, which are then formalized in terms of hyperproperties for deterministic and non-deterministic models in Sect. 4. Section 5 introduces a transformation to control non-determinism in models, and Sect. 6 describes our experimental results. Related work is discussed in Sect. 7.

```
1   init(in ) :=ε
2   init(out):=ε
3   init(wtr):=2
4   init(mut):={⊤,⊥}
5   next(in ) :={ε,req,fill}
6   next(out):=
7   if(in=req&wtr >0):{coff,tea}
8   else         :ε
9   next(wtr):=
10  if   (in=fill ):(mut ? 1 : 2)
11  elif(in=req&wtr >0): wtr−1
12  else              : wtr
13  next(mut):= mut
```

$$\exists\pi\forall\pi'\forall\pi''$$
$$\Box(\neg mut_\pi \wedge mut_{\pi'} \wedge \neg mut_{\pi''}\wedge$$
$$([in=\varepsilon]_\pi \leftrightarrow [in=\varepsilon]_{\pi'} \leftrightarrow [in=\varepsilon]_{\pi''})\wedge$$
$$([in=req]_\pi \leftrightarrow [in=req]_{\pi'}$$
$$\leftrightarrow [in=req]_{\pi''})\wedge$$
$$([in=fill]_\pi \leftrightarrow [in=fill]_{\pi'}$$
$$\leftrightarrow [in=fill]_{\pi''})) \rightarrow$$
$$\Diamond(\neg([o=\varepsilon]_{\pi'} \leftrightarrow [o=\varepsilon]_{\pi''})\vee$$
$$\neg([o=coff]_{\pi'} \leftrightarrow [o=coff]_{\pi''})\vee$$
$$\neg([o=tea]_{\pi'} \leftrightarrow [o=tea]_{\pi''}))$$

(a) Beverage machine with cond. mutant   (b) Hyperproperty expressing killing

(c) Definitely killing test

(d) Spurious test response of mutant

Fig. 1. Beverage machine running example

2   Preliminaries

This section introduces symbolic transition systems as our formalisms for representing discrete reactive systems and provides the syntax and semantics of HyperLTL, a logic for hyperproperties.

2.1   System Model

A symbolic transition system (STS) is a tuple $\mathcal{S} = \langle \mathcal{I}, \mathcal{O}, \mathcal{X}, \alpha, \delta \rangle$, where $\mathcal{I}, \mathcal{O}, \mathcal{X}$ are finite sets of input, output, and state variables, α is a formula over $\mathcal{X} \cup \mathcal{O}$ (the initial conditions predicate), and δ is a formula over $\mathcal{I} \cup \mathcal{O} \cup \mathcal{X} \cup \mathcal{X}'$ (the transition relation predicate), where $\mathcal{X}' = \{x' \mid x \in \mathcal{X}\}$ is a set of primed variables representing the successor states. An input I, output O, state X, and successor state X', respectively, is a mapping of $\mathcal{I}, \mathcal{O}, \mathcal{X}$, and $\mathcal{X}'$, respectively, to values in a fixed domain that includes the elements $\top$ and $\bot$ (representing true and false, respectively). $Y|_\mathcal{V}$ denotes the restriction of the domain of mapping Y to the variables $\mathcal{V}$. Given a valuation Y and a Boolean variable $v \in \mathcal{V}$, $Y(v)$ denotes the value of v in Y (if defined) and $Y[v]$ and $Y[\neg v]$ denote Y with v set to $\top$ and $\bot$, respectively.

We assume that the initial conditions- and transition relation predicate are defined in a logic that includes standard Boolean operators $\neg$, $\wedge$, $\vee$, $\rightarrow$, and $\leftrightarrow$. We omit further details, as our results do not depend on a specific formalism. We write $X, O \models \alpha$ and $I, O, X, X' \models \delta$ to denote that α and δ evaluate to true under an evaluation of inputs I, outputs O, states X, and successor states X'. We assume that every STS has a distinct output O_ε, representing absence of output.

A state X with output O such that $X, O \models \alpha$ are an *initial state* and *initial output*. A state X has a transition with input I to its *successor state* X' with output O iff $I, O, X, X' \models \delta$, denoted by $X \xrightarrow{I,O} X'$. A *trace* of S is a sequence of tuples of concrete inputs, outputs, and states $\langle (I_0, O_0, X_0), (I_1, O_1, X_1), (I_2, O_2, X_2), \ldots \rangle$ such that $X_0, O_0 \models \alpha$ and $\forall j \geq 0$. $X_j \xrightarrow{I_j, O_{j+1}} X_{j+1}$. We require that every state has at least one successor, therefore all traces of S are infinite. We denote by $\mathcal{T}(S)$ the set of all traces of S. Given a trace $p = \langle (I_0, O_0, X_0), (I_1, O_1, X_1), \ldots \rangle$, we write $p[j]$ for (I_j, O_j, X_j), $p[j, l]$ for $\langle (I_j, O_j, X_j), \ldots, (I_l, O_l, X_l) \rangle$, $p[j, \infty]$ for $\langle (I_j, O_j, X_j), \ldots \rangle$ and $p|_\mathcal{V}$ to denote $\langle (I_0|_\mathcal{V}, O_0|_\mathcal{V}, X_0|_\mathcal{V}), (I_1|_\mathcal{V}, O_1|_\mathcal{V}, X_1|_\mathcal{V}), \ldots \rangle$. We lift restriction to sets of traces T by defining $T|_\mathcal{V}$ as $\{ p|_\mathcal{V} \mid t \in T \}$.

S is *deterministic* iff there is a unique pair of an initial state and initial output and for each state X and input I, there is at most one state X' with output O, such that $X \xrightarrow{I,O} X'$. Otherwise, the model is *non-deterministic*.

In the following, we presume the existence of sets of atomic propositions $\mathsf{AP} = \{\mathsf{AP}_\mathcal{I} \cup \mathsf{AP}_\mathcal{O} \cup \mathsf{AP}_\mathcal{X}\}$ (intentionally kept abstract)[1] serving as labels that characterize inputs, outputs, and states (or properties thereof).

For a trace $p = \langle (I_0, O_0, X_0), (I_1, O_1, X_1), \ldots \rangle$ the corresponding trace over AP is $\mathsf{AP}(p) = \langle \mathsf{AP}(I_0) \cup \mathsf{AP}(O_0) \cup \mathsf{AP}(X_0), \mathsf{AP}(I_1) \cup \mathsf{AP}(O_1) \cup \mathsf{AP}(X_1), \ldots \rangle$. We lift this definition to sets of traces by defining $\mathsf{APTr}(S) \stackrel{\text{def}}{=} \{\mathsf{AP}(p) \mid p \in \mathcal{T}(S)\}$.

Example 1. Figure 1a shows the formalization of a beverage machine in SMV [25]. In Fig. 1b, we use atomic propositions to enumerate the possible values of in and out. This SMV model closely corresponds to an STS: the initial condition predicate α and transition relation δ are formalized using integer arithmetic as follows:

$$\alpha \stackrel{\text{def}}{=} \text{out=}\varepsilon \wedge \text{wtr=2}$$

$$\delta \stackrel{\text{def}}{=} \text{wtr>0} \wedge \text{in=req} \wedge \text{out=coff} \wedge \text{wtr'=wtr-1} \vee$$
$$\text{wtr>0} \wedge \text{in=req} \wedge \text{out=tea} \wedge \text{wtr'=wtr-1} \vee$$
$$\text{in=fill} \wedge \neg\text{mut} \wedge \text{out=}\varepsilon \wedge \text{wtr'=2} \vee$$
$$\text{in=fill} \wedge \text{mut} \wedge \text{out=}\varepsilon \wedge \text{wtr'=1} \vee$$
$$\text{in=}\varepsilon \wedge \text{out=}\varepsilon \wedge \text{wtr'=wtr}$$

---

[1] Finite domains can be characterized using binary encodings; infinite domains require an extension of our formalism in Sect. 2.2 with equality and is omitted for the sake of simplicity.

The trace $p = \langle (\varepsilon, \varepsilon, 2), (\text{req}, \varepsilon, 2), (\text{req}, \text{coff}, 1), (\varepsilon, \text{tea}, 0), \ldots \rangle$ is one possible execution of the system (for brevity, variable names are omitted). Examples of atomic propositions for the system are $[\text{in}=\text{coff}], [\text{out}=\varepsilon]$, $[\text{wtr}>0], [\text{wtr}=0]$ and the respective atomic proposition trace of p is $\mathsf{AP}(p) = \langle \{[\text{in}=\varepsilon], [\text{out}=\varepsilon], [\text{wtr}>0]\}, \{[\text{in}=\text{req}], [\text{out}=\varepsilon], [\text{wtr}>0]\}, \{[\text{in}=\text{req}], [\text{out}= \text{coff}], [\text{wtr}>0]\}, \{[\text{in}=\text{req}], [\text{out}=\text{tea}], [\text{wtr}=0]\} \ldots \rangle$.

2.2 HyperLTL

In the following, we provide an overview of the HyperLTL, a logic for hyperproperties, sufficient for understanding the formalization in Sect. 4. For details, we refer the reader to [13]. HyperLTL is defined over atomic proposition traces (see Sect. 2.1) of a fixed STS $\mathcal{S} = \langle \mathcal{I}, \mathcal{O}, \mathcal{X}, \alpha, \delta \rangle$ as defined in Sect. 2.1.

Syntax. Let AP be a set of atomic propositions and let π be a *trace variable* from a set $\mathcal{V}$ of trace variables. Formulas of HyperLTL are defined by the following grammar:

$$\psi ::= \exists \pi . \psi \mid \forall \pi . \psi \mid \quad \varphi$$
$$\varphi ::= a_\pi \quad \mid \quad \neg \varphi \mid \varphi \vee \varphi \mid \bigcirc \varphi \mid \varphi \mathcal{U} \varphi$$

Connectives $\exists$ and $\forall$ are universal and existential trace quantifiers, read as "along some traces" and "along all traces". In our setting, atomic propositions $a \in \mathsf{AP}$ express facts about states or the presence of inputs and outputs. Each atomic proposition is sub-scripted with a trace variable to indicate the trace it is associated with. The Boolean connectives $\wedge$, $\rightarrow$, and $\leftrightarrow$ are defined in terms of $\neg$ and $\vee$ as usual. Furthermore, we use the standard temporal operators *eventually* $\Diamond \varphi \overset{\text{def}}{=} \text{true } \mathcal{U} \varphi$, and *always* $\Box \varphi \overset{\text{def}}{=} \neg \Diamond \neg \varphi$.

Semantics. $\Pi \models_\mathcal{S} \psi$ states that ψ is valid for a given mapping $\Pi : \mathcal{V} \rightarrow \mathsf{APTr}(\mathcal{S})$ of trace variables to atomic proposition traces. Let $\Pi [\pi \mapsto p]$ be as Π except that π is mapped to p. We use $\Pi [i, \infty]$ to denote the trace assignment $\Pi'(\pi) = \Pi(\pi) [i, \infty]$ for all π. The validity of a formula is defined as follows:

$$\Pi \models_\mathcal{S} a_\pi \qquad \text{iff } a \in \Pi(\pi)[0]$$
$$\Pi \models_\mathcal{S} \exists \pi . \psi \qquad \text{iff there exists } p \in \mathsf{APTr}(\mathcal{S}) : \Pi [\pi \mapsto p] \models_\mathcal{S} \psi$$
$$\Pi \models_\mathcal{S} \forall \pi . \psi \qquad \text{iff for all } p \in \mathsf{APTr}(\mathcal{S}) : \Pi [\pi \mapsto p] \models_\mathcal{S} \psi$$
$$\Pi \models_\mathcal{S} \neg \varphi \qquad \text{iff } \Pi \not\models_\mathcal{S} \varphi$$
$$\Pi \models_\mathcal{S} \psi_1 \vee \psi_2 \quad \text{iff } \Pi \models_\mathcal{S} \psi_1 \text{ or } \Pi \models_\mathcal{S} \psi_2$$
$$\Pi \models_\mathcal{S} \bigcirc \varphi \qquad \text{iff } \Pi [1, \infty] \models_\mathcal{S} \varphi$$
$$\Pi \models_\mathcal{S} \varphi_1 \mathcal{U} \varphi_2 \quad \text{iff there exists } i \geq 0 : \Pi [i, \infty] \models_\mathcal{S} \varphi_2$$
$$\text{and for all } 0 \leq j < i \text{ we have } \Pi [j, \infty] \models_\mathcal{S} \varphi_1$$

We write $\models_\mathcal{S} \psi$ if $\Pi \models_\mathcal{S} \psi$ holds and Π is empty. We call $q \in \mathcal{T}(\mathcal{S})$ a π-witness of a formula $\exists \pi . \psi$, if $\Pi [\pi \mapsto p] \models_\mathcal{S} \psi$ and $\mathsf{AP}(q) = p$.

3   Killing Mutants

In this section, we introduce mutants, tests, and the notions of potential and definite killing. We discuss how to represent an STS and its corresponding mutant as a single STS, which can then be model checked to determine killability.

3.1   Mutants

Mutants are variations of a model $\mathcal{S}$ obtained by applying small modifications to the syntactic representation of $\mathcal{S}$. A mutant of an STS $\mathcal{S} = \langle \mathcal{I}, \mathcal{O}, \mathcal{X}, \alpha, \delta \rangle$ (the *original model*) is an STS $\mathcal{S}^m = \langle \mathcal{I}, \mathcal{O}, \mathcal{X}, \alpha^m, \delta^m \rangle$ with equal sets of input, output, and state variables as $\mathcal{S}$ but a deviating initial predicate and/or transition relation. We assume that $\mathcal{S}^m$ is equally input-enabled as $\mathcal{S}$, that is $\mathcal{T}(\mathcal{S}^m)|_{\mathcal{I}} = \mathcal{T}(\mathcal{S})|_{\mathcal{I}}$, i.e., the mutant and model accept the same sequences of inputs. In practice, this can easily be achieved by using self-loops with empty output to ignore unspecified inputs. We use standard mutation operators, such as disabling transitions, replacing operators, etc. Due to space limitations and the fact that mutation operators are not the primary focus of this work, we do not list them here, but refer to the Appendix of [16] and [5]. We combine an original model represented by $\mathcal{S}$ and a mutant $\mathcal{S}^m$ into a *conditional mutant* $\mathcal{S}^{c(m)}$, in order to perform mutation analysis via model checking the combined model.

The conditional mutant is defined as $\mathcal{S}^{c(m)} \stackrel{\text{def}}{=} \langle \mathcal{I}, \mathcal{O}, \mathcal{X} \cup \{\text{mut}\}, \alpha^{c(m)}, \delta^{c(m)} \rangle$, where mut is a fresh Boolean variable used to distinguish states of the original and the mutated STS.

Suppose $\mathcal{S}^m$ replaces a sub-formula δ_0 of δ by δ_0^m, then the transition relation predicate of the conditional mutant $\delta^{c(m)}$ is obtained by replacing δ_0 in δ by $(\text{mut} \wedge \delta_0^m) \vee (\neg\text{mut} \wedge \delta_0)$. We fix the value of mut in transitions by conjoining δ with mut $\leftrightarrow$ mut$'$. The initial conditions predicate of the conditional mutant is defined similarly.

Consequently, for a trace $p \in \mathcal{T}(\mathcal{S}^{c(m)})$ it holds that if $p|_{\{\text{mut}\}} = \{\bot\}^\omega$ then $p|_{\mathcal{I} \cup \mathcal{O} \cup \mathcal{X}} \in \mathcal{T}(\mathcal{S})$, and if $p|_{\{\text{mut}\}} = \{\top\}^\omega$ then $p|_{\mathcal{I} \cup \mathcal{O} \cup \mathcal{X}} \in \mathcal{T}(\mathcal{S}^m)$. Formally, $\mathcal{S}^{c(m)}$ is non-deterministic, since mut is chosen non-deterministically in the initial state. However, we only refer to $\mathcal{S}^{c(m)}$ as non-deterministic if either $\mathcal{S}$ or $\mathcal{S}^m$ is non-deterministic, as mut is typically fixed in the hypertproperties presented in Sect. 4.

Example 1 and Fig. 1a show a conditional mutant as an STS and in SMV.

3.2   Killing

Killing a mutant amounts to finding inputs for which the mutant produces outputs that deviate from the original model. In a reactive, model-based setting, killing has been formalized using conformance relations [29], for example in [4,15], where an implementation *conforms* to its specification if all its input/output sequences are part of/allowed by the specification.

In model-based testing, the model takes the role of the specification and is assumed to be correct by design. The implementation is treated as black box, and therefore mutants of the specification serve as its proxy. Tests (i.e., input/output sequences) that demonstrate non-conformance between the model and its mutant can be used to check whether the implementation adheres to the specification or contains the bug reflected in the mutant. The execution of a test on a system under test fails if the sequence of inputs of the test triggers a sequence of outputs that deviates from those predicted by the test. Formally, tests are defined as follows:

Definition 1 (Test). *A test t of* length n *for S comprises inputs $t|_{\mathcal{I}}$ and outputs $t|_{\mathcal{O}}$ of length n, such that there exists a trace $p \in \mathcal{T}(S)$ with $p|_{\mathcal{I}}[0, n] = t|_{\mathcal{I}}$ and $p|_{\mathcal{O}}[0, n] = t|_{\mathcal{O}}$.*

For non-deterministic models, in which a single sequence of inputs can trigger different sequences of outputs, we consider two different notions of killing. We say that a mutant can be *potentially killed* if there exist inputs for which the mutant's outputs deviate from the original model given an appropriate choice of non-deterministic initial states and transitions. In practice, executing a test that potentially kills a mutant on a faulty implementation that exhibits non-determinism (e.g., a multi-threaded program) may fail to demonstrate non-conformance (unless the non-determinism can be controlled). A mutant can be *definitely killed* if there exists a sequence of inputs for which the behaviors of the mutant and the original model deviate independently of how non-determinism is resolved.

Note potential and definite killability are orthogonal to the folklore notions of weak and strong killing, which capture different degrees of observability. Formally, we define potential and definite killability as follows:

Definition 2 (Potentially Killable). *S^m is potentially killable if*

$$\mathcal{T}(S^m)|_{\mathcal{I} \cup \mathcal{O}} \not\subseteq \mathcal{T}(S)|_{\mathcal{I} \cup \mathcal{O}}$$

Test t for S of length n potentially kills S^m if

$$\{q[0, n] \mid q \in \mathcal{T}(S^m) \wedge q[0, n]|_{\mathcal{I}} = t|_{\mathcal{I}}\}|_{\mathcal{I} \cup \mathcal{O}} \not\subseteq \{p[0, n] \mid p \in \mathcal{T}(S)\}|_{\mathcal{I} \cup \mathcal{O}}.$$

Definition 3 (Definitely Killable). *S^m is definitely killable if there is a sequence of inputs $\vec{I} \in \mathcal{T}(S)|_{\mathcal{I}}$, such that*

$$\{q \in \mathcal{T}(S^m) \mid q|_{\mathcal{I}} = \vec{I}\}|_{\mathcal{O}} \cap \{p \in \mathcal{T}(S) \mid p|_{\mathcal{I}} = \vec{I}\}|_{\mathcal{O}} = \emptyset$$

Test t for S of length n definitely kills S^m if

$$\{q[0, n] \mid q \in \mathcal{T}(S^m) \wedge q[0, n]|_{\mathcal{I}} = t|_{\mathcal{I}}\}|_{\mathcal{O}} \cap$$
$$\{p[0, n] \mid p \in \mathcal{T}(S) \wedge p[0, n]|_{\mathcal{I}} = t|_{\mathcal{I}}\}|_{\mathcal{O}} = \emptyset$$

Definition 4 (Equivalent Mutant). *S^m is equivalent iff S^m is not potentially killable.*

Note that definite killability is stronger than potential killabilty, though for deterministic systems, the two notions coincide.

Proposition 1. *If $\mathcal{S}^m$ is definitely killable then $\mathcal{S}^m$ is potentially killable.*
If $\mathcal{S}^m$ is deterministic then: $\mathcal{S}^m$ is potentially killable iff $\mathcal{S}^m$ is definitely killable.

The following example shows a definitely killable mutant, a mutant that is only potentially killable, and an equivalent mutant.

Example 2. The mutant in Fig. 1a, is definitely killable, since we can force the system into a state in which both possible outputs of the original system (coff, tea) differ from the only possible output of the mutant (ε).

Consider a mutant that introduces non-determinism by replacing line 7 with the code **if**(in=fill):(mut ? {1,2} : 2), indicating that the machine is filled with either 1 or 2 units of water. This mutant is potentially but not definitely killable, as only one of the non-deterministic choices leads to a deviation of the outputs.

Finally, consider a mutant that replaces line 4 with **if**(in=req&wtr>0): (mut ? coff : {coff,tea}) and removes the mut branch of line 7, yielding a machine that always creates coffee. Every implementation of this mutant is also correct with respect to the original model. Hence, we consider the mutant equivalent, even though the original model, unlike the mutant, can output tea.

4   Killing with Hyperproperties

In this section, we provide a formalization of potential and definite killability in terms of HyperLTL, assert the correctness of our formalization with respect to Sect. 3, and explain how tests can be extracted by model checking the Hyper-LTL properties. All HyperLTL formulas depend on inputs and outputs of the model, but are model-agnostic otherwise. The idea of all presented formulas is to discriminate between traces of the original model ($\square\neg\mathrm{mut}_\pi$) and traces of the mutant ($\square\mathrm{mut}_\pi$). Furthermore, we quantify over pairs (π, π') of traces with globally equal inputs ($\square\bigwedge_{i\in\mathrm{AP}_\mathcal{I}} i_\pi \leftrightarrow i_{\pi'}$) and express that such pairs will eventually have different outputs ($\lozenge\bigvee_{o\in\mathrm{AP}_\mathcal{O}} \neg(o_\pi \leftrightarrow o_{\pi'})$).

4.1   Deterministic Case

To express killability (potential and definite) of a deterministic model and mutant, we need to find a trace of the model ($\exists\pi$) such that the trace of the mutant with the same inputs ($\exists\pi'$) eventually diverges in outputs, formalized by ϕ_1 as follows:

$$\phi_1(\mathcal{I}, \mathcal{O}) := \exists\pi\exists\pi'\square(\neg\mathrm{mut}_\pi \wedge \mathrm{mut}_{\pi'} \bigwedge_{i\in\mathrm{AP}_\mathcal{I}} i_\pi \leftrightarrow i_{\pi'}) \wedge \lozenge(\bigvee_{o\in\mathrm{AP}_\mathcal{O}} \neg(o_\pi \leftrightarrow o_{\pi'}))$$

Proposition 2. *For a deterministic model $\mathcal{S}$ and mutant $\mathcal{S}^m$ it holds that*

$$\mathcal{S}^{c(m)} \models \phi_1(\mathcal{I}, \mathcal{O}) \text{ iff } \mathcal{S}^m \text{ is killable.}$$

If t is a π-witness for $\mathcal{S}^{c(m)} \models \phi_1(\mathcal{I}, \mathcal{O})$, then $t[0, n]|_{\mathcal{I} \cup \mathcal{O}}$ kills $\mathcal{S}^m$ (for some $n \in \mathbb{N}$).

4.2 Non-deterministic Case

For potential killability of non-deterministic models and mutants,[2] we need to find a trace of the mutant ($\exists \pi$) such that all traces of the model with the same inputs ($\forall \pi'$) eventually diverge in outputs, expressed in ϕ_2:

$$\phi_2(\mathcal{I}, \mathcal{O}) := \exists \pi \forall \pi' \Box (\text{mut}_\pi \wedge \neg \text{mut}_{\pi'} \bigwedge_{i \in \text{AP}_\mathcal{I}} i_\pi \leftrightarrow i_{\pi'}) \to \Diamond (\bigvee_{o \in \text{AP}_\mathcal{O}} \neg (o_\pi \leftrightarrow o_{\pi'}))$$

Proposition 3. *For non-deterministic $\mathcal{S}$ and $\mathcal{S}^m$, it holds that*

$$\mathcal{S}^{c(m)} \models \phi_2(\mathcal{I}, \mathcal{O}) \text{ iff } \mathcal{S}^m \text{ is potentially killable.}$$

If s is a π-witness for $\mathcal{S}^{c(m)} \models \phi_2(\mathcal{I}, \mathcal{O})$, then for any trace $t \in \mathcal{T}(\mathcal{S})$ with $t|_\mathcal{I} = s|_\mathcal{I}$, $t[0, n]|_{\mathcal{I} \cup \mathcal{O}}$ potentially kills $\mathcal{S}^m$ (for some $n \in \mathbb{N}$).

To express definite killability, we need to find a sequence of inputs of the model ($\exists \pi$) and compare all non-deterministic outcomes of the model ($\forall \pi'$) to all non-deterministic outcomes of the mutant ($\forall \pi''$) for these inputs, as formalized by ϕ_3:

$$\phi_3(\mathcal{I}, \mathcal{O}) := \exists \pi \forall \pi' \forall \pi'' \Box (\neg \text{mut}_\pi \wedge \text{mut}_{\pi'} \wedge \neg \text{mut}_{\pi''} \wedge$$
$$\bigwedge_{i \in \text{AP}_\mathcal{I}} i_\pi \leftrightarrow i_{\pi'} \wedge i_\pi \leftrightarrow i_{\pi''}) \to \Diamond (\bigvee_{o \in \text{AP}_\mathcal{O}} \neg (o_{\pi'} \leftrightarrow o_{\pi''}))$$

In Fig. 1b, we present an instance of ϕ_3 for our running example.

Proposition 4. *For non-deterministic $\mathcal{S}$ and $\mathcal{S}^m$, it holds that*

$$\mathcal{S}^{c(m)} \models \phi_3(\mathcal{I}, \mathcal{O}) \text{ iff } \mathcal{S}^m \text{ is definitely killable.}$$

If t is a π-witness for $\mathcal{S}^{c(m)} \models \phi_3(\mathcal{I}, \mathcal{O})$, then $t[0, n]|_{\mathcal{I} \cup \mathcal{O}}$ definitely kills $\mathcal{S}^m$ (for some $n \in \mathbb{N}$).

To generate tests, we use model checking to verify whether the conditional mutant satisfies the appropriate HyperLTL formula presented above and obtain test cases as finite prefixes of witnesses for satisfaction.

---

[2] The Appendix of [16] covers deterministic models with non-deterministic mutants and vice-versa.

5 Non-deterministic Models in Practice

As stated above, checking the validity of the hyperproperties in Sect. 4 for a given model and mutant enables test-case generation. To the best of our knowledge, MCHYPER [18] is the only currently available HyperLTL model checker. Unfortunately, MCHYPER is unable to model check formulas with alternating quantifiers.[3] Therefore, we are currently limited to checking $\phi_1(\mathcal{I}, \mathcal{O})$ for deterministic models, since witnesses of ϕ_1 may not satisfy ϕ_2 in the presence of non-determinism.

To remedy this issue, we propose a transformation that makes non-determinism *controllable* by means of additional inputs and yields a deterministic STS. The transformed model over-approximates killability in the sense that the resulting test cases only kill the original mutant if non-determinism can also be controlled in the system under test. However, if equivalence can be established for the transformed model, then the original non-deterministic mutant is also equivalent.

5.1 Controlling Non-determinism in STS

The essential idea of our transformation is to introduce a fresh input variable that enables the control of non-deterministic choices in the conditional mutant $\mathcal{S}^{c(m)}$. The new input is used carefully to ensure that choices are consistent for the model and the mutant encoded in $\mathcal{S}^{c(m)}$. W.l.o.g., we introduce an input variable nd with a domain sufficiently large to encode the non-deterministic choices in $\alpha^{c(m)}$ and $\delta^{c(m)}$, and write $nd(X, O)$ to denote a value of nd that uniquely corresponds to state X with output O. Moreover, we add a fresh Boolean variable x^τ to $\mathcal{X}$ used to encode a fresh initial state.

Let $\mathcal{X}_+ \overset{\text{def}}{=} \mathcal{X} \cup \{\text{mut}\}$ and X_+, X'_+, I, O be valuations of $\mathcal{X}_+$, $\mathcal{X}'_+$, $\mathcal{I}$, and $\mathcal{O}$, and X and X' denote $X_+|_{\mathcal{X}}$ and $X'_+|_{\mathcal{X}'}$, respectively. Furthermore, $\psi(X)$, $\psi(X_+, I)$, and $\psi(O, X'_+)$ are formulas uniquely satisfied by X, (X_+, I), and (O, X'_+) respectively.

Given conditional mutant $\mathcal{S}^{c(m)} \overset{\text{def}}{=} \langle \mathcal{I}, \mathcal{O}, \mathcal{X}_+, \alpha^{c(m)}, \delta^{c(m)} \rangle$, we define its controllable counterpart $D(\mathcal{S}^{c(m)}) \overset{\text{def}}{=} \langle \mathcal{I} \cup \{nd\}, \mathcal{O}, \mathcal{X}_+ \cup \{x^\tau\}, D(\alpha^{c(m)}), D(\delta^{c(m)}) \rangle$. We initialize $D(\delta^{c(m)}) \overset{\text{def}}{=} \delta^{c(m)}$ and incrementally add constraints as described below.

Non-deterministic Initial Conditions. Let X be an arbitrary, fixed state. The unique fresh initial state is $X^\tau \overset{\text{def}}{=} X[x^\tau]$, which, together with an empty output, we enforce by the new initial conditions predicate:

$$D(\alpha^{c(m)}) \overset{\text{def}}{=} \psi(X^\tau, O_\varepsilon)$$

We add the conjunct $\neg\psi(X^\tau) \rightarrow \neg x^{\tau\prime}$ to $D(\delta^{c(m)})$, in order to force x^τ evaluating to $\bot$ in all states other than X^τ. In addition, we add transitions

---

[3] While *satisfiability* in the presence of quantifier alternation is supported to some extent [17].

from X^τ to all pairs of initial states/outputs in $\alpha^{c(m)}$. To this end, we first partition the pairs in $\alpha^{c(m)}$ into pairs shared by and exclusive to the model and the mutant:

$$J^\cap \stackrel{\text{def}}{=} \{(O, X_+) \mid X, O \models \alpha^{c(m)}\}$$

$$J^{orig} \stackrel{\text{def}}{=} \{(O, X_+) \mid \neg X_+(\text{mut}) \wedge (X_+, O \models \alpha^{c(m)}) \wedge (X_+[\text{mut}], O \not\models \alpha^{c(m)})\}$$

$$J^{mut} \stackrel{\text{def}}{=} \{(O, X_+) \mid X_+(\text{mut}) \wedge (X_+, O \models \alpha^{c(m)}) \wedge (X_+[\neg\text{mut}], O \not\models \alpha^{c(m)})\}$$

For each $(O, X_+) \in J^\cap \cup J^{mut} \cup J^{orig}$, we add the following conjunct to $D(\delta^{c(m)})$:

$$\psi(X^\tau) \wedge nd(O, X) \to \psi(O, X'_+)$$

In addition, for inputs $nd(O, X)$ without corresponding target state in the model or mutant, we add conjuncts to $D(\delta^{c(m)})$ that represent self loops with empty outputs:

$$\forall (O, X_+) \in J^{orig} : \psi(X^\tau[\text{mut}]) \wedge nd(O, X) \to \psi(O_\varepsilon, X^{\tau'}[\text{mut}])$$

$$\forall (O, X_+) \in J^{mut} : \psi(X^\tau[\neg\text{mut}]) \wedge nd(O, X) \to \psi(O_\varepsilon, X^{\tau'}[\neg\text{mut}])$$

Non-deterministic Transitions. Analogous to initial states, for each state/input pair, we partition the successors into successors shared or exclusive to model or mutant:

$$T^\cap_{(X_+, I)} \stackrel{\text{def}}{=} \{(X_+, I, O, X'_+) \mid X \xrightarrow{I, O} X'\}$$

$$T^{orig}_{(X_+, I)} \stackrel{\text{def}}{=} \{(X_+, I, O, X'_+) \mid \neg X_+(\text{mut}) \wedge (X_+ \xrightarrow{I, O} X'_+) \wedge \neg(X_+[\text{mut}] \xrightarrow{I, O} X'_+)\}$$

$$T^{mut}_{(X_+, I)} \stackrel{\text{def}}{=} \{(X_+, I, O, X'_+) \mid X_+(\text{mut}) \wedge (X_+ \xrightarrow{I, O} X'_+) \wedge \neg(X_+[\neg\text{mut}] \xrightarrow{I, O} X'_+)\}$$

A pair (X_+, I) causes non-determinism if

$$|(T^\cap_{(X_+, I)} \cup T^{orig}_{(X_+, I)})|_{\mathcal{X} \cup \mathcal{I} \cup \mathcal{O} \cup \mathcal{X}'}| > 1 \text{ or } |(T^\cap_{(X_+, I)} \cup T^{mut}_{(X_+, I)})|_{\mathcal{X} \cup \mathcal{I} \cup \mathcal{O} \cup \mathcal{X}'}| > 1.$$

For each pair (X_+, I) that causes non-determinism and each $(X_+, I, O_j, X'_{+j}) \in T^\cap_{(X_+, I)} \cup T^{mut}_{(X_+, I)} \cup T^{orig}_{(X_+, I)}$, we add the following conjunct to $D(\delta^{c(m)})$:

$$\psi(X_+, I) \wedge nd(O_j, X_j) \to \psi(O_j, X'_{+j})$$

Finally, we add conjuncts representing self loops with empty output for inputs that have no corresponding transition in the model or mutant:

$$\forall (X_+, I, O_j, X'_{+j}) \in T^{orig}_{(X_+, I)} : \psi(X_+[\text{mut}], I) \wedge nd(O_j, X_j) \to \psi(O_\varepsilon, X'_{+j}[\text{mut}])$$

$$\forall (X_+, I, O_j, X'_{+j}) \in T^{mut}_{(X_+, I)} : \psi(X_+[\neg\text{mut}], I) \wedge nd(O_j, X_j) \to \psi(O_\varepsilon, X'_{+j}[\neg\text{mut}])$$

The proposed transformation has the following properties:

Proposition 5. *Let S be a model with inputs $\mathcal{I}$, outputs $\mathcal{O}$, and mutant S^m then*

1. $D(S^{c(m)})$ *is deterministic (up to* mut*).*
2. $T(S^{c(m)})|_{\mathcal{X}_+ \cup \mathcal{I} \cup \mathcal{O}} \subseteq T(D(S^{c(m)}))[1, \infty]|_{\mathcal{X}_+ \cup \mathcal{I} \cup \mathcal{O}}.$
3. $D(S^{c(m)}) \not\models \phi_1(\mathcal{I}, \mathcal{O})$ *then* S^m *is equivalent.*

The transformed model is deterministic, since we enforce unique initial valuations and make non-deterministic transitions controllable through input nd. Since we only add transitions or augment existing transitions with input nd, every transition $X \xrightarrow{I,O} X'$ of $S^{c(m)}$ is still present in $D(S^{c(m)})$ (when input nd is disregarded). The potential additional traces of Item 2 originate from the O_ε-labeled transitions for non-deterministic choices present exclusively in the model or mutant. These transitions enable the detection of discrepancies between model and mutant caused by the introduction or elimination of non-determinism by the mutation.

For Item 3 (which is a direct consequence of Item 2), assume that the original non-deterministic mutant is not equivalent (i.e., potentially killable). Then $D(S^{c(m)}) \models \phi_1(\mathcal{I}, \mathcal{O})$, and the corresponding witness yields a test which kills the mutant assuming non-determinism can be controlled in the system under test. Killability purported by ϕ_1, however, could be an artifact of the transformation: determinization potentially deprives the model of its ability to match the output of the mutant by deliberately choosing a certain non-deterministic transition. In Example 2, we present an equivalent mutant which is killable after the transformation, since we will detect the deviating output tea of the model and ε of the mutant. Therefore, our transformation merely allows us to provide a lower bound for the number of equivalent non-deterministic mutants.

5.2 Controlling Non-determinism in Modeling Languages

The exhaustive enumeration of states (J) and transitions (T) outlined in Sect. 5.1 is purely theoretical and infeasible in practice. However, an analogous result can often be achieved by modifying the syntactic constructs of the underlying modeling language that introduce non-determinism, namely:

- *Non-deterministic assignments.* Non-deterministic choice over a finite set of elements $\{x'_1, \ldots x'_n\}$, as provided by SMV [25], can readily be converted into a case-switch construct over nd. More generally, explicit non-deterministic assignments x := ⋆ to state variables x [26] can be controlled by assigning the value of nd to x.
- *Non-deterministic schedulers.* Non-determinism introduced by concurrency can be controlled by introducing input variables that control the scheduler (as proposed in [23] for bounded context switches).

In case non-determinism arises through variables under-specified in transition relations, these variable values can be made inputs as suggested by Sect. 5.1. In general, however, identifying under-specified variables automatically is non-trivial.

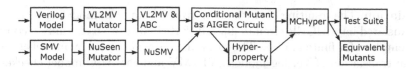

Fig. 2. Tool pipeline of our experiments

Example 3. Consider again the SMV code in Fig. 1a, for which non-determinism can be made controllable by replacing line `if(in=req&wtr>0):{coff,tea}` with lines `if(nd=0&in=req&wtr>0):coff,elif(nd=1&in=req&wtr>0):tea` and adding `init(nd):={0,1}`.

Similarly, the STS representation of the beverage machine, given in Example 1, can be transformed by replacing the first two rules by the following two rules:

$$nd=0 \wedge wtr>0 \wedge in=req \wedge out=coff \wedge wtr'=wtr-1 \vee$$
$$nd=1 \wedge wtr>0 \wedge in=req \wedge out=tea \wedge wtr'=wtr-1 \vee$$

6 Experiments

In this section, we present an experimental evaluation of the presented methods. We start by presenting the deployed tool-chain. Thereafter, we present a validation of our method on one case study with another model-based mutation testing tool. Finally, we present quantitative results on a broad range of generic models.

6.1 Toolchain

Figure 2 shows the toolchain that we use to produce test suites for models encoded in the modeling languages Verilog and SMV. Verilog models are deterministic while SMV models can be non-deterministic.

Variable Annotation. As a first step, we annotate variables as inputs and outputs. These annotations were added manually for Verilog, and heuristically for SMV (partitioning variables into outputs and inputs).

Mutation and Transformation. We produce conditional mutants via a mutation engine. For Verilog, we implemented our own mutation engine into the open source Verilog compiler VL2MV [12]. We use standard mutation operators, replacing arithmetic operators, Boolean relations, Boolean connectives, constants, and assignment operators. The list of mutation operators used for Verilog can be found in the Appendix of [16]. For SMV models, we use the NuSeen SMV framework [5,6], which includes a mutation engine for SMV models. The mutation operators used by NuSeen are documented in [5]. We implemented the transformation presented in Sect. 5 into NuSeen and applied it to conditional mutants.

Translation. The resulting conditional mutants from both modeling formalisms are translated into AIGER circuits [9]. AIGER circuits are essentially a compact representation for finite models. The formalism is widely used by model checkers. For the translation of Verilog models, VL2MV and the ABC model checker are used. For the translation of SMV models, NuSMV is used.

Test Suite Creation. We obtain a test suite, by model checking $\neg\phi_1(\mathcal{I}, \mathcal{O})$ on conditional mutants. Tests are obtained as counter-examples, which are finite prefixes of π-witnesses to $\phi_1(\mathcal{I}, \mathcal{O})$. In case we can not find a counter-example, and use a complete model checking method, the mutant is provably equivalent.

Case Study Test Suite Evaluation. We compare the test suite created with our method for a case study, with the model-based mutation testing tool MoMuT [2,15]. The case study is a timed version of a model of a car alarm system (CAS), which was used in the model-based test case generation literature before [3,4,15].

To this end, we created a test suite for a SMV formulation of the model. We evaluated its strength and correctness on an Action System (the native modeling formalism of MoMuT) formulation of the model. MoMuT evaluated our test suite by computing its mutation score—the ratio of killed- to the total number of- mutants—with respect to Action System mutations, which are described in [15].

This procedure evaluates our test suite in two ways. Firstly, it shows that the tests are well formed, since MoMuT does not reject them. Secondly, it shows that the test suite is able to kill mutants of a different modeling formalism than the one it was created from, which suggests that the test suite is also able to detect faults in implementations.

We created a test suite consisting of 61 tests, mapped it to the test format accepted by MoMuT. MoMuT then measured the mutation score of our translated test suite on the Action System model, using Action System mutants. The measured mutation score is 91% on 439 Action System mutants. In comparison, the test suite achieves a mutation score of 61% on 3057 SMV mutants. Further characteristics of the resulting test suite are presented in the following paragraphs.

Quantitative Experiments. All experiments presented in this section were run in parallel on a machine with an Intel(R) Xeon(R) CPU at 2.00 GHz, 60 cores, and 252 GB RAM. We used 16 Verilog models which are presented in [18], as well as models from opencores.org. Furthermore, we used 76 SMV models that were also used in [5]. Finally, we used the SMV formalism of CAS. All models are available in [1]. Verilog and SMV experiments were run using property driven reachability based model checking with a time limit of 1 h. Property driven reachability based model checking did not perform well for CAS, for which we therefore switched to bounded model checking with a depth limit of 100.

Characteristics of Models. Table 1 present characteristics of the models. For Verilog and SMV, we present average (μ), standard deviation (σ), minimum (Min), and maximum (Max) measures per model of the set of models. For some measurements, we additionally present average (Avg.) or maximum (Max) number over the set of mutants per model. We report the size of the circuits in terms of the number of inputs (#Input), outputs (#Output), state (#State) variables as well as *And* gates (#Gates), which corresponds to the size of the transition relation of the model. Moreover, the row "Avg. Δ # Gates" shows the average size difference (in % of # Gates) of the conditional mutant and the original model, where the average is over all mutants. The last row of the table shows the number of the mutants that are generated for the models.

We can observe that our method is able to handle models of respectable size, reaching thousands of gates. Furthermore, Δ# Gates of the conditional mutants is relatively low. Conditional mutants allow us to compactly encode the original and mutated model in one model. Hyperproperties enable us to refer to and juxtapose traces from the original and mutated model, respectively. Classical temporal logic does not enable the comparison of different traces. Therefore, mutation analysis by model checking classical temporal logic necessitates strictly separating traces of the original and the mutated model, resulting in a quadratic blowup in the size of the input to the classical model-checker, compared to the size of the input to the hyperproperty model-checker.

Table 1. Characteristics of models

Parameters	Verilog				SMV				CAS
	μ	σ	Min	Max	μ	σ	Min	Max	
# Models	16				76				1
# Input	186.19	309.59	4	949	8.99	13.42	0	88	58
# Output	176.75	298.94	7	912	4.49	4.26	1	28	7
# State	15.62	15.56	2	40	-	-	-	-	-
# Gates	4206.81	8309.32	98	25193	189.12	209.59	7	1015	1409
Avg. Δ # Gates	3.98%	14.71%	-10.2%	57.55%	8.14%	8.23%	0.22%	35.36%	0.86%
# Mutants	260.38	235.65	43	774	535.32	1042.11	1	6304	3057

Model Checking Results. Table 2 summarizes the quantitative results of our experiments. The quantitative metrics we use for evaluating our test generation approach are the mutation score (i.e. percentage of killed mutants) and the percentage of equivalent mutants, the number of generated tests, the amount of time required for generating them and the average length of the test cases. Furthermore, we show the number of times the resource limit was reached. For Verilog and SMV this was exclusively the 1 h timeout. For CAS this was exclusively the depth limit 100.

Finally, we show the total test suite creation time, including times when reaching the resource limit. The reported time assumes sequential test suite creation time. However, since mutants are model checked independently, the process can easily be parallelized, which drastically reduces the total time needed to create a test suite for a model. The times of the Verilog benchmark suite are dominated by two instances of the secure hashing algorithm (SHA), which are inherently hard cases for model checking.

We can see that the test suite creation times are in the realm of a few hours, which collapses to minutes when model checking instances in parallel. However, the timing measures really say more about the underlying model checking methods than our proposed technique of mutation testing via hyperporperties. Furthermore, we want to stress that our method is agnostic to which variant of model checking (e.g. property driven reachability, or bounded model checking) is used. As discussed above, for CAS switching from one method to the other made a big difference.

The mutation scores average is around 60% for all models. It is interesting to notice that the scores of the Verilog and SMV models are similar on average, although we use a different mutation scheme for the types of models. Again, the mutation score says more about the mutation scheme than our proposed technique. Notice that we can only claim to report the mutation score, because, besides CAS, we used a complete model checking method (property driven reachability). That is, in case, for example, 60% of the mutants were killed and no timeouts occurred, then 40% of the mutants are provably equivalent. In contrast, incomplete methods for mutation analysis can only ever report lower bounds of the mutation score. Furthermore, as discussed above, the 61.7% of CAS translate to 91% mutation score on a different set of mutants. This indicates that failure detection capability of the produced test suites is well, which ultimately can only be measured by deploying the test cases on real systems.

Table 2. Experimental results

Metrics	Verilog				SMV				CAS
	μ	σ	Min	Max	μ	σ	Min	Max	
Mutation score	56.82%	33.1%	4.7%	99%	64.79%	30.65%	0%	100%	61.7 %
Avg. test-case Len	4.26	1.65	2.21	8.05	15.41	58.23	4	461.52	5.92
Max test-case Len	21.62	49.93	3	207	187.38	1278.56	4	10006	9
Avg. runtime	83.08 s	267.53 s	0.01 s	1067.8 s	1.2 s	5.48 s	-	46.8 s	7.8 s
Equivalent mutants	33.21%	32.47%	0%	95.3%	35.21%	30.65%	0%	100%	0%
Avg. runtime	44.77 s	119.58 s	0s	352.2 s	0.7 s	2.02 s	-	14.9 s	-
# Resource limit	9.96%	27.06%	0%	86.17%	3.8%	19.24%	0%	100%	38.34 %
Total runtime	68.58 h	168.62 h	0 h	620.18 h	0.4 h	1.19 h	0 h	6.79 h	1.15 h

7   Related Work

A number of test case generation techniques are based on model checking; a survey is provided in [19]. Many of these techniques (such as [21,28,30]) differ in abstraction levels and/or coverage goals from our approach.

Model checking based mutation testing using trap properties is presented in [20]. Trap properties are conditions that, if satisfied, indicate a killed mutant. In contrast, our approach directly targets the input/output behavior of the model and does not require to formulate model specific trap properties.

Mutation based test case generation via module checking is proposed in [10]. The theoretical framework of this work is similar to ours, but builds on module checking instead of hyperproperties. Moreover, no experimental evaluation is given in this work.

The authors of [4] present mutation killing using SMT solving. In this work, the model, as well as killing conditions, are encoded into a SMT formula and solved using specialized algorithms. Similarly, the MuAlloy [31] framework enables model-based mutation testing for Alloy models using SAT solving. In this work, the model, as well as killing conditions, are encoded into a SAT formula and solved using the Alloy framework. In contrast to these approaches, we encode only the killing conditions into a formula. This allows us to directly use model checking techniques, in contrast to SAT or SMT solving. Therefore, our approach is more flexible and more likely to be applicable in other domains. We demonstrate this by producing test cases for models encoded in two different modeling languages.

Symbolic methods for weak mutation coverage are proposed in [8] and [7]. The former work describes the use of dynamic symbolic execution for weakly killing mutants. The latter work describes a sound and incomplete method for detecting equivalent weak mutants. The considered coverage criterion in both works is weak mutation, which, unlike the strong mutation coverage criterion considered in this work, can be encoded as a classic safety property. However, both methods could be used in conjunction with our method. Dynamic symbolic execution could be used to first weakly kill mutants and thereafter strongly kill them via hyperproperty model checking. Equivalent weak mutants can be detected with the methods of [7] to prune the candidate space of potentially strongly killable mutants for hyperpropery model checking.

A unified framework for defining multiple coverage criteria, including weak mutation and hyperproperties such as unique-cause MCDC, is proposed in [24]. While strong mutation is not expressible in this framework, applying hyperproperty model checking to the proposed framework is interesting future work.

8   Conclusion

Our formalization of mutation testing in terms of hyperproperties enables the automated model-based generation of tests using an off-the-shelf model checker. In particular, we study killing of mutants in the presence of non-determinism, where test-case generation is enabled by a transformation that makes non-determinism in models explicit and controllable. We evaluated our approach on publicly available SMV and Verilog models, and will extend our evaluation to more modeling languages and models in future work.

References

1. Mutation testing with hyperproperies benchmark models. https://git-service. ait.ac.at/sct-dse-public/mutation-testing-with-hyperproperties. Accessed 25 Apr 2019
2. Aichernig, B., Brandl, H., Jöbstl, E., Krenn, W., Schlick, R., Tiran, S.: MoMuT::UML model-based mutation testing for UML. In: 2015 IEEE 8th International Conference on Software Testing, Verification and Validation (ICST), ICST, pp. 1–8, April 2015
3. Aichernig, B.K., Brandl, H., Jöbstl, E., Krenn, W., Schlick, R., Tiran, S.: Killing strategies for model-based mutation testing. Softw. Test. Verif. Reliab. **25**(8), 716–748 (2015)
4. Aichernig, B.K., Jöbstl, E., Tiran, S.: Model-based mutation testing via symbolic refinement checking (2014)
5. Arcaini, P., Gargantini, A., Riccobene, E.: Using mutation to assess fault detection capability of model review. Softw. Test. Verif. Reliab. **25**(5–7), 629–652 (2015)
6. Arcaini, P., Gargantini, A., Riccobene, E.: NuSeen: a tool framework for the NuSMV model checker. In: 2017 IEEE International Conference on Software Testing, Verification and Validation, ICST 2017, Tokyo, Japan, 13–17 March 2017, pp. 476–483. IEEE Computer Society (2017)
7. Bardin, S., et al.: Sound and quasi-complete detection of infeasible test requirements. In: 8th IEEE International Conference on Software Testing, Verification and Validation, ICST 2015, Graz, Austria, 13–17 April 2015, pp. 1–10 (2015)
8. Bardin, S., Kosmatov, N., Cheynier, F.: Efficient leveraging of symbolic execution to advanced coverage criteria. In: Seventh IEEE International Conference on Software Testing, Verification and Validation, ICST 2014, Cleveland, Ohio, USA, 31 March 2014–4 April 2014, pp. 173–182 (2014)
9. Biere, A., Heljanko, K., Wieringa, S.: AIGER 1.9 and beyond (2011). fmv.jku.at/hwmcc11/beyond1.pdf
10. Boroday, S., Petrenko, A., Groz, R.: Can a model checker generate tests for nondeterministic systems? Electron. Notes Theor. Comput. Sci. **190**(2), 3–19 (2007)
11. Budd, T.A., Lipton, R.J., DeMillo, R.A., Sayward, F.G.: Mutation analysis. Technical report, DTIC Document (1979)
12. Cheng, S.-T., York, G., Brayton, R.K.: VL2MV: a compiler from verilog to BLIF-MV. HSIS Distribution (1993)
13. Clarkson, M.R., Finkbeiner, B., Koleini, M., Micinski, K.K., Rabe, M.N., Sánchez, C.: Temporal logics for hyperproperties. In: Abadi, M., Kremer, S. (eds.) POST 2014. LNCS, vol. 8414, pp. 265–284. Springer, Heidelberg (2014). https://doi.org/10.1007/978-3-642-54792-8_15
14. Clarkson, M.R., Schneider, F.B.: Hyperproperties. J. Comput. Secur. **18**(6), 1157–1210 (2010)
15. Fellner, A., Krenn, W., Schlick, R., Tarrach, T., Weissenbacher, G.: Model-based, mutation-driven test case generation via heuristic-guided branching search. In: Talpin, J.-P., Derler, P., Schneider, K. (eds.) Formal Methods and Models for System Design (MEMOCODE), pp. 56–66. ACM (2017)
16. Fellner, A., Befrouei, M.T., Weissenbacher, G.: Mutation Testing with Hyperproperties. arXiv e-prints, page arXiv:1907.07368, July 2019
17. Finkbeiner, B., Hahn, C., Hans, T.: MGHyper: checking satisfiability of HyperLTL formulas beyond the $\exists^*\forall^*$ fragment. In: Lahiri, S.K., Wang, C. (eds.) ATVA 2018. LNCS, vol. 11138, pp. 521–527. Springer, Cham (2018). https://doi.org/10.1007/978-3-030-01090-4_31

18. Finkbeiner, B., Rabe, M.N., Sánchez, C.: Algorithms for model checking Hyper-LTL and HyperCTL*. In: Kroening, D., Păsăreanu, C.S. (eds.) CAV 2015. LNCS, vol. 9206, pp. 30–48. Springer, Cham (2015). https://doi.org/10.1007/978-3-319-21690-4_3

19. Fraser, G., Wotawa, F., Ammann, P.E.: Testing with model checkers: a survey. Softw. Test. Verification Reliab. **19**(3), 215–261 (2009)

20. Gargantini, A., Heitmeyer, C.: Using model checking to generate tests from requirements specifications. In: Gargantini, A., Heitmeyer, C. (eds.) ACM SIGSOFT Software Engineering Notes, vol. 24, pp. 146–162. Springer, Heidelberg (1999). https://doi.org/10.1145/318774.318939

21. Hong, H.S., Lee, I., Sokolsky, O., Ural, H.: A temporal logic based theory of test coverage and generation. In: Katoen, J.-P., Stevens, P. (eds.) TACAS 2002. LNCS, vol. 2280, pp. 327–341. Springer, Heidelberg (2002). https://doi.org/10.1007/3-540-46002-0_23

22. Howden, W.E.: Weak mutation testing and completeness of test sets. IEEE Trans. Softw. Eng. **8**(4), 371–379 (1982)

23. Lal, A., Reps, T.: Reducing concurrent analysis under a context bound to sequential analysis. Formal Methods Syst. Des. **35**(1), 73–97 (2009)

24. Marcozzi, M., Delahaye, M., Bardin, S., Kosmatov, N., Prevosto, V.: Generic and effective specification of structural test objectives. In: 2017 IEEE International Conference on Software Testing, Verification and Validation, ICST 2017, Tokyo, Japan, 13–17 March 2017, pp. 436–441 (2017)

25. McMillan, K.L.: The SMV system. Technical report, CMU-CS-92-131, Carnegie Mellon University (1992)

26. Nelson, G.: A generalization of Dijkstra's calculus. ACM Trans. Program. Lang. Syst. (TOPLAS) **11**(4), 517–561 (1989)

27. Offutt, A.J.: Investigations of the software testing coupling effect. ACM Trans. Softw. Eng. Methodol. 1(1), 5–20 (1992)

28. Rayadurgam, S., Heimdahl, M.P.E.: Coverage based test-case generation using model checkers. In: Engineering of Computer Based Systems (ECBS), pp. 83–91. IEEE (2001)

29. Tretmans, J.: Test generation with inputs, outputs and repetitive quiescence. Softw.-Concepts Tools **17**(3), 103–120 (1996)

30. Visser, W., Păsăreanu, C.S., Khurshid, S.: Test input generation with Java pathfinder. ACM SIGSOFT Softw. Eng. Notes **29**(4), 97–107 (2004)

31. Wang, K., Sullivan, A., Khurshid, S.: Mualloy: a mutation testing framework for alloy. In: International Conference on Software Engineering: Companion (ICSE-Companion), pp. 29–32. IEEE (2018)

Test Model Coverage Analysis
Under Uncertainty

I. S. W. B. Prasetya$^{(\boxtimes)}$ ⓘ and Rick Klomp

Utrecht University, Utrecht, The Netherlands
s.w.b.prasetya@uu.nl

Abstract. In model-based testing (MBT) we may have to deal with a
non-deterministic model, e.g. because abstraction was applied, or because
the software under test itself is non-deterministic. The same test case may
then trigger multiple possible execution paths, depending on some internal decisions made by the software. Consequently, performing precise test
analyses, e.g. to calculate the test coverage, are not possible. This can be
mitigated if developers can annotate the model with estimated probabilities for taking each transition. A probabilistic model checking algorithm
can subsequently be used to do simple probabilistic coverage analysis.
However, in practice developers often want to know what the achieved
aggregate coverage is, which unfortunately cannot be re-expressed as a
standard model checking problem. This paper presents an extension to
allow efficient calculation of probabilistic aggregate coverage, and moreover also in combination with k-wise coverage.

Keywords: Probabilistic model based testing ·
Probabilistic test coverage · Testing non-deterministic systems

1 Introduction

Model based testing (MBT) is considered as one of the leading technologies for
systematic testing of software [5,6,17]. It has been used to test different kinds
of software, e.g. communication protocols, web applications, and automotive
control systems. In this approach, a model describing the intended behavior of
the system under test (SUT) is first constructed [27], and then used to guide
the tester, or a testing algorithm, to systematically explore and test the SUT's
states. Various automated MBT tools are available, e.g. JTorX [4,26], Phact
[11], OSMO [14], APSL [24], and RT-Tester [17].

There are situations where we end up with a non-deterministic model [13,17,
23], for example when the non-determinism within the system under test, e.g.
due to internal concurrency, interactions with an uncontrollable environment
(e.g. as in cyber physical systems), or use of AI, leads to observable effects at
the model level. Non-determinism can also be introduced as byproduct when
we apply abstraction on an otherwise too large model [20]. Models mined from

© Springer Nature Switzerland AG 2019
P. C. Ölveczky and G. Salaün (Eds.): SEFM 2019, LNCS 11724, pp. 222–239, 2019.
https://doi.org/10.1007/978-3-030-30446-1_12

executions logs [7,21,28] can also be non-deterministic, because log files only provide very limited information about a system's states.

MBT with a non-deterministic model is more challenging. The tester cannot fully control how the SUT would traverse the model, and cannot thus precisely determine the current state of the SUT. Obviously, this makes the task of deciding which trigger to send next to the SUT harder. Additionally, coverage, e.g. in terms of which states in the model have been visited by a series of tests, cannot be determined with 100% certainty either. This paper will focus on addressing the latter problem—readers interested in test cases generation from non-deterministic models are referred to e.g. [13,16,25]. Rather than just saying that a test sequence *may* cover some given state, we propose to *calculate the probability* of covering a given coverage goal, given modelers' estimation on the local probability of each non-deterministic choice in a model.

Given a probabilistic model of the SUT, e.g. in the form of a Markov Decision Process (MDP) [3,22], and a test σ in the form of a sequence of interactions on the SUT, the most elementary type of coverage goal in MBT is for σ to cover some given state s of interest in the model. Calculating the probability that this actually happens is an instance of the probabilistic reachability problem which can be answered using e.g. a probabilistic model checker [3,10,15]. However, in practice coverage goals are typically formulated in an 'aggregate' form, e.g. to cover at least 80% of the states, without being selective on which states to include. Additionally, we may want to know the aggregate coverage over pairs of states (the transitions in the LTS), or vectors of states, as in k-wise coverage [1], as different research showed that k-wise greatly increases the fault finding potential of a test suite [9,18]. Aggregate goals cannot be expressed in LTL or CTL, which are the typical formalisms in model checking. Furthermore, both types of goals (aggregate and k-wise) may lead to combinatorial explosion.

This paper **contributes:** (1) a concept and definition of probabilistic test coverage; as far as we know this has not been covered in the literature before, and (2) an algorithm to calculate probabilistic coverage, in particular of aggregate k-wise coverage goals.

Paper Structure. Section 2 introduces relevant basic concepts. Section 3 introduces the kind of coverage goals we want to be able to express and how their probabilistic coverage can be calculated. Section 4 presents our algorithm for efficient coverage calculation. Section 5 shows the results of our benchmarking. Related work is discussed in Sect. 6. Section 7 concludes.

2 Preliminary: Probabilistic Models and Simple Coverage

As a running example, consider the labelled transition system (LTS) [2] in Fig. 1 as a model of some SUT. The transitions are labelled with actions, e.g. a and b. A non-τ action represents an interaction between the SUT and its environment. In our set up such an action is assumed to occur *synchronously* a la CSP [12] (for an action a to take place, both the SUT and the environment first need to agree on doing a; then they will do a together). The action τ represents an internal action by the SUT, that is not visible to the environment.

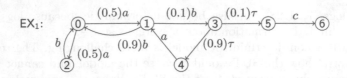

Fig. 1. An example of a probabilistic model of some SUT called EX_1.

To test the SUT, the tester controls the SUT by insisting on which action it wants to synchronize; e.g. if on the state t the SUT is supposed to be able to either do a or b, the tester can insist on doing a. If the SUT fails to go along with this, it is an error. The tester can also test if in this state the SUT can be coerced to do an action that it is not supposed to synchronize; if so, the SUT is incorrect. We will assume a black box setup. That is, the tester cannot actually see the SUT's state, though tester can try to infer this based on information visible to him, e.g. the trace of the external actions done so far. For example after doing a from the state 0 on the SUT EX_1 above, the tester cannot tell whether it then goes to the state 1 or 2. However, if the tester manages to do abc he would on the hind sight know that the state after a must have been 1.

When a state s has multiple outgoing transitions with the same label, e.g. a, this implies non-determinism, since the environment cannot control which a the SUT will take (the environment can only control whether or not it wants to do a). We assume the modeler is able estimate the probability of taking each of these a-transitions and annotate this on each of them. E.g. in Fig. 1 we see that in state 1, two a-transitions are possible, leading to different states, each with the probability of 0.5. Similarly, in state 3 there are two τ-transitions leading to states 4 and 5, with the probability of 0.9 and 0.1 respectively. A probabilistic model such as in Fig. 1 is also called a Markov Decision Process (MDP) [3].

Let M be an MDP model, with finite number of transitions, and a single initial state. Let s, t be states, and a an action. We write $s \in M$ to mean that s is a state in M. The notation $s \xrightarrow{a} t$ denotes a transition that goes from the state s to t and is labelled with a. We write $s \xrightarrow{a} t \in M$ to mean that $s \xrightarrow{a} t$ is a transition in M. $P_M(s \xrightarrow{a} t)$ denotes the probability that M will take this particular transition when it synchronizes over a on the state s.

To simplify calculation over non-deterministic actions, we will assume that M is τ-*normalized* in the following sense. First, a state cannot have a mix of τ and non-τ outgoing transitions. E.g. a state s with two transitions $\{s \xrightarrow{\tau} t, s \xrightarrow{a} u\}$ should first be re-modelled as $\{s \xrightarrow{\tau} t, s \xrightarrow{\tau} s', s' \xrightarrow{a} u\}$ by introducing an intermediate state s', and the modeler should provide estimation on the probability of taking each of the two τ transitions. Second, M should have no state whose all incoming and outgoing transitions are τ transitions. Such a state is considered not interesting for our analyses. Third, M should not contain a cycle that consists of only τ transitions. In a τ-normalized model, non-determinism can only be introduced if there is a state s with multiple outgoing transitions labelled by the same action (which can be τ).

We define an *execution* of the SUT as a finite path ρ through the model starting from its initial state. A *trace* is a finite sequence of external actions.

The trace of ρ, $\mathsf{tr}(\rho)$, is the sequence external actions induced by ρ. A *legal trace* is a trace that can be produced by some execution of the SUT. A *test-case* is abstractly modeled by a trace. We will restrict to test-cases that form legal traces, e.g. *ab*, *aba*, and *ababc* are test cases for Ex1 in Fig. 1. Negative tests can be expressed as legal traces by adding transitions to an error state. A set of test cases is also called a *test suite*.

Since the model can be non-deterministic, the same test case may trigger multiple possible executions which are indistinguishable from their trace. If σ is a trace, $\mathsf{exec}(\sigma)$ denotes the set of all executions ρ such that $\mathsf{tr}(\rho) = \sigma$, and moreover is τ-maximal: it cannot be extended without breaking the property $\mathsf{tr}(\rho) = \sigma$. Assuming τ-maximality avoids having to reason about the probability that ρ, after being observed as σ, is delayed in completing its final τ transitions.

2.1 Representing a Test Case: Execution Model

The probability that a test case σ covers some goal ϕ (e.g. a particular state s) can in principle be calculated by quantifying over $\mathsf{exec}(\sigma)$. However, if M is highly non-deterministic, the size of $\mathsf{exec}(\sigma)$ can be exponential with respect to the length of σ. To facilitate more efficient coverage calculation we will represent σ with the subgraph of M that σ induces, called the *execution model* of σ, denoted by $\mathsf{E}(\sigma)$. $\mathsf{E}(\sigma)$ forms a Markov chain; each branch in $\mathsf{E}(\sigma)$ is annotated with the probability of taking the branch, under the premise that σ has been observed. Since a test case is always of finite length and M is assumed to have no τ-cycle, $\mathsf{E}(\sigma)$ is always acyclic. Typically the size of $\mathsf{E}(\sigma)$ (its number of nodes) is much less than the size of $\mathsf{exec}(\sigma)$. For example, the execution model of the test case *aba* on EX_1 is shown in Fig. 2. An artificial state denoted with $\sharp$ is added so that $\mathsf{E}(\sigma)$ has a single exit node, which is convenient for later.

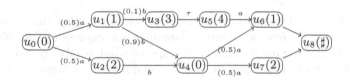

Fig. 2. The execution model of the test case *aba* on EX_1.

To identify the states in $\mathsf{E}(\sigma)$ we assign IDs to them ($u_0...u_8$ in Fig. 2). We write $u.\mathsf{st}$ to denote u's state label, which is the ID of a state in M that u represents (so, $u.\mathsf{st} \in M$); in Fig. 2 this is denoted by the number between brackets in every node.

Importantly, notice that the probability of the transitions in $\mathsf{E}(\sigma)$ may be different than the original probability in M. For example, the transition $u_3 \xrightarrow{\tau} u_5$ in the above execution model has probability 1.0, whereas in the original model EX_1 this corresponds to the transition $3 \xrightarrow{\tau} 4$ whose probability is 0.9. This is because the alternative $3 \xrightarrow{\tau} 5$ could not have taken place, as it leads to an execution whose trace does not correspond to the test case *aba* (which is assumed to have happened).

More precisely, when an execution in the model $E(\sigma)$ reaches a node u, the probability of extending this execution with the transition $u\xrightarrow{\alpha}v$ can be calculated by taking the conditional probability of the corresponding transition in the model M, given that only the outgoing transitions specified by $E(\sigma)$ could happen. So, $P_{E(\sigma)}(u\xrightarrow{\alpha}v)$ is $P_M(u.\text{st}\xrightarrow{\alpha}v.\text{st})$ divided by the the sum of $P_M(u.\text{st}\xrightarrow{\alpha}w.\text{st})$ of all w such that $u\xrightarrow{\alpha}w \in E(\sigma)$.

Let $E = E(\sigma)$. Since E is thus acyclic, the probability that SUT traverses a path/execution ρ in $E(\sigma)$ when it is given σ can be obtained by multiplying the probability of all the transitions in the path:

$$P_E(\rho) = \prod_{s\xrightarrow{\alpha}t\in\rho} P_E(s\xrightarrow{\alpha}t) \tag{1}$$

Simple Coverage Analyses. As an example of a simple analysis, let's calculate the probability that a test case σ produces an execution that passes through a given state s, denoted by $P(\langle s\rangle \mid \sigma)$. This would then just be the sum of the probability of all full executions in $E(\sigma)$ that contain s. So:

$$P(\langle s\rangle \mid \sigma) = \sum_{\rho \text{ s.t. } \rho\in E(\sigma)\wedge s\in\rho} P_{E(\sigma)}(\rho) \tag{2}$$

For example, on the execution model EX_1, $P(\langle 1\rangle \mid aba) = 0.525$, $P(\langle 2\rangle \mid aba) = 0.475$, $P(\langle 4\rangle \mid aba) = 0.05$, whereas $P(\langle 5\rangle \mid aba) = 0$.

3   Coverage Under Uncertainty

Coverage goals posed in practice are however more complex than goals exemplified above. Let us first introduce a language for expressing 'goals'; we will keep it simple, but expressive enough to express what is later called 'aggregate k-wise' goals. A goal of the form $\langle 0, 2, 0\rangle$ is called a *word*, expressing an intent to cover the subpath $\langle 0, 2, 0\rangle$ in the MDP model. We will also allow disjunctions of words and sequences of words (called *sentences*) to appear as goals. For example: $(\langle 0, 2\rangle \vee \langle 1, 0\rangle)$; $\langle 1\rangle$ formulates a goal to first cover the edge $0\rightarrow 2$ or $1\rightarrow 0$, and then (not necessarily immediately) the node 1.

The typical goal people have in practice is to cover at least $p\%$ of the states. This is called an *aggregate goal*. We write this a bit differently: a goal of the form $^1\geq N$ expresses an intent to cover at least N different states. Covering at least $p\%$ can be expressed as $^1\geq \lfloor p * K/100\rfloor$ where K is the number of states in the model. To calculate probabilistic coverage in k-wise testing [1], the goal $^k\geq N$ expresses an intent to cover at least N different words of length k. Formally:

Definition 1. *A coverage goal is a formula ϕ with this syntax:*

$$
\begin{array}{lll}
\phi & ::= S \mid A & \textit{(goal)} \\
S & ::= C \mid C; S & \textit{(sentence)} \\
A & ::= {}^{k}\!\geq N & \textit{(aggregate goal), with } k \geq 1 \\
C & ::= W \mid W \vee C & \textit{(clause)} \\
W & ::= \langle s_0, ..., s_{k-1} \rangle & \textit{(word), with } k \geq 1
\end{array}
$$

A sentence is a sequence $C_0; C_1; ....$ Each C_i is called a *clause*, which in turn consists of one or more words. A *word* is denoted by $\langle s_0, s_1, ... \rangle$ and specifies one or more connected states in an MDP.

Let ρ be an execution. If ϕ is a goal, we write $\rho \vdash \phi$ to mean that ρ covers ϕ. Checking this is decidable. For a word W, $\rho \mid W$ if W is a segment of ρ. For a clause $C = W_0 \vee W_2 \vee ...$, $\rho \vdash C$ if $\rho \vdash W_k$ for some k. Roughly, a sentence $C_0; C_1; ...$ is covered by ρ if all clauses C_i are covered by ρ, and furthermore they are covered in the order as specified by the sentence. We will however define it more loosely to allow consecutive clauses to overlap, as follows:

Definition 2 (Sentence Coverage). *Let S be a sentence. (1) An empty ρ does not cover S. (2) If S is a just a single clause C, then $\rho \vdash S$ iff $\rho \vdash C$. (3) If $S = C; S'$ and a prefix of ρ matches one of the words in C, then $\rho \vdash S$ iff $\rho \vdash S'$. If ρ has no such a prefix, then $\rho \vdash S$ iff $\mathsf{tail}(\rho) \vdash S$.*

An aggregate goal of the form ${}^{k}\!\geq N$ is covered by ρ if ρ covers at least N *different* words of size k. While sentences are expressible in temporal logic, aggregate goals are not. This has an important consequence discussed later.

Let ϕ be a coverage goal and σ a test case. Let's write $P(\phi \mid \sigma)$ to denote the probability that ϕ is covered by σ, which can be calculated analogous to (2) as follows:

Definition 3. *$P(\phi \mid \sigma)$ is equal to $P(\phi \mid E)$ where $E = \mathsf{E}(\sigma)$, $P(\phi \mid E) = \sum_{\rho \; s.t. \; \rho \in \mathsf{exec}(E) \, \wedge \, \rho \vdash \phi} P_E(\rho)$, and where $P_E(\rho)$ is calculated as in (1).*

For example, consider the test case *aba* on the SUT EX_1. Figure 2 shows the execution model of *aba*. $P(\langle 2, 0 \rangle \mid aba)$ is the probability that *aba*'s execution passes through the transition $2 \rightarrow 0$; this probability is 0.5. $P((\langle 2 \rangle \vee \langle 3 \rangle); \langle 1 \rangle \mid aba)$ is the probability that *aba* first visits the state 2 or 3, and sometime later 1; this probability is 0.75. $P({}^{1}\!\geq 4 \mid aba)$ is the probability that the execution of *aba* visits at least four different states; this is unfortunately only 0.05.

Due to non-determinism, the size of $\mathsf{exec}(\sigma)$ could be exponential with respect to the length of σ. Simply using the formula in Definition 3 would then be expensive. Below we present a much better algorithm to do the calculation.

4   Efficient Coverage Calculation

Coverage goals in the form of sentences are actually expressible in Computation Tree Logic (CTL) [3]. E.g. $\langle s, t \rangle; \langle u \rangle$ corresponds to $\mathsf{EF}(s \wedge t \wedge \mathsf{EF}u)$. It follows that the probability of covering a sentence can be calculated through probabilistic CTL model checking [3,10]. Unfortunately, aggregate goals are not expressible in CTL. Later we will discuss a modification of probabilistic model checking to allow the calculation of aggregate goals. We first start with the calculation of *simple sentences* whose words are all of length one.

Let S be a simple sentence, σ a test case, and $E = \mathsf{E}(\sigma)$. In standard probabilistic model checking, $P(S|\sigma)$ would be calculated through a series of multiplications over a probability matrix [3]. We will instead do it by performing labelling on the nodes of E, resembling more to non-probabilistic CTL model checking. This approach is more generalizable to later handle aggregate goals.

Notice that any node u in E induces a unique subgraph, denoted by $E@u$, rooted in u. It represents the remaining execution of σ, starting at u. When we label E with some coverage goal ψ, the labelling will proceed in such a way that when it terminates every node u in E is extended with labels of the form $u.\mathsf{lab}(\psi)$ containing the value of $P(\psi \mid E@u)$. The labelling algorithm is shown in Fig. 3, namely the procedure label(..)—we will explain it below. In any case, after calling $\mathsf{label}(E, S)$, the value of $P(S \mid \sigma)$ can thus be obtained simply by inspecting the $\mathsf{lab}(S)$ of E's root node. This is done by the procedure calcSimple.

1: **procedure** calcSimple(E, S)
2:    label(E, S)
3:    **return** root$(E).\mathsf{lab}(S)$
4: **end procedure**

5: **procedure** label(E, S)
6:    $u_0 \leftarrow$ root(E)
7:    **case** S **of**
8:      $C \quad \rightarrow$ label1(u_0, C)
9:      $C; S' \rightarrow$ label(E, S') ; label1(u_0, S)
10: **end procedure**

11: **procedure** checkClause(u, C)
12:    ▷ *the clause C is assumed to be of this form, with $k \geq 1$:*
13:    **let** $\langle s_0 \rangle \vee ... \vee \langle s_{k-1} \rangle = C$
14:    $isCovered \leftarrow u.\mathsf{st} \in \{s_0, ..., s_{k-1}\}$
15:    **return** $isCovered$
16: **end procedure**

17: **procedure** label1(u, S)
18:    ▷ *recurse to u's successors :*
19:    **forall** $v \in u.\mathsf{next} \rightarrow$ label1(v, S)
20:    ▷ *pre-calculate u's successors' total probability to cover S :*
21:    $q' \leftarrow \sum_{v \in u.\mathsf{next}} u.\mathsf{pr}(v) * v.\mathsf{lab}(S)$
22:    ▷ *calc. u's probability to cover S :*
23:    **case** S **of**
24:      $C \quad \rightarrow$ **if** checkClause(u, C)
            then $q \leftarrow 1$
            else $q \leftarrow q'$
25:      $C; S' \rightarrow$ **if** checkClause(u, C)
            then $q \leftarrow u.\mathsf{lab}(S')$
            else $q \leftarrow q'$
26:    **end case**
27:    ▷ *add the calculated probability as a new label to u :*
28:    $u.\mathsf{lab}(S) \leftarrow q$
29: **end procedure**

Fig. 3. The labeling algorithm to calculate the probability of simple sentences.

Since S is a sentence, it is a sequence of clauses. The procedure label(E, S) first recursively labels E with the tail S' of S (line 9), then we proceed with the labelling of S itself, which is done by the procedure label1. In label1, the following notations are used. Let u be a node in E. Recall that $u.\mathsf{st}$ denotes the ID of the state in M that u represents. We write $u.\mathsf{next}$ to denote the set of

u's successors in E (and not in $M!$). For such a successor v, $u.\text{pr}(v)$ denotes the probability annotation that E puts on the arrow $u{\rightarrow}v$. A label is a pair (ψ, p) where ψ is a coverage goal and p is a probability in $[0..1]$. The notation $u.\text{lab}$ denotes the labels put so far to the node u. The assignment $u.\text{lab}(\psi) \leftarrow p$ adds the label (ψ, p) to u, and the expression $u.\text{lab}(\psi)$ returns now the value of p.

The procedure $\text{label1}(\psi)$ will perform the labelling node by node recursively in the bottom-up direction over the structure of E (line 19). Since E is acyclic, only a single pass of this recursion is needed. For every node $u \in E$, $\text{label1}(u, S)$ has to add a new label (S, q) to the node u where q is the probability that the goal S is covered by the part of executions of σ that starts in u (in other words, the value of $P(S \mid E@u)$). The goal S will be in one of these two forms:

1. S is just a single clause C (line 24). Because S is a simple sentence, C is a disjunction of singleton words $\langle s_0 \rangle \vee ... \vee \langle s_{k-1} \rangle$, where each s_i is an ID of a state in M. If u represents one of these states, the probability that $E@u$ covers C would be 1. Else, it is the sum of the probability to cover C through u's successors (line 20). As an example, Fig. 4 (left) shows how the labeling of a simple sentence $\langle 1 \rangle$ on the execution model in Fig. 2 proceeds.
2. S is a sentence with more than one clause; so it is of the form $C; S'$ (line 25) where C is a clause and S' is the rest of the sentence, we calculate the coverage probability of $E@u$ by basically following the third case in Definition 2. As an example, Fig. 4 (right) shows how the labeling of $S = \langle 0 \rangle;\langle 1 \rangle$ proceeds. At every node u we first check if u covers the first word, namely $\langle 0 \rangle$. If this is the case, the probability that $E@u$ covers S would be the same as the probability that it covers the rest of S, namely $\langle 1 \rangle$. The probability of the later is by now known, calculated by label in its previous recursive call. The result can be inspected in $u.\text{lab}(\langle 1 \rangle)$.

If u does *not* cover S, the probability that $\text{E}(u)$ covers S would be the sum of the probability to cover S through u's successors (calculated in line 21).

Assuming that checking if a node locally covers a clause (the procedure checkClause in Fig. 3) takes a time unit, the time complexity of label1 is $\mathcal{O}(|E|)$, where $|E|$ is the size of E in terms of its number of edges. The complexity of label is thus $\mathcal{O}(|E| * |S|)$, where $|S|$ is the size of the goal S in terms of the number of clauses it has. The size of E is typically just linear to the length of the test case: $\mathcal{O}(N_{sucs} * |\sigma|)$, where N_{sucs} is the average number of successors that each state in M has. This is a significant improvement compared to the exponential run time that we would get if we simply use Definition 3.

4.1 Non-simple Sentences

Coverage goals in k-wise testing would require sentences with words of length $k > 1$ to be expressed. These are thus *non-simple* sentences. We will show that the algorithm in Fig. 3 can be used to handle these sentences as well.

Consider as an example the sentence $\langle 0, 2, 0 \rangle; \langle 4, 1, \sharp \rangle$. The words are of length three, so the sentence is non-simple. Suppose we can treat these words as if they

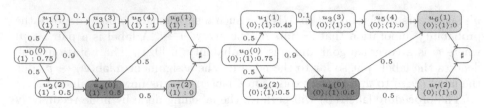

Fig. 4. The **left graph** shows the result of label($\langle 1 \rangle$) on the execution model of aba in Fig. 2. For simplicity, the action labels on the arrows are removed. The probability annotation is kept. In turn, label() calls label1, which then performs the labelling recursively from right to left. The nodes u_6 and u_7 (yellow) are base cases. The probabilities of $\langle 1 \rangle$ on them are respectively 1 and 0. This information is then added as the labels of these nodes. Next, label1 proceeds with the labelling of u_4 and u_5. E.g. on u_4 (orange), because u_4.st is not 1, for u_4 to cover $\langle 1 \rangle$ we need an execution that goes through u_6, with the probability of 0.5. So the probability of $\langle 1 \rangle$ on u_4 is 0.5. The **right graph** shows the result of label($\langle 0 \rangle; \langle 1 \rangle$) on the same execution model. This will first call label($\langle 1 \rangle$), thus producing the labels as shown in the left graph, then proceeds with label1($\langle 0 \rangle; \langle 1 \rangle$). Again, label1 performs the labelling recursively from right to left. The base cases u_6 and u_7 do not cover $\langle 0 \rangle; \langle 1 \rangle$, so the corresponding probability there is 0. Again, this information is added as labels of the corresponding nodes. Node u_4 (orange) has u_4.st = 0. So, any execution that starts from there and covers $\langle 1 \rangle$ would also cover $\langle 0 \rangle; \langle 1 \rangle$. The probability that u_4 covers $\langle 1 \rangle$ is already calculated in the left graph, namely 0.5. So this is also the probability that it covers $\langle 0 \rangle; \langle 1 \rangle$. (Color figure online)

are singletons. E.g. in $\langle 0, 2, 0 \rangle$ the sequence $0, 2, 0$ is treated as a single symbol, and hence the word is a singleton. From this perspective, any non-aggregate goal is thus a simple sentence, and therefore the algorithm in Fig. 3 can be used to calculate its coverage probability. We do however need to pre-process the execution model to align it with this idea.

The only part of the algorithm in Fig. 3 where the size of the words matters is in the procedure checkClause. Given a node u in the given execution model E and a clause C, checkClause(u, C) checks if the clause C is covered by E's executions that start at u. If the words in C are all of length one, C can be immediately checked by knowing which state in M u represents. This information is available in the attribute u.st. Clauses with longer words can be checked in a similar way. For simplicity, assume that the words are all of length k (note: shorter words can be padded to k with wildcards * that match any symbol). We first restructure E such that the st attribute of every node u in the new E contains a word of length k that would be covered if the execution of E arrives at u. We call this restructuring step k-word expansion. Given a base execution model E, the produced new execution model will be denoted by E^k. As an example, the figure below shows the word expansion with $k = 3$ of the execution model in Fig. 2 (for every node v we only show its v.st label, which is an execution segment of length 3). Artificial initial and terminal states are added to the new execution model, labelled with $\sharp$. When a word of length k cannot be formed, because the corresponding segment has reached the terminal state $\sharp$ in E, we pad the word with $\sharp$'s on its the end until its length is k.

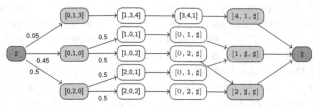

4.2   Coverage of Aggregate Goals

We will only discuss the calculation of aggregate goals of the form $^k \geq N$ where $k = 1$. If $k > 1$ we can first apply a k-word expansion (Sect. 4.1) on the given execution model E, then we calculate $^1 \geq N$ on the expanded execution model.

Efficiently calculating $^1 \geq N$ is more challenging. The algorithm below proceeds along the same idea as how we handled simple sentences, namely by recursing over E. We first need to extend every node u in E with a new label $u.\mathsf{A}$. This label is a set containing pairs of the form $V \mapsto p$ where V is a set of M's states and p is the probability that $E@u$ would cover *all* the states mentioned in V. Only V's whose probability is non-zero need to be included in this mapping. After all nodes in E are labelled like this, the probability $^1 \geq N$ can be calculated from the A of the root node u_0:

$$P(^1{\geq}N \mid \sigma) \;=\; \sum_{V \mapsto p \,\in\, u_0.\mathsf{A}} \text{if } |V| \geq N \text{ then } p \text{ else } 0 \qquad (3)$$

The labelling is done recursively over E as follows:

1. The base case is the terminal node #. The A label of # is just $\emptyset$.
2. For every node $u \in E$, we first recurse to all its successors. Then, we calculate a preliminary mapping for u in the following *multi-set A'*:

$$A' \;=\; \{\, V \cup \{u.\mathsf{st}\} \mapsto p*P_E(u{\to}v) \mid v \in u.\mathsf{next},\; V \mapsto p \in v.\mathsf{A} \,\}$$

As a multi-set note that A' may contain duplicates, e.g. two instances of $V \mapsto p_0$. Additionally, it may contain different maps that belong to the same V, e.g. $V \mapsto p_1$ and $V \mapsto p_2$. All these instances of V need to be merged by summing up their p's, e.g. the above instances is to be merged to $V \mapsto p_0 + p_0 + p_1 + p_2$ The function merge will do this. The label $u.\mathsf{A}$ is then just: $u.\mathsf{A} = \mathsf{merge}(A') = \{V \mapsto \sum_{V \mapsto p \in A'} p \mid V \in \mathsf{domain}(A')\}$, where $\mathsf{domain}(A')$ is the set of all unique V's that appear as $V \mapsto .$ in A'.

The recursion terminates because E is acyclic.

The above algorithm can however perform worse than a direct calculation via Definition 3. The reason is that merge is an expensive operation if we do it literally at every node. If we do not merge at all, and make the A's multi-sets instead of sets, we will end up with $u_0.\mathsf{A}$ that contains as many elements as the number of paths in E, so we are not better of either. Effort to merge is well spent if it delivers large reduction in the size of the resulting set, otherwise the effort is wasted. Unfortunately it is hard to predict the amount of reduction we would get for each particular merge. We use the following merge policy. We only merge on nodes at the $B - 1$-th position of 'bridges' where B is the length of the bridge at hand. A bridge is a sequence of nodes $v_0, ..., v_{B-1}$ such that: (1) every v_i except the last one has only one outgoing edge, leading to v_{i+1}, and (2) the last node v_{B-1} should have more than one successor. A bridge forms thus a deterministic section of E, that leads to a non-deterministic section. Merging on a bridge is more likely to be cost effective. Furthermore, only one merge is needed for an entire bridge. Merging on a non-deterministic node (a node with multiple successors) is risky. This policy takes a conservative approach by not merging at all on such nodes. The next section will discuss the performance of our algorithm.

5   Experimental Results

In the following experiment we benchmark the algorithm from Sect. 4 against the 'brute force' way to calculate coverage using Definition 3. We will use a family of models M_m in Fig. 5. Despite its simplicity, M_m is highly non-deterministic and is designed to generate a large number of executions and words.

We generate a family of execution models $E(i, m)$ by applying a test case tc^i on the model M_m where $m \in \{0, 2, 8\}$. The test case is:

$$tc^i = ac^i ab^i ac^i a$$

The table in Fig. 6 (left) shows the statistics of all execution models used in this experiment. Additionally we also construct $E(i, m)^3$ (applying 3-word expansion). The last column in the table shows the number of nodes in the corresponding $E(i, m)^3$ (the number of executions stays the same, of course).

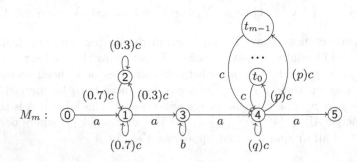

Fig. 5. The model M_m used for the benchmarking. If $m = 0$ then there is no states t_i and $q = 1$. If $m > 0$ then we have states $t_0...t_{m-1}$; $p = 0.3/m$ and $q = 0.7$.

The number of possible executions in the execution models correspond to their degree of non-determinism. The test case tc^i has been designed as such that increasing i exponentially increases the non-determinism of the corresponding execution model (we can see this in Fig. 6 by comparing #paths with the i index of the corresponding $E(i, m)$).

All the models used (M_0, M_2, and M_8) are non-deterministic: M_0 is the least non-deterministic one whereas M_8 is very non-deterministic. This is reflected in the number of possible executions in their corresponding execution models, with $E(i, 8)$ having far more possible executions than $E(i, 0)$.

The following four coverage goals are used:

goal	type	word expansion
$f_1 : \langle 2 \rangle; \langle t_0 \rangle$	simple sentence	no
$f_2 : \langle 1, 1, 1 \rangle; \langle 4, 4, 4 \rangle$	non-simple sentence	3-word
$f_3 : {}^1\!\geq_8$	aggregate	no
$f_4 : {}^3\!\geq_8$	aggregate	3-word

We let our algorithm calculate the coverage of each of the above goals on the execution models $E(5, 0)...E(9, 8)$ and measure the time it takes to finish the calculation. For the merging policy, n is set to 1 when the goal does not need word expansion, and else it is set to be equal to the expansion parameter. The experiment is run on a Macbook Pro with 2,7 GHz Intel i5 and 8 GB RAM. Figure 6 (right) shows the results. For example, we can see that f_1 can be calculated in just a few milli seconds, even on $E(12, m)$ and $E(i, 8)$. In contrast, brute force calculation using Definition 3 on e.g. $E(11, 2), E(12, 2), E(8, 8)$, and

	$|tc|$	#nodes	#paths	#nodes³
$E(5,0)$	20	26	16	103(4)
$E(6,0)$	23	30	32	144(5)
$E(7,0)$	26	34	64	223(7)
$E(8,0)$	29	38	128	381(10)
$E(9,0)$	32	42	256	422(10)
$E(10,0)$	35	46	512	501(11)
$E(11,0)$	38	50	1024	659(13)
$E(12,0)$	41	54	2048	700(13)
$E(5,2)$	20	34	336	185(5)
$E(6,2)$	23	40	1376	306(8)
$E(7,2)$	26	46	5440	435(9)
$E(8,2)$	29	52	21888	695(13)
$E(9,2)$	32	58	87296	944(16)
$E(10,2)$	35	64	349696	1073(17)
$E(11,2)$	38	70	1397760	1333(19)
$E(12,2)$	41	76	5593088	1582(21)
$E(5,8)$	20	58	3600	863(15)
$E(6,8)$	23	70	29984	2760(39)
$E(7,8)$	26	82	175168	4287(52)
$E(8,8)$	29	94	1309824	8261(88)
$E(9,8)$	32	106	8225024	23726(224)

	f_1	f_2	f_3	f_4
$E(5,0)$	0.001	0.002	0.001	0.002
$E(6,0)$	0.001	0.002	0.001	0.002
$E(7,0)$	0.001	0.003	0.001	0.003
$E(8,0)$	0.001	0.004	0.001	0.005
$E(9,0)$	0.001	0.005	0.002	0.006
$E(10,0)$	0.001	0.006	0.003	0.008
$E(11,0)$	0.001	0.008	0.004	0.012
$E(12,0)$	0.001	0.008	0.009	0.024
$E(5,2)$	0.001	0.002	0.002	0.004
$E(6,2)$	0.001	0.004	0.002	0.01
$E(7,2)$	0.001	0.005	0.003	0.039
$E(8,2)$	0.001	0.01	0.005	0.138
$E(9,2)$	0.001	0.014	0.01	0.44
$E(10,2)$	0.001	0.012	0.019	1.09
$E(11,2)$	0.001	0.018	0.041	3.13
$E(12,2)$	0.001	0.023	0.091	10.68
$E(5,8)$	0.001	0.011	0.006	0.032
$E(6,8)$	0.001	0.04	0.034	0.279
$E(7,8)$	0.001	0.076	0.073	1.38
$E(8,8)$	0.002	0.154	0.266	12.04
$E(9,8)$	0.002	0.46	0.539	219

Fig. 6. Left: the execution models used in the benchmark. #nodes and #paths are the number of nodes and full paths (executions) in the corresponding execution model; #nodes³ is the number of nodes in the resulting 3-word expansion model. The number between brackets is #nodes³/#nodes. **Right:** the run time (seconds) of our coverage calculation algorithm on different execution models and coverage goals.

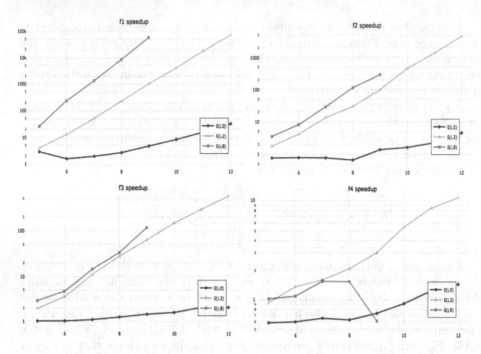

Fig. 7. The graphs show our algorithm's speedup with respect to the brute force calculation on four different goals: f_1 (top left), f_2 (top right), f_3 (bottom left), and f_4 (bottom right). f_1 and f_2 are non-aggregate, whereas f_3 and f_4 are aggregate goals. Calculating f_1 and f_3 does not use word expansion, whereas f_2 and f_4 require 3-word expansion. Each graph shows the speedup with respect to three families of execution models: $E(i, 0)$, $E(i, 2)$, and $E(i, 8)$. These models have increasing degree of non-determinism, with models from $E(i, 8)$ being the most non-deterministic ones compared to the models from other families (with the same i). The horizontal axes represent the i parameter, which linearly influences the length of the used test case. The vertical axes show the speedup in the **logarithmic** scale. (Color figure online)

$E(9, 8)$ would be very expensive, because it has to quantify over more than a million paths in each of these models.

Figure 7 shows the speedup of our algorithm with respect to the brute force calculation—note that the graphs are set in logarithmic scale. We can see that in almost all cases the speedup grows exponentially with respect to the length of the test case, although the growth rate is different in different situations. We can notice that the speed up on $E(i, 0)$ is much lower (though we still have speedup, except for f_4 which we will discuss below). This is because $E(i, 0)$'s are not too non-deterministic. They all induce less than 2100 possible executions. The brute force approach can easily handle such volume. Despite the low speedup, on all $E(i, 0)$'s our algorithm can do the task in just few milli seconds (1–24 ms).

The calculation of f_1 is very fast (less than 2 ms). This is expected, because f_1 is a simple sentence. The calculation of f_2, on the other hand, which is a non-simple sentence, must be executed on the corresponding 3-word expanded execution model, which can be much larger than the original execution model. E.g. $E(9,8)^3$ is over 200 times larger (in the number of nodes) than $E(9,8)$. Despite this we see the algorithm performs pretty well on f_2.

f_3 and f_4 are both aggregate goals. The calculation of f_3 is not problematical, however we see that f_4 becomes expensive on the models $E(12,2), E(8,8)$, and $E(9,8)$ (see Fig. 6 right). In fact, on $E(9,8)$ the calculation of f_4 is even worse than brute force (the dip in the red line in Fig. 7). Recall that $f_4 = {}^3\geq_8$; so, calculating its coverage requires us to sum over different sets of words of size 3 that the different executions can generate. $E(12,2), E(8,8)$, and $E(9,8)$ are large (over 70 states) and highly non-deterministic. Inevitably, they generate a lot of words of size 3, and therefore the number of possible sets of these words explodes. E.g. on $E(8,8)$ and $E(9,8)$ our algorithm ends up with about 1.2M an 6.7M sets of words to sum over. In contrast, the number of full paths in these models are about respectively 1.3M and 8.2M. At this ratio, there is not much to gain with respect to the brute force approach that simply sums over all full paths, whereas our algorithm also has to deal with the overhead of book keeping and merging. Hypothetically, if we always merge, the number of final sets of words can be reduced to respectively about 500K and 2M, so summing over them would be faster. We should not do this though, because merging is expensive, but the numbers do suggest that there is room for improvement if one can figure out how to merge more smartly.

6   Related Work

To the best of our knowledge the concept of probabilistic coverage has not been well addressed in the literature on non-deterministic MBT, or even in the literature on probabilistic automata. A paper by Zu, Hall, and May [30] that provides a comprehensive discussion on various coverage criteria does not mention the concept either. This is a bit surprising since coverage is a concept that is quite central in software testing. We do find its mentioning in literature on statistical testing, e.g. [8,29]. In [29] Whittaker and Thomason discussed the use of Markov chains to encode probabilistic behavioral models. The probabilities are used to model the usage pattern of the SUT. This allows us to generate test sequences whose distribution follows the usage pattern (so-called 'statistical testing'). Techniques from Markov chain are then used to predict properties of the test sequences if we are to generate them in this way, e.g. the probability to obtain a certain level of node or edge coverage, or conversely the expected number of test runs needed to get that level of coverage. In contrast, in our work probabilities are used to model SUT's non-determinism, rather than its usage pattern. We do not concern ourselves with how the tester generates the test sequences, and focuses purely on the calculation of coverage under the SUT's non-determinism. Our coverage goal expressions are more general than [29] by allowing words of arbitrary length (rather than just words of length one or two, which would represent state and respectively edge coverage), clauses, and sentences to be specified as coverage goals. Coverage calculation in both [8, 29] basically comes down to the brute force calculation in Definition 3.

Our algorithm to calculate the coverage of simple sentences has some similarity with the probabilistic model checking algorithm for Probabilistic Computation Tree Logic (PCTL) [10, 15]. Although given a formula f a model checking algorithm tries to decide whether or not f is valid on the given behavior model, the underlying probabilistic algorithm also labels for every state in the model with the probability that any execution that starts from that state would satisfy f. Since we only need to calculate over execution models, which are acyclic, there is no need to do a fixed point iteration as in [15]. From this perspective, our algorithm can be seen as an instance of [15]. However we also add k-word expansion. In addition to simplifying the algorithm when dealing with non-simple sentences, the expansion also serves as a form of memoisation (we do not have to keep calculating the probability for a state u to lead to a word w). In particular the calculation of aggregate coverage goals benefits from this memoisation. Though, the biggest difference between our approach with a model checking algorithm is that the latter does not deal with aggregate properties (there is no concept of aggregate formulas in PCTL). Our contribution can also be seen as opening a way to extend a probabilistic model checking algorithm to calculate such properties. We believe it is also possible to generalize over the aggregation so that the same algorithm can be used to aggregate arbitrary state attributes that admit some aggregation operator (e.g. the cost of staying in various states, which can be aggregated with the '+' operator).

In this paper we have focused on coverage analyses. There are other analyses that are useful to mention. In this paper we abstract away from the data that may have been exchanged during the interactions with the SUT. In practice many systems do exchange data. In this situation we may also want to do data-related analyses as well. E.g. the work by Prasetya [19] discussed the use of an extended LTL to query temporal relations between the data exchanged through the test sequences in a test suite. This is useful e.g. to find test sequences of a specific property, or to check if a certain temporal scenario has been covered. The setup is non-probabilistic though (a query can only tell whether a temporal property holds or not), so an extension would be needed if we are interested in probabilistic judgement. Another example of analyses is risk analyses as in the work by Stoelinga and Timmer [23]. When testing a non-deterministic system, we need to keep in mind that although executing a test suite may report no error, there might still be lurking errors that were not triggered due to internal non-determinism. Stoelinga and Timmer propose to annotate each transition in a model with the estimated probability that it is incorrectly implemented and the entailed cost if the incorrect behavior emerges[1]. This then allows us to calculate

---

[1] We gloss over the complication that the transition might be in a cycle. A test case may thus exercise it multiple times. Each time, exercising it successfully would arguably decrease the probability that it still hides some hidden erroneous behavior. This requires a more elaborate treatment, see [23] for more details.

the probability that a successful execution of a test suite still hides errors, and the expected cost (risk) of these hidden errors.

7   Conclusion

We have presented a concept of probabilistic coverage that is useful to express the coverage of a test suite in model-based testing when the used model is non-deterministic, but has been annotated with estimation on the probability of each non-deterministic choice. Both aggregate and non-aggregate coverage goals can be expressed, and we have presented an algorithm to efficiently calculate the probabilistic coverage of such goals. Quite sophisticated coverage goals can be expressed, e.g. sequence (words) coverage and sequence of sequences (sentences) coverage. We have shown that in most cases the algorithm is very efficient. A challenge still lies on calculating aggregate k-wise test goals on test cases that repeatedly trigger highly non-deterministic parts of the model. Such a situation is bound to generate combinatoric explosion on the possible combinations of words that need to be taken into account. Beyond a certain point, the explosion becomes too much for the merging policy used in our algorithm to handle. Analyses on the data obtained from our benchmarking suggests that in theory there is indeed room for improvement, though it is not yet clear what the best course to proceed. This is left for future work.

References

1. Ammann, P., Offutt, J.: Introduction to Software Testing. Cambridge University Press, Cambridge (2016)
2. Arnold, A.: Finite Transition Systems. International Series in Computer Science (1994)
3. Baier, C., Katoen, J.P., Larsen, K.G.: Principles of Model Checking. MIT Press, Cambridge (2008)
4. Belinfante, A.: JTorX: exploring model-based testing. Ph.D. thesis, University of Twente (2014)
5. Bringmann, E., Krämer, A.: Model-based testing of automotive systems. In: 2008 1st International Conference on Software Testing, Verification, and Validation, pp. 485–493. IEEE (2008)
6. Craggs, I., Sardis, M., Heuillard, T.: AGEDIS case studies: model-based testing in industry. In: Proceedings of 1st European Conference on Model Driven Software Engineering, pp. 129–132 (2003)
7. Dallmeier, V., Lindig, C., Wasylkowski, A., Zeller, A.: Mining object behavior with ADABU. In: Proceedings of the International Workshop on Dynamic Systems Analysis (WODA), pp. 17–24. ACM (2006). https://doi.org/10.1145/1138912.1138918
8. Denise, A., Gaudel, M.C., Gouraud, S.D.: A generic method for statistical testing. In: 15th International Symposium on Software Reliability Engineering ISSRE, pp. 25–34. IEEE (2004)
9. Grindal, M., Offutt, J., Andler, S.F.: Combination testing strategies: a survey. Softw. Test. Verif. Reliab. **15**(3), 167–199 (2005)

10. Hansson, H., Jonsson, B.: A logic for reasoning about time and reliability. Formal Aspects Comput. **6**(5), 512–535 (1994)
11. Heerink, L., Feenstra, J., Tretmans, J.: Formal test automation: the conference protocol with phact. In: Ural, H., Probert, R.L., v. Bochmann, G. (eds.) Testing of Communicating Systems. IAICT, vol. 48, pp. 211–220. Springer, Boston, MA (2000). https://doi.org/10.1007/978-0-387-35516-0_13
12. Hoare, C.A.R.: Communicating Sequential Processes. Prentice Hall, Upper Saddle River (2004)
13. Jard, C., Jéron, T.: TGV: theory, principles and algorithms. Int. J. Softw. Tools Technol. Transf. **7**(4), 297–315 (2005)
14. Kanstrén, T., Puolitaival, O.P.: Using Built-in Domain-Specific Modeling Support to Guide Model-Based Test Generation. Model-Driven Engineering of Information Systems: Principles, Techniques, and Practice, pp. 295–319 (2012)
15. Kwiatkowska, M., Norman, G., Parker, D.: Stochastic model checking. In: Bernardo, M., Hillston, J. (eds.) SFM 2007. LNCS, vol. 4486, pp. 220–270. Springer, Heidelberg (2007). https://doi.org/10.1007/978-3-540-72522-0_6
16. Nachmanson, L., Veanes, M., Schulte, W., Tillmann, N., Grieskamp, W.: Optimal strategies for testing nondeterministic systems. In: ACM SIGSOFT Software Engineering Notes, vol. 29, pp. 55–64. ACM (2004)
17. Peleska, J.: Industrial-strength model-based testing - state of the art and current challenges. In: Proceedings 8th Workshop on Model-Based Testing (MBT), pp. 3–28 (2013). https://doi.org/10.4204/EPTCS.111.1
18. Petke, J., Cohen, M.B., Harman, M., Yoo, S.: Practical combinatorial interaction testing: empirical findings on efficiency and early fault detection. IEEE Trans. Softw. Eng. **41**(9), 901–924 (2015)
19. Prasetya, I.: Temporal algebraic query of test sequences. J. Syst. Softw. **136**, 223–236 (2018)
20. Pretschner, A., Philipps, J.: 10 methodological issues in model-based testing. In: Broy, M., Jonsson, B., Katoen, J.-P., Leucker, M., Pretschner, A. (eds.) Model-Based Testing of Reactive Systems. LNCS, vol. 3472, pp. 281–291. Springer, Heidelberg (2005). https://doi.org/10.1007/11498490_13
21. Schur, M., Roth, A., Zeller, A.: Mining behavior models from enterprise web applications. In: Proceedings of the 9th Joint Meeting on Foundations of Software Engineering, pp. 422–432. ACM (2013). https://doi.org/10.1145/2491411.2491426
22. Stoelinga, M.: An introduction to probabilistic automata. Bull. EATCS **78**(2), 176–198 (2002)
23. Stoelinga, M., Timmer, M.: Interpreting a successful testing process: risk and actual coverage. In: 3rd International Symposium on Theoretical Aspects of Software Engineering TASE, pp. 251–258. IEEE (2009)
24. Tervoort, T., Prasetya, I.S.W.B.: APSL: a light weight testing tool for protocols with complex messages. Hardware and Software: Verification and Testing. LNCS, vol. 10629, pp. 241–244. Springer, Cham (2017). https://doi.org/10.1007/978-3-319-70389-3_20
25. Tretmans, G.J.: A formal approach to conformance testing. Ph.D. thesis, Twente University (1992)
26. Tretmans, J., Brinksma, E.: TorX: automated model-based testing. In: 1st European Conference on Model-Driven Software Engineering (2003)
27. Utting, M., Pretschner, A., Legeard, B.: A taxonomy of model-based testing approaches. Softw. Test. Verif. Reliab. **22**(5), 297–312 (2012)

28. Vos, T., et al.: Fittest: a new continuous and automated testing process for future internet applications. In: 2014 Software Evolution Week-IEEE Conference on Software Maintenance, Reengineering and Reverse Engineering (CSMR-WCRE), pp. 407–410. IEEE (2014)

29. Whittaker, J.A., Thomason, M.G.: A Markov chain model for statistical software testing. IEEE Trans. Softw. Eng. **20**(10), 812–824 (1994)

30. Zhu, H., Hall, P.A., May, J.H.: Software unit test coverage and adequacy. ACM Comput. Surv. **29**(4), 366–427 (1997)

Model Inference

Learning Minimal DFA: Taking Inspiration from RPNI to Improve SAT Approach

Florent Avellaneda$^{(\boxtimes)}$ and Alexandre Petrenko$^{(\boxtimes)}$

Computer Research Institute of Montreal, Montreal, Canada
{florent.avellaneda,alexandre.petrenko}@crim.ca

Abstract. Inferring a minimal Deterministic Finite Automaton (DFA) from a learning sample that includes positive and negative examples is one of the fundamental problems in computer science. Although the problem is known to be NP-complete, it can be solved efficiently with a SAT solver especially when it is used incrementally. We propose an incremental SAT solving approach for DFA inference in which general heuristics of a solver for assigning free variables is replaced by that employed by the RPNI method for DFA inference. This heuristics reflects the knowledge of the problem that facilitates the choice of free variables. Since the performance of solvers significantly depends on the choices made in assigning free variables, the RPNI heuristics brings significant improvements, as our experiments with a modified solver indicate; they also demonstrate that the proposed approach is more effective than the previous SAT approaches and the RPNI method.

Keywords: Machine inference · Machine identification ·
Learning automata · DFA · Grammatical inference · SAT solver

1 Introduction

When we have an unknown system, re-engineering its model brings many advantages. A formal representation of the system allows us to understand how it works. The model can be used to check the properties of the system. Tests could be generated from the model using existing methods for model-based testing.

In this paper we are interested in the inference of a DFA model from observations. As is customary, we follow the principle of parsimony. This principle states that among competing hypotheses, the one with the fewest assumptions should be selected. Addressing the model inference problem, this principle suggests to infer the simplest model consistent with observations. Since the model to infer is an automaton, we generally use the number of states to measure the complexity.

There are two types of approaches for DFA inference, heuristic and exact approaches. Heuristic approaches merge states in an automaton representation of observations until a local minimum is reached. Exact approaches try to find a

© Springer Nature Switzerland AG 2019
P. C. Ölveczky and G. Salaün (Eds.): SEFM 2019, LNCS 11724, pp. 243–256, 2019.
https://doi.org/10.1007/978-3-030-30446-1_13

minimal automaton consistent with observations. The most known heuristic approach is probably the RPNI (Regular Positive and Negative Inference) method [12]. It performs a breadth first search by trying to merge a newly encountered state with states already explored. Effective exact approaches generally formulate constraints and solve them using SAT solvers. Heule and Verwer have proposed an efficient SAT modeling [9]. We proposed an incremental SAT solving approach in the case of FSM inference [3]. The heuristic and exact approaches are generally quite distinct. In this paper we try to combine them together in order to achieve a better performance. The idea is as follows. We know that the efficiency of SAT solvers depends strongly on the order in which the Boolean variables are considered. To choose a "good" order among the Boolean variables SAT solvers use all kinds of generic heuristics which do not exploit the specifics of a particular problem, in our case it is DFA inference. In this paper, we use the RPNI heuristics to define the variable assignment order. Thus, the resulting approach can be viewed as an exact approach, though it uses RPNI to help finding a minimal automaton consistent with observations more quickly.

The paper is organized as follows. Section 2 contains definitions. Section 3 defines the inference problem and provides an overview of passive inference. Section 4 contains our contributions, namely, an incremental SAT solving approach for DFA, and modifications of a SAT solver incorporating the RPNI heuristics for determining the assignment order. Section 5 contains benchmarks. Finally Sect. 6 concludes.

2   Definitions

A *Deterministic Finite Automaton* (DFA) is a sextuplet $\mathcal{A} = (Q, \Sigma, \delta, q_\epsilon, F_A, F_R)$, where Q is a finite set of states, Σ is an alphabet, $\delta : Q \times \Sigma \to Q$ is a transition function, $q_\epsilon \in Q$ is the initial state, and $F_A \subseteq Q$ and $F_R \subseteq Q$ are disjoint sets of marked states, called the *accepting* and *rejecting* states, respectively [6]. We recursively extend the function δ to $Q \times \Sigma^* \to Q$ such that $\delta(q, \epsilon) = q$ and $\delta(q, a.w) = \delta(\delta(q, a), w)$. Also, for simplicity, we will write $(q, a, q') \in \delta$ if $\delta(q, a) = q'$.

A *learning sample* is a pair of finite disjoint sets of positive examples S^+ and negative examples S^-. We say that a DFA $\mathcal{A}$ is *consistent* with $S = (S^+, S^-)$ if $\forall w \in S^+ : \delta(q_\epsilon, w) \in F_A$ and $\forall w \in S^- : \delta(q_\epsilon, w) \in F_R$. If all DFAs with fewer states than $\mathcal{A}$ are not consistent with S, then we say that $\mathcal{A}$ is a *minimal* DFA consistent with S. We say that an example w is *inconsistent* with $\mathcal{A}$ if w is a positive example and $\delta(q_\epsilon, w) \notin F_A$ or w is a negative example and $\delta(q_\epsilon, w) \notin F_R$. We use $Pref(S)$ to denote the set of all prefixes of S^+ and S^-.

A *Prefix Tree Acceptor* (PTA) for a learning sample S, denoted $\mathcal{P}(S)$ is the tree-like DFA consistent with S such that all prefixes in $Pref(S)$ are the states of $\mathcal{P}(S)$ and only they. We denote by q_w the state reached by $\mathcal{P}(S)$ with the word w.

We say that two states $q, q' \in Q$ are *incompatible*, denoted $q \not\cong q'$, if $q \in F_A \wedge q' \in F_R$ or $q \in F_R \wedge q' \in F_A$ or $\exists a \in \Sigma : \delta(q, a) \not\cong \delta(q', a)$. Two states are *compatible* if they are not incompatible.

3 Inference Problem

Given a learning sample $S = (S^+, S^-)$ generated by an unknown DFA, we want to find a minimal DFA $\mathcal{A}$ consistent with S.

The existing approaches merge states in two different ways. The so-called RPNI approach [12] merges states incrementally. It is a heuristic approach, but we know that if the learning sample is large enough then it will find a minimal DFA consistent with S.

Another approach is based on a SAT solver and tries to determine a partition on the set of states of PTA $\mathcal{P}(S) = (Q, \Sigma, \delta, q_\epsilon, F_A, F_R)$ into compatible states such that the number of blocks does not exceed n. Clearly, n should be smaller than $|Q|$. If no partition can be found, it means that the bound n is too low. In this case we increase n and start again.

This approach has the advantage to guarantee that a minimal DFA consistent with S can be found independently of the size of the learning sample.

3.1 RPNI Method

The algorithm RPNI is a popular method for inferring a DFA from a learning sample. A detailed explanation of the RPNI algorithm can be found in [6]. The idea consists in trying to merge states iteratively in a particular order. The algorithm attempts to merge first the states closest to the root state.

In particular, RPNI starts with the PTA determined from S. Then a breadth-first search is performed respecting the lexicographical order. Each time when a new state is found, the algorithm tries to merge it with already explored states (from the earliest to the most recently considered). The algorithm terminates when all states are considered and no more merge can be performed.

A remarkable property of this algorithm is that it identifies in the limit the generator of S. This means that with enough positive and negative examples, the DFA inferred by this algorithm will be the generator.

3.2 SAT Solving Approach

The inference problem can be cast as a constraint satisfaction problem (CSP) [4]. For each state $q \in Q$ of the PTA we introduce an integer variable x_q such that

$$\forall q_i, q_j \in Q : \text{if } q_i \in F_A \wedge q_j \in F_R \text{ then } x_{q_i} \neq x_{q_j}$$
$$\text{if } \exists a \in \Sigma : (q_i, a, q_i'), (q_j, a, q_j') \in \delta \text{ then} \tag{1}$$
$$(x_{q_i} = x_{q_j}) \Rightarrow (x_{q_i'} = x_{q_j'})$$

Let $B = \{0, ..., n-1\}$ be a set of integers representing blocks of a partition. The blocks are ordered following the order of natural numbers. Assuming that the value of x_q is in B for all $q \in Q$, we need to find a solution, i.e., an assignment of values of all variables such that (1) is satisfied. Each assignment implies a partition of n blocks and thus a DFA with at most n states consistent with S.

These CSP formulas can be translated to SAT using unary coding for each integer variable x_q where $q \in Q$: x_q is represented by n Boolean variables $v_{q,0}, v_{q,1}, ..., v_{q,n-1}$. Moreover, Heule and Verwer [9] propose to use auxiliary variables and redundant clauses in order to speed up the solving process. The SAT formulation they propose is as follows.

They define three kinds of variables:

- $v_{q,i}$, $q \in Q$ and $i \in B$. If $v_{q,i}$ is *true*, it means that state q is in block i.
- $y_{a,i,j}$, $i, j \in B$ and $a \in \Sigma$. If $y_{a,i,j}$ is *true*, it means that for any state in block i, the successor reached by symbol a is in block j.
- z_i, $i \in B$. If z_i is *true*, this means that block i becomes an accepting state.

For each state $q \in Q$, we have the clause:

$$v_{q,0} \lor v_{q,1} \lor ... \lor v_{q,n-1} \tag{2}$$

These clauses mean that each state should be in at least one block.
For each state q and every $i, j \in B$ such that $i \neq j$, we have the clauses:

$$\neg v_{q,i} \lor \neg v_{q,j} \tag{3}$$

These clauses mean that each state should be in at most one block.
The clauses 2 and 3 encode the constraint that each state should be in exactly one block.
For every states $q \in F_A, q' \in F_R$ and each $i \in B$, we have the clauses:

$$(\neg v_{q,i} \lor z_i) \land (\neg v_{q',i} \lor \neg z_i) \tag{4}$$

These clauses mean that an accepting state cannot be in the same block as a rejecting state.
For each transition $(q, a, q') \in \delta$ and for every $i, j \in B$:

$$y_{a,i,j} \lor \neg v_{q,i} \lor \neg v_{q',j} \tag{5}$$

This means that if state q is in the block i and its successor q' on symbol a is in the block j then blocks i and j are related for symbol a.
For each transition $(q, a, q') \in \sigma$ and for every $i, j \in B$:

$$\neg y_{a,i,j} \lor \neg v_{q,i} \lor v_{q',j} \tag{6}$$

This means that if blocks i and j are related for symbol a and a state q is in block i, then the successor of q with symbol a have to be in block j.
For each symbol $a \in \Sigma$, for every $i, j, h \in B$ such that $h < j$:

$$\neg y_{a,i,h} \lor \neg y_{a,i,j} \tag{7}$$

This means that each block relation can include at most one pair of blocks for each symbol to enforce determinism. Because of the commutative property of the operator $\lor$, we add the constraint $h < j$ to remove the equivalent clauses.

For each symbol $a \in \Sigma$ and each $i \in B$:

$$y_{a,i,0} \lor y_{a,i,1} \lor ... \lor y_{a,i,n-1} \tag{8}$$

This means that each block relation must include at least one pair of blocks for each symbol.

We represent in Table 1 a summary of the formulas defined by Heule and Verwer.

Table 1. Summary for encoding (1) with clauses from PTA $\mathcal{P}(S) = (Q, \Sigma, \delta, q_\epsilon, F_A, F_R)$ into SAT. n is the maximal number of states in a DFA to infer, $B = \{0, ..., n-1\}$.

Ref	Clauses	Range
(2)	$v_{q,0} \lor v_{q,1} \lor ... \lor v_{q,n-1}$	$q \subset \mathcal{P}(S)$
(3)	$\neg v_{q,i} \lor \neg v_{q,j}$	$q \in \mathcal{P}(S); 0 \le i < j < n$
(4)	$\neg v_{q,i} \lor \neg v_{q',i}$	$q \in F_A, q' \in F_R; i \in B$
(5)	$y_{a,i,j} \lor \neg v_{q,i} \lor \neg v_{q',j}$	$(q, a, q') \in \delta; i, j \in B$
(6)	$\neg y_{a,i,j} \lor \neg v_{q,i} \lor v_{q',j}$	$(q, a, q') \in \delta; i, j \in B$
(7)	$\neg y_{a,i,h} \lor \neg y_{a,i,j}$	$a \in \Sigma; h, i, j \in B; h < j$
(8)	$y_{a,i,0} \lor y_{a,i,1} \lor ... \lor y_{a,i,n-1}$	$a \in \Sigma; i \in B$

It is possible that different assignments for a given SAT formula represents the same solution. In this case, we say that we have symmetry. A good practice is to break this symmetry [1,2,5] by adding constraints such that different assignments satisfying the formula represent different solutions. A formulation can result in a significant amount of symmetry if any permutation of the blocks is allowed. To eliminate this symmetry, Heule and Verwer use the state incompatibility graph which has $|Q|$ nodes and two nodes are connected iff the corresponding states of Q are incompatible. Clearly, each state of a clique (maximal or smaller) must be placed in a distinct block. Hence, they add to the SAT formula clauses for assigning initially each state from the clique to a separate block.

Experiments indicate that the proposed encoding of the constraints (1) is rather compact.

4   Incremental SAT Solving with Domain Specific Heuristics

4.1   Incremental SAT Solving

A disadvantage of the above SAT method is that the bigger a learning sample, the more complex the SAT formula. Thus, it can be expected that the solution time will increase significantly with the size of the learning sample. However, in practice, this becomes detrimental, because we would like to use the largest possible learning sample to increase the chances of inferring a good model.

Addressing this problem, we proposed an iterative method for inferring FSMs [3]. Similar to this method, we propose to generate SAT constraints incrementally for DFAs as well. The idea is to iteratively infer a DFA from constraints generated for a subset (initially it is an empty set) of the learning sample. If the inferred DFA is inconsistent with the full learning sample, then we add more constraints considering an inconsistent example. This idea is in fact used by active inference methods, though active inference rely on a black box as an oracle capable of judging whether or not a word belongs to the model. In our method, the role of an oracle is assigned to a learning sample S. Even if this oracle is restricted since it cannot decide the acceptance for all possible examples, nevertheless, as we demonstrate, it leads to an efficient approach for passive inference from a learning sample.

Our incremental inference method works as follows. Let S be a learning sample (generated by a deterministic DFA). We want to find a minimal DFA consistent with S iteratively. To do that, we search for a DFA $\mathcal{A}$ with at most n states satisfying a growing set of constraints (initially we do not have any constraints). If no solution is found, it means that the bound n is too low. In this case we increase n and start again. If a solution is found and $\mathcal{A}$ is consistent with S, then we return this solution. Otherwise, we find the shortest example w in S inconsistent with $\mathcal{A}$. Then, we formulate a constraint that w has to be consistent with $\mathcal{A}$.

Note that Heule and Verwer's method of using a clique in the incompatibility graph is not applicable in an iterative approach context. Thus, we use an implicit and not explicit symmetry breaking method. In particular, we forbid block permutations by using a total order on the set of states. Let $<$ be a total order over the set of states $Q = \bigcup\limits_{w \in Pref(S)} Q_w$ for all positive and negative examples. Based on a chosen order we add the following clauses excluding permutations. For each $q \in Q$ and each $i \in B$, we have a Boolean formula (which can be translated trivially into clauses):

$$\left(\bigwedge_{q' < q} \neg v_{q',i} \right) \Rightarrow \neg v_{q,i+1} \tag{9}$$

Intuitively, these clauses force to use blocks not already assigned when a state requires a new block.

The SAT formulation from Heule and Verwer is an efficient compact encoding, but determining that two states cannot be merged is a complex task. With our new heuristics, that we will present in Sect. 4.2, the solver will attempt to merge numerous not always compatible states. To reduce the number of such attempts we add more auxiliary (thus redundant) clauses that allow the solver to immediately detect that two states cannot be merged.

In particular, we add new auxiliary variables $E_{q,q'}$ for each pair of states $q, q' \in Q$.

First, we add clauses to encode the constraint that an accepting and a rejecting state cannot be merged. For every states q, q' such that $q \in F_A$ and $q' \in F_R$ we have a Boolean formula:

$$\neg E_{q,q'} \tag{10}$$

Notice that the clauses (4) express the same constraint, but in a less explicit way. In the same vein, we enforce the determinism of solutions by requiring that if two states merged together, their successors for any symbol also have to be merged together. We encode this property by the following formula (which can be translated trivially into clauses). For all $(q, a, p), (q', a, p') \in \delta$ we have a Boolean formula:

$$E_{q,q'} \Rightarrow E_{p,p'} \tag{11}$$

Finally, we encode the propagation of incompatibility to prohibit some mergers by the following formula (which can be translated trivially into clauses). For every states $q, q' \in Q$ and all $i \in \{0, ..., n-1\}$

$$(\neg E_{q,q'} \wedge v_{q,i}) \Rightarrow \neg v_{q',i} \tag{12}$$

It should be noted that we do not only propagate incompatibility here. The aim is to detect a conflict when a wrong merge is done without having to assign more free variables. Obviously the detection of such an error is not always possible without having to assign all free variables, but the above formulas increase the number of cases where this is possible.

Table 2. Summary for additional clauses from the PTA $\mathcal{P}(S) = (Q, \Sigma, \delta, q_\epsilon, F_A, F_R)$.

Ref	Clauses	Range
(9)	$\left(\bigwedge_{q' < q} \neg v_{q',i} \right) \Rightarrow \neg v_{q,i+1}$	$q \in Q, i \in \{0, ..., n-1\}$
(10)	$\neg E_{q,q'}$	$q \in F_A; q' \in F_R$
(11)	$\neg E_{q,q'} \vee E_{p,p'}$	$(q, a, p), (q', a, p') \in \delta$
(12)	$E_{q,q'} \vee \neg v_{q,i} \vee \neg v_{q',i}$	$q, q' \in Q; i \in \{0, ..., n-1\}$

The incremental SAT solving approach is formalized in Algorithm 1. The algorithm refers to Tables 1 and 2 to encode the problem in SAT. Note that in practice we only add clauses not already added to exploit the ability of the SAT solver to operate incrementally.

Theorem 1. *Algorithm 1 returns a DFA consistent with S if it exists and false otherwise.*

Proof. If the algorithm returns a DFA, it means that the condition in line 7 holds, $\mathcal{A}$ is consistent with S. If the algorithm returns *false*, it means that the

---

Algorithm 1. Infer a DFA from a learning sample

Input: A learning sample S and an integer n
Output: A DFA with at most n states consistent with S if it exists
1: Let S' be an empty set
2: $C := v_{q_\epsilon, 0}$
3: $C := C \wedge \bigwedge\limits_{a \in \Sigma,\ 0 \le i < n} (y_{a,i,0} \vee ... y_{a,i,n-1})$ (See Formula 8)
4: $C := C \wedge \bigwedge\limits_{a \in \Sigma,\ 0 \le i,j,h < n,\ h < j} (\neg y_{a,i,h} \vee \neg y_{a,i,j})$ (See Formula 7)
5: **while** C is satisfiable **do**
6:     Let $\mathcal{A}$ be a DFA of a solution of C
7:     **if** $\mathcal{A}$ is consistent with S **then**
8:         **return** $\mathcal{A}$
9:     **end if**
10:     Let w be the shortest example in S inconsistent with $\mathcal{A}$
11:     $S' := S' \cup \{w\}$
12:     Let C be the clauses from the PTA $\mathcal{P}(S')$ using Table 1 and Table 2
13: **end while**
14: **return** $false$

---

formula C is unsatisfiable, and therefore there is no partition of size n for $\mathcal{P}(S')$; hence there is no solution for learning sample S.

The termination of the algorithm is guaranteed by the fact that in each execution of the loop, a new example of S is considered. Thus, when $S' = S$, we know that the condition in line 7 is true.

4.2 Domain Specific Heuristics

The performance of solvers depends strongly on the choices made when assigning free variables. A free variable is a variable not yet assigned to a value $true$ or $false$. Indeed, the resolution time can be significantly longer or shorter depending on these choices. In order to mitigate this problem, solvers use all kinds of heuristics [8,10,11]. These heuristics are generally intended to be comprehensive and try to reduce the resolution time whatever the formulas to solve are.

In this section, we propose to use, instead of the general heuristics, a heuristics specific to the DFA inference to decide which free variable should be assigned next. As the RPNI algorithm does exactly this and identifies in the limit the generator, we propose to use its heuristics to make the variable choices. This is motivated by the observation that RPNI makes state merge choices more and more relevant as the number of examples increases. Thus, we expect that the extra time required by a SAT solver to solve a problem when more examples are added will be compensated by the time saved by our heuristics and by making better choices of next free variables to assign. We know that eventually this will be the case, because all the merging choices made by RPNI are correct choices when the number of examples is large enough.

4.2.1   RPNI Heuristics on Decision Variables

Most of the SAT solvers allow the user to distinguish two types of variables, decision and auxiliary variables. The decision variables are the variables for which we want to know a valid assignment, i.e., the assignment that satisfies the formula. Auxiliary variables are additional variables that can be used to factorize the encoding of a SAT formula or just help a solver find a solution faster. We do not seek generally to find an assignment for these auxiliary variables, since it can be deduced from a valid assignment of the decision variables. In our SAT formula, only variables $v_{q,i}$ will be decision variables. The other variables will be considered by the solver as auxiliary variables. Thus, the SAT solver will terminate when it finds an assignment for all variables $v_{q,i}$.

The RPNI heuristics will be used to decide which variable $v_{q,i}$ should be chosen among the free variables. To do that, each word $w.i$ such that $\delta(q_\epsilon, w) = q$ is assigned to the variable $v_{q,i}$. When the solver must decide which free variable to pick, one of variables $v_{q,i}$ will be chosen according to the lexicographical order on the words associated with variables. Then it will try to assign this variable to *true*.

In fact, this heuristic suggests selecting a state not already assigned to a block and trying to assign it to a block in the ascending order. The order in which the states are selected respects the RPNI strategy, i. e., selecting the state closest in the lexicographical order to the root.

4.2.2   Implementation

Adding the proposed heuristics to a solver, we have slightly modified the solver MiniSAT [7]. In MiniSAT, the variable *order_heap* of type *VarOrderLt* associates a weight of type *Integer* to each free variable. The heuristics used by the solver consists in modifying these weights during the resolution of the formula according to various criteria. Thus, when a free variable assignment must be done, the solver uses *order_heap* to select the free variable according to its weight.

Our modification consists in disabling the default solver heuristics and changing the *VarOrderLt* structure of each variable to a word. Thus, each Boolean variable $v_{q_w,i}$ is associated with the weight $w.i$. As a result, when a free variable has to be assigned the solver returns a variable associated with the shortest word in the lexicographic order.

5   Experimental Evaluation

We have performed a set of benchmarks to evaluate our approach. All DFAs are generated randomly with $|\Sigma| = 4$ and n states. For each state s and each $a \in \Sigma$, we randomly choose a state s' such that $\delta(s, a) = s'$. If the DFA we obtain is not minimal, we start again until we obtain a minimal one. Since generating a random DFA is rather simple, it does not take much time, even if many attempts are required to find a minimal DFA. To generate examples from this DFA, we perform random walks of a random length between 0 and 50.

We compare five algorithms.

- *RPNI*: We use the implementation provided by Stamina competition [13].
- *H&V*: It is the SAT approach elaborated by Heule and Verwer. The method is summarized in Table 1.
- *Incremental SAT*: It is a SAT approach implemented in an incremental way recently proposed by us [3]. This approach corresponds to Algorithm 1, neither using Table 2 for clause generation nor changing the SAT solver.
- *Incremental SAT2*: It is *Incremental SAT* in which we add the additional clauses from Table 2.
- *New algo*: It is our approach described in Sect. 4.

The SAT solver used for this experimentation is MiniSat [7] and we use a VirtualBox with 12 GB of RAM and Intel®Core^{TM} i7-2600K processor.

5.1 Inference Varying the Number of Examples

In this section, we compare the five algorithms on DFAs with five states. We limit the number of states to 5 so that each algorithm is able to solve the problem. DFAs with more states will be considered in the next section. In this experiment, see Fig. 1, we vary the number of examples and determine time it takes to infer a DFA.

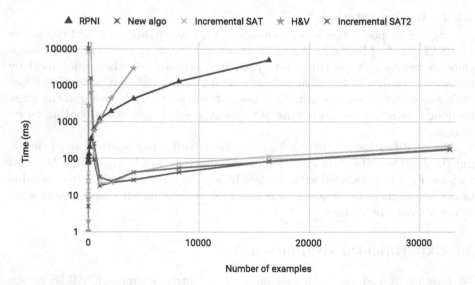

Fig. 1. Average time over 100 instances to infer a DFA with five states vs the number of examples.

We notice that the performances of the *New algo*, *Incremental SAT* and *Incremental SAT2* algorithms are almost the same as well as that they behave best when the learning samples are large enough. The results show that our approach is faster than *H&V* and *RPNI* except in the case where the number of examples is very small.

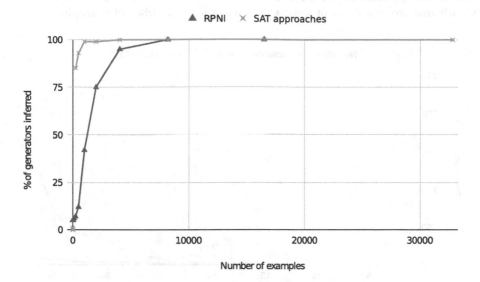

Fig. 2. Percentage of generators inferred correctly vs the number of examples.

To find the reason for that we determine the percentage of generators correctly inferred for SAT and RPNI approaches for learning samples of various sizes, see Fig. 2. We have grouped all the SAT approaches into a single curve because the quality of the obtained solutions is almost the same. This is not surprising because all SAT approaches are focused on finding an optimal solution, i.e., a minimum DFA consistent with observations. The data indicate that longer solution time is the price to pay for a higher percentage of good models inferred by the SAT approaches. After all, RPNI is heuristic, while SAT approaches are deductive. The obtained results indicate that SAT approaches have an important advantage over RPNI. In particular, SAT approaches need about thousand examples to correctly infer almost all generators, while the RPNI approach needs more than ten thousand. In addition, when the RPNI approach does not correctly infer the DFA, the result is generally quite far from the generator and contains hundreds of states.

Thus, the fact that SAT approaches are rather slow when the size of learning samples is only a few dozen is not really important, because with so few examples we are hardly able to infer generators correctly.

5.2   Inference from Learning Samples of Growing Generators

In this section, we focus on experimental comparison of the *Incremental SAT*, *Incremental SAT2* and *New algo* approaches. In the previous section, we saw that they perform similarly when the number of states in generators is fixed to five. Here we will push the algorithms to their limits. Thus we set the number of examples in learning samples at 100,000 and increase the number of generator's states. Comparison with *RPNI* and *H&V* is not possible here because these algorithms are unable to proceed with such a large number of examples.

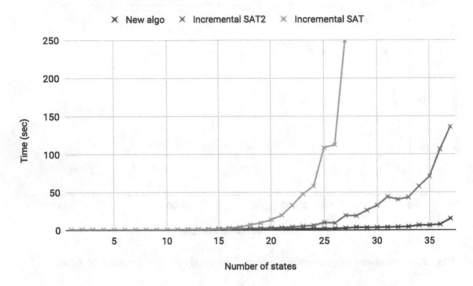

Fig. 3. Average time over 100 instances to infer a DFA vs the number of generator's states

Figure 3 indicates that the three algorithms equally perform when the generators have less than 15 states. However, for generators with more states, our new method has a clear advantage. As an examples, DFAs of 27 states are inferred on average in 2.5 s with our new method while it takes more than 4 min with *Incremental SAT*, and DFAs of 37 states are inferred on average in 15 s with our new method while it takes more than 2 min without the RPNI heuristics on decision variables.

6   Conclusion

In this paper we considered the problem of inferring a minimal DFA from a learning sample that includes positive and negative examples. Among the existing approaches, the heuristic approaches, like RPNI, merge states reaching a local minimum and the exact approaches solve constraints finding a minimal automaton consistent with observations.

In order to improve the scalability of exact inferring approaches, we made the following contributions.

First, we proposed to construct the SAT formula incrementally during the DFA inference, similar to our method for the FSM inference, thus avoiding to deal with a whole (large) learning sample.

Second, we found a way of combining the two approaches such that the result surpasses each of them. In particular, to improve the performance of a SAT solver we proposed to use the RPNI heuristics determining the order in which free variables are assigned.

Finally, we also suggested new auxiliary variables and additional clauses to be used in the traditional SAT encoding which accelerate the process of determining the state incompatibility.

The experimental evaluation of the proposed approach indicates that when a learning sample is large enough, it gives better results than the classical SAT solving approaches and the RPNI algorithm. The experimental results show that the proposed approach is somewhat slower that the latter, but only when the learning sample is too small to correctly infer the generator from it. These experiments seem to confirm that the scalability of the SAT solving approach for DFA inference improves when the SAT formula is built incrementally and a solver is enriched with a problem specific heuristics.

Acknowledgments. This work was partially supported by MEI (Ministère de l'Économie et Innovation) of Gouvernement du Québec and NSERC of Canada.

References

1. Aloul, F.A., Ramani, A., Markov, I.L., Sakallah, K.A.: Solving difficult SAT instances in the presence of symmetry. In: Proceedings of the 39th Annual Design Automation Conference, pp. 731–736. ACM (2002)
2. Aloul, F.A., Sakallah, K.A., Markov, I.L.: Efficient symmetry breaking for Boolean satisfiability. IEEE Trans. Comput. **55**(5), 549–558 (2006)
3. Avellaneda, F., Petrenko, A.: FSM inference from long traces. In: Havelund, K., Peleska, J., Roscoe, B., de Vink, E. (eds.) FM 2018. LNCS, vol. 10951, pp. 93–109. Springer, Cham (2018). https://doi.org/10.1007/978-3-319-95582-7_6
4. Biermann, A.W., Feldman, J.A.: On the synthesis of finite-state machines from samples of their behavior. IEEE Trans. Comput. **100**(6), 592–597 (1972)
5. Brown, C.A., Finkelstein, L., Purdom, P.W.: Backtrack searching in the presence of symmetry. In: Mora, T. (ed.) AAECC 1988. LNCS, vol. 357, pp. 99–110. Springer, Heidelberg (1989). https://doi.org/10.1007/3-540-51083-4_51
6. De la Higuera, C.: Grammatical Inference: Learning Automata and Grammars. Cambridge University Press, Cambridge (2010)
7. Eén, N., Sörensson, N.: An extensible SAT-solver. In: Giunchiglia, E., Tacchella, A. (eds.) SAT 2003. LNCS, vol. 2919, pp. 502–518. Springer, Heidelberg (2004). https://doi.org/10.1007/978-3-540-24605-3_37
8. Freeman, J.W.: Improvements to propositional satisfiability search algorithms. Ph.D. thesis. Citeseer (1995)
9. Heule, M.J.H., Verwer, S.: Software model synthesis using satisfiability solvers. Empir. Softw. Eng. **18**(4), 825–856 (2013)

10. Marques-Silva, J.: The impact of branching heuristics in propositional satisfiability algorithms. In: Barahona, P., Alferes, J.J. (eds.) EPIA 1999. LNCS, vol. 1695, pp. 62–74. Springer, Heidelberg (1999). https://doi.org/10.1007/3-540-48159-1_5

11. Moskewicz, M.W., Madigan, C.F., Zhao, Y., Zhang, L., Malik, S.: Chaff: engineering an efficient sat solver. In: Proceedings of the 38th Annual Design Automation Conference, pp. 530–535. ACM (2001)

12. Oncina, J., Garcia, P.: Inferring regular languages in polynomial updated time. In: Pattern Recognition and Image Analysis: Selected Papers from the IVth Spanish Symposium, pp. 49–61. World Scientific (1992)

13. Walkinshaw, N., Lambeau, B., Damas, C., Bogdanov, K., Dupont, P.: STAMINA: a competition to encourage the development and assessment of software model inference techniques. Empir. Softw. Eng. 18(4), 791–824 (2013)

Incorporating Data into EFSM Inference

Michael Foster[1]([✉]) [iD], Achim D. Brucker[2] [iD], Ramsay G. Taylor[1] [iD],
Siobhán North[1] [iD], and John Derrick[1] [iD]

[1] Department of Computer Science, The University of Sheffield,
Regent Court, Sheffield S1 4DP, UK
{jmafoster1,r.g.taylor,s.north,j.derrick}@sheffield.ac.uk
[2] Department of Computer Science, University of Exeter, Exeter, UK
a.brucker@exeter.ac.uk

Abstract. Models are an important way of understanding software systems. If they do not already exist, then we need to infer them from system behaviour. Most current approaches infer classical FSM models that do not consider data, thus limiting applicability. EFSMs provide a way to concisely model systems with an internal state but existing inference techniques either do not infer models which allow outputs to be computed from inputs, or rely heavily on comprehensive white-box traces to reveal the internal program state, which are often unavailable.

In this paper, we present an approach for inferring EFSM models, including functions that modify the internal state. Our technique uses black-box traces which only contain information visible to an external observer of the system. We implemented our approach as a prototype.

Keywords: EFSM inference · Model inference · Reverse engineering

1 Introduction

Accurate system models are applicable to a broad range of software engineering tasks. They can be used to automate the process of model-based testing [7,15], to detect cyber attacks [16], and to aid the process of requirements capture [4]. Despite their utility, system models can be neglected during development. It is therefore desirable to reverse engineer them from existing systems. One way to do this is to record executions of the system and infer a model from these *traces*.

There is abundant work on the inference of finite state machine (FSM) models from traces [2,10,18], much of which falls into the family of *state merging* algorithms. These begin by constructing the most specific automaton which accepts all of the observed traces, and iteratively consolidate the model by merging states in the FSM which are believed to represent the same program state. The resulting model, as well as being smaller than the original, is often more general. It is able to predict how the system might behave when faced with previously unseen traces. This is a key feature of model inference and differentiates it from automaton minimisation which seeks to reduce the size of a model without changing the language it accepts.

© Springer Nature Switzerland AG 2019
P. C. Ölveczky and G. Salaün (Eds.): SEFM 2019, LNCS 11724, pp. 257–272, 2019.
https://doi.org/10.1007/978-3-030-30446-1_14

Classical FSMs cannot handle data so they struggle to represent systems that exhibit data-dependent behaviour, for example a vending machine which dispenses drinks selected by users. Here, the input of the *select* action determines the output of *dispense*. A classical FSM model of the system would require a separate path for each available drink, so would likely be rather large. Extended Finite State Machines (EFSMs) provide a richer model, featuring a persistent data state, which could be used to store the selected drink, but existing EFSM inference techniques [12,19] do not infer how the data state is used, nor can they capture the *causal* effect of input on output.

This paper presents a technique to infer EFSM models from system traces which explicitly capture this causal relationship. The main contributions are:

1. A technique which uses black-box traces (instead of the more commonly used white-box traces) to infer EFSM models which capture the causal relationship between inputs and outputs.
2. A prototype tool which implements this technique.

The rest of this paper is structured as follows. Section 2 introduces a motivating example and explains how state merging algorithms work. Section 3 presents our EFSM inference technique. Section 4 discusses how we introduce data registers to capture the causal relationship between input and output. Section 5 details how we implemented our technique as a prototype inference tool. Section 6 evaluates our technique with reference to the scenario presented in Sect. 2. Section 7 concludes the paper and discusses possible future works.

2   Background

Reverse engineering models from traces is an inference process which aims to make statements about the overall behaviour of a system by generalising from observations. Consider a simple vending machine which produces traces like those in Fig. 1. Users first *select* a drink by providing its name as an input. The *coin* operation allows users to pay for their drink by inserting coins of a given value, displaying as output the total value inserted so far. Once sufficient payment has been inserted, the *vend* operation is triggered to dispense the drink.

In Fig. 1, we use the notation $methodName(i_1, i_2, \ldots)/[o_1, o_2, \ldots]$ such that $coin(50)/[50]$ represents the event *coin* being called with a single input of 50 and producing a single output of 50. We delimit events with arrows and omit the outputs from events like *select('coke')* which do not produce any.

To infer a classical FSM model from the traces in Fig. 1, we must either remove the data entirely or encode it within the actions by folding input and

$$select(`coke') \rightarrow coin(50)/[50] \rightarrow coin(50)/[100] \rightarrow vend()/[`coke']$$
$$select(`pepsi') \rightarrow coin(50)/[50] \rightarrow coin(50)/[100] \rightarrow vend()/[`pepsi']$$
$$select(`coke') \rightarrow coin(100)/[100] \rightarrow vend()/[`coke']$$

Fig. 1. Exemplary traces of the vending machine.

output values into the transition labels. Taking the latter approach, we represent an event $label(i_1)/[o_1]$ as the atomic action $label\_i_1\_o_1$. The inference process begins by building an automaton which accepts exactly the observed traces. This is usually a tree-shaped automaton called a prefix tree acceptor (PTA), where traces with common prefixes share a common path through the model up to the point of divergence. Figure 2 shows a PTA representing the traces in Fig. 1.

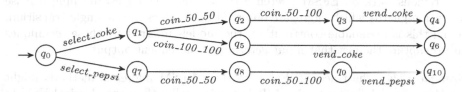

Fig. 2. A classical FSM PTA built from the traces in Fig. 1, in which transition input and output data has been encoded into the transition labels.

We condense the PTA by merging states which we believe represent the same program state, based on the commonality of their outgoing transitions. In Fig. 2, for example, q_3 and q_5 both have an outgoing *vend_coke* transition. The result of merging these two states has two nondeterministic outgoing *vend_coke* transitions. This does not make sense as we merged q_3 and q_5 because we believe their respective outgoing transitions represent the same behaviour, meaning that their destination states should represent the same program state. We merge these states (q_4 and q_6) so the two *vend_coke* transitions are no longer distinct. In this way, branches of a PTA are *zipped* together as we merge successive states.

When the model becomes deterministic again, we search for another pair of states, that might represent the same program state, to merge. This continues until no more pairs of states are believed to represent the same program state. An optimal FSM model which could be inferred from the traces in Fig. 1 is shown in Fig. 3. This is more concise than the PTA in Fig. 2 but is still relatively large and cannot predict the behaviour of the system for unseen inputs.

We cannot expect to infer models of unobserved behaviour but it is not unreasonable to want to predict the outcome of applying the same *action* with different *data*. Classical FSM models cannot separate these, so the transitions *select_coke*

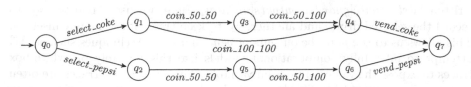

Fig. 3. A classical FSM model of a simple drinks machine, inferred by merging states of the PTA in Fig. 2.

and *select_pepsi* represent different behaviours rather than two instances of *select* with different inputs. This means that small changes in behaviour, like adding additional drinks, have a disproportionate effect on model complexity. EFSMs are a promising solution to this problem. Numerous definitions exist in the literature [3,6,11] but all make use of similar features: parametrised guarded inputs, a persistent data state, and output expressed in terms of input. These features make EFSM models more expressive but also much harder to infer.

Previous work on EFSM inference [12,19] focusses on establishing concise transition guards which aggregate observed data values into a single transition. While this is a valuable contribution, the models inferred by these techniques fail to capture the fact that input *determines* subsequent output.

Example 1. For the traces in Fig. 1, existing EFSM inference methods might produce a model similar to Fig. 4. It is much smaller than the classical FSM in Fig. 3, as we are now able to separate action from data. Here, we have a guard on the *select* transition which requires the first input, i_1, to be either *'coke'* or *'pepsi'*. This is mirrored by the output, o_1, of *vend*. All observed inputs and outputs of *coin* were greater than or equal to 50 so the guard reflects this.

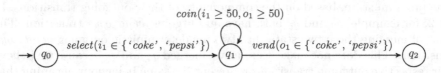

$coin(i_1 \geq 50, o_1 \geq 50)$

$select(i_1 \in \{\,'coke', 'pepsi'\,\})$ $vend(o_1 \in \{\,'coke', 'pepsi'\,\})$

q_0 q_1 q_2

Fig. 4. An EFSM as might be inferred by existing methods. Here, transitions take the form $label(g_1, g_2, \ldots)$ in which inputs are denoted i_n and outputs o_n.

This model summarises the observed values but fails to show how output is computed from input—it is not *computational*. We know that the output of the *vend* transition is either *'coke'* or *'pepsi'* but cannot tell which we will get, much less that it is determined by the input to *select*. Inputs and outputs are both just treated as variables here so there is no explicit link between them.   □

The EFSMs inferred by [12] and [19] use the program variables present in the traces but do not infer *how* individual transitions update variables. An ideal EFSM model of the traces in Fig. 1 is shown in Fig. 5, in which transitions are written $label : arity[guards]/outputs[updates]$. Here, we use a register, r_1, to record the selected drink, and another, r_2, to keep track of the money inserted. This allows us to *compute* the outputs of *vend* and *coin*. Techniques such as [17] attempt to infer fully computational models like this but rely on white-box traces to expose the values of internal variables. Since white-box traces are often unavailable, we would ideally like to use black-box traces, which only contain information available to an external observer of the system.

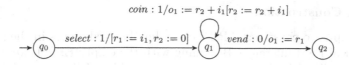

Fig. 5. The ideal EFSM model of the drinks machine.

3   Extending the Inference Process

In this section, we present our technique to infer EFSM models from traces. While there are many different EFSM representations in the literature, [3,11] we use the one we defined in previous work [6].

Definition 1. *An EFSM is a tuple,* (S, s_0, T) *where* S *is a finite non-empty set of states,* $s_0 \in S$ *is the initial state, and* T *is the transition matrix* T : $(S \times S) \to \mathcal{P}(L \times \mathbb{N} \times G \times F \times U)$ *with rows representing origin states and columns representing destination states. In* T, L *is a set of transition labels.* $\mathbb{N}$ *gives the transition arity (the number of input parameters), which may be zero.* G *is a set of Boolean guard functions* $G : (I \times R) \to \mathbb{B}$. F *is a set of output functions* $F : (I \times R) \to O$. U *is a set of update functions* $U : (I \times R) \to R$.

In G, F, *and* U, I *is a tuple* $[i_1, i_2, \ldots, i_m]$ *of values representing the inputs of a transition, which is empty if the arity is zero. Inputs do not persist across states or transitions.* R *is a mapping from variables* $[r_1, r_2, \ldots]$, *representing each register of the machine, to their values. Registers are globally accessible and persist throughout the operation of the machine. All registers are initially undefined until explicitly set by an update expression.* O *is a tuple* $[o_1, o_2, \ldots, o_n]$ *of values, which may be empty, representing the outputs of a transition.*

Syntactic sugar allows transitions from state S_m to state S_n to take the form

$$S_m \xrightarrow{\ label:arity[g_1,\ldots,g_n]/f_1,\ldots,f_n[u_1,\ldots,u_n]\ } S_n$$

The first part of the transition is an atomic *label* naming the event. This is followed by a colon and the *arity* of the transition. Guard expressions $g_1, \ldots, g_n$ are enclosed in square brackets. Next comes a slash, after which $f_1, \ldots, f_n$ define the outputs. Finally, update expressions $u_1, \ldots, u_n$, enclosed in square brackets, define the posterior data state. There should be at most one update function per register per transition to maintain consistency. For transitions without guards, outputs, or updates, the corresponding components are omitted.

Our inference process follows the same basic structure as classical FSM inference algorithms—we build a PTA and then iteratively merge states to form a smaller model. Our technique differs from classical FSM inference in two ways. Firstly, because of the more complex EFSM transitions, attempts to resolve the nondeterminism introduced by merging states might fail, meaning that two states which initially seemed compatible cannot actually be merged. This is not the case in classical FSM inference. We tackle this in Subsect. 3.2. Secondly, the nondeterminism introduced by merging states cannot be resolved by simply merging destination states. We address this in Subsect. 3.3.

3.1   PTA Construction

The first step is to construct a PTA from the observed traces in the same way as for classical FSM inference. Beginning with the empty EFSM, we iteratively attempt to walk each observed trace in the machine. When we reach a point where there is no available transition, we add one. While classical FSMs use an atomic label, EFSMs deal with data so we add guards to test for the observed input values, and outputs which produce the observed values. For example, the event $coin(50)/[50]$ causes the transition $coin : 1[i_1 = 50]/o_1 := 50$ to be added to the machine. The event label is $coin$. It takes one input, which must be equal to the observed input value of 50, and produces the literal output 50.

3.2   Merging States

Like in classical FSM inference, we use a predefined metric to order potential state merges by how strongly we believe that two states represent the same program state. The INFERENCESTEP function in Algorithm 1 merges the first (highest scoring) pair in the list of potential merges and calls RESOLVENONDE-TERMINISM (detailed in the Subsect. 3.3) to resolve any resulting nondetermin-ism. If this succeeds, the merging process begins again with a new list of potential merges, continuing until no more states can be merged. If RESOLVENONDETER-MINISM fails, this indicates that our belief of the two states representing the same program state was false, as we were unable to merge their respective behaviours. We then successively attempt to merge lower scoring state pairs until either one is successful or we run out of possibilities, at which point inference terminates.

Algorithm 1. The top level inference process.

1: **function** LEARN($l, scoringMetric$)
2:     **return** INFER(MAKEPTA(l), $scoringMetric$)

3: **function** INFER($efsm, scoringMetric$)
4:     **switch** INFERENCESTEP($efsm$, SCOREMERGES($efsm, scoringMetric$)) **do**
5:         **case None**
6:             **return** $efsm$
7:         **case Some** new
8:             **return** INFER($new, scoringMetric$)
9: **function** INFERENCESTEP($e, merges$)
10:     **switch** $merges$ **do**
11:         **case** []
12:             **return None**
13:         **case** ((s_1, s_2)#t)
14:             $e' =$ MERGESTATES(s_1, s_2, e)
15:             **switch** RESOLVENONDETERMINISM(NONDETPAIRS(e'), e, e') **do**
16:                 **case Some** new
17:                     **return Some** new
18:                 **case None**
19:                     **return** INFERENCESTEP(e, t)

3.3 Resolving Nondeterminism by Merging Transitions

Classical FSM inference merges duplicate behaviours into a single transition by merging their destination states. Since FSM transitions with the same origin state are only nondeterministic if their labels are equal, there is no need to explicitly merge transitions. This happens "for free" when we merge their destination states. The two transitions then have the same label, origin, and destination so they are no longer distinct. With EFSMs, transitions which express the same behaviour may not be identical. Thus the merging of transitions becomes an explicit step in the algorithm. There is also the possibility that two nondeterministic transitions cannot be merged, which does not occur in classical FSM inference. For example, in Fig. 6b, if r_1 holds value 'coke', there is no observable difference between the behaviour of the two vend transitions and they can be merged. If r_1 holds any value other than 'coke', there is an observable difference in behaviour and the transitions cannot be merged.

Algorithm 2. Resolving nondeterminism.

1: **function** RESOLVENONDETERMINISM($[\,], \_, new$)
2:    **if** DETERMINISTIC(new) **then**
3:       **return** **Some** new
4:    **else**
5:       **return** **None**
6: **function** RESOLVENONDETERMINISM($((from, (d_1, d_2), (t_1, t_2))\#ss), old, new$)
7:    $destMerge \leftarrow$ MERGESTATES(d_1, d_2, new)
8:    **switch** MERGETRANSITIONS($old, destMerge, t_1, t_2$) **do**
9:       **case None**
10:          RESOLVENONDETERMINISM(ss, old, new)
11:       **case Some** $merged$
12:          $newPairs \leftarrow$ NONDETPAIRS($merged$)
13:          **switch** RESOLVENONDETERMINISM($newPairs, old, merged$) **do**
14:             **case Some** new'
15:                **return** **Some** new'
16:             **case None**
17:                RESOLVENONDETERMINISM(ss, old, new)
18: **function** MERGETRANSITIONS($old, destMerge, t_1, t_2$)
19:    **if** DIRECTLYSUBSUMES($old, destMerge,$ ORIGIN(t_1, old)$, t_2, t_1$) **then**
20:       **return** **Some** REPLACETRANSITION($destMerge, t_1, t_2$)
21:    **else if** DIRECTLYSUBSUMES($old, destMerge,$ ORIGIN(t_2, old)$, t_1, t_2$) **then**
22:       **return** **Some** REPLACETRANSITION($destMerge, t_2, t_1$)
23:    **else**
24:       **return** **None**
25: **function** DIRECTLYSUBSUMES($e_1, e_2, s_1, s_2, t_2, t_1$)
26:    **return** ($\forall p$.ACCEPTSTRACE(e_1, p) $\land$ GETSUSTO(s_1, e_1, p) $\implies$
                ACCEPTSTRACE(e_2, p) $\land$ GETSUSTO(s_2, e_2, p) $\implies$
                SUBSUMES($t_2,$ ANTERIORCONTEXT(e_2, p)$, t_1$))
             $\land$ ($\exists c$.SUBSUMES(t_2, c, t_1))

The RESOLVENONDETERMINISM function takes a list of nondeterministic transition pairs and merges the destination states of the first pair. It then calls MERGETRANSITIONS to merge the transitions themselves. If this is successful, RESOLVENONDETERMINISM recurses until all nondeterminism has been resolved. If the transition merge fails, nondeterminism might be resolved by merging a different transition pair. Successive attempts are made until either one is successful or there are no more potential merges. In the latter case, RESOLVENONDETERMINISM fails, indicating that the original state pair should not have been merged.

When merging EFSM transitions, one must *account for* the behaviour of the other. This is conceptualised, for guarded transitions, as *subsumption* in [12] and extended to transitions with data updates in [6] which introduces *contexts* to record constraints on the values of inputs and registers during the execution of an EFSM, for example that a register holds a particular value. The idea of *subsumption in context* formalises the intuition that, in certain contexts, a transition t_2 reproduces the behaviour of t_1 and updates the data state in a manner consistent with t_1 meaning that t_2 can be used in place of t_1 with no observable difference in behaviour. For state s in an EFSM e, we say that a context c is *obtainable* if there exists a trace which is accepted by e, leaving it in state s, and produces c when executed.

Example 2. Consider the EFSM fragments in Fig. 6. Let us call the transitions $q_a \rightarrow q_b$ and $q_c \rightarrow q_d$ in $\mathcal{M}_1$ (Fig. 6a) t_1 and t_2 respectively. Say that the inference process merges states q_a and q_c to form the model in Fig. 6b. This results in nondeterminism between t_1 and t_2 which we would like to resolve.

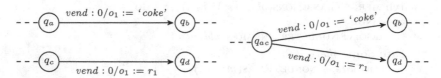

(a) Fragment of $\mathcal{M}_1$ before merging q_a and q_c.   (b) Fragment after merging q_a and q_c.

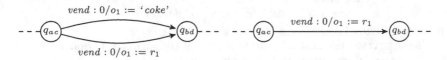

(c) Fragment after merging q_b and q_b to form $\mathcal{M}_2$.   (d) Fragment after merging the two transitions.

Fig. 6. The evolution of an EFSM fragment during the merging process.

We merged states q_a and q_c because we believe that their respective outgoing transitions express the same behaviour. This means that their respective destination states should represent the same program state, so we merge q_b with q_d

to form $\mathcal{M}_2$, shown in Fig. 6c. We then ask if one transition accounts for the behaviour of the other such that they can be merged. This means that in every situation where we could have taken t_1 in $\mathcal{M}_1$, we should now be able to take t_2 in $\mathcal{M}_2$ with no observable difference in behaviour, or vice versa. If r_1 holds value *'coke'*, then t_2 accounts for the behaviour of t_1. □

In Example 2, it is unlikely that r_1 will always hold the value *'coke'* in state q_{ac} but we only need t_2 to account for the behaviour of t_1 in situations where it could be taken in $\mathcal{M}_1$. This means that traces which got us to q_a in $\mathcal{M}_1$ must, when run in $\mathcal{M}_2$, produce contexts in which t_2 subsumes t_1, i.e. contexts in which $r_1 = $ *'coke'*. If this is the case, we say that t_2 *directly subsumes* t_1. This is not presented in [6] and is expressed as the first conjunct of the DIRECTLYSUBSUMES function in Algorithm 2. The second conjunct says that there must exist a context in which t_2 subsumes t_1, which accounts for models with unreachable states, from which any transition would otherwise directly subsume any other transition.

The MERGETRANSITIONS function can only merge transitions where one directly subsumes the other. If this is not the case, then neither can be used in place of the other without risking some observable difference in the behaviour of the model. In this case, MERGETRANSITIONS fails, returning **None**.

4   Introducing Registers

The technique in Sect. 3 allows us to infer deterministic EFSM models from traces by merging transitions where one subsumes the other, but we cannot yet fully capture the causal relationship between input and output. To achieve this, we must infer the use of *internal variables* which store information about the current state for later use. This section explains how we do this.

Example 3. The EFSM in Fig. 7 is the best model of the traces in Fig. 1 that our technique can infer so far. It is, essentially, an EFSM version of Fig. 3. While this is a more *accurate* view of the system—transitions are now expressed as events with parameters rather than atomic actions—it is no more *expressive*.

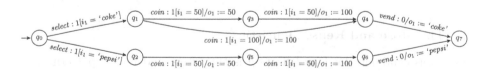

Fig. 7. An EFSM model inferred from the traces in Fig. 1.

The model contains two pairs of identical *coin* transitions which we could merge by *zipping* the path $q_1 \rightarrow q_3 \rightarrow q_4 \rightarrow q_7$ with $q_2 \rightarrow q_5 \rightarrow q_6 \rightarrow q_7$ as discussed in Sect. 2. We cannot do this, though, as it requires the transitions *vend* : $0/o_1 :=$ *'coke'* and *vend* : $0/o_1 :=$ *'pepsi'*, which have different literal outputs, to be merged. Since there is always an observable difference in their behaviour, neither *vend* transition directly subsumes the other so they cannot be merged. This means we cannot condense Fig. 7 any further.

Looking at the bigger picture, the two *vend* transitions do actually exhibit the same behaviour. Both produce, as output, the input of the initial *select* transition. If we could abstract away the concrete inputs and outputs, we could infer a smaller and more general model of the system. □

To this end, we allow the MERGETRANSITIONS function to attempt to introduce internal variables if neither transition directly subsumes the other. The aim here is not to create a "one size fits all" magic oracle, rather to provide a number of smaller heuristics, each of which focusses on a particular *data usage pattern*. We pass a list of heuristics to MERGETRANSITIONS as an additional argument, each of which either successfully returns an EFSM, or fails. If no direct subsumption occurs between two transitions, the heuristics are applied in the supplied order until either one of them succeeds or there are no more left to apply. This approach makes the tool extensible and gives users a degree of control over the characteristics of the final model as they can choose to provide or withhold particular heuristics. If neither transition directly subsumes the other and none of the heuristics are successful, the transition merge fails.

The fact that a heuristic successfully produces an EFSM does not guarantee the model to be acceptable. For example, the heuristic which always returns the empty EFSM resolves any nondeterminism (since a model with no transitions is trivially deterministic) but is clearly unacceptable. We must therefore be suspicious of solutions offered by heuristics if we want our inference process, as a whole, to always return an acceptable model of the original traces.

This leads to the question of how to define whether or not a model is acceptable. Clearly a minimum requirement for models inferred from traces is that they reproduce all of the observed behaviour. Since the original set of traces is finite, we can simply run each one through the model and compare the output to the original. We run this sanity check after each state-merge to ensure that the model still reflects the observed behaviour. If this is not the case, the model is discarded as if the state merge had failed. The remainder of this section details some heuristics which are relevant to our running drinks machine example.

4.1   The Store and Reuse Heuristic

An obvious candidate for generalisation is the "store and reuse" pattern. This manifests itself in Example 3 when the input of *select* is subsequently used as the output of *vend*. Recognising this usage pattern allows us to introduce a *storage register* to abstract away concrete data values and replace two transitions whose outputs differ with a single transition that outputs the content of the register.

The first step is to find *intratrace* matches—instances of data reuse *within* traces. We walk each trace in the current EFSM, recording when the output of a transition matches the input of an earlier transition, to obtain a set of matches for each trace in the form $\{((transition, inputIndex), (transition, outputIndex))\}$.

We then look to see if any of the matches concern the transitions we are trying to merge. If so, we attempt to *generalise* these transitions. This consists of introducing a fresh register to act as storage, adding an update to this register, and dropping the restriction on the relevant input value. The value of this register then becomes the output of the second transition. For example, we generalise the pair $((select : 1[i_1 = \text{'coke'}], 1), (vend : 0/o_1 := \text{'coke'}, 1))$ to $((select : 1/[r_1 := i_1], 1), (vend : 0/o_1 := r_1, 1))$, where r_1 does not already occur in the EFSM.

When multiple transition pairs generalise to the same thing, *between* multiple traces, we call this an *intertrace* match. Finding intertrace matches indicates that the same kind of behaviour occurs across multiple traces, potentially with different data values. This provides evidence in favour of generalising and merging transitions in the model.

4.2   The Increment and Reset Heuristic

Another usage pattern is "increment and reset". In our drinks machine example, the *coin* action outputs the sum of the previous *coin* inputs. This allows customers to use multiple coins to pay for their drink and to observe the total value they have inserted so far. Correctly identifying this usage pattern is not an easy problem to solve, but a naive heuristic is not difficult to implement.

The idea here is that if we want to merge two transitions with identical input values and different numeric outputs, for example $coin : 1[i_1 = 50]/o_1 := 50$ and $coin : 1[i_1 = 50]/o_1 := 100$, then the behaviour must depend on the value of an internal variable. We implement a heuristic which, when faced with such a merge, drops the input guard and adds an update to a fresh register, in this case summing the current register value with the input. For this to work, we must ensure that the register is initialised before our modified transitions are taken. To do this, we augment transitions incident to the origin state with an update function which sets the relevant register to zero. This is the "reset" part of the heuristic which ensures that the register is defined before it is used. A similar principle can be applied to other numeric functions such as subtraction.

4.3   The Same Register Use Heuristic

Heuristics operate on a per-merge basis so it is possible that multiple registers may be introduced to serve the same purpose at different points during the inference process. It is therefore important to recognise this and consolidate register usage to allow transitions which implement the same behaviour with different registers to be merged.

Consider, for example, the transitions $coin : 1/o_1 := r_1 + i_1[r_1 := r_1 + i_1]$ and $coin : 1/o_1 := r_2 + i_1[r_2 := r_2 + i_1]$. Both transitions use a single register and are identical up to the name of this register so it is possible that r_1 and r_2 are just different names for the same register. We therefore try to "merge" the two registers by renaming r_1 to r_2, or vice versa.

5   Implementation

The next task is to code up our technique into an executable program. Unfortunately, some parts of our technique, most notably the DIRECTLYSUBSUMES function, cannot be effectively computed. This section details how we tackled this to produce a prototype inference tool using Isabelle/HOL [14] (henceforth referred to as just "Isabelle"), a proof assistant and programming environment.

Isabelle allows data type and functions to be specified using a Haskell-style syntax, so we can use Isabelle to write programs and to prove that these programs satisfy certain properties. From previous work [6], we already had a formalisation of EFSMs in Isabelle with various proofs. We used this as a starting point for our implementation to avoid the duplication of work. A strength of using Isabelle for implementation is that functions can be expressed at a high level of abstraction, meaning that our Isabelle code is almost identical to the pseudocode in Algorithms 1 and 2.

Since Isabelle code is not directly executable, the built-in *code generator* [8] can be used to automatically convert Isabelle functions and data type to runnable code in a number of conventional programming languages. The code is not particularly well optimised but, assuming correctness of the code generator, properties which hold for the Isabelle formalisation also hold for the generated code. Once we had encoded our technique in Isabelle, we used the code generator to automatically create an executable Scala implementation. This, along with our formalisation, is available at https://github.com/jmafoster1/efsm-inference.

Of course, the code generator cannot generate code for non-computable functions like DIRECTLYSUBSUMES. This leaves us with gaps in our implementation which must be implemented manually. For these, the `code_printing` statement provides the ability to replace functions with custom implementations in the target language. Surprisingly, we were only faced with two problematic functions.

The first of these, NONDETPAIRS, provides details of nondeterministic transitions in an EFSM. For each state, it checks if there is a choice between any pair of outgoing transitions. This involves checking if the conjunction of their guards is satisfiable. We leveraged an existing SMT solver, Z3 [13], to do this for us by converting the guards to an appropriate format at runtime.

Coping with the non-executability of DIRECTLYSUBSUMES was more challenging. This function checks subsumption for all traces which get us to a particular state. The problem here is that there could be an infinite number of traces so we cannot use exhaustive search. Direct subsumption can be proven by induction over traces, on a case by case basis, but this is laborious. We cannot reasonably ask users to do this each time the inference process needs to know whether one transition directly subsumes another.

The solution to this lies in the fact that the inference process only encounters transitions from the original PTA and those introduced by the heuristics. If we can use Isabelle to prove direct subsumption for the various different *families* of transitions the inference process will come across, then the task of checking direct subsumption at runtime becomes a pattern matching exercise. For example, if we merge two states with a pair of identical outgoing transitions, we need to check if a transition directly subsumes itself. Clearly every transition is able to account for its own behaviour, so it does not make sense to check this on a per-merge basis. We proved the *general case* in Isabelle so that at runtime we can simply check to see if the two transitions we are attempting to merge are equal. If they are, then we have direct subsumption. We applied this approach to the other patterns that occur when using the heuristics detailed in Sect. 4.

Different Literal Outputs. If two transitions have outputs which always differ, for example $vend : 0/[o_1 := 'coke']$ and $vend : 0/[o_1 := 'pepsi']$, then there is always an observable difference in behaviour. Along similar lines, transitions which produce different numbers of outputs are always distinguishable. In both of these cases neither transition directly subsumes the other.

Drop Guard Add Update. The "store and reuse" heuristic exchanges a concrete-value guard on an input for an assignment to a fresh storage register. For a pair of transitions, in which one has been generalised and the other has not, for example $select : 1/[r_1 := i_1]$ and $select : 1[i_1 := 'coke']$, if we can ascertain that the relevant register (in this case r_1) is undefined in the origin state, then the general transition directly subsumes the specific one.

Register Output. The "store and reuse" heuristic also replaces a literal output with the content of a register. For a generalised transition to subsume an ungeneralised one, it suffices to show that the relevant register holds the original output value in all relevant contexts which can be obtained in the origin state.

Increment and Reset. The pattern introduced by the "increment and reset" heuristic are more subtle. This heuristic drops a literal guard and introduces an update which *mutates* the data state. We end up testing whether a transition of the form $coin : 1/o_1 := r_2 + i_1[r_2 := r_2 + i_1]$ subsumes a transition of the form $coin : 1[i_1 = n]/o_1 := m$. Neither transition can account for the behaviour of the other here as only one transition changes the data state. The updates are not *consistent* with each other. This means that the increment and reset heuristic only tends to be successful towards the end of the inference process when it is able to replace many transitions of the form $coin : 1[i_1 = n]/o_1 := m$ at once.

Having proved direct subsumption for the various transition families, our executable DIRECTLYSUBSUMES function simply steps through the cases until one matches. If none of the cases match, we have no choice but to ask the user but, for the heuristics detailed in this paper, this is not required. If additional heuristics were used that introduced new kinds of transitions to the model, further cases might be required to avoid queries to the user but, depending on the difficulty of the proofs, this would not be particularly arduous.

5.1   Checking Context Properties

In some of the patterns above, we require obtainable contexts to satisfy certain properties. Even though these are much simpler properties than subsumption, we still cannot exhaustively search all traces, nor can we expect a user to provide an inductive proof for each instance. Instead, we use SAL[1], a model checker with a similar representation to our own EFSM model. This allows us to automatically verify simple properties like "register r is always undefined in state s" in milliseconds. We do sacrifice some of the safety of an inductive proof, but doing so enables us to completely automate the process. Model checkers only work with finite data type, so we can only check a finite subset of all possible inputs. The larger this subset, the more confident we can be of the validity of a merge, but we must balance this with performance. If we are able to check traces over a suitable subset of inputs, then we can be reasonably confident that transition merges made as a result of this are safe.

6   Evaluation

When presented with the traces in Fig. 1, our technique infers the machine in Fig. 5 which we described as "ideal" in Sect. 2. There are many different metrics which could be used to assess this model including size and complexity, predictive power, observance of original behaviour, and correct classification of legal and illegal behaviours. This section provides evaluation and discussion of both the model and the inference process with reference to these metrics.

A common evaluation metric of classical FSM inference techniques [10,18] is the classification of legal and illegal behaviour. This is not suited to techniques that work only with observations of system behaviour which are, by definition, legal behaviours. It is unreasonable to evaluate such techniques with respect to illegal behaviour as examples of this are not available to the inference process.

The main aim of an automated inference is to create models that are easy to understand. This makes smaller models with fewer transitions more desirable. The model in Fig. 5 is both small and simple as it has only three states and three transitions. The original PTA has ten of each. Our model is also smaller than the classical FSM in Fig. 3 which has seven states and nine transitions.

Inferred models should, of course, exhibit all of the originally observed behaviour. This holds for our technique by definition since, at each stage of inference, the new machine is checked to ensure that it accepts all of the originally observed traces. The model in Fig. 5 accepts all of the traces in Fig. 1 and produces all of the originally observed outputs.

An important difference between inference and minimisation is that inference aims to generalise from the observed behaviour. The model we inferred exhibits the same top-level behaviour no matter what drink the user selects or what values of coins the user pays for their drink with. While this inevitably leads to models which *over generalise* the observed behaviour, it enables us to *predict* how the system might behave when faced with unseen inputs.

An advantage of our model over the one in Fig. 4 is that our model is able to *compute* outputs from inputs. For any sequence of inputs to *coin*, we are able to predict the exact value of the output rather than simply constraining it.

---

[1] http://sal.csl.sri.com/.

7   Conclusions and Future Works

This work presents a technique to infer EFSM models from black-box system traces. Building on [6], we have now shown how to infer computational EFSM models from traces by using heuristics which recognise data usage patterns. We defined *direct subsumption* and used it to help us merge transitions. We formalised our technique in Isabelle/HOL and exported it to executable Scala code using Isabelle's built-in code generator where possible.

Most modern inference techniques fit into two categories. Active techniques such as [1,5,9] make use of an oracle, usually the end-user, to guide the inference by classifying traces as either possible or impossible. Assuming the availability of such an oracle, active techniques produce good quality models but are quite labour intensive. By contrast, passive methods such as [2,10,18] sacrifice the oracle in favour of complete automation. These techniques infer models solely from traces of the system under inference so, unlike active methods, they often do not have access to examples of impossible system behaviour in the form of *negative traces* which the system, by definition, is unable to produce.

Classical FSM models use atomic transitions which cannot separate actions from data. They must encode data within the control flow, so struggle with systems that exhibit data-dependent behaviour. EFSM models feature parametrised inputs, guarded transitions, and a persistent data state so are much better suited to modelling data-dependent behaviour. Existing EFSM inference techniques [11,19] focus on inferring transition guards but do not infer models which capture the *causal* relationship between input and output. Attempts have been made to infer computational models [17], but these rely on white-box traces to expose the inner system state. Such traces are often unavailable so the inference of computational EFSM models from black-box traces is a key challenge in EFSM inference. This work presents such a technique.

Future work includes the implementation of further heuristics, such as one to recognise boundary conditions which separate behaviour. Additionally, the tool needs to be run on larger case studies to investigate how well it scales.

References

1. Angluin, D.: Learning regular sets from queries and counterexamples. Inf. Comput. **75**(2), 87–106 (1987). https://doi.org/10.1016/0890-5401(87)90052-6
2. Biermann, A.W., Feldman, J.A.: On the synthesis of finite-state machines from samples of their behavior. IEEE Trans. Comput. **C−21**(6), 592–597 (1972). https://doi.org/10.1109/TC.1972.5009015
3. Cheng, K.T., Krishnakumar, A.S.: Automatic functional test generation using the extended finite state machine model. In: 30th ACM/IEEE Design Automation Conference, pp. 86–91. IEEE (1993). https://doi.org/10.1145/157485.164585
4. Damas, C., Lambeau, B., Dupont, P., Van Lamsweerde, A.: Generating annotated behavior models from end-user scenarios. IEEE Trans. Softw. Eng. **31**(12), 1056–1073 (2005). https://doi.org/10.1109/TSE.2005.138
5. Dupont, P., Lambeau, B., Damas, C., Van Lamsweerde, A.: The QSM algorithm and its application to software behavior model induction. Appl. Artif. Intell. **22**(1–2), 77–115 (2008). https://doi.org/10.1080/08839510701853200

6. Foster, M., Taylor, R.G., Brucker, A.D., Derrick, J.: Formalising extended finite state machine transition merging. In: Sun, J., Sun, M. (eds.) ICFEM 2018. LNCS, vol. 11232, pp. 373–387. Springer, Cham (2018). https://doi.org/10.1007/978-3-030-02450-5_22

7. Fraser, G., Walkinshaw, N.: Behaviourally adequate software testing. In: 2012 IEEE Fifth International Conference on Software Testing, Verification and Validation, pp. 300–309. IEEE (2012). https://doi.org/10.1109/ICST.2012.110

8. Haftmann, F., Bulwahn, L.: Code generation from Isabelle/HOL theories. Part of the Isabelle documentation (2013). http://isabelle.in.tum.de/dist/Isabelle2017/doc/codegen.pdf

9. Isberner, M., Howar, F., Steffen, B.: The TTT algorithm: a redundancy-free approach to active automata learning. In: Bonakdarpour, B., Smolka, S.A. (eds.) RV 2014. LNCS, vol. 8734, pp. 307–322. Springer, Cham (2014). https://doi.org/10.1007/978-3-319-11164-3_26

10. Lang, K.J., Pearlmutter, B.A., Price, R.A.: Results of the Abbadingo one DFA learning competition and a new evidence-driven state merging algorithm. In: Honavar, V., Slutzki, G. (eds.) ICGI 1998. LNCS, vol. 1433, pp. 1–12. Springer, Heidelberg (1998). https://doi.org/10.1007/BFb0054059

11. Lorenzoli, D., Mariani, L., Pezzè, M.: Inferring state-based behavior models. In: Proceedings of the 2006 International Workshop on Dynamic Systems Analysis - WODA 2006, p. 25. ACM Press, New York (2006). https://doi.org/10.1145/1138912.1138919

12. Lorenzoli, D., Mariani, L., Pezzè, M.: Automatic generation of software behavioral models. In: Proceedings of the 30th International Conference on Software Engineering, ICSE 2008, pp. 501–510. ACM, New York (2008). https://doi.org/10.1145/1368088.1368157

13. de Moura, L., Bjørner, N.: Z3: an efficient SMT solver. In: Ramakrishnan, C.R., Rehof, J. (eds.) TACAS 2008. LNCS, vol. 4963, pp. 337–340. Springer, Heidelberg (2008). https://doi.org/10.1007/978-3-540-78800-3_24

14. Nipkow, T., Paulson, L.C., Wenzel, M.: Isabelle/HOL. LNCS, vol. 2283. Springer, Heidelberg (2002). https://doi.org/10.1007/3-540-45949-9. http://link.springer.com/10.1007/3-540-45949-9

15. Taylor, R., Hall, M., Bogdanov, K., Derrick, J.: Using behaviour inference to optimise regression test sets. In: Nielsen, B., Weise, C. (eds.) ICTSS 2012. LNCS, vol. 7641, pp. 184–199. Springer, Heidelberg (2012). https://doi.org/10.1007/978-3-642-34691-0_14

16. Valdes, A., Skinner, K.: Adaptive, model-based monitoring for cyber attack detection. In: Debar, H., Mé, L., Wu, S.F. (eds.) RAID 2000. LNCS, vol. 1907, pp. 80–93. Springer, Heidelberg (2000). https://doi.org/10.1007/3-540-39945-3_6

17. Walkinshaw, N., Hall, M.: Inferring computational state machine models from program executions. In: 2016 IEEE International Conference on Software Maintenance and Evolution (ICSME), pp. 122–132. IEEE (2016). https://doi.org/10.1109/ICSME.2016.74

18. Walkinshaw, N., Lambeau, B., Damas, C., Bogdanov, K., Dupont, P.: STAMINA: a competition to encourage the development and assessment of software model inference techniques. Empir. Softw. Eng. 18(4), 791–824 (2013). https://doi.org/10.1007/s10664-012-9210-3

19. Walkinshaw, N., Taylor, R., Derrick, J.: Inferring extended finite state machine models from software executions. Empir. Softw. Eng. 21(3), 811–853 (2016). https://doi.org/10.1007/s10664-015-9367-7

Ontologies and Machine Learning

Isabelle/DOF: Design and Implementation

Achim D. Brucker[1]([✉]) [iD] and Burkhart Wolff[2]

[1] Department of Computer Science, University of Exeter, Exeter, UK
a.brucker@exeter.ac.uk
[2] LRI, CNRS, Université Paris-Saclay, Paris, France
wolff@lri.fr
http://www.brucker.ch/, http://www.lri.fr/~wolff

Abstract. DOF is a novel framework for *defining* ontologies and *enforcing* them during document development and document evolution. A major goal of DOF is the integrated development of formal certification documents (e. g., for Common Criteria or CENELEC 50128) that require consistency across both formal and informal arguments.

To support a consistent development of formal and informal parts of a document, we provide Isabelle/DOF, an implementation of DOF on top of Isabelle/HOL. Isabelle/DOF is integrated into Isabelle's IDE, which allows for smooth ontology development as well as immediate ontological feedback during the editing of a document.

In this paper, we give an in-depth presentation of the design concepts of DOF's Ontology Definition Language (ODL) and key aspects of the technology of its implementation. Isabelle/DOF is the first ontology language supporting machine-checked links between the formal and informal parts in an LCF-style interactive theorem proving environment.

Sufficiently annotated, large documents can easily be developed collaboratively, while *ensuring their consistency*, and the impact of changes (in the formal and the semi-formal content) is tracked automatically.

Keywords: Ontology · Formal document development · Certification · DOF · Isabelle/DOF

1 Introduction

With the maturation and growing power of interactive proof systems, the body of formalized mathematics and engineering is dramatically increasing. The Isabelle Archive of Formal Proof (AFP) [6], created in 2004, counted in 2015 a total of 215 articles, whereas the count stood at 413 only three years later. An in-depth empirical analysis shows that both complexity and size increased accordingly [11]. Together with the AFP, there is also a growing body on articles concerned with formal software engineering issues such as standardized language definitions (e. g., [15,21]), data-structures (e. g., [14,24]), hardware-models (e. g., [20]), security-related specifications (e. g., [13,26]), or operating systems (e. g., [22,27]).

© Springer Nature Switzerland AG 2019
P. C. Ölveczky and G. Salaün (Eds.): SEFM 2019, LNCS 11724, pp. 275–292, 2019.
https://doi.org/10.1007/978-3-030-30446-1_15

This development raises interest in at least two ways: First, there is a substantial potential of *retrieve* and *reuse* of formal developments, and second, formal techniques allow a deeper checking of documents containing formal specifications, proofs and tests. This paves the way for collaborative, continuously machine-checked developments of certification documents involving both formal as well of informal content evolution.

We are focusing in this paper on the latter aspect. Certification documents have to follow a structure which is relatively strictly defined in certification standards such as [16, 17]. In practice, large groups of developers have to produce a substantial set of documents where the consistency is notoriously difficult to maintain. In particular, certifications are centered around the *traceability* of requirements throughout the entire set of documents. While technical solutions for the traceability problem exists (most notably: DOORS [7]), they are weak in the treatment of formal entities (such as formulas and their logical contexts).

Enforcing a document structure is done by *annotations* with meta-information; the language in which the latter is defined is widely called a *document ontology* (an equivalent term is *vocabulary*) in the semantic web community [3], i. e., a machine-readable form of the structure of a document and the document discourse. Let us consider a set of *text elements* available in a given corpus. These elements may be sentences or paragraphs, figures, tables, definitions or lemmas, code, and, for example, the results of test-executions. By annotation, we make links explicit that may exist between an ontology concept and a document element of the considered corpus. While ontologies as such can be used for a variety of applications, this paper is concerned with the representation of a mixture formal and semi-formal content (as it is, e. g., very common in documents within a software development process). Therefore, we also discuss the mapping to a concrete target document format (e. g., PDF) that, e. g., might be used within a traditional certification process.

In this paper, we present the concepts of our Document Ontology Framework (DOF) designed for building scalable and user-friendly tools on top of interactive theorem provers, and an implementation of DOF called Isabelle/DOF. Isabelle/DOF supports both defining ontologies and documents that conform to one or more ontologies. An example-driven introduction into Isabelle/DOF also presenting details of the user-interaction in the IDE can be found elsewhere [12]. In this paper, we are focusing on the fundamental concepts of its ontology definition language ODL and the more technical issues of its implementation. In particular, we present novel concepts such as *meta-types-as-types*, *class-invariants*, *monitors*, *inner-syntax antiquotations* as well as their interaction.

The rest of the paper is structured as follows: after explicating the underlying assumptions in a generic document model, we present the design of DOF as a language in Sect. 3. It follows a presentation of the implementation of Isabelle/DOF (Sect. 4) and a discussion on related and future work (Sect. 5).

2   Background: The Document Model

In this section, we introduce the assumed document model underlying DOF in general; in particular the concepts *integrated document*, *sub-document*, *text-*

element and *semantic macros* occurring inside text-elements. Furthermore, we assume two different levels of parsers (for *outer* and *inner syntax*) where the inner-syntax is basically a typed λ-calculus and some Higher-order Logic (HOL).

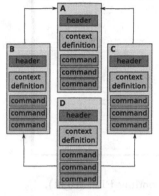

Fig. 1. A theory-graph in the document model.

We assume a hierarchical document model, i. e., an *integrated* document consist of a hierarchy *sub-documents* (files) that can depend acyclically on each other. Sub-documents can have different document types in order to capture documentations consisting of documentation, models, proofs, code of various forms and other technical artifacts. We call the main sub-document type, for historical reasons, *theory*-files. A theory file consists of a *header*, a *context definition*, and a body consisting of a sequence of *commands* (Fig. 1). Even the header consists of a sequence of commands used for introductory text elements not depending on any context. The context-definition contains an `import` and a `keyword` section, for example:

```
theory Example        (* Name of the "theory"               *)
  imports             (* Declaration of "theory" dependencies *)
    Main              (* Imports a library called "Main"     *)
  keywords            (* Registration of keywords defined locally *)
    requirement       (* A command for describing requirements *)
```

where `Example` is the abstract name of the text-file, `Main` refers to an imported theory (recall that the import relation must be acyclic) and `keywords` are used to separate commands from each other.

We distinguish fundamentally two different syntactic levels:

1. the *outer-syntax* (i. e., the syntax for commands) is processed by a lexer-library and parser combinators built on top, and
2. the *inner-syntax* (i. e., the syntax for λ-terms in HOL) with its own parametric polymorphism type checking.

On the semantic level, we assume a validation process for an integrated document, where the semantics of a command is a transformation $\theta \rightarrow \theta$ for some system state θ. This document model can be instantiated with outer-syntax commands for common text elements, e. g., `section⟨...⟩` or `text⟨...⟩`. Thus, users can add informal text to a sub-document using a text command:

```
text⟨This is a description.⟩
```

This will type-set the corresponding text in, for example, a PDF document. However, this translation is not necessarily one-to-one: text elements can be enriched by formal, i. e., machine-checked content via *semantic macros*, called antiquotations:

```
text⟨According to the reflexivity axiom @{thm refl}, we obtain in Γ
    for @{term "fac 5"} the result @{value "fac 5"}.⟩
```

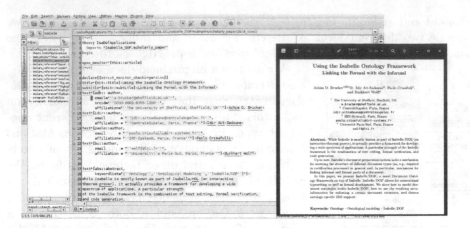

Fig. 2. The Isabelle/DOF IDE (left) and the corresponding PDF (right).

which is represented in the final document (e. g., a PDF) by:

According to the reflexivity axiom $x = x$, we obtain in Γ for fac 5 the result 120.

Semantic macros are partial functions of type $\theta \rightarrow$ `text`; since they can use the system state, they can perform all sorts of specific checks or evaluations (type-checks, executions of code-elements, references to text-elements or proven theorems such as `refl`, which is the reference to the axiom of reflexivity).

Semantic macros establish *formal content* inside informal content; they can be type-checked before being displayed and can be used for calculations before being typeset. They represent the device for linking the formal with the informal.

Implementability of the Assumed Document Model. Batch-mode checkers for DOF can be implemented in all systems of the LCF-style prover family, i. e., systems with a type-checked `term`, and abstract `thm`-type for theorems (protected by a kernel). This includes, e. g., ProofPower, HOL4, HOL-light, Isabelle, as well as Coq and its derivatives. DOF is, however, designed for fast interaction in an IDE. If a user wants to benefit from this experience, only Isabelle and Coq have the necessary infrastructure of asynchronous proof-processing and support by an IDE [10, 18, 28, 29]. For our implementation of DOF, called Isabelle/DOF, we are using the Isabelle platform [25]. Figure 2 shows a screen-shot of an introductory paper on Isabelle/DOF [12] presenting a number of application scenarios and user-interface aspects. On the left, we represented the Isabelle/DOF IDE, while on the right, the generated presentation in PDF is shown.

Isabelle provides, beyond the features required for DOF, a lot of additional benefits. For example, it also allows the asynchronous evaluation and checking of the document content [10, 28, 29] and is dynamically extensible. Its IDE provides a *continuous build, continuous check* functionality, syntax highlighting, and IntelliSense-like auto-completion. It also provides infrastructure for displaying meta-information (e. g., binding and type annotation) as pop-ups, while hovering over sub-expressions. A fine-grained dependency analysis allows the processing of individual parts of theory files asynchronously, allowing Isabelle to interactively process large (hundreds of theory files) documents. Isabelle can group sub-documents into sessions, i.e., sub-graphs of the document-structure that can be "pre-compiled" and loaded instantaneously, i.e., without re-processing.

3   The DOF Design

DOF consists basically of two parts: 1. the declaration of new keywords and new commands allowing for the specification of ontological concepts in our Ontology Definition Language (ODL), and 2. the definition of text-elements that are "ontology-aware," i.e., perform the necessary checks to ensure compliance to an imported ontology. This represents a partial instantiation of the underlying generic document model. The document language can be extended (recall the keywords-section) dynamically, i.e., new *user-defined* can be introduced at run-time. This is similar to the definition of new functions in an interpreter.

We illustrate the design of DOF by modeling a small ontology that can be used for writing formal specifications that, e.g., could build the basis for an ontology for certification documents used in processes such as Common Criteria [17] or CENELEC 50128 [16].[1] Moreover, in examples of certification documents, we refer to a controller of a steam boiler that is inspired by the famous steam boiler formalization challenge [9].

3.1   Ontology Modeling in ODL

Conceptually, ontologies specified in ODL consist of:

- *document classes* (syntactically marked by the doc_class keyword) that describe concepts;
- an optional document base class expressing single inheritance extensions;
- *attributes* specific to document classes, where
  - attributes are typed;
  - attributes of instances of document elements are mutable;
  - attributes can refer to other document classes, thus, document classes must also be HOL-types (such attributes are called *links*);
- a special link, the reference to a super-class, establishes an *is-a* relation between classes;
- classes may refer to other classes via a regular expression in a *where* clause (classes with a where clauses are called *monitor classes*);
- attributes may have default values in order to facilitate notation.

A major design decision of ODL is to denote attribute values by HOL-terms and HOL-types. Consequently, ODL can refer to any predefined type defined in the HOL library, e.g., string or int as well as parameterized types, e.g., _ option, _ list, _ set, or products _ × _. As a consequence of the document

---

[1] The Isabelle/DOF distribution contains an ontology for writing documents for a certification according to CENELEC 50128.

Listing 1.1. An example ontology modeling simple certification documents, including scientific papers such as [12]; also recall Fig. 2.

```
doc_class title  = short_title :: "string option" <= "None"
doc_class author = email       :: "string" <= "''''''"

datatype classification = SIL0 | SIL1 | SIL2 | SIL3 | SIL4

doc_class abstract =
    keywordlist   :: "string list"     <= []
    safety_level  :: "classification"  <= "SIL3"
doc_class text_section =
    authored_by   :: "author set"      <= "{}"
    level         :: "int  option"     <= "None"

type_synonym notion = string

doc_class introduction = text_section +
    authored_by :: "author set"        <= "UNIV"
    uses :: "notion set"
doc_class claim = introduction +
    based_on :: "notion list"
doc_class technical = text_section +
    formal_results  :: "thm list"
doc_class "definition" = technical +
    is_formal :: "bool"
    property  :: "term list"           <= "[]"

datatype kind = expert_opinion | argument | proof

doc_class result = technical +
    evidence   :: kind
    property   :: "thm list"           <= "[]"
doc_class example = technical +
    referring_to :: "(notion + definition) set" <=  "{}"
doc_class "conclusion" = text_section +
    establish   :: "(claim × result) set"
```

model, ODL definitions may be arbitrarily intertwined with standard HOL type definitions. Finally, document class definitions result in themselves in a HOL-types in order to allow *links* to and between ontological concepts.

Listing 1.1 shows an example ontology for mathematical papers (an extended version of this ontology was used for writing [12], also recall Fig. 2). The commands **datatype** (modeling fixed enumerations) and **type_synonym** (defining type synonyms) are standard mechanisms in HOL systems. Since ODL is an add-on, we have to quote sometimes constant symbols (e. g., `"proof"`) to avoid confusion with predefined keywords. ODL admits overriding (such as `authored_by` in the document class `introduction`), where it is set to another library constant, but no overloading. All `text_section` elements have an optional `level` attribute, which will be used in the output generation for the decision if the context is a section header and its level (e. g., chapter, section, subsection). While *within* an inheritance hierarchy overloading is prohibited, attributes may be redeclared freely in independent parts (as is the case for `property`).

3.2   Meta-Types as Types

To express the dependencies between text elements to the formal entities, e. g., `term` (λ-term), `typ`, or `thm`, we represent the types of the implementation language *inside* the HOL type system. We do, however, not reflect the data of these types. They are just declared abstract types, "inhabited" by special constant symbols carrying strings, for example of the format `@{thm <string>}`. When HOL expressions were used to denote values of `doc_class` instance attributes, this requires additional checks after conventional type-checking that this string represents actually a defined entity in the context of the system state θ. For example, the `establish` attribute in the previous section is the power of the ODL: here, we model a relation between *claims* and *results* which may be a formal, machine-check theorem of type `thm` denoted by, for example: `property ="[@{thm ''system_is_safe''}]"` in a system context θ where this theorem is established. Similarly, attribute values like `property = "@{term ⟨A ↔ B⟩}"` require that the HOL-string A ↔ B is again type-checked and represents indeed a formula in θ. Another instance of this process, which we call *second-level type-checking*, are term-constants generated from the ontology such as `@{definition <string>}`. For the latter, the argument string must be checked that it represents a reference to a text-element having the type `definition` according to the ontology in Listing 1.1.

3.3   Annotating with Ontology Meta-Data: Outer Syntax

DOF introduces its own family of text-commands, which allows having side effects of the global context θ and thus to store and manage own meta-information. Among others, DOF provides the commands `section*[<meta-args>]⟨...⟩`, `subsection*[<meta-args>]⟨...⟩`, or `text*[<meta-args>]⟨...⟩`. Here, the argument `<meta-args>` is a syntax for declaring instance, class and attributes for this text element, following the scheme

---

`<ref> :: <class_id>, attr_1 = <expr>, ..., attr_n = <expr>`

The `<class_id>` can be omitted, which represents the implicit superclass `text`, where `attr_i` must be declared attributes in the class and where the HOL `<expr>` must have the corresponding HOL type. Attributes from a class definition may be left undefined; definitions of attribute values *override* default values or values of super-classes. Overloading of attributes is not permitted in DOF.

We can now annotate a text as follows. First, we have to place a particular document into the context of our conceptual example ontology (Listing 1.1):

```
theory Steam_Boiler
  imports
    tiny_cert  (* The ontology defined in Listing 1.1. *)
begin
```

This opens a new document (theory), called `Steam_Boiler` that imports our conceptual example ontology "`tiny_cert`" (stored in a file `tiny_cert.thy`).[2] Now we can continue to annotate our text as follows:

```
title*[a] ⟨The Steam Boiler Controller⟩
abstract*[abs, safety_level="SIL4", keywordlist = "['controller']"]⟨
  We present a formalization of a program which serves to control the
  level of water in a steam boiler.
⟩

section*[intro::introduction]⟨Introduction⟩
text⟨We present ...⟩

section*[T1::technical]⟨Physical Environment⟩
text⟨
  The system comprises the following units
  • the steam-boiler
  • a device to measure the quantity of water in the steam-boiler
  • ...
⟩
```

Where `title*[a ... ]` is a predefined macro for `text*[a::title, ... ]⟨...⟩` (similarly `abstract*`). The macro `section*` assumes a class-id referring to a class that has a `level` attribute. We continue our example text:

```
text*[c1::contrib_claim, based_on="['pumps','steam boiler']" ]⟨
  As indicated in @{introduction "intro"}, we the water level of the
  boiler is always between the minimum and the maximum allowed level.
⟩
```

The first text element in this example fragment *defines* the text entity `c1` and also references the formerly defined text element `intro` (which will be represented in the PDF output, for example, by a text anchor "Section 1" and a hyperlink to its beginning). The antiquotation `@{introduction ... }`, which is automatically generated from the ontology, is immediately validated (the link to `intro` is defined) and type-checked (it is indeed a link to an `introduction` text-element). Moreover, the IDE automatically provides editing and development support such as auto-completion or the possibility to "jump" to its definition by clicking on the antiquotation. The consistency checking ensures, among others,

---

[2] The usual import-mechanisms of the Isabelle document model applies also to ODL: ontologies can be extended, several ontologies may be imported, a document can validate several ontologies.

that the final document will not contain any "dangling references" or references to entities of another type.

DOF as such does not require a particular evaluation strategy; however, if the underlying implementation is based on a declaration-before-use strategy, a mechanism for forward declarations of references is necessary:

```
declare_reference* [<meta-args>]
```

This command declares the existence of a text-element and allows for referencing it, although the actual text-element will occur later in the document.

3.4   Editing Documents with Ontology Meta-Data: Inner Syntax

We continue our running example as follows:

```
text*[d1::definition]⟨
  We define the water level @{term "level"} of a system state
  @{term "σ"} of the steam boiler as follows:
⟩
definition level :: "state → real" where
        "level σ =  level_θ + ... "
update_instance*[d1::definition,
              property += "[@{term ''level σ =  level_θ + ...''}]"]

text*[only::result,evidence="proof"]⟨
  The water level is never lower than @{term "level_θ"}:
⟩
theorem level always_above_level_0: "∀ σ. level σ ≥ level_θ"
  unfolding level_def
  by auto
update_instance*[only::result,
              property += "[@{thm ''level_always_above_level_0''}]"]
```

As mentioned earlier, instances of document classes are mutable. We use this feature to modify meta-data of these text-elements and "assign" them to the property-list afterwards and add results from Isabelle definitions and proofs. The notation A+=X stands for A := A + X. This mechanism can also be used to define the required relation between *claims* and *results* required in the establish-relation required in a summary.

3.5   ODL Class Invariants

Ontological classes as described so far are too liberal in many situations. For example, one would like to express that any instance of a result class finally has a non-empty property list, if its kind is proof, or that the establish relation between claim and result is surjective.

In a high-level syntax, this type of constraints could be expressed, e.g., by:

$$\forall\ x \in \text{result. } x@\text{kind} = \text{proof} \leftrightarrow x@\text{kind} \neq []$$
$$\forall\ x \in \text{conclusion. } \forall\ y \in \text{Domain}(x@\text{establish})$$
$$\rightarrow \exists\ y \in \text{Range}(x@\text{establish}).\ (y,z) \in x@\text{establish}$$
$$\forall\ x \in \text{introduction. finite}(x@\text{authored\_by})$$

where `result`, `conclusion`, and `introduction` are the set of all possible instances of these document classes. All specified constraints are already checked in the IDE of DOF while editing; it is however possible to delay a final error message till the closing of a monitor (see next section). The third constraint enforces that the user sets the `authored_by` set, otherwise an error will be reported.

3.6   ODL Monitors

We call a document class with an accept-clause a *monitor*. Syntactically, an accept-clause contains a regular expression over class identifiers. We can extend our `tiny_cert` ontology with the following example:

```
doc_class article =
    style_id :: string   <= "''CENELEC50128''"
    accepts "(title ~~ {author}}+ ~~ abstract ~~ {introduction}}+  ~~
            {technical || example}}+ ~~ {conclusion}}+)"
```

Semantically, monitors introduce a behavioral element into ODL:

```
open_monitor*[this::article]  (* begin of scope of monitor "this" *)
...
close_monitor*[this]          (* end of scope of monitor "this"  *)
```

Inside the scope of a monitor, all instances of classes mentioned in its accept-clause (the *accept-set*) have to appear in the order specified by the regular expression; instances not covered by an accept-set may freely occur. Monitors may additionally contain a reject-clause with a list of class-ids (the reject-list). This allows specifying ranges of admissible instances along the class hierarchy:

- a superclass in the reject-list and a subclass in the accept-expression forbids instances superior to the subclass, and
- a subclass S in the reject-list and a superclass T in the accept-list allows instances of superclasses of T to occur freely, instances of T to occur in the specified order and forbids instances of S.

Monitored document sections can be nested and overlap; thus, it is possible to combine the effect of different monitors. For example, it would be possible to refine the `example` section by its own monitor and enforce a particular structure in the presentation of examples.

Monitors manage an implicit attribute `trace` containing the list of "observed" text element instances belonging to the accept-set. Together with the concept of ODL class invariants, it is possible to specify properties of a sequence of instances occurring in the document section. For example, it is possible to express that in the sub-list of `introduction`-elements, the first has an `introduction` element with a `level` strictly smaller than the others. Thus, an introduction is forced to have a header delimiting the borders of its representation. Class invariants on monitors allow for specifying structural properties on document sections.

3.7 Document Representation

Up to now, we discussed the support of ontological concepts in the context of an IDE, i. e., a rather dynamic environment that, e. g., allows for interactive querying and displaying of information. Certification processes often require "static" documents, e. g., in a format such as PDF/A that are designed for archiving and long-term preservation of electronic documents, are required.

While many concepts of ODL can easily be mapped to such static formats, more dynamic features (e. g., references) requires additional considerations such as ensuring that references point to text elements that have a unique identifier that is visible in the actual document representation. Currently, the definition of a static document representation is not part of DOF itself and, thus, depends on the underlying implementation. We refer the reader to Sect. 4.6 for details.

4   The Isabelle/DOF Implementation

In this section, we describe the basic implementation aspects of Isabelle/DOF, which is based on the following design-decisions:

- the entire Isabelle/DOF is a "pure add-on," i. e., we deliberately resign on the possibility to modify Isabelle itself.
- we made a small exception to this rule: the Isabelle/DOF package modifies in its installation about 10 lines in the LaTeX generator `thy_output.ML` which greatly simplifies the architecture.[3]
- we decided to make the markup-generation by itself to adapt it as well as possible to the needs of tracking the linking in documents.
- Isabelle/DOF is deeply integrated into the Isabelle's IDE (PIDE) to give immediate feedback during editing and other forms of document evolution.

Semantic macros, as required by our document model, are called *document antiquotations* in the Isabelle literature [30]. While Isabelle's code-antiquotations are an old concept going back to Lisp and having found via SML and OCaml their ways into modern proof systems, special annotation syntax inside documentation comments have their roots in documentation generators such as Javadoc. Their use, however, as a mechanism to embed machine-checked *formal content* is usually very limited and also lacks IDE support.

---

[3] Earlier versions of Isabelle/DOF used an additional LaTeX-to-LaTeX translator that needed to be integrated into the document build process.

4.1 Writing Isabelle/DOF as User-Defined Plugin in Isabelle/Isar

A plugin in Isabelle starts with defining the local data and registering it in the framework. As mentioned before, contexts are structures with independent cells/compartments having three primitives init, extend and merge. Technically this is done by instantiating a functor Generic_Data, and the following fairly typical code-fragment is drawn from Isabelle/DOF:

```
structure Data = Generic_Data
( type T = docobj_tab * docclass_tab * ...
  val empty = (initial_docobj_tab, initial_docclass_tab, ...)
  val extend = I
  fun merge((d1,c1,...),(d2,c2,...)) = (merge_docobj_tab  (d1,d2,...),
                                        merge_docclass_tab(c1,c2,...))
);
```

where the table docobj_tab manages document classes and docclass_tab the environment for class definitions (inducing the inheritance relation). Other tables capture, e. g., the class invariants, inner-syntax antiquotations.

All the text samples shown here have to be in the context of an SML file or in an ML⟨...⟩ command inside a theory file.

Operations follow the model-view-controller paradigm, where Isabelle/Isar provides the controller part. A typical model operation has the type:

```
val opn :: <args_type> -> Context.generic -> Context.generic
```

representing a transformation on system contexts. For example, the operation of declaring a local reference in the context is presented as follows:

```
fun declare_object_local oid ctxt =
let fun decl {tab,maxano} = {tab=Symtab.update_new(oid,NONE) tab,
                             maxano=maxano}
in  (Data.map(apfst decl)(ctxt)
  handle Symtab.DUP _ =>
            error("multiple declaration of document reference"))
end
```

where Data.map is the update function resulting from the instantiation of the functor Generic_Data. This code fragment uses operations from a library structure Symtab that were used to update the appropriate table for document objects in the plugin-local state. Possible exceptions to the update operation were mapped to a system-global error reporting function.

Finally, the view-aspects were handled by an API for parsing-combinators. The library structure Scan provides the operators:

```
op ||     : ('a -> 'b) * ('a -> 'b) -> 'a -> 'b
op --     : ('a -> 'b * 'c) * ('c -> 'd * 'e) -> 'a -> ('b * 'd) * 'e
op >>     : ('a -> 'b * 'c) * ('b -> 'd) -> 'a -> 'd * 'c
op option : ('a -> 'b * 'a) -> 'a -> 'b option * 'a
op repeat : ('a -> 'b * 'a) -> 'a -> 'b list * 'a
```

for alternative, sequence, and piping, as well as combinators for option and repeat. Parsing combinators have the advantage that they can be smoothlessly integrated into standard programs, and they enable the dynamic extension of the grammar. There is a more high-level structure **Parse** providing specific combinators for the command-language Isar:

```
val attribute = Parse.position Parse.name
             -- Scan.optional(Parse.$$$ "=" |-- Parse.!!! Parse.name)"";
val reference = Parse.position Parse.name
             -- Scan.option (Parse.$$$ "::" |-- Parse.!!!
                          (Parse.position Parse.name));
val attributes =(Parse.$$$ "[" |-- (reference
             -- (Scan.optional(Parse.$$$ ","
                  |--(Parse.enum ","attribute)))[]))--| Parse.$$$ "]"
```

The "model" `declare_reference_opn` and "new" `attributes` parts were combined via the piping operator and registered in the Isar toplevel:

```
fun declare_reference_opn (((oid,_),_),_) =
            (Toplevel.theory (DOF_core.declare_object_global oid))
 val _ = Outer_Syntax.command @{command_keyword "declare_reference"}
        "declare document reference"
        (attributes >> declare_reference_opn);
```

Altogether, this gives the extension of Isabelle/HOL with Isar syntax and semantics for the new *command*:

```
declare_reference [lal::requirement, alpha="main", beta=42]
```

The construction also generates implicitly some markup information; for example, when hovering over the `declare_reference` command in the IDE, a popup window with the text: "declare document reference" will appear.

4.2   Programming Antiquotations

The definition and registration of text antiquotations and ML-antiquotations is similar in principle: based on a number of combinators, new user-defined antiquotation syntax and semantics can be added to the system that works on the internal plugin-data freely. For example, in

```
val _ = Theory.setup(
        Thy_Output.antiquotation @{binding docitem}
                                 docitem_antiq_parser
                                 (docitem_antiq_gen default_cid) #>
        ML_Antiquotation.inline @{binding docitem_value}
                                 ML_antiq_docitem_value)
```

the text antiquotation `docitem` is declared and bounded to a parser for the argument syntax and the overall semantics. This code defines a generic antiquotation to be used in text elements such as

```
text⟨as defined in @{docitem ⟨d1⟩} ...⟩
```

The subsequent registration `docitem_value` binds code to a ML-antiquotation usable in an ML context for user-defined extensions; it permits the access to the current "value" of document element, i. e.; a term with the entire update history.

It is possible to generate antiquotations *dynamically*, as a consequence of a class definition in ODL. The processing of the ODL class `definition` also *generates* a text antiquotation @{`definition` ⟨d1⟩}, which works similar to @{`docitem` ⟨d1⟩} except for an additional type-check that assures that `d1` is a reference to a definition. These type-checks support the subclass hierarchy.

4.3   Implementing Second-Level Type-Checking

On expressions for attribute values, for which we chose to use HOL syntax to avoid that users need to learn another syntax, we implemented an own pass over type-checked terms. Stored in the late-binding table `ISA_transformer_tab`, we register for each inner-syntax-annotation (ISA's), a function of type

```
theory -> term * typ * Position.T -> term option
```

Executed in a second pass of term parsing, ISA's may just return `None`. This is adequate for ISA's just performing some checking in the logical context `theory`; ISA's of this kind report errors by exceptions. In contrast, *transforming* ISA's will yield a term; this is adequate, for example, by replacing a string-reference to some term denoted by it. This late-binding table is also used to generate standard inner-syntax-antiquotations from a `doc_class`.

4.4   Programming Class Invariants

For the moment, there is no high-level syntax for the definition of class invariants. A formulation, in SML, of the first class-invariant in Sect. 3.5 is straight-forward:

```
fun check_result_inv oid {is_monitor:bool} ctxt =
  let val kind = compute_attr_access ctxt "kind" oid @{here} @{here}
      val prop = compute_attr_access ctxt "property" oid @{here} @{here}
      val tS = HOLogic.dest_list prop
  in  case kind_term of
      @{term "proof"} => if not(null tS) then true
                         else error("class result invariant violation")
      | _ => false
  end
val _ = Theory.setup (DOF_core.update_class_invariant
                         "tiny_cert.result" check_result_inv)
```

The `setup`-command (last line) registers the `check_result_inv` function into the Isabelle/DOF kernel, which activates any creation or modification of an instance of `result`. We cannot replace `compute_attr_access` by the corresponding antiquotation `@{docitem_value` `kind::oid}`, since `oid` is bound to a variable here and can therefore not be statically expanded.

Isabelle's code generator can in principle generate class invariant code from a high-level syntax. Since class-invariant checking can result in an efficiency problem—they are checked on any edit—and since invariant programming involves a deeper understanding of ontology modeling and the Isabelle/DOF implementation, we backed off from using this technique so far.

4.5   Implementing Monitors

Since monitor-clauses have a regular expression syntax, it is natural to implement them as deterministic automata. These are stored in the `docobj_tab` for monitor-objects in the Isabelle/DOF component. We implemented the functions:

```
val   enabled : automaton -> env -> cid list
val   next    : automaton -> env -> cid -> automaton
```

where `env` is basically a map between internal automaton states and class-id's (`cid`'s). An automaton is said to be *enabled* for a class-id, iff it either occurs in its accept-set or its reject-set (see Sect. 3.6). During top-down document validation, whenever a text-element is encountered, it is checked if a monitor is *enabled* for this class; in this case, the `next`-operation is executed. The transformed automaton recognizing the rest-language is stored in `docobj_tab` if possible; otherwise, if `next` fails, an error is reported. The automata implementation is, in large parts, generated from a formalization of functional automata [23].

4.6   Document Representation

Isabelle/DOF can generate PDF documents, using a LaTeX-backend (for end users there is no need to edit LaTeX-code manually). For PDF documents, a specific representation, including a specific layout or formatting of certain text types (e.g., title, abstract, theorems, examples) is required: for each ontological concept (using the `doc_class`-command), a representation for the PDF output needs to be defined. The LaTeX-setup of Isabelle/DOF provides the `\newisadof` -command and an inheritance-based dispatcher, i.e., if for a concept no LaTeX-representation is defined, the representation of its super-concept is used.

Recall the document class `abstract` from our example ontology (Listing 1.1). The following LaTeX-code (defined in a file `tiny_cert.sty`) defines the representation for abstracts, re-using the the standard `abstract`-environment:

```
\newisadof{tiny_cert.abstract}[reference=,class_id=%
        ,keywordlist=,safety_level=][1]{%
  \begin{isamarkuptext}%
    \begin{abstract}\label{\commandkey{reference}}%
      #1\\ % this is the main text of the abstract
      \ifthenelse{\equal{\commandkey{safety_level}}{}}{}{%
        \medskip\noindent{Safety Level:} \commandkey{safety_level}\\%
      }
      \ifthenelse{\equal{\commandkey{keywordlist}}{}}{}{%
        \medskip\noindent{\textbf{Keywords:}} \commandkey{keywordlist}%
      }
    \end{abstract}%
  \end{isamarkuptext}%
}
```

The \newisadof takes the name of the concept as first argument, followed by a list of parameters that is the same as the parameters used in defining the concept with doc_class. Within the definition section of the command, the main argument (written in the actual document within ‹...›) is accessed using #1. The parameters can be accessed using the \commandkey-command. In our example, we print the abstract within abstract-environment of LaTeX. Moreover, we test if the parameters safety_level and keywordlist are non-empty and, if yes, print them as part of the abstract.

5   Conclusion and Related Work

5.1   Related Work

Our work shares similarities with existing ontology editors such as Protégé [5], Fluent Editor [1], NeOn [2], or OWLGrEd [4]. These editors allow for defining ontologies and also provide certain editing features such as auto-completion. In contrast, Isabelle/DOF does not only allow for defining ontologies, directly after defining an ontological concept, they can also be instantiated and their correct use is checked immediately. The document model of Jupyter Notebooks [8] comes probably closest to our ideal of a "living document."

Finally, the LaTeX that is generated as intermediate step in our PDF generation is conceptually very close to SALT [19], with the difference that instead of writing LaTeX manually it is automatically generated and its consistency is guaranteed by the document checking of Isabelle/DOF.

5.2   Conclusion

We presented the design of DOF, an ontology framework designed for formal documents developed by interactive proof systems. It foresees a number of specific features—such as monitors, meta-types as-types or semantic macros generated from a typed ontology specified in ODL—that support the specifics of such documents linking formal and informal content. As validation of these concepts, we present Isabelle/DOF, an implementation of DOF based on Isabelle/HOL. Isabelle/DOF is unique in at least one aspect: it is an integrated environment that allows both defining ontologies and writing documents that conform to a set of ontological rules, and both are supported by editing and query features that one expects from a modern IDE.

While the batch-mode part of DOF can, in principle, be re-implemented in any LCF-style prover, Isabelle/DOF is designed for fast interaction in an IDE. It is this feature that allows for a seamless development of ontologies together with validation tests checking the impact of ontology changes on document instances. We expect this to be a valuable tool for communities that still have to develop their domain specific ontologies, be it in mathematical papers, formal theories, formal certifications or other documents where the consistency of formal and informal content has to be maintained under document evolution. Today, in some areas such as medicine and biology, ontologies play a vital role for the retrieval of scientific information; we believe that leveraging these ontology-based techniques to the field of formal software engineering can represent a game changer.

Availability. The implementation of the framework is available at https:// git.logicalhacking.com/Isabelle_DOF/Isabelle_DOF/. Isabelle/DOF is licensed under a 2-clause BSD license (SPDX-License-Identifier: BSD-2-Clause).

Acknowledgments. This work has been partially supported by IRT SystemX, Paris-Saclay, France, and therefore granted with public funds of the Program "Investissements d'Avenir".

References

1. Fluent editor (2018). http://www.cognitum.eu/Semantics/FluentEditor/
2. The neon toolkit (2018). http://neon-toolkit.org
3. Ontologies (2018). https://www.w3.org/standards/semanticweb/ontology
4. Owlgred (2018). http://owlgred.lumii.lv/
5. Protégé (2018). https://protege.stanford.edu
6. Archive of formal proofs (2019). https://afp-isa.org
7. Ibm engineering requirements management doors family (2019). https://www.ibm. com/us-en/marketplace/requirements-management
8. Jupyter (2019). https://jupyter.org/
9. Abrial, J.-R.: Steam-boiler control specification problem. In: Abrial, J.-R., Börger, E., Langmaack, H. (eds.) Formal Methods for Industrial Applications. LNCS, vol. 1165, pp. 500–509. Springer, Heidelberg (1996). https://doi.org/10.1007/ BFb0027252
10. Barras, B., et al.: Pervasive parallelism in highly-trustable interactive theorem proving systems. In: Carette, J., Aspinall, D., Lange, C., Sojka, P., Windsteiger, W. (eds.) CICM 2013. LNCS (LNAI), vol. 7961, pp. 359–363. Springer, Heidelberg (2013). https://doi.org/10.1007/978-3-642-39320-4_29
11. Blanchette, J.C., Haslbeck, M., Matichuk, D., Nipkow, T.: Mining the archive of formal proofs. In: Kerber, M., Carette, J., Kaliszyk, C., Rabe, F., Sorge, V. (eds.) CICM 2015. LNCS (LNAI), vol. 9150, pp. 3–17. Springer, Cham (2015). https:// doi.org/10.1007/978-3-319-20615-8_1

12. Brucker, A.D., Ait-Sadoune, I., Crisafulli, P., Wolff, B.: Using the isabelle ontology framework. In: Rabe, F., Farmer, W.M., Passmore, G.O., Youssef, A. (eds.) CICM 2018. LNCS (LNAI), vol. 11006, pp. 23–38. Springer, Cham (2018). https://doi.org/10.1007/978-3-319-96812-4_3

13. Brucker, A.D., Brügger, L., Wolff, B.: Formal network models and their application to firewall policies. Archive of Formal Proofs (2017). http://www.isa-afp.org/entries/UPF_Firewall.shtml

14. Brucker, A.D., Herzberg, M.: The Core DOM. Archive of Formal Proofs (2018). http://www.isa-afp.org/entries/Core_DOM.html

15. Brucker, A.D., Tuong, F., Wolff, B.: Featherweight OCL: a proposal for a machine-checked formal semantics for OCL 2.5. Archive of Formal Proofs (2014). http://www.isa-afp.org/entries/Featherweight_OCL.shtml

16. BS EN 50128:2011: Bs en 50128:2011: Railway applications - communication, signalling and processing systems - software for railway control and protecting systems. Standard, Britisch Standards Institute (BSI) (2014)

17. Common Criteria: Common criteria for information technology security evaluation (version 3.1), Part 3: Security assurance components (2006)

18. Faithfull, A., Bengtson, J., Tassi, E., Tankink, C.: Coqoon - an IDE for interactive-proof development in coq. STTT **20**(2), 125–137 (2018). https://doi.org/10.1007/s10009-017-0457-2

19. Groza, T., Handschuh, S., Möller, K., Decker, S.: SALT - semantically annotated LATEX for scientific publications. In: Franconi, E., Kifer, M., May, W. (eds.) ESWC 2007. LNCS, vol. 4519, pp. 518–532. Springer, Heidelberg (2007). https://doi.org/10.1007/978-3-540-72667-8_37

20. Hou, Z., Sanan, D., Tiu, A., Liu, Y.: A formal model for the SPARCv8 ISA and a proof of non-interference for the LEON3 processor. Archive of Formal Proofs (2016). http://isa-afp.org/entries/SPARCv8.html

21. Hupel, L., Zhang, Y.: CakeML. Archive of Formal Proofs (2018). http://isa-afp.org/entries/CakeML.html

22. Klein, G., et al.: Comprehensive formal verification of an OS microkernel. ACM Trans. Comput. Syst. **32**(1), 2:1–2:70 (2014). https://doi.org/10.1145/2560537

23. Nipkow, T.: Functional automata. Archive of Formal Proofs (2004). http://isa-afp.org/entries/Functional-Automata.html. Formal proof development

24. Nipkow, T.: Splay tree. Archive of Formal Proofs (2014). http://isa-afp.org/entries/Splay_Tree.html. Formal proof development

25. Nipkow, T., Wenzel, M., Paulson, L.C. (eds.): Isabelle/HOL. LNCS, vol. 2283. Springer, Heidelberg (2002). https://doi.org/10.1007/3-540-45949-9

26. Sprenger, C., Somaini, I.: Developing security protocols by refinement. Archive of Formal Proofs (2017). http://isa-afp.org/entries/Security_Protocol_Refinement.html. Formal proof development

27. Verbeek, F., et al.: Formal specification of a generic separation kernel. Archive of Formal Proofs (2014). http://isa-afp.org/entries/CISC-Kernel.html. Formal proof development

28. Wenzel, M.: Asynchronous user interaction and tool integration in Isabelle/PIDE. In: Klein, G., Gamboa, R. (eds.) ITP 2014. LNCS, vol. 8558, pp. 515–530. Springer, Cham (2014). https://doi.org/10.1007/978-3-319-08970-6_33

29. Wenzel, M.: System description: Isabelle/jEdit in 2014. In: Proceedings Eleventh Workshop on User Interfaces for Theorem Provers, UITP 2014, Vienna, Austria, 17th July 2014, pp. 84–94 (2014). https://doi.org/10.4204/EPTCS.167.10

30. Wenzel, M.: The Isabelle/Isar Reference Manual (2017). Part of the Isabelle distribution

Towards Logical Specification
of Statistical Machine Learning

Yusuke Kawamoto(✉)

AIST, Tsukuba, Japan
yusuke.kawamoto.aist@gmail.com

Abstract. We introduce a logical approach to formalizing statistical properties of machine learning. Specifically, we propose a formal model for statistical classification based on a Kripke model, and formalize various notions of classification performance, robustness, and fairness of classifiers by using epistemic logic. Then we show some relationships among properties of classifiers and those between classification performance and robustness, which suggests robustness-related properties that have not been formalized in the literature as far as we know. To formalize fairness properties, we define a notion of counterfactual knowledge and show techniques to formalize conditional indistinguishability by using counterfactual epistemic operators. As far as we know, this is the first work that uses logical formulas to express statistical properties of machine learning, and that provides epistemic (resp. counterfactually epistemic) views on robustness (resp. fairness) of classifiers.

Keywords: Epistemic logic · Possible world semantics · Divergence · Machine learning · Statistical classification · Robustness · Fairness

1 Introduction

With the increasing use of machine learning in real-life applications, the safety and security of learning-based systems have been of great interest. In particular, many recent studies [8,36] have found vulnerabilities on the robustness of deep neural networks (DNNs) to malicious inputs, which can lead to disasters in security critical systems, such as self-driving cars. To find out these vulnerabilities in advance, there have been researches on the formal verification and testing methods for the robustness of DNNs in recent years [22,25,33,37]. However, relatively little attention has been paid to the formal specification of machine learning [34].

To describe the formal specification of security properties, logical approaches have been shown useful to classify desired properties and to develop theories to compare those properties. For example, security policies in temporal systems

This work was supported by JSPS KAKENHI Grant Number JP17K12667, by the New Energy and Industrial Technology Development Organization (NEDO), and by Inria under the project LOGIS.

© Springer Nature Switzerland AG 2019
P. C. Ölveczky and G. Salaün (Eds.): SEFM 2019, LNCS 11724, pp. 293–311, 2019.
https://doi.org/10.1007/978-3-030-30446-1_16

have been formalized as trace properties [1] or hyperproperties [9], which characterize the relationships among various security policies. For another example, epistemic logic [39] has been widely used as formal policy languages (e.g., for the authentication [5] and the anonymity [20,35] of security protocols, and for the privacy of social network [32]). As far as we know, however, no prior work has employed logical formulas to rigorously describe various statistical properties of machine learning, although there are some papers that (often informally) list various desirable properties of machine learning [34].

In this paper, we present a first logical formalization of statistical properties of machine learning. To describe the statistical properties in a simple and abstract way, we employ *statistical epistemic logic* (StatEL) [26], which is recently proposed to describe statistical knowledge and is applied to formalize statistical hypothesis testing and statistical privacy of databases.

A key idea in our modeling of statistical machine learning is that we formalize logical properties in the syntax level by using logical formulas, and statistical distances in the semantics level by using accessibility relations of a Kripke model [28]. In this model, we formalize statistical classifiers and some of their desirable properties: classification performance, robustness, and fairness. More specifically, classification performance and robustness are described as the differences between the classifier's recognition and the correct label (e.g., given by the human), whereas fairness is formalized as the conditional indistinguishability between two groups or individuals by using a notion of counterfactual knowledge.

Our contributions. The main contributions of this work are as follows:

– We show a logical approach to formalizing statistical properties of machine learning in a simple and abstract way. In particular, we model logical properties in the syntax level, and statistical distances in the semantics level.
– We introduce a formal model for statistical classification. More specifically, we show how probabilistic behaviours of classifiers and non-deterministic adversarial inputs are formalized in a distributional Kripke model [26].
– We formalize the classification performance, robustness, and fairness of classifiers by using statistical epistemic logic (StatEL). As far as we know, this is the first work that uses logical formulas to formalize various statistical properties of machine learning, and that provides epistemic (resp. counterfactually epistemic) views on robustness (resp. fairness) of classifiers.
– We show some relationships among properties of classifiers, e.g., different strengths of robustness. We also present some relationships between classification performance and robustness, which suggest robustness-related properties that have not been formalized in the literature as far as we know.
– To formalize fairness properties, we define a notion of certain counterfactual knowledge and show techniques to formalize conditional indistinguishability by using counterfactual epistemic operators in StatEL. This enables us to express various fairness properties in a similar style of logical formulas.

Cautions and limitations. In this paper, we focus on formalizing properties of classification problems and do not deal with the properties of learning algorithms (e.g., fairness through awareness [13]), quality of training data (e.g., sample bias), quality of testing (e.g., coverage criteria), explainability, temporal properties, system level specification, or process agility in system development. It should be noted that all properties formalized in this paper have been known in literatures on machine learning, and the novelty of this work lies in the logical formulation of those statistical properties.

We also remark that this work does not provide methods for checking, guaranteeing, or improving the performance/robustness/fairness of machine learning. As for the satisfiability of logical formulas, we leave the development of testing and (statistical) model checking algorithms as future work, since the research area on the testing and formal/statistical verification of machine learning is relatively new and needs further techniques to improve the scalability. Moreover, in some applications such as image recognition, some formulas (e.g., representing whether an input image is panda or not) cannot be implemented mathematically, and require additional techniques based on experiments. Nevertheless, we demonstrate that describing various properties using logical formulas is useful to explore desirable properties and to discuss their relationships in a framework.

Finally, we emphasize that our work is the first attempt to use logical formulas to express statistical properties of machine learning, and would be a starting point to develop theories of specification of machine learning in future research.

Paper organization. The rest of this paper is organized as follows. Section 2 presents background on statistical epistemic logic (StatEL) and notations used in this paper. Section 3 defines counterfactual epistemic operators and shows techniques to model conditional indistinguishability using StatEL. Section 4 introduces a formal model for describing the behaviours of statistical classifiers and non-deterministic adversarial inputs. Sections 5, 6, and 7 respectively formalize the classification performance, robustness, and fairness of classifiers by using StatEL. Section 8 presents related work and Sect. 9 concludes.

2 Preliminaries

In this section we introduce some notations and recall the syntax and semantics of the *statistical epistemic logic* (StatEL) introduced in [26].

2.1 Notations

Let $\mathbb{R}^{\geq 0}$ be the set of non-negative real numbers, and $[0, 1]$ be the set of non-negative real numbers not greater than 1. We denote by $\mathbb{D}\mathcal{O}$ the set of all probability distributions over a set $\mathcal{O}$. Given a finite set $\mathcal{O}$ and a probability distribution $\mu \in \mathbb{D}\mathcal{O}$, the probability of sampling a value y from μ is denoted by $\mu[y]$. For a subset $R \subseteq \mathcal{O}$ we define $\mu[R]$ by: $\mu[R] = \sum_{y \in R} \mu[y]$. For a distribution μ over a finite set $\mathcal{O}$, its *support* is defined by $\mathsf{supp}(\mu) = \{v \in \mathcal{O} : \mu[v] > 0\}$.

The *total variation distance* of two distributions $\mu, \mu' \in \mathbb{D}\mathcal{O}$ is defined by: $D_{\mathsf{tv}}(\mu \parallel \mu') \stackrel{\text{def}}{=} \sup_{R \subseteq \mathcal{O}} |\mu(R) - \mu'(R)|$.

2.2   Syntax of StatEL

We recall the syntax of the statistical epistemic logic (StatEL) [26], which has two levels of formulas: *static* and *epistemic formulas*. Intuitively, a static formula describes a proposition satisfied at a deterministic state, while an epistemic formula describes a proposition satisfied at a probability distribution of states. In this paper, the former is used only to define the latter.

Formally, let Mes be a set of symbols called *measurement variables*, and Γ be a set of atomic formulas of the form $\gamma(x_1, x_2, \ldots, x_n)$ for a predicate symbol γ, $n \geq 0$, and $x_1, x_2, \ldots, x_n \in$ Mes. Let $I \subseteq [0, 1]$ be a finite union of disjoint intervals, and $\mathcal{A}$ be a finite set of indices (e.g., associated with statistical divergences). Then the formulas are defined by:

Static formulas: $\psi ::= \gamma(x_1, x_2, \ldots, x_n) \mid \neg\psi \mid \psi \wedge \psi$
Epistemic formulas: $\varphi ::= \mathbb{P}_I \psi \mid \neg\varphi \mid \varphi \wedge \varphi \mid \psi \supset \varphi \mid \mathsf{K}_a \varphi$

where $a \in \mathcal{A}$. We denote by $\mathcal{F}$ the set of all epistemic formulas. Note that we have no quantifiers over measurement variables. (See Sect. 2.4 for more details).

The *probability quantification* $\mathbb{P}_I \psi$ represents that a static formula ψ is satisfied with a probability belonging to a set I. For instance, $\mathbb{P}_{(0.95, 1]} \psi$ represents that ψ holds with a probability greater than 0.95. By $\psi \supset \mathbb{P}_I \psi'$ we represent that the conditional probability of ψ' given ψ is included in a set I. The *epistemic knowledge* $\mathsf{K}_a \varphi$ expresses that we knows φ with a confidence specified by a.

As syntax sugar, we use *disjunction* $\vee$, *classical implication* $\rightarrow$, and *epistemic possibility* P_a, defined as usual by: $\varphi_0 \vee \varphi_1 ::= \neg(\neg\varphi_0 \wedge \neg\varphi_1)$, $\varphi_0 \rightarrow \varphi_1 ::= \neg\varphi_0 \vee \varphi_1$, and $\mathsf{P}_a \varphi ::= \neg\mathsf{K}_a \neg\varphi$. When I is a singleton $\{i\}$, we abbreviate $\mathbb{P}_I$ as $\mathbb{P}_i$.

2.3   Distributional Kripke Model

Next we recall the notion of a distributional Kripke model [26], where each possible world is a probability distribution over a set $\mathcal{S}$ of states and each world w is associated with a stochastic assignment σ_w to measurement variables.

Definition 1 (Distributional Kripke model). Let $\mathcal{A}$ be a finite set of indices (typically associated with statistical tests and their thresholds), $\mathcal{S}$ be a finite set of states, and $\mathcal{O}$ be a finite set of data. A *distributional Kripke model* is a tuple $\mathfrak{M} = (\mathcal{W}, (\mathcal{R}_a)_{a \in \mathcal{A}}, (V_s)_{s \in \mathcal{S}})$ consisting of:

- a non-empty set $\mathcal{W}$ of probability distributions over a finite set $\mathcal{S}$ of states;
- for each $a \in \mathcal{A}$, an accessibility relation $\mathcal{R}_a \subseteq \mathcal{W} \times \mathcal{W}$;
- for each $s \in \mathcal{S}$, a valuation V_s that maps each k-ary predicate γ to a set $V_s(\gamma) \subseteq \mathcal{O}^k$.

We assume that each $w \in \mathcal{W}$ is associated with a function $\rho_w : \mathrm{Mes} \times \mathcal{S} \rightarrow \mathcal{O}$ that maps each measurement variable x to its value $\rho_w(x, s)$ observed at a state s. We also assume that each state s in a world w is associated with the assignment $\sigma_s : \mathrm{Mes} \rightarrow \mathcal{O}$ defined by $\sigma_s(x) = \rho_w(x, s)$.

The set $\mathcal{W}$ is called a *universe*, and its elements are called *possible worlds*. All measurement variables range over the same set $\mathcal{O}$ in every world.

Since each world w is a distribution of states, we denote by $w[s]$ the probability that a state s is sampled from w. Then the probability that a measurement variable x has a value v is given by $\sigma_w(x)[v] = \sum_{s \in \mathrm{supp}(w), \sigma_s(x)=v} w[s]$. This implies that, when a state s is drawn from w, an input $\sigma_s(x)$ is sampled from the distribution $\sigma_w(x)$.

2.4 Stochastic Semantics of StatEL

Now we recall the *stochastic semantics* [26] for the StatEL formulas over a distributional Kripke model $\mathfrak{M} = (\mathcal{W}, (\mathcal{R}_a)_{a \in \mathcal{A}}, (V_s)_{s \in \mathcal{S}})$ with $\mathcal{W} = \mathbb{D}\mathcal{S}$.

The interpretation of static formulas ψ at a state s is given by:

$$s \models \gamma(x_1, x_2, \ldots, x_k) \quad \text{iff} \quad (\sigma_s(x_1), \sigma_s(x_2), \ldots, \sigma_s(x_k)) \in V_s(\gamma)$$
$$s \models \neg\psi \quad \text{iff} \quad s \not\models \psi$$
$$s \models \psi \wedge \psi' \quad \text{iff} \quad s \models \psi \text{ and } s \models \psi'.$$

The *restriction* $w|_\psi$ of a world w to a static formula ψ is defined by $w|_\psi[s] = \frac{w[s]}{\sum_{s': s' \models \psi} w[s']}$ if $s \models \psi$, and $w|_\psi[s] = 0$ otherwise. Note that $w|_\psi$ is undefined if there is no state s that satisfies ψ and has a non-zero probability in w.

Then the interpretation of epistemic formulas in a world w is defined by:

$$\mathfrak{M}, w \models \mathbb{P}_I \psi \quad \text{iff} \quad \Pr\left[s \xleftarrow{\$} w : s \models \psi\right] \in I$$
$$\mathfrak{M}, w \models \neg\varphi \quad \text{iff} \quad \mathfrak{M}, w \not\models \varphi$$
$$\mathfrak{M}, w \models \varphi \wedge \varphi' \quad \text{iff} \quad \mathfrak{M}, w \models \varphi \text{ and } \mathfrak{M}, w \models \varphi'$$
$$\mathfrak{M}, w \models \psi \supset \varphi \quad \text{iff} \quad w|_\psi \text{ is defined and } \mathfrak{M}, w|_\psi \models \varphi$$
$$\mathfrak{M}, w \models \mathsf{K}_a \varphi \quad \text{iff} \quad \text{for every } w' \text{ s.t. } (w, w') \in \mathcal{R}_a, \ \mathfrak{M}, w' \models \varphi,$$

where $s \xleftarrow{\$} w$ represents that a state s is sampled from the distribution w.

Then $\mathfrak{M}, w \models \psi_0 \supset \mathbb{P}_I \psi_1$ represents that the conditional probability of satisfying a static formula ψ_1 given another ψ_0 is included in a set I at a world w.

In each world w, measurement variables can be interpreted using σ_w. This allows us to assign different values to different occurrences of a variable in a formula; E.g., in $\varphi(x) \to \mathsf{K}_a \varphi'(x)$, x occurring in $\varphi(x)$ is interpreted by σ_w in a world w, while x in $\varphi'(x)$ is interpreted by $\sigma_{w'}$ in another w' s.t. $(w, w') \in \mathcal{R}_a$.

Finally, the interpretation of an epistemic formula φ in $\mathfrak{M}$ is given by:

$$\mathfrak{M} \models \varphi \quad \text{iff} \quad \text{for every world } w \text{ in } \mathfrak{M}, \ \mathfrak{M}, w \models \varphi.$$

3 Techniques for Conditional Indistinguishability

In this section we introduce some modal operators to define a notion of "counterfactual knowledge" using StatEL, and show how to employ them to formalize conditional indistinguishability properties. The techniques presented here are used to formalize some fairness properties of machine learning in Sect. 7.

3.1   Counterfactual Epistemic Operators

Let us consider an accessibility relation $\mathcal{R}_\varepsilon$ based on a statistical divergence $D(\cdot \parallel \cdot) : \mathbb{DO} \times \mathbb{DO} \to \mathbb{R}^{\geq 0}$ and a threshold $\varepsilon \in \mathbb{R}^{\geq 0}$ defined by:

$$\mathcal{R}_\varepsilon \overset{\text{def}}{=} \{(w, w') \in \mathcal{W} \times \mathcal{W} \mid D(\sigma_w(y) \parallel \sigma_{w'}(y)) \leq \varepsilon\},$$

where y is the measurement variable observable in each world in $\mathcal{W}$. Intuitively, $(w, w') \in \mathcal{R}_\varepsilon$ represents that the probability distribution $\sigma_w(y)$ of the data y observed in a world w is *indistinguishable* from that in another world w' in terms of D.

Now we define the complement relation of $\mathcal{R}_\varepsilon$ by $\overline{\mathcal{R}_\varepsilon} \overset{\text{def}}{=} (\mathcal{W} \times \mathcal{W}) \setminus \mathcal{R}_\varepsilon$, namely,

$$\overline{\mathcal{R}_\varepsilon} = \{(w, w') \in \mathcal{W} \times \mathcal{W} \mid D(\sigma_w(y) \parallel \sigma_{w'}(y)) > \varepsilon\}.$$

Then $(w, w') \in \overline{\mathcal{R}_\varepsilon}$ represents that the distribution $\sigma_w(y)$ observed in w *can be distinguished* from that in w'. Then the corresponding epistemic operator $\overline{\mathsf{K}_\varepsilon}$, which we call a *counterfactual epistemic operator*, is interpreted as:

$$\mathfrak{M}, w \models \overline{\mathsf{K}_\varepsilon}\varphi \text{ iff for every } w' \text{ s.t. } (w, w') \in \overline{\mathcal{R}_\varepsilon}, \text{ we have } \mathfrak{M}, w' \models \varphi \qquad (1)$$

$$\text{iff for every } w' \text{ s.t. } \mathfrak{M}, w' \models \neg\varphi, \text{ we have } (w, w') \in \mathcal{R}_\varepsilon. \qquad (2)$$

Intuitively, (1) represents that if we were located in a possible world w' that looked distinguished from the real world w, then φ would always hold. This means a *counterfactual knowledge*[1] in the sense that, if we had an observation different from the real world, then we would know φ. This is logically equivalent to (2), representing that all possible worlds w' that do not satisfy φ look indistinguishable from the real world w in terms of D.

We remark that the dual operator $\overline{\mathsf{P}_\varepsilon}$ is interpreted as:

$$\mathfrak{M}, w \models \overline{\mathsf{P}_\varepsilon}\varphi \text{ iff there exists a } w' \text{ s.t. } (w, w') \notin \mathcal{R}_\varepsilon \text{ and } \mathfrak{M}, w' \models \varphi. \qquad (3)$$

This means a counterfactual possibility in the sense that it might be the case where we had an observation different from the real world and thought φ possible.

3.2   Conditional Indistinguishability via Counterfactual Knowledge

As shown in Sect. 7, some fairness notions in machine learning are based on conditional indistinguishability of the form (2), hence can be expressed using counterfactual epistemic operators.

Specifically, we use the following proposition, stating that given that two static formulas ψ and ψ' are respectively satisfied in worlds w and w' with probability 1, then the indistinguishability between w and w' can be expressed as $w \models \psi \supset \neg\overline{\mathsf{P}_a}\,\mathbb{P}_1\,\psi'$. Note that this formula means that there is no possible world where we have an observation different from the real world w (satisfying ψ) but we think ψ' possible; i.e., the formula means that if ψ' is satisfied then we have an observation indistinguishable from that in the real world w.

---

[1] Our definition of counterfactual knowledge is limited to the condition of having an observation different from the actual one. More general notions of counterfactual knowledge can be found in previous work (e.g., [38]).

Proposition 1 (Conditional indistinguishability). *Let* $\mathfrak{M} = (\mathcal{W}, (\mathcal{R}_a)_{a \in \mathcal{A}},$ $(V_s)_{s \in \mathcal{S}})$ *be a distributional Kripke model with the universe* $\mathcal{W} = \mathbb{D}\mathcal{S}$. *Let* ψ *and* ψ' *be static formulas, and* $a \in \mathcal{A}$.

(i) $\mathfrak{M} \models \psi \supset \neg\overline{P_a}\,\mathbb{P}_1\,\psi'$ *iff for any* $w, w' \in \mathcal{W}$, $\mathfrak{M}, w \models \mathbb{P}_1\,\psi$ *and* $\mathfrak{M}, w' \models \mathbb{P}_1\,\psi'$ *imply* $(w, w') \in \mathcal{R}_a$.

(ii) *If* $\mathcal{R}_a$ *is symmetric, then* $\mathfrak{M} \models \psi \supset \neg\overline{P_a}\,\mathbb{P}_1\,\psi'$ *iff* $\mathfrak{M} \models \psi' \supset \neg\overline{P_a}\,\mathbb{P}_1\,\psi$.

See Appendix A for the proof.

4   Formal Model for Statistical Classification

In this section we introduce a formal model for statistical classification by using distributional Kripke models (Definition 1). In particular, we formalize a probabilistic behaviour of a classifier C and a non-deterministic input x from an adversary in a distributional Kripke model.

4.1   Statistical Classification Problems

Multiclass classification is the problem of classifying a given input into one of multiple classes. Let L be a finite set of *class labels*, and $\mathcal{D}$ be the finite set of *input data* (called *feature vectors*) that we want to classify. Then a *classifier* is a function $C : \mathcal{D} \to$ L that receives an input datum and predicts which class (among L) the input belongs to. Here we do *not* model how classifiers are constructed from a set of training data, but deal with a situation where some classifier C has already been obtained and its properties should be evaluated.

Let $f : \mathcal{D} \times$ L $\to \mathbb{R}$ be a *scoring function* that gives a score $f(v, \ell)$ of predicting the class of an input datum (feature vector) v as a label ℓ. Then for each input $v \in \mathcal{D}$, we denote by $H(v) = \ell$ to represent that a label ℓ maximizes $f(v, \ell)$. For example, when the input v is an image of an animal and ℓ is the animal's name, then $H(v) = \ell$ may represent that an oracle (or a "human") classifies the image v as ℓ.

4.2   Modeling the Behaviours of Classifiers

Classifiers are formalized on a distributional Kripke model $\mathfrak{M} = (\mathcal{W}, (\mathcal{R}_a)_{a \in \mathcal{A}},$ $(V_s)_{s \in \mathcal{S}})$ with $\mathcal{W} = \mathbb{D}\mathcal{S}$ and a real world $w_{\mathsf{real}} \in \mathcal{W}$. Recall that each world $w \in \mathcal{W}$ is a probability distribution over the set $\mathcal{S}$ of states and has a stochastic assignment $\sigma_w : \mathtt{Mes} \to \mathbb{D}\mathcal{O}$ that is consistent with the deterministic assignments σ_s for all $s \in \mathcal{S}$ (as explained in Sect. 2.3).

We present an overview of our formalization in Fig. 1. We denote by $x \in \mathtt{Mes}$ an input to the classifier C, and by $y \in \mathtt{Mes}$ a label output by C. We assume that the input variable x (resp. the output variable y) ranges over the set $\mathcal{D}$ of input data (resp. the set L of labels); i.e., the deterministic assignment σ_s at each state $s \in \mathcal{S}$ has the range $\mathcal{O} = \mathcal{D} \cup$ L and satisfies $\sigma_s(x) \in \mathcal{D}$ and $\sigma_s(y) \in$ L.

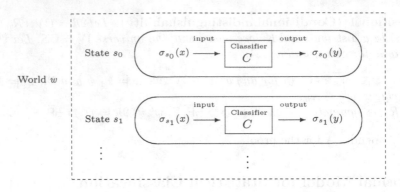

Fig. 1. A world w is chosen non-deterministically. With probability $w[s_i]$, the world w is in a deterministic state s_i where the classifier C receives the input value $\sigma_{s_i}(x)$ and returns the output value $\sigma_{s_i}(y)$.

A key idea in our modeling is that we formalize logical properties in the syntax level by using logical formulas, and statistical distances in the semantics level by using accessibility relations $\mathcal{R}_a$. In this way, we can formalize various statistical properties of classifiers in a simple and abstract way.

To formalize a classifier C, we introduce a static formula $\psi(x, y)$ to represent that C classifies a given input x as a class y. We also introduce a static formula $h(x, y)$ to represent that y is the actual class of an input x. As an abbreviation, we write $\psi_\ell(x)$ (resp. $h_\ell(x)$) to denote $\psi(x, \ell)$ (resp. $h(x, \ell)$). Formally, these static formulas are interpreted at each state $s \in \mathcal{S}$ as follows:

$$s \models \psi(x, y) \ \text{ iff } \ C(\sigma_s(x)) = \sigma_s(y).$$
$$s \models h(x, y) \ \text{ iff } \ H(\sigma_s(x)) = \sigma_s(y).$$

4.3 Modeling the Non-deterministic Inputs from Adversaries

As explained in Sect. 2.3, when a state s is drawn from a distribution $w \in \mathcal{W}$, an input value $\sigma_s(x)$ is sampled from the distribution $\sigma_w(x)$, and assigned to the measurement variable x. Since x denotes the input to the classifier C, the input distribution $\sigma_w(x)$ over $\mathcal{D}$ can be regarded as the *test dataset*. This means that each world w corresponds to a test dataset $\sigma_w(x)$. For instance, $\sigma_{w_{\text{real}}}(x)$ in the real world w_{real} represents the actual test dataset. The set of all possible test datasets (i.e., possible distributions of inputs to C) is represented by $\Lambda \overset{\text{def}}{=} \{\sigma_w(x) \mid w \in \mathcal{W}\}$. Note that Λ can be an infinite set.

For example, let us consider testing the classifier C with the actual test dataset $\sigma_{w_{\text{real}}}(x)$. When C assigns a label ℓ to an input x with probability 0.2, i.e., $\Pr\left[\, v \xleftarrow{\$} \sigma_{w_{\text{real}}}(x) : C(v) = \ell \,\right] = 0.2$, then this can be expressed by:

$$\mathfrak{M}, w_{\text{real}} \models \mathbb{P}_{0.2}\, \psi_\ell(x).$$

We can also formalize a non-deterministic input x from an adversary in this model as follows. Although each state s in a possible world w is assigned the probability $w[s]$, each possible world w itself is not assigned a probability. Thus, each input distribution $\sigma_w(x) \in \Lambda$ itself is also not assigned a probability, hence our model assumes no probability distribution over Λ. In other words, we assume that a world w and thus an adversary's input distribution $\sigma_w(x)$ are non-deterministically chosen. This is useful to model an adversary's malicious inputs in the definitions of security properties, because we usually do not have a prior knowledge of the distribution of malicious inputs from adversaries, and need to reason about the worst cases caused by the attack. In Sect. 6, this formalization of non-deterministic inputs is used to express the robustness of classifiers.

Finally, it should be noted that we cannot enumerate all possible adversarial inputs, hence cannot construct $\mathcal{W}$ by collecting their corresponding worlds. Since $\mathcal{W}$ can be an infinite set and is unspecified, we do not aim at checking whether or not a formula is satisfied in all possible worlds of $\mathcal{W}$. Nevertheless, as shown in later sections, describing various properties using StatEL is useful to explore desirable properties and to discuss relationships among them.

5   Formalizing the Classification Performance

In this section we show a formalization of classification performance using StatEL (See Fig. 2 for basic ideas). In classification problems, the terms *positive/negative* represent the result of the classifier's prediction, and the terms *true/false* represent whether the classifier predicts correctly or not. Then the following terminologies are commonly used:

(*tp*) *true positive* means both the prediction and actual class are positive;

(*tn*) *true negative* means both the prediction and actual class are negative;

(*fp*) *false positive* means the prediction is positive but the actual class is negative;

(*fn*) *false negative* means the prediction is negative but the actual class is positive.

These terminologies can be formalized using StatEL as shown in Table 1. For example, when an input x shows true positive at a state s, this can be expressed as $s \models \psi_\ell(x) \land h_\ell(x)$. True negative, false positive (Type I error), and false negative (Type II error) are respectively expressed as $s \models \neg\psi_\ell(x) \land \neg h_\ell(x)$, $s \models \psi_\ell(x) \land \neg h_\ell(x)$, and $s \models \neg\psi_\ell(x) \land h_\ell(x)$.

Then the *precision* (*positive predictive value*) is defined as the conditional probability that the prediction is correct given that the prediction is positive; i.e., $precision = \frac{tp}{tp+fp}$. Since the test dataset distribution in the real world w_{real} is expressed as $\sigma_{w_{\text{real}}}(x)$ (as explained in Sect. 4.3), the precision being within an interval I is given by:

$$\Pr\left[v \xleftarrow{\$} \sigma_{w_{\text{real}}}(x) \;:\; H(v) = \ell \;\middle|\; C(v) = \ell \right] \in I,$$

Table 1. Logical description of the table of confusion

| | Actual class | | Prevalence$_{\ell,I}(x) \overset{\text{def}}{=}$ | Accuracy$_{\ell,I}(x) \overset{\text{def}}{=}$ |
	positive $h_\ell(x)$	negative $\neg h_\ell(x)$	$\mathbb{P}_I(tp(x) \vee fn(x))$	$\mathbb{P}_I(tp(x) \vee tn(x))$
Positive prediction $\psi_\ell(x)$	$tp(x) \overset{\text{def}}{=}$ $\psi_\ell(x) \wedge h_\ell(x)$	$fp(x) \overset{\text{def}}{=}$ $\psi_\ell(x) \wedge \neg h_\ell(x)$	Precision$_{\ell,I}(x) \overset{\text{def}}{=}$ $\psi_\ell(x) \supset \mathbb{P}_I h_\ell(x)$	FDR$_{\ell,I}(x) \overset{\text{def}}{=}$ $\psi_\ell(x) \supset \mathbb{P}_I \neg h_\ell(x)$
Negative prediction $\neg\psi_\ell(x)$	$fn(x) \overset{\text{def}}{=}$ $\neg\psi_\ell(x) \wedge h_\ell(x)$	$tn(x) \overset{\text{def}}{=}$ $\neg\psi_\ell(x) \wedge \neg h_\ell(x)$	FOR$_{\ell,I}(x) \overset{\text{def}}{=}$ $\neg\psi_\ell(x) \supset \mathbb{P}_I h_\ell(x)$	NPV$_{\ell,I}(x) \overset{\text{def}}{=}$ $\neg\psi_\ell(x) \supset \mathbb{P}_I \neg h_\ell(x)$
	Recall$_{\ell,I}(x) \overset{\text{def}}{=}$ $h_\ell(x) \supset \mathbb{P}_I \psi_\ell(x)$	FallOut$_{\ell,I}(x) \overset{\text{def}}{=}$ $\neg h_\ell(x) \supset \mathbb{P}_I \psi_\ell(x)$		
	MissRate$_{\ell,I}(x) \overset{\text{def}}{=}$ $h_\ell(x) \supset \mathbb{P}_I \neg\psi_\ell(x)$	Specificity$_{\ell,I}(x) \overset{\text{def}}{=}$ $\neg h_\ell(x) \supset \mathbb{P}_I \neg\psi_\ell(x)$		

which can be written as:

$$\Pr\left[s \overset{\$}{\leftarrow} w_{\mathsf{real}} : s \models h_\ell(x) \mid s \models \psi_\ell(x) \right] \in I.$$

By using StatEL, this can be formalized as:

$$\mathfrak{M}, w_{\mathsf{real}} \models \mathsf{Precision}_{\ell,I}(x) \quad \text{where} \quad \mathsf{Precision}_{\ell,I}(x) \overset{\text{def}}{=} \psi_\ell(x) \supset \mathbb{P}_I h_\ell(x). \quad (4)$$

Note that the precision depends on the test data sampled from the distribution $\sigma_{w_{\mathsf{real}}}(x)$, hence on the real world w_{real} in which we are located. Hence the measurement variable x in $\mathsf{Precision}_{\ell,I}(x)$ is interpreted using the stochastic assignment $\sigma_{w_{\mathsf{real}}}$ in the world w_{real}.

Symmetrically, the *recall* (*true positive rate*) is defined as the conditional probability that the prediction is correct given that the actual class is positive; i.e., $recall = \frac{tp}{tp+fn}$. Then the recall being within I is formalized as:

$$\mathsf{Recall}_{\ell,I}(x) \overset{\text{def}}{=} h_\ell(x) \supset \mathbb{P}_I \psi_\ell(x). \quad (5)$$

In Table 1 we show the formalization of other notions of classification performance using StatEL.

6   Formalizing the Robustness of Classifiers

Many studies have found attacks on the robustness of statistical machine learning [8]. An input data that violates the robustness of classifiers is called an *adversarial example* [36]. It is designed to make a classifier fail to predict the actual class ℓ, but is recognized to belong to ℓ from human eyes. For example, in computer vision, Goodfellow et al. [18] create an image by adding undetectable noise to a panda's photo so that humans can still recognize the perturbed image as a panda, but a classifier misclassifies it as a gibbon.

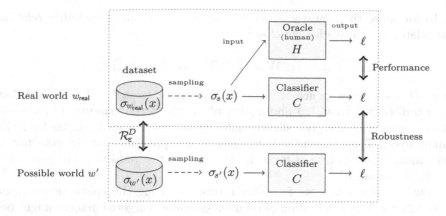

Fig. 2. The classification performance compares the conditional probability of the human H's output with that by the classifier C's. On the other hand, the robustness compares the conditional probability in the real world w_{real} with that in a possible world w' that is close to w_{real} in terms of $\mathcal{R}_\varepsilon^D$. Note that an adversary's choice of the test dataset $\sigma_{w'}(x)$ is formalized by the non-deterministic choice of the possible world w'.

In this section we formalize robustness notions for classifiers by using epistemic operators in StatEL (See Fig. 2 for an overview of the formalization). In addition, we present some relationships between classification performance and robustness, which suggest robustness-related properties that have not been formalized in the literature as far as we know.

6.1 Total Correctness of Classifiers

We first note that the *total correctness* of classifiers could be formalize as a classification performance (e.g., precision, recall, or accuracy) in the presence of all possible inputs from adversaries. For example, the total correctness could be formalized as $\mathfrak{M} \models \mathsf{Recall}_{\ell,I}(x)$, which represents that $\mathsf{Recall}_{\ell,I}(x)$ is satisfies in all possible worlds of $\mathfrak{M}$.

In practice, however, it is not possible or tractable to check whether the classification performance is achieved for all possible dataset and for all possible inputs, e.g., when $\mathcal{W}$ is an infinite set. Hence we need a weaker form of correctness notions, which may be verified in a certain way. In the following sections, we deal with robustness notions that are weaker than total correctness.

6.2 Probabilistic Robustness Against Targeted Attacks

When a robustness attack aims at misclassifying an input as a specific target label, then it is called a *targeted attack*. For instance, in the above-mentioned attack by [18], a gibbon is the target into which a panda's photo is misclassified.

To formalize the robustness, let $\mathcal{R}_\varepsilon^D \subseteq \mathcal{W} \times \mathcal{W}$ be an accessibility relation that relates two worlds having closer inputs, i.e.,

$$\mathcal{R}_\varepsilon^D \stackrel{\text{def}}{=} \{(w, w') \in \mathcal{W} \times \mathcal{W} \mid D(\sigma_w(x) \parallel \sigma_{w'}(x)) \leq \varepsilon\},$$

where D is some divergence or distance. Intuitively, $(w, w') \in \mathcal{R}_\varepsilon^D$ implies that the two distributions $\sigma_w(x)$ and $\sigma_{w'}(x)$ of inputs to the classifier C are close data in terms of D (e.g., two slightly different images that look pandas from the human' eyes). Then an epistemic formula $\mathsf{K}_\varepsilon^D \varphi$ represents that the classifier C is confident that φ is true as far as it classifies the test data that are perturbed by a level ε of noise[2].

Now we discuss how we formalize robustness using the epistemic operator K_ε^D as follows. A first definition of robustness against targeted attacks might be:

$$\mathfrak{M}, w_{\text{real}} \models h_{\text{panda}}(x) \supset \mathsf{K}_\varepsilon^D \mathbb{P}_0 \, \psi_{\text{gibbon}}(x),$$

which represents that a panda's photo x will not be recognized as a gibbon at all after the photo is perturbed by noise. However, this does not express probability or cover the case where the human cannot recognize the perturbed image as a panda, for example, when the image is perturbed by a transformation such as rescaling and rotation [2]. Instead, for some $\delta \in [0, 1]$, we formalize a notion of *probabilistic robustness against targeted attacks* by:

$$\mathsf{TargetRobust}_{\text{panda}, \delta}(x, \text{gibbon}) \stackrel{\text{def}}{=} \mathsf{K}_\varepsilon^D \left(h_{\text{panda}}(x) \supset \mathbb{P}_{[0,\delta]} \, \psi_{\text{gibbon}}(x) \right).$$

Since L_p-norms are often regarded as reasonable approximations of human perceptual distances [6], they are used as distance constraints on the perturbation in many researches on targeted attacks (e.g. [6, 18, 36]). To represent the robustness against these attacks in our model, we should take a metric D defined by $D(\sigma_w(x) \parallel \sigma_{w'}(x)) = \max_{v, v'} \|v - v'\|_p$ where v and v' range over the datasets $\mathsf{supp}(\sigma_w(x))$ and $\mathsf{supp}(\sigma_{w'}(x))$ respectively.

6.3 Probabilistic Robustness Against Non-targeted Attacks

Next we formalize *non-targeted attacks* [30, 31] in which adversaries try to misclassify inputs as some arbitrary incorrect labels (i.e., not as a specific label like a gibbon). Compared to targeted attacks, this kind of attacks are easier to mount, but harder to defend.

A notion of *probabilistic robustness against non-targeted attacks* can be formalized for some $I = [1 - \delta, 1]$ by:

$$\mathsf{TotalRobust}_{\ell, I}(x) \stackrel{\text{def}}{=} \mathsf{K}_\varepsilon^D \left(h_\ell(x) \supset \mathbb{P}_I \, \psi_\ell(x) \right) = \mathsf{K}_\varepsilon^D \, \mathsf{Recall}_{\ell, I}(x). \tag{6}$$

---

[2] This usage of modality relies on the fact that the value of the measurement variable x can be different in different possible worlds.

Then we derive that $\mathsf{TotalRobust}_{\mathsf{panda},I}(x)$ implies $\mathsf{TargetRobust}_{\mathsf{panda},\delta}(x,\mathsf{gibbon})$, namely, robustness against non-targeted attacks is not weaker than robustness against targeted attacks.

Next we note that by (6), robustness can be regarded as recall in the presence of perturbed noise. This implies that for each property φ in Table 1, we could consider $\mathsf{K}^D_\varepsilon\varphi$ as a property related to robustness although these have not been formalized in the literature of robustness of machine learning as far as we recognize. For example, $\mathsf{K}^D_\varepsilon\,\mathsf{Precision}_{\ell,i}(x)$ represents that in the presence of perturbed noise, the prediction is correct with a probability i given that it is positive. For another example, $\mathsf{K}^D_\varepsilon\,\mathsf{Accuracy}_{\ell,i}(x)$ represents that in the presence of perturbed noise, the prediction is correct (whether it is positive or negative) with a probability i.

Finally, note that by the reflexivity of $\mathcal{R}^D_\varepsilon$, $\mathfrak{M}, w_{\mathsf{real}} \models \mathsf{K}^D_\varepsilon\,\mathsf{Recall}_{\ell,I}(x)$ implies $\mathfrak{M}, w_{\mathsf{real}} \models \mathsf{Recall}_{\ell,I}(x)$, i.e., robustness implies recall without perturbation noise.

7   Formalizing the Fairness of Classifiers

There have been researches on various notions of fairness in machine learning. In this section, we formalize a few notions of fairness of classifiers by using StatEL. Here we focus on the fairness that should be maintained in the *impact*, i.e., the results of classification, rather than the *treatment*[3].

To formalize fairness notions, we use a distributional Kripke model $\mathfrak{M} = (\mathcal{W}, (\mathcal{R}_a)_{a \in \mathcal{A}}, (V_s)_{s \in \mathcal{S}})$ where $\mathcal{W}$ includes a possible world w_d having a dataset d from which an input to the classifier C is drawn. Recall that x (resp. y) is a measurement variable denoting the input (resp. output) of the classifier C. In each world w, $\sigma_w(x)$ is the distribution of C's input over $\mathcal{D}$, i.e., the test data distribution, and $\sigma_w(y)$ is the distribution of C's output over L. For each group $G \subseteq \mathcal{D}$ of inputs, we introduce a static formula $\eta_G(x)$ representing that an input x belongs to G. We also introduce a formula ξ_d representing that d is the dataset that the input to C is drawn from. Formally, these formulas are interpreted as follows:

- For each state $s \in \mathcal{S}$, $s \models \eta_G(x)$ iff $\sigma_s(x) \in G$.
- For each world $w \in \mathcal{W}$, $w \models \xi_d$ iff $\sigma_w(x) = d$.

Now we formalize three popular notions of fairness of classifiers by using counterfactual epistemic operators (introduced in Sect. 3) as follows.

7.1   Group Fairness (Statistical Parity)

The *group fairness* formulated as *statistical parity* [13] is the property that the output distributions of the classifier are identical for different groups. Formally,

---

[3] For instance, *fairness through awareness* [13] requires that protected attributes (e.g., race, religion, or gender) are not explicitly used in the prediction process. However, StatEL may not be suited to formalizing such a property in treatment.

for each $b = 0, 1$ and a group $G_b \subseteq \mathcal{D}$, let μ_{G_b} be the distribution of the output (over L) of the classifier C when the input is sampled from a dataset d and belongs to G_b. Then the statistical parity is formalized using the total variation D_{tv} by $D_{\mathsf{tv}}(\mu_{G_0} \| \mu_{G_1}) \leq \varepsilon$.

To express this using StatEL, we define an accessibility relation $\mathcal{R}_\varepsilon^{\mathsf{tv}}$ in $\mathfrak{M}$ by:

$$\mathcal{R}_\varepsilon^{\mathsf{tv}} \stackrel{\text{def}}{=} \{(w, w') \in \mathcal{W} \times \mathcal{W} \mid D_{\mathsf{tv}}(\sigma_w(y) \| \sigma_{w'}(y)) \leq \varepsilon\}. \tag{7}$$

Intuitively, $(w, w') \in \mathcal{R}_\varepsilon^{\mathsf{tv}}$ represents that the two probability distributions $\sigma_w(y)$ and $\sigma_{w'}(y)$ of the outputs by the classifier C respectively in w and in w' are close in terms of D_{tv}. Note that $\sigma_w(y)$ and $\sigma_{w'}(y)$ respectively represent μ_{G_0} and μ_{G_1}.

Then the statistical parity w.r.t. groups G_0, G_1 means that in terms of $\mathcal{R}_\varepsilon^{\mathsf{tv}}$, we cannot distinguish a world having a dataset d and satisfying $\eta_{G_0}(x) \wedge \psi(x, y)$ from another world satisfying $\xi_d \wedge \eta_{G_1}(x) \wedge \psi(x, y)$. By Proposition 1, this is expressed as:

$$\mathfrak{M}, w_d \models \mathsf{GrpFair}(x, y)$$

where $\mathsf{GrpFair}(x, y) \stackrel{\text{def}}{=} (\eta_{G_0}(x) \wedge \psi(x, y)) \supset \neg \overline{\mathsf{P}_\varepsilon^{\mathsf{tv}}} \, \mathbb{P}_1(\xi_d \wedge \eta_{G_1}(x) \wedge \psi(x, y))$.

7.2   Individual Fairness (as Lipschitz Property)

The *individual fairness* formulated as a Lipschitz property [13] is the property that the classifier outputs similar labels given similar inputs. Formally, let μ_v and $\mu_{v'}$ be the distributions of the outputs (over L) of the classifier C when the inputs are $v \in \mathcal{D}$ and $v' \in \mathcal{D}$, respectively. Then the individual fairness is formalized using some divergence $D : \mathbb{DL} \times \mathbb{DL} \rightarrow \mathbb{R}^{\geq 0}$, some metric $r : \mathcal{D} \times \mathcal{D} \rightarrow \mathbb{R}^{\geq 0}$, and a threshold $\varepsilon \in \mathbb{R}^{\geq 0}$ by $D(\mu_v \| \mu_{v'}) \leq \varepsilon \cdot r(v, v')$.

To express this using StatEL, we define an accessibility relation $\mathcal{R}_\varepsilon^{r,D}$ in $\mathfrak{M}$ for the metric r and the divergence D as follows:

$$\mathcal{R}_\varepsilon^{r,D} \stackrel{\text{def}}{=} \left\{ (w, w') \in \mathcal{W} \times \mathcal{W} \mid \begin{array}{l} v \in \mathsf{supp}(\sigma_w(x)), \ v' \in \mathsf{supp}(\sigma_{w'}(x)), \\ D(\sigma_w(y) \| \sigma_{w'}(y)) \leq \varepsilon \cdot r(v, v') \end{array} \right\}. \tag{8}$$

Intuitively, $(w, w') \in \mathcal{R}_\varepsilon^{r,D}$ represents that, when inputs are closer in terms of the metric r, the classifier C outputs closer labels in terms of the divergence D.

Then the individual fairness w.r.t. r and D means that in terms of $\mathcal{R}_\varepsilon^{r,D}$, we cannot distinguish two worlds where $\psi(x, y)$ is satisfied, i.e., the classifier C outputs y given an input x. By Proposition 1, this is expressed as:

$$\mathfrak{M}, w_d \models \mathsf{IndFair}(x, y)$$

where $\mathsf{IndFair}(x, y) \stackrel{\text{def}}{=} \psi(x, y) \supset \neg \overline{\mathsf{P}_\varepsilon^{r,D}} \, \mathbb{P}_1(\xi_d \wedge \psi(x, y))$.

This represents that when we observe the distribution of the classifier's output y, we can less distinguish two worlds w and w' when their inputs $\sigma_w(x)$ and $\sigma_{w'}(x)$ are closer.

7.3 Equal Opportunity

Equal opportunity [21,40] is the property that the recall (true positive rate) is the same for all the groups. Formally, given an advantage class $\ell \in L$ (e.g., not defaulting on a loan) and a group $G \subseteq \mathcal{D}$ of inputs with a protected attribute (e.g., race), a classifier C is said to satisfy equal opportunity of ℓ w.r.t. G if we have:

$$\Pr[C(x) = \ell \mid x \in G,\ H(x) = \ell] = \Pr[C(x) = \ell \mid x \in \mathcal{D} \setminus G,\ H(x) = \ell].$$

If we allow the logic to use the universal quantification over the probability value i, then the notion of equal opportunity could be formalized as:

$$\mathsf{EqOpp}(x) \stackrel{\text{def}}{=} \forall i \in [0,1].\ (\xi_d \wedge \eta_G(x) \supset \mathsf{Recall}_{\ell,i}(x)) \leftrightarrow (\xi_d \wedge \neg\eta_G(x) \supset \mathsf{Recall}_{\ell,i}(x)).$$

However, instead of allowing for this universal quantification, we can use the modal operators $\overline{\mathsf{P}^{\mathsf{tv}}_\varepsilon}$ (defined by (7)) with $\varepsilon = 0$, and represent equal opportunity as the fact that we cannot distinguish a world having a dataset d and satisfying $\eta_G(x) \wedge \psi(x,y)$ from another world satisfying $\xi_d \wedge \neg\eta_G(x) \wedge \psi(x,y)$ as follows:

$$\mathsf{EqOpp}(x) \stackrel{\text{def}}{=} (\eta_G(x) \wedge \psi(x,y)) \supset \neg\overline{\mathsf{P}^{\mathsf{tv}}_0}\,\mathbb{P}_1(\xi_d \wedge \neg\eta_G(x) \wedge \psi(x,y)).$$

Then equal opportunity can be regarded as a special case of statistical parity.

8 Related Work

In this section, we provide a brief overview of related work on the specification of statistical machine learning and on epistemic logic for describing specification.

Desirable properties of statistical machine learning. There have been a large number of papers on attacks and defences for deep neural networks [8,36]. Compared to them, however, not much work has been done to explore the formal specification of various properties of machine learning. Seshia et al. [34] present a list of desirable properties of DNNs (deep neural networks) although most of the properties are presented informally without mathematical formulas. As for robustness, Dreossi et al. [11] propose a unifying formalization of adversarial input generation in a rigorous and organized manner, although they formalize and classify attacks (as optimization problems) rather than define the robustness notions themselves. Concerning the fairness notions, Gajane [16] surveys the formalization of fairness notions for machine learning and present some justification based on social science literature.

Epistemic logic for describing specification. Epistemic logic [39] has been studied to represent and reason about knowledge [14,19,20], and has been applied to describe various properties of systems.

The *BAN logic* [5], proposed by Burrows, Abadi and Needham, is a notable example of epistemic logic used to model and verify the authentication in cryptographic protocols. To improve the formalization of protocols' behaviours, some epistemic approaches integrate process calculi [7,10,23].

Epistemic logic has also been used to formalize and reason about privacy properties, including anonymity [17,20,27,35], receipt-freeness of electronic voting protocols [24], and privacy policy for social network services [32]. Temporal epistemic logic is used to express information flow security policies [3].

Concerning the formalization of fairness notions, previous work in formal methods has modeled different kinds of fairness involving timing by using temporal logic rather than epistemic logic. As far as we know, no previous work has formalized fairness notions of machine learning using counterfactual epistemic operators.

Formalization of statistical properties. In studies of philosophical logic, Lewis [29] shows the idea that when a random value has various possible probability distributions, then those distributions should be represented on distinct possible worlds. Bana [4] puts Lewis's idea in a mathematically rigorous setting. Recently, a modal logic called statistical epistemic logic [26] is proposed and is used to formalize statistical hypothesis testing and the notion of differential privacy [12]. Independently of that work, French et al. [15] propose a probability model for a dynamic epistemic logic in which each world is associated with a subjective probability distribution over the universe, without dealing with non-deterministic inputs or statistical divergence.

9   Conclusion

We have shown a logical approach to formalizing statistical classifiers and their desirable properties in a simple and abstract way. Specifically, we have introduced a formal model for probabilistic behaviours of classifiers and non-deterministic adversarial inputs using a distributional Kripke model. Then we have formalized the classification performance, robustness, and fairness of classifiers by using StatEL. Moreover, we have also clarified some relationships among properties of classifiers, and relevance between classification performance and robustness. To formalize fairness notions, we have introduced a notion of counterfactual knowledge and shown some techniques to express conditional indistinguishability. As far as we know, this is the first work that uses logical formulas to express statistical properties of machine learning, and that provides epistemic (resp. counterfactually epistemic) views on robustness (resp. fairness) of classifiers.

In future work, we are planning to include temporal operators in the specification language and to formally reason about system-level properties of learning-based systems. We are also interested in developing a general framework for the formal specification of machine learning associated with testing methods and possibly extended with Bayesian networks. Our future work also includes an extension of StatEL to formalize machine learning other than classification problems. Another possible direction of future work would be to clarify the relationships between our counterfactual epistemic operators and more general notions of counterfactual knowledge in previous work such as [38].

A   Proof for Proposition 1

Proposition 1 (Conditional indistinguishability). *Let* $\mathfrak{M} = (\mathcal{W}, (\mathcal{R}_a)_{a \in \mathcal{A}}, (V_s)_{s \in \mathcal{S}})$ *be a distributional Kripke model with the universe* $\mathcal{W} = \mathbb{DS}$. *Let* ψ *and* ψ' *be static formulas, and* $a \in \mathcal{A}$.

(i) $\mathfrak{M} \models \psi \supset \neg \overline{P_a} \mathbb{P}_1 \psi'$ *iff for any* $w, w' \in \mathcal{W}$, $\mathfrak{M}, w \models \mathbb{P}_1 \psi$ *and* $\mathfrak{M}, w' \models \mathbb{P}_1 \psi'$ *imply* $(w, w') \in \mathcal{R}_a$.

(ii) *If* $\mathcal{R}_a$ *is symmetric, then* $\mathfrak{M} \models \psi \supset \neg \overline{P_a} \mathbb{P}_1 \psi'$ *iff* $\mathfrak{M} \models \psi' \supset \neg \overline{P_a} \mathbb{P}_1 \psi$.

Proof. We first prove the claim (i) as follows. We show the direction from left to right. Assume that $\mathfrak{M} \models \psi \supset \neg \overline{P_a} \mathbb{P}_1 \psi'$. Let $w, w' \in \mathcal{W}$ such that $\mathfrak{M}, w \models \mathbb{P}_1 \psi$ and $\mathfrak{M}, w' \models \mathbb{P}_1 \psi'$. Then $w|_\psi = w$. By $\mathfrak{M}, w \models \psi \supset \neg \overline{P_a} \mathbb{P}_1 \psi'$, we obtain $\mathfrak{M}, w|_\psi \models \neg \overline{P_a} \mathbb{P}_1 \psi'$, which is logically equivalent to $\mathfrak{M}, w|_\psi \models \overline{K_a} \neg \mathbb{P}_1 \psi'$. By the definition of $\overline{K_a}$, for every $w'' \in \mathcal{W}$, $\mathfrak{M}, w'' \models \mathbb{P}_1 \psi'$ implies $(w|_\psi, w'') \in \mathcal{R}_a$. Then, since $w|_\psi = w$ and $\mathfrak{M}, w' \models \mathbb{P}_1 \psi'$, we obtain $(w, w') \in \mathcal{R}_a$.

Next we show the other direction as follows. Assume the right hand side. Let $w \in \mathcal{W}$ such that $\mathfrak{M}, w \models \mathbb{P}_1 \psi$. Then for every $w' \in \mathcal{W}$, $\mathfrak{M}, w' \models \mathbb{P}_1 \psi'$ implies $(w, w') \in \mathcal{R}_a$. By the definition of $\overline{K_a}$, we have $\mathfrak{M}, w \models \overline{K_a} \neg \mathbb{P}_1 \psi'$, which is equivalent to $\mathfrak{M}, w \models \neg \overline{P_a} \mathbb{P}_1 \psi'$. By $\mathfrak{M}, w \models \mathbb{P}_1 \psi$, we have $w|_\psi = w$, hence $\mathfrak{M}, w|_\psi \models \neg \overline{P_a} \mathbb{P}_1 \psi'$. Therefore $\mathfrak{M}, w \models \psi \supset \neg \overline{P_a} \mathbb{P}_1 \psi'$.

Finally, the claim (ii) follows from the claim (i) immediately.   □

References

1. Alpern, B., Schneider, F.B.: Defining liveness. Inf. Process. Lett. **21**(4), 181–185 (1985). https://doi.org/10.1016/0020-0190(85)90056-0

2. Athalye, A., Engstrom, L., Ilyas, A., Kwok, K.: Synthesizing robust adversarial examples. In: Proceedings of the ICML, pp. 284–293 (2018)

3. Balliu, M., Dam, M., Guernic, G.L.: Epistemic temporal logic for information flow security. In: Proceedings of PLAS, p. 6 (2011). https://doi.org/10.1145/2166956.2166962

4. Bana, G.: Models of objective chance: an analysis through examples. In: Hofer-Szabó, G., Wroński, L. (eds.) Making it Formally Explicit. ESPS, vol. 6, pp. 43–60. Springer, Cham (2017). https://doi.org/10.1007/978-3-319-55486-0_3

5. Burrows, M., Abadi, M., Needham, R.M.: A logic of authentication. ACM Trans. Comput. Syst. **8**(1), 18–36 (1990). https://doi.org/10.1145/77648.77649

6. Carlini, N., Wagner, D.A.: Towards evaluating the robustness of neural networks. In: Proceedings Security and Privacy, pp. 39–57 (2017). https://doi.org/10.1109/SP.2017.49

7. Chadha, R., Delaune, S., Kremer, S.: Epistemic logic for the applied pi calculus. In: Proceedings of FMOODS/FORTE, pp. 182–197 (2009).https://doi.org/10.1007/978-3-642-02138-1_12

8. Chakraborty, A., Alam, M., Dey, V., Chattopadhyay, A., Mukhopadhyay, D.: Adversarial attacks and defences: a survey. CoRR abs/1810.00069 (2018). http://arxiv.org/abs/1810.00069

9. Clarkson, M.R., Schneider, F.B.: Hyperproperties. In: Proceedings of CSF, pp. 51–65. IEEE (2008). https://doi.org/10.1109/CSF.2008.7

10. Dechesne, F., Mousavi, M., Orzan, S.: Operational and epistemic approaches to protocol analysis: bridging the gap. In: Proceedings of LPAR, pp. 226–241 (2007)

11. Dreossi, T., Ghosh, S., Sangiovanni-Vincentelli, A.L., Seshia, S.A.: A formalization of robustness for deep neural networks. In: Proceedings of VNN (2019)

12. Dwork, C.: Differential privacy. In: Proceedings of ICALP, pp. 1–12 (2006)

13. Dwork, C., Hardt, M., Pitassi, T., Reingold, O., Zemel, R.S.: Fairness through awareness. In: Proceedings of ITCS, pp. 214–226. ACM (2012)

14. Fagin, R., Halpern, J., Moses, Y., Vardi, M.: Reasoning About Knowledge. The MIT Press, Cambridge (1995)

15. French, T., Gozzard, A., Reynolds, M.: Dynamic aleatoric reasoning in games of bluffing and chance. In: Proceedings of AAMAS, pp. 1964–1966 (2019)

16. Gajane, P.: On formalizing fairness in prediction with machine learning. CoRR abs/1710.03184 (2017). http://arxiv.org/abs/1710.03184

17. Garcia, F.D., Hasuo, I., Pieters, W., van Rossum, P.: Provable anonymity. In: Proceedings of FMSE, pp. 63–72 (2005). https://doi.org/10.1145/1103576.1103585

18. Goodfellow, I.J., Shlens, J., Szegedy, C.: Explaining and harnessing adversarial examples. In: Proceedings of ICLR (2015)

19. Halpern, J.Y.: Reasoning About Uncertainty. The MIT press, Cambridge (2003)

20. Halpern, J.Y., O'Neill, K.R.: Anonymity and information hiding in multiagent systems. J. Comput. Secur. 13(3), 483–512 (2005)

21. Hardt, M., Price, E., Srebro, N.: Equality of opportunity in supervised learning. In: proceedings of NIPS, pp. 3315–3323 (2016)

22. Huang, X., Kwiatkowska, M., Wang, S., Wu, M.: Safety verification of deep neural networks. In: Proceedings of CAV, pp. 3–29 (2017). https://doi.org/10.1007/978-3-319-63387-9_1

23. Hughes, D., Shmatikov, V.: Information hiding, anonymity and privacy: a modular approach. J. Comput. Secur. 12(1), 3–36 (2004)

24. Jonker, H.L., Pieters, W.: Receipt-freeness as a special case of anonymity in epistemic logic. In: Proceedings of Workshop On Trustworthy Elections (WOTE 2006), June 2006

25. Katz, G., Barrett, C.W., Dill, D.L., Julian, K., Kochenderfer, M.J.: Reluplex: an efficient SMT solver for verifying deep neural networks. In: Proceedings of CAV, pp. 97–117 (2017). https://doi.org/10.1007/978-3-319-63387-9_5

26. Kawamoto, Y.: Statistical epsitemic logic. CoRR abs/1412.4451 (2019). https://arxiv.org/pdf/1907.05995.pdf

27. Kawamoto, Y., Mano, K., Sakurada, H., Hagiya, M.: Partial knowledge of functions and verification of anonymity. Trans. Japan Soc. Ind. Appl. Math. 17(4), 559–576 (2007). https://doi.org/10.11540/jsiamt.17.4_559

28. Kripke, S.A.: Semantical analysis of modal logic i normal modal propositional calculi. Math. Logic Q. 9(5–6), 67–96 (1963)

29. Lewis, D.: A subjectivist's guide to objective chance. In: Studies in Inductive Logic and Probability, Vol. II, pp. 263–293. University of California Press, Berkeley (1980)

30. Madry, A., Makelov, A., Schmidt, L., Tsipras, D., Vladu, A.: Towards deep learning models resistant to adversarial attacks. In: Proceedings of ICLR (2018)

31. Moosavi-Dezfooli, S., Fawzi, A., Frossard, P.: Deepfool: A simple and accurate method to fool deep neural networks. In: Proceedings of CVPR, pp. 2574–2582 (2016). https://doi.org/10.1109/CVPR.2016.282
32. Pardo, R., Schneider, G.: A formal privacy policy framework for social networks. In: Proceedings of SEFM, pp. 378–392 (2014). https://doi.org/10.1007/978-3-319-10431-7_30
33. Pei, K., Cao, Y., Yang, J., Jana, S.: Deepxplore: automated whitebox testing of deep learning systems. In: Proceedings of SOSP, pp. 1–18 (2017). https://doi.org/10.1145/3132747.3132785
34. Seshia, S.A., et al.: Formal specification for deep neural networks. In: Lahiri, S.K., Wang, C. (eds.) ATVA 2018. LNCS, vol. 11138, pp. 20–34. Springer, Cham (2018). https://doi.org/10.1007/978-3-030-01090-4_2
35. Syverson, P.F., Stubblebine, S.G.: Group principals and the formalization of anonymity. In: Wing, J.M., Woodcock, J., Davies, J. (eds.) FM 1999. LNCS, vol. 1708, pp. 814–833. Springer, Heidelberg (1999). https://doi.org/10.1007/3-540-48119-2_45
36. Szegedy, C., Zaremba, W., Sutskever, I., Bruna, J., Erhan, D., Goodfellow, I.J., Fergus, R.: Intriguing properties of neural networks. In: Proceedings of ICLR (2014)
37. Tian, Y., Pei, K., Jana, S., Ray, B.: Deeptest: automated testing of deep-neural-network-driven autonomous cars. In: Proceedings of ICSE, pp. 303–314 (2018). https://doi.org/10.1145/3180155.3180220
38. Williamson, T.: Philosophical knowledge and knowledge of counterfactuals. Grazer Philosophische Studien **74**, 89 (2007)
39. von Wright, G.H.: An Essay in Modal Logic. North-Holland Pub. Co., Amsterdam (1951)
40. Zafar, M.B., Valera, I., Gomez-Rodriguez, M., Gummadi, K.P.: Fairness beyond disparate treatment and disparate impact: Learning classification without disparate mistreatment. In: Proceedings of WWW, pp. 1171–1180 (2017). https://doi.org/10.1145/3038912.3052660

Operating Systems

Efficient Formal Verification for the Linux Kernel

Daniel Bristot de Oliveira[1,2,3](✉) [iD], Tommaso Cucinotta[2] [iD],
and Rômulo Silva de Oliveira[3] [iD]

[1] RHEL Platform/Real-time Team, Red Hat, Inc., Pisa, Italy
daniel@bristot.me
[2] RETIS Lab, Scuola Superiore Sant'Anna, Pisa, Italy
tommaso.cucinotta@santannapisa.it
[3] Department of Systems Automation, UFSC, Florianópolis, Brazil
romulo.deoliveira@ufsc.br

Abstract. Formal verification of the Linux kernel has been receiving
increasing attention in recent years, with the development of many models, from memory subsystems to the synchronization primitives of the
real-time kernel. The effort in developing formal verification methods
is justified considering the large code-base, the complexity in synchronization required in a monolithic kernel and the support for multiple
architectures, along with the usage of Linux on critical systems, from
high-frequency trading to self-driven cars. Despite recent developments
in the area, none of the proposed approaches are suitable and flexible
enough to be applied in an efficient way to a running kernel. Aiming to
fill such a gap, this paper proposes a formal verification approach for the
Linux kernel, based on automata models. It presents a method to auto-
generate verification code from an automaton, which can be integrated
into a module and dynamically added into the kernel for efficient on-the-
fly verification of the system, using in-kernel tracing features. Finally, a
set of experiments demonstrate verification of three models, along with
performance analysis of the impact of the verification, in terms of latency
and throughput of the system, showing the efficiency of the approach.

Keywords: Verification · Linux kernel · Automata · Testing

1 Introduction

Real-time variants of the Linux operating system (OS) have been successfully
used in many safety-critical and real-time systems belonging to a wide spectrum
of applications, going from sensor networks [19], robotics [39], factory automation [17] to the control of military drones [11] and distributed high-frequency
trading systems [10,13], just to mention a few. However, for a wider adoption of
Linux in next-generation cyber-physical systems, like self-driving cars [42], automatic testing and formal verification of the code base is increasingly becoming
a non-negotiable requirement. One of the areas where it is mostly difficult and

© Springer Nature Switzerland AG 2019
P. C. Ölveczky and G. Salaün (Eds.): SEFM 2019, LNCS 11724, pp. 315–332, 2019.
https://doi.org/10.1007/978-3-030-30446-1_17

non-trivial to adopt such techniques is the one of the kernel, due to its inherent complexity. This need has fomented the development of many formal models for the Linux kernel, like the Memory Model [2] and formal verification of spinlock primitives [28]. However, Linux lacks a methodology for runtime verification that can be applied broadly throughout all of the in-kernel subsystems.

Some complex subsystems of Linux have been recently modeled and verified by using automata. For example, modeling the synchronization of threads in the PREEMPT_RT Linux kernel achieved practical results in terms of problems spotted within the kernel [33] (and fixes being proposed afterwards). As a consequence, the kernel community provided positive feedback, underlining that the *event* and *state* abstractions used in automata look natural to the modeling of the kernel behavior, because developers are already accustomed to using and interpreting event traces in these terms [30,31].

The problem, however, is that the previously proposed approach [33] relies on tracing events into an in-kernel buffer, then moving the data to user-space where it is saved to disk, for later post-processing. Although functional, when it comes to tracing high-frequency events, the act of in-kernel recording, copying to user-space, saving to disk and post-processing the data related to kernel events profoundly influences the timing behavior of the system. For instance, tracing scheduling and synchronization-related events can generate as many as 900000 events per second, and more than 100 MB per second of data, per CPU, making the approach non-practical, especially for big muti-core platforms.

An alternative could be hard-coding the verification in the Linux kernel code. This alternative, however, is prone not to become widely adopted in the kernel. It would require a considerable effort for acceptance of the code on many subsystems. Mainly because complex models can easily have thousands of states. A second alternative would be maintaining the verification code as an external *patchset*, requiring the users to recompile the kernel before doing the checking, what would inhibit the full utilization of the method as well. An efficient verification method for Linux should unify the flexibility of using the dynamic tracing features of the kernel while being able to perform the verification with low overheads.

Paper Contributions. This paper proposes an efficient automata-based verification method for the Linux kernel, capable of verifying the correct sequences of in-kernel events as happening at runtime, against a theoretical automata-based model that has been previously created. The method starts from an automata-based model, as produced through the well-known Supremica modeling tool, then it auto-generates C code with the ability of efficient transition look-up time in $O(1)$ for each hit event. The generated code embedding the automaton is compiled as a module, loaded *on-the-fly* into the kernel and dynamically associated with kernel tracing events. This enables the run-time verification of the observed in-kernel events, compared to the sequences allowed by the model, with any mismatch being readily identified and reported. The verification is carried out in kernel space way more efficiently than it was possible to do in user-space, because there is no need to store and export the whole trace of occurred events.

Indeed, results from performance analysis of a kernel under verification show that the overhead of the verification of kernel operations is very limited, and even lower than merely activating tracing for all of the events of interest.

2 Background

This section provides the background for the two main concepts used for the verification of Linux: the automata-based formal method used for modeling, and the tracing mechanism within the kernel at the basis of the verification process.

2.1 Automata and Discrete Event System

A *Discrete Event System* (DES) can be described in various ways, for example using a *language* (that represents the valid sequences of events that can be observed during the evolution of the system). Informally speaking, an automaton is a formalization used to model a set of well-defined rules that define such a language.

The evolution of a DES is described with all possible sequence of events $e_1, e_2, e_3, ...e_n$, $e_i \in E$, defining the language $\mathcal{L}$ that describes the system.

There are many possible ways to describe the language of a system. For example, it is possible to use regular expressions. For complex systems, more flexible modeling formats, like automaton, were developed.

Automata are characterized by the typical directed graph or state transition diagram representation. For example, consider the event set $E = \{a, b, g\}$ and the state transition diagram in Fig. 1, where nodes represent system states, labeled arcs represent transitions between states, the arrow points to the initial state and the nodes with double circles are *marked states*, i.e., safe states of the system.

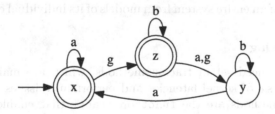

Fig. 1. State transitions diagram (based on Fig. 2.1 from [7]).

Formally, a deterministic automaton, denoted by G, is a tuple

$$G = \{X, E, f, x_0, X_m\} \tag{1}$$

where:

- X is the set of states

- E is the finite set of events
- $f : X \times E \to X$ is the transition function. It defines the state transition in the occurrence of a event from E in the state X.
- x_0 is the initial state
- $X_m \subseteq X$ is the set of marked states

For instance, the automaton G shown in Fig. 1 can be defined as follows:

- $X = \{x, y, z\}$
- $E = \{a, b, g\}$
- $f : (x, a) = x; (y, a) = x; (z, b) = z; (x, g) = z; (y, b) = y; (z, a) = (z, g) = y.$
- $x_0 = x$
- $X_m = \{x, z\}$

The automaton starts from the initial state x_0 and moves to a new state $f(x_0, e)$ upon the occurrence of an event e. This process continues based on the transitions for which f is defined.

Informally, following the graph of Fig. 1 it is possible to see that the occurrence of event a, followed by event g and a will lead from the initial state to state y. The language $\mathcal{L}(G)$ generated by an automaton $G = \{X, E, f, x_0, X_m\}$ consists of all possible chains of events generated by the state transition diagram starting from the initial state.

Given a set of *marked states*, i.e., possible final or safe states when modeling a system, an important language generated by an automaton is the *marked language*. This consists of the set of words in $\mathcal{L}(G)$ that lead to marked states, and it is also called the language *recognized* by the automaton.

Automata theory also enables operations among automata. An important operation is the *parallel composition* of two or more automata that are combined to compose a single, augmented-state, automaton. This allows for merging two or more automata models into one single model, constituting the standard way of building a model of an entire system from models of its individual components [7].

2.2 Linux Tracing

Linux has an advanced set of tracing methods, which are mainly applied in the runtime analysis of kernel latencies and performance issues [27]. The most popular tracing methods are the `function tracer` that enables the trace of kernel functions [38], and the `tracepoint` that enables the tracing of hundreds of events in the system, like the *wakeup* of a new thread or the occurrence of an interrupt. But there are many other methods, like `kprobes` that enable the creation of `dynamic tracepoints` in arbitrary places in the kernel code [22], and composed arrangements like using the `function tracer` and `tracepoints` to examine the code path from the time a task is woken up to when it is scheduled.

An essential characteristic of the Linux tracing feature is its efficiency. Nowadays, almost all Linux based operating systems (OSes) have these tracing methods enabled and ready to be used in production kernels. Indeed, these methods

```
sh-2038  [002] d... 16230.043339: ttwu_do_wakeup <-try_to_wake_up
sh-2038  [002] d... 16230.043339: check_preempt_curr <-ttwu_do_wakeup
sh-2038  [002] d... 16230.043340: resched_curr <-check_preempt_curr
sh-2038  [002] d... 16230.043343: sched_wakeup: comm=cat pid=2040 prio=120 target_cpu=003
```

Fig. 2. Ftrace output.

have nearly zero overhead when disabled, thanks to the extensive usage of run-time code modification techniques, that allow for a greater efficiency than using conditional jumps when tracing is disabled. For instance, when the `function tracer` is disabled, a `no-operation` assembly instruction is placed right at the beginning of all traceable functions. When the `function tracer` is enabled, the `no-operation` instruction is overwritten with an instruction that calls a function that will *trace* the execution, for instance by appending information into an in-kernel trace buffer. This is done at runtime, without any need for a reboot. A `tracepoint` works similarly, but using a jump label [14]. The mentioned tracing methods are implemented in such a way that it is possible to specify how an event will be handled dynamically, at runtime. For example, when enabling a `tracepoint`, the function responsible to handle the event is specified through a proper in-kernel API.

Currently, there are two main interfaces by which these features can be accessed from user-space: `perf` and `Ftrace`. Both tools can hook to the trace methods, processing the events in many different ways. The most common action is to record the occurrence of events into a trace-buffer for post-processing or human interpretation of the events. Figure 2 shows the output of the `Ftrace` tracing functions and `tracepoints`. The recording of events is optimized by the usage of *per-cpu* lock-less trace buffers. Furthermore, it is possible to take actions based on events. For example, it is possible to record a *stacktrace*.

These tracing methods can also be leveraged for other purposes. Similarly to `perf` and `Ftrace`, other tools can also hook a function to a tracing method, non-necessarily for the purpose of providing a trace of the system execution to the user-space. For example, the Live Patching feature of Linux uses the `function tracer` to hook and deviate the execution of a problematic function to a revised version of the function that fixes a problem [36].

3   Related Work

This section overviews major prior works related to the technique introduced in this paper, focusing on automata-based modeling of various Linux kernel subsystems, use of formal methods for other OS kernels, and finally the use of other formal methods to assess the correctness of various Linux kernel functions.

3.1   Automata-Based Linux Modelling

A number of works exist making use of automata-based models to verify correctness of Linux kernel code. The work presented in [29] uses trace and automata to verify conditions in the kernel. The paper presents models for SYN-flood, escaping from a chroot jail, validation of locking and of real-time constraints. The LTTng tracer [41] is used to compare the models to the kernel execution. The models are very simple and presented as proof of concept. There are only five states in the largest model, which is related to locking validation. There are only two states in the real-time constraints model. Despite its simplicity, this paper corroborates the idea of connecting automata to tracing as a layer of translation from kernel to formal methods, including aspects of Linux real-time features.

State-aware/Stateful robustness testing [26] is an important area that uses formal system definition. Robust testing is also used in the OS context as a fault tolerance technique [37]. A case study of state-based robustness testing is presented in [15] that includes the OS states of a real-time version of Linux. The results show that the OS state plays a significant role in testing for corner cases that are not covered by traditional robustness verification. Another relevant project for Linux is SABRINE [16], an approach using tracing and automata for *state-aware robustness testing* of OSes. SABRINE works as follows: It traces the interactions among components of the OS in the first step. The software then extracts state models from the traces automatically. The traces are processed in this phase in order to find sequences of similar functions, to be grouped, forming a pattern. Later, similar patterns are grouped into clusters. The last step is the generation of the behavioral model from the clusters. A behavioral model consists of event-connected states in the finite-state automata (FSA) format.

The ability to extract models from the operating system depends on the operating system components specification and their interfaces. The paper targets not a system component, but the set of mechanisms used to synchronize NMI, IRQ, and thread operations. The analyzed events are present in most subsystems, such as disabling interruptions and preemption, or locks.

SABRINE was later improved by the TIMEOUT approach [40] which records the time spent in each state. The FSA is then created using timed automata. The worst-case execution time observed during the profiling phase is used as the Timed-FSA's timing parameter, so timing errors can also be detected.

3.2 Formal Methods and OS Kernels

Verification of an operating system kernel, with its various components, is a particularly challenging area.

Some works that addressed this issue include the BLAST tool [21], where control flow automata were used, combining existing state-space reduction techniques based on verification and counter-example-driven refinement with *lazy abstraction*. This enables on-demand refinement of specification parts by selecting more specific predicates to add to the model while the model checker is running, without the need to revisit parts of the state space that are not affected by the refinements. Interestingly, for the Linux and Microsoft Windows NT kernels, authors applied the technique to verify the security properties of OS drivers. The technique required instrumentation of the original drivers, inserting a conditional jump to an error handler, and a model of the surrounding kernel behavior to enable the verification that the faulty code could ever be reached.

The SLAM [4] static code analyzer shares major goals with BLAST, enabling C programs to be analyzed to detect violations of certain conditions. SLAM is also used within the Static Driver Verifier (SDV) framework [3] to check Microsoft Windows device drivers against a set of rules. For example, it has been used to detect improper use of the Windows XP kernel API in some drivers. SATABS [5] and CBMC [24] are verification tools used within the DDVerify [43] framework to check synchronization constructs, interrupts and deferred tasks.

MAGIC [8] is a tool for automatic verification of sequential C programs that uses finite state machine specifications. The tool can analyze a direct acyclic graph of C functions by extracting a finite state model from the source code and then reducing the verification to a problem of boolean satisfiability (SAT). The verification is performed by checking the specification against an increasingly refined sequence of abstractions until either it is verified or a counter-example is found. This allows the technique to be used with relatively large models, along with its modular approach, avoiding the need to enumerate the state-space of the entire system. MAGIC was used to verify the correctness of a number of functions involved in system calls handling mutexes, sockets and packet handling in the Linux kernel. The tool was also later extended to handle concurrent software systems [9], although authors focused on verifying correctness and liveness in presence of message-passing based concurrency without variable sharing. Authors were able to find a bug in the source code of Micro-C/OS, although the bug had already been fixed in a new release when they notified the developers.

Other remarkable works have also been carried out evaluating the formal correctness of a whole micro-kernel, such as seL4 [23], regarding the adherence of the compiled code to its expected behavior stated in formal terms. seL4 also includes precise worst-case execution time analysis [6]. These findings were possible thanks to the simplicity of the seL4 micro-kernel, e.g. semi-preemptability.

3.3   Formal Methods and the Linux Kernel Community

The adoption of formal methods is not new to the Linux kernel community, especially in the kernel development and debugging workflow.

Indeed, the `lockdep` mechanism [12] built into the Linux kernel is a remarkable work in this area. By observing the order of execution and the calling context of lock calls, Lockdep is able to identify errors in the use of locking primitives that could eventually lead to deadlocks. The mechanism includes detecting errors in the acquisition order of multiple (nested) locks across multiple kernel code paths, and detecting common errors in handling spinlocks across the IRQ handler vs process context, such as acquiring a spinlock from the process context with enabled IRQs as well as from an IRQ handler. By applying the technique based on locking classes instead of individual locks, the number of different lock states that the kernel must keep is reduced.

A formal memory model is introduced in [2] to automate the verification of the consistency of core kernel synchronization operations, across a wide range of supported architectures and associated memory consistency models. The Linux memory model ended up being part of the official Linux release, adding the Linux Kernel Memory Consistency Model (LKMM) subsystem, an array of tools that formally describe the Linux memory consistency model, and also producing "litmus tests" in the form of kernel code that can be executed and tested directly.

The TLA+ formalism [25] has also been successfully applied to discover bugs in the Linux kernel. Examples of problems discovered or confirmed by using TLA+ include the correctness of memory management locking during a context switch and fairness properties of the arm64 ticket spinlock implementation [28].

These recent results created interest in the potential of using formal methods in Linux development. Therefore, the present paper describes our proposed technique for validation at *runtime* of allowed kernel events sequences, as specified through an automata-based model. As highlighted above, the technique fills an empty spot in the related literature, focusing on *efficient* verification that is achieved by: (1) tracking relevant kernel events at a proper abstraction level, leveraging the `perf` and `Ftrace` subsystems, but (2) without any need to actually collect a full trace of the relevant events from the kernel to user-space for further analysis: events sequences are directly checked inside the kernel leveraging efficient code automatically generated from the automata-based model, characterized by a $O(1)$ event processing time adding very small overheads, even lower than those arising merely for *tracing* the relevant events. This will be shown through experimental results in Sect. 5.

4   Efficient Formal Verification for the Linux Kernel

An overarching view of the approach being proposed in this paper is displayed in Fig. 3. It has three major phases. First, the behavior of a part of the Linux kernel is modeled using automata, using the set of events that are available in the tracing infrastructure[1]. The model is represented using the *.dot* `Graphviz` format [20]. The *.dot* format is open and widely used to represent finite-state machines and automata. For example, the Supremica modeling tool [1] supports exporting automata models using this format.

Figure 4 presents the example of an automaton for the verification of in-kernel scheduling-related events. The model specifies that the event *sched_waking* cannot take place while preemption is enabled, in order not to cause concurrency issues with the scheduler code (see [33] for more details).

In the second step, the `.dot` file is translated into a C data structure, using the `dot2c` tool[2]. The auto-generated code follows a naming convention that allows it to be linked with a kernel module skeleton that is already able to refer to the generated data structures, performing the verification of occurring events in the

---

[1] These can be obtained for example by running: `sudo cat /sys/kernel/debug/tracing/available_events`.

[2] The tools, the verification modules, the BUG report, high-resolution figures and FAQ are available in the companion page [32].

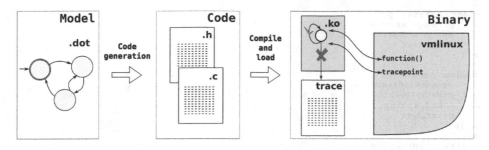

Fig. 3. Verification approach.

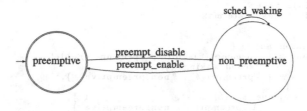

Fig. 4. Wake-up In preemptive (*WIP*) Model.

kernel, according to the specified model. For example, the automaton in Fig. 4 is transformed into the code in Fig. 5.

The **enum states** and **events** provide useful identifiers for states and events. As the name suggests, the **struct automaton** contains the automaton structure definition. Its corresponding C version contains the same elements of the formal definition. The most critical element of the structure is **function**, a matrix indexed in constant time $O(1)$ by **curr_state** and **event** (as shown in the **get_next_state()** function in Fig. 6). Likewise, for debugging and reporting reasons, it is also possible to translate the event and state indexes into strings in constant time, using the **state_names** and **event_names** vectors.

Regarding scalability, although the matrix is not the most efficient solution with respect to the memory footprint, in practice, the values are reasonable for nowadays common computing platforms. For instance, the Linux Task Model Automata presented in [33], with 9017 states and 20103 transitions, resulted in a binary object of less than 800 KB, a reasonable value even for nowadays Linux-based embedded systems. The automaton structure is static, so no element changes are allowed during the verification. This simplifies greatly the needed synchronization for accessing it. The only information that changes is the variable that saves the *current state* of the automata, so it can easily be handled with atomic operations, that can be a single variable for a model that represents the entire system. For instance, the model in Fig. 4 represents the state of a CPU (because the preemption enabling status is a *per-cpu* status variable in Linux), so there is a *current state* variable *per-cpu*, with the cost of (*1 Byte * the number of CPUs of the system*). The simplicity of automaton defini-

```
1  enum states {
2    preemptive = 0,
3    non_preemptive ,
4    state_max
5  };
6
7  enum events {
8    preempt_disable = 0,
9    preempt_enable ,
10   sched_waking ,
11   event_max
12 };
13
14 struct automaton {
15   char *state_names [state_max];
16   char *event_names [event_max];
17   char function [state_max][event_max];
18   char initial_state ;
19   char final_states [state_max];
20 };
21
22 struct automaton aut = {
23   .event_names = { "preempt_disable", "preempt_enable",
24                    "sched_waking" },
25   .state_names = { "preemptive", "non_preemptive" },
26   .function = {
27     { non_preemptive ,          -1,               -1 },
28     {                  -1, preemptive , non_preemptive },
29   },
30   .initial_state = preemptive ,
31   .final_states = { 1, 0 }
32 };
```

Fig. 5. Auto-generated code from the automaton in Fig. 4.

```
1  char get_next_state (struct automaton *aut, enum states curr_state ,
2                       enum events event) {
3    return aut->function [curr_state][event];
4  }
```

Fig. 6. Helper functions to get the next state.

tion is a crucial factor for this method: all verification functions are $O(1)$, the definition itself does not change during the verification and the sole information that changes has a minimal footprint.

In the last step, the auto-generated code from the automata, along with a set of helper functions that associate each automata event to a kernel event, are compiled into a kernel module (a .ko file). The model in Fig. 4 uses only **tracepoints**. The *preempt_disable* and *preempt_enable* automaton events are connected to the **preemptirq:preempt_disable** and **preemptirq:preempt_enable** kernel events, respectively, while the *sched_waking* automaton event is connected to the **sched:sched_waking** kernel event. The Sleeping While in Atomic (*SWA*) model in Fig. 7 also uses tracepoints for *preempt_disable* and *enable*, as well as for *local_irq_disable* and *enable*. But the *SWA* model also uses **function tracers**.

One common source of problems in the **PREEMPT_RT** Linux is the execution of functions that might put the process to sleep, while in a non-preemptive code section [34]. The event *might_sleep_function* represents these functions. At initialization time, the *SWA* module *hooks* to a set of functions that are known to eventually putting the thread to sleep.

Note that another noteworthy characteristic of the proposed framework is that, by using user-space probes [18], it is also possible to perform an integrated automata-based verification of both user and kernel-space events, without requiring code modifications.

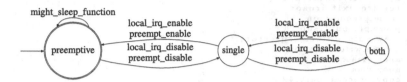

Fig. 7. Sleeping While in Atomic (*SWA*) model.

The kernel module produced as just described can be loaded at any time during the kernel execution. During initialization, the module connects the functions that handle the automaton events to the kernel tracing events, and the verification can start. The verification keeps going on until it is explicitly disabled at runtime by unloading the module.

The verification output can be observed via the tracing file regularly produced by Ftrace. As performance is a major concern for runtime verification, debug messages can be disabled of course. In this case, the verification will produce output only in case of problems.

An example of output is shown in Fig. 8. In this example, in Line 1 a *debug* message is printed, notifying the occurrence of the event *preempt_enable*, moving the automaton from the state *non_preemptive* to *preemptive*. In Line 2, *sched_waking* is not expected in the state *preemptive*, causing the output of the *stack trace*, to report the code path in which the problem was observed.

The problem reported in Fig. 8 is the output of a *real bug* found in the kernel while developing this approach. The bug was reported to the Linux kernel mailing list, including the verification module as the test-case for reproducing the problem (see footnote 2).

5   Performance Evaluation

Being efficient is a key factor for a broader adoption of a verification method. Indeed, an efficient method has the potential to increase its usage among Linux developers and practitioners, mainly during development, when the vast majority of complex testing takes place. Therefore, this section focuses on the performance of the proposed technique, by presenting evaluation results on a real platform verifying models, in terms of the two most important performance metrics for Linux kernel (and user-space) developers: *throughput* and *latency*.

```
1   bash−1157   [003]  ....2..     191.199172: process_event: non_preemptive −>
        preempt_enable = preemptive safe!
2   bash−1157   [003] dN..5..      191.199182: process_event: event
        sched_waking not expected in the state preemptive
3   bash−1157   [003] dN..5..      191.199186: <stack trace>
4   => process_event
5   => __handle_event
6   => ttwu_do_wakeup
7   => try_to_wake_up
8   => irq_exit
9   => smp_apic_timer_interrupt
10  => apic_timer_interrupt
11  => rcu_irq_exit_irqson
12  => trace_preempt_on
13  => preempt_count_sub
14  => _raw_spin_unlock_irqrestore
15  => __down_write_common
16  => anon_vma_clone
17  => anon_vma_fork
18  => copy_process.part.42
19  => _do_fork
20  => do_syscall_64
21  => entry_SYSCALL_64_after_hwframe
```

Fig. 8. Example of output from the proposed verification module, as occurring when a problem is found.

The measurements were conducted on an HP ProLiant BL460c G7 server, with two six-cores Intel Xeon L5640 processors and 12 GB of RAM, running a Fedora 30 Linux distribution. The kernel selected for the experiments is the Linux PREEMPT_RT version *5.0.7-rt5*. The real-time kernel is more sensible for synchronization as the modeled preemption and IRQ-related operations occur more frequently than in the mainline kernel.

5.1   Throughput Evaluation

Throughput evaluation was made using the *Phoronix Test Suite* benchmark [35], and its output is shown in Fig. 9. The same experiments were repeated in three different configurations. First, the benchmark was run in the system *as-is*, without any tracing nor verification running. Then, it was run in the system after enabling verification of the *SWA* model. Finally, a run was made with the system being traced, only limited to the events used in the verified automaton. It is worth mentioning that tracing in the experiments means only recording the events. The complete verification in user-space would still require the copy of data to user-space and the verification itself, which would add further overhead.

On the CPU bound tests (Crypto, CPU Stress and Memory Copying), both trace and verification have a low impact on the system performance. In contrast, the benchmarks that run mostly on kernel code highlights the overheads of both methods. In all cases, the verification performs better than tracing. The reason is that, despite the efficiency of tracing, the amount of data that has to be manipulated costs more than the simple operations required to do the verification, essentially the cost of looking up the next state in memory in $O(1)$, and storing the next state with a single memory write operation.

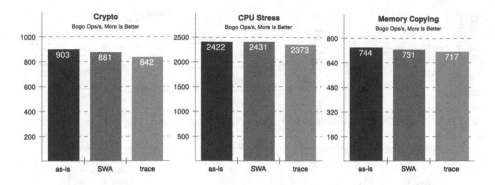

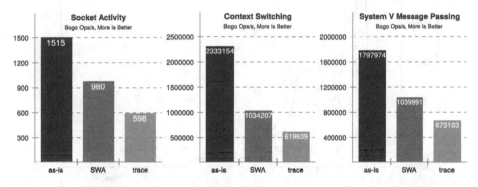

Fig. 9. Phoronix Stress-NG Benchmark Results: *as-is* is the system without tracing nor verification; *SWA* is the system while verifying *Sleeping While in Atomic* automata in Fig. 11 and with the code in Fig. 5; and the *trace* is the system while tracing the same events used in the *SWA* verification.

5.2 Latency Evaluation

Latency is the main metric used when working with the PREEMPT_RT kernel. The latency of interest is defined as the delay the highest real-time priority thread suffers from, during a new activation, due to in-kernel synchronization. Linux practitioners use the `cyclictest` tool to measure this latency, along with `rteval` as background workload, generating intensive kernel activation.

Two models were used in the latency experiment. Similarly to Sect. 5.1, the *SWA* model was evaluated against the kernel *as-is*, and the kernel simply tracing the same set of events. In addition, the *Need Re-Schedule* (*NRS*) model in Fig. 10 was evaluated. It describes the synchronization events that influence the latency, and it is part of the model previously described in [33][3]. The *NRS* measurements were made on the same system but configured as a single CPU[4].

---

[3] Note that supporting the full model in [33] is not yet possible with the tool being presented in this paper, due to additional changes needed within the kernel. Therefore, this is still work in progress.

[4] This is a restriction from [33].

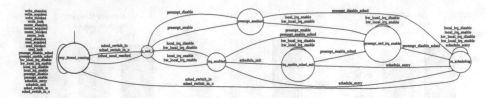

Fig. 10. Need Re-Sched forces Scheduling (*NRS* model) from [33] (see footnote 2).

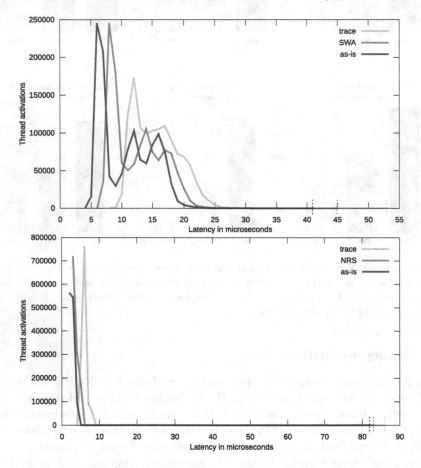

Fig. 11. Latency evaluation, using the *SWA* model (top) and the *NRS* model (bottom).

Consistently with the results obtained in the throughput experiments, the proposed verification mechanism is more efficient than the sole tracing of the same events. This has the effect that the `cyclictest` latency obtained under the proposed method, shown in Fig. 11 (*SWA/NRS* curves), is more similar to the one of the kernel *as-is* than what is obtained while just tracing the events.

6   Conclusions and Future Work

The increasing complexity of the Linux kernel code-base, along with its increasing usage in safety-critical and real-time systems, pushed towards a stronger need for applying formal verification techniques to various kernel subsystems. Nonetheless, two factors have been placing a barrier in this regard: (1) The need of complex setups, even including modifications and re-compilation of the kernel; (2) The excessively poor performance exhibited by the kernel while under tracing, for collecting data needed in the verification, typically carried out in user-space.

The solution for both problems seemed to be controversial: the usage of in-kernel tracing along with user-space post-processing reduces the complexity of the setup, but incurs the problem of having to collect, transfer to user-space and process large amounts of data. On the other hand, the inclusion of verification code "hard-coded" in the kernel requires more complex setups, with the need for applying custom patches and recompiling the kernel, with said patches being quite cumbersome to maintain as the kernel evolves over time.

This paper tackles these two problems by using the standard tracing infrastructure available in the Linux kernel to dynamically attach verification code to a non-modified running kernel, by exploiting the mechanism of dynamically loadable kernel modules. Furthermore, the verification code is semi-automatically generated from standard automata description files, as can be produced with open editors. The presented benchmark results show that the proposed technique overcomes standard tracing and user-space processing of kernel events to be verified in terms of performance. Moreover, the proposed technique is more efficient than merely tracking the events of interest just using tracing features available in the kernel.

Regarding possible future work on the topic, the usage of parametric and timed-automata would open the possibility of using more complex and complete verification methods, not only addressing the logical and functional behavior, but also dealing with the timing behavior. In terms of efficiency of the implementation, a hot-topic in the Linux kernel tracing community is the in-kernel processing of data via *eBPF*, as established already with in-kernel packet processing. This might be a worthwhile avenue to explore and compare with the current method of using a dynamically loadable module, in which part of the code has been auto-generated.

References

1. Akesson, K., Fabian, M., Flordal, H., Malik, R.: Supremica - an integrated environment for verification, synthesis and simulation of discrete event systems. In: 2006 8th International Workshop on Discrete Event Systems, pp. 384–385, July 2006. https://doi.org/10.1109/WODES.2006.382401
2. Alglave, J., Maranget, L., McKenney, P.E., Parri, A., Stern, A.: Frightening small children and disconcerting grown-ups: concurrency in the Linux Kernel. In: Proceedings of the Twenty-Third International Conference on Architectural Support for Programming Languages and Operating Systems, ASPLOS 2018, pp. 405–418. ACM, New York (2018). https://doi.org/10.1145/3173162.3177156

3. Ball, T., Cook, B., Levin, V., Rajamani, S.K.: Technical Report MSR-TR-2004-08 - SLAM and Static Driver Verifier: Technology Transfer of Formal Methods inside Microsoft - Microsoft Research, January 2004. https://www.microsoft.com/en-us/research/wp-content/uploads/2016/02/tr-2004-08.pdf

4. Ball, T., Rajamani, S.K.: The SLAM project: debugging system software via static analysis. In: Proceedings of the 29th ACM SIGPLAN-SIGACT Symposium on Principles of Programming Languages, POPL 2002, pp. 1–3. ACM, New York (2002). https://doi.org/10.1145/503272.503274

5. Basler, G., Donaldson, A., Kaiser, A., Kroening, D., Tautschnig, M., Wahl, T.: SATABS: a bit-precise verifier for C programs. In: Flanagan, C., König, B. (eds.) TACAS 2012. LNCS, vol. 7214, pp. 552–555. Springer, Heidelberg (2012). https://doi.org/10.1007/978-3-642-28756-5_47

6. Blackham, B., Shi, Y., Chattopadhyay, S., Roychoudhury, A., Heiser, G.: Timing analysis of a protected operating system kernel. In: Proceedings of the 32nd IEEE Real-Time Systems Symposium (RTSS11), Vienna, Austria, pp. 339–348, November 2011

7. Cassandras, C.G., Lafortune, S.: Introduction to Discrete Event Systems, 2nd edn. Springer, Heidelberg (2010)

8. Chaki, S., Clarke, E.M., Groce, A., Jha, S., Veith, H.: Modular verification of software components in C. IEEE Trans. Softw. Eng. **30**(6), 388–402 (2004). https://doi.org/10.1109/TSE.2004.22

9. Chaki, S., Clarke, E., Ouaknine, J., Sharygina, N., Sinha, N.: Concurrent software verification with states, events, and deadlocks. Formal Aspects Comput. **17**(4), 461–483 (2005). https://doi.org/10.1007/s00165-005-0071-z

10. Chishiro, H.: RT-Seed: real-time middleware for semi-fixed-priority scheduling. In: 2016 IEEE 19th International Symposium on Real-Time Distributed Computing (ISORC) (2016)

11. Condliffe, J.: U.S. military drones are going to start running on Linux, July 2014. https://gizmodo.com/u-s-military-drones-are-going-to-start-running-on-linu-157 2853572

12. Corbet, J.: The kernel lock validator, May 2006. https://lwn.net/Articles/185666/

13. Corbet, J.: Linux at NASDAQ OMX, October 2010. https://lwn.net/Articles/411064/

14. Corbet, J.: Jump label, October 2010. https://lwn.net/Articles/412072/

15. Cotroneo, D., Di Leo, D., Natella, R., Pietrantuono, R.: A case study on state-based robustness testing of an operating system for the avionic domain. In: Flammini, F., Bologna, S., Vittorini, V. (eds.) SAFECOMP 2011. LNCS, vol. 6894, pp. 213–227. Springer, Heidelberg (2011). https://doi.org/10.1007/978-3-642-24270-0_16

16. Cotroneo, D., Leo, D.D., Fucci, F., Natella, R.: SABRINE: state-based robustness testing of operating systems. In: Proceedings of the 28th IEEE/ACM International Conference on Automated Software Engineering, ASE 2013, Piscataway, NJ, USA, pp. 125–135. IEEE Press (2013). https://doi.org/10.1109/ASE.2013.6693073

17. Cucinotta, T., et al.: A real-time service-oriented architecture for industrial automation. IEEE Trans. Ind. Inform. **5**(3), 267–277 (2009). https://doi.org/10.1109/TII.2009.2027013

18. Dronamraju, S.: Linux kernel documentation - uprobe-tracer: Uprobe-based event tracing, May 2019. https://www.kernel.org/doc/Documentation/trace/uprobetracer.txt

19. Dubey, A., Karsai, G., Abdelwahed, S.: Compensating for timing jitter in comput-
    ing systems with general-purpose operating systems. In: 2009 IEEE International
    Symposium on Object/Component/Service-Oriented Real-Time Distributed Com-
    puting, pp. 55–62, March 2009. https://doi.org/10.1109/ISORC.2009.28
20. Ellson, J., Gansner, E., Koutsofios, L., North, S.C., Woodhull, G.: Graphviz—open
    source graph drawing tools. In: Mutzel, P., Jünger, M., Leipert, S. (eds.) GD 2001.
    LNCS, vol. 2265, pp. 483–484. Springer, Heidelberg (2002). https://doi.org/10.
    1007/3-540-45848-4_57
21. Henzinger, T.A., Jhala, R., Majumdar, R., Sutre, G.: Lazy abstraction. In: Pro-
    ceedings of the 29th ACM SIGPLAN-SIGACT Symposium on Principles of Pro-
    gramming Languages, POPL 2002, pp. 58–70. ACM, New York (2002). https://
    doi.org/10.1145/503272.503279
22. Hiramatsu, M.: Linux tracing technologies: Kprobe-based event tracing, May 2019.
    https://www.kernel.org/doc/html/latest/trace/kprobetrace.html
23. Klein, G., et al.: seL4: formal verification of an OS Kernel. In: Proceedings of the
    ACM SIGOPS 22nd Symposium on Operating Systems Principles, SOSP 2009, pp.
    207–220. ACM, New York (2009). https://doi.org/10.1145/1629575.1629596
24. Kroening, D., Tautschnig, M.: CBMC – C bounded model checker. In: Ábrahám,
    E., Havelund, K. (eds.) TACAS 2014. LNCS, vol. 8413, pp. 389–391. Springer,
    Heidelberg (2014). https://doi.org/10.1007/978-3-642-54862-8_26
25. Lamport, L.: The temporal logic of actions. ACM Trans. Program. Lang. Syst.
    16(3), 872–923 (1994). https://doi.org/10.1145/177492.177726
26. Lei, B., Liu, Z., Morisset, C., Li, X.: State based robustness testing for components.
    Electron. Notes Theoret. Comput. Sci. **260**, 173–188 (2010). https://doi.org/10.
    1016/j.entcs.2009.12.037
27. Linux Kernel Documentation: Linux tracing technologies, May 2019. https://www.
    kernel.org/doc/html/latest/trace/index.html
28. Marinas, C.: Formal methods for kernel hackers (2018). https://linuxplumbersconf.
    org/event/2/contributions/60/attachments/18/42/FormalMethodsPlumbers2018.
    pdf
29. Matni, G., Dagenais, M.: Automata-based approach for kernel trace analysis. In:
    2009 Canadian Conference on Electrical and Computer Engineering, pp. 970–973,
    May 2009. https://doi.org/10.1109/CCECE.2009.5090273
30. de Oliveira, D.B.: How can we catch problems that can break the preempt_rt
    preemption model? November 2018. https://linuxplumbersconf.org/event/2/
    contributions/190/
31. de Oliveira, D.B.: Mind the gap between real-time linux and real-time theory,
    November 2018. https://www.linuxplumbersconf.org/event/2/contributions/75/
32. de Oliveira, D.B.: Companion page: Efficient formal verification for the linux kernel,
    May 2019. http://bristot.me/efficient-formal-verification-for-the-linux-kernel/
33. de Oliveira, D.B., Cucinotta, T., de Oliveira, R.S.: Untangling the intricacies of
    thread synchronization in the PREEMPT_RT Linux Kernel. In: Proceedings of
    the IEEE 22nd International Symposium on Real-Time Distributed Computing
    (ISORC), Valencia, Spain, May 2019
34. de Oliveira, D.B., de Oliveira, R.S.: Timing analysis of the PREEMPT_RT Linux
    kernel. Softw.: Pract. Exp. **46**(6), 789–819 (2016). https://doi.org/10.1002/spe.
    2333
35. Phoronix Test Suite: Open-source, automated benchmarking, May 2019. www.
    phoronix-test-suite.com
36. Poimboeuf, J.: Introducing kpatch: dynamic kernel patching, February 2014.
    https://www.redhat.com/en/blog/introducing-kpatch-dynamic-kernel-patching

37. Pullum, L.L.: Software Fault Tolerance Techniques and Implementation. Artech House Inc., Norwood (2001)
38. Rostedt, S.: Secrets of the Ftrace function tracer. Linux Weekly News, January 2010. http://lwn.net/Articles/370423/. Accessed 09 May 2017
39. San Vicente Gutiérrez, C., Usategui San Juan, L., Zamalloa Ugarte, I., Mayoral Vilches, V.: Real-time Linux communications: an evaluation of the Linux communication stack for real-time robotic applications, August 2018. https://arxiv.org/pdf/1808.10821.pdf
40. Shahpasand, R., Sedaghat, Y., Paydar, S.: Improving the stateful robustness testing of embedded real-time operating systems. In: 2016 6th International Conference on Computer and Knowledge Engineering (ICCKE), pp. 159–164, October 2016. https://doi.org/10.1109/ICCKE.2016.7802133
41. Spear, A., Levy, M., Desnoyers, M.: Using tracing to solve the multicore system debug problem. Computer **45**(12), 60–64 (2012). https://doi.org/10.1109/MC.2012.191
42. The Linux Foundation: Automotive grade Linux, May 2019. https://www.automotivelinux.org/
43. Witkowski, T., Blanc, N., Kroening, D., Weissenbacher, G.: Model checking concurrent Linux device drivers. In: Proceedings of the Twenty-second IEEE/ACM International Conference on Automated Software Engineering, ASE 2007, pp. 501–504. ACM, New York (2007).https://doi.org/10.1145/1321631.1321719

Reproducible Execution of **POSIX** Programs with **DiOS**

Petr Ročkai[✉], Zuzana Baranová, Jan Mrázek, Katarína Kejstová,
and Jiří Barnat

Faculty of Informatics, Masaryk University, Brno, Czech Republic
{xrockai,xbaranov,xmrazek7,xkejstov,barnat}@fi.muni.cz

Abstract. In this paper, we describe DiOS, a lightweight model operating system which can be used to execute programs that make use of POSIX APIs. Such executions are fully reproducible: running the same program with the same inputs twice will result in two exactly identical instruction traces, even if the program uses threads for parallelism.

DiOS is implemented almost entirely in portable C and C++: although its primary platform is DiVM, a verification-oriented virtual machine, it can be configured to also run in KLEE, a symbolic executor. Finally, it can be compiled into machine code to serve as a user-mode kernel.

Additionally, DiOS is modular and extensible. Its various components can be combined to match both the capabilities of the underlying platform and to provide services required by a particular program. New components can be added to cover additional system calls or APIs.

The experimental evaluation has two parts. DiOS is first evaluated as a component of a program verification platform based on DiVM. In the second part, we consider its portability and modularity by combining it with the symbolic executor KLEE.

1 Introduction

Real-world software has a strong tendency to interact with its execution environment in complex ways. To make matters worse, typical environments in which programs execute are often extremely unpredictable and hard to control. This is an important factor that contributes to high costs of software validation and verification. Even the most resilient verification methods (those based on testing) see substantial adverse effect.

In automated testing, one of the major criteria for a good test case is that it gives reliable and reproducible results, without intermittent failures. This is especially true in the process of debugging: isolating a fault is much harder when it cannot be consistently observed. For this reason, significant part of the effort involved in testing is spent on controlling the influence of the environment on the execution of test cases.

This work has been partially supported by the Czech Science Foundation grant No. 18-02177S and by Red Hat, Inc.

P. C. Ölveczky and G. Salaün (Eds.): SEFM 2019, LNCS 11724, pp. 333–349, 2019.
https://doi.org/10.1007/978-3-030-30446-1_18

The situation is even worse with more rigorous verification methods – for instance, soundness of verification tools based on dynamic analysis strongly depends on the ability to fully control the execution of the system under test.

In this paper, we set out to design and implement a small and sufficiently self-contained model operating system that can provide a realistic environment for executing POSIX-based programs. Since this environment is fully virtualised and isolated from the host system, program execution is always fully reproducible. As outlined above, such reproducibility is valuable, sometimes even essential, in testing and program analysis scenarios. Especially dynamic techniques, like software model checking or symbolic execution, rely on the ability to replay interactions of the program and obtain identical outcomes every time.

1.1 Contribution

The paper describes our effort to implement a compact operating system on top of existing verification frameworks and virtual machines (see Sect. 3). Despite its minimalist design, the current implementation covers a wide range of POSIX APIs in satisfactory detail (see also Sect. 4.3). The complete source code is available online,[1] under a permissive open-source licence. Additionally, we have identified a set of low-level interfaces (see Sect. 2) with two important qualities:

1. the interfaces are lightweight and easy to implement in a VM,
2. they enable an efficient implementation of complex high-level constructs.

Minimal interfaces are a sound design principle and lead to improved modularity and re-usability of components. In our case, identification of the correct interfaces drives both *portability* and *compactness of implementation*.

Finally, the design that we propose improves robustness of verification tools. A common implementation strategy treats high-level constructs (e.g. the `pthread` API) as primitives built into the execution engine. This ad-hoc approach often leads to implementation bugs which then compromise the soundness of the entire tool. Our design, on the other hand, emphasises clean separation of concerns and successfully reduces the amount of code which forms the trusted execution and/or verification core.

1.2 Design Goals

We would like our system to have the following properties:

1. Modularity: minimise the interdependence of the individual OS components. It should be as easy as possible to use individual components (for instance `libc`) without the others. The kernel should likewise be modular.

---

[1] https://divine.fi.muni.cz/2019/dios/.

2. Portability: reduce the coupling to the underlying platform (verification engine), making the OS useful as a pre-made component in building verification and testing tools.
3. Veracity: the system should precisely follow POSIX and other applicable standardised semantics. It should be possible to port realistic programs to run on the operating system with minimal effort.

Since the desired properties are hard to quantify, we provide a qualitative evaluation in Sect. 5. To demonstrate the viability of our approach, we show that many UNIX programs, e.g. `gzip` or a number of programs from the GNU `coreutils` suite can be compiled for DiOS with no changes and subsequently analysed using an explicit-state model checker.

1.3   Related Work

Execution reproducibility is a widely studied problem. A number of tools capture *provenance*, or history of the execution, by following and recording program's interactions with the environment, later using this information to reproduce the recorded execution. For instance, ReproZip [4] bundles the environment variables, files and library dependencies it observes so that the executable can be run on a different system. Other programs exist, that instead capture the provenance in form of logs [7], or sometimes more complex structures – provenance graphs in case of ES3 [5].

SCARPE [7] was developed for Java programs and captures I/O, user inputs and interactions with the database and the filesystem into a simple event log. The user has to state which interactions to observe by annotating the individual classes that make up the program, since the instrumentation introduces substantial overhead, and recording all interactions may generate a considerable amount of data (for example, capturing a large portion of the database).

Another common approach to dealing with the complexity of interactions with the execution environment is *mocking* [14,15]: essentially, building small models of the parts of the environment that are relevant in the given test scenario. A *mock object* is one step above a stub, which simply accepts and discards all requests. A major downside of using mock objects in testing is that sufficiently modelling the environment requires a lot of effort: either the library only provides simple objects and users have to model the system themselves, or the mock system is sophisticated, but the user has to learn a complex API.

Most testing frameworks for mainstream programming languages offer a degree of support for building mock objects, including mock objects which model interaction with the operating system. For instance the `pytest` tool [11] for Python allows the user to comfortably mock a database connection. A more complex example of mocking would be the filesystem support in Pex [10], a symbolic executor for programs targeting the .NET platform. KLEE is a symbolic executor based on LLVM and targets C (and to some degree C++) programs with a different approach to environment interaction. Instead of modelling the file system or other operating system services, it allows the program to directly interact with the host operating system, optionally via a simple adaptation layer which provides a degree of isolation based on symbolic file models.

This latter approach, where system calls and even library calls are forwarded to the host operating system is also used in some runtime model checkers, most notably Inspect [19] and CHESS [16]. However, those approaches only work when the program interacts with the operating system in a way free from side effects, and when external changes in the environment do not disturb verification.

One approach to lifting the non-interference requirement is *cache-based* model checking [13], where initially, the interactions with the environment are directly performed and recorded in a cache. If the model checker then needs to revisit one of the previous states, the cache component takes over and prevents inconsistencies from arising along different execution paths. This approach is closely related to our *proxy* and *replay* modes (Sect. 4.1), though in the case of cache-based model checking, both activities are combined into a single run of the model checker. Since this approach is focused on piece-wise verification of distributed systems, the environment mainly consists of additional components of the same program. For this reason, the cache can be realistically augmented with process checkpointing to also allow backtracking the environment to a certain extent.

Finally, standard (offline) model checkers rarely support more than a handful of interfaces. The most widely supported is the POSIX threading API, which is modelled by tools such as Lazy-CSeq [6] and its variants, by Impara [18] and by a few other tools.

2   Platform Interface

In this section, we will describe our expectations of the execution or verification platform and the low-level interface between this platform and our model operating system. We then break down the interface into a small number of areas, each covering particular functionality.

2.1   Preliminaries

The underlying platform can have different characteristics. We are mainly interested in platforms or tools based on dynamic analysis, where the program is at least partially interpreted or executed, often in isolation from the environment. If the platform itself isolates the system under test, many standard facilities like file system access become unavailable. In this case, the role of DiOS is to provide a substitute for the inaccessible host system.

If, on the other hand, the platform allows the program to access the host system, this easily leads to inconsistencies, where executions explored first can interfere with the state of the system observed by executions explored later. For instance, files or directories might be left around, causing unexpected changes in the behaviour[2] of the system under test. In cases like those, DiOS can serve to

---

[2] If execution A creates a file and leaves it around, execution B might get derailed when it tries to create the same file, or might detect its presence and behave differently.

insulate such executions from each other. Under DiOS, the program can observe the effects of its actions along a single execution path – for instance, if the program creates a file, it will be able to open it later. However, this file never becomes visible to another execution of the same program, regardless of the exploration order.

Unfortunately, not all facilities that operating systems provide to programs can be modelled entirely in terms of standard C. To the contrary, certain areas of high-level functionality that the operating system is expected to implement strongly depend on low-level aspects of the underlying platform. Some of those are support for thread scheduling, process isolation, control flow constructs such as `setjmp` and C++ exceptions, among others. We will discuss those in more detail in the following sections.

2.2 Program Memory

An important consideration when designing an operating system is the semantics of the memory subsystem of its execution platform. DiOS is no exception: it needs to provide a high-level memory management API to the application (both the C `malloc` interface and the C++ `new`/`delete` interface). In principle, a single flat array of memory is sufficient to implement all the essential functionality. However, it lacks both in efficiency and in robustness. Ideally, the platform would provide a memory management API that manages individual memory objects which in turn support an in-place resize operation. This makes operations more efficient by avoiding the need to make copies when extra memory is required, and the operating system logic simpler by avoiding a level of indirection.

If the underlying platform is memory-safe and if it provides a supervisor mode to protect access to certain registers or to a special memory location, the remainder of kernel isolation is implemented by DiOS itself, by withholding addresses of kernel objects from the user program. In this context, memory safety entails bound checks and an inability to overflow pointers from one memory object into another.

2.3 Execution Stack

Information about active procedure calls and about the local data of each procedure are, on most platforms, stored in a special *execution stack*. While the presence of such a stack is almost universal, the actual representation of this stack is very platform-specific. On most platforms that we consider,[3] it is part of standard program memory and can be directly accessed using standard memory operations. If both reading and modifications of the stack (or stacks) is possible, most of the operations that DiOS needs to perform can be implemented without special assistance from the platform itself. Those operations are:

---

[3] The main exception is KLEE, where the execution stack is completely inaccessible to the program under test and only the virtual machine can access the information stored in it. See also Sect. 3.2.

- creation of a new execution stack, which is needed in two scenarios: isolation of the kernel stack from the user-space stack and creation of new tasks (threads, co-routines or other similar high-level constructs),
- stack unwinding, where stack frames are traversed and removed from the stack during exception propagation or due to setjmp/longjmp.

Additionally, DiOS needs a single operation that must be always provided by the underlying platform: it needs to be able to transfer control to a particular stack frame, whether within a single execution stack (to implement non-local control flow) or to a different stack entirely (to implement task switching).

In some sense, this part of the platform support is the most complex and the hardest to implement. Fortunately, the features that rely on the above operations, or rather the modules which implement those features, are all optional in DiOS.

2.4   Auxiliary Interfaces

There are three other points of contact between DiOS and the underlying platform. They are all optional or can be emulated using standard C features, but if available, DiOS can use them to offer additional facilities mainly aimed at software verification and testing with fault injection.

Indeterminate values. A few components in DiOS use, or can be configured to use, values which are not a priori determined. The values are usually subject to constraints, but within those constraints, each possible value will correspond to a particular interaction outcome. This facility is used for simulating interactions that depend on random chance (e.g. thread scheduling, incidence of clock ticks relative to the instruction stream), or where the user would prefer to not provide specific input values and instead rely on the verification or testing platform to explore the possibilities for them (e.g. the content of a particular file).

Nondeterministic choice. A special case of the above, where the selection is among a small number of discrete options. In those cases, a specific interface can give better user experience or better tool performance. If the choice operator is not available but indeterminate values are, they can be used instead. Otherwise, the sequence of choices can be provided as an input by the user, or they can be selected randomly. The choice operation is used for scheduling choices and for fault injection (e.g. simulation of malloc failures).

Host system call execution. Most POSIX operating systems provide an indirect system call facility, usually as the C function syscall(). If the platform makes this function accessible from within the system under test, DiOS can use it to allow real interactions between the user program and the host operating system to take place and to record and then replay such interactions in a reproducible manner.

3 Supported Platforms

In the previous section, we have described the target platform in generic, abstract terms. In this section, we describe 3 specific platforms which can execute DiOS and how they fit with the above abstract requirements.

3.1 DiVM

DiVM [17] is a verification-oriented virtual machine based on LLVM. A suite of tools based on DiVM implement a number of software verification techniques, including explicit-state, symbolic and abstraction-based model checking. DiVM is the best supported of all the platforms, since it has been specifically designed to delegate responsibility for features to a model operating system. All features available in DiOS are fully supported on this platform.

In DiVM, the functionality that is not accessible through standard C (or LLVM) constructs is provided via a set of *hypercalls*. These hypercalls form the core of the platform interface in DiOS and whenever possible, ports to other platforms are encouraged to emulate the DiVM hypercall interface using the available platform-native facilities.

3.2 KLEE

KLEE [3] is a symbolic executor based on LLVM, suitable both for automated test generation and for exhaustive exploration of bounded executions. Unlike DiVM, KLEE by default allows the program under test to perform external calls (including calls to the host operating system), with no isolation between different execution branches. Additionally, such calls must be given concrete arguments, since they are executed as native machine code (i.e. not symbolically). However, if the program is linked to DiOS, both these limitations are lifted: DiOS code can be executed symbolically like the rest of the program, and different execution branches are isolated from each other.

However, there is also a number of limitations when KLEE is considered as a platform for DiOS. The two most important are as follows:

1. KLEE does not currently support in-place resizing of memory objects. This is a design limitation and lifting it requires considerable changes. A workaround exists, but it is rather inefficient.
2. There is only one execution stack in KLEE, and there is no support for non-local control flow. This prevents DiOS from offering threads, C++ exceptions and setjmp when executing in KLEE.

Additionally, there is no supervisor mode and hence no isolation between the kernel and the user program. However, in most cases, this is not a substantial problem. Non-deterministic choice is available via indeterminate symbolic values, and even though KLEE can in principle provide access to host syscalls, we have not evaluated this functionality in conjunction with DiOS. Finally, there are a few minor issues that are, however, easily corrected:[4]

1. KLEE does not support the va_arg LLVM instruction and relies on emulating platform-specific mechanisms instead, which are absent from DiOS,
2. it handles certain C functions specially, including the malloc family, the C++ new operator, the errno location and functions related to assertions and program termination; this interferes with the equivalent functionality provided by DiOS libc, and finally
3. global constructors present in the program are unconditionally executed before the entry function; since DiOS invokes constructors itself, this KLEE behaviour also causes a conflict.

3.3 Native Execution

The third platform that we consider is native execution, i.e. the DiOS kernel is compiled into machine code, like a standard user-space program, to execute as a process of the host operating system. This setup is useful in testing or in stateless model checking, where it can provide superior execution speed at the expense of reduced runtime safety. The user program still uses DiOS libc and the program runs in isolation from the host system. The platform-specific code in DiOS uses a few hooks provided by a shim which calls through into the host operating system for certain services, like the creation and switching of stacks. The design is illustrated in Fig. 1.

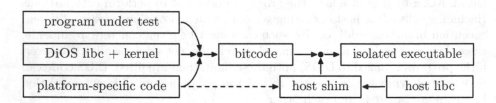

Fig. 1. Architecture of the native execution platform.

Like in KLEE, the native port of DiOS does not have access to in-place resizing of memory objects, but it can be emulated slightly more efficiently using the mmap host system call. The native port, however, does not suffer from the single-stack limitations that KLEE does: new stacks can be created using mmap calls, while stack switching can be implemented using host setjmp and longjmp functions.[5] The host stack unwinding code is directly used (the DiVM platform code implements the same libunwind API that most POSIX systems also use).

---

[4] A version of KLEE with fixes for those problems is available online, along with other supplementary material, from https://divine.fi.muni.cz/2019/dios/.

[5] The details of how this is done are discussed in the online supplementary material at https://divine.fi.muni.cz/2019/dios/.

On the other hand, non-deterministic choice is not directly available. It can be simulated by using the `fork` host system call to split execution, but this does not scale to frequent choices, such as those arising from scheduling decisions. In this case, a random or an externally supplied list of outcomes are the only options.

4 Design and Architecture

This section outlines the structure of the DiOS kernel and userspace, their components and the interfaces between them. We also discuss how the kernel interacts with the underlying platform and the user-space libraries stacked above it. A high-level overview of the system is shown in Fig. 2. The kernel and the user-mode parts of the system under test can be combined using different methods; even though they can be linked into a single executable image, this is not a requirement, and the kernel can operate in a separate address space.

Like with traditional operating systems, kernel memory is inaccessible to the program and libraries executing in user-mode. In DiOS, this protection is optional, since not all platforms provide supervisor mode or sufficient memory safety; however, it does not depend on address space separation between the kernel and the user mode.

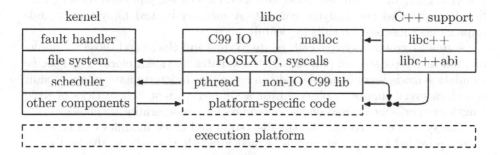

Fig. 2. The architecture of DiOS.

4.1 Kernel Components

The decomposition of the kernel to a number of components serves multiple goals: first is resource conservation – some components have non-negligible memory overhead even when they are not actively used. This may be because they need to store auxiliary data along with each thread or process, and the underlying verification tool then needs to track this data throughout the execution or throughout the entire state space. The second is improved portability to platforms which do not provide sufficient support for some of the components, for instance thread scheduling. Finally, it allows DiOS to be reconfigured to serve in new contexts by adding a new module and combining it with existing code.

The components of the kernel are organised as a stack, where upper components can use services of the components below them. While this might appear to
be a significant limitation, in practice this has not posed substantial challenges,
and the stack-organised design is both efficient and simple. A number of pre-
made components are available, some in multiple alternative implementations:

Task scheduling and process management. There are 4 scheduler implementations: the simplest is a *null* scheduler, which only allows a single task and does
not support any form of task switching. This scheduler is used on KLEE. Second
is a synchronous scheduler suitable for executing software models of hardware
devices. The remaining two schedulers both implement asynchronous, thread-
based parallelism. One is designed for verification of safety properties of parallel
programs, while the other includes a fairness provision and is therefore more
suitable for verification of liveness properties.

In addition to the scheduler, there is an optional process management component. It is currently only available on the DiVM platform, since it heavily relies
on operations which are not available elsewhere. It implements the `fork` system
call and requires one of the two asynchronous schedulers.

POSIX System Calls. While a few process-related system calls are implemented
in the components already mentioned, the vast majority is not. By far the largest
coherent group of system calls deals with files, directories, pipes and sockets, with
file descriptors as the unifying concept. A memory-backed filesystem module
implements those system calls by default.

A smaller group of system calls relate to time and clocks and those are implemented in a separate component which simulates a system clock. The specific
simulation mode is configurable and can use either indeterminate values to shift
the clock every time it is observed, or a simpler variant, where ticks of fixed
length are performed based on the outcome of a nondeterministic choice.

The system calls covered by the filesystem and clock modules can be alter-
nately provided by a *proxy* module, which forwards the calls to the host operating system, or by a *replay* module which replays traces captured by the *proxy*
module.

Auxiliary modules. There is a small number of additional modules which do not
directly expose functionality to the user program. Instead, they fill in support
roles within the system. The two notable examples are the *fault handler* and the
system call stub component.

The fault handler takes care of responding to error conditions indicated by the
underlying platform. It is optional, since not all platforms can report problems
to the system under test. If present, the component allows the user to configure
which problems should be reported as counterexamples and which should be
ignored. The rest of DiOS also uses this component to report problems detected
by the operating system itself, e.g. the `libc` uses it to flag assertion failures.

The stub component supplies fallback implementations of all system calls
known to DiOS. This component is always at the bottom of the kernel

configuration stack – if any other component in the active configuration implements a particular system call, that implementation is used. Otherwise, the fallback is called and raises a runtime error, indicating that the system call is not supported.

4.2 Thread Support

One of the innovative features of DiOS is that it implements the POSIX threading API using a very simple platform interface. Essentially, the asynchronous schedulers in DiOS provide an illusion of thread-based parallelism to the program under test, but only use primitives associated with coroutines – creation and switching of execution stacks (cf. Sect. 2.3).

However, an additional external component is required: both user and library code needs to be instrumented with *interrupt points*, which allow thread preemption to take place. Where to insert them can be either decided statically (which is sufficient for small programs) or dynamically, allowing the state space to be reduced using more sophisticated techniques.[6] The implementation of the interrupt point is, however, supplied by DiOS: only the insertion of the function call is done externally.

The scheduler itself provides a very minimal internal interface – the remainder of thread support is implemented in user-space libraries (partly libc and partly libpthread, as is common on standard POSIX operating systems). Even though the implementation is not complete (some of the rarely-used functions are stubbed out), all major areas are well supported: thread creation and cancellation, mutual exclusion, condition variables, barriers, reader-writer locks, interaction with fork, and thread-local storage are all covered. Additionally, both C11 and C++11 thread APIs are implemented in terms of the pthread interface.

4.3 System Calls

The system call interface of DiOS is based on the ideas used in *fast system call* implementations on modern processors.[7] A major advantage of this approach is that system calls can be performed using standard procedure calls on platforms which do not implement supervisor mode.

The list of system calls available in DiOS is fixed:[8] in addition to the kernel-side implementation, which may or may not be available depending on the active

---

[6] In DIVINE [1], a model checker based on DiVM, interrupt points are dynamically enabled when the executing thread performs a visible action. Thread identification is supplied by the scheduler in DiOS using a platform-specific (hypercall) interface.

[7] For instance, on contemporary x86-64 processors, this interface is available via the syscall and sysret instructions.

[8] The list of system calls is only fixed relative to the host operating system. To allow the system call proxy component to function properly, the list needs to match what is available on the host. For instance, creat, uname or fdatasync are system calls on Linux but standard libc functions on OpenBSD.

configuration, each system call has an associated user-space C function, which is declared in one of the public header files and implemented in libc.

The available system calls cover thread management, sufficient to implement the pthread interface (the system calls themselves are not standardised by POSIX), the fork system call, kill and other signal-related calls, various process and process group management calls (getpid, getsid, setsid, wait, and so on). Notably, exec is currently not implemented, and it is not clear whether adding it is feasible on any of the platforms. The thread- and process- related functionality was described in more detail in Sect. 4.2.

Another large group of system calls cover files and networking, including the standard suite of POSIX calls for opening and closing files, reading and writing data, creating soft and hard links. This includes the *at family introduced in POSIX.1 which allows thread-safe use of relative paths. The standard BSD socket API is also implemented, allowing threads or processes of the program under test to use sockets for communication. Finally, there are system calls for reading (clock_gettime, gettimeofday) and setting clocks (clock_settime, settimeofday).

4.4   The C Library

DiOS comes with a complete ISO C99 standard library and the C11 thread API. The functionality of the C library can be broken down into the following categories:

- Input and output. The functionality required by ISO C is implemented in terms of the POSIX file system API. Number conversion (for formatted input and output) is platform independent and comes from pdclib.
- The string manipulation and character classification routines are completely system-independent. The implementations were also taken from pdclib.
- Memory allocation: new memory needs to be obtained in a platform-dependent way. Optionally, memory allocation failures can be simulated using a non-deterministic choice operator. The library provides the standard assortment of functions: malloc, calloc, realloc and free.
- Support for errno: this variable holds the code of the most recent error encountered in an API call. On platforms with threads (like DiOS), errno is thread-local.
- Multibyte strings: conversion of Unicode character sequences to and from UTF-8 is supported.
- Time-related functions: time and date formatting (asctime) is supported, as is obtaining and manipulating wall time. Interval timers are currently not simulated, although the relevant functions are present as simple stubs.
- Non-local jumps. The setjmp and longjmp functions are supported on DiVM and native execution, but not in KLEE.

In addition to ISO C99, there are a few extensions (not directly related to the system call interface) mandated by POSIX for the C library:

- Regular expressions. The DiOS libc supports the standard regcomp & regexec APIs, with implementation based on the TRE library.
- Locale support: A very minimal support for POSIX internationalisation and localisation APIs is present. The support is sufficient to run programs which initialise the subsystem.
- Parsing command line options: the getopt and getopt_long functions exist to make it easy for programs to parse standard UNIX-style command switches. DiOS contains an implementation derived from the OpenBSD code base.

Finally, C99 mandates a long list of functions for floating point math, including trigonometry, hyperbolic functions and so on. A complete set of those functions is provided by DiOS via its libm implementation, based on the OpenBSD version of this library.

4.5   C++ Support Libraries

DiOS includes support for C++ programs, upto and including the C++17 standard. This support is based on the libc++abi and libc++ open-source libraries maintained by the LLVM project. The versions bundled with DiOS contain only very minor modifications relative to upstream, mainly intended to reduce program size and memory use in verification scenarios.

Notably, the exception support code in libc++abi is unmodified and works both in DiVM and when DiOS is executing natively as a process of the host operating system. This is because libc++abi uses the libunwind library to implement exceptions. When DiOS runs natively, the host version of libunwind is used, the same as with setjmp. When executing in DiVM, DiOS supplies its own implementation of the libunwind API, as described in [20].

4.6   Binary Compatibility

When dealing with verification of real-world software, the exact layout of data structures becomes important, mainly because we would like to generate native code from verified bitcode files (when using either KLEE or DiVM). To this end, the layouts of relevant data structures and values of relevant constants are automatically extracted from the host operating system[9] and then used in the DiOS libc. As a result, the native code generated from the verified bitcode can be linked to host libraries and executed as usual. The effectiveness of this approach is evaluated in Sect. 5.3.

---

[9] This extraction is performed at DiOS build time, using hostabi.pl, which is part of the DiOS source distribution. The technical details are discussed in the online supplementary material.

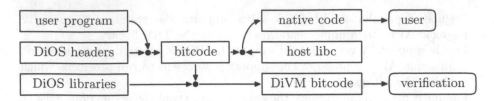

Fig. 3. Building verified executables with DiOS.

5   Evaluation

We have tested DiOS in a number of scenarios, to ensure that it meets the goals that we describe in Sect. 1.2. The first goal – modularity – is hard to quantify in isolation, but it was of considerable help in adapting DiOS for different use cases. We have used DiOS with success in explicit-state model checking of parallel programs [1], symbolic verification of both parallel and sequential programs [12], for verification of liveness (LTL) properties of synchronous C code synthesized from Simulink diagrams, and for runtime verification of safety properties of software [9]. DiOS has also been used for recording, replaying and fuzzing system call traces [8].

5.1   Verification with DiVM

In this paper, we report on 3 sets of tests that we performed particularly to evaluate DiOS. The first is a set of approximately 2200 test programs[10] which cover various aspects of the entire verification platform. Each of them was executed in DiOS running on top of DiVM and checked for a number of safety criteria: lack of memory errors, use of uninitialized variables, assertion violations, deadlocks and arithmetic errors. In the case of parallel programs (about 400 in total), all possible schedules were explored. Additionally, approximately 700 of the test programs depend on one or more input values (possibly subject to constraints), in which case symbolic methods or abstraction are used to cover all feasible paths through the program. The tests were performed on two host operating systems: Linux 4.19 with `glibc` 2.29 and on OpenBSD 6.5, with no observed differences in behaviour.

The majority (1300) of the programs are written in C, the remainder in C++, while a third of them (700) were taken from the SV-COMP [2] benchmark suite. Roughly half of the programs contain a safety violation, the location of which is annotated in the source code. The results of the automated analysis are in each case compared against the annotations. No mismatches were found in the set.

---

[10] All test programs are available online at http://divine.fi.muni.cz/2019/dios/, including scripts to reproduce the results reported in this and in the following sections.

5.2   Portability

To evaluate the remaining ports of DiOS, we have taken a small subset (370 programs, or 17%) of the entire test suite and executed the programs on the other two platforms currently supported by DiOS. The subset was selected to fall within the constraints imposed by the limitations of our KLEE port – in particular, lack of support for threads and for C++ exceptions. We have focused on filesystem and socket support (50 programs) and exercising the standard C and C++ libraries shipped with DiOS. The test cases have all completed successfully, and KLEE has identified all the annotated safety violations in these programs.

5.3   API and ABI Coverage and Compatibility

Finally to evaluate our third goal, we have compiled a number of real-world programs against DiOS headers and libraries and manually checked that they behave as expected when executed in DiOS running on DiVM, fully isolated from the host operating system. The compilation process itself exercises source-level (API) compatibility with the host operating system.

We have additionally generated native code from the bitcode that resulted from the compilation using DiOS header files (see Fig. 3) and which we confirmed to work with DiOS libraries. We then linked the resulting machine code with the libc of the host operating system (glibc 2.29 in this case). We have checked that the resulting executable program also behaves as expected, confirming a high degree of binary compatibility with the host operating system. The programs we have used in this test were the following (all come from the GNU software collection):

- coreutils 8.30, a collection of 107 basic UNIX utilities, out of which 100 compiled successfully (we have tested a random selection of those),
- diffutils 3.7, programs for computing differences between text files and applying the resulting patches – the diffing programs compiled and diff3 was checked to work correctly, while the patch program failed to build due to lack of exec support on DiOS,
- sed 4.7 builds and works as expected,
- make 4.2 builds and can parse makefiles, but it cannot execute any rules due to lack of exec support,
- the wget download program failed to build due to lack of gethostbyname support, the cryptographic library nettle failed due to deficiencies in our compiler driver and mtools failed due to missing langinfo.h support.

6   Conclusions and Future Work

We have presented DiOS, a POSIX-compatible operating system designed to offer reproducible execution, with special focus on applications in program verification. The larger goal of verifying unmodified, real-world programs requires the cooperation of many components, and a model of the operating system is an important piece of the puzzle. As the case studies show, the proposed approach is a viable way forward. Just as importantly, the design goals have been fulfilled: we have shown that DiOS can be successfully ported to rather dissimilar platforms, and that its various components can be disabled or replaced with ease.

Implementation-wise, there are two important future directions: further extending the coverage and compatibility of DiOS with real operating systems, and improving support for different execution and software verification platforms. In terms of design challenges, the current model of memory management for multi-process systems is suboptimal, and there are currently no platforms on which the `exec` family of system calls could be satisfactorily implemented. We would like to rectify both shortcomings in the future.

References

1. Baranová, Z., et al.: Model checking of C and C++ with DIVINE 4. In: D'Souza, D., Narayan Kumar, K. (eds.) ATVA 2017. LNCS, vol. 10482, pp. 201–207. Springer, Cham (2017). https://doi.org/10.1007/978-3-319-68167-2_14
2. Beyer, D.: Reliable and reproducible competition results with BenchExec and witnesses (Report on SV-COMP 2016). In: Chechik, M., Raskin, J.-F. (eds.) TACAS 2016. LNCS, vol. 9636, pp. 887–904. Springer, Heidelberg (2016). https://doi.org/10.1007/978-3-662-49674-9_55
3. Cadar, C., Dunbar, D., Engler, D.R.: KLEE: unassisted and automatic generation of high-coverage tests for complex systems programs. In: OSDI, pp. 209–224. USENIX Association (2008)
4. Chirigati, F., Shasha, D., Freire, J.: Reprozip: using provenance to support computational reproducibility. In: Proceedings of the 5th USENIX Workshop on the Theory and Practice of Provenance, TaPP 2013, Berkeley, CA, USA, pp. 1:1–1:4. USENIX Association (2013). http://dl.acm.org/citation.cfm?id=2482949.2482951
5. Frew, J., Metzger, D., Slaughter, P.: Automatic capture and reconstruction of computational provenance. Concurr. Comput. Pract. Exper. **20**(5), 485–496 (2008). https://doi.org/10.1002/cpe.v20:5. ISSN 1532–0626
6. Inverso, O., Nguyen, T.L., Fischer, B., Torre, S.L., Parlato, G.: Lazy-CSeq: a context-bounded model checking tool for multi-threaded C-programs. In: 2015 30th IEEE/ACM International Conference on Automated Software Engineering (ASE), pp. 807–812 (2015). https://doi.org/10.1109/ASE.2015.108
7. Joshi, S., Orso, A.: Scarpe: a technique and tool for selective capture and replay of program executions. In: 2007 IEEE International Conference on Software Maintenance, pp. 234–243 (2007). https://doi.org/10.1109/ICSM.2007.4362636. ISBN 978-1-4244-1256-3
8. Kejstová, K.: Model checking with system call traces. Master's thesis, Masarykova univerzita, Fakulta informatiky, Brno (2019). http://is.muni.cz/th/tukvk/
9. Kejstová, K., Ročkai, P., Barnat, J.: From model checking to runtime verification and back. In: Lahiri, S., Reger, G. (eds.) RV 2017. LNCS, vol. 10548, pp. 225–240. Springer, Cham (2017). https://doi.org/10.1007/978-3-319-67531-2_14

10. Kong, S., Tillmann, N., de Halleux, J.: Automated testing of environment-dependent programs-a case study of modeling the file system for Pex. In: 2009 Sixth International Conference on Information Technology: New Generations, pp. 758–762. IEEE (2009). https://doi.org/10.1109/ITNG.2009.80

11. Krekel, H., Oliveira, B., Pfannschmidt, R., Bruynooghe, F., Laugher, B., Bruhin, F.:. Pytest 4.5 (2004). https://github.com/pytest-dev/pytest

12. Lauko, H., Štill, V., Ročkai, P., Barnat, J.: Extending DIVINE with symbolic verification using SMT. In: Beyer, D., Huisman, M., Kordon, F., Steffen, B. (eds.) TACAS 2019. LNCS, vol. 11429, pp. 204–208. Springer, Cham (2019). https://doi.org/10.1007/978-3-030-17502-3_14. ISBN 978-3-030-17502-3

13. Leungwattanakit, W., Artho, C., Hagiya, M., Tanabe, Y., Yamamoto, M., Takahashi, K.: Modular software model checking for distributed systems. IEEE Trans. Softw. Eng. **40**(5), 483–501 (2014). https://doi.org/10.1109/TSE.2013.49

14. Mackinnon, T., Freeman, S., Craig, P.: Extreme Programming Examined. Chapter Endo-testing: Unit Testing with Mock Objects, pp. 287–301. Addison-Wesley Longman Publishing Co. Inc., Boston (2001). http://dl.acm.org/citation.cfm?id=377517.377534. ISBN 0-201-71040-4

15. Mostafa, S., Wang, X.: An empirical study on the usage of mocking frameworks in software testing. In: 2014 14th International Conference on Quality Software, pp. 127–132 (2014). https://doi.org/10.1109/QSIC.2014.19

16. Musuvathi, M., Qadeer, S., Ball, T., Basler, G., Nainar, P.A., Neamtiu, I.: Finding and reproducing heisenbugs in concurrent programs. In: Symposium on Operating Systems Design and Implementation, USENIX (2008)

17. Ročkai, P., Štill, V., Černá, I., Barnat, J.: DiVM: model checking with LLVM and graph memory. J. Syst. Softw. **143**, 1–13 (2018). https://doi.org/10.1016/j.jss.2018.04.026. ISSN 0164-1212

18. Wachter, B., Kroening, D., Ouaknine, J.: Verifying multi-threaded software with impact. In: Formal Methods in Computer-Aided Design, pp. 210–217. IEEE (2013). https://doi.org/10.1109/FMCAD.2013.6679412

19. Yang, Y., Chen, X., Gopalakrishnan, G.: Inspect: a runtime model checker for multithreaded c programs. Technical report (2008)

20. Štill, V., Ročkai, P., Barnat, J.: Using off-the-shelf exception support components in C++ verification. In: Software Quality, Reliability and Security (QRS), pp. 54–64 (2017)

Program Analysis

Using Relational Verification for Program Slicing

Bernhard Beckert[1]([✉]), Thorsten Bormer[1], Stephan Gocht[2], Mihai Herda[1]([✉]),
Daniel Lentzsch[1], and Mattias Ulbrich[1]([✉])

[1] Karlsruhe Institute of Technology, Karlsruhe, Germany
{beckert,herda,ulbrich}@kit.edu
[2] KTH Royal Institute of Technology, Stockholm, Sweden

Abstract. Program slicing is the process of removing statements from a program such that defined aspects of its behavior are retained. For producing precise slices, i.e., slices that are minimal in size, the program's semantics must be considered. Existing approaches that go beyond a syntactical analysis and do take the semantics into account are not fully automatic and require auxiliary specifications from the user. In this paper, we adapt relational verification to check whether a slice candidate obtained by removing some instructions from a program is indeed a valid slice. Based on this, we propose a framework for precise and automatic program slicing. As part of this framework, we present three strategies for the generation of slice candidates, and we show how dynamic slicing approaches – that interweave generating and checking slice candidates – can be used for this purpose. The framework can easily be extended with other strategies for generating slice candidates. We discuss the strengths and weaknesses of slicing approaches that use our framework.

Keywords: Program slicing · Relational verification

1 Introduction

Program slicing, introduced by Weiser [40], is a technique to reduce the size of a program while preserving a certain part of its behavior. Different kinds of slicing approaches have been developed [31]. A *static slice* preserves the program's behavior for all inputs, while a *dynamic slice* preserves it only for a particular single input. A *backward slice* keeps only those parts of the program that influence the value of certain variables at a certain location in the program, while a *forward slice* keeps those program parts whose behavior is influenced by the variables' values. The form of slicing introduced by Weiser is now known as *static backward slicing* and is the form of slicing which is pursued in this paper. Slicing techniques can be used to optimize the results of compilers. Slicing is also a powerful tool for challenges in software engineering such as code comprehension, debugging, refactoring, and fault localization [8], as well as in information-flow security [19].

© Springer Nature Switzerland AG 2019
P. C. Ölveczky and G. Salaün (Eds.): SEFM 2019, LNCS 11724, pp. 353–372, 2019.
https://doi.org/10.1007/978-3-030-30446-1_19

```
1   int f(int h, int N){    1   int f(int h, int N){    1   int f(int h, int N){
2     int i = 0;            2     int i = 0;            2     int i = 0;
3     int x = 0;            3     int x = 0;            3     int x = 0;
4     while(i < N) {        4     while(i < N) {        4     while(i < N) {
5       if(i < N - 1)       5       if(i < N - 1)       5       if(i < N - 1)
6         x = h;            6         skip;             6         skip;
7       else                7       else                7       else
8         x = 42;           8         x = 42;           8         skip;
9       i++;                9       i++;                9       i++;
10    }                     10    }                     10    }
11    return x;             11    return x;             11    return x;
12  }                       12  }                       12  }
```

Fig. 1. (a) Original program, (b) slice w.r.t. variable x at line 11, (c) incorrect slice candidate

All applications of slicing can benefit from small and precise slices. Most existing slicing approaches, however, are only syntactical, i.e., they do not take the semantics of the various program operations into account. On the other hand, many existing approaches that do take the semantics into account are not fully automatic and require auxiliary specifications from the user (e.g., precomputed or user-provided functional loop invariants are used in [4, 22]).

Figure 1 shows an example of static backward slicing. The goal is to slice the program in Fig. 1a w.r.t. a slicing criterion which requires the value of x at the statement in line 11 to be preserved. A valid slice for this criterion is shown in Fig. 1b: The assignment in line 6 of the program has been removed. This line has no effect on the value of x, as it is always set to 42 in the last loop iteration. In fact, the statement is not completely removed but replaced with an effect free *skip* statement to keep the program's structure similar to that of the input program. To show that this program is a valid slice, a syntactical analysis is insufficient, as it would not be able to see that in the *last* iteration variable x is overwritten. A semantic analysis is required to determine that the last loop iteration always executes the else-branch. The slicing procedure needs to reason about loops and path conditions, and in this paper we use relational verification for this purpose.

Relational verification approaches that consider the program's semantics and automatically reason about loops have become available in the last couple of years, e.g. [13, 24, 38]. These approaches can efficiently and automatically show the equivalence of two programs – provided that the two programs have a similar structure. Since slices are constructed by removing program statements, they have a similar structure to the original program and are a good use case for relational verification. In this paper we make the following *contributions*:

1. We provide an extensible framework for precise and automatic slicing of programs written in a low level *intermediate representation* language, as well as a semantics therefor. The slicing approaches using this framework need no (auxiliary) specification other than the slicing criterion.
2. We adapt a relational verifier to check if a slice candidate obtained by removing instructions from a program is a valid slice.
3. We adapt a dynamic slicing algorithm and use it to generate slice candidates.

The feasibility of our framework has been shown in a tool paper [5] describing an implementation. Here, we focus on the theoretical background of the framework.

Structure of the Paper. In Sect. 2, we formally describe the programs which we handle and define what a valid slice is. We introduce relational verification in Sect. 3 and extend it to prove the validity of a slice candidate. The framework itself, as well as three slicing approaches based on this framework are described in Sect. 4. Section 5 consists of a discussion of the framework. We present related work in Sect. 6 and conclude in Sect. 7.

2   Static Backward Slicing

Static backward slicing as introduced by Weiser [40] reduces a program by removing instructions in a way that preserves a specified subset of the program's behavior. The *slicing criterion* – the specification of the behavioral aspects that must be retained – is given in form of a set of program variables and a location within the program. Instructions may be removed if and only if they have no effect (a) on the value of the specified program variables at the specified location whenever it is reached and (b) on how often the location is reached.

High level programming languages are feature rich, increasing the effort needed for a program analysis. A solution for dealing with language complexity is to perform the analysis on a simpler, intermediate representation. While the implementation of our slicing framework [5] works on LLVM IR [1] programs, to keep the definitions in this paper easy to understand, we here use a language whose computational model is similar to that of LLVM IR but that has only four instructions: *skip*, *halt*, *assign*, and *jnz*. We formalize the notions of *slice candidate*, *slicing criterion* and *valid slice* using a computation model based on a register machine with an unbounded number of registers. Thus we do not have high-level constructs such as *if* or *while* statements but instead branching and looping are done using conditional jump instructions. The advantage of using such a language is the fact that the control flow is reduced to jumps, and, in the context of slicing, a program remains executable no matter what statements are removed. Figure 2 shows the examples from Fig. 1 written in our simple IR language. The criterion location is now 12, the criterion variable is still x.

```
0    assign i 0           0    assign i 0           0    assign i 0
1    assign x 0           1    assign x 0           1    assign x 0
2    assign c1 (i >= N)   2    assign c1 (i >= N)   2    assign c1 (i >= N)
3    jnz c1 12            3    jnz c1 12            3    jnz c1 12
4    assign t1 (N - 1)    4    assign t1 (N - 1)    4    assign t1 (N - 1)
5    assign c2 (i >= t1)  5    assign c2 (i >= t1)  5    assign c2 (i >= t1)
6    jnz c2 9             6    jnz c2 9             6    jnz c2 9
7    assign x h           7    skip                 7    skip
8    jnz 1 10             8    jnz 1 10             8    jnz 1 10
9    assign x 42          9    assign x 42          9    skip
10   assign i (i + 1)     10   assign i (i + 1)     10   assign i (i + 1)
11   jnz 1 2              11   jnz 1 2              11   jnz 1 2
12   halt                 12   halt                 12   halt
```

Fig. 2. The three examples from Fig. 1 translated into our IR language.

$$\frac{P[pc] = skip}{(s, pc) \rightsquigarrow (s, pc+1)}$$

$$\frac{pc > len(P)}{(s, pc) \rightsquigarrow (end, pc)}$$

$$\frac{P[pc] = halt}{(s, pc) \rightsquigarrow (end, pc)}$$

$$(end, pc) \rightsquigarrow (end, pc)$$

$$\frac{P[pc] = jnz \; v \; target \qquad s(v) = 0}{(s, pc) \rightsquigarrow (s, pc+1)}$$

$$\frac{P[pc] = assign \; v \; exp \qquad x = s(exp)}{(s, pc) \rightsquigarrow (s[v \backslash x], pc+1)}$$

$$\frac{P[pc] = jnz \; v \; target \qquad s(v) \neq 0}{(s, pc) \rightsquigarrow (s, target)}$$

Fig. 3. The semantics of our programming language for a fixed program P

We will now define the semantics of our IR language. Let Var be the set of program variables, S the set of states, where a state is a function $s : Var \rightarrow \mathbb{N}$, and $pc \in \mathbb{N}$ the program counter. An instruction I is an atomic operation that can be executed by the machine. Let $\mathcal{I}$ be the set of all four instructions provided by our IR language. When an instruction is executed, the system changes its state and program counter as determined by the transition function $\rho : S \times \mathbb{N} \times \mathcal{I} \rightarrow S \times \mathbb{N}$. A program P is a finite sequence of instructions: $\langle I_0, I_1, \ldots I_n \rangle$. We denote a location i of program P as $P[i]$ with $P[i] = I_i$ for any $i \in \{0, 1, \ldots n\}$ with $0 \leq i \leq len(P) - 1$, where $len(P)$ is the length of the program.

The semantics of the four instructions in our IR language is shown in Fig. 3. The instruction $skip$ increments the program counter and has no other effects. To obtain a slice candidate, instructions in the original program are replaced with $skip$. To model the termination of programs we introduce a special state, end, such that once the system reaches this state, it will remain in this state forever. The instruction $halt$ is used to bring the system to the end state. The assignment instruction, $assign$, takes a variable v and an integer expression exp as arguments. After the execution of this instruction, the value of the variable v in the new state is updated with the result x of the expression exp and the program counter is incremented. To obtain precise slices, we restrict exp to only one operator. The conditional jump instruction, jnz, allows the register machine to support branching and looping. The instruction gets a variable v and an integer expression $target$ as arguments. If the variable v evaluates to zero in the state in which jnz is executed, then the program counter is incremented, otherwise the program counter is set to the value of $target$. We will now define program traces:

Definition 1 (Program trace). *A trace T of a program P is a possibly infinite sequence of state and program counter pairs $\langle (s_0, pc_0), (s_1, pc_1), \ldots \rangle$ such that:*

1. *$pc_0 = 0$*
2. *For each trace index i but the last, $(s_i, pc_i) \rightsquigarrow (s_{i+1}, pc_{i+1})$*

We use $T^s[i]$ and $T^{pc}[i]$ to denote respectively the ith state and the ith program counter of a trace. Also we use $len(T) \in \mathbb{N} \cup \{\omega\}$ to denote the length of trace T; note that it can be infinite. We define F_T^l to be the sequence comprised of those states $T^s[i]$ for which $T^{pc}[i] = l$, in the same order as they appear in T^s. We define the notions of a slicing criterion, slice candidate and valid slice:

Definition 2 (Slicing Criterion). *A slicing criterion C for a program P is a pair (i_C, Var_C) where i_C is a location in P and $Var_C \subseteq Var$.*

Definition 3 (Slice Candidate). *A slice candidate for a program P_o is a program P_L that is constructed by replacing the instructions at some locations in P_o with the skip instruction. That is, given a set L of locations of program P_o:*

$$P_L[i] = \begin{cases} skip, & i \in L \\ P_o[i], & i \notin L \end{cases}$$

Definition 4 (Valid Slice). *Given a slicing criterion (i_C, Var_C), a slice candidate P_s for a program P_o is a valid slice for P_o if, for any two traces T_s of P_s and T_o of P_o with $T_s[0] = T_o[0]$, the following holds:*

1. *$len(F_{T_o}^{i_C}) = len(F_{T_s}^{i_C})$,*
2. *$F_{T_o}^{i_C}[i](v) = F_{T_s}^{i_C}[i](v)$ for every $v \in Var_C$ and every i with $0 \leq i < len(F_{T_o}^{i_C})$.*

The first requirement ensures that the criterion location is reached in both the original program and the slice candidate the same number of times. The second requirement ensures that the criterion variables have the same values every time the criterion location is reached in the original program and in the slice candidate.

Weiser [40] deals with the feature-richness of programming languages by working on flow graphs, and slices are constructed by removing nodes from the flow-graph. In his approach, however, only nodes with a single successor can be removed while we can remove conditional jumps. Definition 4 is similar to the concept of observation windows in [40]; however, we do not require the original program to terminate. Thus, we extend the definition of Weiser to nonterminating programs, as opposed to many other slicing approaches (as stated in [34]) that are not termination sensitive. Compared to other extensions of the definition of Weiser, e.g. the one in [3], Definition 4 allows for slices which are not *quotients* of the original program, i.e., it allows the removal of conditional jumps while preserving the instructions which are in the program locations between the conditional jump and the jump target. The program

```
0   assign x 42
1   halt
```

is thus a valid slice of the program shown in Fig. 2a, according to Definition 4. Not requiring the slice to be a quotient allows the removal of additional statements. However, the structure of a slice may differ significantly from that of the original program. When using slicing with the goal of program optimization a further reduction of the program is a clear advantage. If the goal is program comprehension, however, then the slice not being a quotient of the original program presents both advantages and disadvantages. One the one hand, a significantly different structure of the slice compared to that of the original program, may cause the user to have difficulties understanding the behavior of the original program. On the other hand, the fact that some conditional jump statements are not in the slice may indicate to the user that certain program branches are irrelevant with respect to the given slicing criterion and help him better understand the program behavior.

3   Relational Verification of Slice Candidates

Relational verification is an approach for establishing a formal proof that if a relational precondition holds on two respective pre-states of two programs P and Q then the respective post-states of P and Q will fulfill a relational postcondition. For two complex programs that yet are similar to each other, much less effort is required to prove their equivalence than to prove that they both satisfy a complex functional specification. The effort for proving equivalence mainly depends on the difference between the programs and not on their overall size and complexity. This is particularly beneficial for the verification of slice candidates, because the candidates are obtained by replacing program instructions with *skip* and thus have a structure similar to the original program.

We formally define the property that is checked by a relational verifier. To that end, we call a predicate π a transition predicate for a program P if for any two states, s and s', $\pi(s, s')$ holds if and only if program P when started in state s terminates in state s'. Thus, for two programs, P and Q, a relational verifier checks the validity of the following proof obligation:

$$Pre(s_P, s_Q) \wedge \pi(s_P, s'_P) \wedge \rho(s_Q, s'_Q) \rightarrow Post(s'_P, s'_Q),$$

where π and ρ are transition predicates for P and Q, respectively, and *Pre* and *Post* are respectively the relational precondition and postcondition.

However, a relational verifier that only checks this property is of limited use for checking slice candidates. For the case in which the location of the slicing criterion refers to the post-state (in Fig. 2a that corresponds to location 12 that contains the *halt* instruction), relational verification can be used to check whether a slice candidate is a valid slice. For a slice candidate Q obtained from a program P, this is done by setting *Pre* to require equal pre-states s_P and s_Q and *Post* to require the criterion variables to evaluate to the same values in the post-states s'_P and s'_Q. However, a successful proof shows the validity of the slice candidates only for inputs for which both P and Q terminate, as the transition predicates may be false for certain pre-states. In the rest of this section we show how a relational verifier can be adapted to support slicing on locations other than the end of the program and how to use relational verification to also show that

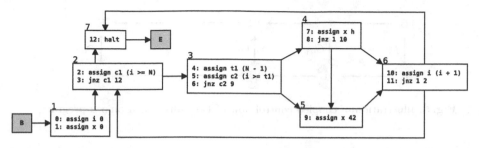

Fig. 4. The CFG for the program in Fig. 2a

the program and candidate run in lockstep (i.e. the two executions run through corresponding states), ensuring thus mutual termination.

Our slicing framework is based on the LLRêVE [14,24] relational verifier, which works on programs written in LLVM IR. It analyzes the control flow graphs (CFGs) of the programs and reduces the validity of the relational specification to the satisfiability of a set M of Horn-constraints over uninterpreted predicates. The satisfiability of the Horn-constraints in M can be checked with state of the art SMT solvers such as Z3 [32] and ELDARICA [35].

If the analyzed programs contain loops, their CFGs contain cycles, which constitute a challenge for verification because the number of iterations is unknown. LLRêVE handles cycles by using so called *synchronization points*, at which the program state is abstracted by means of predicates. The paths between synchronization points are cycle free and can be handled easily. Synchronization points are defined by labeling basic blocks of the CFG with unique numbers. The entry and the exit of a function are considered special synchronization points B and, respectively, E. Additionally, the user can also define synchronization points at any location of the analyzed programs. The user must ensure that there is a synchronization point for each basic block of the CFG of the two programs, and has to match them appropriately. In general, it is difficult to find matching synchronization points for two programs; however, in the case of program slicing this can be done automatically by keeping the CFG of the original program. Figure 4 shows the CFG for the program in Fig. 2a and each basic block is labeled with the number of a synchronization point. In the CFG of the slice in Fig. 2b, the *assign* instruction in block 4 is replaced with *skip*, the synchronization points remain the same, and matching them is trivial. If a conditional jump is replaced with *skip*, we only remove the edge to the block containing the jump target, thus keeping the same synchronization points for the slice candidate.

Given one synchronization point per basic block, the CFG can be viewed as a set of linear paths $\langle n, \pi, m \rangle$, where n and m denote the starting and end synchronization points of the path, and $\pi(s, s')$ is the transition predicate between the two synchronization points, with s and s' being the states before and, respectively, after the transition. Because the linear paths consists of assignments only, the transition predicates can be easily computed. For two programs with a similar structure, it is expected that there exist coupling predicates that describe

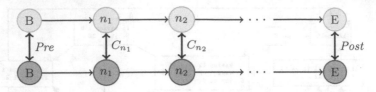

Fig. 5. Illustration of coupled control flow of two fully synchronized programs

the relation between the program states at two corresponding synchronization points. For two programs P and Q we introduce an uninterpreted coupling predicate $C_n(s_p, s_q)$ for each synchronization point n, as shown in Fig. 5. The relational precondition *Pre* and postcondition *Post* are the coupling predicates for the special synchronization points B and E, respectively. The set M consists of Horn-constraints over these coupling predicates. For two linear paths between synchronization points n and m in programs P and Q characterized by the two transition predicates π and ρ, respectively, this constraint is added to M:

$$C_n(s_p, s_q) \wedge \pi(s_p, s_p') \wedge \rho(s_q, s_q') \rightarrow C_m(s_p', s_q') \tag{1}$$

To ensure that there is no divergence from lockstep, for every two paths $\langle n, \pi, m \rangle$ and $\langle n, \rho, k \rangle$ in programs P and Q, respectively, with $m \neq k, m \neq n, n \neq k$ the following constraint is added to M:

$$C_n(s_p, s_q) \wedge \pi(s_p, s_p') \wedge \rho(s_q, s_q') \rightarrow \textit{false} \tag{2}$$

Note, that even though the synchronization points m and k do not appear in Eq. 2, they respectively determine the transition predicates π and ρ.

Theorem 1. *Let P and Q be programs specified with the relational precondition Pre and postcondition Post, for which matching synchronization points have been found. Let M be the set of constraints generated according to 1 and 2. If M is satisfiable, then for every pair of pre-states satisfying Pre:*

1. The synchronization points are reached in the same order in P and Q,
2. If P terminates, then so does Q and Post holds for the two post-states.

Proof. For distinct synchronization points n, m, k, the fact that constraint 2 has a model implies that *(case 1)* π or ρ is *false*, meaning that the execution of P or Q cannot reach respectively m or k from n, or *(case 2)* C_n is false meaning that n is not reachable in P or Q, or per (chaining of) constraint 1 the pre-states do not satisfy the precondition. Thus, P and Q reach the synchronization points (including E, thus implying mutual termination) in the same order. For two synchronization points n, m, the fact that constraint 1 has a model implies that *(case 1)* m cannot be reached from n in P or Q, or *(case 2)* C_n is false and n is not reachable or the pre-states do not satisfy the precondition, or *(case 3)* starting in n with C_n holding, both programs reach m and C_m holds there. The constraints generated according to 1 are thus interpolants that show the validity of the relational specification. $\qquad\square$

To check the validity of a slice candidate for the cases in which the criterion location is in the middle of the program, we adapt the constraints generated by the relational specification. The relational precondition *Pre* still requires equal pre-states, while the relational postcondition *Post* is set to *true*. We ensure a synchronization point n_C exists in the program and slice candidate at the location of the criterion instruction. For example Fig. 2a n_C is the synchronization point 5 in Fig. 4. If the criterion location is part of a basic block with more than one instruction, we split that basic block up such that we obtain a block containing only the criterion location. For a program P with a slice candidate Q and a given slicing criterion (i_C, V_C) with a synchronization point n_C we add the following constraint:

$$C_{n_C}(s_P, s_Q) \rightarrow \forall x \in V_C \; s_P(x) = s_Q(x) \tag{3}$$

Theorem 2. *Let P be a program and Q a slice candidate specified with the relational precondition Pre requires equal pre-states and postcondition Post is true. Let M be the set of constraints generated according to 1, 2 and 3. If M is satisfiable, then for every pair of pre-states that fulfill Pre:*

1. *The criterion location is reached equally often in P and Q,*
2. *At the i-th time (for $i \geq 1$) the criterion instruction is reached in P and in Q, the criterion variables are equal in P and Q,*
3. *If P terminates, then so does Q.*

Proof. From Theorem 1 results that P and Q run in lockstep with respect to the synchronization points. The instruction at the criterion location has its own synchronization point. As a consequence of this, the criterion instruction is executed in both P and Q the same number of times and the candidate terminates iff the original program terminates. Due to Constraint 3, the coupling predicate corresponding to the criterion locations ensures that each time the criterion location is reached, the criterion variables have the same values. □

Thus, for a program P with a slice candidate Q and a slicing criterion (i_C, V_C), if the set M containing the constraints 1, 2 and 3 for every synchronization point is satisfiable, then Q is a valid slice according to Definition 4. Moreover, if the set M is unsatisfiable, then the SMT solver returns an unsatisfiability proof that contains a counterexample with two concrete inputs for which the slice property is violated – provided the SMT solver does not time out.

4   A Framework for Automatic Slicing

Being able to use relational verification to check whether a slice candidate is valid, we construct a framework for automatic program slicing. The framework consists of two components which interact with each other. The first component, the candidate generation engine, generates the slice candidates and sends them to the second component, the relational verifier (in this case LLRêve).

The relational verifier transmits one of three possible answers to the candidate generation engine: (1) the candidate is a valid slice, (2) the candidate is not valid along with an input that leads to a violation of the slice property (Definition 4), or (3) a timeout. The candidate generation engine can use the answer to adapt its candidate generation strategy.

An advantage of the framework is that the candidate generation engine does not need to care about the correctness of the slice candidates it generates – as this is taken care of by the relational verifier. The framework can easily be extended with candidate generation strategies other than those that we present in this paper. Thus, it provides a platform for relational verification based slicing for the software slicing community.

We distinguish between two types of candidate generation strategies. On the one hand there are strategies that generate candidates by replacing program instructions by *skip* according to some heuristics without using any information from the relational verifier other than the existence of a counterexample. Examples for such properties are described in Sect. 4.1. On the other hand there are strategies that also consider the values from the counterexample when generating the next slice candidates. We present one such strategy, *counterexample guided slicing*, in Sect. 4.2.

4.1 Removing Instructions Based on Heuristics

The *brute forcing* (BF) strategy generates all possible slice candidates. As their number is exponential w.r.t. the number of instructions in the original program, it is clear that this strategy does not scale for large programs. Nevertheless, this strategy has the benefit of generating the smallest possible slice with our framework. Brute forcing can be used as part of a divide and conquer strategy to slice parts of programs which are small enough. As an improvement, this strategy can start by generating the candidates in ascending order with respect to their size, i.e. the number of instructions that the candidate retains from the original program. Once a candidate is shown to be a valid slice, no further candidates need to be checked, as their size cannot be smaller than that of the found slice.

The *single statement elimination* (SSE) strategy successively replaces a single instruction of the original program with `skip`, and checks whether the obtained program is a valid slice. If this is the case, the strategy attempts to successively remove every other instruction as well. The strategy requires, in the worst case, quadratically many calls to the relational verifier, which occurs when in each iteration the last candidate is shown to be a valid slice. Although this approach scales better than BF, it finds only slices in which program instructions can be removed individually. Groups of instructions such as `assign x (x + 50)` and `assign x (x - 50)` where the removal of a single instruction results in an invalid slice candidate, but removing the entire group would result in a valid slice cannot be removed. The SSE strategy can be generalized to support the removal of groups of up to a given number of instructions.

4.2   Counterexample Guided Slicing

The *counterexample guided slicing* (CGS) strategy uses *dynamic slicing* to generate slice candidates. Dynamic slicing was first introduced in [27], and a survey on dynamic slicing approaches can be found in [28]. For the CGS strategy we adapted the dynamic slicing algorithm from [2], which is a syntactic approach based on the Program Dependence Graph (PDG) [15]. The PDG is a directed graph in which nodes represent program instructions, conditions, or input parameters, and edges represent possible dependencies between the nodes. An edge from node n_1 to node n_2 encodes that n_1 may depend on n_2. There are roughly two types of dependencies in the PDG. On one hand data dependencies arise when one node uses program variables which are defined in another node. Control dependencies, on the other hand, arise when the execution of a node depends on the other, control, node (e.g. an instruction may be executed only if the condition of a conditional jump is *true*). Whether an edge exists between two nodes in the PDG is determined syntactically by analyzing the CFG. Because the CFG represents an over-approximation of the possible program executions, the PDG edges also represent an over-approximation of the real dependencies in the program. Using the PDG, a backward slice is computed by finding all nodes that are reachable from a node representing the criterion location. On the most basic level, the algorithm in [2], which receives the PDG and an execution trace as inputs, works by computing the subgraph of the PDG which contains only the nodes corresponding to those instructions which have been executed in the program trace. The dynamic slice is computed using this subgraph and further optimizations are possible, as it has to be valid only for a single input.

A PDG node can depend on multiple other nodes, but some of these dependencies are determined by the execution path of the program (e.g. a variable can be assigned on more than one branch, resulting in multiple dependencies for instructions that use that variable). Unlike static slicing, for dynamic slicing only one execution path is relevant – the one corresponding to the input for which the dynamic slice is computed. Thus, PDG edges representing dependencies that are relevant only for other inputs can be removed. A similar situation arises with loops: at different loop iterations, a node inside the loop body may have different dependencies. When performing dynamic slicing, the number of iterations done by a loop is known (assuming the program terminates for the input), and the PDG can be extended with nodes representing the body instructions at different iterations, which also leads to an increased precision of the dynamic slice. The extended PDG is called a *dynamic dependence graph* (DDG) in [2]. Based on the observation that the nodes inside the loop body can depend on only a finite number of other nodes, a new node is added to the PDG just for those iterations in which the corresponding instruction has different dependencies than in all previous iterations. These optimizations give rise to the *reduced dynamic dependence graph* (RDDG). Thus, by ignoring dependencies caused by other inputs than the one for which the dynamic slice is computed, additional instructions can be removed than in the case of static slicing. To ensure compatibility with the slicing property from Definition 4, we adapt this algorithm to support cri-

Data: Program P, Slicing criterion (i_C, V_C)
Result: Program Slice P_s
$P_s \leftarrow \Phi$; $s \leftarrow \bar{0}$; $b \leftarrow$ *false*;
repeat
    | $P_d \leftarrow$ *dynamicSlice*$(P, s, (i_C, V_C))$;
    | $P_s \leftarrow SDS(P_s, P_d)$;
    | $(b, s) \leftarrow$ *relationalVerification*$(P, P_s, (i_C, V_C))$;
until $b \vee$ *timeout*;
if *timeout* **then**
    | $P_s \leftarrow P$;
end
return P_s;

Algorithm 1. The CGS Strategy

terion locations other than the end of the program. For this, when computing the dynamic slice with the RDDG we do not mark the `return` statement, as is done in [2], but rather all nodes that correspond to the criterion location. If the criterion location is inside a loop, then multiple nodes are marked.

The adapted RDDG dynamic slicing algorithm is purely syntactical and thus scales much better than a semantic approach. Thus we can use it as part of the candidate generation strategy, as relational verification of slice candidates remains the bottleneck of our framework.

For the CGS strategy we wish to merge several dynamic slices $P_{d_1}, \ldots, P_{d_n}$ for the respective input states $s_1, \ldots, s_n$ into a single dynamic slice P_u that is a valid for all inputs $s_1, \ldots, s_n$. In general, the union slice of dynamic slices (which contains all program instructions that are in at least one dynamic slice) is not a correct dynamic slice for all respective inputs of the given dynamic slices. A solution to this was presented in [18] in the form of an iterative algorithm called *simultaneous dynamic slicing (SDS)*, which computes a single dynamic slice valid for each input in a given set.

We can now present the CGS strategy, shown in Algorithm 1. It starts with an initialization of the slice candidate P_s with a program Φ, in which all instructions have been replaced with *skip*, of an arbitrary initial state s, e.g. one in which all variables are set to 0 and of the variable b which will be set to true when a valid slice will be found. The strategy uses the initial state s with the criterion (i_C, V_C) to compute a dynamic slice P_d. The instructions from P_d are then added to the slice candidate P_s which is checked for validity by the relational verifier. If P_s is a valid slice candidate, the variable b is set to *true* and the strategy returns P_s. Otherwise, the relational verifier delivers a counterexample, which is used as the initial state s in the next iteration. Both the dynamic slicer and relational verifier may timeout, in which case the strategy returns the original program P.

Theorem 3. *Let P be a program and P_d be a dynamic slice for all initial states $s \in S_d$, and s_{ce} be the counterexample obtained when checking whether P_d is a valid slice of P. Then the following holds:*

1. $s_{ce} \notin S_d$.
2. The dynamic slice P_{ce} for the initial state s_{ce} contains at least one instruction which is not in P_d.

Proof. Both properties follow from the correctness of the relational verifier and of the dynamic slicer and of the SDS algorithm. (1) If $s_{ce} \in S_d$ then the relational verifier delivered a spurious counterexample, the dynamic slicer delivered an invalid dynamic slice, or the SDS algorithm computed a wrong simultaneous dynamic slice. (2) If P_{ce} contains no additional instruction compared to P_d, then $P_d \cup P_{ce} = P_d$ which means that P_d is a dynamic slice for s_{ce}. This implies that the relational verifier delivered a spurious counterexample. □

Theorem 3 guarantees that the CGS strategy adds at least one instruction back after each iteration. Thus, the number of calls of the relational verifier is linear in the number of program instructions. The SDS algorithm is needed for this theorem to hold. The validity of the slice computed with CGS, however, is guaranteed by the relational verifier. Thus, if the CGS algorithm computes the simple union of dynamic slices, the relational verifier my return a counterexample that it already provided in a previous CGS iteration. In this case the CGS algorithm needs to terminate and return the original program. Given the fact that computing the union of dynamic slices is much easier than computing the simultaneous dynamic slice, the user of the framework must make a choice between performance and completeness. Our implementation of CGS computes the union of dynamic slices.

The CGS strategy has the least number of calls to the relational verifier compared with the other strategies presented in this paper. Nevertheless, it comes with some disadvantages. First, the program needs to be executed at each iteration, which – depending on the analyzed program – can cause performance issues and for some inputs the program may not even terminate. Second, the CGS strategy is vulnerable to timeouts of the relational verifier. If a timeout occurs, then the strategy fails entirely and must return the original program as the slice candidate, while the BF and SSE strategies could continue their search for a valid slice candidate. Third, the precision of CGS depends on the precision of the dynamic slicing approach used in the candidate generation. Even though the used dynamic slicing approach can remove more statements than static syntactic slicing approaches, the dynamic slices it computes are still over-approximations.

5   Discussion

We start the discussion by reiterating the evaluation results [6] of the prototypical implementation of the framework consisting of the tool SEMSLICE [5,7], as shown in Table 1. For the evaluation, we used a collection of small but intricate examples (e.g., the example of Fig. 1 or a routine in which the same value is first added and then subtracted), each focusing on a particular challenge which cannot be handled by syntactic state of the art slicers. Some examples are taken from slicing literature [4,9,16,22,39]. The second column indicates the source of

Table 1. Evaluation

Original			BF			SSE			CGS		
Example	Source	#stmts	time (s)	#stmts	#calls	time (s)	#stmts	#calls	time (s)	#stmts	#calls
count_occurrence_error	self	50				13	42	11			
count_occurrence_result	self	50				16	44	13			
dead_code_after_ssa	[39]	4	< 1	2	4	< 1	2	4	< 1	2	1
dead_code_unused_variable	self	3	< 1	2	2	< 1	2	3	< 1	2	1
identity_not_modifying	[16]	8	< 1	3	3	< 1	7	5	< 1	6	1
identity_plus_minus_50	[4]	5	< 1	2	4	< 1	5	4	< 1	5	1
iflow_cyclic	[39]	18	62	14	2197	< 1	16	6	< 1	17	1
iflow_dynfamic_override	self	15	23	8	1298	< 1	11	8	< 1	12	1
iflow_endofloop (Fig. 1)	self	19	118	15	4065	< 1	16	7	< 1	18	2
intermediate	self	13	4	11	129	< 1	12	5	< 1	12	2
requires_path_sensitivity	[22]	20	647	16	26894	< 1	17	10	< 1	18	3
single_pass_removal	self	13	< 1	3	7	< 1	6	11	< 1	8	1
unchanged_over_itteration	self	20	29	9	932	1	15	14	< 1	20	2
unreachable_code_nested	self	10	< 1	2	1	< 1	9	1	< 1	4	1
whole_loop_removable	self	20	15	8	469	< 1	17	5	< 1	17	2

each example, the third the number of LLVM-IR statements in the program. For each example, the third the number of LLVM-IR statements in the program. For each slice candidate generation-strategy from Sect. 4 (BF, SSE, and CGS), the table lists the number of statements in the smallest slice found by SEMSLICE, the (wall) time needed by the tool, and the number of calls to the relational verifier. The experiments were conducted on a machine with an Intel Core I5-6600K CPU and 16 GB RAM. The exponential BF approach works satisfactorily fast on functions with up to 20 statements, and while it requires more time than the other approaches it computes more precise slices. For examples with less than 10 statements the brute-force approach takes less than one second. The other two approaches achieved slices of similar precision (to each other) and required less than one second for most examples. The evaluation shows that the framework can handle programs that require a large number of calls to the relational verifier, e.g. the program *requires_paths_sensitivity* with the BF strategy called the relational verifier almost 27000 times and took about 10 minutes to find the slice. The BF strategy serves as a *worst-case* scenario when using the slicing framework to automatically slice programs. Other strategies need fewer calls. For this example the other strategies were still able to remove some instructions with fewer less calls to the relational verifier and therefore they could scale to larger programs. Thus, the scalability of our slicing approach can be increased by using candidate generation strategies that do not call relational verifier often. Another way to ensure that our approach to slicing scales to large programs is to apply it to individual program functions (as opposed to applying it to the entire program). Our current prototypical implementation supports only a subset of the LLVM IR instruction set, which is the main reason we did not evaluate it on large, real-life programs.

Our slicing approach works on an intermediate representation language. This is beneficial for the implementation of the approach, as it does not need to handle all features of a modern high level programming language. However, one of the uses for program slicing is to help the user debug and comprehend a program written in a high level language. It is possible to perform relational verification of such programs, the early version of LLRêve was in fact working on a simple *while* language in [14], LLVM-IR was later chosen [24] to increase the practicability of LLRêve. We believe the current framework can be adapted for slicing high level languages by either (1) attempting to translate back the IR slice to the high level language, or (2) by defining the slicing candidate in the high level language and then translating both the original program and the slice candidate into the IR and then using the extended relational verifier. For the first option we expect that only an over-approximation of the IR slice can be obtained by translating it back into the high level language, similar to what was done in [20]. As for the second solution, the CFGs of the original program and slice candidate in the IR may be so different that our approach would no longer be able to automatically find matching synchronization points. A solution to this would be to automatically annotate the original program and its slice candidate in the high level language, thus marking the synchronization points and using these marks in the IR translation. A further solution for supporting a high-level language would be to extend the work in [14] with the ideas of this paper. Thus, Definition 4 of a valid slice would need to be adapted for high-level programming languages and the weakest liberal precondition calculus from [14] would need to be extended such that it supports slicing in the case in which the criterion location is in the middle of the program. By working on the high-level programming language we would lose the advantages of working on an intermediate representation, i.e. relative language independence and existing support for various code optimizations, but our approach to slicing would become more suitable for program debugging and comprehension.

The IR language that we used to present our approach is not inter-procedural. While we could consider all programs as having been inlined beforehand, recursive procedures would not be supported. The relational verifier supports dealing with function calls using mutual function summaries [24] which abstract two matching function calls using coupling predicates. In general it is difficult to find matching function calls, but for checking the validity of slice candidates this can be done automatically, similar to finding matching synchronization points. Thus, our approach can be extended to support recursive functions; however the function calls themselves may not be removed, otherwise the mutual function summaries cannot be used.

In the semantics that we provided in Sect. 2 we assume that an error (e.g. a division by zero) causes the system to transition to the end state. An interesting question in the context of program slicing is whether instructions which may cause errors can be removed from the program. While some approaches (e.g. [33,34]) keep the error prone instructions in the slice, others (e.g. [29]) allow the removal of such statements but at the cost of a weaker soundness property (i.e., what constitutes a valid slice) which is nonetheless still useful in certain application scenarios such as software verification. With our slicing approach, we keep error prone instructions in the slice. However, because we take the semantics of the program instructions into account, we can remove error prone instructions which will never cause an error, e.g. a division where the divisor will never be zero.

The completeness of our approach, i.e. whether a valid slice according to Definition 4 is deemed as such, is limited in practice by two factors. First, the relational verifier is required to automatically infer the coupling predicates needed to verify the validity of a slice candidate. The relational verifier works well when the needed coupling predicates are limited to linear arithmetics [26]. The second factor limiting completeness is the requirement that the original program and the slice candidate must run in lockstep. This is needed to ensure the mutual termination and that the criterion location is executed the same number of times. Thus, whereas we can remove instructions from inside a loop, we are not able to remove the loop itself (in our case the conditional jump instruction), even if it is empty – i.e. it loops over *skip* instructions.

6   Related Work

Static slicing is an active area of research and many approaches have been developed. We present those that are most similar to our work.

Assertion based slicing [4] also takes the semantics of the program into consideration. Program methods must be specified with a contract, which also represents the slicing criterion, i.e. statements are removed such that the reduced program still fulfills the contract. Unlike in our approach, loop invariants are required and only groups of instructions that are at consecutive program locations can be removed. This approach improves and combines older approaches [10,11], an implementation also exists [12]. The approach in [30] also uses a method's contract as the slicing criterion. However, the program parts that are deemed irrelevant are not removed, but replaced with an abstraction. Thus, the slice candidate over-approximates the behavior of the original program. If the contract is proved for the slice candidate, then it is also valid for the original program.

Path sensitive backward slicing [22] is another slicing approach that takes the program's semantics into consideration. The main idea is to symbolically execute the program and check the satisfiability of the path condition of every execution path. Only the satisfiable paths are used for computing the slice. The approach handles loops by using abstract interpretation to generate loop invariants, which can lead to an over-approximated description of the loop behavior. Thus, while the approach offers an increased precision when compared to syntactic approaches, it is not able slice the program in Fig. 1a. An implementation of this approach is available in the tool Tracer [23]. The idea of discarding dependencies that can only occur on infeasible program paths has also been explored in other works e.g. [9,36]. For these approaches, a compromise between the precision and scalability had to be found.

Abstract program slicing [17] is an approach which makes use of the program's semantics, however a different slicing criterion is used. Instead of preserving those instructions that affect the exact values of the criterion variables at the criterion location, this approach preserves the statements that affect a property of the criterion variable. The properties pursued in this approach are whether the variables belong to a given abstract domain, e.g. the positive integers. Using abstract interpretation, for some operations the abstract domain of the output is known – provided the abstract domains of the inputs are also known. Thus some dependencies modeled in the PDG can be removed. This approach can generate slices which are not valid according to Definition 4.

The Frama-C framework [25] for software analysis provides components that support abstract interpretation and program slicing (based on program dependence graphs). Abstract interpretation can be used to improve the precision of the slicing component by identifying some infeasible branches. Abstract interpretation can automatically handle loops, but it does this by over-approximating their effects.

In [33] a different notion of semantic dependence between program statements is defined. In that work it is assumed that each node in the CFG of a program has an assigned function that represents the computation performed by that node. Thus, a statement s is semantically dependent on a statement s' if the interpretation of the function computed by s' affects the execution behavior of s. Consider a program that contains the instruction `assign x (x + 0)` followed by the criterion location and x as a criterion variable. According to the definition from [33] the assignment would be in the slice, because if the interpretation of the symbol + changes (e.g. to multiplication) then so would the value of x at the criterion location. In our approach, on the other hand, we consider the semantics of the program instructions to be fix, and can remove the statement from the slice, as it leaves the value of x unchanged.

Other, syntactic, slicing approaches have been surveyed in [41] and in [37], and a survey of dynamic slicing techniques can be found in [28].

7   Conclusion and Future Work

We extended a relational verification approach such that it can check whether a slice candidate is indeed a valid slice. Based on this, we built a framework for precise and automatic static slicing which consists of a candidate generation engine and the extended relational verifier. We presented three strategies to compute slice candidates, of which *counterexample guided slicing* is more sophisticated. It uses the counterexample provided by the relational verifier to refine the slice candidate with a dynamic slicer.

We plan to improve the precision of the slices by performing an additional analysis on empty loops to check whether they terminate. If this is the case, they can be safely removed. Furthermore, we plan to improve the performance of the relational verifier by using PDGs to simplify the programs that need to be checked for equivalence, using the fact that two programs with isomorphic PDGs are equivalent, as shown in [21]. We will also investigate how the results (e.g. coupling invariants) of the relational verifier can be reused when checking another slice candidate, constructed from the same original program.

References

1. LLVM language reference manual. https://llvm.org/docs/LangRef.html. Accessed 06 Feb 2019
2. Agrawal, H., Horgan, J.R.: Dynamic program slicing. In: Proceedings of the ACM SIGPLAN 1990 Conference on Programming Language Design and Implementation, PLDI 1990, pp. 246–256. ACM, New York (1990). https://doi.org/10.1145/93542.93576
3. Barraclough, R.W., et al.: A trajectory-based strict semantics for program slicing. Theoret. Comput. Sci. **411**(11), 1372–1386 (2010). https://doi.org/10.1016/j.tcs.2009.10.025
4. Barros, J.B., da Cruz, D., Henriques, P.R., Pinto, J.S.: Assertion-based slicing and slice graphs. Formal Aspects Comput. **24**(2), 217–248 (2012). https://doi.org/10.1007/s00165-011-0196-1
5. Beckert, B., Bormer, T., Gocht, S., Herda, M., Lentzsch, D., Ulbrich, M.: SEMSLICE: exploiting relational verification for automatic program slicing. In: Polikarpova, N., Schneider, S. (eds.) IFM 2017. LNCS, vol. 10510, pp. 312–319. Springer, Cham (2017). https://doi.org/10.1007/978-3-319-66845-1_20
6. Beckert, B., Bormer, T., Gocht, S., Herda, M., Lentzsch, D., Ulbrich, M.: Evaluation data of SemSlice (2019). https://doi.org/10.5281/zenodo.3334571
7. Beckert, B., Bormer, T., Gocht, S., Herda, M., Lentzsch, D., Ulbrich, M.: Implementation of the SemSlice tool (2019). https://doi.org/10.5281/zenodo.3334553
8. Binkley, D., Harman, M.: A survey of empirical results on program slicing. In: Advances in Computers, vol. 62, pp. 105–178. Elsevier (2004). https://doi.org/10.1016/S0065-2458(03)62003-6
9. Canfora, G., Cimitile, A., Lucia, A.D.: Conditioned program slicing. Inf. Softw. Technol. **40**(11–12), 595–607 (1998). https://doi.org/10.1016/S0950-5849(98)00086-X
10. Chung, I.S., Lee, W.K., Yoon, G.S., Kwon, Y.R.: Program slicing based on specification. In: Proceedings of the 2001 ACM Symposium on Applied Computing, SAC 2001, pp. 605–609. ACM, New York (2001). https://doi.org/10.1145/372202.372784
11. Comuzzi, J.J., Hart, J.M.: Program slicing using weakest preconditions. In: Gaudel, M.-C., Woodcock, J. (eds.) FME 1996. LNCS, vol. 1051, pp. 557–575. Springer, Heidelberg (1996). https://doi.org/10.1007/3-540-60973-3_107
12. da Cruz, D., Henriques, P.R., Pinto, J.S.: GamaSlicer: an online laboratory for program verification and analysis. In: Proceedings of the Tenth Workshop on Language Descriptions, Tools and Applications, LDTA 2010, pp. 3:1–3:8. ACM, New York (2010). https://doi.org/10.1145/1868281.1868284
13. De Angelis, E., Fioravanti, F., Pettorossi, A., Proietti, M.: Relational verification through horn clause transformation. In: Rival, X. (ed.) SAS 2016. LNCS, vol. 9837, pp. 147–169. Springer, Heidelberg (2016). https://doi.org/10.1007/978-3-662-53413-7_8
14. Felsing, D., Grebing, S., Klebanov, V., Rümmer, P., Ulbrich, M.: Automating regression verification. In: Proceedings of the 29th ACM/IEEE International Conference on Automated Software Engineering, ASE 2014, pp. 349–360. ACM (2014). https://doi.org/10.1145/2642937.2642987
15. Ferrante, J., Ottenstein, K.J., Warren, J.D.: The program dependence graph and its use in optimization. ACM Trans. Program. Lang. Syst. **9**(3), 319–349 (1987). https://doi.org/10.1145/24039.24041

16. Field, J., Ramalingam, G., Tip, F.: Parametric program slicing. In: Proceedings of the 22nd ACM SIGPLAN-SIGACT Symposium on Principles of Programming Languages, POPL 1995, pp. 379–392. ACM, New York (1995). https://doi.org/10.1145/199448.199534

17. Halder, R., Cortesi, A.: Abstract program slicing on dependence condition graphs. Sci. Comput. Program. **78**(9), 1240–1263 (2013). https://doi.org/10.1016/j.scico.2012.05.007

18. Hall, R.J.: Automatic extraction of executable program subsets by simultaneous dynamic program slicing. Autom. Softw. Eng. **2**(1), 33–53 (1995). https://doi.org/10.1007/BF00873408

19. Hammer, C., Snelting, G.: Flow-sensitive, context-sensitive, and object-sensitive information flow control based on program dependence graphs. Int. J. Inf. Secur. **8**(6), 399–422 (2009). https://doi.org/10.1007/s10207-009-0086-1

20. Herda, M., Tyszberowicz, S., Beckert, B.: Using dependence graphs to assist verification and testing of information-flow properties. In: Dubois, C., Wolff, B. (eds.) TAP 2018. LNCS, vol. 10889, pp. 83–102. Springer, Cham (2018). https://doi.org/10.1007/978-3-319-92994-1_5

21. Horwitz, S., Prins, J., Reps, T.: On the adequacy of program dependence graphs for representing programs. In: Proceedings of the 15th ACM SIGPLAN-SIGACT Symposium on Principles of Programming Languages, POPL 1988, pp. 146–157. ACM, New York (1988). https://doi.org/10.1145/73560.73573

22. Jaffar, J., Murali, V., Navas, J.A., Santosa, A.E.: Path-sensitive backward slicing. In: Miné, A., Schmidt, D. (eds.) SAS 2012. LNCS, vol. 7460, pp. 231–247. Springer, Heidelberg (2012). https://doi.org/10.1007/978-3-642-33125-1_17

23. Jaffar, J., Murali, V., Navas, J.A., Santosa, A.E.: TRACER: a symbolic execution tool for verification. In: Madhusudan, P., Seshia, S.A. (eds.) CAV 2012. LNCS, vol. 7358, pp. 758–766. Springer, Heidelberg (2012). https://doi.org/10.1007/978-3-642-31424-7_61

24. Kiefer, M., Klebanov, V., Ulbrich, M.: Relational program reasoning using compiler IR - combining static verification and dynamic analysis. J. Autom. Reason. **60**(3), 337–363 (2017). https://doi.org/10.1007/s10817-017-9433-5

25. Kirchner, F., Kosmatov, N., Prevosto, V., Signoles, J., Yakobowski, B.: Frama-c: a software analysis perspective. Formal Aspects Comput. **27**(3), 573–609 (2015). https://doi.org/10.1007/s00165-014-0326-7

26. Klebanov, V., Rümmer, P., Ulbrich, M.: Automating regression verification of pointer programs by predicate abstraction. Formal Methods Syst. Des. **52**(3), 229–259 (2018). https://doi.org/10.1007/s10703-017-0293-8

27. Korel, B., Laski, J.W.: Dynamic program slicing. Inf. Process. Lett. **29**(3), 155–163 (1988). https://doi.org/10.1016/0020-0190(88)90054-3

28. Korel, B., Rilling, J.: Dynamic program slicing methods. Inf. Softw. Technol. **40**(11–12), 647–659 (1998). https://doi.org/10.1016/S0950-5849(98)00089-5

29. Léchenet, J.-C., Kosmatov, N., Le Gall, P.: Cut branches before looking for bugs: sound verification on relaxed slices. In: Stevens, P., Wąsowski, A. (eds.) FASE 2016. LNCS, vol. 9633, pp. 179–196. Springer, Heidelberg (2016). https://doi.org/10.1007/978-3-662-49665-7_11

30. Liu, T., Tyszberowicz, S., Herda, M., Beckert, B., Grahl, D., Taghdiri, M.: Computing specification-sensitive abstractions for program verification. In: Fränzle, M., Kapur, D., Zhan, N. (eds.) SETTA 2016. LNCS, vol. 9984, pp. 101–117. Springer, Cham (2016). https://doi.org/10.1007/978-3-319-47677-3_7

31. Lucia, A.D.: Program slicing: methods and applications. In: Proceedings First IEEE International Workshop on Source Code Analysis and Manipulation, pp. 142–149, November 2001. https://doi.org/10.1109/SCAM.2001.972675
32. de Moura, L., Bjørner, N.: Z3: an efficient SMT solver. In: Ramakrishnan, C.R., Rehof, J. (eds.) TACAS 2008. LNCS, vol. 4963, pp. 337–340. Springer, Heidelberg (2008). https://doi.org/10.1007/978-3-540-78800-3_24
33. Podgurski, A., Clarke, L.A.: A formal model of program dependences and its implications for software testing, debugging, and maintenance. IEEE Trans. Softw. Eng. **16**(9), 965–979 (1990). https://doi.org/10.1109/32.58784
34. Ranganath, V.P., Amtoft, T., Banerjee, A., Hatcliff, J., Dwyer, M.B.: A new foundation for control dependence and slicing for modern program structures. ACM Trans. Program. Lang. Syst. **29**(5) (2007). https://doi.org/10.1145/1275497.1275502
35. Rümmer, P., Hojjat, H., Kuncak, V.: Disjunctive interpolants for horn-clause verification. In: Sharygina, N., Veith, H. (eds.) CAV 2013. LNCS, vol. 8044, pp. 347–363. Springer, Heidelberg (2013). https://doi.org/10.1007/978-3-642-39799-8_24
36. Snelting, G., Robschink, T., Krinke, J.: Efficient path conditions in dependence graphs for software safety analysis. ACM Trans. Softw. Eng. Methodol. **15**(4), 410–457 (2006). https://doi.org/10.1145/1178625.1178628
37. Tip, F.: A survey of program slicing techniques. Technical report, Amsterdam, The Netherlands, The Netherlands (1994). https://www.franktip.org/pubs/jpl1995.pdf
38. Verdoolaege, S., Janssens, G., Bruynooghe, M.: Equivalence checking of static affine programs using widening to handle recurrences. ACM Trans. Program. Lang. Syst. **34**(3), 11:1–11:35 (2012). https://doi.org/10.1145/2362389.2362390
39. Ward, M.: Properties of slicing definitions. In: 2009 Ninth IEEE International Working Conference on Source Code Analysis and Manipulation, pp. 23–32, September 2009. https://doi.org/10.1109/SCAM.2009.12
40. Weiser, M.: Program slicing. In: Proceedings of the 5th International Conference on Software Engineering, ICSE 1981, Piscataway, NJ, USA, pp. 439–449. IEEE Press (1981). http://dl.acm.org/citation.cfm?id=800078.802557
41. Xu, B., Qian, J., Zhang, X., Wu, Z., Chen, L.: A brief survey of program slicing. SIGSOFT Softw. Eng. Notes **30**(2), 1–36 (2005). https://doi.org/10.1145/1050849.1050865

Local Nontermination Detection
for Parallel C++ Programs

Vladimír Štill[(✉)] and Jiří Barnat

Faculty of Informatics, Masaryk University, Brno, Czech Republic
divine@fi.muni.cz

Abstract. One of the key problems with parallel programs is ensuring that they do not hang or wait indefinitely – i.e., there are no deadlocks, livelocks and the program proceeds towards its goals. In this work, we present a practical approach to detection of nonterminating sections of programs written in C or C++, and its implementation into the DIVINE model checker. This complements the existing techniques for finding safety violations such as assertion failures and memory errors. Our approach makes it possible to detect partial deadlocks and livelocks, i.e., those situations in which some of the threads are progressing normally while the others are waiting indefinitely. The approach is also applicable to programs that do not terminate (such as daemons with infinite control loops) as it can be configured to check only for termination of selected sections of the program. The termination criteria can be user-provided; however, DIVINE comes with the set of built-in termination criteria suited for the analysis of programs with mutexes and other common synchronisation primitives.

1 Introduction

Assessing correctness of parallel programs is a hard task even for experienced programmers. Therefore, the standard program development includes a bunch of quality assurance activities such as testing. Unfortunately, the nondeterministic nature of thread scheduling and concurrency makes it quite hard for testing to achieve good guarantees of quality in the case of parallel programs. Formal methods, on the other hand, provide a more systematic approach and in some cases may even prove the absence of erroneous behaviours. However, they are not used very often in practice due to the extra effort required for their application or simply because they are not powerful enough to handle the overall complexity and size of real-world programs. Nevertheless, continuous improvement in formal methods is desirable to cover the corner cases of their use and to allow them to become more usable in software development.

Especially beneficial techniques are those that can be directly applied to programs written in mainstream programming languages. Such techniques significantly lower the barrier towards their usage by programmers. However, the

This work has been partially supported by the Czech Science Foundation grant No. 18-02177S.

© Springer Nature Switzerland AG 2019
P. C. Ölveczky and G. Salaün (Eds.): SEFM 2019, LNCS 11724, pp. 373–390, 2019.
https://doi.org/10.1007/978-3-030-30446-1_20

```
// can be used for synchronization      int main() {
std::atomic< int > x = 0;                  // start thread running worker
                                           std::thread t( worker );
void worker() {                            x = 42; // let worker run
  while ( x != 0 ) { } // wait             // ...
  do_work();                               t.join();
}                                        }
```

Fig. 1. A simple C++ code snippet with two threads, it uses C++ standard threading support and atomic variables. A programmer's intention was that the worker function first waits until x becomes non-zero, and then proceeds with do_work. However, the waiting condition (at the first line of the worker function) is incorrectly just the opposite. Therefore, if main executes x = 42 before waiting in worker starts, the wait will never end (assuming x is never set to 0 again). Note that none of safety checks is able to detect that the program might hang. For the rest of the paper, we will omit the std:: namespace to simplify the notation.

development of these techniques is extremely demanding due to numerous specific features the real-world programming languages exhibit. As a result, many techniques introduced and implemented stay at the level of prototypes without being mature enough to be applicable outside the scientific community – e.g., they might be missing features such as pointer arithmetic, functionality of the standard libraries or the concept of exceptions. See the Software-Verification Competition (SV-COMP) [6], to find some examples of tools aiming at verification of real-world programs written in C.

A significant limitation of many existing tools for analysis of parallel programs in programming languages such as C and C++ is that they are only concerned with safety checking – they check that a bad state of the program is unreachable. Most common examples of bad states include assertion failures and memory errors (such as invalid memory accesses and memory leaks). Unfortunately, this is far from being sufficient in practice. See, for example, the code given in Fig. 1. That piece of code easily passes any safety checks; however, when executed in reality, it often hangs and does not terminate.

In this paper, we report about our new technique for checking nontermination for parallel programs written in C and C++ that may be applied to programs with arbitrary synchronisation primitives. In particular, we can check that a *specified part* of a program finishes whenever its execution has been started, which in turn enables us to check for problems such as partial deadlocks or local nontermination. Note that our technique does not require the program under analysis to terminate at all. Therefore, it is also applicable to programs that do not terminate but have some parts that are supposed to finish. It does; however, require that the program has a finite state space because our technique is built on top of a state space exploration. Note that even for a finite state space, a program may exhibit infinite behaviour.

The main observation is that a program often has sections which once entered should also be left: for example critical sections, certain function calls (such as a pop from a queue, which can wait for an element to become available; or a thread join, etc.), or parts of code which wait for a resource or an action (waiting for a mutex, waiting on a barrier, waiting until a variable is set to a given value). If the analysis of the program focuses on such sections, it is possible to detect when these sections are started, but do not terminate. This covers partial deadlock and partial livelock detection in which such sections participate. We also provide a global nontermination detection mode that decides if the program as a whole terminates, nevertheless this is not the primary goal of our approach.

Our technique is built on top of explicit-state model checking. We believe that while explicit-state model checking is prone to state space explosion, it is well suited for the detection of problems related to infinite runs of parallel programs which cannot be handled by techniques such as bounded model checking or stateless model checking. While our approach is closely related to checking for properties written in temporal logic such as LTL or CTL*, our *local nontermination* technique cannot be substituted equivalently with CTL* model checking. One of the reasons is that these logics are unable to relate to entities which are dynamically created during the execution of the program, and there is no bound to their number. For example, there is no way to express in CTL* that for all mutexes it holds that if they are locked, they are also eventually unlocked unless all the mutexes are enumerated beforehand. This is an essential concern for realistic programs where mutexes and other synchronisation primitives can be created dynamically at runtime, and their number can depend on the computation of the program itself. Furthermore, to avoid counterexamples which are unrealistic with practical thread schedulers, we need a form of *fairness* of process scheduling different from the fairness constraints used typically with LTL model checking.

The approach described in this paper is implemented in a modified version of the DIVINE model checker [3,13]. The implementation, as well as all the examples, can be found on the paper webpage[1].

The rest of the paper is structured as follows: Sect. 2 gives a short overview of related work and Sect. 3 gives definitions and preliminaries needed for the rest of the work. In Sect. 4 we define our *local nontermination* property, in Sect. 5 we discuss how it can be checked and the implementation in DIVINE, and it Sect. 6 we evaluate it. Finally, Sect. 7 concludes this work.

2   Related Work

For the related work, we consider only results which go beyond safety checking. There are many approaches to find problems such as assertion violations or memory safety violations, but they are fundamentally limited to properties concerning finite runs of the program, and we are focusing here on an infinite behaviour, namely on the absence of termination. Similarly, we do not mention techniques which specialise on checking sequential programs and have no support

---

[1] https://divine.fi.muni.cz/2019/lnterm/.

for parallelism, as well as techniques which are tailored to a specific modelling language and cannot be applied in general.

Several techniques for checking properties other than safety exist – indeed usage of various temporal logics, such as Linear Temporal Logic (LTL) [2, Chapter 5] and Computation Tree Logic (CTL) [2, Chapter 6] in the context of model checking dates way back to the beginning of research in formal methods. Unfortunately, these techniques are not often applied to programs written in real-world programming languages such as C and C++.

As for techniques which detect nontermination, both static and dynamic techniques exist for the detection of deadlocks caused by circular waiting for mutexes [1,5,7]. However, these techniques specialise on mutexes and do not allow general nontermination detection, and it is unlikely that they could be naturally extended to cover it. There are also techniques that detect deadlocks of the whole program (i.e., a program state from which the program cannot move) [8,9], but these techniques cannot find cases in which only some threads of the program are making progress, while other threads are blocked forever. Also, these global deadlock detection techniques are inadequate in the presence of synchronisation mechanisms which causes busy waiting instead of blocking (for example spin locks) or in the cases when normally blocking operations are implemented using busy waiting (which can be easier to handle for the verifier in some cases). A somewhat different approach based on communicating channels is proposed in [11], but this approach is aiming at the Go programming language which primarily uses shared channels for communication between threads. Overall, neither of these techniques is applicable in general for the detection of nontermination in programs which use a combination of synchronisation primitives in shared memory.

3   Preliminaries

In this section, we shortly describe necessary details about representation of programs, their state space, and resource sections so that we can define local nontermination.

3.1   State Space of a Program

The *state space* of a program is a directed multigraph with labelled edges. The vertices of the state space multigraph are called *states* (of the program). Each state represents a snapshot of the program (its memory, program counters and stacks of all its threads, . . .). States v_1, v_2 are connected by an edge in the state space if v_2 can be reached from v_1 in an atomic step, which is a sequence of instructions that executes at most one action which can interfere with any action executed in parallel with it. In DIVINE, the state space generator attempts to make the longest possible atomic step while ensuring that the generation of the edge terminates. Edges are labelled, and the labels can be used to indicate accepting edges and error edges. Error edges are edges on which safety violation occurs (e.g., an assertion violation or memory error). The notion of accepting edges was taken initially from transition-based Büchi automata and used for LTL model checking, but in general, it is a way to mark an edge as interesting for the verification algorithm, but not erroneous. These labels are set by the verified program, which can be instrumented to influence edge labelling or by DIVINE when it detects an error.

The state space of a program can be an infinite graph. However, in DIVINE, we are primarily concerned with programs which have finite state space. If the state space is infinite, DIVINE might find an error if it is present there, or it might compute until its resources are exhausted. Please note that programs with finite state space can have infinite behaviour as they can loop through the same set of states indefinitely.

3.2 Resource Sections

A *resource section* of a program is a block of code with an identifier of a resource and type of the resource section. Each resource section is delimited in the source code by section start and section end annotations. Examples of such sections are a mutex-waiting section that denotes a block of code in which a thread is waiting for the acquisition of a mutex. Mutex-waiting section is identified by a mutex and the thread which waits for it. Another example can be a critical section, which is identified by a mutex (there is no need to use a thread for the identification, as a mutex can be owned by at most one thread at any point in time). Resource section can also be bound to a function – in this case, it is identified by the stack frame of the function and by the program counter of its beginning. Regardless of the identification, the idea for a resource section is that once it is entered, it should also be exited.

As a resource section can be entered repeatedly (for example when it is on a cycle or in a function which is called multiple times) we will define a *resource section instance* to be a particular execution of a resource section with the given identifier. The author of annotations which define resource sections should ensure that the same resource section is not entered again before it is left. Please note that this does not limit the usage of function-associated resource sections to non-recursive functions – each such section is also identified by the stack frame, and therefore resource sections corresponding to different recursion depths are different resource sections. Similarly, a program can be in multiple resource sections which wait for the same mutex at the same time, each of them corresponding to a different waiting thread.

4 Local Nontermination

With our local nontermination property, we aim at detection of resource section instances which are entered but are never left – *nonterminating resource section instances*. We will first use examples of terminating and nonterminating resource section instances, and then we will define them precisely.

```
mutex m;

  void thread0() {
    unique_lock lock(m); // Error
    while (true) {
      do_work();
    }
  } // unlock

  void thread1() {
    while (true) {
      unique_lock lock(m);
      do_other_work();
    } // unlock
  }
```

```
mutex m;

  void thread0() {
    while (true) {
      unique_lock lock(m); // Fixed
      do_work();
    } // unlock
  }

  void thread1() {
    while (true) {
      unique_lock lock(m);
      do_other_work();
    } // unlock
  }
```

Fig. 2. A program with a nonterminating critical section (in `thread0`) and a deadlock (if `thread0` enters its critical section, `thread1` will wait infinitely). Please note that in C++ it is possible to use scope-based locks: the critical section belonging to mutex m is entered when `unique_lock lock(m)` is executed and left at the end of the scope in which the `lock` variable was defined (at the matching curly brace; also marked with comment `// unlock`).

Fig. 3. A fixed version of the program from Fig. 2 (the start of the critical section was moved from the position `// Error` in the left code to `// Fixed` and therefore the critical section can end now). Intuitively, each critical section in this program terminates. However, as we can see in Fig. 4, it is possible to find an infinite path in the state space of this program that infinitely waits for one of the critical sections. To make matters worse, this path can respect weak fairness.

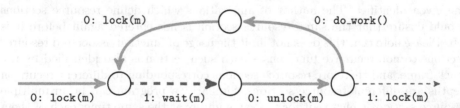

Fig. 4. A fragment of state space of program in Fig. 3 with starving lasso marked with bold edges. Each edge is marked by the thread it belongs to and the action of this thread. Furthermore, to ease the orientation, actions belonging to `thread0` are marked with continuous red edges while actions belonging to `thread1` are marked with dashed blue edges. We can see that both threads participate in the repeated part of the counterexample and `thread0` is denied the possibility (starves) to execute after `0: unlock(m)` (the thin blue dashed edge). (Color figure online)

A simple example can be seen in Fig. 2. There we have a mutex which is locked, but never unlocked as the corresponding critical section contains an infinite loop. We have four different resource sections in this example. Two of them corresponds to the critical sections guarded by the mutex, and two of them are hidden inside unique_lock, where they implement waiting until the mutex is unlocked. Nonterminating resource section instances are the instances corresponding to the critical section in thread0 and any instances corresponding to waiting for the mutex in thread1 that is executed after the critical section in thread0 is entered. We can fix this example by putting the critical section in thread0 inside the infinite loop, as shown in Fig. 3.

Suppose that we have defined nonterminating section as one in which it is possible to stay indefinitely (i.e., for the specific case of waiting for m in thread1, termination could be expressed by LTL formula $\mathbf{G}(wait\text{-}m\text{-}t1\text{-}start \implies \mathbf{F}\,wait\text{-}m\text{-}t1\text{-}end)$). We can witness the existence of such nonterminating section in a program with a finite state space by a lasso-shaped path. Such the nontermination witness can also be found for the program in Fig. 3, even though the code might intuitively seem to terminate. First thread0 executes its lock action, then thread1 starts waiting. If thread0 always executes unlock and lock before thread1 is allowed to run, thread1 will never be able to finish waiting. The counterexample is illustrated in Fig. 4 and is valid also under weak fairness assumptions.

In general, if a thread waits for some condition which is both infinitely often true and infinitely often false, there can be a run in which the waiting thread is only allowed to run at those moments when the condition is false. This type of run is present in any program that uses busy waiting, which is very common in practice. For this practical reason, we cannot rely on the definition of nontermination as expressed with the LTL formula above, and we need a different way to describe nonterminating sections.

Definition 1 (Nonterminating resource section instance). *A resource section instance is nonterminating if and only if it can reach a point from which it is not possible to reach its end.*

For a particular resource section (e.g., again waiting for m in thread1), checking for absence of nonterminating resource section instances can be expressed using a CTL* property

$$\mathbf{AG}\,(wait\text{-}m\text{-}t1\text{-}start \implies \mathbf{A}[(\mathbf{EF}\,wait\text{-}m\text{-}t1\text{-}end)\,\mathbf{W}\,wait\text{-}m\text{-}t1\text{-}end])$$

(where **W** is the weak until operator).

In general, the CTL* approach cannot be used, as it requires the set of resource sections to be known before the analysis starts, so that the formula can be created as a conjunction of formulas for each resource section. This is hard to do if resource sections can be created at runtime, which is often the case when dealing with programs in languages such as C and C++ – the number of objects such as threads, mutexes, or function invocations which are used to identify resource sections might be hard to determine without exploration of all the runs of the program.

```
mutex m1, m2;
{
  unique_lock l1(m1);
  do_work_1();
  {
    unique_lock l2(m2);
    do_work_2();
  } // unlock(m2)
} // unlock(m1)
```

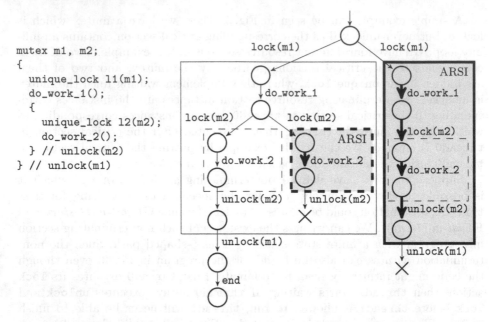

Fig. 5. A small example of a program with two resource section instances (on the left-hand side) and its state space, which shows active resource section instances (ARSIs; on the right-hand side). Please note that, in order to keep the state space simple, this example program is sequential and deterministic; the nondeterminism is caused only by the construction which gives rise to ARSIs. The resource section instances belonging to the critical section of mutex m1 are wrapped in a solid rectangle in the image, while resource section instances belonging to m2 are wrapped in a dashed rectangle. ARSIs are denoted by thick frame and yellow background and accepting edges in the state space are marked by thick arcs. Please recall that active resource section instances cannot be nested. Crosses at the end of edges denote points where exploration of the state space was terminated due to reaching the end of an active resource section instance. (Color figure online)

5   Detection of Nontermination

The detection of nonterminating resource section instances in the context of explicit-state model checking proceeds as follows. The basic idea behind the detection of nonterminating resource section instances is that the model checker focuses on them one at a time. Every time a resource section instance is about to be entered during the state space exploration, the algorithm introduces a nondeterministic branching to the state space graph. In one branch the resource section instance remains inactive, in which case the state space exploration proceeds as usual to discover other resource sections. However, in the other branch, the instance becomes active. Under this branch the resource section instance is checked for being nonterminating. Note that the nondeterministic branching happens only outside of active resource sections, which means the *active resource section instances* (ARSIs) cannot be nested. Once the state space graph in the active branch reaches a state that is out of the scope of an ARSI, the state space exploration within this branch is stopped (a state with no successors is generated outside the ARSI). Active resource section instances cannot be nested, but for any instance of a resource section nested in an active section instance, there is also an instance which is nested in an inactive section instance, and therefore can become active elsewhere in the state space. As a result of this construction, for every nonterminating resource section in the original program, there is a corresponding ARSI in the augmented state space graph. To let the exploration algorithm know that it is exploring a part of the state space that is within an ARSI, we mark all edges within ARSIs as accepting. An illustration of a state space graph augmented with nondeterministic choices and accepting edges is given in Fig. 5. This augmentation of the state space can be performed by a program instrumentation. Now to discover ARSIs which are nonterminating according to Definition 1, it is enough to detect terminal strongly connected components made of accepting edges only.

5.1   Detection Algorithm

Henceforward, we assume the state space graph is finite, and if the program to be verified terminates then this fact is reflected by a state with no successors in the underlying state space graph. Note that the program may terminate even within a resource section instance. An ARSI terminates either by reaching the end of the section instance, or by the termination of the whole underlying program. In both cases, this means a state with no successors is generated and reachable from the ARSI entrance point. Finally, we assume that any waiting is implemented in nonblocking way; in particular we require that waiting operations give rise to cycles in the state space of the waiting thread.[2] As a result, the detection of nonterminating ARSIs can be performed as a search for an accepting terminal strongly connected component in the state space graph.

Definition 2 (Terminal Strongly Connected Component). *A strongly connected component S is* terminal[3] *if for each state v in S all successors of v are in S (there are no edges out of S).*

Definition 3 (Fully Accepting Terminal SCC). *A terminal strongly connected component of the state space is* fully accepting *(fully accepting terminal SCC, or FATSCC) if and only if it is nontrivial and all its edges are accepting.*

Theorem 1. *A program contains a nonterminating resource section instance if and only if its state space graph contains a fully accepting terminal strongly connected component.*

---

[2] This is not a problem in practice as any blocking synchronisation (such as waiting for a mutex) can be simulated by a busy waiting loop.

[3] Also sometimes called bottom strongly connected components, or closed communicating classes, especially in the area of probabilistic system analysis [12].

Proof. Assume the program contains a nonterminating ARSI $\mathcal{A}$. Then there must exist a set of states in $\mathcal{A}$ from which neither program end nor the corresponding resource section end can be reached. Among these states, there must be a subset which can be repeated indefinitely and cannot be left – a nontrivial terminal SCC which is part of an ARSI and therefore it is fully accepting – a FATSCC in the state space.

For the other direction let us assume that there is an FATSCC in the state space graph. Since any edge which enters or leaves an ARSI is not accepting (which follows directly from the construction of the state space graph), all states that are part of the FATSCC must be states within a single ARSI. Since the component is terminal and non-trivial, it cannot be left. Furthermore, a program termination point cannot be part of the FATSCC as it has no successors and an ARSI end cannot be part the FATSCC as edges going to it are not accepting. Therefore, it is impossible to reach either a program termination point or a state that would be outside of the resource section instance from the FATSCC, therefore, the FATSCC witnesses a resource section instance that does not terminate.   □

To detect the presence of a FATSCC in the state space graph we employ the standard Tarjan's algorithm for finding strongly connected components. To decide if an SCC is terminal, it suffices to check that there are no edges going from it to any different SCC. Finally, to detect if a terminal component is nontrivial and fully accepting it is enough to check that the component contains at least one state with some successors (it is nontrivial) and that all states of the component have only accepting outgoing edges (it is fully accepting). These are minor modifications of the algorithm. Furthermore, it is possible to extend the algorithm to also perform safety checking while checking for nontermination – when a new edge with an error label is traversed, the exploration can be terminated immediately with a safety counterexample. This way any need for separate safety checking is eliminated.

Note that it is also possible to define *global nontermination* using Definition 1. In this case we only need to treat the whole program as a single active resource section instance.

5.2   Scheduling and Fairness

To provide further context, we also want to discuss the relation of our nontermination property to LTL model checking with fairness. Fairness constraints [2, Chapter 3.5] are needed in analysis of temporal properties of parallel systems to avoid reporting of unrealistic counterexamples, such as those in which an enabled thread never gets the chance to make an action. Basically, even if we use LTL formula to describe nontermination and allow for LTL model checking under weak fairness, we still may obtain counterexamples that are totally unrealistic. This is because a weakly-fair scheduler[4] admits runs in which the context switches that happen among participating threads are very regular, hence unrealistic.

The nontermination as defined in Definition 1 can be seen as a manifestation of an additional assumption about the thread scheduler. It claims that the scheduler is in the essence somehow irregular, i.e., it will not allow for a context switch always after a fixed number of instructions or at a specific location in the code. Another way of looking at this is to assume that the scheduler is probabilistic and assigns some non-zero probability to interruption between any two instructions. With a probabilistic scheduler, we can equivalently define nonterminating resource section instance as a section instance which can get to the point when there is zero probability of reaching its end. Under the probabilistic view we can also say that programs we denote as correct, i.e., without nonterminating sections, have zero probability of looping forever.

5.3 Implementation and Usage

We have implemented our nontermination detection approach in a branch of the DIVINE model checker. Resource sections can be specified by annotations in the source code of the program to be analysed by the user of the tool. Furthermore, DIVINE provides predefined resource sections for various POSIX thread (`pthread`) synchronisation primitives, namely for mutexes (including recursive and reader-writer mutexes), condition variables, barriers, and joining of threads. Since C++ threading support in DIVINE uses the libc++ library which uses POSIX threads, these resource sections are also used for native C++ threading.

User-defined annotations can be given in one of the following categories: exclusive section, waiting for an event, and waiting for function end. For user-defined resource sections, DIVINE provides C and C++ interface which can be found on the web page accompanying this publication.[5] To make it possible to specify which resource section types should be considered for analysis, we use program instrumentation, which enables resource sections based on commandline arguments (for more details see the accompanying web page). The instrumentation also ensures that edges which are part of an ARSI are accepting.

The detection of nonterminating resource sections in DIVINE uses Tarjan's algorithm for finding strongly connected components. The algorithm runs on-the-fly, which means that it generates the state space graph as needed, and therefore, it can terminate before the entire state space graph is explored. The algorithm finishes if it finds a fully accepting terminal strongly connected component, if it discovers a safety error (to avoid the need for a separate safety verification), or once the entire state space is explored.

---

[4] For our purposes, a weakly-fair scheduler is a scheduler which ensures that on every accepting cycle in the state space all threads which existed during the execution of this cycle were also executed at least once on the cycle.

[5] https://divine.fi.muni.cz/2019/lnterm.

5.4   Interaction with Other Features of DIVINE

Since DIVINE is a research tool not all the features implemented within the tool are expected to run together. In this case there are some features of DIVINE which interfere with local nontermination detection in a not so obvious way.

Counterexamples. When an error is found DIVINE has support to show a counterexample and walk through it using an interactive simulator [3]. For safety properties, this counterexample is a sequence of states which ends with an error. For verification of properties described by LTL or Büchi automata (which are partially supported by DIVINE), the counterexample is a lasso-shaped trace. For nontermination, the part of the state space to be reported consists of a fully accepting terminal strongly connected component and a path that leads to it. However, it is not practical to output the information about the whole SCC, as it can be large. For this reason, DIVINE gives only a trace to the first state of the FATSCC (i.e., the first state from which end of the given resource section instance is not reachable).

Spurious Wakeups. Condition variables are often used in parallel programs to block threads until some event occurs (e.g., a shared queue becomes non-empty). They provide a function which blocks the current thread (`wait`) and a function which signals the condition variable and causes waiting threads to proceed (`signal`). In most implementations, including C++ standard APIs and platform-specific APIs on Windows and Linux, `wait` is allowed to return before it is signalled: this behaviour is called *spurious wakeup* and programmers must take it into account when using condition variables.

To help with the discovery of bugs caused by spurious wakeup, DIVINE simulates spurious wakeup using nondeterministic choice. For nontermination detection, it is necessary to ensure that any spurious wakeup does not hide nontermination – we want to report resource section instances which can be only left by spurious wakeup as nonterminating. This can be done by careful implementation of the `wait` function in DIVINE – it first nondeterministically decides if a spurious wakeup will happen, and then, if it is not happening, it enters resource section which waits for `signal` and cannot be woken up spuriously. If the spurious wakeup is simulated, it behaves as if the thread was blocked and allows other threads to run. Once the waiting thread is used again for generation of successor states, it is unblocked and `wait` returns spuriously. The exhaustive enumeration of possible thread interleavings ensures that other threads can run arbitrarily long.

Data Nondeterminism and Symbolic Data. To make it possible to verify programs that depend on input data, DIVINE has support for symbolic values [10]. In an analysis of programs with symbolic values, the computation can be split when a branch depends on a symbolic value. This splitting can cause problems for nontermination detection if leaving some resource section instance requires a particular value of an input variable. Therefore, in the presence of symbolic

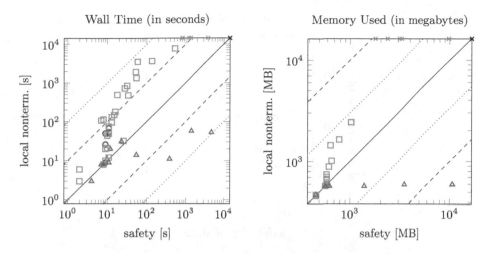

Fig. 6. Scatter plots which compare local nontermination detection with safety checking as implemented in DIVINE. Please note that both axes use a logarithmic scale. The dashed and dotted lines in wall time graphs signify 10× and 100× difference respectively. For graphs of memory usage, the dotted lines signify 3× difference and the dashed 10× difference. Green squares correspond to benchmarks which were error-less in both modes and blue circles correspond to benchmarks which contained errors in both cases. Red triangles correspond to benchmarks which contained a nonterminating section. The crosses on the outer edge of the plot correspond to timeouts and out-of-memory errors. All the failures for local/global nontermination were due to timeouts, benchmarks which failed with out-of-memory did so in all cases. (Color figure online)

data, nontermination checking might miss some instances of nontermination. We defer this problem to future work.

Relaxed Memory Models. DIVINE has support for analysis of parallel programs under the x86-TSO memory model of Intel and AMD CPUs [14], which allows the program to exhibit behaviour not present under the interleaving semantics of threads. One of the main problems in interaction between nontermination and relaxed memory is that relaxed memory models over-approximate the possible behaviours of the system to cover all possibilities of contemporary processors of a given architecture. As nontermination is checking for *absence of termination*, it can spuriously hide nontermination if the state space of the program is over-approximated. Again, we defer this problem to future work.

6   Evaluation

To our best knowledge there is no suitable benchmark set that would cover termination in parallel programs, therefore, we had to develop a suitable benchmark on our own. We naturally wanted to analyse performance of our verification method on real-world data structures. Unfortunately, it is hard to reuse any

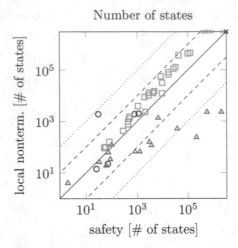

Fig. 7. A comparison of state space sizes for local nontermination and safety. The dashed and dotted lines signify 10× and 100× difference respectively. The meaning of the marks in the graph is the same as in Fig. 6.

existing real-world test cases of parallel data structures for verification, as these tests are usually developed as stress tests. Stress tests use large amounts of data and are supposed to be run for a long time in order to maximise a chance that a parallelism-related bug is found during the testing period. For the purpose of application of a formal verification tool such as DIVINE, the mentioned approach to testing of parallel programs is inappropriate. Since a model checker explores systematically all interleavings of the program within a single execution, further repeated executions, such as the ones within a stress test, are useless and only add to the complexity of the verification task. For these reasons, the tests we included in our benchmark are tests we created or adapted and modified specifically for the purpose of nontermination detection we wanted to evaluate.

To preserve some diversity at least, we opted for the following tests to be included in our benchmark. First, to cover some real-world scenarios, we created some tests for the Thread library from widely used C++ Boost[6] (35 test cases). Second, we used some tests from DIVINE project itself (8 test cases), and finally we developed a couple of specific tests for small programs demonstrating behaviour of local nontermination with various synchronisation primitives (16 test cases). Overall, the benchmark covered usage of lockfree and mutex guarded parallel data structures (e.g. parallel queues), synchronised variables, less-used synchronisation primitives such as reader-writer locks, or a single-producer-single-consumer queue and the parallel hashset from [4].

To evaluate our verification approach we let each test run with a 4 hours timeout and 16 GB memory limit. We measured runtime and memory requirements for the three following configurations of our tool:

---

[6] https://www.boost.org/doc/libs/1_69_0/doc/html/thread.html.

Safety. A baseline configuration, in which the tool merely generates the state space of the program and checks for the standard safety issues, such as assertion violation, invalid memory access, etc. In this mode no nontermination can be detected.

Local Nontermination. The configuration in which the nonterminating resource section detection is used. Under this configuration, the state space of the original program is expanded with every entrance to the resource section as described in Sect. 4.

Global Nontermination. The configuration that treats the whole program as a single resource section and detects if it terminates according to Definition 1. Since this configuration does not introduce additional nondeterminism, the state space of the program is roughly the same size as for *safety*.

The difference between local and global nontermination configurations is in the shape of the state space; both use the same algorithm (Tarjan's algorithm for SCC decomposition). Thanks to this difference, local nontermination can be applied to programs which should not terminate, to check if each of its resource sections terminate.

Comparison of safety and local nontermination can be seen in Fig. 6. We evaluate wall time and memory consumption – in practice heavy duty tools like DIVINE are likely to be used in long-running overnight tests (preferably only if anything relevant for the test changed since the last run), therefore longer runtimes might not be a big problem up to some point, but it is important to test that the verification tasks fit in some reasonable amount of memory. As we can see, the time overhead of local nontermination configuration is quite significant (up to 59×) especially for larger programs which are correct. As for memory consumption, we can see that total overhead is less then threefold, which is mostly due to the state space compression employed by DIVINE.

The wall time blow-up is due to extra nondeterminism introduced by active resource sections – the state space can grow by a factor that is related to the number of resource section instances encountered in the original state space. Note that many resource sections are likely to be very short. For programs that were invalid, i.e., contained some nonterminating resource sections, the verification usually exited faster under the local nontermination configuration than under the safety configuration, which means that once a nonterminating section is encountered, it is checked relatively quickly. Further insight into the comparison of safety and local nontermination can be seen in Fig. 7, which compares sizes of state spaces for these two configurations. Here, we can see that the overhead in the size of the state space is lower than the time overhead (less than 10×). The extra time overhead is likely caused by inefficiencies in DIVINE. For example, when DIVINE nondeterministically chooses from N values, it will re-execute instructions between the last remembered state and the point of the nondeterministic choice N times.

Figure 8 shows a comparison of local nontermination with global nontermination and safety with global nontermination. Here, we can see that global nontermination behaves similarly to safety, with some time overhead caused by the

Wall Time (in seconds)

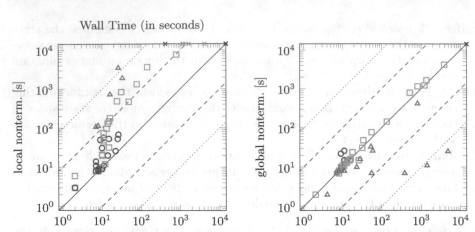

Fig. 8. The first scatter plot compares local nontermination checking with checking if the whole program terminates (global nontermination). In this comparison, the red triangles correspond to benchmarks which did not end, but for which all resource sections terminated. Finally, in the second graph, we compare global nontermination checking with safety. Here, the red triangles correspond to benchmarks which did not terminate but were safe. See Fig. 6 for the general description of the plot layouts. (Color figure online)

somewhat more involved algorithm. This is well in line with our expectations, as global nontermination does not introduce any extra nondeterminism compared to safety and Tarjan's algorithm runs in linear time with respect to the size of the state space, and so does reachability. This further highlights that the overwhelming part of the time overhead of local nontermination is in the increase of the state space size. It is important to note that local nontermination can be applied to programs which are intended to run infinitely (but have finite state space) – it can detect if there is a nonterminating resource section in such a program. As state space sizes and memory consumption are almost the same for safety and for global nontermination, we omit memory and state space size comparisons for the later two pairs of configurations.

Errors Found. No errors were found in the C++ Boost tests. On the other hand, all the errors we artificially implanted in the test cases were found. As for the errors which were not deliberately introduced in the tests, we have found one error in a test of a lock-free queue from an older version of DIVINE. The test was part of DIVINE's test suite for a long time and was used to test that the queue works when it is continuously fed with elements while keeping its size bounded. This means that the test was deliberately nonterminating and the intention was that all the operations executed by main loops of the test's two threads terminate, which was not the case – a variable which was supposed to keep track of the size of the queue was not maintained properly, and therefore it could have happened that the reader thread would wait indefinitely, attempting to read from an empty queue which would never fill up. So far the test case was run under DIVINE with the safety algorithm only, therefore the error did not manifest and remained undetected.

7   Conclusion

We have presented a novel approach to detection of parts of real-world programs written in C and C++ which do not terminate. Our method allows for detection of partial deadlocks (and livelocks) caused by misuse of synchronisation, but it is not limited to any particular mode of parallel programming (such as lock-based synchronisation, or programs with communication channels) and indeed allows any combination of synchronisation allowed by C++ itself. To achieve this, it is necessary to provide simple annotations for parts of the code which are to be checked for termination. Our implementation in the DIVINE model checker ships with these annotations already prepared for verification of programs which use C++ blocking synchronisation primitives (mutexes, condition variables), or similar synchronisation primitives from the POSIX threads library (`pthreads`). Due to the universality of these synchronisation primitives, our annotations allow for checking of most programs which use blocking synchronisation out of the box. For lock-free programs, users have to annotate functions or blocks of code which are required to be exited once they were entered.

We have implemented our technique in an open-source model checker DIVINE, and evaluated it on a set of benchmarks including our tests of the Thread library from widely used C++ Boost. The evaluation shows that while the time overhead of local nontermination checking can be quite significant (up to 59× compared to safety checking on our benchmarks), the memory overhead is quite modest (under 3×). During the evaluation, we have discovered a hidden bug that remained in the code for a couple of years, even though the code was subject to intensive safety checking.

Our technique enables checking nontermination in parallel programs, including detection of partial deadlocks and livelocks. It also supports detection of cases when infinitely-running programs contain sections which are supposed to terminate but do not terminate. We believe that even the overhead shown in our evaluation is worth paying for the additional guarantees over safety checking. While related to verification of properties written in temporal logics such as CTL*, our technique cannot be subsumed into CTL* verification, as CTL* cannot quantify over objects which can be created while the program runs.

For future work, it is crucial to further investigate interactions between nontermination checking and relaxed memory, and nontermination and symbolic data representation, as the presence of either of these features can lead to programs being reported as terminating even if they are not in the current situation. Nevertheless, even in the presence of relaxed memory or symbolic data, any reported nonterminating section of the program is indeed a case when the program cannot proceed past the given point. We would also like to investigate better algorithms for detection of local nontermination that might avoid adding nondeterminism to the program under analysis.

References

1. Agarwal, R., et al.: Detection of deadlock potentials in multithreaded programs. IBM J. Res. Dev. **54**(5), 3:1–3:15 (2010)
2. Baier, C., Katoen, J.-P.: Principles of Model Checking (Representation and Mind Series). The MIT Press, Cambridge (2008)
3. Baranová, Z., et al.: Model Checking of C and C++ with DIVINE 4. In: D'Souza, D., Narayan Kumar, K. (eds.) ATVA 2017. LNCS, vol. 10482, pp. 201–207. Springer, Cham (2017). https://doi.org/10.1007/978-3-319-68167-2_14
4. Barnat, J., Ročkai, P., Štill, V., Weiser, J.: Fast, dynamically-sized concurrent hash table. In: Fischer, B., Geldenhuys, J. (eds.) SPIN 2015. LNCS, vol. 9232, pp. 49–65. Springer, Cham (2015). https://doi.org/10.1007/978-3-319-23404-5_5
5. Bensalem, S., Havelund, K.: Scalable dynamic deadlock analysis of multi-threaded programs. In: 2005 Parallel and Distributed Systems: Testing and Debugging (2005)
6. Beyer, D.: Automatic verification of C and Java programs: SV-COMP 2019. In: Beyer, D., Huisman, M., Kordon, F., Steffen, B. (eds.) TACAS 2019. LNCS, vol. 11429, pp. 133–155. Springer, Cham (2019). https://doi.org/10.1007/978-3-030-17502-3_9
7. Cai, Y., Chan, W.K.: Magiclock: scalable detection of potential deadlocks in large-scale multithreaded programs. IEEE Trans. Softw. Eng. **40**(3), 266–281 (2014)
8. Chaki, S., Clarke, E., Ouaknine, J., Sharygina, N., Sinha, N.: Concurrent software verification with states, events, and deadlocks. Formal Aspects Comput. **17**(4), 461–483 (2005)
9. Demartini, C., Iosif, R., Sisto, R.: A deadlock detection tool for concurrent Java programs. Softw.: Pract. Exp. **29**(7), 577–603 (1999)
10. Lauko, H., Ročkai, P., Barnat, J.: Symbolic computation via program transformation. In: Fischer, B., Uustalu, T. (eds.) ICTAC 2018. LNCS, vol. 11187, pp. 313–332. Springer, Cham (2018). https://doi.org/10.1007/978-3-030-02508-3_17
11. Ng, N., Yoshida, N.: Static deadlock detection for concurrent go by global session graph synthesis. In: Proceedings of the 25th International Conference on Compiler Construction, CC 2016, pp. 174–184. ACM, New York (2016)
12. Norris, J.R.: Markov Chains. Cambridge Series in Statistical and Probabilistic Mathematics. Cambridge University Press, Cambridge (1997)
13. Ročkai, P., Štill, V., Černá, I., Barnat, J.: DiVM: model checking with LLVM and graph memory. J. Syst. Softw. **143**, 1–13 (2018). https://divine.fi.muni.cz/2017/divm/
14. Štill, V., Barnat, J.: Model checking of C++ programs under the x86-TSO memory model. In: Sun, J., Sun, M. (eds.) ICFEM 2018. LNCS, vol. 11232, pp. 124–140. Springer, Cham (2018). https://doi.org/10.1007/978-3-030-02450-5_8

Relating Models and Implementations

An Implementation Relation for Cyclic Systems with Refusals and Discrete Time

Raluca Lefticaru[1], Robert M. Hierons[1(✉)], and Manuel Núñez[2]

[1] Department of Computer Science, The University of Sheffield,
Sheffield SD1 4DP, UK
{r.lefticaru,r.hierons}@sheffield.ac.uk
[2] Departamento de Sistemas Informáticos y Computación,
Universidad Complutense de Madrid, Madrid, Spain
mn@sip.ucm.es

Abstract. This paper explores a particular type of model, a cyclic model, in which there are sequences of observable actions separated by discrete time intervals, introduces a novel implementation relation and studies some properties of this relation. Implementation relations formalise what it means for an unknown model of the system under test (SUT) to be a correct implementation of a specification. Many implementation relations are variants of the well known ioco implementation relation, and this includes several timed versions of ioco. It transpires that the timed variants of ioco are not suitable for cyclic models. Our implementation relation encapsulates the discrete nature of time in cyclic models and takes into account not only the actions that models can perform but also the ones that they can refuse at each point of time. We prove that our implementation relation is a conservative extension of trace containment and present two alternative characterisations.

1 Introduction

Robotic systems form the basis for advances in a number of areas such as manufacturing, healthcare, and transport but also in home assistance. In fact, their use is steadily increasing in all sectors: sales increased by 30% in 2017, a new peak for the fifth year in a row [12], and according to a UK government report[1] it is expected that the value of the global market for robotics and autonomous systems will be £13 billion by 2025. A number of the areas where robotic systems are becoming ubiquitous are safety-critical and so there is a need for robotic systems that are safe, reliable and trusted.

---

[1] https://tinyurl.com/nyf64av.

This work has been supported by EPSRC grant EP/R025134/2 RoboTest: Systematic Model-Based Testing and Simulation of Mobile Autonomous Robots, the Spanish MINECO-FEDER (grant numbers DArDOS, TIN2015-65845-C3-1-R and FAME, RTI2018-093608-B-C31) and the Region of Madrid (grant number FORTE-CM, S2018/TCS-4314).

© Springer Nature Switzerland AG 2019
P. C. Ölveczky and G. Salaün (Eds.): SEFM 2019, LNCS 11724, pp. 393–409, 2019.
https://doi.org/10.1007/978-3-030-30446-1_21

In practice, developers of robotic systems produce a state-based model and then separately develop a simulation model, which is used to validate the original model and potentially also to test the system developed. Concerning time, these simulations have discrete time and are cyclic in nature, with each time slot containing a sequence of actions (see, for example, [19]). Unfortunately, there is no guarantee that the simulation model is consistent with the original model. In addition, the actual choice of simulations (test cases) to run is typically ad hoc.

This paper relates to a line of research regarding the development process for robotic systems. As usual, a state-based model (in a language, RoboChart [16], similar to those used by roboticists) is produced but the model is given a formal semantics. The model is also automatically mapped to a simulation model, in a language called RoboSim [4], that is consistent with the original model. The simulation models are also given a formal semantics, making it possible to automatically analyse or reason about them. A formal semantics for RoboSim [5] is given by mapping a RoboSim model to a variant of CSP, called tock-CSP [20, Chapter 14]. One of the benefits of this approach is that we can analyse the semantics of a RoboSim model using formal tools and methodologies available for CSP. In particular, and this is the main goal of this paper, we can formally define when an SUT conforms to a specification of the system, in this case the robot, that we would like to build. It will then be possible to systematically and automatically derive test cases from a tock-CSP model, which provides the semantics of a RoboSim model, and map it back to define simulation runs (test cases) for the simulation. As a result, we would obtain systematic test generation algorithms for automating the validation of specifications of robotic systems through simulation. This should make the development of robotic systems more efficient and effective, through removing the need for several manual, error prone activities.

The above is motivated by the observation that software testing [1,17] is the main validation technique to increase the reliability of software governing the behaviour of systems. Initially, testing was considered to be an *informal* activity but it is currently well-known that formal methods and testing can be successfully combined. There are many complementary approaches to testing, supported by tools [15,22], with a formal basis [2,6,10,11]. Formal approaches to testing usually rely on state-based models, that is, models that are in the form of labelled transition systems (LTSs); these models have states and labelled transitions between the states. LTSs have typically been used to define the operational semantics of a number of specification languages including different variants of CSP [20]. In testing from an LTS, it is normal to assume that the SUT behaves like an unknown LTS (this is called the *test hypothesis* [13]) and so testing involves comparing two LTSs. More generally, if we want to reason about the correctness of one model (a design) with respect to another model (specification) then we need to define what we mean by correctness and such notions are described as *implementation relations*. There are many implementation relations for LTSs, with different implementation relations typically differing in the observational power of the observer [7]. An observer might only be allowed to observe the actions in which the system participates. However, we can increase the capabilities of the observers. For example, we might consider situations in which they are also able to observe the *refusal* of a set of actions; it is possible that the system cannot participate in some set X of actions. In the scope of testing, this is a well-known and classical approach [18] and typically a refusal of a set X is observed through the tester only offering the actions in X and a deadlock occurring.

In this paper we present an implementation relation for timed systems where time is discrete, we are interested in using refusals while testing and do not assume that SUTs are input-enabled. Essentially, this is the framework underlying the LTSs generated by the operational semantics of tock-CSP [20] which, in turn, is the formal language to which RoboSim descriptions are translated [5]. We consider an LTS corresponding to tock-CSP rather than just RoboSim in order to aid generality. For example, there is potential to adapt the research reported in this paper for use with other simulation languages and also languages, such as Statecharts [8], that have a cyclic nature and a step semantics. The work should thus be relevant to the testing of many classes of control systems.

The rest of the paper is organised as follows. In Sect. 2 we explain the testing context and discuss related work. In Sect. 3 we introduce the main definitions and give a preliminary implementation relation: trace inclusion. In Sect. 4 we introduce our implementation relation and show that it is strictly stronger than trace inclusion. In Sect. 5 we present two alternative characterisations of our implementation relation. Finally, in Sect. 6 we give our conclusions and describe some lines for future work.

2 Testing Context and Related Work

In testing we distinguish between inputs and outputs since these play different roles and this has led to additional implementation relations. The best known implementation relation is ioco [23]. In classical ioco, there is only one type of refusal, called *quiescence*, that can be observed if the system is in a state where it cannot evolve via an internal action and, in addition, the system cannot produce an output without first receiving an input. If we are testing an SUT, then quiescence is typically observed through a timeout. Note that there is an extension of ioco to include refusals [9] that we will discuss later on.

While implementation relations such as ioco are widely used, they usually do not take into account time. Time is not a *normal* action: it is not like an input, since the tester does not control it, and it is not like an output since the SUT does not control it (the SUT cannot, for example, stop time). As a result, there are now several timed variants of ioco (all are typically called tioco) [3,14,21]. The versions of tioco differ in a number of ways, including whether quiescence is a possible observation. However, time is typically continuous and these implementation relations either do not consider refusals or they only consider one simple type of refusal (quiescence).

As previously mentioned, we were motivated by an interest in certain types of simulations (in the context of robotics). These simulations are cyclic, where each cycle is of the form of a finite sequence of observations followed by the passing of a unit of time. In addition, outputs are urgent: time cannot pass if an output is possible. An agent (robot) might potentially be in a situation in which it cannot engage in certain actions and it is desirable to model this, which can be achieved through using refusals. As a result of the above factors, we require that time is discrete and refusals can be observed. The observation of the refusal of a set A is typically represented by the situation in which the environment chooses to only engage in the actions in A and the composition of the environment and SUT deadlocks. The observation of a deadlock takes time and is usually observed through a timeout, similar to what is usually done to observe quiescence. As a result, the observation of a deadlock (and so also a refusal) should precede a duration (an action representing a unit of time passing). In this paper we develop implementation relations for timed LTSs that capture the scenario described above.

A last point of divergence with respect to ioco and its variants is that they usually assume that the SUT is *input-enabled*. Essentially, this means that the SUT should be able to react to any input provided by the tester. This assumption makes sense for a range of systems and is based on the observation that the SUT will not block input. However, there are also systems that are not input-enabled and where this is deliberate. For example, certain options/fields might be greyed-out on a webpage or simply not available; consider, for instance, the options available to an editor and to an author in a journal's manuscript system. In the context of autonomous systems, and more related to the topic of this paper, a system might switch off sensors and, in addition, sensors might fail. It is well-known that one might convert a model that is not input-enabled into one that is. However, in the type of systems that we are considering in this paper, such a completed model would less appropriately model an SUT in which certain inputs are disabled and could lead to the generation of test cases that either do not make sense from a testing perspective or contain redundancy.

Concerning related work, it might be possible to use some versions of tioco with discrete time and in some situations this will be sufficient but we prefer a *native* discrete time tioco (in addition, previous work does not consider refusals). There is a variant of ioco that we initially considered because it includes refusals and systems need not be input-enabled [9]. We depart from this work in several lines (in addition to including time). First, our refusals are observed only in stable states[2] and this has some implications. Specifically, an *internal choice* between outputs is equivalent to the same external choice while if we consider inputs then we obtain semantically different processes. Using a process algebraic notation, we have $(\tau; !o_1; stop) + (\tau; !o_2; stop) \sim (!o_1; stop) + (!o_2; stop)$ while $(\tau; ?i_1; stop) + (\tau; ?i_2; stop) \not\sim (?i_1; stop) + (?i_2; stop)$, where actions preceded by ? and ! denote, respectively, an input and an output, and τ denotes an internal action. Second, their notion of input-enabledness is more restrictive than ours: at a certain port, either all the inputs are enabled or none of them is. In their

---

[2] We will say that a state is stable if it is not possible to take a transition whose label is an output or an internal action.

notation, we have only one port and we allow several inputs to be enabled and several to not be.

3 Background and Models

In this section we define the models and notation used in this paper.

3.1 Traces and Automata

Observations made in testing will be in the form of sequences and we use ϵ for the empty sequence. Given a set A, A^* denotes the set of finite sequences of elements from A and A^ω denotes the set of infinite sequences of elements from A.

A system will interact with its environment through inputs and outputs. Throughout the paper, I and O will represent the (disjoint) input and output alphabets and we let $L = I \cup O$ denote the set of actions.

The basic, untimed, type of model we consider is an automaton in which, as usual in Automata Theory and in contrast to the standard notion of LTS, we have the concept of a final state.

Definition 1 (Automaton). *We say that* $p = (Q, q_0, L, T, F)$ *is an automaton where*

- Q *is a countable, non-empty set of states;*
- $q_0 \in Q$ *is the initial state;*
- L *is a countable set of actions;*
- $T \subseteq Q \times (L \cup \{\tau\}) \times Q$ *is the transition relation, where* $\tau \notin L$ *represents an internal action;*
- $F \subseteq Q$ *is the set of final states.*

At any time, an automaton p is in a particular state $q \in Q$. If $(q, a, q') \in T$ for action $a \in L \cup \{\tau\}$ then p can move to state q' through action a. We will sometimes use an alternative notation: a transition $(q, a, q') \in T$ can be expressed as $q \xrightarrow{a} q'$. We will also write $q \xrightarrow{a}\!\!\!\!\!/\,$ if there does not exist q' such that $(q, a, q') \in T$. The transition relation can be extended as follows.

Definition 2. *Let* $p = (Q, q_0, L, T, F)$ *be an automaton with states* $q, q' \in Q$, *visible actions* $a, a_1, \ldots, a_n \in L$, *with* $n > 1$, *and sequence of visible actions* $\sigma \in L^*$.

$$q \xRightarrow{\epsilon} q' \Leftrightarrow_{\text{def}} q = q' \text{ or } \exists q_1, \ldots, q_{n-1} \in Q : q \xrightarrow{\tau} q_1 \xrightarrow{\tau} \ldots q_{n-1} \xrightarrow{\tau} q'$$

$$q \xRightarrow{a} q' \Leftrightarrow_{\text{def}} \exists q_1, q_2 \in Q : q \xRightarrow{\epsilon} q_1 \xrightarrow{a} q_2 \xRightarrow{\epsilon} q'$$

$$q \xRightarrow{a_1 \ldots a_n} q' \Leftrightarrow_{\text{def}} \exists q_1, \ldots, q_{n-1} \in Q : q \xRightarrow{a_1} q_1 \xRightarrow{a_2} \ldots q_{n-1} \xRightarrow{a_n} q'$$

$$q \xRightarrow{\sigma} \Leftrightarrow_{\text{def}} \exists q' \in Q : q \xRightarrow{\sigma} q'$$

$$q \xRightarrow{\sigma}\!\!\!\!\!/\, \Leftrightarrow_{\text{def}} \nexists q' \in Q : q \xRightarrow{\sigma} q'$$

$$p \xRightarrow{\sigma} \Leftrightarrow_{\text{def}} q_0 \xRightarrow{\sigma}$$

As usual, we will not always distinguish between a model and its initial state. If $p = (Q, q_0, L, T, F)$, then we will identify p with its initial state q_0, and, for example, we will usually write $p \overset{\sigma}{\Longrightarrow}$ instead of $q_0 \overset{\sigma}{\Longrightarrow}$. The automaton $p = (Q, q_0, L, T, F)$ defines the language $L(p)$ of finite sequences that take p to a final state.

Definition 3. *Given automaton $p = (Q, q_0, L, T, F)$, the language $L(p) \subseteq L^*$ is defined as $L(p) = \{\sigma \in L^* | \exists q \in F : q_0 \overset{\sigma}{\Longrightarrow} q\}$.*

3.2   Timed Models

We now describe our timed model, which is an LTS in which there is a special action, $\ominus$, that denotes the passing of a unit of time. We call this action 'tock' in order to be consistent with tock-CSP [20, Chapter 14].

Definition 4 (tockLTS, timed traces). *A labelled transition system with tock (or tockLTS) is a tuple $p = (Q, q_0, I, O, T)$ where*

- *Q is a countable, non-empty set of states;*
- *$q_0 \in Q$ is the initial state;*
- *I and O are countable disjoint sets of inputs and outputs respectively, with $L = I \cup O$ being the set of visible actions;*
- *$T \subseteq Q \times (L \cup \{\tau, \ominus\}) \times Q$ is the transition relation, where $\tau \notin L$ represents the internal action, and $\ominus$ represents a tock action denoting the passage of a unit of time.*

We use $TockLTS(I, O)$ to denote the set of tockLTS with input set I and output set O.

The definition of the $\overset{\sigma}{\Longrightarrow}$ relation is similar to the one given in Definition 2, with the only difference that $\sigma \in (L \cup \{\ominus\})^*$ and, therefore, we omit it. The set of timed traces of p is defined as

$$Ttraces(p) = \{\sigma \in (L \cup \{\ominus\})^* \mid p \overset{\sigma}{\Longrightarrow}\}$$

As usual, we expect processes to have certain properties. First, processes should not have *forced inputs*, that is, for each state of a process there exists at least an outgoing transition that is not an input. Second, we should have the *urgency* of internal actions and outputs (to be consistent with how simulations operate). Third, processes should not show *Zeno behaviour*, that is, processes in which an infinite sequence of actions can occur in finite time should not be allowed. Finally, processes should have *time determinism*: processes do not branch as a result of time passing (a $\ominus$), though a process can branch through internal actions that occur after a $\ominus$.

Definition 5 (No forced inputs, urgency, Zeno behaviour, time determinism). *Let $p = (Q, q_0, I, O, T)$ be a tockLTS. Then*

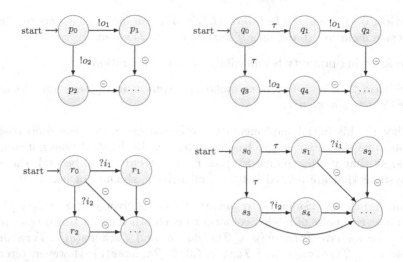

Fig. 1. Models related by (refusal) timed trace inclusion

- p *has no forced inputs if for all* $q \in Q$ *there exists* $a \in O \cup \{\tau, \ominus\}$ *such that* $q \xrightarrow{a}$.
- p *has urgent internal actions and output if for all* $q \in Q$ *and* $a \in O \cup \{\tau\}$, *if* $q \xrightarrow{a}$ *then* $q \xrightarrow{\ominus} \!\!\!\!\!/\,$.
- p *has Zeno behaviour if there exists a state* $q \in Q$ *and an infinite path from* q *with finitely many* tock *actions.*

  p *has time determinism if for all states* $q_1, q_2, q_3 \in Q$ *we have that* $q_1 \xrightarrow{\ominus}$ $q_2 \wedge q_1 \xrightarrow{\ominus} q_3$ *implies* $q_2 = q_3$.

If a tockLTS fulfills the previous properties then it also has a very interesting property: processes cannot *stop time*. In other words, it is always possible for time to progress (though certain actions might first happen). The proof of the following is a straightforward consequence of the absence of Zeno behaviour and the assumption of no forced inputs.

Proposition 1. *Let* $p = (Q, q_0, I, O, T)$ *be a tockLTS. We have that for all* $q \in Q$ *there exists an infinite path* $\sigma = \mu_1 \ominus \mu_2 \ominus \mu_3 \ldots \in ((I \cup O)^*\{\ominus\})^\omega$ *such that* $q \xRightarrow{\sigma}$ *and* $\forall i, \mu_i \in (I \cup O)^*$.

3.3   A First Implementation Relation

If the environment can only observe traces of visible actions and time (i.e. it cannot observe refusals) then we have one natural implementation relation: the requirement that all observations (traces) that can be made when interacting with the SUT are also observations that can be made when interacting with the specification.

Definition 6. *Let p and q be two tockLTSs. We say that p conforms to q under timed trace inclusion if and only if* $Ttraces(p) \subseteq Ttraces(q)$.

The following property is immediate from the definition.

Proposition 2. *The timed trace inclusion relation is reflexive and transitive but need not be symmetric.*

Although this initial implementation relation has some nice properties, in addition to its simplicity, it also has some drawbacks. First, it does not consider refusals, so that its discriminatory power can be enhanced. Second, there are some systems that are related but that, intuitively, should not be.

Example 1. Let us consider the fragments of models given in Fig. 1(top and bottom). These two pairs of models conform to each other under timed trace inclusion because we have $Ttraces(p) \subseteq Ttraces(q)$ and $Ttraces(q) \subseteq Ttraces(p)$, $Ttraces(r) \subseteq Ttraces(s)$ and $Ttraces(s) \subseteq Ttraces(r)$. However, often we will want to be able to distinguish between such processes. On the one hand, we expect both conformances between p and q because outputs cannot be controlled by the environment. In other words, a choice between outputs should work exactly as the corresponding internal choice. For example, even though $?o_1$ and $?o_2$ are available at p_0, a user/tester cannot choose which of them will be performed (testers cannot block output). On the other hand, r and s should not be equivalent. The issue is that the tester or user can choose between two inputs in the same way that one can choose among the available options in a vending machine. If we have the corresponding internal choice and we reach, for example, state s_1 then input $?i_2$ is not available. The implementation relation that we present in the next section satisfies all of these properties.

4   An Implementation Relation Including Refusals

So far, the discussion has only allowed inputs, outputs, and the passing of time to be observed. In this section we explore the notion of refusals in our setting and how they can be added as observations, with this leading to a stronger implementation relation.

Recall that we are interested in models that are cyclic/have a step semantics: a sequence of actions occurs without time (in the model) passing and then there is a tock action. A refusal of a set $X \subseteq L$ is typically observed through the tester only being willing to engage in the actions in X and the composition of the tester and the SUT deadlocking. Since deadlocks are observed (in testing) through timeouts, the observation of a refusal takes time and so we only allow a refusal to be observed immediately before a tock action. Since outputs and internal actions are urgent, this means that a refusal can only be observed in a stable state. Note that we might have combined a refusal with the $\ominus$ that follows this; we chose not to because this is not the usual use of refusals and also because we would like to have the potential to extend the work to allow an observation to end with a refusal.

Definition 7 (Stable state). *Let* $p = (Q, q_0, I, O, T)$ *be a tockLTS, with* $L = I \cup O$. *We say that the state* $q \in Q$ *is* stable *if for all* $a \in O \cup \{\tau\}$ *we have that* $q \not\xrightarrow{a}$.

Given a set $X \subseteq L$ *of actions, we use* $R(X)$ *to denote the refusal of set* X. *Further, we let* $\mathcal{R}(L) = \{R(X) | X \subseteq L\}$ *denote the set of all possible refusals.*

We can extend the transition relation of a tockLTS with refusals as follows.

Definition 8 (Refusal). *Let* $p = (Q, q_0, I, O, T)$ *be a tockLTS and* $X \subseteq I \cup O$. *For all* $q \in Q$ *we write* $q \xrightarrow{R(X)} q$ *if the following hold:*

1. q is stable and
2. for all $x \in X$ *we have that* $q \not\xrightarrow{x}$.

This constitutes the observation of the refusal $R(X)$, *that is, at a given stable state the model cannot perform the actions belonging to* X.

It follows that the observation of a refusal $R(X)$ implies that no element $a \in X \cup O \cup \{\tau\}$ can be accepted in state q: $q \not\xrightarrow{a}$.

Note also that the second condition from the definition implies that we include $R(X)$ as a refusal if all the actions in X can be refused, even if there are other actions from $L \setminus X$ that can be refused. Therefore, we do not only include *maximal* refusals. In fact, doing this would lead to some undesirable effects (this will be clearer after we give our implementation relation using refusals).

We can then give the set of refusal traces of a tockLTS in which, as we already said, $p \xrightarrow{\sigma}$ is defined in terms of $p \xrightarrow{x}$, in the usual way. Recall, however, that a refusal can only be observed immediately before a tock action. We therefore obtain a set of potential refusal traces (those that satisfy this condition) and we call these *timed refusal traces*. Also note that a timed refusal trace cannot end in a refusal since the observation of a refusal takes time (and so must be followed by a $\ominus$). As a result, this set is not prefix closed.

Definition 9 (Timed refusal traces). *Let* L *be a set of actions. We define the set of* timed refusal traces *over* L *as* $RT(L) = (L^* \cup (\mathcal{R}(L)\{\ominus\}))^*$.

Let $p = (Q, q_0, I, O, T)$ *be a tockLTS, with* $L = I \cup O$. *The set of* timed refusal traces *of* p *is defined as*

$$TRtraces(p) = \{\sigma \in (L \cup \{\ominus\} \cup \mathcal{R}(L))^* | p \xrightarrow{\sigma}\} \cap RT(L)$$

We then obtain a second implementation relation in the natural way: we do not require the inclusion of (timed) traces but the inclusion of timed refusal traces.

Definition 10. *Let* I *and* O *be countable disjoint sets of inputs and outputs, respectively. Let* p *and* q *be two elements of* $TockLTS(I, O)$. *We say that* p *conforms to* q *under* timed refusal trace inclusion *if and only if* $TRtraces(p) \subseteq TRtraces(q)$.

First, we present an example showing some relations between models and why maximal refusals do not provide the expected implementation relation.

Example 2. Consider again the fragments of models p and q given in Fig. 1(top). We have that we cannot add refusals to traces in states p_0, q_0, q_1 and q_3 because they are not stable. Therefore, we have $TRtraces(p) \subseteq TRtraces(q)$ and $TRtraces(q) \subseteq TRtraces(p)$.

Consider now r and s given in Fig. 1(bottom). Assuming that $I = \{?i_1, ?i_2\}$ and $O = \emptyset$, we have that s has the timed refusal traces $R(\{?i_1\})\ominus$ and $R(\{?i_2\})\ominus$ and these are not timed refusal traces of r. Essentially, the τ transitions mean that s moves to a state in which it can refuse one input ($?i_2$ in s_1 and $?i_1$ in s_2) before performing a $\ominus$.

We have $TRtraces(r) \subseteq TRtraces(s)$, so that r conforms to s under timed refusal trace inclusion, but the converse is not the case. This shows that an external choice between inputs is a good implementation of the internal choice between the same inputs.

These last two fragments are also useful to show why we cannot restrict ourselves to compute only maximal refusal sets. If we would do this, we would have that the timed refusal traces of r would be the same but the ones corresponding to s would be $R(\{?i_2\})?i_1 \cdots, R(\{?i_1\})?i_2 \cdots, R(\{?i_1\})\ominus, R(\{?i_2\})\ominus, \ldots$ and we would not have timed trace inclusion.

We can now compare this implementation relation with trace inclusion introduced in Definition 6. The proof of the following result follows from the fact that, for a process r, $Ttraces(r) = TRtraces(r) \cap L^*$.

Proposition 3. *Let I and O be countable disjoint sets of inputs and outputs, respectively. Let p and q be two elements of $TockLTS(I, O)$. If p conforms to q under timed refusal trace inclusion then p conforms to q under timed trace inclusion.*

However, the converse is not the case as the following result shows.

Proposition 4. *Let I and O be countable disjoint sets of inputs and outputs, respectively. There exist p and q in $TockLTS(I, O)$ such that p conforms to q under timed trace inclusion but p does not conform to q under timed refusal trace inclusion.*

Proof. In order to prove this it is sufficient to give an example of such tockLTSs. Consider r and s depicted in Fig. 1(bottom). In Example 1 we showed that $Ttraces(r) = Ttraces(s)$. Therefore, s conforms to r under timed trace inclusion. On the contrary, in Example 2 we showed that $TRtraces(s) \not\subseteq TRtraces(r)$. Therefore, s does not conform to s under refusal timed trace inclusion.

To summarise, r conforms to s under timed trace inclusion but not under timed refusal trace inclusion. The result therefore holds.

We therefore obtain the following.

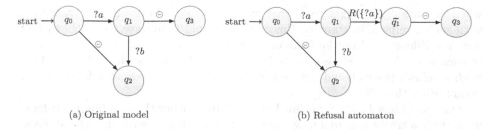

(a) Original model   (b) Refusal automaton

Fig. 2. A refusal can only happen immediately before a duration or tock $\ominus$

Theorem 1. *Timed refusal trace inclusion is strictly stronger than timed trace inclusion.*

This tells us that if we can observe timed refusal traces in testing then we have a more powerful implementation relation than just timed trace inclusion. It is also the case that if the environment (e.g. the user) can observe timed refusal traces (through, for example, the refusal of actions being observed as a result of options not being available on a screen) then it is insufficient to test for trace inclusion: the user might consider an SUT p to be faulty with respect to a specification q even though they have the same sets of timed traces.

5   Alternative Characterisations

In this section we provide two alternative characterisations of timed refusal trace inclusion. First, we develop an approach in which a tockLTS p is transformed into an automaton whose language describes the set of timed refusal traces of p. This gives us the potential to use automata theory and algorithms when reasoning about timed refusal trace inclusion. We then show how we can model timed refusal trace inclusion in terms of observers and the observations they can make. This shows that our definition of timed refusal trace inclusion corresponds to what can be observed, with respect to the SUT, in our setting and so confirms that it is the right implementation relation for our context.

5.1   Using an Automaton

Trace inclusion corresponds to a relation between the languages defined by the automata corresponding to two LTS. The benefit is that it is possible to use standard results and algorithms from formal language theory. This is particularly useful if the processes are deterministic finite state automata since there are efficient algorithms for many standard problems, including language inclusion (that is, trace inclusion in our setting). We now show how we can generate an automaton whose traces are exactly the timed refusal traces of a tockLTS q.

In order to explore one approach that might be used to achieve this, consider the fragment of a model in Fig. 2(a). This can refuse all actions other than $?b$

when in state q_1. It might seem that we can simply add a self-loop transition, with such a refusal, in state q_1. However, we would then have the problem that such a self-loop need not be followed by a $\ominus$ action. For example, the inclusion of such a self-loop in state q_1 would allow refusal traces such as $?aR(\{?a\})?b$. Such a refusal trace should not be allowed since it has a refusal followed by an action other than $\ominus$.

One possible solution is outlined in Fig. 2(b). Rather than adding a self-loop, we include a transition, to a new state $\tilde{q}_1$, that is labelled with the refusal. From $\tilde{q}_1$ there is only one possible action, which is $\ominus$. We also require that $\tilde{q}_1$ is not a final state of the automaton. As a result, any path that reaches a final state and includes the transition from q_1 to $\tilde{q}_1$ must follow this transition by a transition with label $\ominus$. Note that we require the notion of a final state and so the model is an *automaton* and not a tockLTS.

We now formally define the automaton $\mathcal{M}(p)$ that includes these refusals.

Definition 11. *Let $p = (Q, q_0, I, O, T)$ be a tockLTS. Let us consider the subset of states that can evolve by performing $\ominus$, that is, $Q_\ominus = \{q \in Q | q \xrightarrow{\ominus}\}$. We define a set of fresh states $\tilde{Q} = \{\tilde{q} | q \in Q_\ominus\}$ (i.e. $Q \cap \tilde{Q} = \emptyset$). The new set of states $\tilde{Q}$ has a state for each state of $Q_\ominus$.*

We let $\mathcal{M}(p)$ denote the automaton $(Q \cup \tilde{Q}, q_0, I \cup O \cup \mathcal{R}(L), T', F)$ where

- $T' = T \cup \{(q, R(X), \tilde{q}) | q \in Q_\ominus \wedge q \xrightarrow{R(X)}\} \cup \{(\tilde{q}, \ominus, q') | q \in Q_\ominus \wedge q \xrightarrow{\ominus} q'\}$.
- $F = Q$.

The following result shows that the previous construction is correct.

Theorem 2. *Let $p = (Q, q_0, I, O, T)$ be a tockLTS. We have that $TRtraces(p) = L(\mathcal{M}(p))$.*

Proof. First, observe that both sets are subsets of $RT(L)$, where $L = I \cup O$. We will prove a slightly stronger result than the one stated before. Specifically, we will prove that for all $\sigma \in RT(L)$, we have that σ takes p to state q if and only if q is a final state of $\mathcal{M}(p)$ and σ takes $\mathcal{M}(p)$ to state q.

We use proof by induction on the length of σ. The base case, with σ being the empty sequence, is immediate.

Inductive hypothesis: the result holds if σ has length less than k ($k > 0$). Let us suppose that σ has length k and σ takes one of p and $\mathcal{M}(p)$ to state q. By the definition of $RT(L)$, $\sigma = \sigma_1 a$ for some $a \in L \cup \{\ominus\}$ (i.e. sequences in $RT(L)$ cannot end in refusals). There are two cases to consider. First, if σ_1 does not end with a refusal then, by the inductive hypothesis, we have that σ_1 reaches the same states in p and $\mathcal{M}(p)$. In addition, by construction we have that a takes p and $\mathcal{M}(p)$ to the same state and so the result follows. The second case is where σ_1 ends in a refusal and so $\sigma = \sigma_2 R(X)\ominus$ for some $X \subseteq L$ and $\sigma_2 \in RT(L)$. By the inductive hypothesis, σ_2 takes p and $\mathcal{M}(p)$ to the same state q_1. By construction, $R(X)\ominus$ takes p and $\mathcal{M}(p)$ to the same state q and so the result follows.

5.2 Using Observers

Implementation relations should correspond to the ability of the environment, or a tester, to distinguish between processes, with it typically being the case that we require that all observations that can be made of the SUT are also observations that can be made when interacting with the specification (see, for example, [23]). In this section we define the notion of an observer, in our context, and how such an observer interacts with a tockLTS. This will provide an alternative, but equivalent, characterisation of timed refusal trace inclusion.

We follow the classical approach of ioco [23], in which a special action θ is included in an observer to denote the observation of a refusal. An observer will be placed in parallel with the SUT, with the two synchronising on common actions in $I \cup O \cup \{\ominus\}$; θ synchronises with refusals. Before we include a formal definition, we informally explain the properties we expect an observer to have in order to observe the refusal of X in state u.

1. There is a transition from u labelled by θ, with the parallel composition being defined so that the other transitions are given priority over this (if the SUT and observer are both able to take an action $a \neq \theta$ then they take such an action, in preference to communicating through a θ).
2. For all $x \in X$, there is a transition from u that has label x. This ensures that if p can engage in an action $x \in X$ when in the current state then the parallel composition of p and the observer can engage in action x and so a refusal will not be observed (since x is given priority over θ).
3. For all $a \in O$, there is a transition from u labelled with u. Similar to the previous case, the prioritisation of such actions over θ means that this ensures that a θ transition cannot occur if p can perform an internal action or an output. As a result, if the process (with which u is interacting) is not in a stable state then a refusal cannot happen.
4. There are no transitions from u labelled with an action from $L\backslash(X \cup O)$. This ensures that the observer can only change state by engaging in an action from X or through taking a transition with label θ.

The combination of the above ensures that the observer can only take the transition with label θ if the process p is in a stable state and also no actions from X are possible - i.e. if and only if p can refuse X. In order to ensure that a refusal can only be observed in a stable state we will require observers to have the following property.

Definition 12 (Observer). *Let I and O be countable disjoint sets of inputs and outputs, respectively. An observer u is an automaton with action set $L = I \cup O \cup \{\ominus, \theta\}$ that satisfies the following properties for each state q of u:*

1. *$q \not\xrightarrow{\tau}$;*
2. *if $q \not\xrightarrow{\theta}$ then for all $a \in O$ we have that $q \xrightarrow{a}$;*
3. *if $q \xrightarrow{\ominus}$ then for all $a \in O$ we have that $q \not\xrightarrow{a}$;*
4. *if (q, θ, q') is a transition of u then $\ominus$ is the only action available in state q'.*

We let $\mathcal{U}(I, O)$ denote the set of observers with input set I and output set O.

The last rule ensures that a refusal must be followed by a $\ominus$. The second rule is the standard condition that a tester is able to observe outputs; the exception is because the observation of a refusal takes time and so a θ must be followed by a $\ominus$.

We can now define a parallel composition operator $\,]\!|\,$ between a process $p \in TockLTS(I, O)$ and an observer $u \in \mathcal{U}(I, O)$. This is similar to the operators for LTS [23] but we choose to enrich the observations made with refusal sets.

Definition 13 (Synchronised parallel communication). *Let I and O be countable disjoint sets of inputs and outputs, respectively. Let $p = (Q, q_0, I, O, T) \in TockLTS(I, O)$ and $u = (Q', q_0', I \cup O \cup \{\ominus, \theta\}, T', Q') \in \mathcal{U}(I, O)$. The composition of the observer u and the model p, denoted by $u \,]\!|\, p$, is an automaton $(Q \times Q', (q_0, q_0'), I \cup O \cup \mathcal{R}(I \cup O) \cup \{\ominus\}, T'', F)$ in which $F = Q \times Q'$ and T'' is defined as follows:*

- *If $(q_1, \tau, q_2) \in T$ then for all $q' \in Q'$ we have $((q_1, q'), \tau, (q_2, q')) \in T''$.*
- *If $(q_1, a, q_2) \in T$ and $(q_1', a, q_2') \in T'$, with $a \in I \cup O \cup \{\ominus\}$, then we have $((q_1, q_1'), a, (q_2, q_2')) \in T''$.*
- *Let $X \subseteq I \cup O$. If $(q_1, \ominus, q_2) \in T$, $(q_1', \theta, q_2') \in T'$ then $((q_1, q_1'), \mathcal{R}(X), (q_1, q_2')) \in T''$ is the case if the following conditions hold:*
  - *for all $a \in I \cup O$ we have that either there does not exist q_3 such that $(q_1, a, q_3) \in T$ or there does not exist q_3' such that $(q_1', a, q_3') \in T'$.*
  - *for all $a \in X$ we have that there exists q_3' such that $(q_1', a, q_3') \in T'$.*

Note that, since $p \in TockLTS(I, O)$ and $(q_1, \ominus, q_2) \in T$, we know that q_1 is a stable state.

The sets of observations that the observer u can make of p, denoted by $obs^\theta(u, p)$, are given by the following:

$$obs^\theta(u, p) =_{def} \{\sigma \in (I \cup O \cup \mathcal{R}(L) \cup \{\ominus\})^* \mid u \,]\!|\, p \stackrel{\sigma}{\Longrightarrow}\}$$

Note that in the last rule of the composition, since q_1 may evolve via $\ominus$ then we have that it must be a stable state (for all $a \in O \cup \{\tau\}$ we have that $q_1 \not\stackrel{a}{\rightarrow}$); this follows from the fact that p is a tockLTS and tockLTSs have urgent outputs and internal actions (Definition 5). In this rule, also note that we *discard* the state reached after the performance of $\ominus$ from q_1: the composition makes p remains in the same state, according to how refusals are added as transitions to tockLTSs (Definition 8).

The following shows how observations relate to timed refusal traces and is a result of the definition of $u \,]\!|\, p$ and the definition of timed refusal traces (Definition 9).

Proposition 5. *Let I and O be countable disjoint sets of inputs and outputs, respectively. Given $\sigma \in (I \cup O \cup \{\ominus\} \cup \mathcal{R}(L))^*$ and p in $TockLTS(I, O)$, there is an observer $u \in \mathcal{U}(I, O)$ such that $\sigma \in obs^\theta(u, p)$ if and only if σ is a prefix of a timed refusal trace of p.*

Note that in the above result σ need not be a timed refusal trace of p since σ could end in a refusal; to make this a timed refusal trace it would be necessary to add the $\ominus$ that follow this refusal. The following result is immediate from Proposition 5.

Theorem 3. *Let I and O be countable disjoint sets of inputs and outputs, respectively. Given p and q in $TockLTS(I,O)$ we have that p conforms to q under timed refusal trace inclusion if and only if, for all $u \in \mathcal{U}(I,O)$ we have that $obs^\theta(u,p) \subseteq obs^\theta(u,q)$.*

Since the observers capture the observations that can be made, this tells us that timed refusal trace inclusion is a suitable implementation relation for our scenario.

6   Conclusions and Future Work

There has been significant interest in testing from formal models since this brings the potential for automated systematic testing. In order to test from a formal model one requires an implementation relation that says what it means for the system under test (SUT) to be a correct implementation of the specification. This paper considered cyclic models, in which behaviours are of the form of sequences of observable actions separated by discrete time intervals. The work was motivated by the use of cyclic simulators in a number of areas, including robotic systems.

Although many implementation relations are variants of the well known ioco implementation relation, ioco and its timed versions were not suitable for cyclic models. As a result, there was a need to define novel implementation relations that take into account the discrete nature of time in cyclic models and also not only the actions that models can perform but also the ones that they can refuse at each point of time. We introduced the notion of a timed refusal trace and also our main implementation relation: timed refusal trace inclusion. We introduced two alternative characterisations of timed refusal trace inclusion. First, we showed how one can define an automaton whose language is exactly the set of timed refusal traces of a model; this allows one to express correctness in terms of formal language containment for automata. We also showed how one can define timed refusal trace inclusion in terms of the observations that can be made by an observer interacting with processes (the specification and SUT); this demonstrates that timed refusal trace inclusion corresponds to the notion of observation for our models.

There are several possible lines of future work. It should be possible to extend classical test generation algorithms to test for timed refusal trace inclusion. There is also the potential to enrich models to include, for example, probabilities or continuous variables (i.e. hybrid systems). Finally, we plan to carry out case studies with robotic systems.

References

1. Ammann, P., Offutt, J.: Introduction to Software Testing, 2nd edn. Cambridge University Press, Cambridge (2017)
2. Binder, R.V., Legeard, B., Kramer, A.: Model-based testing: where does it stand? Commun. ACM **58**(2), 52–56 (2015)
3. Briones, L.B., Brinksma, E.: A test generation framework for *quiescent* real-time systems. In: Grabowski, J., Nielsen, B. (eds.) FATES 2004. LNCS, vol. 3395, pp. 64–78. Springer, Heidelberg (2005). https://doi.org/10.1007/978-3-540-31848-4_5
4. Cavalcanti, A., Ribeiro, P., Miyazawa, A., Sampaio, A., Conserva Filho, M., Didier, A.: RoboSim reference manual. Technical report, University of York (2019)
5. Cavalcanti, A., et al.: Verified simulation for robotics. Sci. Comput. Program. **174**, 1–37 (2019)
6. Cavalli, A.R., Higashino, T., Núñez, M.: A survey on formal active and passive testing with applications to the cloud. Ann. Telecommun. **70**(3–4), 85–93 (2015)
7. van Glabbeek, R.: The linear time-branching time spectrum I. The semantics of concrete, sequential processes. In: Bergstra, J.A., Ponse, A., Smolka, S.A. (eds.) Handbook of Process Algebra, chapter 1, North Holland (2001)
8. Harel, D.: Statecharts: a visual formulation for complex systems. Sci. Comput. Program. **8**(3), 231–274 (1987)
9. Heerink, L., Tretmans, J.: Refusal testing for classes of transition systems with inputs and outputs. In: 19th Joint International Conference on Protocol Specification, Testing, and Verification and Formal Description Techniques, FORTE/PSTV 1999, pp. 23–38. Chapman & Hall (1997)
10. Hierons, R.M., et al.: Using formal specifications to support testing. ACM Comput. Surv. **41**(2), 9:1–9:76 (2009)
11. Hierons, R.M., Bowen, J.P., Harman, M. (eds.): Formal Methods and Testing. LNCS, vol. 4949. Springer, Heidelberg (2008). https://doi.org/10.1007/978-3-540-78917-8
12. World Robotics 2018: International Federation of Robotics. Statistical Department (2018)
13. ISO/IEC JTCI/SC21/WG7, ITU-T SG 10/Q.8: Information Retrieval, Transfer and Management for OSI; Framework: Formal Methods in Conformance Testing. Committee Draft CD 13245–1, ITU-T proposed recommendation Z.500. ISO - ITU-T (1996)
14. Krichen, M., Tripakis, S.: Conformance testing for real-time systems. Form. Methods Syst. Des. **34**(3), 238–304 (2009)
15. Marinescu, R., Seceleanu, C., Le Guen, H., Pettersson, P.: A research overview of tool-supported model-based testing of requirements-based designs. In: Advances in Computers, chapter 3, vol. 98, pp. 89–140. Elsevier (2015)
16. Miyazawa, A., Ribeiro, P., Li, W., Cavalcanti, A., Timmis, J., Woodcock, J.: RoboChart: modelling and verification of the functional behaviour of robotic applications. Softw. Syst. Model. (2019, to appear)
17. Myers, G.J., Sandler, C., Badgett, T.: The Art of Software Testing, 3rd edn. Wiley, Hoboken (2011)
18. Phillips, I.: Refusal testing. Theor. Comput. Sci. **50**(3), 241–284 (1987)
19. Rohmer, E., Singh, S.P., Freese, M.: V-REP: aversatile and scalable robot simulation framework. In: 26th IEEE/RSJ International Conference on Intelligent Robots and Systems, IROS 2013, vol. 1, pp. 1321–1326. IEEE Computer Society (2013)

20. Roscoe, A.W.: Understanding Concurrent Systems. Texts in Computer Science. Springer, London (2010). https://doi.org/10.1007/978-1-84882-258-0
21. Schmaltz, J., Tretmans, J.: On conformance testing for timed systems. In: Cassez, F., Jard, C. (eds.) FORMATS 2008. LNCS, vol. 5215, pp. 250–264. Springer, Heidelberg (2008). https://doi.org/10.1007/978-3-540-85778-5_18
22. Shafique, M., Labiche, Y.: A systematic review of state-based test tools. Int. J. Softw. Tools Technol. Transf. **17**(1), 59–76 (2015)
23. Tretmans, J.: Model based testing with labelled transition systems. In: Hierons, R.M., Bowen, J.P., Harman, M. (eds.) Formal Methods and Testing. LNCS, vol. 4949, pp. 1–38. Springer, Heidelberg (2008). https://doi.org/10.1007/978-3-540-78917-8_1

Modular Indirect Push-Button Formal Verification of Multi-threaded Code Generators

Anton Wijs[✉] and Maciej Wiłkowski

Eindhoven University of Technology, 5600 MB Eindhoven, The Netherlands
a.j.wijs@tue.nl, m.wilkowski@student.tue.nl

Abstract. In model-driven development, the automated generation of a multi-threaded program based on a model specifying the intended system behaviour is an important step. Verifying that such a generation step semantically preserves the specified functionality is hard. In related work, code generators have been formally verified using theorem provers, but this is very time-consuming work, should be done by an expert in formal verification, and is not easily adaptable to changes applied in the generator. In this paper, we propose, as an alternative, a push-button approach, combining equivalence checking and code verification with previous results we obtained on the verification of generic code constructs. To illustrate the approach, we consider our SLCO framework, which contains a multi-threaded Java code generator. Although the technique can still only be applied to verify individual applications of the generator, its push-button nature and efficiency in practice makes it very suitable for non-experts.

1 Introduction

Model-driven software development (MDSD) [23] aims to make the software development process more transparent and less error-prone. In an MDSD workflow, Domain Specific Languages (DSLs) are used to model the system under development, and model transformations are applied to initially refine the model, and finally generate source code that either fully or partially implements the program. The development of concurrent software is particularly complex, and techniques to support developers are sorely needed. Formal verification can play a vital role in that regard, to ensure that the artifacts produced in an MDSD workflow are functionally correct.

The correctness of models and source code has been investigated for many years, for instance see [8,19,21,25,46]. On the other hand. the *transformation* of a model to another model or code has received less attention [2]. To ensure that the final program is correct, it must be proven that the source code captures the intended functionality as specified by the models.

Verifying model tranformations, that transform an artifact into another artifact, is fundamentally more complex than verifying the artifacts themselves [2].

P. C. Ölveczky and G. Salaün (Eds.): SEFM 2019, LNCS 11724, pp. 410–429, 2019.
https://doi.org/10.1007/978-3-030-30446-1_22

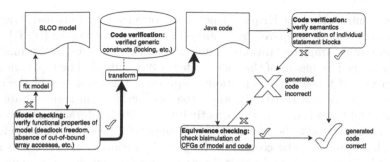

Fig. 1. Model-to-code verification workflow.

This is particularly true for model-to-code transformations (or code generators), due to the usual difference in abstraction level between input model and output source code, and the usual lack of formal semantics of the target programming language. Still, in recent years, techniques have been developed to *directly* verify code generators (and compilers) [7,9,24,26,27]. These techniques use theorem provers [6,15,30,37]. Their advantage is that they can establish that the generators are guaranteed to provide correct output, but their drawback is the effort that is required to construct the proofs, the expertise needed to do so, and their inflexibility when the requirements of the generator change.

Alternatively, *indirect* approaches try to prove for a concrete input model that a generator produces correct output, every time the generator is applied. This is in practice often good enough, as the programs produced by generators are deployed, not the generators themselves, and it is much less complex to verify the output of a transformation rather than the transformation itself [2,7]. However, most existing indirect approaches do not support multi-threaded code, have limited scalability, or check the preservation of particular properties, as opposed to full semantics preservation [1,13,33,38–40].

In this paper, we propose an indirect technique to verify semantics preservation for generators of multi-threaded code. Its main features are that (1) it is push-button, requiring no additional input from the user when the generator is applied, and (2) it is modular, meaning that it scales linearly as the program size increases. We demonstrate our technique in the context of the *Simple Language of Communicating Objects* (SLCO) framework [35], which includes a generator for multi-threaded Java code, but the technique can be adapted to other DSLs and programming languages.

An overview of the technique workflow is given in the Activity diagram of Fig. 1. Initially, a given model is formally verified, by means of the MCRL2 model checker [11], to determine whether it satisfies a list of desired properties (for more information on this, see [35]). If it does, it can be subjected to code generation. Verification of this step is the topic of the current paper, and is done in two procedures that can be performed independently. In one procedure, for each state machine in the model, corresponding with one thread in the source code, a *control flow graph* (CFG) is extracted from both the model and the code. These

CFGs are interpreted as Kripke structures, converted to Labelled Transition Systems, and finally compared by means of *bisimulation checking* [16,31]. In the other procedure, implementations of individual state changes in the model are formally verified by means of the code verifier VERCORS [8]. The separation logic specifications of those implementations, expressing the semantics of the model, are automatically generated. Together, the two verification results imply that the individual threads have been correctly implemented. Interaction between the threads is guaranteed to be correct, since the generator uses a mechanism for this that we have proven to be correct in the past, by means of the VERIFAST code verifier [21,47]. All in all, we exploit the strengths of model checking, equivalence checking, and code verification to achieve verified MDSD.

Structure of the Paper. Section 2 presents the preliminary concepts. SLCO and code generation are discussed in Sect. 3. In this section, the formal semantics of SLCO and an updated code generator are presented for the first time. Our code generator verification technique is explained in Sect. 4. Its implementation and experimental results are discussed in Sect. 5. Related work is considered in Sect. 6, and finally, Sect. 7 contains our conclusions.

2   Preliminaries

The semantics of a system can be formally expressed by a Labelled Transition System (LTS) as presented in Definition 1.

Definition 1 (Labelled Transition System). *An LTS $\mathcal{G}$ is a tuple $(\mathcal{S}, \mathcal{A}, \mathcal{T}, \hat{s})$, with*

- $\mathcal{S}$ *a finite set of states;*
- $\mathcal{A}$ *a set of action labels;*
- $\mathcal{T} \subseteq \mathcal{S} \times \mathcal{A} \times \mathcal{S}$ *a transition relation;*
- $\hat{s} \in \mathcal{S}$ *the initial state.*

Action labels in $\mathcal{A}$ are denoted by a, b, c, etc. A transition $(s, a, s') \in \mathcal{T}$, or $s \xrightarrow{a} s'$ for short, denotes that LTS $\mathcal{G}$ can move from state s to state s' by performing the a-action.

To compare LTSs, we use strong bisimulation, which is an equivalence relation, i.e., it is reflexive, symmetric and transitive.

Definition 2 (Strong bisimulation). *A binary relation B between two LTSs $\mathcal{G}_1 = (\mathcal{S}_1, \mathcal{A}_1, \mathcal{T}_1, \hat{s}_1)$ and $\mathcal{G}_2 = (\mathcal{S}_2, \mathcal{A}_2, \mathcal{T}_2, \hat{s}_2)$ is a strong bisimulation iff for all $s \in \mathcal{S}_1$ and $t \in \mathcal{S}_2$, $s \, B \, t$ implies:*

1. *if $s \xrightarrow{a} s'$ then $t \xrightarrow{a} t'$ and $s' \, B \, t'$;*
2. *if $t \xrightarrow{a} t'$ then $s \xrightarrow{a} s'$ and $s' \, B \, t'$.*

Two states s, t are (strongly) bisimilar, denoted by $s \leftrightarrow t$, iff there is a bisimulation relation B such that $s \, B \, t$. Two LTSs $\mathcal{G}_1 = (\mathcal{S}_1, \mathcal{A}_1, \mathcal{T}_1, \hat{s}_1)$, $\mathcal{G}_2 = (\mathcal{S}_2, \mathcal{A}_2, \mathcal{T}_2, \hat{s}_2)$ are (strongly) bisimilar, denoted by $\mathcal{G}_1 \leftrightarrow \mathcal{G}_2$, iff $\hat{s}_1 \leftrightarrow \hat{s}_2$.

An alternative way to define the semantics of systems is by means of a *Kripke structure*, which is labelled on the states as opposed to the transitions.

Definition 3 (Kripke structure). *A Kripke structure is a tuple* $\mathcal{K} = (\mathcal{S}, \mathcal{P}, \mathcal{T}, \mathcal{L}, \hat{s})$, *with*

- $\mathcal{S}$ *a finite set of states;*
- $\mathcal{P}$ *a finite set of atomic propositions;*
- $\mathcal{T} \subseteq \mathcal{S} \times \mathcal{S}$ *a total transition relation;*
- $\mathcal{L} : \mathcal{S} \to 2^{\mathcal{P}}$ *a state labelling function.*
- $\hat{s} \in \mathcal{S}$ *the initial state.*

With $s \to t$, we denote that $(s, t) \in \mathcal{T}$. We refer to the domain of LTSs as **LTS**, and to the domain of Kripke structures as **KS**.

In [29,36], a translation from Kripke structures to LTSs is defined that preserves bisimilarity.[1]

Definition 4 (Kripke structure into LTS embedding). *The embedding* **lts** : **KS** $\to$ **LTS** *is defined as* **lts**$(K) = (\mathcal{S}', \mathcal{A}, \mathcal{T}, \hat{s})$ *for arbitrary Kripke structures* $K = (\mathcal{S}, \mathcal{P}, \mathcal{T}, \mathcal{L}, \hat{s})$, *where*

- $\mathcal{S}' = \mathcal{S} \cup \{\bar{s} \mid s \in \mathcal{S}\}$, *with for all* $s \in \mathcal{S}$, *we have* $\bar{s} \notin \mathcal{S}$;
- $\mathcal{A} = 2^{\mathcal{P}} \cup \{\perp\}$;
- $\mathcal{T} \subseteq \mathcal{S}' \times \mathcal{A} \times \mathcal{S}'$ *is the least relation satisfying the following rules for all* $s, t \in \mathcal{S}$:

$$\frac{}{s \xrightarrow{\perp} \bar{s}} \qquad \frac{}{\bar{s} \xrightarrow{\mathcal{L}(s)} s} \qquad \frac{s \to t}{s \xrightarrow{\mathcal{L}(t)} t}$$

The fresh symbol $\perp$ is used to indicate that from the target state of a $\perp$-transition, an outgoing transition will be present with the original (Kripke) label of the target state of the latter transition.

3   SLCO and the Generation of Java Code

Figure 2 presents the meta-model of version 2.0 of SLCO. An SLCO model consists of a number of *classes*, instances of those classes called *objects*, multiple *channels* via which these objects can communicate with each other, and user-defined *actions*. Each class specifies the potential behaviour of a system component, and consists of a finite number of *state machines*, a set of *object-local variables* that can be accessed by each state machine in the class, and *ports* that are connected to channels, via which state machines can communicate with state machines in other objects. Variables can be of type *Boolean*, *Integer* or *Byte*, or Array of any of those types.

A state machine consists of a number of *states*, including one *initial state*, and *transitions* between those states, indicating possible state changes. Furthermore, a state machine may have a finite number of *state machine-local variables*,

---

[1] We omit a definition of bisimilarity for Kripke structures. For the details, see [36]. Also, in contrast to [29,36], the translation as defined here does not treat transitions between equally labelled states as internal LTS steps, since no such transitions are present in our Kripke structures (see Sect. 4.2).

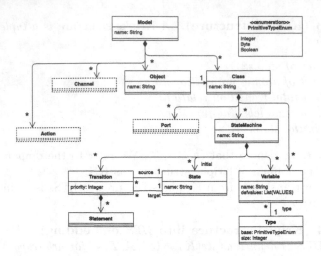

Fig. 2. The metamodel of SLCO 2.0.

and with each transition, a (possibly empty) sequence (or *block*) of *statements* is associated. Those statements can access (read and update) both the state machine-local variables and the variables of the instance (object) of the class in which the state machine resides. A transition can be *fired* if the current state of the state machine is the source state of the transition, and the associated block is *enabled*. A block is enabled iff its first statement is enabled. The order in which the outgoing transitions of a particular state should be considered for firing can be specified using *transition priorities*, but we do not consider these in the current paper. Here, we consider three types of statement:

- **Expression**: a statement evaluating to either **true** or **false**, e.g. x = 0. It is enabled iff it evaluates to **true**.
- **Assignment**: a statement assigning a value to either a state machine-local or object-local variable, e.g. x := 1. It is always enabled.
- **Composite**: a sequence of assignments, optionally preceded by an expression, e.g. [x = 0; x := 1]. It is enabled iff its first substatement is enabled.

In the current paper, we do not consider channels and ports (hence those concepts are marked with dashed lines in Fig. 2), focussing instead completely on concurrent behaviour represented by multiple state machines within a class. Hence, in the following, we do not discuss channels, nor do we consider actions. For more information on these concepts, see the SLCO tool paper [35]. The complete SLCO language also has the statements **send** and **receive**, for sending and receiving messages over channels. Nevertheless, in Sect. 4, we explain that including channels (and hence **send** and **receive** statements), actions and transition priorities actually requires only a minor extension of our verification approach. In other words, the fragment of SLCO that we focus on in this paper is sufficient to demonstrate our approach.

$$\text{assign}\ \frac{s \Rightarrow (x := e)s' \land \downarrow_\sigma (x := e)}{\langle\sigma, s\rangle \xrightarrow{x:=e} \langle\sigma[\xi_\sigma(e)/x], s'\rangle} \qquad \text{expr}\ \frac{s \Rightarrow (e)s' \land \xi_\sigma(e)}{\langle\sigma, s\rangle \xrightarrow{e} \langle\sigma, s'\rangle}$$

$$\text{comp}\ \frac{s \Rightarrow ([e; x_1 := e_1; \ldots; x_n := e_n])s' \land \xi_\sigma(e) \land \downarrow_\sigma (x_1 := e_1; \ldots; x_n := e_n)}{\langle\sigma, s\rangle \xrightarrow{[e;x_1:=e_1;\ldots;x_n:=e_n]} \langle\sigma[\xi_\sigma(e_1)/x_1] \cdots [\xi_\sigma(e_n)/x_n], s'\rangle}$$

$$\text{nonterm}\ \frac{s \Rightarrow (E)s' \land \uparrow_\sigma (E)}{\langle\sigma, s\rangle \xrightarrow{E} \lightning} \qquad \text{par}\ \frac{\langle\sigma, s, S\rangle \xrightarrow{E} \langle\sigma', s', S'\rangle}{\langle\sigma, s||t, S, T\rangle \xrightarrow{E} \langle\sigma', s'||t, S', T\rangle}$$

$$\langle\sigma, t||s, S, T\rangle \xrightarrow{E} \langle\sigma', t||s', S', T\rangle$$

Fig. 3. SLCO SOS rules for assignment, expression, and composite statements

When a transition is fired, its block of statements is executed. The formal semantics of this for *basic* SLCO, a version of SLCO in which each transition has up to one statement, is presented by means of SOS rules in Fig. 3. SLCO models can be transformed to basic SLCO models by introducing additional states and transitions, and breaking up multiple-statement transitions into single-statement transition sequences. For the SOS rules, we denote with $s \Rightarrow (E)s'$ that in the state machine, there is a transition with statement E from state s to state s'. Furthermore, we reason about the current state of an SLCO model by means of *situations*. A situation is a tuple $\langle\sigma, s_1|| \ldots ||s_n\rangle$, with σ a total function mapping the variables in the model to values of the appropriate types, and $s_1|| \ldots ||s_n$ the combination of the current states $s_1, \ldots, s_n$ of state machines 1 to n. The conclusions of the SOS rules are transitions in an LTS capturing the semantics of an SLCO model, where the LTS states represent situations of the model.

The predicate $\downarrow_\sigma (E)$ evaluates to **true** iff execution of statement E under σ (i.e., the variables have the values defined by σ) successfully terminates. In particular, no out-of-bound accesses of array variables occur. The negation of this is denoted by $\uparrow_\sigma (E)$ and whenever this is applicable, trying to execute E results in reaching the *error situation* $\lightning$ (rule **nonterm**). Function $\xi_\sigma(e)$ is used to evaluate expression e, and in case e is of type Boolean, $\xi_\sigma(e)$ holds iff $\downarrow_\sigma (e)$ and e evaluates to **true**, and $\sigma[\xi_\sigma(e)/x]$ denotes an updated σ, in which $\xi_\sigma(e)$ has been assigned to variable x, the latter not being of type Array (but possibly an element of an array).

As indicated by SOS rule **par**, SLCO has an interleaving semantics. If, in a given situation with a state s, a statement E can be fired, then so can it be fired in a situation consisting of the parallel composition of several states including s. Furthermore, note that the rules define that the execution of individual statements is *atomic*, i.e., cannot be interrupted by the execution of other statements.

Generation of Multi-threaded Java Code. The SLCO framework includes a generator for multi-threaded Java code, in which each state machine in a given SLCO model is transformed into a separate thread. Figure 4 presents part of an example SLCO model, named RE, on the left, and part of the translation of state machine SM1, contained in RE, on the right. Checking for the code-equivalent of enabled transitions and executing associated statement translations is done in the method exec as part of the SM1 Java thread. Depending on the current

```
                                       1   ...
                                       2   public void exec() {
                                       3     // variable to store non-deterministic choices
                                       4     int j_choice;
                                       5     while(true) {
 1    model RE {                        6       switch(j_currentState) {
 2      classes                         7       case S0:
 3      P {                             8         j_choice = j_randomGenerator.nextInt(2);
 4        variables Boolean[3] x        9         switch(j_choice) {
 5        state machines               10         case 0:
 6        SM1 {                        11           if (execute_S0_0()) {
 7          variables Integer i        12             j_currentState = RE.j_State.S1;
 8          initial S0 states S1       13           }
 9          transitions               14           break;
10            S0 -> S1 {              15         case 1:
11              [not x[i]; x[i+1]:=x[i]] 16           if (execute_S0_1()) {
12            }                        17             j_currentState = RE.j_State.S1;
13            S0 -> S1 {}              18           }
14            S1 -> S0 {              19           break;
15              i := (i+1) % 2;        20         }
16            }                        21       case S1:
17          }                          22         if (execute_S1_0()) {
18        SM2 { ... }                  23           j_currentState = RE.j_State.S0;
19      }                              24         }
20      objects p: P(x:=[False,True,True]) 25       break;
21    }                                26       default:
                                       27         return;
                                       28       }
                                       29     }
                                       30   }
                                       31   ...
```

Fig. 4. An example SLCO model (left) and part of its Java implementation (right)

state (j_currentState), the execution of the statements of a translated outgoing transition is attempted, and if successful, the associated state change is applied. Non-determinism is translated by the code generator by using a random number generator (line 8 in the code) to randomly select the code of an outgoing transition. Note that for each SLCO transition, a dedicated *transition method* is implemented that executes a translation of the block associated to the transition.

In Fig. 5, implementations of the transition methods execute_S0_0 and execute_S1_0 are given, which map one-to-one on the blocks in RE. Each method returns a Boolean value reflecting whether or not the statement block was successfully executed. Note that for shared (object-local) variables, a locking mechanism is required, to ensure that no inconsistent behaviour occurs due to multiple threads accessing and updating the same variables simultaneously. This locking mechanism is based on the concept of *ordered locking* [18]: each variable is associated with a separate lock, the locks are sorted, and acquiring locks should be done in that specified order. In the example, each element of array x has its own lock, and the locks for x[i] and x[i + 1] both need to be acquired before the update can be performed. After adding the lock IDs to an array java_lockIDs (lines 3–4 in method execute_S0_0), and sorting the IDs (line 5), the locks are requested from the Java object java_kp (line 6). After evaluation and/or execution of the statement, the locks are released (lines 8 and 12).

Finally, instances of the java_Keeper class, such as java_kp in Fig. 5, manage the locks of the implementation of an SLCO object in an array of reentrant locks; given a number of lock IDs in an array l, a lock method tries to acquire the locks in the specified order, and an unlock method releases the locks in that order.

```
1   boolean execute_S0_0() {
2       // [not x[i]; x[i + 1] := x[i]]
3       java_lockIDs[0] = 0 + i;
4       java_lockIDs[1] = 0 + i + 1;
5       Arrays.sort(java_lockIDs,0,2);
6       java_kp.lock(java_lockIDs, 2);
7       if (!(!(x[i]))) {
8           java_kp.unlock(java_lockIDs, 2);
9           return false;
10      }
11      x[i + 1] = x[i];
12      java_kp.unlock(java_lockIDs, 2);
13      return true;
14  }
```

```
1   boolean execute_S1_0() {
2       // i := (i + 1) % 2
3       i = (i + 1) % 2;
4       return true;
5   }
```

Fig. 5. Methods execute_S0_0 and execute_S1_0 for RE

4   Verification of Code Generation

4.1   Verification Overview

Figure 1 presents an Activity diagram of our workflow for the verification of the code generator. In the current section, we discuss the various steps from the *transform* activity onwards, and reason about the fact that together, these steps provide a correctness proof for individual applications of the code generator. As input, we expect an SLCO model that is functionally correct, i.e., that has the desired functional properties and the absence of out-of-bound array accesses.

The code generator uses a library of *generic* constructs that can be reused each time the generator is applied on a model. In general, the content of such a library is DSL-specific. For SLCO, we have added implementations for the *channel* construct, and the ordered locking scheme. Implementations of generic constructs can be formally verified once, and then safely reused in each application of the generator. In the past, we have verified both constructs using the VERIFAST code verifier [21,47]. For the ordered locking scheme, we have verified that no deadlocks can be introduced by locking, and that the scheme ensures that atomicity of the statements is preserved. Hence, as long as the generated code adheres to the scheme it is guaranteed that concurrent executions of statements do not interfere with each other, and that no deadlocks occur when trying to acquire locks. It is straightforward to check this for our generated code, since the locks are only accessed via generic lock and unlock methods that are part of the verified ordered locking scheme implementation, and that have been proven to implement lock acquisition and release correctly, using VERIFAST.

Isolating the locking scheme has multiple advantages for the remaining verification task. First of all, the locking steps can be ignored, and we can focus on the behavioural aspects specified by the model. Second of all, it makes the remaining verification task modular; as the shared variables are the only means for the state machines in the model to communicate, the interaction of the corresponding threads in the program is guaranteed to be correct. Furthermore, as statement atomicity is preserved, we know that no inconsistent system states can be reached when the threads execute in parallel. What remains is to prove that each individual state machine is correctly translated into a thread.

```
data Ins = Conditional Expr Block
         | Switch Expr [(Expr, Block)]
         | Nondeterm [Block]
         | Loop Expr Block
         | Assign VariableRef Expr
         | MethodInv MethodCall
```

Fig. 6. Definition of the BIR main concepts

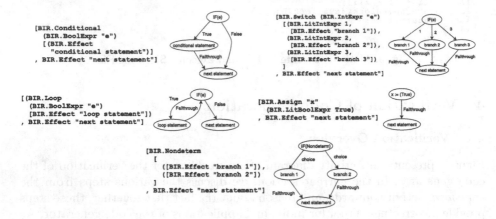

Fig. 7. Translating BIR to CFG

To do the latter, each time the generator is applied on a given SLCO model, two verification steps can be performed independently: checking for equivalence of the CFGs of each state machine and its corresponding Java thread, to determine whether they have equivalent control flows, and verifying semantics preservation when the blocks of individual transitions are translated to Java methods, to determine whether the individual steps in the control flows are equivalent. In Sect. 4.2, we discuss the former. The latter is addressed in Sect. 4.3.

The two steps nicely complement each other, together addressing the semantics (Fig. 3). The CFG equivalence checking step establishes that in all reachable program states, each transition method will be considered for execution iff the corresponding transition is an outgoing transition of the corresponding model state. The transition method verification step establishes that execution of a transition method indeed has the intended effect on the current state, i.e., all transition methods correctly implement the block of their transition. In Sect. 4.4, we discuss what is required to support the complete SLCO language, including the use of channels, actions, and transition priorities.

4.2   Constructing and Comparing CFGs

To extract accurate CFGs from SLCO state machines and Java threads, we have defined the *Behaviour Intermediate Representation* (BIR) language. This language has enough concepts to capture both types of CFGs: on the one hand, it can reflect how the Java code implements the statements of an SLCO model,

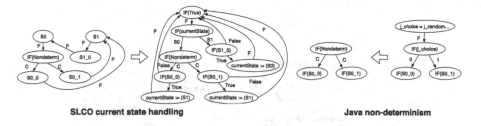

SLCO current state handling   **Java non-determinism**

Fig. 8. Transforming the SLCO and Java CFGs of RE.

and therefore support if-then, switch, and loop constructs. On the other hand, it supports modelling concepts such as non-deterministic choice.

Figure 6 lists a definition of the main BIR instructions. An `Expr` can be evaluated and a `Block` is a sequence of instructions. Furthermore:

- A `Conditional` guards a `Block` with an `Expr` condition. If the latter evaluates to `true`, the `block` can be executed. It can be used to represent `if-then` Java constructs.
- A `Loop` expresses that execution of the involved `Block` should be repeated as long as the involved `Expr` condition evaluates to `true`.
- A `Switch` branches to multiple instructions, where the branches represent the different possible outcomes of evaluating the first `Expr` instruction. It can be used to represent Java `switch` constructs.
- A `Nondeterm` branches to multiple instructions non-deterministically. It can represent non-deterministic choice in SLCO models.
- An `Assign` expresses that the evaluation of the `Expr` instruction should be assigned to the given variable reference.
- A `MethodInv` represents a method invocation.

BIR descriptions of state machines and threads can be represented by CFGs. How partial CFGs are derived from the various BIR instructions is shown in Fig. 7. For the `Conditional`, `Switch`, `Loop`, `Assign` and `Nondeterm` instructions, direct translations are given (`MethodInv` is processed similar to `Assign`), with `BIR.Effect` being used as a placeholder for nested instructions that need to be translated recursively. In addition, there are various types of expression, to reflect their type and whether they are literals or more complex expressions. In the CFGs, nodes are labelled with BIR instructions, and edges are either labelled with `Fallthrough`, representing unconditional flow of execution, `choice`, representing an option for a non-deterministic choice, or some value, representing the result of an evaluation for a branching instruction (IF-node).

While the CFG of a Java program can be directly obtained by transforming all constructs to BIR instructions, the transformation of SLCO models is more involved: first, each statement block is transformed, after which for each state machine state, an additional instruction is created, and those state instructions are connected with each other via the BIR representations of the blocks. On the

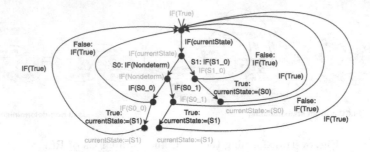

Fig. 9. The LTS produced for the RE example, both for the model and the code.

left in Fig. 8, the CFG of SM1 (Fig. 4) is given, where F is short for `Fallthrough`, C is short for `choice`, and S0_0, S0_1 and S1_0 represent the various transitions.

Once the CFGs of an SLCO model and corresponding generated Java code have been constructed, some transformations have to be applied on them to bring them semantically together. First of all, nodes representing SLCO blocks must have the same label as their corresponding Java translations (their actual semantic equivalence is addressed in Sect. 4.3). Besides this, we apply two other transformations: (1) we introduce a mechanism on the SLCO side to keep track of the current state, as this is also done on the Java side, and (2) we directly introduce nondeterminism on the Java side by means of the `Nondeterm` instruction. We have proven manually that both transformations are semantics preserving. Figure 8 presents the application of those transformations on the RE example. On the SLCO side, the nodes representing state machine states are removed, and the control flow is replaced by a `switch` instruction involving a new variable `currentState`, to keep track of the current state, inside a `Loop` instruction with condition `true`, i.e., an infinite loop. The instructions representing the various blocks are turned into IF-nodes, and are connected to the new `switch` instruction via the appropriate value of `currentState`. After each block instruction, the current state is updated if execution of the block was successful. Otherwise, the state machine remains in the same state.

On the Java side, every occurrence of the `j_choice` variable, which involves obtaining a new random value followed by a `switch` instruction using `j_choice`, is replaced by a new `Nondeterm` instruction.

When the CFGs have been transformed, what remains is to remove the edge labelling, such that the CFGs can be interpreted as Kripke structures. Labels `Fallthrough` and `choice` can be safely removed, but the conditional labels need to be preserved, in order to maintain the guarded control flow. As the nested instructions inside `Conditional`, `Switch` and `Loop` all have exactly one incoming edge, coming from an IF-node (Fig. 7), we can move the conditional edge labels to the target nodes of those edges. For instance, in case of `Switch` in Fig. 7, we relabel the `branch 1` node to `1: branch 1`, and so on.

Finally, we transform the resulting Kripke structures to LTSs (Definition 4), and check whether the LTSs are strongly bisimilar (Definition 2). In case of the RE example, the two LTSs are in fact identical. Figure 9 presents one of those LTSs. For ease of presentation, each state $\hat{s}$ (black circle) in Fig. 9 in fact represents a state s together with a companion state $\bar{s}$, connected via a $\bot$-transition from s to $\bar{s}$ and a transition labelled with the associated grey label in Fig. 9 back from $\bar{s}$ to s. All in- and outgoing transitions of a state $\hat{s}$ in Fig. 9 are connected to s (as opposed to $\bar{s}$). The top state in the figure is the initial state. This is indicated by the large incoming arrow head.

4.3   Verification of Transition Methods

To verify the transformation of each SLCO block, we use the VERCORS tool set [8]. With it, we can check whether Java code satisfies a specification written in permission-based separation logic [4]. Its verification engine is VIPER [28].

```
1   /*@
2   pure boolean updated_S0_0_x(int x_index, int i0, boolean b1,
3       boolean x_old) {
4           return ((x_index == i0) ? b1 : x_old);
5   }
6
7   given int i;
8   given boolean[] x;
9   given boolean b0;
10  given int i0;
11  given boolean b1;
12  invariant x != null;
13  context (\forall* int slco_i ; 0 <= slco_i < x.length ;
14      Perm(x[slco_i],write));
15  ensures b0 ==> \result == true;
16  ensures !b0 ==> \result == false;
17  ensures b0 ==> (\forall* int slco_i ; 0 <= slco_i < x.length ;
18      x[slco_i] == updated_S0_0_x(slco_i, i0, b1, \old(x[slco_i])));
19  ensures !b0 ==> (\forall* int slco_i ; 0 <= slco_i < x.length ;
20      x[slco_i] == \old(x[slco_i]));
21  @*/
22  boolean execute_S0_0() {
23      // SLCO statement: [not x[i]; x[i + 1] := x[i]]
24      /*@ assume 0 <= i < x.length; @*/
25      /*@ b0 = !(x[i]); @*/
26      if (!(!(x[i]))) { return false; }
27      /*@ assume 0 <= i + 1 < x.length; @*/
28      /*@ assume 0 <= i < x.length; @*/
29      /*@ i0 = i + 1; b1 = x[i]; @*/
30      x[i + 1] = x[i];
31      return true;
32  }
33
34  /*@
35  given int i;
36  given boolean[] x;
37  given int i_old;
38  invariant x != null;
39  ensures \result == true;
40  ensures (i == (i_old + 1) % 2);
41  @*/
42  boolean execute_S1_0() {
43      // SLCO statement: i := (i + 1) % 2
44      /*@ i_old = i; @*/
45      i = (i + 1) % 2;
46      return true;
47  }
```

Fig. 10. Methods execute_S0_0 and execute_S1_0 for RE, with VERCORS specifications.

We have extended our SLCO-to-Java code generator with a feature to generate a list of the transition methods implementing the SLCO blocks of a given SLCO model, with VERCORS specifications. In Fig. 10, methods execute_S0_0 and execute_S1_0 of the RE example model are listed with their specifications. The specifications formally express the effect of executing SLCO statements, as defined by the corresponding SOS rules (Fig. 3). Note the absence of locking, as this can be abstracted away safely, making it easier to construct VERCORS specifications.

To isolate the methods from the complete program, we specify which variables each method can access (the given ... statements at lines 7–8 and 35–36). Furthermore, for all arrays, we specify that they have been properly initialised (invariant x != null, lines 12 and 38), and in case array elements are updated by the method, appropriate write permission is given (lines 13–14).

To properly express postconditions, ghost variables are used. In case of an SLCO Assignment translation, such as execute_S1_0, the old value of the updated variable (here i) is stored (in a variable i_old), which allows us to specify the effect (line 40). Furthermore, we specify that **true** is returned (line 39).

In case a Composite statement is translated (execute_S0_0), the specification is more elaborate, as multiple variables can be updated, and there is optionally a guard. Ghost variables are used to store all intermediate results, such that they can be referred to in the specification. Note that before each array access, an assumption has been added to specify that no out-of-bound array accesses can be performed, relying on the SLCO model having been verified in this regard. Depending on the evaluation of the guard, the method either returns **true** or **false** (lines 15–16), and the array is either updated or not (lines 17–20). Finally, when an array is updated in a Composite statement, an auxiliary function is defined (for example, see lines 2–5), since array elements may be updated multiple times in a single Composite, and in general, when expressions are used to compute array indices, this cannot be detected statically. In case an element is updated multiple times, only the final update should be specified in the postcondition, and the auxiliary function allows us to relate each element to their final update.

The final case, not applicable in the example, is that a method implements an SLCO Expression. The postcondition of such a method addresses that **true** is returned iff a guard implementing the Expression evaluates to **true**.

4.4 Supporting the Complete SLCO Language

The approach, as presented in the previous sections, verifies that a model written in a specific fragment of the SLCO language is correctly transformed into multithreaded Java code. To support the complete SLCO language, the verification approach needs to be extended in a number of ways. In this section, we discuss these extensions, which require only minor changes to the approach as it exists currently. Implementing those extensions is planned for future work.

1. SLCO has the concept of *channel* to model the communication between state machines of different objects by means of message passing. In earlier work, we

have formally verified that a (lock protected) Java channel correctly implements the semantics of the SLCO channel [10]. This implementation is now part of our library of generic constructs. To support channels, the verification approach proposed in the current paper only needs to be extended to match **send** and **receive** statements in the CFGs of SLCO state machines and their corresponding Java threads. As those statements are implemented using the verified **send** and **receive** methods of the generic implementation of SLCO channel, the actual *effect* of sending and receiving a message via a channel does not need to be verified anymore.

2. User-defined *actions* are SLCO statements that allow the definition of model-specific instructions. For instance, these can refer to calling standard Java library methods. Our verification approach can be extended straightforwardly to match the actions in the CFGs of the state machines and their corresponding Java threads.

3. Finally, SLCO supports *transition priorities* that allow the user to specify the order in which transitions should be fired. In Java, this order is implemented by placing implementations of the associated statements inside `if-then-else` constructs. First of all, the BIR language (more specifically, the `Nondeterm` instruction) must be extended with priorities. Second of all, a transformation needs to be defined to transform `if-then-else` constructs implementing those priorities in Java to `Nondeterm` instructions, similar to how implementations of non-determinism are transformed to such instructions in the current approach.

5   Implementation and Experiments

The SLCO framework has been developed in PYTHON 3, using TEXTX [14] for meta-modelling and JINJA2[2] for model transformations. Hence, the generation of VERCORS specifications has also been implemented in PYTHON. The CFG extractor, including the transformations from CFG to Kripke structures and from Kripke structures to LTSs, has been written in HASKELL. For bisimulation checking of LTSs, we use the MCRL2 toolset, which has a tool called *ltscompare* that implements efficient bisimulation checking with complexity $\mathcal{O}(m \log n)$, with n the number of states and m the number of transitions in an LTS [16,31].

To validate the effectiveness of our approach, we ran a number of experiments on a MacBook Pro with a 3.1 GHz Intel Core i5 processor and 16 GB RAM, running macOS Mojave. We selected 50 models from the BEEM benchmark suite [32]. These models stem from well-known examples and case studies, modelling mutual exclusion algorithms, communication protocols, controllers, leader election algorithms, planning and scheduling problems, and puzzles. Originally written in the DVE language, the models have first been translated to SLCO using a model transformation. This is a straightforward task, as all language concepts of DVE can be translated to similar concepts in SLCO. In most cases, a model contains a single object with one or more state machines. Furthermore,

---

[2] http://jinja.pocoo.org.

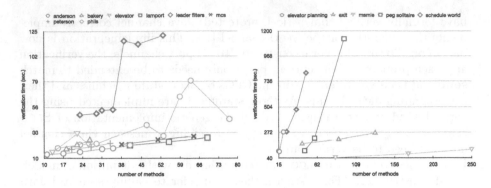

Fig. 11. VERCORS verification runtimes

in many cases, thousands of lines of code were produced when translating the models to Java code. The largest instance overall that we considered, msmie.4, resulted in 12,157 lines of source code, implementing a program with ten threads.

Due to the modular approach of our verification procedure, allowing us to isolate individual state machines, the CFG equivalence checking step never required more than 0.5 s to process, given a model, all its state machines and their translations. Regarding the time required for the verification of transition methods, Fig. 11 presents the runtime results for VERCORS for a representative selection of 13 models. For each model, we have processed multiple instances, between three and eight, that are all part of the BEEM benchmark set. This allows us to investigate how the runtime scales as the number of transition methods is increased. For the other models, similar scalability results have been obtained. As expected, in most cases, the runtime scales linearly, but not to the same degree for all models. For instance, for the msmie instances, although they have many methods, the verification time is very short, since the methods are not complex, most of them containing only unguarded assignments. On the other hand, the peg solitaire instances have transition methods with guards and relatively complex expressions to refer to array elements, resulting in the runtime increasing much more rapidly as the number of methods is increased. For a few models, such as phils, this phenomenon results in the runtime not linearly increasing as the number of methods is increased. Some instances have more methods than others, yet fewer of those are guarded, or involve array accesses.

Concluding, the CFG equivalence checking step scales very well, and can be used to reason about the CFGs of large models and programs. Moreover, for the verification of transition methods, VERCORS is very suitable, but to improve scalability, we will have to work on reducing the amount of verification work, for instance by detecting functional duplicates among the transition methods. In case of the BEEM models, many models contain such duplicates. In those cases, the involved state machines are all very similar, specifying the same computation to be performed on different data. In future work, we plan to exploit that.

6   Related Work

Equivalence checking has been applied in the past to directly verify semantics preservation of model transformation rules, for instance see [5,20,34,44]. This approach requires that a model transformation can be formally defined, and hence that both the source and target modelling language has a formal semantics. Furthermore, programming languages describe systems at a much lower abstraction level than modelling languages, making equivalence checking more directly suitable for model-to-model than for model-to-code transformations. In the current paper, we use equivalence checking as well, but we also apply CFG transformations and code verification to bridge the gap between abstraction levels.

For an overview of applying formal verification on model-to-code transformations, see [2]. Formal verification of a statechart-to-Java generation algorithm using the Isabelle/HOL theorem prover [30] is described in [7]. Similar to our approach, their proof aims to demonstrate bisimulation between model and code, but their modelling language does not support variables. They prove once that the generator algorithm is correct, but note that for full verification, it may be more suitable to verify on a case-by-case basis, like we do, to ensure that the implementation of the generator algorithm is correct as well.

In [39], a Java code generator framework based on QVT is presented. The KIV theorem prover [15] is used to prove particular security properties. Staats and Heimdahl [38], on the other hand, apply model checking on both the model and the code to verify the preservation of selected LTL properties. In [40], DSL-generated C code is checked using the SPIN model checker [19]. A PROMELA model is generated in which the generated C code is embedded, and LTL properties are formulated for checking. Pnueli et al. [33] propose the CVT tool that uses refinement checking to detect whether properties, proven to be satisfied by a given Statemate model, have been preserved in generated C code. In [13], the preservation of properties is verified by means of transforming Event-B models [3] to specifications for the Dafny code verification tool [25].

In contrast to all the approaches above, we check for the preservation of the complete model semantics. In our view, a list of concrete properties can serve to verify that a model is correct, although the question always remains whether such a list completely covers the intended functionality. For a code generation step, on the other hand, it must be guaranteed that the generated code exactly implements what the model specifies. If this is the case, then any property satisfied by the model will be preserved by the code generator. Additionally, most of the above approaches do not support the generation of multi-threaded code, even though constructing such programs is particularly error-prone.

Ab Rahim and Whittle [1] propose an interactive technique in which the user initially supplies assertions about generated code that are later added automatically to code using a separate model tranformation. A software model checker is applied to verify that assertions hold in generated code. Our technique, on the other hand, does not require additional user input, and due to its modular approach, scales much better than one directly using model checking.

Techniques for compiler verification are similar to code generator verification techniques, and can be used to further strengthen the development workflow to verify that code is correctly compiled into an executable. In [26,27], the Coq theorem prover [6] is used to both implement and verify a C compiler. A compiler for the block diagram language LUSTRE[17] is verified using Coq in [9]. Finally, Kumar et al. [24] use the HOL4 theorem prover [37] to verify that programs described in their language, called CakeML, are compiled correctly. These results are impressive, yet we question how flexible the techniques are when the code generation or compilation procedure needs to be updated.

Finally, software model checking techniques, such as [12,22], offer another approach to verify code. Tools such as Java PathFinder [41] could be useful to verify parts of the generated code. We plan to investigate how such techniques can be applied effectively in the near future.

7   Conclusions

In this paper, we have presented a push-button formal verification technique to indirectly verify generators of multi-threaded code, that can be automatically performed each time the generator is applied. Besides its push-button nature, its main strength is its modularity, which is enabled by our earlier results [10,47] on verifying generic constructs that are used to implement the communication between threads. This allows us to focus the technique proposed in the current paper to focus on individual threads in isolation. Due to this, it can verify the generation of thousands of lines of code in a few minutes. Furthermore, it can be easily adapted to changes, and made applicable to other DSLs and programming languages, as long as mappings to CFGs via our BIR language and the generation of separation logic specifications are constructed and updated accordingly.

Concerning future work, we have so far proven manually that transformations, such as the ones illustrated in Fig. 8, are correct. We will work on formally proving this using a theorem prover. Furthermore, as the current performance bottleneck is transition methods verification, we will work on the detection of functionally equivalent transitions, to reduce the amount of verification work. Furthermore, we will extend our method with support for the complete SLCO language, and further extensions including timed behaviour [42,43,45]. Finally, we will also apply the same approach to other DSLs and programming languages, in particular for the generation of software for graphics processors.

References

1. Ab Rahim, L., Whittle, J.: Verifying semantic conformance of State Machine-to-Java code generators. In: Petriu, D.C., Rouquette, N., Haugen, Ø. (eds.) MODELS 2010. LNCS, vol. 6394, pp. 166–180. Springer, Heidelberg (2010). https://doi.org/10.1007/978-3-642-16145-2_12
2. Ab Rahim, L., Whittle, J.: A survey of approaches for verifying model transformations. Softw. Syst. Model. 14, 1003–1028 (2013)

3. Abrial, J.R.: Modeling in Event-B: System and Software Engineering. Cambridge University Press, Cambridge (2010)
4. Amighi, A., Haack, C., Huisman, M., Hurlin, C.: Permission-based separation logic for multithreaded Java programs. Log. Methods Comput. Sci. **11**(1–2), 1–66 (2015)
5. Baldan, P., Corradini, A., Ehrig, H., Heckel, R., König, B.: Bisimilarity and behaviour-preserving reconfigurations of open Petri Nets. In: Mossakowski, T., Montanari, U., Haveraaen, M. (eds.) CALCO 2007. LNCS, vol. 4624, pp. 126–142. Springer, Heidelberg (2007). https://doi.org/10.1007/978-3-540-73859-6_9
6. Bertot, Y., Castéran, P.: Interactive Theorem Proving and Program Development: Coq' Art: The Calculus of Inductive Constructions. Springer, Heidelberg (2004). https://doi.org/10.1007/978-3-662-07964-5
7. Blech, J., Glesner, S., Leitner, J.: Formal verification of Java code generation from UML models. Fujaba Days **2005**, 49–56 (2005)
8. Blom, S., Darabi, S., Huisman, M., Oortwijn, W.: The VerCors tool set: verification of parallel and concurrent software. In: Polikarpova, N., Schneider, S. (eds.) IFM 2017. LNCS, vol. 10510, pp. 102–110. Springer, Cham (2017). https://doi.org/10.1007/978-3-319-66845-1_7
9. Bourke, T., Brun, L., Dagand, P.E., Leroy, X., Pouzet, M., Rieg, L.: A formally verified compiler for Lustre. In: PLDI, ACM SIGPLAN Notices, vol. 52, pp. 586–601. ACM (2017)
10. Bošnački, D., et al.: Towards modular verification of threaded concurrent executable code generated from DSL models. In: Braga, C., Ölveczky, P.C. (eds.) FACS 2015. LNCS, vol. 9539, pp. 141–160. Springer, Cham (2016). https://doi.org/10.1007/978-3-319-28934-2_8
11. Bunte, O., et al.: The mCRL2 toolset for analysing concurrent systems. In: Vojnar, T., Zhang, L. (eds.) TACAS 2019. LNCS, vol. 11428, pp. 21–39. Springer, Cham (2019). https://doi.org/10.1007/978-3-030-17465-1_2
12. Chaki, S., Clarke, E., Groce, A., Jha, S., Veith, H.: Modular verification of software components in C. In: ICSE, pp. 385–395. IEEE (2003)
13. Dalvandi, M., Butler, M., Rezazadeh, A.: From Event-B models to Dafny code contracts. In: Dastani, M., Sirjani, M. (eds.) FSEN 2015. LNCS, vol. 9392, pp. 308–315. Springer, Cham (2015). https://doi.org/10.1007/978-3-319-24644-4_21
14. Dejanović, I., Vaderna, R., Milosavljević, G., Vuković, Ž.: TextX: a Python tool for domain-specific languages implementation. Knowl.-Based Syst. **115**, 1–4 (2017). https://doi.org/10.1016/j.knosys.2016.10.023
15. Ernst, D., Pfähler, J., Schellhorn, G., Haneberg, D., Reif, W.: KIV: overview and verifythis competition. Int. J. Softw. Tools Technol. Transf. **17**(6), 677–694 (2015)
16. Groote, J., Jansen, D., Keiren, J., Wijs, A.: An O(m log n) algorithm for computing stuttering equivalence and branching bisimulation. ACM Trans. Comput. Log. **18**(2), 13:1–13:34 (2017)
17. Halbwachs, N., Caspi, P., Raymond, P., Pilaud, D.: The synchronous data flow programming language LUSTRE. Proc. IEEE **79**(9), 1305–1320 (1991)
18. Havender, J.: Avoiding deadlock in multitasking systems. IBM Syst. J. **7**(2), 74–84 (1968)
19. Holzmann, G.: The SPIN Model Checker: Primer and Reference Manual. Addison-Wesley Professional (2003)
20. Hülsbusch, M., König, B., Rensink, A., Semenyak, M., Soltenborn, C., Wehrheim, H.: Showing full semantics preservation in model transformation - a comparison of techniques. In: Méry, D., Merz, S. (eds.) IFM 2010. LNCS, vol. 6396, pp. 183–198. Springer, Heidelberg (2010). https://doi.org/10.1007/978-3-642-16265-7_14

21. Jacobs, B., Smans, J., Philippaerts, P., Vogels, F., Penninckx, W., Piessens, F.: VeriFast: a powerful, sound, predictable, fast verifier for C and Java. In: Bobaru, M., Havelund, K., Holzmann, G.J., Joshi, R. (eds.) NFM 2011. LNCS, vol. 6617, pp. 41–55. Springer, Heidelberg (2011). https://doi.org/10.1007/978-3-642-20398-5_4

22. Jhala, R., Majumdar, R.: Software model checking. ACM Comput. Surv. **41**(4), 21:1–21:54 (2009)

23. Kleppe, A., Warmer, J., Bast, W.: MDA Explained: The Model Driven Architecture: Practice and Promise. Addison-Wesley Professional (2005)

24. Kumar, R., Myreen, M., Norrish, M., Owens, S.: CakeML: a verified implementation of ML. In: POPL, ACM SIGPLAN Notices, vol. 49, pp. 179–191. ACM (2014)

25. Leino, K.R.M.: Dafny: an automatic program verifier for functional correctness. In: Clarke, E.M., Voronkov, A. (eds.) LPAR 2010. LNCS (LNAI), vol. 6355, pp. 348–370. Springer, Heidelberg (2010). https://doi.org/10.1007/978-3-642-17511-4_20

26. Leroy, X.: Formal verification of a realistic compiler. Commun. ACM **52**(7), 107–115 (2009)

27. Leroy, X.: Formal proofs of code generation and verification tools. In: Giannakopoulou, D., Salaün, G. (eds.) SEFM 2014. LNCS, vol. 8702, pp. 1–4. Springer, Cham (2014). https://doi.org/10.1007/978-3-319-10431-7_1

28. Müller, P., Schwerhoff, M., Summers, A.J.: Viper: a verification infrastructure for permission-based reasoning. In: Jobstmann, B., Leino, K.R.M. (eds.) VMCAI 2016. LNCS, vol. 9583, pp. 41–62. Springer, Heidelberg (2016). https://doi.org/10.1007/978-3-662-49122-5_2

29. De Nicola, R., Vaandrager, F.: Action versus state based logics for transition systems. In: Guessarian, I. (ed.) LITP 1990. LNCS, vol. 469, pp. 407–419. Springer, Heidelberg (1990). https://doi.org/10.1007/3-540-53479-2_17

30. Nipkow, T., Paulson, L., Wenzel, M.: Isabelle/HOL: A Proof Assistant for Higher-Order Logic. Springer, Heidelberg (2002). https://doi.org/10.1007/3-540-45949-9

31. Paige, R., Tarjan, R.: Three partition refinement algorithms. SIAM J. Comput. **16**(6), 973–989 (1987)

32. Pelánek, R.: BEEM: benchmarks for explicit model checkers. In: Bošnački, D., Edelkamp, S. (eds.) SPIN 2007. LNCS, vol. 4595, pp. 263–267. Springer, Heidelberg (2007). https://doi.org/10.1007/978-3-540-73370-6_17

33. Pnueli, A., Shtrichman, O., Siegel, M.: The code validation tool CVT: automatic verification of a compilation process. Int. J. Softw. Tools Technol. Transf. **2**(2), 192–201 (1998)

34. de Putter, S., Wijs, A.: A formal verification technique for behavioural model-to-model transformations. Formal Aspects Comput. **30**(1), 3–43 (2018)

35. de Putter, S., Wijs, A., Zhang, D.: The **SLCO** framework for verified, model-driven construction of component software. In: Bae, K., Ölveczky, P.C. (eds.) FACS 2018. LNCS, vol. 11222, pp. 288–296. Springer, Cham (2018). https://doi.org/10.1007/978-3-030-02146-7_15

36. Reniers, M., Schoren, R., Willemse, T.: Results on embeddings between state-based and event-based systems. Comput. J. **57**(1), 73–92 (2014)

37. Slind, K., Norrish, M.: A brief overview of HOL4. In: Mohamed, O.A., Muñoz, C., Tahar, S. (eds.) TPHOLs 2008. LNCS, vol. 5170, pp. 28–32. Springer, Heidelberg (2008). https://doi.org/10.1007/978-3-540-71067-7_6

38. Staats, M., Heimdahl, M.P.E.: Partial translation verification for untrusted code-generators. In: Liu, S., Maibaum, T., Araki, K. (eds.) ICFEM 2008. LNCS, vol. 5256, pp. 226–237. Springer, Heidelberg (2008). https://doi.org/10.1007/978-3-540-88194-0_15

39. Stenzel, K., Moebius, N., Reif, W.: Formal verification of QVT transformations for code generation. In: Whittle, J., Clark, T., Kühne, T. (eds.) MODELS 2011. LNCS, vol. 6981, pp. 533–547. Springer, Heidelberg (2011). https://doi.org/10.1007/978-3-642-24485-8_39

40. Sulzmann, M., Zechner, A.: Model checking DSL-generated C source code. In: Donaldson, A., Parker, D. (eds.) SPIN 2012. LNCS, vol. 7385, pp. 241–247. Springer, Heidelberg (2012). https://doi.org/10.1007/978-3-642-31759-0_18

41. Visser, W., Havelund, K., Brat, G., Park, S., Lerda, F.: Model checking programs. Autom. Softw. Eng. **10**(2), 203–232 (2003)

42. Wijs, A.: Achieving discrete relative timing with untimed process algebra. In: ICECCS, pp. 35–46. IEEE (2007)

43. Wijs, A.: What to do next?: Analysing and optimising system behaviour in time. Ph.D. thesis, VU University Amsterdam (2007)

44. Wijs, A., Engelen, L.: Efficient property preservation checking of model refinements. In: Piterman, N., Smolka, S.A. (eds.) TACAS 2013. LNCS, vol. 7795, pp. 565–579. Springer, Heidelberg (2013). https://doi.org/10.1007/978-3-642-36742-7_41

45. Wijs, A., Fokkink, W.: From χ_t to μCRL: combining performance and functional analysis. In: ICECCS, pp. 184–193. IEEE (2005)

46. Wijs, A., Neele, T., Bošnački, D.: GPUexplore 2.0: unleashing GPU explicit-state model checking. In: Fitzgerald, J., Heitmeyer, C., Gnesi, S., Philippou, A. (eds.) FM 2016. LNCS, vol. 9995, pp. 694–701. Springer, Cham (2016). https://doi.org/10.1007/978-3-319-48989-6_42

47. Zhang, D., et al.: Verifying atomicity preservation and deadlock freedom of a generic shared variable mechanism used in model-to-code transformations. In: Hammoudi, S., Pires, L.F., Selic, B., Desfray, P. (eds.) MODELSWARD 2016. CCIS, vol. 692, pp. 249–273. Springer, Cham (2017). https://doi.org/10.1007/978-3-319-66302-9_13

Runtime Verification

An Operational Guide to Monitorability

Luca Aceto[1,2](✉), Antonis Achilleos[2](✉), Adrian Francalanza[3](✉),
Anna Ingólfsdóttir[2](✉), and Karoliina Lehtinen[4](✉)

[1] Gran Sasso Science Institute, L'Aquila, Italy
[2] Reykjavik University, Reykjavik, Iceland
{luca,antonios,anna}@ru.is
[3] University of Malta, Msida, Malta
adrian.francalanza@um.edu.mt
[4] University of Liverpool, Liverpool, UK
k.lehtinen@liverpool.ac.uk

Abstract. Monitorability underpins the technique of Runtime Verification because it delineates what properties can be verified at runtime. Although many monitorability definitions exist, few are defined *explicitly* in terms of the operational guarantees provided by monitors, *i.e.*, the computational entities carrying out the verification. We view monitorability as a spectrum, where the fewer guarantees that are required of monitors, the more properties become monitorable. Accordingly, we present a monitorability hierarchy based on this trade-off. For regular specifications, we give syntactic characterisations in Hennessy–Milner logic with recursion for its levels. Finally, we map existing monitorability definitions into our hierarchy. Hence our work gives a unified framework that makes the operational assumptions and guarantees of each definition explicit. This provides a rigorous foundation that can inform design choices and correctness claims for runtime verification tools.

1 Introduction

Runtime Verification (RV) [12] is a lightweight verification technique that checks for a specification by analysing the current execution exhibited by the system under scrutiny. Despite its merits, the technique is limited in certain respects: any sufficiently expressive specification language contains properties that cannot be monitored at runtime [2,3,19,24,30,39,41]. For instance, the *satisfaction* of a safety property ("bad things never happen") cannot, in general, be determined by observing the (finite) behaviour of a program up to the current execution point; its *violation*, however, can. *Monitorability* [12,41] concerns itself

This research was supported by the Icelandic Research Fund projects "TheoFoMon: Theoretical Foundations for Monitorability" (№:163406-051) and "Epistemic Logic for Distributed Runtime Monitoring" (№:184940-051), by the BMBF project "Aramis II" (№:01IS160253), the EPSRC project "Solving parity games in theory and practice" (№:EP/P020909/1), and project BehAPI, funded by the EU H2020 RISE programme under the Marie Skłodowska-Curie grant agreement №:778233.

© Springer Nature Switzerland AG 2019
P. C. Ölveczky and G. Salaün (Eds.): SEFM 2019, LNCS 11724, pp. 433–453, 2019.
https://doi.org/10.1007/978-3-030-30446-1_23

with the delineation between properties that are monitorable and those that are not. Besides its importance from a foundational perspective, monitorability is paramount for a slew of RV tools, such as those described in [9,17,23,40,42], that synthesise monitors from specifications expressed in a variety of logics. These monitors are executed with the system under scrutiny to produce verdicts concerning the satisfaction or violation of the specifications from which they were synthesised.

Monitorability is crucial for a principled approach because it disciplines the construction of RV tools. It should espouse the separation of concerns between the specification of a correctness property on the one hand, and the method used to verify it on the other [30]. It defines, either explicitly or implicitly, a notion of *monitor correctness* [27,28,31,38], which then guides the automated synthesis of monitors from specifications. It also delimits the monitorable fragment of the specification logic on which the synthesis is defined: monitors need not be synthesised for non-monitorable specifications. In some settings, a syntactic characterisation of monitorable properties can be identified [1,3,30], and used as a *core calculus* for studying optimisations of the synthesis algorithm. More broadly, monitorability boundaries may guide the design of *hybrid* verification strategies, which combine RV with other verification techniques (see the work in [2] for an example of this approach).

In spite of its importance, there is *no* generally accepted notion of monitorability to date. The literature contains a number of definitions, such as the ones proposed in [3,14,25,30,32,41]. These differ in aspects such as the adopted specification formalism, *e.g.*, LTL, Street automata, RECHML *etc.*,, the operational model, *e.g.*, testers, automata, process calculi *etc.*, and the semantic domain, *e.g.*, infinite traces, finite and infinite (finfinite) traces or labelled transition systems. Even after these differences are normalised, many of these definitions are *not* in agreement: there are properties that are monitorable according to some definitions but *not* monitorable according to others. More alarmingly, as we will show, frequently cited definitions of monitorability contain serious errors.

This discrepancy between definitions raises the question of *which one* to adopt when designing and implementing an RV tool, and *what effect* this choice has on the behaviour of the resulting tool. A difficulty in informing this choice is that few of those definitions make explicit the relationship between the operational model, *i.e.*, the behaviour of a monitor, and the monitored properties. In other words, it is not clear what the guarantees provided by the various monitors mentioned in the literature are, and how they differ from each other.

Example 1. Consider the runtime verification of a system exhibiting (only) three events over finfinite traces: failure (f), success (s) and recovery (r). One property we may require is that *"failure never occurs and eventually success is reached"*, otherwise expressed in LTL fashion as $(G \neg f) \wedge (F s)$. According to the definition of monitorability attributed to Pnueli and Zaks [41] (discussed in Sect. 7), this property is monitorable. However, it is not monitorable according to others, including Schneider [44], Viswanathan and Kim [45], and Aceto *et al.* [3], whose definition of monitorability coincides with some subset of *safety properties.* ∎

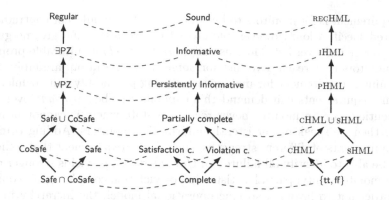

Fig. 1. The monitorability hierarchy of regular properties

Contributions. To our mind, this state of the art is unsatisfactory for tool construction. More concretely, an RV tool broadly relies on the following ingredients:

1. the *input* of the tool in terms of the formalism used to describe the specification properties;
2. the executable description of monitors that are the tool's *output* and
3. the *mapping* between the inputs and outputs, *i.e.,* the synthesis function of monitors from specifications.

Any account on monitorability should, in our view, shed light on those three aspects, particularly on what it means for the synthesis function and the monitors it produces to be *correct*. This involves establishing the relationship between *the truth value* of a specification, given by a two-valued semantics, and *what the runtime analysis tells us about it*, given by the operational behaviour exhibited by the monitor; ideally, the specification and operational descriptions should also be described independently of one another, in order to ensure the aforementioned separation of concerns.[1] In addition, any account on monitorability should also be flexible enough to incorporate a variety of relationships between specification properties and the expected behaviour of monitors. This is essential for it be of use to the tool implementors, acting as a principled foundation to guide their design decisions.

For these reasons, we take the view that monitorability comes on a *spectrum*. There is a trade-off between the guarantees provided by monitors and the properties that can be monitored with those guarantees. We argue that considering different requirements gives rise to a *hierarchy of monitorability*—depicted in Fig. 1 (middle)—which classifies properties according to what types of guarantees RV can give for them. At one extreme, anything can be monitored if the

---

[1] In RV, it is commonplace to see the expected monitor behaviour described via an intermediary n-valued logic semantics [13,14,32] (*e.g.,* mapping finite traces into the three verdicts called accepting, rejecting and inconclusive). Although convenient in certain cases, the approach goes against our tenet for the separation of concerns.

only requirement is for monitors to be *sound i.e.,* they should not contradict the monitored specification. However, monitors that are *just* sound give no guarantees of ever giving a verdict. More usefully, *informatively* monitorable properties enjoy monitors that reach a verdict for *some* finite execution; arguably, this is the minimum requirement for making monitoring potentially worthwhile. More stringent requirements can demand this capability to be *invariant* over monitor executions, *i.e.,* a monitor never reaches a state where it cannot provide a verdict; then we speak of persistently informative monitors. Adding completeness requirements of different strengths, such as the requirement that a monitor should be able to identify all failures and/or satisfactions, yields stronger definitions of monitorability: partial, satisfaction or violation complete, and complete.

In order not to favour a specific operational model, the hierarchy in Fig. 1 (middle) is cast in terms of abstract behavioural requirements for monitors. We then provide an instantiation that concretises those requirements into an *operational* hierarchy, establishing operational counterparts for each type of monitorability over regular properties. To this end, we use the operational framework developed in [3], that uses finite-state monitors and in which partial and complete monitorability were already defined. We show this framework to be, in a suitable technical sense, maximally general (Theorem 2) for regular properties. This shows that our work is equally applicable to other operational models for monitoring regular properties.

In order for a tool to synthesise monitors from specifications, it is useful to have *syntactic characterisations* of the properties that are monitorable with the required guarantees: synthesis can then directly operate on the syntactic fragment. We offer monitorability characterisations as fragments of RECHML [6, 37] (a variant of the modal μ-calculus [34]) interpreted over finfinite traces—see Fig. 1 (right). The logic is expressive enough to capture all regular properties— the focus of nearly all existing definitions of monitorability—and subsumes more user-friendly but less expressive specification logics such as LTL. Partial and complete monitorability already enjoy monitor synthesis functions and neat syntactic characterisations in RECHML [3]; related synthesis functions based on syntactic characterisations for a branching-time setting [29, 30] have already been implemented in a tool [8, 9]. Here, we provide the missing syntactic characterisation for informative monitorability, and for a fragment of persistently informative monitorability.

Finally, we show that the proposed hierarchy accounts for existing notions of monitorability. See Fig. 1 (left). Safety, co-safety and their union correspond to partial monitorability and its two components, satisfaction- and violation-monitorability; Pnueli and Zaks's definition of monitorability can be interpreted in two ways, of which one ($\exists$PZ) maps to informative monitorability, and the other ($\forall$PZ) to persistently informative monitorability. We also show that the definitions of monitorability proposed by Falcone *et al.* [25], contrary to their claim, do *not* coincide with safety and co-safety properties. To summarise, our principal contributions are:

1. A unified operational perspective on existing notions of monitorability, clarifying what operational guarantees each provides, see Theorems 1, 6 and 7;
2. An extension to the syntactic characterisations of monitorable classes from [3], mapping all but one of these classes to fragments in RECHML, which can be viewed as a target byte-code for higher-level logics, see Theorems 4 and 5.

2   Preliminaries

Traces. We assume a *finite* set of actions, $a, b, \ldots \in \mathrm{ACT}$. The metavariables $t, u \in \mathrm{ACT}^\omega$ range over *infinite* sequences of actions. *Finite traces*, denoted as $s, r \in \mathrm{ACT}^*$, represent *finite* prefixes of system runs. Collectively, finite and infinite traces $\mathrm{ACT}^\infty = \mathrm{ACT}^\omega \cup \mathrm{ACT}^*$ are called *finfinite* traces. We use $f, g \in \mathrm{ACT}^\infty$ to range over finfinite traces and $F \subseteq \mathrm{ACT}^\infty$ to range over sets of finfinite traces. A (finfinite) trace with action a at its head is denoted as af. Similarly, a (finfinite) trace with a prefix s and continuation f is denoted as sf. We write $s \preceq f$ to denote that the finite trace s is a prefix of f, *i.e.*, $\exists g$ such that $f = sg$.

Properties. A *property* over finfinite (*resp.,* infinite) traces, denoted by the variable P, is a subset of ACT^∞ (*resp.,* of ACT^ω). In general, a *property* refers to a finfinite property, unless stated otherwise. A finite trace s *positively determines* a property $P \subseteq \mathrm{ACT}^\infty$ when $sf \in P$ for *every* continuation $f \in \mathrm{ACT}^\infty$; analogously, s *negatively determines* P when $sf \notin P$ for every $f \in \mathrm{ACT}^\infty$. The same terms apply similarly when $P \subseteq \mathrm{ACT}^\omega$. We call a property *regular* if it is the union of a regular property $P_{\mathrm{fin}} \subseteq \mathrm{ACT}^*$ and an ω-regular property $P_{\mathrm{inf}} \subseteq \mathrm{ACT}^\omega$.

3   A Monitor-Oriented Hierarchy

From a tool-construction perspective, it is important to give concrete, implementable definitions of monitors; we do so in Sect. 4. To understand the guarantees that these monitors will provide, we first discuss the general notion of monitor and monitoring system. Already in this general setting, we are able to identify the various requirements that give rise to the hierarchy of monitorability, depicted in the middle part of Fig. 1. Section 4 will then provide operational semantics to this hierarchy, in the setting of regular properties.

We consider a monitor to be an entity that analyses finite traces and (at the very least) identifies a set of finfinite traces that it *accepts* and a set of finfinite traces that it *rejects*. We consider two postulates. Firstly, an acceptance or rejection verdict has to be based on a finite prefix of a trace, Definition 1. 1: verdicts are thus given for *incomplete* traces. Secondly, verdicts must be *irrevocable*, Definition 1. 2. These postulates make explicit two features shared by most monitorability definitions in the literature.

Definition 1. *A* monitoring system *is a triple* $(M, \mathbf{acc}, \mathbf{rej})$*, where M is a nonempty set of monitors,* $\mathbf{acc}, \mathbf{rej} \subseteq M \times \mathrm{ACT}^\infty$*, and for every $m \in M$ and $f \in \mathrm{ACT}^\infty$:*

1. $\big(\textbf{acc}(m,f)$ *implies* $\exists s \cdot (s \preceq f$ *and* $\textbf{acc}(m,s))\big)$ *and* $\big(\textbf{rej}(m,f)$ *implies* $\exists s \cdot (s \preceq f$ *and* $\textbf{rej}(m,s))\big)$;
2. $\big(\textbf{acc}(m,s)$ *implies* $\forall f \cdot \textbf{acc}(m,sf)\big)$ *and* $\big(\textbf{rej}(m,s)$ *implies* $\forall f \cdot \textbf{rej}(m,sf)\big)$. ∎

Remark 1. Finite automata do not satisfy the requirements of Definition 1 since their judgement can be revoked. Standard Büchi automata are not good candidates either, since they need to read the entire infinite trace to accept or reject. ∎

We define a notion of maximal monitoring system for a collection of properties; for each property P in that set, such a system must contain a monitor that reaches a verdict for all traces that have some prefix that determines P.

Definition 2. *A monitoring system* $(M, \textbf{acc}, \textbf{rej})$ *is* maximal *for a collection of properties* $C \subseteq 2^{\mathrm{ACT}^{\infty}}$ *if for every* $P \in C$ *there is a monitor* $m_P \in M$ *such that*

(i) $\textbf{acc}(m_P, f)$ *iff trace* f *has a prefix that positively determines* P;
(ii) $\textbf{rej}(m_P, f)$ *iff trace* f *has a prefix that negatively determines* P. ∎

In Sect. 4, we present an instance of such a maximal monitoring system for regular properties. This shows that, for regular properties at least, the maximality of a monitoring system is a reasonable requirement. Unless otherwise stated, we assume a fixed maximal monitoring system $(M, \textbf{acc}, \textbf{rej})$ throughout the rest of the paper. For $m \in M$ to monitor for a property P, it needs to satisfy some requirements. The most important such requirement is *soundness*.

Definition 3 (Soundness). *Monitor* m *is* sound *for property* P *if for all* f:

– $\textbf{acc}(m,f)$ *implies* $f \in P$, *and*
– $\textbf{rej}(m,f)$ *implies* $f \notin P$. ∎

Lemma 1. *If* m *is sound for* P *and* $\textbf{acc}(m,s)$ *(resp.,* $\textbf{rej}(m,s)$*), then* s *positively (resp., negatively) determines* P.

Lemma 2. *For every* $P \subseteq \mathrm{ACT}^{\infty}$: *(i)* m_P *is sound for* P; *and (ii) if* m *is a sound monitor for* P *and* $\textbf{acc}(m,f)$ *(resp.,* $\textbf{rej}(m,f)$*), then it is also the case that* $\textbf{acc}(m_P, f)$ *(resp.,* $\textbf{rej}(m_P, f)$*).*

The dual requirement to soundness, *i.e.*, *completeness*, entails that the monitor detects *all* violating and satisfying traces. Unfortunately, this is only possible for trivial properties in the finfinite[2] domain—see Proposition 1. Instead, monitors may be required to accept all satisfying traces, or reject all violating traces.

Definition 4 (Completeness). *Monitor* m *is* satisfaction-complete *for* P *if* $f \in P$ *implies* $\textbf{acc}(m,f)$ *and* violation-complete *for* P *if* $f \notin P$ *implies* $\textbf{rej}(m,f)$. *It is* complete *for* P *if it is both* satisfaction- *and* violation-complete *for* P *and* partially-complete *if it is either* satisfaction- *or* violation-complete. ∎

---

[2] In the infinite domain more properties *are* completely monitorable, see Sect. 8.

Proposition 1. *If m is sound and complete for P then $P = \mathrm{ACT}^\infty$ or $P = \emptyset$.*

Proof. If $\varepsilon \in P$, then $\mathbf{acc}(m, \varepsilon)$, so from Definition 1, $\forall f \in \mathrm{ACT}^\infty.\ \mathbf{acc}(m, f)$. Due to the soundness of m, $P = \mathrm{ACT}^\infty$. Similarly, $P = \emptyset$ when $\varepsilon \notin P$. $\square$

We define monitorability in terms of the guarantees that the monitors are expected to give. Soundness is not negotiable. Given the consequences of requiring completeness, as evidenced by Proposition 1, we consider weaker forms of completeness. The weaker the completeness guarantee, the more properties can be monitored.

Definition 5 (Complete Monitorability). *Property P is completely monitorable when there exists a monitor that is sound and complete for P. It is monitorable for satisfactions (resp., violations) when there exists a monitor m that is sound and satisfaction (resp., and violation) complete for P. It is partially (-complete) monitorable when it is monitorable for satisfactions or violations.*

A class of properties $C \subseteq 2^{\mathrm{ACT}^\infty}$ is satisfaction, violation, partially, or completely monitorable, when every property $P{\in}C$ is, respectively, satisfaction, violation, partially or completely monitorable. We denote the class of all satisfaction, violation, partially, and completely monitorable properties by maximal monitoring systems as SCmp, VCmp, PCmp, and Cmp, respectively. ∎

Since even partial monitorability, the weakest form in Definition 5, renders a substantial number of properties unmonitorable [3], one may consider even weaker forms of completeness that only flag a subset of satisfying (or violating) traces. Sound denotes monitorability *without* completeness requirements. Arguably, however, the weakest guarantee for a sound monitor of a property P to be of use is the one that pledges to flag at least *one* trace. One may then further strengthen this requirement and demand that this guarantee is *invariant* throughout the analysis of a monitor: for every prefix observed the monitor is still able to flag at least once (possibly after observing more actions).

Definition 6 (Informative Monitorability[3]). *Monitor m is satisfaction- (resp., violation-) informative if $\exists f \cdot \mathbf{acc}(m, f)$ (resp., $\mathbf{rej}(m, f)$). It is satisfaction- (resp., violation-) persistently informative if $\forall s \exists f \cdot \mathbf{acc}(m, sf)$ (resp., $\mathbf{rej}(m, sf)$). We simply say that m is informative (resp., persistently informative) when we do not distinguish between satisfactions or violations.* ∎

Definition 7 (Informative Monitorability). *We say that property P is informatively (resp., persistently informatively) monitorable if there is an informative (resp., a persistently informative) monitor that is sound for P. A class of properties $C \subseteq 2^{\mathrm{ACT}^\infty}$ is informatively (resp., persistently informatively) monitorable, when all its properties are informatively (resp., persistently informatively) monitorable. The class of all informatively (resp., persistently informatively) monitorable properties by maximal monitoring systems is denoted as ICmp*

---

[3] These are *not* related to the *informative prefixes* from [35] or to *persistence* from [43].

$$\varphi, \psi \in \text{RECHML} ::= \text{tt} \qquad | \text{ ff} \qquad | \ \varphi \vee \psi \qquad | \ \varphi \wedge \psi$$
$$\qquad | \ \langle a \rangle \varphi \qquad | \ [a]\varphi \qquad | \ \min X.\varphi \qquad | \ \max X.\varphi \qquad | \ X$$

$$[\![\text{tt}, \sigma]\!] \stackrel{\text{def}}{=} \text{ACT}^{\infty} \qquad\qquad\qquad\qquad [\![\text{ff}, \sigma]\!] \stackrel{\text{def}}{=} \emptyset$$
$$[\![\varphi_1 \vee \varphi_2, \sigma]\!] \stackrel{\text{def}}{=} [\![\varphi_1, \sigma]\!] \cup [\![\varphi_2, \sigma]\!] \qquad\qquad [\![\varphi_1 \wedge \varphi_2, \sigma]\!] \stackrel{\text{def}}{=} [\![\varphi_1, \sigma]\!] \cap [\![\varphi_2, \sigma]\!]$$
$$[\![[a]\varphi, \sigma]\!] \stackrel{\text{def}}{=} \{f \mid f = ag \text{ implies } g \in [\![\varphi, \sigma]\!]\} \quad [\![\langle a \rangle \varphi, \sigma]\!] \stackrel{\text{def}}{=} \{af \mid f \in [\![\varphi, \sigma]\!]\}$$
$$[\![\min X.\varphi, \sigma]\!] \stackrel{\text{def}}{=} \bigcap \{F \mid [\![\varphi, \sigma[X \mapsto F]\!]] \subseteq F \}$$
$$[\![\max X.\varphi, \sigma]\!] \stackrel{\text{def}}{=} \bigcup \{F \mid F \subseteq [\![\varphi, \sigma[X \mapsto F]\!]] \} \qquad\qquad [\![X, \sigma]\!] \stackrel{\text{def}}{=} \sigma(X)$$

Fig. 2. RECHML syntax and (finfinite) linear-time semantics

(resp., *PICmp*). *A property P is persistently informatively monitorable for sat-isfaction (resp., for violation) if there is a satisfaction- (resp., violation-) per-sistently informative monitor that is sound for P. We revisit this definition in Sect. 4.* ∎

Example 2. The property *"f never occurs and eventually s is reached"* (Exam-ple 1) is *not* partially monitorable but *is* persistently informatively monitorable.

The property requiring that *"r only appears a finite number of times"* is *not* informatively monitorable. For if it were, the respective sound informative monitor m should at least accept or reject one trace. If it accepts a trace f, by Definition 1, it must accept some prefix $s \preceq f$. Again, by Definition 1, all continuations, including sr^{ω}, must be accepted by m. This makes it unsound, which is a contradiction. Similarly, if m rejects some f, it must reject some finite $s \preceq f$ that necessarily contains a finite number of r actions, making it unsound. ∎

Theorem 1 (Monitorability Hierarchy). *The monitorability classes given in Definitions 5 and 7 form the inclusion hierarchy depicted in Fig. 1.*

Proof. The hardest inclusion to show from Fig. 1 is PCmp = SCmp∪VCmp ⊆ PICmp. Pick a property $P \in$ VCmp. Let $s \in$ ACT*. If $\exists f \cdot sf \notin P$ then by Definition 4 we have $\textbf{rej}(m_P, sf)$. Otherwise, $\forall f \cdot sf \in P$, mean-ing that s positively determines P, and by Definition 2 we have $\textbf{acc}(m_P, sf)$. By Definition 6, we deduce that m_P is persistently informative since $\forall s \exists f \cdot \textbf{acc}(m_P, sf)$ or $\textbf{rej}(m_P, sf)$. Thus, by Definition 7, it follows that $P \in$ PICmp. The case for $P \in$ SCmp is dual. □

4 An Instantiation for Regular Properties

We provide a concrete maximal monitoring system for regular properties. This monitoring system gives an operational interpretation to the levels of the moni-torability hierarchy, and enables us to find syntactic characterisations for them in RECHML [3,37]. Since this logic is a reformulation of the modal μ-calculus [34], it is expressive enough to describe all regular properties and to embed specification formalisms such as LTL, (ω-)regular expressions, Büchi automata, and Street automata, used in the state of the art on monitorability.

The Logic. The syntax of RECHML is defined by the grammar in Fig. 2, which assumes a countable set of logical variables $X, Y \in \text{LVar}$. Apart from the standard constructs for truth, falsehood, conjunction and disjunction, the logic is equipped with existential ($\langle a \rangle \varphi$) and universal ($[a] \varphi$) modal operators, and *two* recursion operators expressing least and greatest fixpoints (*resp.*, $\min X . \varphi$ and $\max X . \varphi$). The semantics is given by the function $[\![-]\!]$ defined in Fig. 2. It maps a (possibly open) formula to a set of (finfinite) traces [3] by induction on the formula structure, using valuations that map logical variables to sets of traces, $\sigma : \text{LVar} \to \mathcal{P}(\text{Act}^\infty)$, where $\sigma(X)$ is the set of traces assumed to satisfy X. An existential modality $\langle a \rangle \varphi$ denotes all traces with a prefix action a and a continuation that satisfies φ, whereas a universal modality $[a] \varphi$ denotes all traces that are either *not* prefixed by a or are of the form ag for some g that satisfies φ. The sets of traces satisfying the least and greatest fixpoint formulae, $\min X . \varphi$ and $\max X . \varphi$, are the least and the greatest fixpoints, respectively, of the function induced by the formula φ. For closed formulae, we use $[\![\varphi]\!]$ in lieu of $[\![\varphi, \sigma]\!]$ (for some σ). Formulae are generally assumed to be closed and guarded [36]. In the discussions we occasionally treat formulae, φ, as the properties they denote, $[\![\varphi]\!]$.

LTL [20] is the specification logic of choice for many RV approaches. As a consequence, it is also the logic used by a number of studies in monitorability (*e.g.*, see [13,14,32]). Our choice of logic, RECHML, is not limiting in this regard.

Example 3. The characteristic LTL operators can be encoded in RECHML as:

$$\mathsf{X}\varphi \overset{\text{def}}{=} \bigvee_{a \in \text{Act}} \langle a \rangle \varphi \qquad \varphi \, \mathsf{U} \, \psi \overset{\text{def}}{=} \min Y . (\psi \vee (\varphi \wedge \mathsf{X}\, Y)) \qquad \mathsf{F}\varphi \overset{\text{def}}{=} \mathsf{tt}\, \mathsf{U}\, \varphi$$
$$\varphi \, \mathsf{R} \, \psi \overset{\text{def}}{=} \max Y . ((\psi \wedge \varphi) \vee (\psi \wedge \mathsf{X}\, Y)) \qquad\qquad\qquad \mathsf{G}\varphi \overset{\text{def}}{=} \mathsf{ff}\, \mathsf{R}\, \varphi$$

In examples, atomic propositions a and $\neg a$ resp., denote $\langle a \rangle \mathsf{tt}$ and $[a] \mathsf{ff}$. ∎

RECHML allows us to consider monitorable properties that may be misses by previous approaches. For instance, it is well known that logics such as the modal μ-calculus (and variants such as RECHML) can describe properties that are *not* expressible in popular specification languages like LTL [46].

Example 4. Recall the system discussed in Example 1 where $\text{Act} = \{\mathsf{f}, \mathsf{s}, \mathsf{r}\}$. Consider the property requiring that *"success (s) occurs on every even position"*. Although this is *not* expressible in LTL [46], it can be expressed in RECHML as:

$$\varphi_{\text{even}} = \max X . \left(\bigvee_{a \in \{\mathsf{f}, \mathsf{s}, \mathsf{r}\}} \langle a \rangle \langle \mathsf{s} \rangle X \right)$$

The weaker property *"success (s) occurs on every even position until the execution ends"* still cannot be expressed in LTL, but can be expressed in RECHML:

$$\varphi_{\text{evenW}} = \max X . \left(\bigwedge_{a \in \{\mathsf{f}, \mathsf{s}, \mathsf{r}\}} [a] \, ([\mathsf{s}] X \wedge [\mathsf{f}] \mathsf{ff} \wedge [\mathsf{r}] \mathsf{ff}) \right) \qquad\qquad ∎$$

$$m, n \in \text{MON} ::= v \quad | \ a.m \quad | \ m + n \quad | \ m \otimes n \quad | \ m \oplus n \quad | \ \mathsf{rec}\, x.m \quad | \ x$$
$$v, u \in \text{VERD} ::= \mathsf{end} \quad | \ \mathsf{no} \quad | \ \mathsf{yes}$$

$$\text{MAcT} \frac{}{a.m \xrightarrow{a} m} \qquad \text{MVER} \frac{}{v \xrightarrow{a} v} \qquad \text{MREC} \frac{m[\mathsf{rec}\, x.m/x] \xrightarrow{a} n}{\mathsf{rec}\, x.m \xrightarrow{a} n}$$

$$\text{MSELL} \frac{m \xrightarrow{a} m'}{m + n \xrightarrow{a} m'} \qquad \text{MPAR} \frac{m \xrightarrow{a} m' \quad n \xrightarrow{a} n'}{m \odot n \xrightarrow{a} m' \odot n'}$$

$$\text{MTauL} \frac{m \xrightarrow{\tau} m'}{m \odot n \xrightarrow{\tau} m' \odot n} \qquad \text{MVrE} \frac{}{\mathsf{end} \odot \mathsf{end} \xrightarrow{\tau} \mathsf{end}} \qquad \text{MVrC1} \frac{}{\mathsf{yes} \otimes m \xrightarrow{\tau} m}$$

$$\text{MVrC2} \frac{}{\mathsf{no} \otimes m \xrightarrow{\tau} \mathsf{no}} \qquad \text{MVrD1} \frac{}{\mathsf{no} \oplus m \xrightarrow{\tau} m} \qquad \text{MVrD2} \frac{}{\mathsf{yes} \oplus m \xrightarrow{\tau} \mathsf{yes}}$$

Fig. 3. Monitor syntax and labelled-transition semantics

For better readability and familiarity, we use LTL for the examples that can be encoded accordingly. Note that since we operate in the finfinite domain, X should be read as a *strong* next operator, in line with Example 3.

The Monitors. We consider the operational monitoring system of [3, 30], summarised in Fig. 3 (symmetric rules for binary operators are omitted). The full system is given in [3]. Monitors are states of a transition system where $m + n$ denotes an (external) choice and $m \odot n$ denotes a composite monitor where $\odot \in \{\oplus, \otimes\}$. There are three distinct *verdict* states, yes, no, and end, although only the first two are relevant to monitorability.

This semantics gives an operational account of how a monitor in state m incrementally analyses a sequence of actions $s = a_1 \ldots a_k$ to reach a new state n; the monitor m accepts (*resp.*, rejects) a trace f, $\mathbf{acc}(m, f)$ (*resp.*, $\mathbf{rej}(m, f)$), when it can transition to the verdict state yes (*resp.*, no) while analysing a prefix $s \preceq f$ (*i.e.*, s denotes an incomplete trace). Since verdicts are irrevocable (rule MVER in Fig. 3), it is not hard to see that this operational framework satisfies the conditions for a monitoring system of Definition 1. The monitoring system of Fig. 3 is also maximal for regular properties, according to Definition 2. This concrete instance thus demonstrates the realisability of the abstract definitions in Sect. 3.

Theorem 2. *For all $\varphi \in \text{RECHML}$, there is a monitor $m \in \text{MON}$ that is sound for φ and accepts all finite traces that positively determine φ and rejects all finite traces that negatively determine φ.*

As a corollary of Theorem 2, from Lemma 1 we deduce that for any arbitrary monitoring system $(M, \mathbf{acc}, \mathbf{rej})$, if $m \in M$ is sound for some $\varphi \in \text{RECHML}$, then there is a monitor $n \in \text{MON}$ from Fig. 3 that accepts (*resp.*, rejects) all traces f that m accepts (*resp.*, rejects). In the sequel, we thus assume that the fixed monitoring system is $(\textsc{Mon}, \textbf{acc}, \textbf{rej})$ of Fig. 3, as it subsumes all others.

5 A Syntactic Characterisation of Monitorability

We present syntactic characterizations for the various monitorability classes as fragments of $\textsc{RecHML}$.

Partial Monitorability, Syntactically. In [3], Aceto *et al.* identify a maximal partially monitorable syntactic fragment of $\textsc{RecHML}$.

Theorem 3. (Partially-Complete Monitorability [3]). *Consider the syntactic fragments:*

$$\varphi, \psi \in \textsc{sHML} ::= \textsf{tt} \mid \textsf{ff} \mid [a]\varphi \mid \varphi \wedge \psi \mid \max X.\varphi \mid X \text{ and}$$
$$\varphi, \psi \in \textsc{cHML} ::= \textsf{tt} \mid \textsf{ff} \mid \langle a \rangle \varphi \mid \varphi \vee \psi \mid \min X.\varphi \mid X.$$

The fragment $\textsc{sHML}$ *is monitorable for violation whereas* $\textsc{cHML}$ *is monitorable for satisfaction. Furthermore, if* $\varphi \in \textsc{RecHML}$ *is monitorable for satisfaction (resp., for violation) by some* $m \in \textsc{Mon}$, *it is expressible in* $\textsc{cHML}$ *(resp.,* $\textsc{sHML}$*), i.e.,* $\exists \psi \in \textsc{cHML}$ *(resp.,* $\psi \in \textsc{sHML}$*), such that* $[\![\varphi]\!] = [\![\psi]\!]$.

As a corollary of Theorem 3 we obtain *maximality*: any $\varphi \in \textsc{RecHML}$ that is monitorable for satisfaction (*resp.*, for violation) can also be expressed as some $\psi \in \textsc{cHML}$ (*resp.*, $\psi \in \textsc{sHML}$) where $[\![\varphi]\!] = [\![\psi]\!]$. For this fragment, the following automated synthesis function, which is readily implementable, is given in [3].

$$
\begin{aligned}
\mathsf{m}(\textsf{ff}) &\stackrel{\text{def}}{=} \textsf{no} & \mathsf{m}(\varphi_1 \wedge \varphi_2) &\stackrel{\text{def}}{=} \mathsf{m}(\varphi_1) \otimes \mathsf{m}(\varphi_2) & \mathsf{m}(\max X.\varphi) &\stackrel{\text{def}}{=} \textsf{rec}\, x.\mathsf{m}(\varphi) \\
\mathsf{m}(\textsf{tt}) &\stackrel{\text{def}}{=} \textsf{yes} & \mathsf{m}(\varphi_1 \vee \varphi_2) &\stackrel{\text{def}}{=} \mathsf{m}(\varphi_1) \otimes \mathsf{m}(\varphi_2) & \mathsf{m}(\min X.\varphi) &\stackrel{\text{def}}{=} \textsf{rec}\, x.\mathsf{m}(\varphi) \\
\mathsf{m}([a]\varphi) &\stackrel{\text{def}}{=} a.\mathsf{m}(\varphi) + \textstyle\sum_{b \in \textsc{Act} \setminus \{a\}} b.\textsf{yes} & & & \mathsf{m}(X) &\stackrel{\text{def}}{=} x \\
\mathsf{m}(\langle a \rangle \varphi) &\stackrel{\text{def}}{=} a.\mathsf{m}(\varphi) + \textstyle\sum_{b \in \textsc{Act} \setminus \{a\}} b.\textsf{no} & & &
\end{aligned}
$$

Informative Monitorability, Syntactically. We proceed to identify syntactic fragments of $\textsc{RecHML}$ that correspond to informative monitorability.

Definition 8. *The informative fragment is* $\textsc{iHML} = \textsc{siHML} \cup \textsc{ciHML}$ *where*

$$\textsc{siHML} = \{\varphi_1 \wedge \varphi_2 \in \textsc{RecHML} \mid \varphi_1 \in \textsc{sHML} \text{ and } \textsf{ff} \text{ appears in } \varphi_1\},$$
$$\textsc{ciHML} = \{\varphi_1 \vee \varphi_2 \in \textsc{RecHML} \mid \varphi_1 \in \textsc{cHML} \text{ and } \textsf{tt} \text{ appears in } \varphi_1\} \qquad \blacksquare$$

Theorem 4. *For* $\varphi \in \textsc{RecHML}$, φ *is informatively monitorable if and only if there is some* $\psi \in \textsc{iHML}$, *such that* $[\![\psi]\!] = [\![\varphi]\!]$.

The maximality results of Theorems 3 and 4 permits tool constructions to concentrate on the syntactic fragments identified when synthesising monitors. Theorems 3 and 4 also serve as a lightweight (syntactic) check to determine when a property is monitorable (according to the monitorability classes in Fig. 1).

Example 5. The property $\varphi_{\text{even}}W$ from Example 4 is monitorable for violation; this can be easily determined since it is expressible in sHML. By contrast, φ_{even} from Example 4 cannot be expressed in either sHML or cHML. In fact, it is *not* partially-complete monitorable: it cannot be satisfaction complete because the trace $(\text{rs})^\omega \in [\![\varphi_{\text{even}}]\!]$ but no prefix can be accepted since they all violate the property; it cannot be violation complete either, since the trace $\epsilon \notin [\![\varphi_{\text{even}}]\!]$ but is can be extended by $(\text{rs})^\omega$ which makes (persistent) rejection verdicts unsound. The property $\mathsf{G}\neg\mathsf{f} \wedge \mathsf{F}\mathsf{s}$ from Example 2 (expressed here in LTL) is a siHML property, as $\mathsf{G}\neg\mathsf{f}$ can be written in sHML as $\max X.[\mathsf{f}]\mathsf{ff} \wedge [\mathsf{s}]X \wedge [\mathsf{r}]X$. In contrast, $\mathsf{F}\mathsf{G}\neg\mathsf{r}$ cannot be written in iHML since it is not informatively monitorable. ∎

Remark 2. In siHML and ciHML, φ_1 describes an informative part of the formula, that is, a formula with at least one path to tt (or ff), which indicates that the corresponding finite trace determines the property. Monitor synthesis from these fragments can use this part of the formula to synthesize a monitor that detects the finite traces that satisfy (violate) φ_1. The value of the synthesised monitor then depends on φ_1. It is therefore important to have techniques to extract some φ_1 that will retain as much monitoring information as possible. This extraction is outside the scope of this paper and left as future work. ∎

Persistently Informative Monitorability, Syntactically. We also give a syntactic characterization of the RECHML properties that are informatively monitorable for satisfaction or violation. As the requirements for persistently informative monitors are subtler than for informative monitors, the fragments we present are more involved than those for informative monitorability.

Definition 9. *We define* EHML, *the explicit fragment of* RECHML:

$$\varphi \in \text{EHML} ::= \mathsf{tt} \quad | \; \mathsf{ff} \quad | \; \min X.\varphi \quad | \; \max X.\varphi \quad | \; X$$
$$| \; \varphi \vee \psi \quad | \; \varphi \wedge \psi \quad | \; \bigvee_{\alpha \in \text{ACT}} \langle \alpha \rangle \varphi_\alpha \quad | \; \bigwedge_{\alpha \in \text{ACT}} [\alpha]\varphi_\alpha. \quad \blacksquare$$

Example 6. Formula $[\mathsf{f}][\mathsf{s}]\mathsf{ff}$ is not explicit, but, assuming that $\text{ACT} = \{\mathsf{f}, \mathsf{s}, \mathsf{r}\}$, it can be rewritten as the explicit formula $[\mathsf{f}]([\mathsf{s}]\mathsf{ff} \wedge [\mathsf{f}]\mathsf{tt} \wedge [\mathsf{r}]\mathsf{tt}) \wedge [\mathsf{s}]\mathsf{tt} \wedge [\mathsf{r}]\mathsf{tt}$. ∎

Roughly, the following definition captures whether tt and ff are reachable from subformulae (where the binding of a variable is reachable from the variable).

Definition 10. *Given a closed* sHML *(resp.,* cHML*) formula* φ, *we define for a subformula* ψ *that it can refute (resp., verify) in 0 unfoldings, when* ff *(resp., tt) appears in* ψ, *and that it can refute (resp., verify) in* $k+1$ *unfoldings, when it can refute (resp., verify) in* k *unfoldings, or* X *appears in* ψ *and* ψ *is in the scope of a subformula* $\max X.\psi'$ *(resp.,* $\min X.\psi'$) *that can refute (resp., verify) in* k *unfoldings. We simply say that* ψ *can refute (resp., verify) when it can refute (resp., verify) in* k *unfoldings, for some* $k \geq 0$. ∎

Example 7. For formula $\max X.[\mathsf{s}]X \wedge [\mathsf{f}]\mathsf{ff} \wedge [\mathsf{r}]\mathsf{ff}$, subformula $[\mathsf{s}]X \wedge [\mathsf{f}]\mathsf{ff} \wedge [\mathsf{r}]\mathsf{ff}$ can refute in 0 unfoldings. In contrast, $[\mathsf{s}]X$ cannot refute in 0 unfoldings, but it can refute in 1, because X appears in it and $\max X.[\mathsf{s}]X \wedge [\mathsf{f}]\mathsf{ff} \wedge [\mathsf{r}]\mathsf{ff}$ can refute in 0 unfoldings. Therefore, all subformulae of $\max X.[\mathsf{s}]X \wedge [\mathsf{f}]\mathsf{ff} \wedge [\mathsf{r}]\mathsf{ff}$ can refute. ∎

We now define the fragments of RECHML corresponding to RECHML properties that are persistently informatively monitorable for satisfaction or violation.

Definition 11. *We define the fragment* PHML = SPHML ∪ CPHML *where:*

$$\mathrm{SPHML} = \left\{ \varphi_1 \wedge \varphi_2 \in \mathrm{RECHML} \;\middle|\; \begin{array}{l} \varphi_1 \in \mathrm{SHML} \cap \mathrm{EHML} \text{ and every} \\ \text{subformula of } \varphi_1 \text{ can refute} \end{array} \right\}$$

$$\mathrm{CPHML} = \left\{ \varphi_1 \vee \varphi_2 \in \mathrm{RECHML} \;\middle|\; \begin{array}{l} \varphi_1 \in \mathrm{CHML} \cap \mathrm{EHML} \text{ and every} \\ \text{subformula of } \varphi_1 \text{ can verify} \end{array} \right\} \quad ∎$$

Theorem 5. *For* $\varphi \in$ RECHML, φ *is persistently informatively monitorable for violation (resp., for satisfaction) if and only if there is some* $\psi \in$ SPHML *(resp.,* $\psi \in$ CPHML*), such that* $[\![\psi]\!] = [\![\varphi]\!]$.

Remark 3. To the best of our efforts, a syntactic characterisation of persistently informative monitorability would involve pairs of equivalent formulae with parts from SHML and CHML that together become, in some sense, explicit. We leave such a characterization as future work. ∎

6   Safety and Co-safety

The classic (and perhaps the most intuitive) definition of monitorability consists of (some variation of) *safety* properties [3,7,25,32,44,45]. There are, however, subtleties associated with how exactly safety properties are defined—particularly over the finfinite domain—and how decidable they need to be to qualify as truly monitorable. For example, Kim and Viswanathan [45] argued that only recursively enumerable safety properties are monitorable (they restrict themselves to infinite, rather than finfinite traces). By and large, however, most works on monitorability restrict themselves to regular properties, as we do in Sect. 4.

We adopt the definition of safety that is intuitive for the context of RV: a property can be considered monitorable if its failures can be identified by a finite prefix. This is equivalent to Falcone *et al.*'s definition of safety properties [25, Def. 4] and, when restricted to infinite traces, to other work such as [7,16,32].

Definition 12 (Safety). *A property* $P \subseteq \mathrm{ACT}^\infty$ *is a safety property if every* $f \notin P$ *has a prefix that determines* P *negatively. The class of safety properties is denoted as* **Safe** *in Fig. 1.* ∎

Pnueli and Zaks, and Falcone *et al.* (among others) argue that it makes sense to monitor both for violation and satisfaction. Hence, if safety is monitorable for violations, then the dual class, co-safety (a.k.a. guarantee [25], reachability [15]), is monitorable for satisfaction. That is, every trace that satisfies a co-safety property can be positively determined by a finite prefix.

Definition 13 (Co-safety). *A property* $P \subseteq \text{ACT}^\infty$ *is a* co-safety property *if every* $f \in P$ *has prefix that determines* P *positively. The class of co-safety properties is denoted as* CoSafe, *also represented in Fig. 1.*   ∎

Example 8. *"Eventually* s *is reached", i.e.,* F s, *is a co-safety property whereas* "f *never occurs", i.e.,* G ¬f, *is a safety property.* The property "s *occurs infinitely often", i.e.,* G F s, *is neither safety nor co-safety.* The property only holds over infinite traces so it cannot be positively determined by a finite trace. Dually, there is *no* finite trace that determines that there cannot be an infinite number of s occurrences in a continuation of the trace. Similarly, φ_{even} from Example 4 is neither a safety nor a co-safety property, but φ_{even}W is a safety property.   ∎

Safety and Co-safety, Operationally. It should come as no surprise that safety and co-safety coincide with an equally natural operational definition. Here, we establish the correspondence with the denotational definition of safety (co-safety), completing three correspondences amongst the monitorability classes of Fig. 1.

Theorem 6. *VCmp* = *Safe and SCmp* = *CoSafe.*

Proof. We treat the case for safety, as the case for co-safety is similar. If P is a safety property, then for every $f \in \text{ACT}^\infty \setminus P$, there is some finite prefix s of f that negatively determines P. Therefore, m_P is sound (Lemma 2) and violation-complete (Definition 2) for P. The other direction follows from the fact that whenever $P \subseteq \text{ACT}^\infty$ is monitorable for violation, every $f \in \text{ACT}^\infty \setminus P$ has a finite prefix that negatively determines it.

Aceto *et al.* [3] already show the correspondence between violation (dually, satisfaction) monitorability over finfinite traces and properties expressible in sHML (dually, cHML). As a corollary of Theorem 6, we obtain a syntactic characterisation for the Safe and CoSafe monitorability classes; see Fig. 1.

Remark 4. Falcone *et al.* [25, Def. 17, Thm. 3] propose definitions of monitorability over finfinite traces that are claimed to coincide with the classes Safe, CoSafe and their union. However, this claim is incorrect. The properties, "the trace is finite" and G F s from Example 8 are neither safety nor co-safety properties. On the other hand, they are monitorable according to the alternative monitorability definition given in [25, Def. 17]. If the results claimed in [25, Thm. 3] held true, this would contradict the fact that those properties are neither safety nor co-safety properties. See [4] for further details.   ∎

7   Pnueli and Zaks

The work on monitorability due to Pnueli and Zaks [41] is often cited by the RV community [12]. The often overlooked particularity of their definitions is that they only define monitorability of a property *with respect to a (finite) sequence.*

Definition 14. ([41]). *Property* P *is* s-monitorable, *where* $s \in \text{ACT}^*$, *if there is some* $r \in \text{ACT}^*$ *such that* P *is positively or negatively determined by* sr.   ∎

Example 9. The property $(f \wedge F r) \vee (F G s)$ is s-monitorable for any finite trace that begins with f, *i.e.*, fs, since it is determined by the extension fsr. It is *not* s-monitorable for finite traces that begin with an action other than f.   ∎

Monitorability over properties—rather than over property–sequence pairs—can then be defined by either quantifying *universally* or *existentially* over finite traces: a property is monitorable either if it is s-monitorable for all s, or for some s. We address both definitions, which we call ∀PZ- and ∃PZ-monitorability respectively. ∀PZ-monitorability is the more standard interpretation: it appears for example in [13, 25] where it is attributed to Pnueli and Zaks. However, the original intent seems to align more with ∃PZ-monitorability: in [41], Pnueli and Zaks refer to a property as non-monitorable if it is not monitorable for *any* sequence. This interpretation coincides with *weak monitorability* used in [18].

Definition 15. (∀PZ-monitorability). *A property P is (universally Pnueli–Zaks) ∀PZ-monitorable if it is s-monitorable for all finite traces s. The class of all ∀PZ-monitorable properties is denoted ∀PZ.*   ∎

Definition 16. (∃PZ-monitorability). *A property is (existentially Pnueli–Zaks) ∃PZ-monitorable if it is s-monitorable for some finite trace s, i.e., if it is ε-monitorable. The class of ∃PZ-monitorable properties is written ∃PZ.*   ∎

The apparently innocuous choice between existential and universal quantification leads to different monitorability classes ∀PZ and ∃PZ.

Example 10. Consider the property *"Either s occurs before f, or r happens infinitely often"*, expressed in LTL fashion as $((\neg f) U s) \vee (G F r)$. This property is ∃PZ-monitorable because the trace s positively determines the property. However, it is *not* ∀PZ-monitorable because no extension of the trace f positively or negatively determines that property. Indeed, all extensions of f violate the first disjunct and, as we argued in Example 8, there is no finite trace that determines the second conjunct positively or negatively. Property φ_{even} from Example 4 is ∀PZ-monitorable: any prefix of the form $a_0 s \ldots a_n s$ or $a_0 s \ldots a_n$ (including ε), where $n \geq 0$ and every $a_i \in \{s, f, r\}$, can be extended to a prefix that negatively determines it (*e.g.*, by extending it with ff).   ∎

From Definitions 15 and 16, it follows immediately that ∀PZ $\subset$ ∃PZ.

Proposition 2. *All properties in Safe $\cup$ CoSafe are ∀PZ-monitorable.*

Proof. Let $P \in$ Safe and pick a finite trace s. If there is an f such that $sf \notin P$ then, by Definition 12, there exists $r \preceq sf$ that negatively determines P, meaning that s has an extension that negatively determines P. Alternatively, if there is *no* f such that $sf \notin P$, s itself positively determines P. Hence P is s-monitorable, for *every* s, according to Definition 14. The case for $P \in$ CoSafe is dual.   □

Pnueli and Zaks, Operationally. ∃PZ-monitorability coincides with informative monitorability: ∃PZ-monitorable properties are those for which some monitor can reach a verdict on some finite trace. For similar reasons, ∀PZ-monitorability coincides with informative monitorability. See Fig. 1.

Theorem 7. $\exists PZ = ICmp$ *and* $\forall PZ = PICmp$.

Proof. Since the proofs of the two claims are analogous, we simply outline the one for $\forall PZ = PICmp$. Let $P \in \forall PZ$ and pick a finite trace $s \in ACT^*$. By Lemma 2, m_P is sound for P. By Definition 6 we need to show that there exists an f such that $\mathbf{acc}(m_P, sf)$ or $\mathbf{rej}(m_P, sf)$. From Definition 15 and 14 we know that there is a finite r such that sr positively or negatively determines P. By Definition 2 we know that $\mathbf{acc}(m_P, sr)$ or $\mathbf{rej}(m_P, sr)$. Thus $P \in PICmp$, which is the required result.

Conversely, assume $P \in PICmp$, and pick some $s \in ACT^*$. By Definitions 15 and 14, we need to show that there is an extension of s that positively or negatively determines P. From Definitions 6 and 7, there exists some f such that $\mathbf{acc}(m_P, sf)$ or $\mathbf{rej}(m_P, sf)$. By Definition 1, there is a finite extension of s, say sr, that is a prefix of sf such that $\mathbf{acc}(m_P, sr)$ or $\mathbf{rej}(m_P, sr)$. By Definition 2, we know that sr either positively or negatively determines P. Thus $P \in \forall PZ$.

8 Monitorability in Other Settings

We have shown how classical definitions of monitorability fit into our hierarchy and provided the corresponding operational interpretations and syntactic characterisations, focusing on regular finfinite properties over a finite alphabet and monitors with irrevocable verdicts. Here we discuss how different parameters, both within our setting and beyond, affect what is monitorable.

Monitorability with respect to the Alphabet. The monitorability of a property can depend on ACT. For instance, if ACT has at least two elements $\{a, b, \ldots\}$, property $\{a^\omega\}$, which can be represented as $\max X.\langle a \rangle X$, is s-monitorable for every sequence s, as s can be extended to sb, which negatively determines the property. On the other hand, assume that $ACT = \{a\}$. In this case, $\{a^\omega\}$ is neither $\exists PZ$- nor $\forall PZ$-monitorable. Indeed, no string $s = a^k$, $k \geq 0$, determines $\{a^\omega\}$ positively or negatively as s does not satisfy it but its extension a^ω does. On the other hand, when restricted to infinite traces, $\{a^\omega\}$ is again $\exists PZ$-monitorable.

So far, we only considered finite alphabets; how an infinite alphabet, which may encode integer data for example, affects monitorability is left as future work.

Monitoring with Revocable Verdicts. Early on, we postulated that verdicts are irrevocable. Although this is a typical (implicit) assumption in most work on monitorability, some authors have considered monitors that give revocable judgements when an irrevocable one is not appropriate. This approach is taken by Bauer *et al.* when they define a finite-trace semantics for LTL, called RV-LTL [13]. Falcone *et al.* [25] also have a definition of monitorability based on this idea (in addition to those discussed in Remark 4). It uses the four-valued domain $\{\mathsf{yes}, \mathsf{no}, \mathsf{yes}_c, \mathsf{no}_c\}$ (c for *currently*). Finite traces that do not determine a property yield a (revocable) verdict yes_c or no_c that indicates whether the trace observed so far satisfies the property; yes and no are still irrevocable. This definition allows *all* finfinite properties to be monitored since it does not require verdicts to be irrevocable.

This type of monitoring does not give any guarantees beyond soundness: there are properties that are monitorable according to this definition for which no sound monitor ever reaches an irrevocable verdict: F G s for the system from Example 1 has no sound informative monitor, yet can be monitored according to Falcone *et al.* 's four-valued monitoring. This type of monitorability is complete, in the sense of providing at least a *revocable* verdict for all traces.

Monitorability in the Infinite and Finite. Bauer *et al.* use ∀PZ-monitorability in their study of runtime verification for LTL [14] and attribute it to Pnueli and Zaks. However, unlike Falcone *et al.*, Pnueli and Zaks [41] and ourselves, they focus on properties over *infinite* traces. There are some striking differences that arise if there is no risk of an execution ending. Aceto *et al.* show that, unlike in the finfinite domain, a set of non-trivial properties becomes completely monitorable: HML [33] (a.k.a. modal logic) is both satisfaction- and violation-monitorable over infinite traces [3]. Furthermore, some properties, like $\{a^\omega\}$ over ACT $= \{a\}$, that were not ∃PZ- or ∀PZ-monitorable on the finfinite domain, are ∃PZ- or even ∀PZ-monitorable on the infinite domain. The full analysis of how the hierarchy in Fig. 1 changes for the infinite domain is left for future work.

Havelund and Peled recently presented a related classification of infinitary properties [32]. Their classification consists of safety and co-safety properties, (there called AFS and AFR), and properties that are not positively or not negatively determined by any sequence (NFS and NFR) and properties where some, but not all prefixes have an extention that determines the property positively, and their negations (SFS and SFR). They show that several of their classes contain both ∀PZ-monitorable and non-∀PZ-monitorable properties. In contrast, in our classification, ∀PZ-monitorability is not orthogonal to other types of monitorability; rather, it is part of a spectrum that reflects the trade-offs between the strengths of the guarantees a monitor can provide and the specifications that can be monitored with these guarantees.

Barringer *et al.* [11] consider monitoring of properties over *finite* traces. In this domain, all properties are monitorable if, as is the case in [11], the end of a trace is *observable*; in this setting the question of monitorability is less relevant.

Monitoring Non-regular Properties. Although we have focussed on the monitorability of regular properties, the monitorability hierarchy of Sect. 3 is not restricted to this setting. Indeed, although non-regular properties require richer monitors, for example monitors with a stack or registers, the same concerns of soundness and degress of completeness remain relevant. Barringer *et al.* consider a specification logic that allows for context-free properties [11]. In [26], Ferrier *et al.* consider monitors with registers (*i.e.,* infinite state monitors) to verify safety properties that are not regular. Characterising (*e.g.,* syntactically) the different classes of monitorability for non-regular properties is left as future work.

Beyond Monitorability. Stream-based monitoring systems such as [21,22] are more concerned with producing (revocable) aggregate outputs and transforming traces to satisfy properties, employing more powerful monitors than the ones considered here (*e.g.,* transducers). Instead of monitorability, *enforceability* [5, 25] is a criterion that is better suited for these settings.

9   Conclusion

We have proposed a unified, operational view on monitorability. This allows us to clearly state the implicit operational guarantees of existing definitions of monitorability. For instance, recall Example 1 from the introduction: since $(G \neg f) \wedge (F s)$ is $\exists$PZ- and $\forall$PZ-monitorable but it is neither a safety nor a co-safety property, we know there is a monitor which can recognise some violations and satisfactions of this property, but there is no monitor that can recognise *all* satisfactions or *all* violations. Although we focussed on regular, finfinite properties, the definitions of monitorability in Sect. 3, and, more fundamentally, the methodology that systematically puts the relationship between monitor behaviour and specification centre stage, are equally applicable to other settings.

The emphasis our approach places on the explicit guarantees provided by the different types of monitorability should clarify the role of monitorability in the design of RV tools which, depending on the setting, may have different requirements. Indeed, a monitor that checks that the output of a module does not violate the preconditions of the next module had better be violation-complete; on the other hand, it is probably sufficient that a monitor be informative when it is used as a light-weight, best-effort part of a hybrid verification strategy.

References

1. Aceto, L., Achilleos, A., Francalanza, A., Ingólfsdóttir, A.: Monitoring for silent actions. In: Lokam, S., Ramanujam, R. (eds.) FSTTCS. LIPIcs, vol. 93, pp. 7:1–7:14. Schloss Dagstuhl-Leibniz-Zentrum fuer Informatik, Dagstuhl, Germany (2017)
2. Aceto, L., Achilleos, A., Francalanza, A., Ingólfsdóttir, A.: A framework for parameterized monitorability. In: Baier, C., Dal Lago, U. (eds.) FoSSaCS 2018. LNCS, vol. 10803, pp. 203–220. Springer, Cham (2018). https://doi.org/10.1007/978-3-319-89366-2_11
3. Aceto, L., Achilleos, A., Francalanza, A., Ingólfsdóttir, A., Lehtinen, K.: Adventures in monitorability: from branching to linear time and back again. Proc. ACM Program. Lang. 3(POPL), 52:1–52:29 (2019). https://dl.acm.org/citation.cfm?id=3290365
4. Aceto, L., Achilleos, A., Francalanza, A., Ingólfsdóttir, A., Lehtinen, K.: An operational guide to monitorability. CoRR abs/1906.00766 (2019). http://arxiv.org/abs/1906.00766
5. Aceto, L., Cassar, I., Francalanza, A., Ingólfsdóttir, A.: On runtime enforcement via suppressions. In: 29th International Conference on Concurrency Theory, CONCUR 2018. LIPIcs, vol. 118, pp. 34:1–34:17. Schloss Dagstuhl (2018). https://doi.org/10.4230/LIPIcs.CONCUR.2018.34

6. Aceto, L., Ingólfsdóttir, A., Larsen, K.G., Srba, J.: Reactive Systems: Modelling, Specification and Verification. Cambridge University Press, New York (2007)
7. Alpern, B., Schneider, F.B.: Defining liveness. Inf. Process. Lett. **21**(4), 181–185 (1985)
8. Attard, D.P., Cassar, I., Francalanza, A., Aceto, L., Ingolfsdottir, A.: A runtime monitoring tool for actor-based systems. In: Gay, S., Ravara, A. (eds.) Behavioural Types: From Theory to Tools, pp. 49–74. River Publishers (2017)
9. Attard, D.P., Francalanza, A.: A monitoring tool for a branching-time logic. In: Falcone, Y., Sánchez, C. (eds.) RV 2016. LNCS, vol. 10012, pp. 473–481. Springer, Cham (2016). https://doi.org/10.1007/978-3-319-46982-9_31
10. Baier, C., Tinelli, C. (eds.): Tools and Algorithms for the Construction and Analysis of Systems - 21st International Conference, TACAS 2015, LNCS, vol. 9035. Springer, Heidelberg (2015). https://doi.org/10.1007/978-3-662-46681-0
11. Barringer, H., Rydeheard, D., Havelund, K.: Rule systems for run-time monitoring: from Eagle to RuleR. J. Log. Comput. **20**(3), 675–706 (2008)
12. Bartocci, E., Falcone, Y., Francalanza, A., Reger, G.: Introduction to runtime verification. In: Bartocci, E., Falcone, Y. (eds.) Lectures on Runtime Verification. LNCS, vol. 10457, pp. 1–33. Springer, Cham (2018). https://doi.org/10.1007/978-3-319-75632-5_1
13. Bauer, A., Leucker, M., Schallhart, C.: Comparing LTL semantics for runtime verification. J. Log. Comput. **20**(3), 651–674 (2010)
14. Bauer, A., Leucker, M., Schallhart, C.: Runtime verification for LTL and TLTL. ACM Trans. Softw. Eng. Methodol. **20**(4), 14:1–14:64 (2011). https://doi.org/10.1145/2000799.2000800
15. Bérard, B., et al.: Systems and Software Verification: Model-checking Techniques and Tools. Springer, Heidelberg (2013). https://doi.org/10.1007/978-3-662-04558-9
16. Chang, E., Manna, Z., Pnueli, A.: Characterization of temporal property classes. In: Kuich, W. (ed.) ICALP 1992. LNCS, vol. 623, pp. 474–486. Springer, Heidelberg (1992). https://doi.org/10.1007/3-540-55719-9_97
17. Chen, F., Rosu, G.: Mop: an efficient and generic runtime verification framework. In: Gabriel, R.P., Bacon, D.F., Lopes, C.V., Steele Jr., G.L. (eds.) Proceedings of the 22nd Annual ACM SIGPLAN Conference on Object-Oriented Programming, Systems, Languages, and Applications, OOPSLA 2007, pp. 569–588. ACM (2007). https://doi.org/10.1145/1297027.1297069
18. Chen, Z., Wu, Y., Wei, O., Sheng, B.: Poster: deciding weak monitorability for runtime verification. In: 2018 IEEE/ACM 40th International Conference on Software Engineering: Companion (ICSE-Companion), pp. 163–164, May 2018
19. Cini, C., Francalanza, A.: An LTL proof system for runtime verification. In: Baier and Tinelli [10], pp. 581–595. https://doi.org/10.1007/978-3-662-46681-0_54
20. Clarke, E.M., Grumberg, O., Peled, D.: Model Checking. MIT press (1999)
21. Convent, L., Hungerecker, S., Leucker, M., Scheffel, T., Schmitz, M., Thoma, D.: TeSSLa: temporal stream-based specification language. In: Massoni, T., Mousavi, M.R. (eds.) SBMF 2018. LNCS, vol. 11254, pp. 144–162. Springer, Cham (2018). https://doi.org/10.1007/978-3-030-03044-5_10
22. D'Angelo, B., et al.: LOLA: runtime monitoring of synchronous systems. In: 12th International Symposium on Temporal Representation and Reasoning (TIME 2005), pp. 166–174. IEEE Computer Society Press, June 2005
23. Decker, N., Leucker, M., Thoma, D.: jUnit^{RV}–adding runtime verification to jUnit. In: Brat, G., Rungta, N., Venet, A. (eds.) NFM 2013. LNCS, vol. 7871, pp. 459–464. Springer, Heidelberg (2013). https://doi.org/10.1007/978-3-642-38088-4_34

24. Diekert, V., Leucker, M.: Topology, monitorable properties and runtime verification. Theor. Comput. Sci. **537**, 29–41 (2014). https://doi.org/10.1016/j.tcs.2014.02.052

25. Falcone, Y., Fernandez, J.C., Mounier, L.: What can you verify and enforce at runtime? Int. J. Softw. Tools Technol. Transf. **14**(3), 349–382 (2012)

26. Ferrère, T., Henzinger, T.A., Saraç, N.E.: A theory of register monitors. In: Dawar, A., Grädel, E. (eds.) Proceedings of the 33rd Annual ACM/IEEE Symposium on Logic in Computer Science, LICS 2018, pp. 394–403. ACM (2018). https://doi.org/10.1145/3209108.3209194

27. Francalanza, A.: A theory of monitors (extended abstract). In: Jacobs, B., Löding, C. (eds.) FoSSaCS 2016. LNCS, vol. 9634, pp. 145–161. Springer, Heidelberg (2016). https://doi.org/10.1007/978-3-662-49630-5_9

28. Francalanza, A.: Consistently-detecting monitors. In: 28th International Conference on Concurrency Theory (CONCUR). LIPIcs, vol. 85, pp. 8:1–8:19. Schloss Dagstuhl (2017). https://doi.org/10.4230/LIPIcs.CONCUR.2017.8

29. Francalanza, A., et al.: A foundation for runtime monitoring. In: Lahiri, S., Reger, G. (eds.) RV 2017. LNCS, vol. 10548, pp. 8–29. Springer, Cham (2017). https://doi.org/10.1007/978-3-319-67531-2_2

30. Francalanza, A., Aceto, L., Ingólfsdóttir, A.: Monitorability for the Hennessy-Milner logic with recursion. Form. Methods Syst. Des. **51**(1), 87–116 (2017). https://doi.org/10.1007/s10703-017-0273-z

31. Francalanza, A., Seychell, A.: Synthesising correct concurrent runtime monitors. Form. Methods Syst. Des. (FMSD) **46**(3), 226–261 (2015). https://doi.org/10.1007/s10703-014-0217-9

32. Havelund, K., Peled, D.: Runtime verification: from propositional to first-order temporal logic. In: Colombo, C., Leucker, M. (eds.) RV 2018. LNCS, vol. 11237, pp. 90–112. Springer, Cham (2018). https://doi.org/10.1007/978-3-030-03769-7_7

33. Hennessy, M., Milner, R.: Algebraic laws for nondeterminism and concurrency. J. ACM **32**(1), 137–161 (1985). https://doi.org/10.1145/2455.2460

34. Kozen, D.C.: Results on the propositional μ-calculus. Theor. Comput. Sci. **27**, 333–354 (1983)

35. Kupferman, O., Vardi, M.Y.: Model checking of safety properties. Form. Methods Syst. Des. **19**(3), 291–314 (2001)

36. Kupferman, O., Vardi, M.Y., Wolper, P.: An automata-theoretic approach to branching-time model checking. J. ACM **47**(2), 312–360 (2000)

37. Larsen, K.G.: Proof systems for satisfiability in Hennessy-Milner logic with recursion. Theor. Comput. Sci. **72**(2), 265–288 (1990). https://doi.org/10.1016/0304-3975(90)90038-J

38. Laurent, J., Goodloe, A., Pike, L.: Assuring the guardians. In: Bartocci, E., Majumdar, R. (eds.) RV 2015. LNCS, vol. 9333, pp. 87–101. Springer, Cham (2015). https://doi.org/10.1007/978-3-319-23820-3_6

39. Manna, Z., Pnueli, A.: Completing the temporal picture. Theor. Comput. Sci. **83**(1), 97–130 (1991). https://doi.org/10.1016/0304-3975(91)90041-Y

40. Neykova, R., Bocchi, L., Yoshida, N.: Timed runtime monitoring for multiparty conversations. Form. Asp. Comput. **29**(5), 877–910 (2017). https://doi.org/10.1007/s00165-017-0420-8

41. Pnueli, A., Zaks, A.: PSL model checking and run-time verification via testers. In: Misra, J., Nipkow, T., Sekerinski, E. (eds.) FM 2006. LNCS, vol. 4085, pp. 573–586. Springer, Heidelberg (2006). https://doi.org/10.1007/11813040_38

42. Reger, G., Cruz, H.C., Rydeheard, D.E.: MarQ: monitoring at runtime withQEA. In: Baier and Tinelli [10], pp. 596–610. https://doi.org/10.1007/978-3-662-46681-0_55

43. Rosu, G.: On safety properties and their monitoring. Sci. Ann. Comput. Sci. **22**(2), 327–365 (2012)

44. Schneider, F.B.: Enforceable security policies. ACM Trans. Inf. Syst. Secur. **3**(1), 30–50 (2000)

45. Viswanathan, M., Kim, M.: Foundations for the run-time monitoring of reactive systems – *Fundamentals of the MaC Language*. In: Liu, Z., Araki, K. (eds.) ICTAC 2004. LNCS, vol. 3407, pp. 543–556. Springer, Heidelberg (2005). https://doi.org/10.1007/978-3-540-31862-0_38

46. Wolper, P.: Temporal logic can be more expressive. Inf. Control **56**(1/2), 72–99 (1983). https://doi.org/10.1016/S0019-9958(83)80051-5

Let's Prove It Later—Verification at Different Points in Time

Martin Ring[1] and Christoph Lüth[1,2(✉)]

[1] Deutsches Forschungszentrum für Künstliche Intelligenz, Bremen, Germany
christoph.lueth@dfki.de
[2] FB 3—Mathematics and Computer Science, Universität Bremen,
Bremen, Germany

Abstract. The vast majority of cyber-physical and embedded systems today is deployed without being fully formally verified during their design. Postponing verification until after deployment is a possible way to cope with this, as the verification process can benefit from instantiating operating parameters which were unknown at design time. But there exist many interesting alternatives between early verification (at design time) and late verification (at runtime). Moreover, this decision also has an impact on the specification style. Using a case study of the safety properties of an access control system, this paper explores the implications of different points in time chosen for verification, and points out the respective benefits and trade-offs. Further, we sketch some general rules to govern the decision when to verify a system.

1 Introduction

Contemporary embedded and cyber-physical systems have become so commonplace that we, almost unconsciously, rely on their correct functioning—we just expect our smartphone to work. This is contrary to the fact that these systems have reached a complexity where the verification of their correct behaviour becomes prohibitively expensive. Subsequently, a full correctness proof is only ever done for the most safety-critical systems. For all other devices, errors during the design process may remain undetected in the final product. This is due to the way these systems are currently designed.

The current design flow for embedded and cyber-physical systems is (idealized) as follows: we first *specify* the system's intended behaviour, then construct a *model* of the system and finally an executable *implementation*. Some of these steps may be conflated or missing; e.g. in model-based specification, the specification is the model, or one may generate an implementation from the model. In this design flow, *verification* refers to all activities which show that the implementation of the system satisfies its specification [1].

Current verification techniques such as theorem proving, model checking, static analysis or testing are conducted at design time and finished before deployment, for two reasons: firstly, we want to make sure the system has no errors

© Springer Nature Switzerland AG 2019
P. C. Ölveczky and G. Salaün (Eds.): SEFM 2019, LNCS 11724, pp. 454–468, 2019.
https://doi.org/10.1007/978-3-030-30446-1_24

before putting it into operation, and secondly, it is not entirely clear how to conduct verification at runtime. But this approach has the drawback that the time for verification is limited; errors which are not caught by the time the system is going into operation will remain undetected and may later on have unintended, unpleasant, or even catastrophic consequences.

On the other hand, verification does not necessarily need to terminate with the end of the development. In *runtime verification*, we check whether a particular run of the system satisfies desired properties. This has the advantage that we do not need to stop verification if we deploy the system, and checking whether a specific run of the system satisfies the desired property is of lower complexity compared to model-checking [2]. The drawbacks are that it may be costly to continuously monitor the behaviour of the system at runtime, and once we find an error, it may be too late to do anything about it. This is particularly true for hardware, and systems where the split between hardware and software is decided rather late in the development process.

The idea of *self-verification* is to investigate the middle ground in between: verify properties of the system as soon as practically possible, but as late as necessary. In other words, verification does not terminate with deployment, but is also not kept until the last moment. The present paper investigates the idea of self-verification as proposed in [3,4] further. The key contribution is to examine the implication of self-verification on the development process. We do so by means of a case study, an access control system, which is simple to understand yet offers subtle effects and is easy to visualize.

The paper is structured as follows. Section 2 introduces the basic concepts of self-verification, which are elaborated more concretely in Sect. 3 using the case study, an access control system. Section 4 shows our approach to realizing self-verifying systems, and Sect. 5 concludes with a general discussion of the wider applicability.

2 Self-verification

Modern cyber-physical systems are designed to be versatile, such that they are able to handle numerous operating contexts and operate in many different environments. Thus, they have a large number of parameters which become instantiated at runtime. The key advantage of self-verification is that after deployment, the concrete values of these parameters may become known for verification. Some may be instantiated early on after deployment, and not change after that at all, or only very infrequently; others may change, but not that often; and even others may be sensor data which are read in small intervals, but where the rate of change may be limited. All of this information may be utilized at runtime for more efficient verification.

This observation hinges on the fact that proving a property ϕ depends, *inter alia*, on the number of free variables in ϕ, and that parameters as mentioned above usually occur as free (or universally quantified) variables in ϕ. Then, proving $\phi\left[\frac{t}{x}\right]$ with a ground term t instantiated for x is typically orders of magnitude easier than proving ϕ.

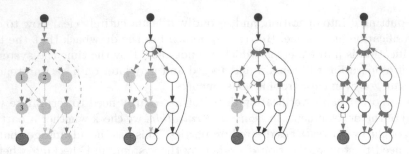

Fig. 1. Four different points in time chosen for verification, from design time (leftmost) to runtime (rightmost). Trigger transitions are marked with small boxes; they trigger verification tasks which show that every possible path through the state space which does not include other trigger transitions is safe. Green boxes mark successful verification, and red boxes mark failed verification tasks. The solid red state is unsafe; it violates the safety property ϕ. Grayed-out states are not reachable, because they come after a failed verification (open red box). Design time verification (on the left) would identify the system as erroneous and prohibit its execution. Second to left, the system is verified early after deployment and thus is allowed to execute only a small fraction (6 transitions) of the system, blocking two transitions and leaving 6 transitions unreachable. Third to left, most of the system is executable (11 transitions) but two transitions are blocked and one transition is not reachable. The rightmost example allows all but one transition. Note that in the last example the system gets deadlocked in state 4 when taking the leftmost path. (Color figure online)

Self-verification provides some challenges. At runtime, we do not have as many resources in terms of memory and computing power as at design time, and we need to transport the proof obligations derived from the specification into the runtime environment. So, self-verification needs a design flow to support it: a format and logic in which to encode the properties at design time, and light-weight proof engines which run under the resource constraints of an embedded system. We will show in Sect. 4 how such a design flow can be implemented.

However, the focus of the present paper is to investigate the effects of self-verification on the development. That is, we want to explore *when* to prove properties and which ones, and we want to investigate how self-verification interacts with the development process.

Comparing self-verification to runtime and *a priori* design time verification on a more abstract level, we consider specific runs of the system $\langle \sigma_i \rangle_{i \in \mathbb{N}}$, consisting of states σ_i, and a safety property ϕ. Usual design time verification proves the general property that for all runs, $\forall i. \phi(\sigma_i)$, i.e. the safety property holds for all states. In OCL and related formalisms, this is achieved by an inductive argument, showing that we start in a safe state, $\phi(\sigma_0)$, and that from a safe state we can only get to a safe state, $\phi(\sigma_i)$ implies $\phi(\sigma_{i+1})$. Runtime verification, on the other hand, considers whether a specific run satisfies $\forall i. \phi(\sigma_i)$ and does not restrict the transitions of the system; unsafe states can be reached, but this is always detected. In self-verification, instead of restricting transitions, we classify them into trigger transitions and ordinary transitions. The idea is that when the system goes through a trigger transition $\sigma_i \rightarrow \sigma_{i+1}$, self-verification shows that all states σ_k reachable with ordinary transitions from σ_{i+1} are safe, i.e. $\phi(\sigma_k)$. If another trigger transition is reached, the self-verification is run again. Note that the classification of trigger transitions and ordinary transitions depends on the particular ϕ, and is a design decision (see Sect. 3 below). A priori and runtime verification can be seen as extreme cases of self-verification: in design time verification only one transition (the one leading to the initial state of the system) is classified as a trigger transition, while in runtime verification every transition is a trigger transition. Figure 1 illustrates the effect of different sets of trigger transitions for one system. Because the effort to state and prove ϕ increases with the number of states we want to cover, self-verification allows us to strike a balance: we may prove ϕ with little effort for a small number of states, and so have to reprove it more often, or we may prove ϕ for more states, but with more effort.

When we specify the desired behaviour of the system with design time verification, we need to state the required preconditions very precisely—they need to be strong enough to be able to actually show that the system globally satisfies the specified properties, and to preclude unwanted behaviour, but weak enough to still allow all desired implementation. If we move verification into runtime, we can relax preconditions at design time, allowing for more readable specifications and speeding up the development process. Consider Fig. 1 again: to make the system usable as well as correct, one would have to, e.g. refine the specification (or the implementation) to exclude the transitions from states 1 and 2 to 3. With self-verification, we can allow a more liberal specification or implementation and still remain safe, making the development process easier.

Thus, in essence specification becomes easier and faster to write, and moreover we are liberated from having to prove everything a priori, and can instead adapt the proving strategy to the problem at hand.

3   Case Study

In the following, we will demonstrate our methodology in a case study (building loosely on Abrial [5]). The case study is simple enough to be easily understood, yet complex enough to show the subtle effects of verification at different points in time.

3.1   Informal Description

To motivate our case study, think of a building where fine-grained access control is needed for security or safety reasons, e.g. a nuclear power plant, but which also needs to be able to be evacuated very fast in the case of an emergency. In that case, we want to be able to eliminate access control (to allow fast evacuation) and just open some of the doors in such a way that all users are able to get out, but no user gains access to a room where they are not allowed to enter.

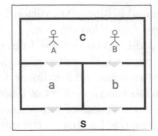

Fig. 2. Example of a very simple building. The user with card A is authorized for room a, user B is authorized for room b, both are authorized for rooms c and s. Room s is the only safe room (it is the outside). The situation shown violates the safety property.

More precisely, we have a *building* consisting of several *rooms*. The rooms are connected by *doors*, which are unidirectional (think of turnstiles; normal two-way doors are an obvious generalization). Thus, doors lead from one room to another one, which is equivalent to each room having a set of entries and exits.

Users are represented in the system by *cards* which regulate the access to rooms. (In the following, we use cards and users interchangeably; the formal specification only has cards.) Each card authorizes access to a set of rooms, by restricting passage through the doors. The access control system operates in two modes: in normal mode, a door may only be passed (using a card) if the card authorizes access to the room the door is leading to. However, we can declare an emergency for the whole building; in that modus, some doors are opened, allowing anyone to pass through.

Opening doors in an emergency is subject to two *safety properties*: firstly, it should allow any user (card) to eventually arrive in a safe room, and secondly, it should not allow any user to enter a room they are not authorized to. A subset of rooms is considered to be *safe*; in the simplest case, this can just be the outside modelled as a room. As an example for the necessity of the safety properties, take the nuclear power plant: even in case of an emergency, one would not want anybody to exit through the reactor core.

This rather innocuous specification allows some subtle effects. Consider the simple building in Fig. 2; the depicted situation violates the safety property, as in case of an emergency, we cannot disable access control and open the doors in such a fashion that neither user A or user B are allowed to access rooms they are not authorized to (rooms b and a, respectively), and both are able to get to a safe room (s).

Hence, we need to prevent a situation like this from happening. This could be done by

- either restricting the layout of the building in such a way that situations like this do not happen (this is what is usually done, with layouts were corridors are the default escape route, and users do not have to traverse long sequences of rooms);

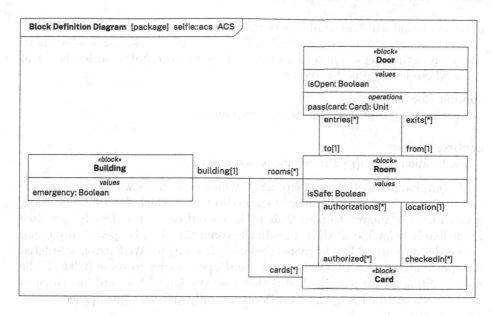

Fig. 3. Formal specification of an access control system.

- or by restricting the authorizations of the cards in such a way that a situation like above does not happen;
- or by checking that *before* a users enters a room no situation violating the safety property like above is created.

3.2 Formal Specification

We can now give a formal specification of our access control system. We will use a subset of SysML [6] and OCL [7], where block definition diagrams (BDDs, the SysML equivalent to UML class diagrams) model the structure of the system, and OCL constrains the dynamic behaviour.

In Fig. 3, we can see blocks modelling the building, doors, rooms and cards respectively. The building has a Boolean attribute *emergency*. A door leads from exactly one to another room, but a room may have many (or no) entries and exits. A door may only connect rooms which are part of the same building:

context Door
  inv: from.building = to.building

Furthermore cards are also associated to buildings and may only authorize access to rooms which belong to the same building:

context Card
  inv: authorizations→forall(r | r.building = **self**.building)

Cards have a set of *authorizations* (rooms which the holder of the card is allowed to enter) and exactly one *location*, which determines the current location of the card, and which must always be contained in the set of authorizations. On the other hand, rooms have a set of *authorized* cards (those cards which have the room in their set of authorizations), and a set of *checkedIn* cards (the set of cards whose location is this room).

context Room
  inv: checkedIn→forall(p | authorized→contains(p))

context Card
  inv: location→forall(r | authorizations→contains(r))

Rooms have a Boolean attribute *isSafe* which determines whether the room is safe during an emergency. A door has a method *pass*, which determines whether a given card is allowed to pass. This is the case if either the door is open (see immediately below), or if the card is in the room this door is opening from, and the card is authorized for the room the door is opening to. We have encapsulated this precondition as an OCL function *mayPass* in order to reuse it later. The postcondition of the *pass* method is that the *location* of the card has changed to the room the door is opening to. Doors are only allowed to be opened in case of an emergency.

context Door
  def: mayPass(card: Card): Boolean =
    isOpen **or** from.building.emergency
    and card.authorizations→contains(to)
  inv: isOpen **implies** from.building.emergency

context Door::pass(card: Card)
  pre: mayPass(card) **and** card.location = from
  post: card.location = to

We now want to formalize the safety property: in an emergency, users can always reach a safe room, yet no user has access to a room they are not authorized to. To formalize a user being able to reach a room, we formalize the notion of recursive *access*, which models the traversal along a sequence of connected rooms: users have access to the room they are currently in, and recursively to all rooms which can be reached through doors which may be passed (i.e. rooms which have an entry from an accessable room that this card has access to). We formulate this notion as an OCL function *hasAccess* which for a given room determines whether a given card has access to this room. Since OCL does not allow non-terminating functions we pass the set of already traversed rooms to the helper function *hasAccess$* such that we do not traverse cycles:

context Room
  def: hasAccess(card: Card): Boolean = hasAccess$(card,Set{})
  def: hasAccess$(card: Card, visited: Set(Room)): Boolean =
    card.location = **self or**
    visited.excludes(**self**) **and** entries→exists(e |

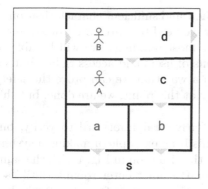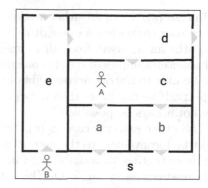

Fig. 4. Situations which are safe. On the left, user B cannot enter room c until user A has left. On the right, a similar situation, but user B may have taken the long path through room e and d quite unnecessarily before not being able to proceed further.

> e.mayPass(card) **and**
> e.from.hasAccess$(card, visited→including(**self**)))

We can now specify the safety properties: firstly, that users can always reach a safe room, and secondly, that users only have access to rooms they are authorized for:

context Card:
  inv safe1: building.rooms→exists(r |
    r.isSafe **and** r.hasAccess(**self**))
  inv safe2: building.rooms→forall(r |
    not r.authorized→contains(**self**) **implies not** r.hasAccess(**self**)))

3.3 When to Verify

In order to preclude an unsafe situation as in Fig. 2, we have to show our system satisfies the safety property. Of course, in full generality—universally quantified over all buildings and all authorizations—the safety property does not hold; we can easily find counterexamples (such as Fig. 2). If we want to show the safety property at design time, we have to formalize conditions which are sufficient for the safety property (i.e. preclude unsafe buildings).

With self-verification, we can show the safety property after deployment, at different points in time:

(a) right after deployment to a specific building, for all possible cards, authorizations and allocations of users to rooms; or
(b) after authorization has changed, for a specific building, but for all possible allocations of users to rooms; or
(c) when a user requests access to a different room: if the new configuration of the user in this different room is unsafe, access is not granted.

In case (a), we would either need an explicit and sufficient characterization of "every user always has a safe exit route", or we need to search a lot of instances (all paths for all users from all rooms). For most buildings, we will be able to find counterexamples of unsafe configurations of users and access rights, but we may be able to restrict access rights in such a way that we can prove the safety property. If we can prove the safety property at this point, we are done, but this may not always be possible.

The other extreme case is (c); this is fairly straightforward to verify, but might be inconvenient to the user. (Thus, this is an example of making a system safe by restricting its availability.) Consider the situation in Fig. 4 with the same authorizations as in Fig. 2. On the left, user B cannot enter room c until user A has left, because otherwise we would have the situation from Fig. 2 which is not safe. This might result in situations like on the right of Fig. 4, where user B might take a long tour through room e to room d only to find they cannot proceed any further.

A good compromise is case (b): we verify the safety property each time the authorizations change, for a specific building and specific authorizations. In most cases, this should be reasonably efficient—the search space is through all possible allocations of users to rooms—but still precludes unsafe allocations.

Note how self-verification allows us to relax the development process: because we can prove the safety property at runtime, we do not need to specify all its preconditions at design time (here, we do not need to characterize the preconditions to make buildings and authorizations safe). This makes the development process more *agile* without compromising safety.

4   Realization

4.1   A Design Flow for Self-verification

Our design flow targets hardware-software co-design for embedded and cyber-physical systems. As demonstrated in Sect. 3, we use a subset of SysML (block definition diagrams and state machine diagrams[1]) together with OCL as a specification formalism. Block definition diagrams and state machine diagrams can be given a formal semantics (which is not the case for all SysML diagrams), so our specifications have a mathematically well-defined, formal meaning. This is indispensable if we want to perform formal correctness proofs. Figure 5 sketches the design flow.

We have developed a textual representation of block definition diagrams and state machine diagrams (in the spirit of USE [8]), which we use in our design flow. Figure 6 shows an excerpt; parts of the corresponding OCL specifications have been shown in Sect. 3 above. We can also use commercial tools like Astah SysML, but their OCL support tends to be not as sophisticated. Instead, we make use of the OCL implementation of the Eclipse Modelling Foundation. Moreover, our

---

[1] The case study only uses block definition diagrams.

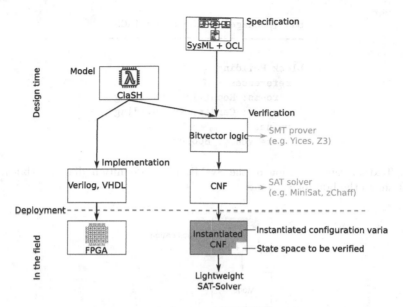

Fig. 5. A design flow for self-verification.

textual representation makes the design flow fairly light-weight, allowing users to employ any editor and versioning system at their disposal.

The implementation is given as an executable *system model*. To stay independent of a specific programming language, we use the functional hardware description language CλaSH [9] as our modelling language, since it allows us to simulate the system as well as synthesize an implementation in VHDL or VeriLog. Another possibility with more commercial traction would be SystemC, but that has less clear semantics and it is embedded in C++, technically a lot more awkward to handle (in CλaSH, adding proof support was merely a question of adding an additional backend; in SystemC, we do not even have an explicit representation of the model to start from).

Our tool chain reads the SysML and OCL specification, performs the appropriate type checks, reads the CλaSH model, and generates the corresponding first-order proof obligations in bitvector format (first-order logic with limited width integers as datatypes). The proof obligations are essentially obtained by taking a representation of the system model in bitvector logic, and showing they satisfy the OCL constraints (pre/postconditions and invariants). They can be either processed at design time by an SMT prover such as Yices or Z3, or transferred to runtime. Proving at runtime is either performed by an SMT prover running on the target system, if the latter is powerful enough, or by converting the proof obligations into conjunctive normal form (e.g. using the Yices prover) before transferring it to the target system, and using a SAT solver at runtime (either as a lightweight software SAT solver [10] or even a hardware SAt solver [11]). We have evaluated this design flow using a ZedBoard (which consists of a

```
bdd [package] selfie::acs [ACS]
--------------------------------

block Building
   references
      rooms: Room[*] <- building
      cards: Card[*] <- building
   values
      emergency: Boolean
```

Fig. 6. Textual representation of the SysML block definition diagram (bdd). The excerpt shows the bdd for Building.

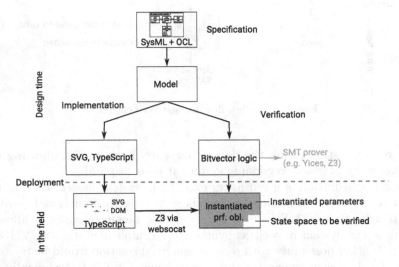

Fig. 7. Design flow adapted to our demonstrator.

Xilinx FPGA controlled by an ARMv7 core), see [4]. Our evaluation has shown that verification at runtime can cope with systems where *a priori* verification fails, precisely because of the reduction in search space by instantiating parameters which become known at runtime.

4.2 The Demonstrator

If we implement the case study in our usual design flow, we derive a hardware implementation, e.g. on an FPGA. In order to explore the implications of proving at different points in time, and to demonstrate the effects of self-verification in an easily accessible setting, we implemented the case study as an interactive demonstrator.

Simulating the hardware turned out to be very slow, so instead we chose to adapt our flow: the implementation is an interactive SVG, with the dynamic behaviour implemented in TypeScript. The core of the system is generated as implementation stubs, using an adapted form of our design flow (see Fig. 7). We have chosen TypeScript [12] as the target language (TypeScript is like JavaScript, but with added type security), because it allows us to dynamically modify the abstract syntax tree (the DOM) of the SVG. This allows the demonstrator to be displayed and run on any recent web browser. In addition to the specified behaviour we manually implemented means to add and remove cards and change their access rights, and reading building topologies from a non-interactive SVG. We have implemented access cards (and implicitly their owners) as automated agents which randomly roam the building. This allows us to observe the implications of the different points in time of the verification; for example, the behaviours mentioned for case (c) in Sect. 3 above manifest themselves in agents hovering in one place unable to proceed because of the violation of the safety property this would incur.

The generated SMT proof obligations are a general equivalence proof which can be processed by an SMT prover at design time. As mentioned above, the prover quickly finds counter examples since our specification can easily be violated in general. By adding runtime information in the form of assertions, we refine the instance on the fly. This was realized by establishing a WebSocket connection between the SVG and the Z3 prover. For this, we use the *websocat* utility, which wraps a WebSocket server around a command-line program. This allows us to load the general proof and then incrementally send assertions restricting the state space.

Technically, the arbitrarily mutable state of our simulation is in principle not compatible with the monotonous nature of adding assertions: assertions can only add information but not change or remove. Fortunately, SMT-LIB (the common language used by most SMT provers) allows us to use scopes (with the commands *push* and *pop*) for this. In order for this to work, we introduce a fixed order in which information is added, which is based on the order of execution in the system, ideally corresponding to the frequency of change. First we add the general building topology, then the access rights, and after that, the tracked locations of the card holders. Between every assertion, we save the current size of the assertion stack with the *push* command. If any information changes, we remove the assertion with the now outdated information as well as any assertion which came afterwards. Then we only need to add the updated assertions. Depending on the point in time chosen, we can check satisfiability anywhere between.

An interesting feature of our implementation is that we did not implement any algorithm which opens the doors. Instead, we use the prover to give us a model of the existentially quantified safety property, which states that there must be a safe way to exit (i.e. a set of doors to open in case of emergency). Through self-verification not only did we not have to characterize buildings, access rights or safe paths through the building, we even did not have to implement a path finding algorithm at all.

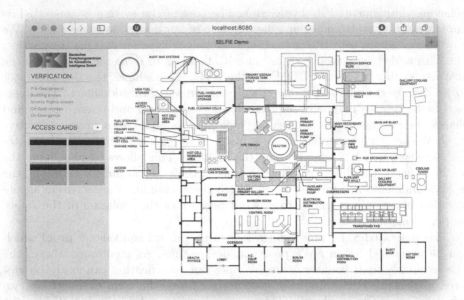

Fig. 8. The demonstrator is implemented as an interactive SVG document, displayed here in a web browser.

The demonstrator is shown in Fig. 8. It connects the implementation to the proof engine running the SMT instance. We can manually choose one of the three different information levels for the proof, which result in different assertions being added as well as different triggers for the proof.

Users can explore the consequences of the different points in time for the self-verification. For example, if they choose to verify early on (after a new card has been added or access rights change) and add a lot of cards, they will notice a considerable slow-down when adding new cards or changing access rights. If they choose to verify late (before a user enters a room), and construct situations like in Fig. 4, they will realize how users congregate in front of a room unable to get in. (The demonstrator is intended to be used together with additional interactive explanation, not stand-alone, as situations like this will have to be constructed consciously.)

The source code of the demonstrator is publicly available on GitHub.[2]

5   Discussion and Conclusions

This paper has elaborated on earlier proposals of self-verification—systems which are not verified *a priori*, during the design phase, but where the proof obligations incurred during the development are postponed until after deployment,

---

[2] https://github.com/DFKI-CPS/selfie-demo.

and are proven at runtime. This makes proofs easier, as we can instantiate a number of the parameters of the system which are unknown at design time, but become known at runtime. This reduces the state space, turning the exponential growth of the state space—the bane of model-checking—into exponential reduction. Self-verification is supported by a tool chain we have developed, which allows specification in SysML/OCL, system modelling in CλaSH, and verification using SMT provers and SAT checkers.

It should be noted that self-verification is in no way intended to *replace* design time verification. If proof obligations can be shown at design time, they should by all means be discharged; however, self-verification offers a different way to tackle proof obligations which can *not* be shown at design time, supplementing design time verification, and offering the designer to pick the best of all possible worlds.

5.1   When to Prove

The focus of the present paper has been to investigate the implications and consequences of the point in time at which the proof of safety properties take place at runtime. Generally, the earlier we can prove, the more general the proven safety property, but the larger the search space becomes and subsequently the longer it will take. How to pick the right points in time depends on the actual system and is very much a design decision. In future work, we want to further investigate how the designer can be assisted in this decision; in particular, the system should suggest which variables offer the most reduction in proof time when instantiated.

However, we have made a number of observations which can help to assist in finding the right set of trigger transitions. The set of trigger transitions should be large enough such that verification tasks can be completed in a timely manner (again, acceptable verification times depend on the concrete use case), but reduced in a way such that no critical transition is included. Trigger transitions might be prohibited by self-verification in case the specification is violated (fails to verify in the concrete instance), so critical transitions should not be included in the set of trigger transitions: e.g. if we verify the existence of an escape route in case of an emergency it is clearly too late to handle failure. On the other hand administrative operations like changing access rights are far better suited to be included as trigger transitions, since a potential failure is presented to a trained user of the system. Lastly, one should avoid transient states (e.g. a user is inside a security gate) which can only be left through trigger transitions since self-verification may lead to a system dead-locked there, as in Fig. 1.

5.2   Conclusions

The vehicle of our investigations was a case study consisting of an access control system, which is parameterized in many dimensions (the building under control, the access rights, the users) that can be instantiated at different points in time. In order to make our results concrete and tangible, we have developed a demonstrator—the access control system implemented as an interactive SVG, which can be viewed and run in any web browser. Users can directly experience the effect of choosing different verification triggers.

The demonstrator also exhibits the general applicability of self-verification and the versatility of our tool chain, which could be adapted to support a different implementation platform (SVG and TypeScript instead of CλaSH) with moderate effort.

This raises the question of the general applicability of the approach. As presented here, some kinds of safety-critical systems could not be addressed adequately, namely fail-safe systems, where there is no default safe state which we can always revert to if self-verification does not succeed. On the other hand, an attractive avenue for further exploration is "just-in-time verification", where one tries to prove properties at run time as they are needed.

References

1. IEEE: IEEE std 1012–2016. IEEE standard for software verification and validation. Technical report. IEEE (2016)
2. Leucker, M., Schallhart, C.: A brief account of runtime verification. J. Log. Algebraic Program. **78**(5), 293–303 (2009)
3. Lüth, C., Ring, M., Drechsler, R.: Towards a methodology for self-verification. In: 2017 6th International Conference on Reliability, Infocom Technologies and Optimization (Trends and Future Directions) (ICRITO), 11–15 September 2017 (2017)
4. Ring, M., Bornebusch, F., Lüth, C., Wille, R., Drechsler, R.: Better late than never – verification of embedded systems after deployment. In: 2019 Design, Automation Test in Europe Conference Exhibition (DATE), pp. 890–895, March 2019
5. Abrial, J.R.: System study: method and example (1999)
6. OMG: Systems Modeling Language (SysML), Version 1.5, May 2017
7. OMG: Object Constraint Language (OCL), Version 2.4, February 2014
8. Gogolla, M., Richters, M.: Development of UML descriptions with USE. In: Shafazand, H., Tjoa, A.M. (eds.) EurAsia-ICT 2002. LNCS, vol. 2510, pp. 228–238. Springer, Heidelberg (2002). https://doi.org/10.1007/3-540-36087-5_27
9. Baaij, C., Kooijman, M., Kuper, J., Boeijink, W., Gerards, M.: ClaSH: structural descriptions of synchronous hardware using haskell. In: Proceedings of the 13th EUROMICRO Conference on Digital System Design: Architectures, Methods and Tools, United States, IEEE Computer Society, pp. 714–721, September 2010
10. Bornebusch, F., Wille, R., Drechsler, R.: Towards lightweight satisfiability solvers for self-verification. In: 7th International Symposium on Embedded Computing and System Design (ISED). IEEE (2017)
11. Ustaoglu, B., Huhn, S., Große, D., Drechsler, R.: SAT-lancer: a hardware SAT-solver for self-verification. In: 28th ACM Great Lakes Symposium on VLSI (GLVLSI) (2018)
12. Hejlsberg, A.: Typescript (2012)

Security

Using Threat Analysis Techniques to Guide Formal Verification: A Case Study of Cooperative Awareness Messages

Marie Farrell[1]([✉]), Matthew Bradbury[2], Michael Fisher[1], Louise A. Dennis[1], Clare Dixon[1], Hu Yuan[2], and Carsten Maple[2]

[1] Department of Computer Science, University of Liverpool, Liverpool, UK
marie.farrell@liverpool.ac.uk
[2] Cyber Security Centre, WMG, University of Warwick, Coventry, UK

Abstract. Autonomous robotic systems such as Connected and Autonomous Vehicle (CAV) systems are both safety-and security-critical, since a breach in system security may impact safety. Generally, safety and security concerns for such systems are treated separately during the development process. In this paper, we consider an algorithm for sending Cooperative Awareness Messages (CAMs) between vehicles in a CAV system and the use of CAMs in preventing vehicle collisions. We employ threat analysis techniques that are commonly used in the cyber security domain to guide our formal verification. This allows us to focus our formal methods on those security properties that are particularly important and to consider both safety and security in tandem. Our analysis centres on identifying STRIDE security properties and we illustrate how these can be formalised, and subsequently verified, using a combination of formal tools for distinct aspects, namely Promela/SPIN and Dafny.

1 Introduction

Emerging applications of autonomous robotic systems include Connected and Autonomous Vehicle (CAV) systems where self-driving vehicles communicate with each other in order to safely travel between different locations. This communication typically occurs over a wireless network that is vulnerable to attacks and these attacks could potentially impede the safety of the passengers. Therefore, ensuring that both cyber security and safety issues are properly addressed during the software development process is crucial for these CAV systems. While a recent survey on formal verification techniques for autonomous robotic systems identified a number of challenges for applying formal methods to these systems [19], cyber security as a distinct challenge for formal methods has often been overlooked. In particular, identifying which cyber security properties to verify is often difficult for formal methods practitioners.

This work is supported by grant EP/R026092 (FAIR-SPACE Hub) through UKRI under the Industry Strategic Challenge Fund (ISCF) for Robotics and AI Hubs in Extreme and Hazardous Environments.

P. C. Ölveczky and G. Salaün (Eds.): SEFM 2019, LNCS 11724, pp. 471–490, 2019.
https://doi.org/10.1007/978-3-030-30446-1_25

In this paper, we present a simple case study that employs (informal) threat analysis techniques from the cyber security domain to guide our verification effort of the Cooperative Awareness Message (CAM) protocol, used in vehicle-to-vehicle communications [26]. CAMs are heartbeat messages that are periodically broadcast by each vehicle to its neighbours to provide basic vehicle status information including position, velocity, acceleration, heading, etc. [26]. Since these vehicles communicate over an unsecured network, ensuring that CAMs are secure is crucial as we move toward driverless cars. This is also relevant in other areas where autonomous vehicles communicate with each other, such as a group of vehicles in orbit or rovers mapping an unknown and hazardous environment.

To this end, we contribute a basic methodology for security-minded formal verification and a case study demonstrating our approach using existing formal methods and STRIDE threat analysis. The threat analysis will identify threats that fall into specific aspects of the six categories specified by STRIDE. Since CAMs are for use in CAV systems, which are inherently cyber-physical, we see this case study as an experiment on how to combine threat analysis and formal verification and our approach could be used in the development of other cyber-physical systems.

This paper is structured as follows. In the remainder of Sect. 1 we outline our basic methodology for security-guided formal verification. Then, Sect. 2 describes the relevant background material and related work. In Sect. 3, we present our threat analysis of the CAM protocol using the STRIDE classification. In Sect. 4, we present our results of analysing how a spoofing attack can impact the safety of a simple, three vehicle CAV system by devising an abstract system model in Promela and using the SPIN model-checker for verification. Section 5 presents a Dafny implementation of the CAM protocol and illustrates how we can verify properties related to Denial of Service and Repudiation. Finally, we conclude and outline future work in Sect. 6.

1.1 Methodology

In order to enhance the software engineering process and encourage collaboration between cyber security and formal methods practitioners we followed the high-level methodology outlined in Fig. 1. We started by analysing the available documentation that informally describes the CAM messaging protocol [1]. Then we independently carried out threat analysis and construction of formal models of the CAM protocol.

In particular, we constructed two formal models of the protocol. The first is a high-level system model that is written in Promela and verified using the SPIN model-checker which we use to investigate a spoofing attack. The second is an algorithm-level model of the CAM protocol, written in Dafny, which we use to analyse properties related to denial of service and non-repudiation. Finally, we defined formal properties, based on the threat analysis that was carried out, that we then encoded and verified with respect to our formal models of the CAM protocol.

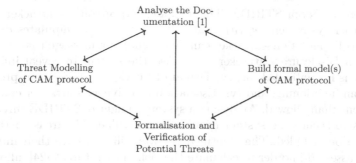

Fig. 1. Our high-level methodology for security-guided formal verification of the CAM protocol involved independently carrying out threat analysis and formal modelling based on the available documentation. Then we used the identified threats to guide our formal verification effort.

In the event that errors or discrepancies were found in either the threat analysis or formal verification, we returned to the documentation for clarification. This is indicated by the arrows in Fig. 1 and allowed us to discern whether the errors were in our modelling of the protocol and/or if the correct level of abstraction was captured by our formal models. By following this methodology we were able to foster cooperation and combine expertise from both the cyber security and formal methods domains. This kind of collaboration can be easily integrated into the development process and can potentially save time since formal verification and security analysis can be combined and used in a complementary fashion.

In practice, the system might be modified as mechanisms are put in place to prevent attacks that were exposed by threat analysis. When this occurs, developers should revise and reverify their models in light of this new behaviour.

2   Background and Related Work

In this section, we present the relevant background material under three distinct headings. First, we describe the threat analysis techniques that we have used, then we discuss formal verification and introduce the tools and techniques that we use throughout the remainder of this paper. We also provide concrete details about Cooperative Awareness Messages (CAMs) as contained in the standard documentation [1]. Finally, we briefly describe related work in this area.

Threat Analysis: When engineering security-critical systems, developers often employ threat analysis techniques to help to identify security vulnerabilities so that targeted mitigations can be put in place. One such technique is the STRIDE [15] classification. In fact, there are many other techniques for threat modelling, and our approach works equally well with any of them (e.g. CIA which stands for Confidentiality, Integrity and Availability [31]), but for ease of explanation, we adopt STRIDE. This includes: (i) Spoofing - attacker pretends to be another system entity, (ii) Tampering - attacker manipulates data maliciously, (iii) Repudiation - attacker can deny sending a message that it sent, (iv) Information Disclosure - attacker can cause the system to reveal information to those it is not intended for, (v) Denial of Service - attacker can prevent the system from functioning, and (vi) Escalation of Privilege - attacker can perform more actions than allowed. Analysing a system in light of STRIDE threats helps developers to secure the system by identifying vulnerable areas so that mitigations can be included. The identified threats will also have their impact and likelihood assessed in order to calculate the risk of each threat [24], allowing the prioritisation of developing mitigations for threats with a higher risk.

Formal Verification: In order to assure the correctness of a software system, formal methods provide an array of mathematically-based tools and techniques for proving properties about a system. Formal methods are predominantly used in safety-critical systems where a software failure can potentially cause harm. In this paper, we employ two distinct formal methods; Promela/SPIN [10] and Dafny [17] to verify properties about the CAM protocol. In each case, we model the CAM protocol at a different abstraction level; Promela for system-level modelling and Dafny for algorithm-level verification. Since these systems are typically very complex, the use of multiple formal methods is necessary [8], and cyber security threat analysis techniques help us to highlight the most relevant security properties.

Promela is a general purpose programming language, particularly developed for protocol verification, while the patterns of temporal behaviour that can be verified can be complex and varied [9]. SPIN is a model-checker that automatically checks temporal properties over system models encoded in the Promela programming language [9,10]. Essentially, SPIN explores all possible runs of Promela input models and assesses these against an automaton capturing temporal behaviour that should *never* occur. If all runs have been explored without finding a violation of the temporal properties then the model is valid. If a violation is found, it is returned as a counter-example[1].

Dafny is a programming language that facilitates the use of specification constructs that allow the user to specify pre-and post-conditions as well as loop invariants and variants [17]. Dafny is used in the static verification of the functional correctness of programs. Dafny programs are translated into the Boogie intermediate verification language [3] and then the Z3 automated theorem prover discharges the associated proof obligations [7]. We chose Dafny for this case study because of its similarity to other programming languages making it easy to communicate the verified solution to security engineers that are unfamiliar with formal methods[2].

Cooperative Awareness Messages (CAMs): As outlined briefly in Sect. 1, CAM are heartbeat messages that are sent between vehicles in a CAV system. The

---

[1] We used version 6.4.6 of SPIN.
[2] We used version 2.2.0 of Dafny.

CAM standard documentation is contained in [1] and we briefly summarise this here in order to give the reader an understanding of the nature of the CAM protocol. In autonomous vehicles, the CA Basic Service is a facilities layer that is responsible for operating the CAM protocol which is composed of two services: (1) the sending of CAMs, including their generation and transmission, and, (2) the receiving of CAMs and the modification of the receiving vehicle's state in light of the received messages. The CA Basic Service is in control of how frequently CAMs are sent and it interfaces to a number of other services, such as the SF-SAP which provides a number of basic security services (including digital signatures and certificates) for CAM [1, §5.1].

CAMs are sent in plain text as they are intended for all vehicles within range of the sender. This also means that time expensive encryption and decryption is not required. However, to ensure the authenticity of the sender (that a message sent from vehicle v actually came from vehicle v), digital signatures are used as they allow a receiver to use the contents of the message, the signature and the public key of the sender to verify its origin. Note that in this paper we are primarily concerned with the protocol for sending and receiving CAMs and the threats that can be identified at this level rather than detailed cryptographic protocols and digital signing.

Once CAMs are received by surrounding vehicles, the receivers can modify their own state based on the received messages. In particular, if a vehicle receives a message from one proceeding it which indicates that the leading vehicle is slowing down, then the vehicle that received this CAM should also slow down in order to avoid collision.

Related Work: iUML-B and refinement in Event-B have been used to analyse a known security flaw called double tagging in a network protocol [30]. Other related work includes the use of the TAMARIN prover to formally analyse and identify one known functional correctness flaw and one unknown authentication flaw for a revocation protocol [33]. Here, the revocation is of malicious or misbehaving vehicles from a vehicular networking system. Our work differs to these in that we use threat analysis to guide our verification rather than use formal methods to identify previously known bugs.

Vanspauwen and Jacobs have devised an approach to the static verification of cryptographic protocol implementations using their symbolic model of cryptography formalised in VeriFast [32]. They attach contracts to the primitives in an existing cryptography library. Their focus is on the verification of cryptographic protocols whereas we focus on using cyber security techniques to guide verification rather than verifying cryptographic protocol implementations.

Huang and Kang [11] use a probabilistic extension of the Clock constraint specification language (Ccsl) to analyse safety and security properties related to timing constraints for a cooperative automotive system. They specified a number of safety constraints as well as a number of security constraints including spoofing, secrecy, tampering and availability. Their work facilitates the verification, using the UPPAAL model-checker, of safety and security properties related to timing constraints. It does not, however, integrate results from a security engineering perspective in order to define these properties and only focuses on those properties related to timing.

Other related work includes the use of the CSP process algebra for protocol verification [27–29]. Their focus is on authentication [28] and non-repudiation protocols [27]. Their approach involves specifying the relevant protocol, agents and environment in CSP [29]. Notably, they remark that, by modelling the protocol in CSP, they could provide a formal and verified specification of the protocol which allowed them to clarify the, usually, informal protocol description.

Kamali et al. [14] have used formal verification of an autonomous vehicle platooning system to demonstrate the use of different formal techniques for distinct system subcomponents. In this case, autonomous decision-making, real-time properties and spatial aspects. Our approach, presented in this paper uses different formal methods to verify distinct security-related properties of the CAM protocol at different levels of abstraction.

3   Threat Analysis of CAM

In this section, we describe our threat analysis of the CAM protocol. Threat analysis is important for ensuring the security of a system since it is used to identify all of the potential threats to the system. There are a variety of different threat modelling methods including STRIDE, SAHARA, HARA, TARA and others that are suggested in multiple industry standards (i.e. ISO26262, SAE J3061). In this paper, we use the STRIDE classification outlined earlier [15].

3.1   Specialising STRIDE for CAM

CAMs (formatted using ASN.1 as specified in [1, Annex A]) are a vital aspect of a safe CAV system, as they are used by each vehicle to inform surrounding vehicles of their current status. Each vehicle needs to trust that the values contained within a CAM are timely and accurate. If this is not the case then autonomous vehicles could make incorrect and even unsafe decisions. Note that we focus here on CAMs generated by On-Board Units (OBU) in vehicles rather than Road Side Units (RSU) as the OBU algorithm for CAM generation is more complex and thus more interesting from a formal methods perspective. In terms of the CAM protocol, we specialise the STRIDE threats:

Spoofing: attacker sends messages masquerading as another vehicle.
Tampering: attacker tampers with a message sent by another vehicle.
Repudiation: a vehicle can deny sending a message that it has actually sent.
Information Disclosure: vehicles only receive messages intended for them.
Denial of Service: messages are not sent within a reasonable time frame.
Escalation of Privilege: attacker can send more CAMs than permitted.

The threat modelling contained in Table 1 was carried out by examining each piece of information that could be sent via CAMs and considering which STRIDE

Table 1. This table contains our threat analysis of the CAM protocol. Here, 'Requirement' corresponds to the information that the vehicle must sense about itself in order to know the value of the corresponding 'Message Element' on the left. Furthermore, the 'Threats' correspond to those identified using STRIDE.

Message type	Message element	Requirement	Attack surfaces	Threats
Vehicle information [20]	Vehicle type	Originating station (RSU), vehicle length, vehicle width	Data system, planning system, wireless comms	S, I, D
	Position	Reference position		
	Lane position	Current lane position	Sensing: lidar, radar, camera, ultrasonic	S, T, R, I, D
	Speed	Vehicle velocity		
	Acceleration	Longitudinal, lateral, vertical		
	Heading	Heading	Positioning system: GPS, A-GPS	
	Driving model	Acceleration control		
	GPS	Preceding vehicle GPS, following vehicle GPS	Wireless comms	
Traffic notification [1]	Warning	Emergency vehicle, crash, collision.	Controlling centre infrastructures, Wireless comms	D, E
	Indication	Speed limits, traffic light		

threats an attacker might exploit. The information contained in Table 1 is based on the C-ITS standard messages elements, a summary of threats [5, 6, 12, 18, 22, 25]. We summarise the information contained in Table 1 as follows.

For CAM, there are two distinct kinds of 'Message Type'. In particular, 'Vehicle information' CAMs include the vehicle type and its state information (speed, position, GPS, etc.). Conversely, 'Traffic notification' CAMs provide emergency warnings and traffic indications. For each kind of CAM, 'Message Element' indicates the specific components that are included in the messages. For each message element, its corresponding 'Requirement' refers to the information that the vehicle must sense/have access to in order to populate the corresponding message element field. In cyber security, an 'Attack Surface' is the region of the system that an adversary can exploit to attack the system. Finally, the possible 'Threats' for CAM are modelled based on STRIDE.

For example, in order to include GPS information we require the GPS information of both the leader and following vehicles. Here, the attack surface is the positioning system (GPS/A-GPS) and possible threats are Repudiation [25] or Spoofing [5].

The threat analysis contained in Table 1 has identified potential points of attack and we consider them in more detail in the next subsection. Note that, in the remainder of this paper, we focus on 'Vehicle information' CAMs but we have included 'Traffic notification' messages in Table 1 for illustrative purposes. These Decentralised Environment Notification Messages (DENM) are generated using a different protocol which we are not focusing on in this work.

3.2   Considering the Threats

We have identified a number of threats in Table 1 and, as part of the threat analysis process, we examine them in more detail here which allows us to identify which are the most likely to occur/cause the most damage.

In Table 1, we have identified Tampering as a threat for some of the state information contained in CAMs. However, in practice, Tampering is prevented via digital signatures and certificates, the verification of which is beyond the scope of this paper but details can be found in [16]. In particular, the CA Basic Service, which is responsible for operating the CAM protocol, interfaces with the SF-SAP security entity as described in [1, §5.1 & §6.2.2] which provides access to security services for CAM such as digital signing and certificates. Here, certificates are used to indicate the holder's privileges for sending CAMs. In this way, incoming CAMs are accepted if the sender's certificate is valid and is consistent with their privileges.

As CAMs are intended for all who receive them, we do not analyse Information Disclosure properties. Escalation of Privilege attacks could enable an attacker to send more messages than allowed, but in general all vehicles have the same level of authority so we do not consider this attack here.

Based on our analysis, we conclude that Spoofing, Denial of Service and Repudiation threats are the most relevant/important threats pertaining to this case study. To our knowledge, no formal, mathematical definition of the STRIDE properties exists since they are to be specialised for a given system. However, if we wish to include these in our formal verification of CAM then we must more closely consider those properties that we are interested in (Spoofing, Denial of Service and Repudiation). We explore these in more detail as follows:

Spoofing: an attacker pretends to be another vehicle and sends false information about that vehicle (e.g. speed) in CAMs. This could potentially cause vehicles to collide and we analyse this using Promela/SPIN in Sect. 4 by modelling an attacker of the system.

Denial of Service: a compromised vehicle does not send CAMs within a reasonable amount of time. If a vehicle sends too many CAMs then the network becomes overloaded. Conversely, if a vehicle does not send CAMs frequently enough then the most recent CAMs sent may be deemed out of date and thus ignored. In particular, a replay attack could occur where an attacker or a compromised vehicle resends CAMs that have already been sent causing a network overload. If suitable measures are not put in place to ensure that the time that the message was sent was not too far in the past then vehicles may react to an out of date message. We address this using Dafny in Sect. 5 by verifying an availability property of the algorithm for sending CAMs.

Repudiation: we can reduce the possibility of a vehicle denying that it has sent a CAM by requiring that CAMs are stored in a sequence and not providing functionality to remove CAMs from this sequence. Another repudiation related attack could result in an attacker or compromised vehicle claiming to have sent a CAM when in fact it has not sent one. In this case, vehicles could potentially forward CAMs to other vehicles. This is a particular condition that is prohibited in the documentation [1] and our Dafny implementation of the algorithm for receiving CAMs in Sect. 5 considers this.

These are the threats that, based on our threat analysis, we consider to be the most relevant/likely with respect to the CAM protocol and we use these to guide our formal verification effort[3].

4   Model-Checking with Promela/SPIN

In this case study, it is easy to see that safety and security are inextricably linked. For CAV systems, the most important safety property to consider is that collisions should be avoided at all costs. Therefore, an attacker of the system who is attempting to cause harm will likely target security vulnerabilities that have the potential to violate this safety property. A key aspect of the threat analysis process is the identification of a suitable attacker. To this end, we recognise that there may be malicious vehicles on the road that are attempting to cause vehicles to collide, perhaps a disgruntled taxi driver who is unemployed due to the adoption of autonomous vehicles. Such a collision could be caused by spoofing the CAMs sent between vehicles. Our analysis of spoofing and how it can impact the safety of the CAV system is captured here in a SPIN analysis of a simplified scenario involving CAMs between vehicles in a platoon/convoy.

4.1   Basic Scenario: Safety

We investigated message passing between multiple vehicles by applying SPIN to an abstracted Promela model for sending and receiving CAMs. Figure 2 contains three vehicles travelling in a platoon/convoy: one leader; one middle; and one tail vehicle. The leader and tail send CAMs to the middle vehicle, and it follows a simple protocol.

- If no CAMs are received then it continues unchanged.
- If it receives exactly one CAM then sets its own speed to half the speed in the CAM[4].
- If it receives two CAMs then it sets its own speed to be the average of the two speeds (rounded down).

---

[3] Artefacts available at: https://github.com/mariefarrell/CAMVerification.git.

[4] This only occurs at initialisation when the speed of the other vehicle is 0.

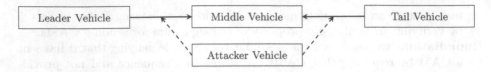

Fig. 2. Our three vehicle model where CAMs are sent from the leader and tail vehicles to the middle vehicle. The attacker executes a Spoofing attack.

We used the following default conditions to analyse this Promela model with SPIN: (1) the leader chooses a random discrete speed 10, 20, 30, 40, 50, 60 or 70 at each time step, (2) the tail similarly chooses a random discrete speed at each time step, and (3) we ran the system for 100 time steps with a round-robin interleaving concurrency between vehicles.

The simple safety property that we verified is that the speed of the middle vehicle is never *much* different to the speed of the leader or of the tail, for more than one step. Here, *much different* means a difference of more than '51' in speed. We formalise: it is always the case that, if the speed of the middle vehicle is *much different* then it will not be in the next state. We write this in temporal logic as:

$$\Box(big\_speed\_difference \Rightarrow \bigcirc \neg big\_speed\_difference)$$

where '$\Box$' and '$\bigcirc$' are LTL's [23] "always" and "in the next state" operators, respectively. Although we have only written $\bigcirc$ here for ease of presentation, in the actual implementation the property is that the difference has been corrected after twelve next steps – this is because SPIN treats next as the next instruction execution, which includes print states used for understandability and debugging purposes not as the next tick of the internal clock. In SPIN, we negate this property and so the "never claim" (or safety property [4]) that we implement is

$$\Diamond(big\_speed\_difference \land \bigcirc big\_speed\_difference)$$

where '$\Diamond$' is LTL's [23] "eventually" operator. Here, *big_speed_difference* is **true** when any of the following inequalities hold

- middle vehicle speed > (leader vehicle speed + 51)
- middle vehicle speed < (leader vehicle speed − 51)
- middle vehicle speed > (tail vehicle speed + 51)
- middle vehicle speed < (tail vehicle speed − 51)

We have successfully verified that this safety property holds of our model using the SPIN model-checker. Next, we use this model to investigate how a Spoofing attack could lead to an unsafe scenario for the vehicle platoon.

```
0    proctype attacker(chan l_in, t_in){    /* attacker */
1      printf("attacker: starting\n");
2      bool head = 0;
3      bool tl = 0;
4      A:    (clock > 10); /* wait until under way */
5        if
6        :: (head = 0) -> printf("attacker: inserting vspeed of 10\n");
7              l_in!10; l_in!10; head = 1; goto A;
8              ...
9        :: (head = 0) -> printf("attacker: inserting vspeed of 70\n");
10             l_in!70; l_in!70; head = 1; goto A;
11       :: (tl = 0) -> printf("attacker: inserting tspeed of 10\n");
12             t_in!10; t_in!10; tl = 1; goto A;
13             ...
14       :: (tl = 0) -> printf("attacker: inserting tspeed of 70\n");
15             t_in!70; t_in!70; tl = 1; goto A;
16       :: (clock <= 100) -> goto A;
17       :: (clock > 100) -> goto FIN;
18     fi;
19   FIN:   printf("attacker: finishing\n")
20   }
```

Fig. 3. Promela model of the attacker.

4.2 Investigating Spoofing

Inspired by the threat analysis contained in Table 1, we have modelled a Spoofing attack in Promela for the above scenario. In order to analyse this kind of threat, we add a process to our Promela model to describe an attacker of the system. The behaviour of this attacker (as illustrated in Figs. 2 and 3) is as follows:

– At one point in the execution trace the attacker may insert two speed messages into the channel between the leader and middle vehicle stating that the leader's speed is 10, 20, 30, … or 70 (lines 6–10 of Fig. 3).
– At one point in the execution trace the attacker may insert two speed messages into the channel between the tail and the middle vehicle stating that the leader's speed is 10, 20, 30, … or 70 (lines 11–15 of Fig. 3).

We note that in each of the above cases, both the speed, whether to insert a message and the time that the message is inserted are chosen at random. Running SPIN with this attacker model and the initial model described above, we can see that our $\square(big\_speed\_difference \Rightarrow \bigcirc \neg big\_speed\_difference)$ property has been violated. It is important to note that this is a deliberately simple example but scales up to more complex versions of such Spoofing attacks.

4.3 Discussion

In Sect. 3, cyber security threat analysis focused the whole vehicle security area to scenarios, such as the one illustrated in Fig. 2, that were identified as high risk. In particular, this threat that was identified following STRIDE and analysed using Promela/SPIN could potentially lead to an unsafe scenario causing vehicles to collide. Note that whilst the above example deals with modelling and verification of aspects of a platoon/convoy, where a group of vehicles drive together with a leader, this could be generalised to messages between autonomous vehicles driving without a platoon.

The evidence that we have collected above illustrates how a spoofing attack on this system can negatively impact its safe operation. We have focused on speed, but using model-checking, we can explore whether spoofing of other attributes, as identified in Table 1, can impact safety. These results can help to strengthen the argument as to why mitigations should be put in place against specific threats. Our simple attacker model has allowed us to identify that a spoofing attack is indeed possible for this scenario. In practice, mitigations would be put in place against this kind of attack. Then, our simple model would be refined to add these mitigations and would then undergo further verification.

In particular, those implementing the CAM protocol should consider the possibility that malicious vehicles may join the platoon with the sole aim of causing collisions. Based on our formal Promela model, runtime monitors could be synthesised to monitor the CAMs being sent between vehicles so that this spoofing attack could be recognised and prevent it from causing harm.

Our Promela model that describes an attacker and three vehicles is only one scenario that could occur, particularly as there may be many more vehicles in a real world scenario. To our knowledge, there is no systematic way of identifying all possible models of the system that include a spoofing attack. However, we can systematically work through the attributes that have been identified in Table 1 as likely to be vulnerable to spoofing to examine how spoofing attacks can influence safe system behaviour.

5   Deductive Verification with Dafny

In this section, we construct and verify a CAM send and receive implementation using Dafny. Our Dafny implementation of CAM contains two basic methods; sendCAM (Fig. 4) and receiveCAM (Fig. 5). We have formalised the specification of CAM using the available documentation [1, §6.1.3] and followed its nomenclature. As is to be expected when following the associated documentation, quite some time was taken when constructing the formal specification from the informal, English-language description of the CAM protocol contained in [1].

Our verification of sendCAM and receiveCAM in Dafny focuses on the Denial of Service and Repudiation security threats, this time at the algorithmic level. In our implementation we have simplified the structure of CAMs from the ASN.1 encoding to focus on the semantic contents of the message as follows:

```
CAM(id:int, time:int, heading:int, speed:int, position:int)
```

Here, id refers to the vehicle that is sending the CAM and time is the timestamp at which the CAM was sent. These attributes are required by the documentation [1]. As mentioned earlier, CAMs are sent periodically, or when any of the status information (e.g. speed) contained in the message has changed since the last message was sent.

```
0   method sendCAM(T_CheckCamGen:int, T_GenCam_DCC:int)
1   returns (msgs:seq<CAM>, now:int)
2   requires 0 < T_CheckCamGen ≤ T_GenCamMin;
3   requires T_GenCamMin ≤ T_GenCam_DCC ≤ T_GenCamMax;
4   ensures T_GenCam_DCC * |msgs| ≤ now ≤ T_GenCamMax * |msgs|;
5   ensures |msgs| ≥ 2 ⟹ ∀ i: int • 1 ≤ i < |msgs| ⟹
6      T_GenCam_DCC ≤ (msgs[i].time - msgs[i-1].time) ≤ T_GenCamMax;
7   ensures |msgs| = MaxMsgs;
8   {
9     var T_GenCam, T_GenCamNext, j := T_GenCamMax, T_GenCamMax, GetId();
10    var N_GenCam, trigger_two_count := N_GenCamDefault, 0;
11    msgs, now := [], 0;
12    var LastBroadcast, PrevLastBroadcast,prevsent := now, now, msgs;
13    var heading, speed, pos := GetHeading(), GetSpeed(), GetPosition();
14    var prevheading, prevspeed, prevpos, statechanged := -1, -1, -1, false;
15
16    while (|msgs| < MaxMsgs)
17    decreases MaxMsgs - |msgs|;
18    invariant 0 ≤ |msgs| ≤ MaxMsgs ∧ 0 < N_GenCam ≤ N_GenCamMax;
19    invariant T_GenCamMin ≤ T_GenCamNext ≤ T_GenCamMax;
20    invariant T_GenCamMin ≤ T_GenCam ≤ T_GenCamMax;
21    invariant 0 ≤ PrevLastBroadcast ≤ now ∧ now = LastBroadcast;
22    invariant now - T_GenCamMax ≤ PrevLastBroadcast ≤ LastBroadcast;
23    invariant |msgs| ≥ 1 ⟹ msgs[|msgs|-1].time = LastBroadcast;
24    invariant |msgs| ≥ 2 ⟹ msgs[|msgs|-2].time = PrevLastBroadcast;
25    invariant now > 0 ⟹ T_GenCam_DCC ≤ LastBroadcast - PrevLastBroadcast ≤
           T_GenCamMax;
26    invariant now > 0 ⟹ CAM(j,now,heading,speed,pos) in msgs;
27    invariant now > 0 ⟹ |prevsent| + 1 = |msgs|;
28    invariant |msgs| ≥ 2 ⟹ ∀ i: int • 1 ≤ i < |msgs| ⟹
29       T_GenCam_DCC ≤ (msgs[i].time - msgs[i-1].time) ≤ T_GenCamMax;
30    invariant T_GenCamMin * |msgs| ≤ T_GenCam_DCC * |msgs| ≤ now;
31    invariant now > 0 ⟹ now ≤ T_GenCamMax * |msgs|;
32    {
33      prevsent, PrevLastBroadcast := msgs, LastBroadcast;
34      T_GenCam, statechanged := T_GenCamNext, false;
35      now := now + T_GenCam_DCC;
36
37      while (true)
38      decreases LastBroadcast + T_GenCam - now;
39      invariant now - LastBroadcast ≤ max(T_GenCam_DCC, T_GenCam);
40      {
41        heading, speed, pos := GetHeading(), GetSpeed(), GetPosition();
42        statechanged := abs(heading - prevheading) ≥ headingthreshold ∨
43                        abs(speed - prevspeed) ≥ speedthreshold ∨
44                        abs(pos - prevpos) ≥ posthreshold.Floor;
45
46        if (statechanged ∨ now - LastBroadcast ≥ T_GenCam) { break; }
47        else { now := now + T_CheckCamGen; }
48      }
49      msgs := msgs + [CAM(j,now,heading,speed,pos)];
50
51      if (statechanged) {
52        T_GenCamNext, trigger_two_count := now - LastBroadcast, 0;
53      }
54      else if (now - LastBroadcast ≥ T_GenCam){
55        trigger_two_count := trigger_two_count + 1;
56        if (trigger_two_count = N_GenCam) { T_GenCamNext := T_GenCamMax; }
57      }
58      LastBroadcast := now;
59      prevheading, prevspeed, prevpos := heading, speed, pos;
60    }
61    return msgs, now;
62  }
```

Fig. 4. Dafny implementation of the sendCAM algorithm. We have specified the Denial of Service property as a postcondition on lines 4–5.

5.1 Sending CAMs

Figure 4 contains the verified Dafny code corresponding to the sendCAM algorithm which is responsible for generation and transmission of CAMs. We describe the key components of the Dafny algorithm in Fig. 4 as follows:

Lines 0–3: Since CAMs should be sent periodically within time bounds specified by the CA Basic Service, this method takes two variables as input. T_CheckCamGen describes how often to check if another CAM should be sent and T_GenCam_DCC which describes the minimum time interval between two consecutive CAM generations. It returns a sequence of CAMs that have been sent, denoted by msgs, and the current time given by the variable, now. The preconditions, indicated by the requires keyword on lines 2 and 3, provide constraints on these variables. In particular, T_GenCam_DCC is required to be between T_GenCamMin (100 ms) and T_GenCamMax (1000 ms) [1, §6.1.3].

Lines 4–7: The postconditions on lines 4–7, indicated by the ensures keyword, specify that the expected number of CAMs have been sent and that these messages were sent within the required time bounds. This corresponds to the Denial of Service threat by ensuring that messages are sent on time and arrive within specified time bounds. In particular, line 4 provides constraints on the value of the current time. This is necessary because Dafny does not support real-time systems so we had to manually keep track of time. The postcondition on line 5 specifies that the interval between any two consecutive CAMs is between T_GenCam_DCC and T_GenCamMax as described in [1]. For the purpose of discretising the system, the postcondition on line 7 ensures that the maximum number (MaxMsgs := 100) of CAMs are sent[5].

Lines 8–14: Here, we initialise the relevant local variables. In particular, we set msgs to the empty sequence and now to 0 (line 11). Some of these variables are specified in the CAM documentation but others are not and we include them for implementation purposes. In particular, T_GenCam as defined on line 9 represents the current upper limit of the CAM generation interval, by default this is equal to T_GenCam_Max [1, §6.1.3]. We also assume the existence of verified helper functions for GetHeading(), GetSpeed() and GetPosition() as used on line 13.

Lines 16–17: The method loops until MaxMsgs number of CAMs have been sent. In order to prove termination of the loop, we specify the loop variant as indicated by the decreases keyword on line 17.

Lines 18–25: We specify these loop invariants to ensure that the relevant variables stay within the allowable bounds during loop execution. In particular, the invariant on line 18 relates to the postcondition on line 7 by specifying that the number of CAMs sent so far is less than or equal to MaxMsgs.

Lines 26–27: These invariants ensure that once time has begun then at least one CAM has been sent.

Lines 28–31: These invariants relate to the postcondition on lines 4–6 and thus relate to the availability property described earlier.

---

[5] We chose 100 as a value but we could easily have chosen some other value.

```
0   method receiveCAM(fromid: int, cams: seq<CAM>, now: int) returns (brake: bool)
1   requires 0 ≤ fromid < |cams|;
2   requires fromid = cams[fromid].id;
3   ensures !(now - cams[fromid].time > T_GenCamMax)
4           ∧ Sign(Magnitude(cams[fromid].heading)) = Sign(Magnitude(GetHeading
            (now)))
5           ∧ GetSpeed(now) - cams[fromid].speed < 0 ⟹ brake;
6   ensures now - cams[fromid].time > T_GenCamMax ⟹ !brake;
7   {
8     var speeddiff := 0;
9
10    if (now - cams[fromid].time > T_GenCamMax){
11        brake := false;
12      }
13    else if(Sign(Magnitude(cams[fromid].heading)) = Sign(Magnitude(GetHeading
          (now))))
14    {
15      speeddiff := GetSpeed(now) - cams[fromid].speed;
16
17      if (speeddiff < 0){
18        brake:=true;
19      }
20    }
21  }
```

Fig. 5. Dafny implementation of the `receiveCAM` algorithm.

Lines 32–36: During each loop iteration we update the appropriate variables. Note that we increment the current time, now, by T_GenCam_DCC to allow time to advance until the earliest time that the next CAM can be sent.

Lines 37–50: This inner loop checks if any state information has changed and updates the `statechanged` variable accordingly. Note that the variables `headingthreshold`, `speedthreshold` and `posthreshold` are global and their values are controlled by the CA Basic Service [1] as described in Sect. 2. If the autonomous vehicle's state has changed or it is time to send another CAM then we break from this inner loop. Otherwise, nothing has changed so we keep looping to allow time to advance until either the state has changed or sufficient time has passed since the last CAM was sent. Once we have exited this inner loop then a CAM is sent.

Lines 51–57: Based on the reason that the CAM was sent, i.e. whether the state changed or it was simply time to send a CAM, this if-else statement updates the relevant variables as described in [1, §6.1.3].

Lines 58–62: Finally, we update and return the appropriate variables.

In this way, the Dafny algorithm illustrated in Fig. 4 is verified with respect to the STRIDE Denial of Service threat (or Availability property). We also verified other correctness properties that were derived from the documentation [1]. As mentioned above, it was necessary to discretise some components of the specification. In fact, discretising the continuous features of autonomous systems is a common challenge for formal methods [19]. As already discussed, the CA Basic Service also facilitates the receiving of CAMs and we describe our Dafny implementation of the receive method in the next subsection.

5.2 Receiving CAMs

Figure 5 contains our Dafny implementation of the `receiveCAM` algorithm which takes as input the id of the vehicle sending the CAM (`fromid`), the sequence of CAMs that have been sent (`cams`) and the current time (`now`).

We have used this to verify a simple Non-Repudiation property as specified by the preconditions on lines 1–2. We assume that CAMs are uploaded to a sequence that can then be accessed by the other vehicles nearby. The latest CAM for each car is stored at a position in the sequence that matches its vehicle id number. We express the non-repudiation property by requiring that the received CAM did indeed come from a vehicle with a valid id and that the vehicle claiming to have sent the CAM did actually send one. §6.1.1 of [1] specifies that any received CAMs should not be forwarded to other vehicles in the intelligent transport system and our preconditions capture this by requiring that the sender did actually send a CAM.

Of course, CAMs are used by the receiving vehicles to modify their state with respect to the information that they receive. For example, if a leader vehicle decreases their speed then a vehicle that is travelling behind it should also reduce their speed, provided that they are travelling in the same direction. To this end, our `receiveCAM` implementation in Fig. 5 also describes when the vehicle should brake. We specify this safety property as a postcondition on lines 3–6. In particular, if the current vehicle and the one that sent the CAM are travelling in the same direction and the current vehicle has a greater speed than the one in front, then the brake should be engaged.

Without the security property on line 1–2, the safety property can still be verified. However, if the security property is violated and an attacker is sending a false message to the receiving vehicle, potentially that the leader has not slowed down when they have, then there could be a collision even though the safety property on lines 3–6 is preserved. This illustrates the importance of considering security properties alongside safety for these complex and connected systems where security violations can impact safety. In reality, the braking mechanism would be more complex than simply toggling a boolean flag as we have done above, however, the same basic properties apply.

5.3 Discussion

One advantage of Dafny for this case study is that we were able to run tests in Visual Studio to complement the formal verification results presented above. Crucially, Dafny is relatively easy to communicate to security practitioners since it more closely resembles the implementation language than other formal methods such as Promela/SPIN (Sect. 4). However, since it is not a language that can be used for the final implementation, some discrepancies may exist between our implementation and the one used in the fully implemented system. In particular, a more realistic version of this algorithm would keep track of whether the receiving vehicle are getting closer to the vehicle in front or not rather than just focusing on the speed part of the CAM and this could be seen as a refinement of our original model.

Note that the Denial of Service property that we have verified in the sendCAM method only applies if the attacker is trying to flood the network with CAMs, and does not address the scenario when they might use other kinds of messages. However, our approach could be extended to other message types in vehicle-to-vehicle communications, such as DENM [26].

An open question in software verification is in ensuring that the verified models faithfully capture what happens in the fully implemented systems. This "reality gap" is difficult to traverse and will almost always exist when building abstract models of program behaviour [8,19]. Since all real world implementations of CAM should comply to the specification outlined in [1], we chose it as our starting point for modelling this protocol. We could potentially run the Dafny implementation alongside a real world implementation and check that they exhibit the same behaviour but this was out of the scope of this work.

6 Conclusions and Future Work

This paper presents a case study showing how cyber security threat analysis techniques can be used to guide formal methods practitioners in verifying security properties, particularly as they may impact safety. Previously, we discussed the need for the use of integrated formal methods in the robotics domain and the example that we present here is no different [8].

We carried out STRIDE threat analysis of the CAM protocol for sending and receiving messages between autonomous vehicles. This resulted in the identification of spoofing, denial of service and repudiation as attacks that may occur. We modelled spoofing by specifying the behaviour of an attacker in our Promela model. Denial of service was considered via an availability property in the Dafny implementation of the algorithm for sending CAMs. Finally, repudiation was addressed as a property to be verified of the Dafny algorithm for receiving CAMs.

By modelling the system at different levels of abstraction; system-level in Promela/SPIN and algorithm-level in Dafny, we were able to investigate and to verify properties related to STRIDE threat analysis. In particular, model-checking with Promela/SPIN is useful for examining high-level temporal properties. Conversely, the use of theorem proving with Dafny allowed us to examine properties of an implementation of the CAM protocol. Our use of distinct tools allowed us to examine different properties of the CAM protocol at different levels of abstraction. Future analysis of CAM with various tools will likely provide a better understanding of which STRIDE properties should be checked using different kinds of formal methods.

An important aspect here is that, although it could be useful, the individual formal analyses do not need to be combined as in holistic/compositional formal approaches [2,13,21]. Instead, formal methods are used to focus security analysis on to specific areas/scenarios highlighted by informal cyber security analysis as being of "high risk". However, an interesting avenue of future work might involve proving that the independent formal models do, in fact, capture the same system.

This work is a first step toward a detailed methodology of how STRIDE properties should be treated in formal verification. Therefore, our future work aims to define a more general methodology for combining threat analysis techniques and formal methods. Of course, our use of Promela/SPIN and Dafny has been motivated by our familiarity with these tools and it is certainly the case that other formal methods may have been a better choice for our study. We intend to investigate this further in future work.

References

1. Intelligent Transport Systems (ITS): Vehicular Communications, Basic Set of Applications. Part 2: Specification of Cooperative Awareness Basic Service. Standard Draft ETSI EN 302 637-2, European Telecommunications Standards Institute, November 2018. V1.4.0 (2018–08)
2. Back, R.-J.: A calculus of refinements for program derivations. Acta Informatica 25(6), 593–624 (1988)
3. Barnett, M., Chang, B.-Y.E., DeLine, R., Jacobs, B., Leino, K.R.M.: Boogie: a modular reusable verifier for object-oriented programs. In: de Boer, F.S., Bonsangue, M.M., Graf, S., de Roever, W.-P. (eds.) FMCO 2005. LNCS, vol. 4111, pp. 364–387. Springer, Heidelberg (2006). https://doi.org/10.1007/11804192_17
4. Ben-Ari, M.: Principles of the Spin model checker. Springer, Cham (2008). https://doi.org/10.1007/978-1-84628-770-1
5. Bittl, S., Gonzalez, A.A., Myrtus, M., Beckmann, H., Sailer, S., Eissfeller, B.: Emerging attacks on VANET security based on GPS time spoofing. In: IEEE Conference on Communications and Network Security, pp. 344–352. IEEE (2015)
6. Choi, J., Jin, S.: Security threats in connected car environment and proposal of in-vehicle infotainment-based access control mechanism. In: Park, J.J., Loia, V., Choo, K.-K.R., Yi, G. (eds.) MUE/FutureTech -2018. LNEE, vol. 518, pp. 383–388. Springer, Singapore (2019). https://doi.org/10.1007/978-981-13-1328-8_49
7. de Moura, L., Bjørner, N.: Z3: an efficient SMT solver. In: Ramakrishnan, C.R., Rehof, J. (eds.) TACAS 2008. LNCS, vol. 4963, pp. 337–340. Springer, Heidelberg (2008). https://doi.org/10.1007/978-3-540-78800-3_24
8. Farrell, M., Luckcuck, M., Fisher, M.: Robotics and integrated formal methods: necessity meets opportunity. In: Furia, C.A., Winter, K. (eds.) IFM 2018. LNCS, vol. 11023, pp. 161–171. Springer, Cham (2018). https://doi.org/10.1007/978-3-319-98938-9_10
9. Fisher, M.: An Introduction to Practical Formal Methods Using Temporal Logic. Wiley, Hoboken (2011)
10. Holzmann, G.J.: The Spin Model Checker: Primer and Reference Manual. Addison-Wesley, Reading (2003)
11. Huang, L., Kang, E.-Y.: Formal verification of safety and security related timing constraints for a cooperative automotive system. In: Fundamental Approaches to Software Engineering. LNCS, vol. 11424, pp. 210–227. Springer, Cham (2019). https://doi.org/10.1007/978-3-030-16722-6_12
12. Jagielski, M., Jones, N., Lin, C.-W., Nita-Rotaru, C., Shiraishi, S.: Threat detection for collaborative adaptive cruise control in connected cars. In: ACM Conference on Security & Privacy in Wireless and Mobile Networks, pp. 184–189. ACM (2018)

13. Jones, C.B.: Tentative steps toward a development method for interfering programs. ACM Trans. Program. Lang. Syst. **5**(4), 596–619 (1983)
14. Kamali, M., Linker, S., Fisher, M.: Modular verification of vehicle platooning with respect to decisions, space and time. In: Artho, C., Ölveczky, P.C. (eds.) FTSCS 2018. CCIS, vol. 1008, pp. 18–36. Springer, Cham (2019). https://doi.org/10.1007/978-3-030-12988-0_2
15. Kohnfelder, L., Garg, P.: The threats to our products (April 1999). https://adam.shostack.org/microsoft/The-Threats-To-Our-Products.docx. Accessed 10 Dec 2018
16. Langenstein, B., Vogt, R., Ullmann, M.: The use of formal methods for trusted digital signature devices. In: Florida Artificial Intelligence Research Society, pp. 336–340. AAAI Press (2000)
17. Leino, K.R.M.: Dafny: an automatic program verifier for functional correctness. In: Clarke, E.M., Voronkov, A. (eds.) LPAR 2010. LNCS (LNAI), vol. 6355, pp. 348–370. Springer, Heidelberg (2010). https://doi.org/10.1007/978-3-642-17511-4_20
18. Liu, J., Yan, C., Xu, W.: Can you trust autonomous vehicles: contactless attacks against sensors of self-driving vehicles. In: DEFCON24 (2016). http://bit.ly/2EQNOLs
19. Luckcuck, M., Farrell, M., Dennis, L., Dixon, C., Fisher, M.: Formal Specification and Verification of Autonomous Robotic Systems: A Survey. ACM Computing Surveys, US (2019). accepted
20. Michele Rondinone, A.C.: Deliverable (d) no: 5.1 definition of v2x message sets. report, Universidad Miguel Hernandez, V1.0 27/08/2018 (August 2018)
21. Morgan, C., Robinson, K., Gardiner, P.: On the Refinement Calculus. Springer, Cham (1988). https://doi.org/10.1007/978-1-4471-3273-8
22. Petit, J., Stottelaar, B., Feiri, M., Kargl, F.: Remote attacks on automated vehicles sensors: experiments on camera and lidar. Black Hat Eur. **11**, 2015 (2015)
23. Pnueli, A.: The temporal logic of programs. In: 18th Symposium on the Foundations of Computer Science, pp. 46–57. IEEE (1977)
24. Ross, R.S.: Guide for conducting risk assessments. Technical report, National Institute of Standards and Technology. SP 800–30 Rev. 1 (September 2012)
25. Ruddle, A., et al.: Security requirements for automotive on-board networks based on dark-side scenarios. EVITA Deliverable D **2**, 3 (2009)
26. Santa, J., Pereñíguez, F., Moragón, A., Skarmeta, A.F.: Vehicle-to-infrastructure messaging proposal based on CAM/DENM specifications. In: Wireless Days (WD), IFIP, pp. 1–7. IEEE (2013)
27. Schneider, S.: Formal analysis of a non-repudiation protocol. In: Computer Security Foundations Workshop, pp. 54–65. IEEE (1998)
28. Schneider, S.: Verifying authentication protocols in CSP. IEEE Trans. Softw. Eng. **24**(9), 741–758 (1998)
29. Schneider, S., Delicata, R.: Verifying security protocols: an application of CSP. In: Abdallah, A.E., Jones, C.B., Sanders, J.W. (eds.) Communicating Sequential Processes. The First 25 Years. LNCS, vol. 3525, pp. 243–263. Springer, Heidelberg (2005). https://doi.org/10.1007/11423348_14
30. Snook, C., Hoang, T.S., Butler, M.: Analysing security protocols using refinement in iUML-B. In: Barrett, C., Davies, M., Kahsai, T. (eds.) NFM 2017. LNCS, vol. 10227, pp. 84–98. Springer, Cham (2017). https://doi.org/10.1007/978-3-319-57288-8_6
31. Stallings, W., Brown, L., Bauer, M.D., Bhattacharjee, A.K.: Computer Security: Principles and Practice. Pearson, Upper Saddle River (2012)

32. Vanspauwen, G., Jacobs, B.: Verifying protocol implementations by augmenting existing cryptographic libraries with specifications. In: Calinescu, R., Rumpe, B. (eds.) SEFM 2015. LNCS, vol. 9276, pp. 53–68. Springer, Cham (2015). https://doi.org/10.1007/978-3-319-22969-0_4

33. Whitefield, J., et al.: Formal analysis of V2X revocation protocols. In: Livraga, G., Mitchell, C. (eds.) STM 2017. LNCS, vol. 10547, pp. 147–163. Springer, Cham (2017). https://doi.org/10.1007/978-3-319-68063-7_10

Towards Detecting Trigger-Based Behavior in Binaries: Uncovering the Correct Environment

Dorottya Papp[1,2]([✉])[iD], Thorsten Tarrach[2][iD], and Levente Buttyán[1][iD]

[1] CrySyS Lab, Department of Networked Systems and Services, BME,
Budapest, Hungary
{dpapp,buttyan}@crysys.hu
[2] AIT Austrian Institute of Technology GmbH, Vienna, Austria
thorsten.tarrach@ait.ac.at

Abstract. In this paper, we present our first results towards detecting trigger-based behavior in binary programs. A program exhibits trigger-based behavior if it contains undocumented, often malicious functionality that is executed only under specific circumstances. In order to determine the inputs and environment required to trigger such behavior, we use directed symbolic execution and present techniques to overcome some of its practical limitations. Specifically, we propose techniques to overcome the environment problem and the path selection problem. We implemented our techniques and evaluated their performance on a real malware sample that launches denial-of-service attacks upon receiving specific remote commands. Thanks to our techniques, our implementation was able to determine those specific commands and all other requirements needed to trigger the malicious behavior in reasonable time.

Keywords: Directed symbolic execution ·
Trigger-based behavior · Software verification

1 Introduction

Trigger-based behavior is the execution of undocumented, potentially malicious features in an application upon reception of some inputs that satisfy pre-defined criteria. Such inputs are referred to as *trigger inputs*. The pre-defined criteria are

The presented research has been partially supported by the SETIT Project (no. 2018-1.2.1-NKP-2018-00004), which has been implemented with the support provided from the National Research, Development and Innovation Fund of Hungary, financed under the 2018-1.2.1-NKP funding scheme, and by the European Union, co-financed by the European Social Fund (EFOP-3.6.2-16-2017-00013, Thematic Fundamental Research Collaborations Grounding Innovation in Informatics and Infocommunications). It has also been supported by the SECREDAS project, which receives funding from ECSEL Joint Undertaking under Grant Agreement No 783119. This Joint Undertaking received support from the European Unions Horizon 2020 Research and Innovation Programme.

© Springer Nature Switzerland AG 2019
P. C. Ölveczky and G. Salaün (Eds.): SEFM 2019, LNCS 11724, pp. 491–509, 2019.
https://doi.org/10.1007/978-3-030-30446-1_26

hard-coded into the application in the form of checks and their semantic meaning can encompass all sorts of external requirements, e.g. specific system time or location, special text entered or message received. While not all instances of trigger-based behavior are malicious (take, for example, software easter eggs[1]), such behavior is often used by malware. For example, malware can evade in-depth analysis by scanning its environment and ceasing malicious activities if it finds hints of an analysis framework[2]. Trigger-based behavior also includes backdoors, a behavior prevalent in firmware images [9], in which case, special access is granted, if a specific string is received as input. These examples show that in many cases, the application to be analyzed is only available in binary form. Therefore, in this paper, we consider applications available as binaries. Due to the often malicious intent behind the implementation of trigger-based behavior, its detection is important. However, the combination of inputs required to trigger the hidden behavior is known only to its author, therefore, uncovering such behavior via testing is challenging.

Previous work in this field [4,10,12] have demonstrated the usefulness of symbolic execution [3] to uncover trigger-based behavior. Symbolic execution was originally developed to automate testing by analyzing execution paths and generating test cases, which lead execution down the analyzed execution path. In order to uncover trigger-based behavior, we need to analyze the application's interaction with its environment and how the environment influences its behavior. If data from the environment is replaced with symbolic variables, symbolic execution can analyze this interaction and can obtain the hard-coded conditions together with the trigger input values satisfying those conditions.

However, using symbolic execution has a limitation: the more symbolic variables are introduced into the analysis, the more execution paths must be analyzed, leading to the *path explosion problem*. Previous work addressed this problem by considering only a subset of potential trigger input types. In [4], for example, the human analyst is required to select possible trigger input types in advance. However, as only the malware author knows the exact trigger inputs, there is a chance that the human analyst fails to select all necessary types of input. In [10], the authors describe a technique that works on Android Bytecode but only consider time, location and SMS objects as trigger inputs. In [12], a lightweight version of symbolic execution is performed over JavaScript code, which analyzes the effects of potential values in the navigator's fields.

In this paper, we want to overcome the path explosion problem without limiting the trigger input types. Our goal is to develop an approach, which can consider all external data as potential trigger inputs while relying on symbolic execution to calculate the inputs and environment required to reach a selected program point. The overview of our main idea is shown in Fig. 1. We assume that the analyzed binary is deterministic and interacts with the environment through the operating system and its API (system calls). Therefore, we consider invoked

---

[1] https://electrek.co/2017/12/23/tesla-christmas-easter-egg/.

[2] https://www.fireeye.com/blog/threat-research/2011/01/the-dead-giveaways-of-vm-aware-malware.html.

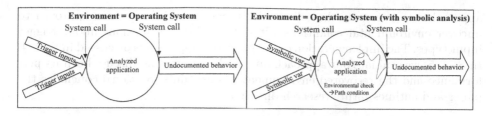

Fig. 1. Symbolic execution for uncovering trigger-based behavior

library functions as part of the analyzed binary. In real-life execution, the binary would invoke multiple system calls and the return values from a subset of those system calls would be interpreted by the binary as trigger inputs. The binary would then proceed to match those return values against the pre-defined criteria hard-coded into its logic and execute the potentially malicious behavior only if the result of the comparison(s) is a match. In order to analyze this interaction, the return values of system calls that return data from external sources must be replaced with fresh symbolic variables. Then, symbolic execution can be used to analyze this interaction.

Our contributions in this paper are the following:

(1) We present an approach for uncovering trigger-based behavior in binaries, which is capable of considering all external data sources as trigger input types. Our approach replaces system calls with symbolic summary functions, which return fresh symbolic variables instead of external data.

(2) Our approach relies on directed symbolic execution [14] to guide analysis towards a selected program point. However, directed symbolic execution expects a semantically correct and complete interprocedural control-flow graph. The generation of such a control-flow graph is a challenge for binary programs, mainly due to indirect jumps. Our approach is designed such that directed symbolic execution can be performed even if the interprocedural control-flow graph has incorrect/missing edges and/or nodes.

(3) We implement our approach in angr [18]: we model 36 system calls for Linux and discuss modifications to angr's workflow in order to make our approach feasible in practice.

(4) We evaluate our approach on a real malware sample compiled for the ARM platform, which is known to exhibit trigger-based behavior. The program logic of the selected sample contains elements known to be challenging for symbolic execution and its execution relies on multiple sources of environmental input. Our approach is able to reach program points deep in the binary and obtain the environmental conditions required to trigger their execution. In addition, our analysis time is in the order of hours, which is a reasonable performance considering the complexity of the analyzed sample and the generality of our approach.

The paper is structured as follows. Section 2 provides an overview of symbolic execution: the main idea behind the technique, its limitations and current approaches to overcome those limitations. Section 3 discusses our approach to uncover environmental conditions without a priori assumptions about trigger input types. The implementation of the proposed approach is discussed in Sect. 4. In Sect. 5, we evaluate our approach on a real malware and discuss both its performance and the recovered environmental constraints. Section 6 concludes the paper and outlines future research directions.

2   Background

In this section, we discuss the concept of symbolic execution. The techniques has been well-researched over the years and as such, a full survey of the field is out of scope for this paper. We only summarize its main characteristics and discuss the challenges it poses for our research. Readers interested in a full overview of this field are kindly referred to [3] and [17].

Symbolic execution is an analysis technique originally proposed to automatically generate test cases and increase code coverage during software testing. During symbolic analysis, registers and memory addresses do not store exact values but instead special symbols called symbolic variables. When first introduced into the analysis, symbolic variables may take on any value, i.e. they are *unconstrained*. When analysis reaches a branch in the analyzed software, two execution paths are spawned for both sides of the branch, i.e. it *forks*. In each spawned execution path, constraints are placed on the symbolic variables to represent the chosen path. The set of constraints collected on an execution path is the *path constraint*. An execution path is *satisfiable*, if there exists an assignment to its symbolic variables such that the path constraint is satisfied. If no such assignment exists, the execution path is said to be *unsatisfiable*.

The challenges of performing symbolic execution on arbitrary software in binary form are manifold. Firstly, tools implementing the technique have to model the execution state on the platform the analyzed software is supposed to run on, including instruction set, registers, memory, interrupts, calling conventions, flags, etc. Tools implementing symbolic execution, e.g. DART [11], KLEE [5], S2E [8], MAYHEM [7] and angr [18], come with such a model of the target platform. Secondly, symbolic execution can only reason about code it analyzes and has no knowledge about library functions, system calls and their side effects. This challenge is better known as the *environment problem* and is typically tackled using summary functions, which are pieces of code that summarize the effects of the missing piece of code. Thirdly, as symbolic execution spawns execution paths to pursue at each encountered branch; the number of execution paths to analyze is exponential with respect to the number of conditional branches in the analyzed software. This challenge is known as the *path explosion problem* and it results in symbolic execution not being able to exhaustively explore all execution paths in all but the simplest of cases. This challenge is partially tackled by specifying which parts of the software are of interest to the analysis and only executing those parts symbolically. In such scenarios, the analysis engine keeps track of not only the symbolic state, but the concrete execution state as well, earning the name mixed concrete and symbolic execution. Lastly, since not all execution paths can be explored during symbolic execution, analysis has to decide which paths to pursue. This challenge is known as the *path selection problem* and it is usually tackled using a heuristic exploration strategy. The depth-first strategy explores an execution path to its completion before backtracking to the second deepest branch. The breadth-first strategy, on the other hand, seeks to explore all execution paths in parallel. There are also randomized approaches, where the next pursued path is selected randomly or with some probability. In certain application domains of symbolic execution, path selection algorithms have been tailored for a specific goal, e.g. maximizing coverage [5, 13] or reaching a certain program point [14, 16].

We use angr, which is capable of mixed concrete and symbolic execution and has a model for the ARM platform. However, angr in itself does not solve the environment and the path selection problems. A major part of our work was to address these problems, and in Sect. 3, we describe how we did so.

3   Methodology

Our methodology focuses on how to calculate the correct environmental conditions such that a certain behavior implemented by the analyzed malware can be triggered. We assume that the human analyst has a specific program point of interest and wishes to uncover the inputs required to trigger its execution. Towards this end, we employ two techniques:

(1) Symbolic summary functions capturing the behavior of invoked system calls in order to introduce a model of environmental data to the analysis, and
(2) Shortest-distance symbolic execution [14], a path selection strategy to guide analysis towards the selected program point.

We elaborate on these techniques in Sects. 3.1 and 3.2, respectively.

3.1   Symbolic Summary Functions

As mentioned before, the environment is represented by operating system services, and the environment manifests itself as the result of invoking system calls. Therefore, we need symbolic summaries of system calls which model their effects. Such symbolic summary functions allow us to simulate the environment for the analyzed application and enable mixed concrete and symbolic execution to analyze how returned data influences execution.

Our summaries are semantically equivalent to the system calls they replace with two major exceptions. Firstly, if the system call writes into the environment (e.g. sends packets or writes in a file), the summary always returns with success. This allows us to contain the path explosion problem: if we simulated both success and failure, we would need to simulate the various conditions for failure, which would further increase the number of execution paths to analyze. However, we acknowledge the possibility of system call failures being used as triggers.

Secondly, if the system call returns data from the environment (e.g. assigned process ID, system time, messages over the network), the summary function returns fresh symbolic variables instead. Using the fresh symbolic variables, the influence of the environment on the application can be analyzed.

Symbolic summaries can be written based on the semantic information available about the system calls in the operating system's documentation. These summaries need to be written only once for a particular platform. As an example, let us consider the Linux system call fork, responsible for duplicating processes. On success, it returns the PID of the child process in the parent and 0 in the child. On failure, it returns −1 to the parent, creates no child process and sets errno appropriately. In order to explore how the invocation of fork influences the analyzed binary, we need to replace its return value with a fresh symbolic variable. According to its manpage[3], its return value has the type pid_t which is a signed integer. On the ARM platform, a signed integer is 32 bits long, therefore, the model of this system call for analyzing ARM binaries must return a 32-bit long symbolic variable. The variable must be constrained as written in the documentation: it can be a positive number, 0 or −1. Two further constraints must be added to the model to capture its behavior faithfully. Firstly, if the return value is greater then 0, than semantically, analysis continues in the child process. Therefore, the PID and the parent PID of the execution state must be updated accordingly. Secondly, if the return value is −1, then semantically, the system call failed and a new symbolic variable is required to represent the error condition, and its value must be constrained to one of the potential error codes.

3.2   Approach to Symbolic Execution

Symbolic summary functions only introduce the model of environmental data in the form of fresh symbolic variables. The actual conditions required to trigger a specific behavior in the analyzed binary are encoded in its instructions. In order to calculate the correct environmental values, we need to recover and solve these conditions. To this end, we use mixed concrete and symbolic execution, capable of both recovering these conditions as path conditions and solving them thanks to Satisfiability Modulo Theory solvers. Specifically, we employ shortest-distance symbolic execution (SDSE) [14], designed to prioritize execution paths which are closer to a selected target according to some metric.

SDSE was originally proposed to solve the line reachability problem: how to reach a target line in the source code? It requires the interprocedural control-flow graph in order to guide symbolic execution towards the targeted line. The approach first translates execution paths to control-flow graph nodes, then computes the shortest distance from said nodes to the node corresponding to the target line. The computed metric is used as scores to prioritize execution paths. At branches, SDSE selects the execution path with the lowest score among all available paths for analysis.

---

[3] http://man7.org/linux/man-pages/man2/fork.2.html.

Our scenario is similar to the one SDSE was developed for in the sense that we need a solution for the reachability problem in order to recover constraints placed on environmental data. However, there are key differences as well. Firstly, SDSE was originally proposed and implemented at the source code level, while we apply it at the binary level. As a result, instead of a target line, we aim to reach a target binary instruction. Secondly, as stated in [14], SDSE can only work correctly, if the interprocedural control-flow graph recovered from the binary does not have mismatching calls and returns. Otherwise, semantically incorrect or infeasible paths may be computed as shortest paths, resulting in incorrect scores and priorities. In order to generate a semantically correct control-flow graph whose structure properly captures function calls and returns encountered during execution, the generator algorithm has to consider a lot of context-related information, including call sites, return sites and the call stack. There exist algorithms capable of handling that information [6,18], however, their usage in practice poses a challenge. As more context-related information is taken into consideration, the time and space required to generate and store the resulting control-flow graph also increases exponentially. Instead of generating such a control-flow graph, we implemented a heuristic algorithm to discard edges whose inclusion in the shortest path calculation might result in incorrect paths. This heuristic allows us to keep the required contextual information at a minimum by taking into consideration potential changes to the call stack at edges that result in semantically correct function calls and returns. We discuss the implementation of this heuristic in Sect. 4.2.

4   Implementation

We implemented our approach in angr (version 7.8.2.21), an open-source binary analysis tool written in Python, capable of analyzing binary formats of major operating systems, such as ELF, PE and Mach-0 files. The tool implements many analyses for binary code, including mixed concrete and symbolic execution, constraint solving, control-flow graph generation, program slicing, dependency analysis, etc. These analyses are performed over the intermediate representation (IR) of valgrind [15], called VEX, to provide platform independence. VEX translates a sequence of binary instructions into a block of IR instructions. As a result, most analyses are not performed on a per instruction basis, but rather on a per IR block basis. Our implementation uses the following features of angr:

(1) mixed concrete and symbolic execution engine with a constraint solver,
(2) control-flow graph generation, and
(3) model of execution states, including registers, memory, and elements from POSIX, such as files and sockets.

There were cases, in which we needed to modify the workflow and execution of angr. We discuss these modifications in the rest of this section.

4.1   Symbolic Summaries for System Calls

angr supports system call invocations during mixed concrete and symbolic execution. However, developers focus more on defining the environment at the library level and therefore, the tool has more symbolic summaries for standard libc functions than it has for system calls. As a result, many system calls invoked during our tests were missing and had to be added to the tool manually. The list of 36 system calls we had to create symbolic summaries for is shown in Table 1.

Table 1. System calls on Linux for which symbolic summaries were created

_newselect	arm_set_tls	brk	clone	close	connect
exit	exit_group	fcntl	fcntl64	fork	futex
geteuid32	getgid32	getpid	getppid	gettimeofday	getuid32
ioctl	kill	mmap2	nanosleep	open	read
recv	rt_sigaction	rt_sigprocmask	sendto	setrlimit	setsockopt
socket	time	ugetrlimit	uname	wait4	write

4.2   Control Flow Graph

There are two algorithms to generate an interprocedural control-flow graph in angr. The first algorithm is called CFGFast and it relies on heuristics and assumptions to greatly decrease the time required for generation. The second algorithm is called CFGAccurate (CFGEmulated in later versions) and it performs lightweight symbolic execution to generate the control-flow graph, increasing accuracy. In our implementation, we used CFGAccurate as accuracy is important for using SDSE.

Extending the Control Flow Graph. There are program constructs which pose a challenge during control-flow graph generation, e.g. indirect jumps. We encountered scenarios where CFGAccurate detected the indirect jumps but it was unable to accurately determine the address the analyzed code jumped to. The limitation is caused by the lightweight nature of its symbolic execution: if a read or write operation involves an operand which could be assigned multiple values, that operand is skipped and a fresh, unconstrained symbolic variable is used instead. However, angr's symbolic execution has an upper limit on the number of successor states it generates when analyzing an execution state. If the instruction pointer of the analyzed execution state has more than 256 solutions (by default), then the tool assumes that the instruction pointer was overwritten with unconstrained data, and flags the execution state as one producing unconstrained successors.[4] As a result, CFGAccurate may fail to analyze certain parts

---

[4] This assumption is included in angr's documentation together with the fact that it is not sound in general.

of the binary due to the inaccurate execution state used during construction. This scenario is illustrated with the following two instructions:

```
ldr r4, [r3, #4]     ; load function address from memory
blx r4               ; call function
```

The code includes a call to the address contained in r4, whose value is loaded from memory. The address from where the value is to be loaded is influenced by r3. If r3 holds an operand with multiple potential values while control-flow recovery analyzes this code segment, then analysis has to read a multi-valued operand from the register. However, as discussed before, instead of performing the read, the recovery algorithm creates a fresh, unconstrained symbolic variable to represent the result of the read operations. As a result, r4 will also hold an unconstrained symbolic variable when the recovery algorithm tries to determine the jump address. Because the unconstrained symbolic variable has more than 256 solutions, the state is flagged as one producing unconstrained successors and address resolution fails.

Normal mixed concrete and symbolic execution, however, never skips operands and is much less likely to run into such a scenario. Execution states have operands with semantically correct values and correct path constraints. If control-flow graph generation is resumed from such a state, CFGAccurate can accurately identify the indirect jump addresses, if the value of r4 has less than 256 solutions. Therefore, during control-flow graph generation, we take note of addresses where unconstrained successors were computed as potential extension points of the control-flow graph. When normal mixed concrete and symbolic execution reaches such an address, we use the accurate execution state to extend the control-flow graph on the fly.

Shortest Path Calculation. The accuracy of CFGAccurate is influenced by its level of context-sensitivity. This parameter captures how deep the call stack is taken into consideration when determining the calling context of any given control-flow graph node. By default, the algorithm analyzes each address only once per distinct calling context. As a result, different levels of context sensitivity result in different graph structures, which in turn influence the available paths computed by generic shortest path algorithms. Figure 2 shows the different contexts in which functions are analyzed at different levels of context sensitivity. Because of the different contexts, functions may be replicated multiple times in the control-flow graph. Note, that we demonstrate the effect of context sensitivity at the source code level only for ease of understanding, but our techniques work at the binary level.

In order for generic shortest path algorithms to compute semantically correct paths in the interprocedural control-flow graph, edges connecting mismatched call sites and return sites must be discarded. CFGAccurate can record the execution state from which a specific control-flow graph node was created, allowing access to its call stack. The algorithm also annotates edges with attributes recovered by VEX during lightweight symbolic execution. One of these attributes is

```
void c(){
    printf("Executing function c");
}
void b(){
    printf("Executing function b");
    c();
}
void a(){
    printf("Executing function a");
    c();
}
int main(int argc, void* argv) {
    a();
    b();
    return 0;
}
```

	0-context sensitivity	1-context sensitivity	2-context sensitivity
a	a	main→a	(library init)→main→a
b	b	main→b	(library init)→main→b
c	c	a→c b→c	main→a→c main→b→c
printf	printf	a→printf b→printf c→printf	main→a→printf main→b→printf a→c→printf b→c→printf

Fig. 2. Different contexts of functions during control-flow graph generation

the semantic meaning of the jump at the end of each IR block (e.g. function call, return, etc.). Inspired by the control-flow graph model of [2], a visibly push-down automaton which keeps track of the calling context of functions, we rely on the call stack and the edge annotation to implement a heuristic that discards semantically incorrect paths violating the following rules:

1. The call stack depth difference between the source node and the destination can only change by −1, 0 or 1, corresponding to returning, staying in the function or calling another function, respectively.
2. In case of calls and returns, the edge's attributes must support the deduction made from the call stack depth difference. For example, if the call stack depth

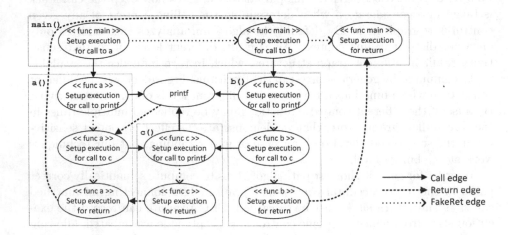

Fig. 3. Fake return edges in an interprocedural control-flow graph

difference is 1, then the edge's attributes must state that the edge represents a function invocation.

If any of the above rules is violated, the edge is discarded during the shortest path calculation.

Our approach can rely on generic shortest path algorithms thanks to special, so called *fake return* edges. These edges are directed edges from the call site to the return site and are automatically added by angr whenever a call is encountered. Their importance is highlighted in Fig. 3, which shows the fake return edges in the interprocedural control-flow graph of the source code shown in Fig. 2 when context sensitivity level is set to 0. For the sake of clarity, the actual instructions responsible for setting up the execution state for calling functions were omitted. By default, CFGAccurate analyzes each IR block once per distinct calling context. With 0 context sensitivity level, the calling context is only the currently analyzed function, which leads to each function being present in the graph exactly once. For each analyzed block, angr adds a call edge to the called function and a fake return edge to the return site. These special edges mainly serve the purpose of ensuring connectivity in the graph. Because each block is analyzed once per distinct calling context, each function has only 1 return edge. For example, consider the printf function. Even tough it is called from a, b and c, it is analyzed only once, the first time it is encountered when called from a. As a result, printf has only 1 return edge, leading to its return site in a. Without fake return edges, printf's call site in b would not be connected to its return site in b.

Our edge discarding heuristic can also lead to loss of connectivity without fake return edges. For example, our heuristic discards the call edge between c and printf because the control-flow graph nodes' call stack depth does not support a function call. The call site has the context main→a→c, while printf has a the context main→a→printf. Because the call stack depth difference is 0, the edge should indicate staying in the function instead of calling another function. Without the discarded call edge, generic shortest path algorithms must rely on the fake return edge to calculate shortest paths. However, even if the fake return edge is used, simulation must execute the function represented by the said edge. In order to faithfully capture the cost of calling a function, we assign weights to fake return edges: the smallest number of IR blocks simulated between the call and return sites throughout analysis, i.e. the shortest path mixed concrete and symbolic execution uncovered. Thanks to this heuristic, we are able to keep context sensitivity at level 1.

4.3   Call Stack Management

During our work, we discovered mismatches between how the call stack is managed in CFGAccurate and how it is managed during mixed concrete and symbolic execution. The discrepancies between the algorithms hinders us in translating execution states into control-flow graph nodes.

In case of mixed concrete and symbolic execution, function calls are detected by statically looking at the semantic information about the jump at the end of the analyzed IR block. Function returns, on the other hand, are detected by looking at the stack pointer. The function returns if either the stack pointer has a lower value than it had at the call (which is the convention in e.g. Intel platforms) or execution has reached the return address recorded at the call and the stack pointer has the same value as it had at the call (which is the convention in platforms like ARM where the return address is stored in the link register).

CFGAccurate uses the same approach with an additional feature. For each IR block address encountered during CFG construction, it checks with angr's loader whether the address corresponds to a symbol. If it does, it forcefully simulates a call to that symbol. This approach has the advantage of providing more meaningful nodes in the control-flow graph. However, it hinders us from accurately matching execution states to control-flow graph nodes as the calling contexts are different. As an example, consider the following instructions:

```
000105a4 <getspoof>:
    ...
    105bc: eb0022aa  bl 1906c <rand>
    ...
0001906c <rand>:
    1906c: ea000065  b 19208 <__GI_random>
    ...
00019208 <__GI_random>:
    ...
```

The getspoof function at 0x105bc calls rand, which immediately jumps to __GI_random. In case of symbolic execution, the execution state at 0x19208 has the calling context getspoof→rand, while the control-flow graph node representing 0x19208 has the context getspoof→rand→__GI_random, because 0x19208 corresponds to a symbol. Due to the different calling contexts, the execution state cannot be translated to the control-flow graph node. Thus, we removed the forceful simulation of function calls from CFGAccurate.

We have also encountered call stack management issues in scenarios where mixed concrete and symbolic execution forks in functions with only one of the paths returning. The issues are caused by angr running its call stack management code before adding path constraints to the state. We illustrate the problem with an example. Consider the following snippet from the strcasecmp_l function.

```
179c4: lsl r3, r3, #1     ; increment index for string1
179c8: lsl r0, r0, #1     ; increment index for string2
179cc: ldrsh r3, [lr, r3] ; load next char of string1
179d0: ldrsh r0, [lr, r0] ; load next char of string2
179d4: subs r0, r3, r0    ; compare the chars
179d8: popne {pc} ; (ldrne pc, [sp], #4)
179dc: ldrb r3, [ip], #1
```

The function iterates over two strings character by character to check whether they are equal. The comparison between two characters is implemented using subtraction. If the result of the subtraction is 0, i.e. the characters are the same and the function continues, otherwise, it returns. If any of the input strings consists of symbolic variables as characters, the comparison has two outcomes: equals and not equals. At the end of simulating the block starting at 0x179c4, angr forks and creates the two successor states, one at 0x179dc and another at the return site. It then proceeds to check whether any of these states returned. However, the path condition has not been added to the successors yet, therefore, the stack pointer of the state at the return site is a symbolic expression encoding both staying in the function and returning. As a result, the call stack management code cannot deduce that the state returned and fails to pop strcasecmp_1 from the call stack. To overcome this issue, we concretize the stack pointer after forks and re-run the call stack management code to get correct call stacks.

4.4 Model of the Execution State

In order to model the side effects of system calls and any additional data they might return, we extended the original execution state model provided by angr. The extended model includes additional POSIX elements on a per-path basis, such as group ID, thread ID and parent process ID.

We also modified how system time is tracked throughout mixed concrete and symbolic execution. Originally, angr used a monotonically increasing, global symbolic variable to model system time which is suitable for the default breadth-first exploration strategy. However, SDSE's prioritization strategy can backtrack to an earlier execution state, which semantically means taking us "back in time". In order to support such a backward flow of time, we model system time on a per-path basis with local symbolic variables.

Throughout mixed concrete and symbolic execution, we also monitor the execution state to detect whether branches are the result of references to uninitialized memory addresses. This scenario can be the result of a bug in the analyzed binary, but might also signal missing side-effects of system call models. As a result, we do not pursue such paths any further, but keep them separated from the rest of execution states for further analysis.

5 Evaluation

We evaluated our approach on a slightly modified sample from the Kaiten[5] malware family. Kaiten variants are Trojan horses which open backdoors on various platforms and perform malicious tasks when remotely instructed to do so. Our sample implements its own IRC protocol parser and expects remote commands to be delivered as IRC private messages. Some commands are used to launch denial-of-service attacks, execute shell commands and download files.

---

[5] https://www.symantec.com/security-center/writeup/2015-102008-3612-99?tabi
d=2.

We chose this sample because its execution relies heavily on its environment. In order to trigger any malicious behavior, the sample must be able to communicate over the network. It needs to connect to the IRC server at the preprogrammed address and log into the also preprogrammed IRC channel. The sample uses randomly generated strings as nick and user name in the IRC communication; the seed is calculated from the system time, the process ID and the parent process ID. Once connection to the IRC channel has been established, the correct IRC private message must be received in order to trigger any behavior implemented in the sample.

Our chosen sample poses two challenges. Firstly, due to our assumptions and the sample's implementation, a vast number of execution paths are available for analysis. There are three main sources for such a high number of paths:

(1) Environmental data. The sample relies on the system time, process IDs and communication over the network. As we assume no prior knowledge about its functionality, our analysis has to analyze all those inputs using symbolic variables, leading to many branches.
(2) String handling. The sample implements an IRC protocol parser and uses standard libc functions such as `strlen`, `strtok` and `strcasecmp` to manipulate the string messages received over the network. These functions typically loop over the string character by character. As their inputs are returned from the kernel, our analysis must consider each of the characters as symbolic variables. Such loops are known to contribute to the path explosion problem.
(3) Infinite loop. The sample is implemented to run in an infinite loop, continuously listening for messages from the IRC server and trying to reconnect in cases of communication failure. As a result, exploring all execution paths cannot be done in a finite amount of time.

Another challenge is in the sample's logic. In case of receiving a well-formed IRC message, the sample dispatches the message to the appropriate handler function via jump tables. These jump tables are represented in the control-flow graph by nodes with many call edges leading to different handler functions. The use of jump tables decreases the accuracy of shortest path calculation, as the shortest path is always to take the correct call edge, even if said edge is infeasible.

5.1   Setting Up Our Experiment

Modifications to the Sample. Before we applied our implementation to the chosen sample, we made a few modifications to it which we describe here. First, we downloaded its publicly available source code[6]. Then, we shortened all strings in the jump tables of the source code to contain only a single character and the terminating null. With this modification, we can contain the path explosion of looping over strings to a certain extent. Note, however, that the modified sample still includes multiple jump tables organized into layers with each layer requiring

---

[6] https://packetstormsecurity.com/files/25575/kaiten.c.html.

multiple characters with specific values. Therefore, even with this modification, the sample still requires a string with multiple characters to invoke the necessary handler functions. We also set the address of the IRC server to 127.0.0.1 in order to avoid symbolically analyzing a DNS lookup. Finally, we recompiled the modified source code for the ARM platform and performed our analysis on the resulting binary. Both the original and the modified source code are available as supplementary materials [1].

Target Behavior. As the target behavior, we selected one of the functions launching denial-of-service attacks (tsunami in the source code). The attack is executed in a child process and sends spoofed packets to the target IP specified in the command. We inserted a call to the kill libc function before the child process is created and set the underlying kill system call as our target. Note, that this system call is used in other functions as well, therefore, we only accept reaching it, if it is done via the tsunami function.

In order to reach this function, mixed concrete and symbolic execution has to simulate the communication with the IRC server and "send" a specific string to the sample. The string must meet the following requirements:

(1) The sample must interpret its first part as an IRC private message, i.e. it must start with the corresponding code from the jump table of IRC message-handling functions (4 in our case).
(2) It must contain the preprogrammed name of the IRC channel to which the sample logged into (# in our modification).
(3) It must be intended for the sample, either by specifically mentioning the sample's IRC nick (randomly generated) or by using a wildcard character.
(4) The sample must interpret its last part as a command for launching the DoS attack implemented in tsunami, i.e. it must contain the corresponding code from the jump table of command-handling functions (0 in our case).

Unfortunately, while generating the control-flow graph with context sensitivity level 1, angr did not flag the IR blocks implementing the jump tables as producing unconstrained successors. As a result, jump tables were not treated as potential extension points, forcing us to specify the missing edges manually.

Parameters of the Machine. We ran the sample on a machine with two Xeon E5-2680 CPUs of 10 cores each, running at 2.8 GHz. The machine has 378 Gb of RAM available. Note that angr is not multithreaded and uses only a single core. We also restricted angr to run with 100 Gb of memory.

5.2 Results

Runtime Performance. Table 2 shows the performance of our prototype implementation on the modified Kaiten binary sample. The execution path reaching the targeted program point at the source code level is available as supplementary material [1]. The execution time of a single run consists of four components:

Table 2. Runtime performance of each stage of approach on modified Kaiten binary sample

Stage	Runtime (hh:mm:ss)
Control-flow graph generation and extension	0:10:42
Simulation of execution paths	19:08:54
Shortest distance calculation	8:05:44
Other management tasks	5:05:11

(1) generation and extension of the control-flow graph,
(2) simulating execution paths,
(3) calculating scores during backtracking, and
(4) other management tasks, e.g. concretizing stack pointers when necessary, logging events, checking if our target was reached, etc.

The measured execution time of our analysis was 32.5 h. Most of the time was spent with either simulating execution paths or calculating shortest distances.

The execution time of simulating execution paths can be accredited to the logic of the sample. During our tests, analysis encountered addresses, whose simulation took hours for mixed concrete and symbolic execution. These addresses were part of libc, including **rand** and multiple string-manipulating functions whose simulation involved computations with complex symbolic values. **rand** is used by the modified sample to generate random 1-character-long strings for communication with the IRC server. While the generated string for the nick has to be analyzed in order to reach the target system call, its value does not matter: the symbolic string representing network input either matches it, or it does not. Therefore, we replaced **rand** with angr's built-in symbolic summary and used a fresh, unconstrained symbolic variable to represent its result. However, the results of string manipulations contribute directly to the execution path leading towards the selected target behavior: they affect how long the symbolic string representing network input is and what constraints are placed on its characters. Therefore, we did not influence the execution of string manipulations and settled for the increased execution time.

Recovered Path Condition. The execution state which first reached the target system call had 76 constraints, encoding the network conditions and the remote command required to trigger the target behavior. We checked their correctness manually by looking at the source code.

Depending on their complexity, some constraints are intuitive to interpret. For example, <Bool socket_retval_23127_32 == 0x3> can be interpreted as the requirement for successfully creating sockets. socket_retval_23127_32 is the symbolic variable introduced in the socket system call. The two numbers are appended by angr: the first is a unique identifier, while the second is the length of the variable in bits. The return value of socket in case of success is a file descriptor (positive integer) and -1 in case of failure, it is -1. Given that the right-hand side of the equation is positive, we can deduct that the sample invoked the system call to create a socket which had to be completed successfully.

The human interpretation of other constraints, however, is quite challenging due to their complexity. For example, our modified sample sets an upper limit of 4096 on the number of characters it reads from a socket in one go. Therefore, our symbolic summary of `recv` returns a 4096-character-long string made up of symbolic variables. The sample then invokes multiple string manipulating functions which loop over the string character by character. The corresponding binary instructions are conditional in many cases, which means that in real life, the CPU would execute them only if necessary. During simulation, however, one of their operands is a symbolic character and therefore, they cannot be skipped. Instead, when possible, their results are encoded into `If-Then-Else` structures: if the flag evaluates to true, then the result is the `Then` value, else the `Else` value. These structures can be nested into each other, leading to constraints whose evaluation is tedious manually. In such cases, the constraint solver can be used to calculate the assigned values, giving the inputs required to trigger the targeted program point.

6   Conclusion

In this paper, we proposed an approach to determine what inputs and environmental conditions must be met in order to trigger undocumented, hidden behaviors in binary programs. Our approach consists of two techniques. Firstly, we model the environment at the operating system level by providing symbolic summary functions of system calls. Our summary functions have the same number and type of arguments as their real-world counterparts, but introduce fresh symbolic variables in order to model the effects of system calls. Secondly, we use shortest-distance symbolic execution to find a feasible path to a selected program point and collect the constraints along said path to acquire insight into the required input values and environmental settings. This technique relies on a semantically correct, complete inter-procedural control-flow graph, which is often unavailable for binary programs due to indirect jumps. Therefore, our approach is designed to allow for incorrect/missing edges and/or nodes.

We implemented our approach using angr and evaluated it on a sample from the Kaiten malware family. The sample implements an IRC bot client, which, among other things, launches denial-of-service attacks when remotely instructed to do so. The logic of the chosen sample poses additional challenges as many of its implementation details are known to be hard to analyze symbolically. Nevertheless, our approach successfully found a feasible path within reasonable time. The path condition along that path gave additional insight as to what kind of environment is needed to trigger a specific attack.

The manual interpretation of conditions can be tedious, so we recommend to automate this process as much as possible, but we leave the details of such automated evaluation of trigger conditions for future work. Another possible future research direction is to alleviate the task of manually finding program points whose trigger condition is of interest to the human analyst. Our recommendation is to identify patterns of suspicious behaviors in an off-line manner, e.g. by syntactic analysis. Given a set of such patterns, their presence in the analyzed sample could be determined by automated static analysis and the corresponding program points could be listed as targets for our approach described in this paper. We also leave as future work the evaluation of our approach on a larger sample set. We envision a study of other malware families and their variants, studying the differences in their environmental requirements.

References

1. Supplementary materials. https://www.crysys.hu/~dpapp/publications/files/Pap pTB2019sefm.zip
2. Babić, D., Martignoni, L., McCamant, S., Song, D.: Statically-directed dynamic automated test generation. In: Proceedings of the 2011 International Symposium on Software Testing and Analysis, ISSTA 2011, pp. 12–22. ACM, New York (2011). https://doi.org/10.1145/2001420.2001423
3. Baldoni, R., Coppa, E., D'elia, D.C., Demetrescu, C., Finocchi, I.: A survey of symbolic execution techniques. ACM Comput. Surv. 51(3), 1–39 (2018). https://doi.org/10.1145/3182657
4. Brumley, D., Hartwig, C., Liang, Z., Newsome, J., Song, D., Yin, H.: Automatically identifying trigger-based behavior in malware. In: Lee, W., Wang, C., Dagon, D. (eds.) Botnet Detection. Advances in Information Security, pp. 65–88. Springer, Boston (2008). https://doi.org/10.1007/978-0-387-68768-1_4
5. Cadar, C., Dunbar, D., Engler, D.: Klee: unassisted and automatic generation of high-coverage tests for complex systems programs. In: Proceedings of the 8th USENIX Conference on Operating Systems Design and Implementation, OSDI 2008, pp. 209–224. USENIX Association, Berkeley (2008). http://dl.acm.org/citation.cfm?id=1855741.1855756
6. Caselden, D., Bazhanyuk, A., Payer, M., McCamant, S., Song, D.: HI-CFG: construction by binary analysis and application to attack polymorphism. In: Crampton, J., Jajodia, S., Mayes, K. (eds.) ESORICS 2013. LNCS, vol. 8134, pp. 164–181. Springer, Heidelberg (2013). https://doi.org/10.1007/978-3-642-40203-6_10
7. Cha, S.K., Avgerinos, T., Rebert, A., Brumley, D.: Unleashing mayhem on binary code. In: Proceedings of the 2012 IEEE Symposium on Security and Privacy, SP 2012, pp. 380–394. IEEE Computer Society, Washington, DC (2012). https://doi.org/10.1109/SP.2012.31
8. Chipounov, V., Kuznetsov, V., Candea, G.: S2E: a platform for in-vivo multi-path analysis of software systems. In: Proceedings of the Sixteenth International Conference on Architectural Support for Programming Languages and Operating Systems, ASPLOS XVI, pp. 265–278. ACM, New York (2011). https://doi.org/10.1145/1950365.1950396
9. Costin, A., Zaddach, J., Francillon, A., Balzarotti, D.: A large-scale analysis of the security of embedded firmwares. In: 23rd USENIX Security Symposium (USENIX Security 2014), pp. 95–110. USENIX Association, San Diego (2014). https://www.usenix.org/conference/usenixsecurity14/technical-sessions/presentation/costin

10. Fratantonio, Y., Bianchi, A., Robertson, W., Kirda, E., Kruegel, C., Vigna, G.: Triggerscope: towards detecting logic bombs in android applications. In: 2016 IEEE Symposium on Security and Privacy (SP), pp. 377–396, May 2016. https://doi.org/10.1109/SP.2016.30

11. Godefroid, P., Klarlund, N., Sen, K.: Dart: directed automated random testing. In: Proceedings of the 2005 ACM SIGPLAN Conference on Programming Language Design and Implementation, PLDI 2005, pp. 213–223. ACM, New York (2005). https://doi.org/10.1145/1065010.1065036

12. Kolbitsch, C., Livshits, B., Zorn, B., Seifert, C.: Rozzle: de-cloaking internet malware. In: 2012 IEEE Symposium on Security and Privacy, pp. 443–457, May 2012. https://doi.org/10.1109/SP.2012.48

13. Li, Y., Su, Z., Wang, L., Li, X.: Steering symbolic execution to less traveled paths. In: Proceedings of the 2013 ACM SIGPLAN International Conference on Object Oriented Programming Systems Languages & #38; Applications, OOPSLA 2013, pp. 19–32. ACM, New York (2013). https://doi.org/10.1145/2509136.2509553

14. Ma, K.-K., Yit Phang, K., Foster, J.S., Hicks, M.: Directed symbolic execution. In: Yahav, E. (ed.) SAS 2011. LNCS, vol. 6887, pp. 95–111. Springer, Heidelberg (2011). https://doi.org/10.1007/978-3-642-23702-7_11

15. Nethercote, N., Seward, J.: Valgrind: a framework for heavyweight dynamic binary instrumentation. In: Proceedings of the 28th ACM SIGPLAN Conference on Programming Language Design and Implementation, PLDI 2007, pp. 89–100, ACM, New York (2007). https://doi.org/10.1145/1250734.1250746

16. Parvez, R., Ward, P.A.S., Ganesh, V.: Combining static analysis and targeted symbolic execution for scalable bug-finding in application binaries. In: Proceedings of the 26th Annual International Conference on Computer Science and Software Engineering, CASCON 2016, pp. 116–127. IBM Corp., Riverton (2016). http://dl.acm.org/citation.cfm?id=3049877.3049889

17. Schwartz, E.J., Avgerinos, T., Brumley, D.: All you ever wanted to know about dynamic taint analysis and forward symbolic execution (but might have been afraid to ask). In: 2010 IEEE Symposium on Security and Privacy, pp. 317–331, May 2010. https://doi.org/10.1109/SP.2010.26

18. Shoshitaishvili, Y., et al.: Sok: (state of) the art of war: offensive techniques in binary analysis. In: 2016 IEEE Symposium on Security and Privacy (SP), pp. 138–157, May 2016. https://doi.org/10.1109/SP.2016.17

Verification

Formal Verification of Rewriting Rules for Dynamic Fault Trees

Yassmeen Elderhalli[1(✉)], Matthias Volk[2], Osman Hasan[1],
Joost-Pieter Katoen[2], and Sofiène Tahar[1]

[1] Electrical and Computer Engineering, Concordia University, Montréal, Canada
{y_elderh,o_hasan,tahar}@ece.concordia.ca
[2] Software Modeling and Verification, RWTH Aachen University, Aachen, Germany
{matthias.volk,katoen}@cs.rwth-aachen.de

Abstract. Dynamic Fault Trees (DFTs) model the failure behavior of systems dynamics. Several rewriting rules have been recently developed, which allow the simplification of DFTs prior to a formal analysis with tools such as the STORM model checker. To ascertain the soundness of the analysis, we propose to formally verify these rewriting rules using higher-order-logic (HOL) theorem proving. We first present the formalization in HOL of commonly used DFT gates, i.e., AND, OR and PAND, with an arbitrary number of inputs. Then we describe our formal specification of the rewriting rules and the verification of their intended behavior using the HOL4 theorem prover.

Keywords: Dynamic Fault Trees · Rewriting rules ·
Theorem proving · HOL4

1 Introduction

Dynamic Fault Trees (DFTs) graphically model the dynamically changing failure dependencies between system components [15,16]. The modeling starts by a top event that represents an undesired event, like the failure of a system or subsystem. Then, the different relationships between the system basic events that lead to the failure of the top event are modeled using DFT gates. DFTs are more suitable to model real-world situations that cannot be captured using static fault trees (SFTs). For example, DFTs models have been used to provide the safety analysis for autonomous cars [8].

DFTs are directed acyclic graphs (DAG) with typed nodes (AND, OR, etc.). Successors of a node v in the DAG are *inputs* of v. Some commonly used DFT elements are shown in Fig. 1. Nodes without inputs are *basic events* (BE, Fig. 1(a)) that represent atomic components, which can fail according to a failure distribution. Special cases of BEs are *constant failed* elements (CONST($\top$), Fig. 1(b)), which are always failed and *constant fail-safe* elements (CONST($\bot$), Fig. 1(c)),

This work is partially supported by the DFG RTG 2236 UnRAVeL.

P. C. Ölveczky and G. Salaün (Eds.): SEFM 2019, LNCS 11724, pp. 513–531, 2019.
https://doi.org/10.1007/978-3-030-30446-1_27

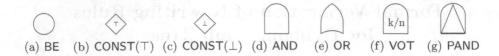

(a) BE   (b) CONST(⊤) (c) CONST(⊥) (d) AND   (e) OR   (f) VOT   (g) PAND

Fig. 1. Some DFT elements

which can never fail. DFT *gates* are nodes with inputs and are used to model the state dependencies and redundancies among system components. Some commonly used DFT gates include SFT gates (AND, OR and VOT-gates) as well as the Priority-AND (PAND) DFT gate. The output event of the AND-gate (Fig. 1(d)) fails when both input events fail. The OR-gate (Fig. 1(e)) requires that at least one of its input events fails for the output event to fail. The output of the VOT_k-gate (k out of n gate) (Fig. 1(f)) fails when at least k out of the n inputs fail. The PAND-gate (Fig. 1(g)) acts in a similar way to the AND-gate, i.e., it requires that both input events fail. However, an additional condition is needed, where the inputs should fail in sequence, usually from left to right. There are also other DFT gates that are used to model the dynamic behavior in systems, like the Functional-DEPendency (FDEP) and spare gates. In this paper, we only consider DFTs with AND, OR, VOT and PAND-gates.

Traditionally, DFTs are analyzed quantitatively by converting the given DFT model into a Markov chain (MC) [1,3,17], where the latter can be analyzed analytically or using simulation. Recently, an algebra has been proposed to provide the analysis of DFTs analytically without the need to use MC models [12]. In the algebraic approach, temporal operators are defined to capture the failure dependency between system components. The DFT gates are modeled using these temporal operators and their probabilities of failure are expressed based on these operators. Moreover, the DFT algebra provides several simplification properties that allow reducing the structure of a given DFT for a simpler analysis.

In order to ensure a complete and sound analysis, formal methods have also been explored for analyzing DFTs. Probabilistic model checkers, such as STORM [2], have been used for the probabilistic analysis of DFTs via MCs. For example, STORM supports the analysis of DFTs, among other probabilistic models, and allows the verification of the probability of failure and the Mean-Time-To-Failure (MTTF) of the top event of a given DFT. The scalability of this analysis can be significantly improved by DFT rewriting rules [10] that facilitate simplifying a DFT before analysis. Simplification of the DFT is achieved by transforming the underlying graph of the DFT according to the rewrite rules. Experimental evaluation in [10] showed that rewriting heavily improves the performance of the DFT analysis. For example, while originally 68% of the 183 DFTs in [10] could be solved within 2 h, applying the rewriting beforehand allowed to solve 95% of the DFTs. Moreover, the total analysis time was reduced from 41 h to 18 h when using rewriting. Simplifying DFTs by rewriting enables the analysis of DFTs that could not be analyzed before, and can lead to speed-ups and memory savings of up to two orders of magnitude [10].

The rewrite rules are generic for n-ary gates and can be implemented in any tool that supports DFT analysis. Proving the correctness of the rewrite rules as done in [11] is an involved manual and error-prone process. To the best of our knowledge, a rigorous, mechanically checkable proof of correctness of these rewriting rules has not been done. Thus, their usage in a formal analysis raises soundness concerns especially when dealing with the analysis of safety-critical systems, like transportation or healthcare. On the other hand, higher-order logic (HOL) theorem proving has been recently used to formalize DFT gates and operators [6] based on the algebra presented in [12]. Several simplification theorems are formally verified using the HOL4 theorem prover [9], which enable formally verifying a reduced form of a DFT. Moreover, the probabilistic behaviors of DFT gates are formally verified based on the HOL4 probability and Lebesgue integral theories [13,14]. However, this formalization does not support n-ary gates, which are required to model generic failure scenarios. In addition, the VOT-gate has not been formalized in HOL.

In this paper, we propose to use the recent HOL DFT formalization to verify the DFT rewriting rules of [10] using the HOL4 theorem prover. This requires extending the DFT gates definitions in [6] for an arbitrary number of inputs and defining the VOT-gate. Our main contributions are summarized as follows:

- Higher-order logic formalization of AND, OR, PAND and VOT_k (k out of n) gates for arbitrary number of inputs. This allows a formal reasoning about generic DFT constructs.
- A mechanized verification in HOL4 of the correctness of the DFT rewrite rules of [10] that are concerned with DFTs with AND, OR, VOT and PAND-gates. This proves that all these rules preserve reliability and MTTF.

These contributions provide the assurance of correctness of the rewrite rules and thus adds the confidence to tools, that exploit these rules in their DFT analysis.

The rest of the paper is structured as follows: Sect. 2 describes the DFT rewrite rules. We review the HOL4 DFT theory (library) in Sect. 3. In Sect. 4, we present the HOL formalization of n-ary gates. The formal verification details of the rewrite rules are presented in Sect. 5. Finally, we conclude the paper in Sect. 6.

2   DFT Rewrite Rules

In the following, we recap the rewrite rules for DFTs as presented by Junges *et al.* [10]. The simplification of DFTs is performed by graph rewriting [4] on the underlying graph of the DFT. We represent a DFT as a labelled graph by extending the induced graph with labels encoding the type of the DFT element and the ordering of the inputs. The graph transformation on the labelled graph is performed by applying a chain of rewrite rules.

2.1 Rewrite Framework

A rewrite rule is specified by two (sub-)DFTs: the left-hand side capturing the (sub-)DFT before applying the rewrite rule and the right-hand side depicting the resulting (sub-)DFT after the graph rewrite. An example of a rewrite rule is given in Fig. 2. The rule depicts the subsumption of OR-gates by AND-gates.

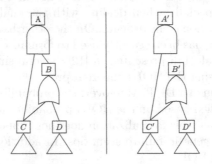

Fig. 2. Subsumption of OR-gates by AND-gates [10, Rewrite rule 8]

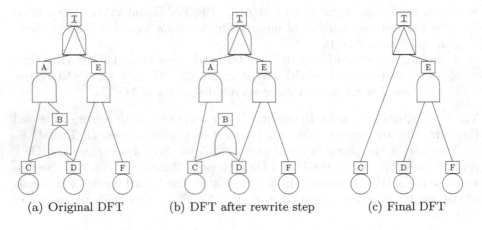

(a) Original DFT   (b) DFT after rewrite step   (c) Final DFT

Fig. 3. Example application of rewrite rule (Color figure online)

A rewrite rule can be applied whenever a (sub-)DFT can be matched with the left-hand side of the rule. Elements represented by a triangle in the rewrite rule match every gate type. Matched elements might have additional ingoing and outgoing edges not matched by the rewrite rule. These edges are retained during the rewriting step. Applying a rewrite rule replaces the matched part with the right-hand side of the rule. All non-matched parts remain unchanged during the rewriting step. Note that in general, rewrite rules might lead to inconsistent graphs with dangling edges or DFTs that are no longer well-formed (e.g., cyclic DFTs). In these cases, the rewrite rule cannot be applied. It is important to note also that most of the rewrite rules can also be applied from right to left.

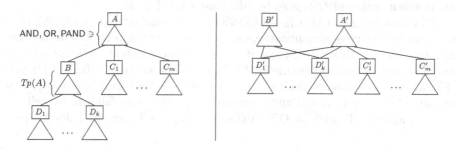

Fig. 4. Left-flattening of gates [10, Rewrite rule 5]

An example application of the given subsumption rule is depicted in Fig. 3. Figure 3(a) depicts the original DFT used as input. The subsumption rule from Fig. 2 can be applied and the matched sub-DFT is highlighted in blue. Applying the rule removes the connection between AND-gate A and OR-gate B and yields the rewritten DFT in Fig. 3(b). Further simplification by applying additional rewrite rules results in the final DFT in Fig. 3(c). Using the rewrite rules leads to a simpler DFT, which is considerably smaller—and easier to understand.

During rewriting multiple rules might be applicable for the current DFT or different sub-DFTs match the left-hand side of a rewrite rule. The sequence of rewrite steps is chosen by a rewrite strategy. As the rewrite framework is not confluent, the strategy heavily influences the size of the resulting DFTs and a heuristic approach is used. For further details, see [10].

2.2   Rewrite Rules

In the following we consider 22 rules of the 29 rewrite rules given in [10]. Of the remaining 7 rules, one rule gives the Shannon expansion for VOT_k-gates, which deals with variables as Boolean, whereas generally DFTs, as formalized in HOL, treat variables as real numbers representing time to failure functions. The other 6 rules apply to FDEPs and SPAREs; both gate types are not considered here. We recap a selection of the rewrite rules and use the same rule enumeration as in [10, Sect. 5.3].

General Rewrite Rules. The first rewrite rules 1–7 consider structural identities such as commutativity of static gates, removal of gates with a single successor or no predecessor, and left-flattening of gates. As an example, the rewrite rule for left-flattening is given in Fig. 4. The rule can only be applied if the top element of the (sub-)DFT is an AND-, OR- or PAND-gate, and the first input is of the same gate type as the top element ($Tp(B) = Tp(A)$). Applying the left-flattening rule adds the inputs of B as first inputs of A. Gate B is not removed as it might still have connections to other parts of the DFT.

Rules 8–10 capture standard axioms from Boolean algebra on the static gates such as subsumption of OR-gates by AND-gates (cf. Fig. 2).

DFTs containing constant failed CONST($\top$) or constant fail-safe CONST($\bot$) events can lead to large simplifications as often complete sub-DFTs can be evaluated to constant. Rules 11–14 specifically consider constant elements and we exemplary present the rewrite rule for AND-/PAND-gates with CONST($\bot$) inputs in Fig. 5. If at least one of the inputs of an AND-/PAND-gate is fail-safe, it is impossible for the gate to fail and therefore it can be set to fail-safe as well.

Encoding of VOT-gates by OR-/AND-gates is given in rewrite rules 15–16.

Rewrite Rules for PAND-gates. So far, the rewrite rules mostly captured simplifications of static gates, which are based on the corresponding properties in Boolean algebra. The remaining rules 18–23 consider PAND-gates where the order of failures is crucial. As an example, consider the rewrite rule for conflicting PAND-gates with independent successors in Fig. 6. PAND-gate D_1 requires that input B fails strictly before C or simultaneously with C. If C fails strictly before B, D_1 becomes fail-safe. D_2 requires the opposite behavior. If both elements B and C are independent, they will not fail simultaneously. Thus, either PAND-gate D_1 or D_2 will become fail-safe. As the PAND-gates can never both fail, A is fail-safe and can be replaced by CONST($\bot$).

Note that the rewrite rule can only be applied if B and C are independent—and at most one input is CONST($\top$). Otherwise, a common cause failure can let both B and C fail simultaneously, both PAND-gates fail and A fails as well. The independence assumption in this rewrite rule is a *context restriction*, which prevents the application of the rule for certain DFTs.

2.3   Non-structural Rules

There are two additional rules that are not present in the rewrite framework as they go beyond structural rules and are not captured by graph transformations.

Removing BEs. The BEs that have no connection to other DFT elements (and are not the top level element) are called *dispensable*. Dispensable BEs can be removed from the DFT as they do not influence the analysis results. An example is given in Fig. 7. In the original DFT in Fig. 7(a), BE C is dispensable and can be removed yielding the DFT in Fig. 7(b).

Merging BEs. In our analysis we are only interested in the reliability or MTTF of the top level element. The state of other elements is not important for this analysis. Thus, we can simplify a DFT by merging multiple BEs into a single BE. Consider the example DFT in Fig. 7(b). Both BEs A and B have an exponential failure distribution with failure rates λ_A and λ_B, respectively. The failure

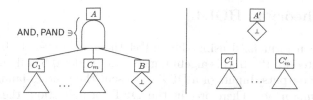

Fig. 5. AND-/PAND-gate with CONST($\perp$) successor [10, Rewrite rule 13]

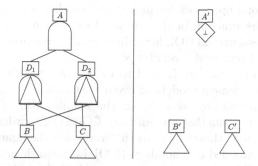

Fig. 6. Conflicting PAND–gates with independent successors [10, Rewrite rule 19]

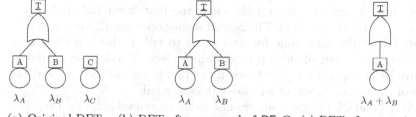

(a) Original DFT   (b) DFT after removal of BE C (c) DFT after merging of BEs

Fig. 7. Example application of non-structural rules

distribution of an OR-gate is the minimum over its inputs and is exponentially distributed as well. Thus, we can replace multiple BEs $A_1, \ldots, A_n$ under an OR-gate by a single BE A' with failure rate $\lambda_{A'} = \sum_{i=1}^{n} \lambda_{A_i}$. In our example, merging both BEs leads to the final DFT in Fig. 7(c). The resulting OR-gate with a single input can be simplified further by applying the rewrite framework.

After presenting the details of DFT rewrite rules, in the sequel, we present our efforts in formally verifying them using HOL theorem proving. For some of these rules, such as Rule 5, it is required to formally model DFT gates for arbitrary number of inputs. In the next sections, we first review the DFT theory developed in HOL4 and then introduce the new HOL definitions of n-ary gates.

3   DFT Theory in HOL4

DFTs have been formalized using the HOL4 theorem prover [6] based on the algebra presented in [12]. In this algebra, gates are modeled based on the time of failure of their outputs. Inputs of a DFT represent the time-to-failure functions of systems components. Therefore, in the DFT formalization, these functions are defined as lambda abstracted functions that allow them to be treated later as random variables for conducting the probabilistic analysis of DFTs. Identity elements and temporal operators are introduced to allow expressing and manipulating the structure function of the top level element of a given DFT. Their mathematical expressions and HOL formalization are presented in Table 1, where PosInf is the HOL4 representation of $+\infty$.

The Always identity element is used to model an event that fails from time 0, whereas the Never element models an event that fails at $+\infty$, i.e., it can never fail. These two elements are necessary in the simplification process of DFTs, when there are input events that are fail-safe ($\mathsf{CONST}(\bot)$) or have already failed ($\mathsf{CONST}(\top)$). Therefore, these functions that represent the inputs and outputs of DFT gates return extended-real numbers (HOL4 extreal theory), which are real numbers and $\pm\infty$. Three temporal operators are introduced in [12] to model the failure dependency among system components. The Before operator ($\lhd$) models a situation where one system component fails before the other. This operator accepts two inputs and its output fails when the first input fails before the second, otherwise it can never fail. The Simultaneous operator (Δ) requires that both inputs fail at the same time for its output to fail. If this condition does not hold, then the output of this operator fails at $+\infty$. Finally, the output of the Inclusive Before operator ($\unlhd$) fails when the first input fails before or at the same time of the second input, otherwise it does not fail.

The AND ($\cdot$) and OR ($+$) gates are similar to the ones used in SFTs. However, it is required to define them in a way compatible with the rest of the definitions of DFT gates. Table 2 [6] lists the formal definitions of these gates, where max and min are HOL4 functions that return the maximum and minimum values of their input arguments, respectively. The output of the AND-gate (Fig. 1(d)) is modeled using the maximum (max) time of failure of the inputs. The OR-gate

Table 1. Definitions of identity elements and temporal operators

Element/Operator	Mathematical expression	Formalization
Always element	$d(ALWAYS) = 0$	$\vdash$ ALWAYS = (λs. (0:extreal))
Never element	$d(NEVER) = +\infty$	$\vdash$ NEVER = (λs. PosInf)
Before	$d(A \lhd B) = \begin{cases} d(A), & d(A) < d(B) \\ +\infty, & d(A) \geq d(B) \end{cases}$	$\vdash \forall$ A B. D_BEFORE A B = (λs. if A s < B s then A s else PosInf)
Simultaneous	$d(A \Delta B) = \begin{cases} d(A), & d(A) = d(B) \\ +\infty, & d(A) \neq d(B) \end{cases}$	$\vdash \forall$ A B. D_SIMULT A B = (λs. if A s = B s then A s else PosInf)
Inclusive Before	$d(A \unlhd B) = \begin{cases} d(A), & d(A) \leq d(B) \\ +\infty, & d(A) > d(B) \end{cases}$	$\vdash \forall$ A B. D_INCLUSIVE_BEFORE A B = (λs. if A s $\leq$ B s then A s else PosInf)

Table 2. DFT gates

Gate	Mathematical expression	Formalization
AND	$d(A \cdot B) = max(d(A), d(B))$	⊢ ∀ A B. D_AND A B = (λs. max (A s)(B s))
OR	$d(A + B) = min(d(A), d(B))$	⊢ ∀ A B. D_OR A B = (λs. min (A s)(B s))
PAND	$d(Q_{PAND}) = \begin{cases} d(B), & d(A) \leq d(B) \\ +\infty, & d(A) > d(B) \end{cases}$	⊢ ∀ A B. PAND A B = (λs. if A s ≤ B s then B s else PosInf)

(Fig. 1(e)) requires that at least one of its input events fails. Therefore, the time of failure of its output is modeled using the minimum (min) time of failure of its inputs. The PAND-gate (Fig. 1(g)) is modeled using the extreal comparison operator ($\leq$) and if statements. The time of failure of its output equals the time of the second input if the first input fails before or at the same time of the second input, otherwise, the output can never fail (PosInf). It is worth mentioning that the DFT gates accept inputs that are time-to-failure functions, which allows constructing complex DFT models. The structure function of a given DFT can be expressed using the AND, OR and temporal operators. For example, the PAND-gate can be expressed as: $Y \cdot (X \trianglelefteq Y)$. Several simplification properties are introduced in [12] that allow simplifying the structure function of a given DFT in order to facilitate the analysis, such as the commutativity and idempotence properties of the OR and AND-gates. These simplification properties are formally verified using HOL4 [7], which ensures their correctness. The verification of these properties is based mainly on the definitions of the operators and the properties of extreal numbers. For example, D_OR X X = X, is verified based on the definition of the OR gate and the properties of the extreal min function. However, since the DFT operators of this algebra are binary operators, the simplification properties cannot support rewriting DFTs with n-ary gates. Thus, they cannot support the simplification of generic DFTs, which is the scope of the current work.

4   HOL Formalization of n-ary DFT Gates

In order to verify the DFT rewriting rules, presented in [10], we need to handle DFT gates with an arbitrary number of inputs. Therefore, we extend the definitions of DFT gates of [6]. In these definitions, we utilize lists to represent the arbitrary number of inputs. In other words, the input of an n-ary gate is a list of arbitrary size of time-to-failure functions that represent inputs of a DFT gate. We formally define the n-ary AND-gate as:

Definition 1.   ⊢ ∀L. n_AND L = FOLDR (λ a b. D_AND a b) ALWAYS L

where FOLDR is used to apply a binary (2-input) function over a list from right to left. The function in our case here is the binary D_AND that accepts two inputs and returns their result of the DFT AND operation between them. FOLDR requires including an element that is used to apply the function to the last element of the input list. We use ALWAYS in this case as it is the identity element of the AND and does not affect its behavior. L represents the list of inputs to be ANDed. For example, n_AND [X; Y; Z] equals D_AND X (D_AND Y (D_AND Z ALWAYS)).

In a similar manner, we formally define the n-ary OR as:

Definition 2. $\vdash \forall$L. n_OR L = FOLDR (λ a b. D_OR a b) NEVER L

D_OR is the function used with FOLDR in this definition. We use NEVER in this case as it is the identity element for the OR, i.e., NEVER will not affect the behavior of the OR-gate. It is worth mentioning that FOLDL can be used with these definitions as well, since the order of applying the OR and AND-gates does not matter if it starts from the left or from the right.

We formally define the n-ary PAND-gate as:

Definition 3. $\vdash \forall$L. n_PAND L = FOLDL (λ a b. P_AND a b) ALWAYS L

This is similar to the previous definitions. However, since the PAND-gate requires that the input events fail from left to right, we use FOLDL in this case. We use ALWAYS as it does not affect the behavior of the PAND-gate, i.e., for any input X that is greater than or equal to 0, PAND ALWAYS X = X.

The VOT$_k$ (k out of n) gate can be defined using the n_OR and n_AND gates. Firstly, we need to get the combinations that lead to the failure of the VOT-gate. For example, a (2/3) VOT-gate requires having all possible pairs out of the three inputs. Therefore, we first need to get all the possible k elements of the input list. We define k_out that accepts a list and a number k, which identifies the number of elements to be retrieved from the input list.

Definition 4. $\vdash \forall$k L. k_out k L = $\{$s| s $\subseteq$ (set L) $\wedge$ (CARD s = k)$\}$

where set L returns a set with the elements in list L, and CARD is a HOL function that returns the cardinality (number of elements) of a given set. This definition basically returns a set of sets, where the inner sets are subsets of set L. This means that these inner subsets contain elements from the input list L. The added condition is that the cardinality of each of these sets equals k. As a result, we get all possible combinations of the input list that have k elements.

We use k_out to define the VOT-gate by ANDing the elements of each inner set, then ORing the result of this ANDing. We need to recall that the n_AND and n_OR accept inputs as lists not sets. Therefore, we apply a function that converts a set into a list (SET_TO_LIST). We formally define the VOT-gate as:

Definition 5. $\vdash \forall$k L. k_out_n_gate k L =
    n_OR (MAP (λa. n_AND (SET_TO_LIST a)) (SET_TO_LIST (k_out k L)))

where SET_TO_LIST is a HOL4 function that accepts a set and returns a list of the elements of this set. MAP is used to map a function over a list and returns a list of the mapped elements. In this definition, we first convert the outer set of k_out to a list using SET_TO_LIST (k_out k L). Then, we apply n_AND to each element of this list using MAP and convert each inner set to a list. Finally, the n_OR is applied to the result of the MAP, i.e., the result will be the OR of ANDs and each AND has only k elements of the input list. We verify several properties for k_out and the VOT-gate, such as the finiteness of the inner and outer sets, besides other properties that are useful in the verification of the DFT rewriting rules. The HOL4 script can be accessed from [5].

5   Formal Verification of Rewriting Rules

We list the verification details of some of the rewrite rules described in Sect. 2. The details of verifying the rest of the rules can be accessed from [5].

General Rewrite Rules. The structural rewrite rules 1–5 and 7 are verified based on the definitions of n-ary gates and some list and extreal number theories properties, whereas rule 6 is implemented implicitly in the DFT formalization.

Commutativity of static gates (Rule 1)
Theorem 1. ⊢ $\forall L_1\ L_2$. PERM $L_1\ L_2$ ⇒ (n_AND L_1 = n_AND L_2)
Theorem 2. ⊢ $\forall L_1\ L_2$. PERM $L_1\ L_2$ ⇒ (n_OR L_1 = n_OR L_2)
Theorem 3. ⊢ $\forall L_1\ L_2$ k.
PERM $L_1\ L_2$ ⇒(k_out_n_gate k L_1 = k_out_n_gate k L_2)

The commutativity property indicates that the order of the inputs of any static gate will not affect its behavior, i.e., the time of failure for the output of the gate remains the same. We use the permutation of two lists (PERM $L_1\ L_2$) to add the condition that L_1 and L_2 have the same inputs but with different orders. We verify the commutativity of the n_AND and n_OR gates using induction, FOLDR definition and some properties of the 2-input AND and OR-gates, defined in Sect. 3, such as associativity and commutativity. The proof of the commutativity property for the VOT-gate is mainly based on the following lemma:

Lemma 1. ⊢ $\forall L_1\ L_2$ k. PERM $L_1\ L_2$ ⇒ (k_out k L_1 = k_out k L_2)

which states that the sets returned by k_out are the same for two lists that have the same elements with different orders.

Gate with a single successor (Rule 3)
Theorem 4. ⊢ $\forall$x. rv_gt0 [x] ⇒ (n_AND [x] = x)
Theorem 5. ⊢ $\forall$x. n_OR [x] = x
Theorem 6. ⊢ $\forall$x. rv_gt0 [x] ⇒ (k_out_n_gate 1 [x] = x)
Theorem 7. ⊢ $\forall$x. rv_gt0 [x] ⇒ (n_PAND [x] = x)

For the static gates and the n_PAND gate, if the input list consists of only one element, then the output fails once the single input fails. The function rv_gt0 ensures that the inputs of the gates are greater than or equal to 0, which is valid as we are dealing with time-to-failure functions. We recursively define rv_gt0 as:

Definition 6. *rv_gt0*

(rv_gt0 [] = T) $\wedge$ ($\forall$h t. rv_gt0 (h::t) = ($\forall$s. 0 $\leq$ h s) $\wedge$ rv_gt0 t)

For n_AND and n_OR, rule 3 is verified based on some properties of the D_AND and D_OR gates. For VOT-gate, we use the VOT $(1/n)$ property (Theorem 25) that replaces the VOT-gate with the n_OR gate. Finally, we verify rule 3 for n_PAND using its definition and some list and extreal numbers properties.

Left-flattening of AND-/OR-/PAND-gates (Rule 5)

Theorem 8. $\vdash$ $\forall L_1$ L_2.

rv_gt0 $(L_1$ ++ $L_2)$ $\Rightarrow$ (n_AND (n_AND L_2::L_1) = n_AND $(L_2$ ++ L_1))

Theorem 9. $\vdash$ $\forall L_1$ L_2. n_OR (n_OR L_2::L_1) = n_OR $(L_2$ ++ L_1)

Theorem 10. $\vdash$ $\forall L_1$ L_2.

rv_gt0 $(L_1$ ++ $L_2)$ $\Rightarrow$(n_PAND (n_PAND L_2::L_1) = n_PAND $(L_2$ ++ L_1))

In order to verify Theorem 8, we first verify the n_AND append property that would split the AND of two appended lists as:

Lemma 2. $\vdash$ $\forall L_1$ L_2.

rv_gt0 $(L_1$ ++ $L_2)$ $\Rightarrow$ (n_AND $(L_1$ ++ $L_2)$ = D_AND (n_AND L_1)(n_AND L_2))

where ++ is a list operator used to append two lists. We verify Theorem 8 by first rewriting n_AND L_2::L_1 as [n_AND L_2]++L_1, where :: is a list operator used to add an element to a list, which in the considered case is n_AND L_2. Then, we use Lemma 2 to rewrite the left hand side of Theorem 8 to D_AND (n_AND [n_AND L2])(n_AND L_1) and use Theorem 4 to verify Theorem 8. In a similar way, we verify Theorem 9 by verifying a lemma for appending two lists with n_OR as:

Lemma 3. $\vdash$ $\forall L_1$ L_2. n_OR $(L_1$ ++ $L_2)$ = D_OR (n_OR L_1)(n_OR L_2)

For the left-flattening property of the n_PAND gate, we first verify a lemma that rv_gt0 L$\Rightarrow$ $\forall$s. 0 $\leq$ n_PAND L s, which states that the output of the n_PAND gate is greater than or equal to 0 if the inputs follow the same condition. Theorem 10 is then verified based on the previous lemma, induction on the list argument and some P_AND and list properties.

Identical leftmost successors of AND, OR or PAND (Rule 7)

Theorem 11. $\vdash$ $\forall$x L. n_AND (x::x::L) = n_AND (x::L)

Theorem 12. $\vdash$ $\forall$x L. n_OR (x::x::L) = n_OR (x::L)

Theorem 13. $\vdash$ $\forall$x L. rv_gt0 [x] $\Rightarrow$ (n_PAND (x::x::L) = n_PAND (x::L))

Theorems 11 and 12 are verified based on the definitions of n_AND and n_OR with the associativity and idempotence of D_AND and D_OR gates. Theorem 13 requires verifying that the output of a 2-input PAND-gate (P_AND defined in Sect. 3) with an input that already failed (ALWAYS) as the left input fails with the failure of the second (right) input.

Lemma 4. $\vdash \forall X.$ $(\forall s.$ $0 \le X$ $s)$ $\Rightarrow$ (P_AND ALWAYS X = X)

Finally, we verify the idempotence property of the P_AND gate.

Lemma 5. $\vdash \forall X.$ P_AND X X = X

Subsumption of OR-gates by AND-gates (Rule 8)

Theorem 14. $\vdash \forall X$ Y. D_AND X (D_OR X Y) = X

Subsumption of AND-gates by OR-gates (Rule 9)

Theorem 15. $\vdash \forall X$ Y. D_OR X (D_AND X Y) = X

Distributing OR-gates over AND-gates (Rule 10)

Theorem 16. $\vdash \forall X$ Y Z. D_OR (D_AND X Y)(D_AND Y Z) = D_AND (D_OR X Z) Y

We verify the rules 8–10 that are concerned with the standard axioms of Boolean algebra based on basic properties of D_AND and D_OR gates, such as the commutativity and distributivity of the AND over the OR.

OR-gates with fail-safe (NEVER) successors (Rule 11)

Theorem 17. $\vdash \forall L_1$ $L_2.$ n_OR $(L_1$ ++ [NEVER] ++ $L_2)$ = n_OR $(L_1$ ++ $L_2)$

OR-gates with already failed (ALWAYS) successors (Rule 12)

Theorem 18. $\vdash \forall L_1$ $L_2.$
rv_gt0 $(L_1$ ++ $L_2)$ $\Rightarrow$ (n_OR $(L_1$ ++ [ALWAYS] ++ $L_2)$ = ALWAYS)

Rewrite rules 11–14 deal with scenarios that include fail-safe (NEVER) or CONST($\bot$), and failed (ALWAYS) or CONST($\top$).

For Theorem 17, we use Lemma 3 and the definition of n_OR with the property stating that $\forall X.$ D_OR X NEVER = X. We verify Theorem 18 based on Lemma 3 and the definition of n_OR along with the following lemma:

Lemma 6. $\vdash \forall X.$ $(\forall s.$ $0 \le X$ $s)$ $\Rightarrow$ (D_OR X ALWAYS = ALWAYS)

Then, we verify that the output of the n_OR is greater than or equal to 0 if the inputs are all greater than or equal to 0. Theorem 18 is then verified using the previous lemmas and some properties of the D_OR gate.

AND-gate with a fail-safe (NEVER) successor (Rule 13)

Theorem 19. $\vdash \forall L_1$ $L_2.$
rv_gt0 $(L_1$ ++ $L_2)$ $\Rightarrow$(n_AND $(L_1$ ++ [NEVER] ++ $L_2)$ = NEVER)

Theorem 20. $\vdash \forall L.$ rv_gt0 L $\Rightarrow$ (n_PAND (L ++ [NEVER]) = NEVER)

Theorem 21. $\vdash \forall L.$ rv_gt0 L $\Rightarrow$ (n_PAND (NEVER::L) = NEVER)

Theorem 22. $\vdash \forall L_1$ $L_2.$
rv_gt0 $(L_1$ ++ $L_2)$ $\Rightarrow$(n_PAND $(L_1$ ++ [NEVER] ++ $L_2)$ = NEVER)

We verify Theorem 19 using Lemma 2 and some properties for the D_AND, such as the commutativity property and ANDing with NEVER.

We verify this rule for PAND-gate by verifying two cases. Firstly, we verify that the output of the PAND cannot fail if the NEVER input is the rightmost input (Theorem 20). This is mainly verified based on some list properties to manipulate rv_gt0 along with the left flattening property of the PAND (Theorem 10). Similarly, we verify the second case when the left most input of the PAND-gate is fail-safe (Theorem 21). Finally, we verify a generic property, where the fail-safe input can be at any position (Theorem 22).

AND-gate with a failed (ALWAYS) element as successor (Rule 14)

Theorem 23. $\vdash \forall L.$ rv_gt0 L $\Rightarrow$ (n_AND (ALWAYS::L) = n_AND L)

Theorem 24. $\vdash \forall L.$ rv_gt0 L $\Rightarrow$ (n_PAND (ALWAYS::L) = n_PAND L)

Theorem 23 is verified using the definition of the n_AND gate with the property that the output of the gate is greater than or equal to 0 if the inputs satisfy the same condition. We verify Theorem 24 based on the definition of the n_PAND and the idempotence property of the PAND-gate.

The VOT-gate can behave as an OR-gate, when $k = 1$ (Rule 15), and as an AND-gate, when k equals the number of its inputs (Rule 16). The verification details of these rules are listed below.

Voting (1/n) is an OR-gate (Rule 15)

Theorem 25. $\vdash \forall L.$

ALL_DISTINCT L $\wedge$ rv_gt0 L $\Rightarrow$ (k_out_n_gate 1 L = n_OR L)

As mentioned previously, the voting gate is defined as the OR of a list and each element in the list is the AND of another list of k elements. In order to verify Theorem 25, we need to use the commutativity property of the n_OR gate (Theorem 2), i.e, we need to verify that the list of the n_OR in the voting gate definition (MAP (λa. n_AND (SET_TO_LIST a))(MAP (λa. {a}) L)) and the input list L possess the permutation property when $k = 1$. Therefore, we first verify that the list generated from k_out 1 L is the permutation of the list MAP (λa. {a}) L. We need to recall that MAP (λa. {a}) L generates another list that has all elements from the input list L but as sets. Then, we verify that the list generated from applying the n_AND to the list of k_out 1 L is the permutation of applying n_AND to MAP (λa. {a}) L. We also verify the following property:

Lemma 7. $\vdash \forall L.$ rv_gt0 L $\Rightarrow$

PERM (MAP (λa. n_AND (SET_TO_LIST a)) (MAP (λa. {a}) L)) L

Finally, we use these verified properties of permutation and the commutativity property of n_OR to verify Theorem 25.

Voting (n/n) is an AND-gate (Rule 16)

Theorem 26. ⊢ ∀L.
ALL_DISTINCT L ⇒ (k_out_n_gate (LENGTH L) L = n_AND L)

Theorem 26 is used when k equals the length of the input list (LENGTH L), i.e., VOT (n/n), and n is the number of inputs of the gate. In this case, the VOT-gate acts as an AND-gate. We verify this by first rewriting using the VOT-gate and k_out definitions. Then, we verify that {s| s ⊆ set L ∧ (CARD s = LENGTH L)} = {set L}. This way the original expression of the VOT-gate can be reduced to n_OR [n_AND (SET_TO_LIST (set L))]. Then, we verify that PERM L (SET_TO_LIST (set L)), which means that the original list and the list generated from the set of the original list are the permutation of each other. This is a consequence of using set L in the formal definition of the VOT-gate, which requires the added condition that the elements in the original list are distinct, i.e., they are not equal or repeated. This condition is added using the HOL predicate ALL_DISTINCT L. Finally, we verify Theorem 26 using the commutativity property of the AND (Theorem 1) and the definition of n_OR.

Rewrite Rules for PAND-gates. Rules 18–23 deal with PAND-gates that require considering the order of the inputs.

Representing AND-gate using OR- and PAND-gates (Rule 18)

Theorem 27. ⊢ ∀X Y. D_AND X Y = D_OR (P_AND X Y) (P_AND Y X)

Conflicting PAND-gates with independent successors (Rule 19)

Theorem 28. ⊢ ∀X Y.
(∀s. ALL_DISTINCT [X s; Y s]) ⇒ (D_AND (P_AND X Y) (P_AND Y X) = NEVER)

We verify Theorems 27 and 28 based on the definitions of D_AND, D_OR and P_AND gates and some properties of the extreal numbers. Note that the added condition for rule 19 is that the inputs are distinct (ALL_DISTINCT), i.e., they cannot fail simultaneously. This results from the fact that the inputs are independent (there is no common cause of failure) and they possess continuous failure distributions. Therefore, rule 19 cannot be applied unless this context restriction is ensured using this assumption.

PAND-gate with a PAND-successor (Rule 20)

Theorem 29. ⊢ ∀B C_1 C_2 L. rv_gt0 (L ++ [B; C_1; C_2]) ⇒
(n_PAND ([B; P_AND C_1 C_2] ++ L) =
D_AND (P_AND C_1 C_2) (n_PAND ([B; C_2] ++ L)))

We verify Theorem 29 based on manipulating the input lists and the PAND appended with a single element lemma, which we verify as:

Lemma 8. $\vdash \forall x\ L.\ \text{rv\_gt0}\ L \Rightarrow (\text{n\_PAND}\ (L\ ++\ [x]) = \text{P\_AND}\ (\text{n\_PAND}\ L)\ x)$

Based on Lemma 8 and list induction and manipulation, we verify that the left-hand-side of Theorem 29 equals: $\text{P\_AND}(\text{D\_AND}(\text{P\_AND}\ \text{C1}\ \text{C2})(\text{n\_PAND}$ $(\text{B::C2::L})))$ x, where x is the additional element generated through induction. Then, we verify a property stating that the time of failure of the PAND-gate should be greater than or equal to the failure time of any of its inputs, since it is required that the failure to occur from left to right.

PAND-gate with a first OR-successor (Rule 21)

Theorem 30. $\vdash \forall X\ Y\ L.\ \text{rv\_gt0}\ [X;\ Y] \Rightarrow$
$(\text{n\_PAND}\ (\text{D\_OR}\ X\ Y::L) = \text{D\_OR}\ (\text{n\_PAND}\ (X::L))\ (\text{n\_PAND}\ (Y::L))$

To verify Theorem 30, we first apply induction to the input argument and rewrite using the rule of n_PAND with a single successor. Then, we use the definitions of the P_AND, n_PAND and some simplification theorems, such as P_AND ALWAYS X = X. Using some list properties, such as applying a function to two appended list using FOLDL (we need to recall that the definition of n_PAND is based on FOLDL), we reach a point where the whole goal is similar to and can be verified using the following lemma:

Lemma 9. $\vdash \forall X\ Y\ Z.\ \text{P\_AND}\ (\text{D\_OR}\ X\ Y)\ Z = \text{D\_OR}\ (\text{P\_AND}\ X\ Z)(\text{P\_AND}\ Y\ Z)$

PAND-gate with ALWAYS as non-first successor (Rule 23)

Theorem 31. $\vdash \forall L_1.\ L_1 \neq []\ \wedge\ (\forall x.\ \text{MEM}\ x\ L_1 \Rightarrow \forall s.\ 0 < x\ s) \Rightarrow$
$\forall L_2.\ \text{n\_PAND}\ (L_1\ ++\ [\text{ALWAYS}]\ ++\ L_2) = \text{NEVER}$

Theorem 31 shows that if the inputs to the left of the input that already failed (ALWAYS) do not fail from the beginning, i.e., their time of failure is greater than 0, then the output of the n_PAND can never fail. Therefore, we add the condition that the inputs to the left (list L_1) are greater than 0 using $\forall x.\ \text{MEM}\ x\ L_1 \Rightarrow$ $\forall s.\ 0 < x\ s$. We verify Theorem 31 using induction over list L_1. After some basic list and extreal theory based reasoning, we reach the step for the left-hand-side:
FOLDL $(\lambda a\ b.\ \text{P\_AND}\ a\ b)$
   $(\text{P\_AND}\ (\text{FOLDL}(\lambda a\ b.\ \text{P\_AND}\ a\ b)\ h\ L_1)\ \text{ALWAYS})\ L_2$
where h is the appended element that results from induction. We verify that P_AND $(\text{FOLDL}(\lambda a\ b.\ \text{P\_AND}\ a\ b)\ h\ L_1)$ ALWAYS = NEVER, which can be done if the first input of the P_AND is greater than 0. We verify the following property:

Lemma 10. $\vdash \forall s\ L.\ (\forall x.\ \text{MEM}\ x\ L \Rightarrow \forall s.\ 0 < x\ s) \Rightarrow$
$\forall h.\ 0 < h\ s \Rightarrow 0 < \text{FOLDL}\ (\lambda a\ b.\ \text{P\_AND}\ a\ b)\ h\ L\ s$

This lemma basically means that if we have a list of inputs and an additional element, h, that are greater than 0, then the result of applying P_AND using FOLDL is also greater than 0. Using this lemma, the left hand side is reduced to FOLDL (λa b. P_AND a b) NEVER L_2. Finally, we use the following lemma to verify the Theorem 31.

Lemma 11. ⊢ ∀L. FOLDL (λa b. P_AND a b) NEVER L = NEVER

This lemma indicates that if we apply P_AND to a list of inputs with an element NEVER at the beginning, then the output equals NEVER

Non-structural Rules. The BEs that are not connected to the given DFT can be safely removed. This is already implicitly embedded in the current DFT formalization, as we are verifying the rewrite rules by proving that the time of failure before and after rewriting remains the same. Therefore, if the BEs are not connected to the DFT, this means that they are not affecting the time of failure of the top element and thus they can be removed in the verification process. Since DFT gates are modeled as time-to-failure functions, merging BEs is also already embedded in the DFT formalization. For example, the OR-gate is modeled using the min function. This means that the inputs of the OR-gate are merged and the output of the OR-gate can be replaced with the min function.

We illustrate the usage of the verified rules on the example of Fig. 3:

Theorem 32. ⊢ ∀. c d f
P_AND (D_AND c (D_OR c d))(D_AND d f) ▪ P_AND c (D_AND d f)

In this section, we presented the formal definitions and proofs of the rewriting rules in [10], which we believe is a novel contribution as details about how to mathematically conduct these proofs are not available in [10]. In fact, in [10], the correctness of the rewrite rules is described inexplicitly based on the behavior of DFT gates rather than their formal mathematical models as presented in this paper. It is worth noting that our formal definitions and verified lemmas allowed verifying several DFT rewriting rules that can be used with tools that simplify DFTs prior to the analysis. In addition, verifying these rules represent the first step towards formally verifying tools, such as STORM, that support DFT analysis and use these rewriting rules. The HOL4 script for these rules and their lemmas is comprised of about 1500 lines and required about 80 h to develop. The script is available at [5].

6   Conclusions

In this paper, we provided the formal verification of DFT rewriting rules using the HOL4 theorem prover. These rules enable simplifying DFTs before performing the analysis through tools, such as the STORM model checker. In order to verify the rules, we formally defined n-ary gates, such as AND, OR, PAND and VOT-gates and verified several lemmas based on these definitions and the available DFT theory in HOL4. We mainly verified DFT rules that deal with the static gates (AND, OR & VOT-gates) and the PAND-gate. The rules include some known properties, such as the commutativity of the static gates. Moreover, we verified some more complex rules that deal with PAND with different input scenarios. The formal verification of the rewriting rules in the DFTs analysis adds the confidence level of the results of the tools that use them. We plan to extend this work to verify rewriting rules that include Functional DEPendency (FDEP) and Spare gates as well. This work can be considered as a first milestone for formally verifying automated DFT analysis tools such as STORM.

Acknowledgments. The authors would like to thank Sebastian Junges, from RWTH Aachen University, for the discussions and comments on the rewrite rules.

References

1. Boudali, H., Crouzen, P., Stoelinga, M.: Dynamic fault tree analysis using input/output interactive Markov chains. In: Proceedings of DSN, pp. 708–717. IEEE (2007)
2. Dehnert, C., Junges, S., Katoen, J.-P., Volk, M.: A STORM is coming: a modern probabilistic model checker. In: Majumdar, R., Kunčak, V. (eds.) CAV 2017. LNCS, vol. 10427, pp. 592–600. Springer, Cham (2017). https://doi.org/10.1007/978-3-319-63390-9_31
3. Dugan, J.B., Bavuso, S.J., Boyd, M.A.: Fault trees and sequence dependencies. In: Proceedings of RAMS, pp. 286–293 (1990)
4. Ehrig, H., Ehrig, K., Prange, U., Taentzer, G.: Fundamentals of Algebraic Graph Transformation. Monographs in Theoretical Computer Science. An EATCS Series. Springer, Heidelberg (2006). https://doi.org/10.1007/3-540-31188-2
5. Elderhalli, Y.: DFT rewriting rules: HOL4 script, Concordia University, Montreal, QC, Canada (2019). http://hvg.ece.concordia.ca/code/hol/DFT-rewrite/index.php
6. Elderhalli, Y., Ahmad, W., Hasan, O., Tahar, S.: Probabilistic analysis of dynamic fault trees using HOL theorem proving. J. Appl. Log. **6**, 467–509 (2019)
7. Elderhalli, Y., Hasan, O., Ahmad, W., Tahar, S.: Formal dynamic fault trees analysis using an integration of theorem proving and model checking. In: Dutle, A., Muñoz, C., Narkawicz, A. (eds.) NFM 2018. LNCS, vol. 10811, pp. 139–156. Springer, Cham (2018). https://doi.org/10.1007/978-3-319-77935-5_10
8. Ghadhab, M., Junges, S., Katoen, J., Kuntz, M., Volk, M.: Safety analysis for vehicle guidance systems with dynamic fault trees. Reliab. Eng. Syst. Saf. **186**, 37–50 (2019)
9. HOL4 (2019). https://hol-theorem-prover.org/
10. Junges, S., Guck, D., Katoen, J., Rensink, A., Stoelinga, M.: Fault trees on a diet: automated reduction by graph rewriting. Form. Asp. Comput. **29**(4), 651–703 (2017)
11. Junges, S.: Simplifying dynamic fault trees by graph rewriting. Master thesis, RWTH Aachen University (2015)
12. Merle, G.: Algebraic modelling of dynamic fault trees, contribution to qualitative and quantitative analysis. Ph.D. thesis, ENS Cachan, France (2010)

13. Mhamdi, T., Hasan, O., Tahar, S.: On the formalization of the lebesgue integration theory in HOL. In: Kaufmann, M., Paulson, L.C. (eds.) ITP 2010. LNCS, vol. 6172, pp. 387–402. Springer, Heidelberg (2010). https://doi.org/10.1007/978-3-642-14052-5_27

14. Mhamdi, T., Hasan, O., Tahar, S.: Formalization of entropy measures in HOL. In: van Eekelen, M., Geuvers, H., Schmaltz, J., Wiedijk, F. (eds.) ITP 2011. LNCS, vol. 6898, pp. 233–248. Springer, Heidelberg (2011). https://doi.org/10.1007/978-3-642-22863-6_18

15. Ruijters, E., Stoelinga, M.: Fault tree analysis: a survey of the state-of-the-art in modeling, analysis and tools. Comput. Sci. Rev. **15–16**, 29–62 (2015)

16. Stamatelatos, M., Vesely, W., Dugan, J., Fragola, J., Minarick, J., Railsback, J.: Fault Tree Handbook with Aerospace Applications. NASA Office of Safety and Mission Assurance (2002)

17. Volk, M., Junges, S., Katoen, J.P.: Fast dynamic fault tree analysis by model checking techniques. IEEE Trans. Ind. Inform. **14**(1), 370–379 (2018)

Partially Bounded Context-Aware Verification

Luka Le Roux[✉] and Ciprian Teodorov[✉]

Lab-STICC, MOCS, CNRS UMR 6285, ENSTA Bretagne, Brest, France
{luka.leroux,ciprian.teodorov}@ensta-bretagne.fr

Abstract. Model-checking enables the formal verification of software systems. Powerful and automated, this technique suffers, however, from the state-space explosion problem because of the exponential growth in the number of states with respect to the number of interacting components. To address this problem, the Context-aware Verification (CaV) approach decomposes the verification problem using environment-based guides. This approach improves the scalability but it requires an acyclic specification of the verification guides, which are difficult to specify without losing completeness.

In this paper, we present a new verification strategy that generalises CaV while ensuring the decomposability of the state-space. The approach relies on a language for the specification of the arbitrary guides, which relaxes the acyclicity requirement, and on a partially-bounded verification procedure.

The effectiveness of our approach is showcased through a case-study from the aerospace domain, which shows that the scalability is maintained while easing the conception of the verification guides.

1 Introduction

Since its introduction in the early 1980s, model-checking [11,23] provides an automated formal approach for the verification of complex requirements of hardware and software systems. This technique relies on the exhaustive analysis of all states in the system to check if it correctly implements the specifications, usually expressed using temporal logics. However, because of the internal complexity of the studied systems, model-checking is often challenged with an unmanageable large state-space, a problem known as the state-space explosion problem [8,21]. Numerous techniques [1,7,9,12,28,31] have been proposed to reduce the impact of this problem effectively pushing the inherent limits of model-checking further and further.

Amongst these techniques, the Context-aware Verification (CaV) approach [12,14,16] proposes to separately capture the open system and its environment. From the specifications, the first step of CaV is to formally capture the open system and its *contexts* (environment and property). Each context and the open system are the inputs to a verification task. From there, if one or several tasks

© Springer Nature Switzerland AG 2019
P. C. Ölveczky and G. Salaün (Eds.): SEFM 2019, LNCS 11724, pp. 532–548, 2019.
https://doi.org/10.1007/978-3-030-30446-1_28

do not scale, CaV offers different automated context-driven techniques for further problem decomposition [13] and for efficient memory management during reachability [26].

This approach was applied to realistic case studies from the medical [5], automotive [25], and aerospace [15,24] domains with very promising results. However, the CaV approach imposes an acyclicity constraint on the verification contexts, which limits expressiveness and renders the approach difficult to use in practice. This limitation impacts the verification engineers who need to manually extract and validate an acyclic model from the environment model. In many cases, the environment behaviours are inherently cyclic and require a verbose and error-prone manual unrolling up to an arbitrarily-chosen depth. Furthermore, when an acyclic model is available, the designer needs to prove its completeness with respects to the complete environment model, problem which is not addressed in the CaV literature.

In this paper, we address these problems through a new verification strategy that generalises CaV. Most notably it enables the specification of cyclic interaction scenarios and uses the closed system as its entry point. The approach is based on an eXtended Guide Description Language (xGDL) and on a partially-bounded verification strategy. The later automatically unrolls these cyclic *verification guides* (previously referred as *context*[1]) to an arbitrary depth. Through this approach the verification engineer is relieved of two tedious tasks: *(a)* extracting the acyclic interaction scenarios from a previously defined environment model, and *(b)* proving the completeness of the extracted scenarios with respect to the full environment model. Moreover, this approach explicitly exposes the *unrolling depth of the verification guides* as a sufficient completeness criteria for the verification. Showing that this bound is sufficient for completeness may be simpler than proving that the length of all paths is sufficient. The core of any model-checking strategy, the reachability analysis, up to the reachability diameter of the system, is necessary for the verification of safety and bounded-liveness properties. In general, our approach aims at the verification of arbitrary properties, however, in the context of this paper we focus on the reachability analysis.

The approach is validated on an aircraft Landing Gear System (LGS), introduced in [6]. Through this case-study we emphasis: *(a)* the usage of xGDL for modelling verification guides, used for closing the system for verification, and for guiding the reachability procedure; *(b)* a state-space decomposition procedure based on the syntactic rewriting of the verification guides, and; *(c)* some reachability results, obtained through the complementarity of our partially-bounded reachability analysis in conjunction with the CaV state-space decomposition strategies.

Section 2 introduces the related work focusing on the CaV approach and its similarities to Bounded Model Checking (BMC). Section 3 describes our main

---

[1] **Contexts and guides:** CaV uses the open system (no environment) and a *context* as an entry point. The generalisation presented in this paper uses the closed system instead and restrict its environment through a [verification] *guide.*

contribution, the semantics of the guide description language, the partially-bounded verification procedure and discusses the completeness conditions. Section 4 presents LGS system and the associated xGDL model along with the obtained results. Section 5 concludes this study introducing some future research directions.

2   Background and Related Work

Model checking is a technique that relies on building a finite model of a system of interest, and checking that a desired property, typically specified as a temporal logic formula, holds for that model. Since the introduction of model-checking in the early 1980s [23], several model-checker tools have been developed to help the verification of concurrent systems [2,18,31].

However, while model-checking provides an automated rigorous framework for formal system validation and verification, and has successfully been applied on industrial systems it suffers from the state-space explosion problem. This is due to the exponential growth of the number of reacheable states with respect to the number of interacting components. To enable the verification of ever larger systems, numerous research efforts are focused on reducing the impact of the state-space explosion problem. Some of these approaches use efficient data-structures such as BDD [7] for achieving compact state-space representation. Other approaches prune the state-space using techniques such as partial-order reduction [17,22,28] and symmetry reduction [9] that exploit fine-grain transition interleaving symmetries and global system symmetries respectively.

Complementary to these, are techniques based on the specification of environments relevant to the studied system [20,24,27,30]. These approaches propose tools that generate environments, based either on assumptions on the system and its interactions with the environment [20,27], or on the properties that need to be verified [30]. Amongst these, the *Context-aware Verification* (CaV) provides a structured approach for capturing the verification problem through a number of independent *verification contexts* (referred simply as contexts in the following), which explicitly represent the restricted model behaviours along with the requirements to be verified. The model is decomposed in two components: the system-under-study and the environment. While the system specification is viewed as a black-box that never changes during the verification, the environment model is decomposed in multiple *acyclic interaction scenarios*, expressed with the Context Definition Language (CDL). The verification contexts are created by associating to each interaction scenario the relevant properties. The verification process iteratively composes these contexts with the system to verify the associated properties. The CaV approach imposes a formal, methodical decomposition and classification of large requirements sets, a first step in overcoming the state-space explosion problem. To guarantee the exhaustiveness of the analysis, the verification should be accompanied by a completeness proof showing that all behaviours unrolled by the guide are sufficient.

CaV relies on CDL formalism to specify the verification guides separately from the system. The core concept of the CDL language is the *context*, which associates the requirements to be verified to a verification guide (an acyclic component communicating asynchronously with the system). The interaction of the system with the environment is specified through a number of interaction scenarios. The interleaving of these interaction scenarios generates a transition system representing all the bounded behaviours of the environment, which can be fed as input to model-checkers. Moreover, CDL enables the specification of requirements about the system's behaviour as properties that are verified by the OBP Observation Engine. These properties expressed through property-pattern definitions [14] are based on events (e.g. variable x changed), predicates, and synchronous observers.

Techniques such as bounded model checking [10] (BMC) exploit the observation that in many practical settings the property verification can be done with only a bounded reachability analysis. Hence, in the absence of a full-coverage proof, these approaches cannot guarantee the absence of errors, but only their presence. The usage of explicit acyclic behaviors, and the CaV approach can be considered as the explicit-state equivalent of symbolic BMC. Moreover, as opposed to BMC, the usage of acyclic behaviors offers more flexibility for specifying the "bounds" of the analysis, and the context can be seen as a high-level skeleton which drives the analysis through a complex state-space partition.

The xGDL language, introduced in this study focuses on the specification of the verification guides. This study generalizes the CaV approach by enabling the specification of cyclic verification guides, which releases the need of extracting acyclic models from the environment. Moreover, as opposed to the guide specification in the CDL language, the xGDL specifications are semantically decoupled from the system. During verification, the xGDL specifications are synchronously composed with the system through a labeling function.

By enabling the definition of acyclic verification guides, this study improves the applicability of the CaV approach. Prior to the verification step the verification guides are unrolled to a predefined bound, similarly to BMC. The main difference stems however in the scope of the bound. For BMC the bound is global over the system and its environment, in our approach the bound is partial, applying only to the verification guide.

3   A Language for Context Guided Reachability: xGDL

The approach proposed in this paper supposes a closed transition system as an entry point. By definition, a closed system includes behaviours from both the verification target and its environment. This ensures compatibility with a wide range of verification techniques with the same entry point, independently of the formalism used for property specification.

In addition, our approach requires a labelling function (a total and deterministic relation) over the closed system transitions with the co-domain in $A \cup \{\tau\}$, where A is the set of observable actions involving the environment (referred later as *interactions*) and where τ denotes the lack thereof.

A xGDL specification defines a language over A or a subset of A. The synchronous composition of the closed system and a xGDL specification thus restricts the sequences of possible interactions to those accepted by the specified language.

Section 3.1 provides the abstract syntax of xGDL, Sect. 3.2 provides its operational semantics through inference rules, Sect. 3.3 explicitly defines the compilation of a xGDL specification to a verification guide (a deterministic finite automaton, DFA), Sect. 3.4 details how a verification guide and the closed transition system to be verified are synchronously composed.

3.1   xGDL Abstract Syntax

A xGDL verification guide defines a language of interactions. Those are drawn from a finite alphabet A. The syntax of xGDL is given by the following BNF-style grammar:

$$\bot \mid a \mid C;C \mid C \square C \mid C \| C \mid$$
$$C ::= \; C? \mid C+ \mid C* \mid C\{i,j\} \mid$$
$$\{i,j\} \; of \; [C_1,...,C_n]$$

C ranges over the set $\mathcal{E}$ of terms of the xGDL language, a ranges over the alphabet A of observable interactions, and $i,j \in \mathbb{N}$ with $i \leq j$.

According to the previous grammar, an xGDL specification is one of the following: $- \bot$, the empty term; $- a$, an observable interaction; $- C;C$, a sequential composition of two terms; $- C\square C$, a non-deterministic choice between two terms; $- C\|C$, a parallel composition, by unrestricted interleaving of two terms; $- C?$, an optional term $- C+$, an unbounded replication of a term, with at least one occurrence; $- C*$, an unbounded replication of a term, with potentially 0 occurrences; $- C\{i,j\}$, a bounded replication of the a term with at least i occurrences and at most j; $- \{i,j\} \; of \; [C_1,...,C_n]$, possible permutations of length at least i to at most j among a set of terms.

3.2   xGDL Operational Semantics

xGDL operational semantics is defined via inference rules. The notation $C \xrightarrow{a} C'$ denotes a tuple $(C,a,C') \in \mathcal{E} \times \{A \cup \tau\} \times \mathcal{E}$, where A is the alphabet of interactions (observable actions initiated by the closed system's environment), τ denotes the lack thereof and $\mathcal{E}$ is the set of all possible terms. If $C \xrightarrow{a} C'$ with $a \neq \tau$, then C can be translated into C' upon *executing* the interaction a. If $C \xrightarrow{\tau} C'$, then C and C' can be said to be semantically equivalent.

$$\frac{a \in A^+}{a \xrightarrow{a} \bot} \; [\text{atom}] \qquad \frac{a \in A^+}{a;C \xrightarrow{a} C} \; [\text{seq}_1] \qquad \frac{C_1 \xrightarrow{a} C_1' \wedge C_1 \neq a}{C_1;C_2 \xrightarrow{a} C_1';C_2} \; [\text{seq}_2]$$

$$\frac{}{C_1 \square C_2 \xrightarrow{\tau} C_1} \; [\text{alt}_1] \qquad \frac{}{C_1 \square C_2 \xrightarrow{\tau} C_2} \; [\text{alt}_2] \qquad \frac{C_1 \xrightarrow{a_1} C_1'}{C_1 \| C_2 \xrightarrow{a_1} C_1' \| C_2} \; [\text{par}_1]$$

$$\frac{C_2 \xrightarrow{a_2} C_2'}{C_1 \| C_2 \xrightarrow{a_2} C_1 \| C_2'} \; [\text{par}_2] \qquad \frac{}{\bot \| C \xrightarrow{\tau} C} \; [\text{par}_3] \qquad \frac{}{C \| \bot \xrightarrow{\tau} C} \; [\text{par}_4]$$

Atom, Sequence, Alternative and Parallelism. If the term is a single **interaction** a, it is *executed* and it results in the empty term $\bot$ ($a \xrightarrow{a} \bot$, rule *atom*).

If the term is a **sequence** of the form $a; C$, the interaction a is *executed* and it results in the term C ($a; C \xrightarrow{a} C$, rule *seq$_1$*). If the term is a sequence of the form $C_1; C_2$ such that C_1 is not a single interaction and such that $\exists (a, C_1') \in \{A \cup \tau\} \times \mathcal{E}$, $C_1 \xrightarrow{a} C_1'$, then the interaction a is *executed* and it results in the term $C_1'; C_2$ ($C_1; C_2 \xrightarrow{a} C_1'; C_2$, rule *seq$_2$*).

If the term is a **non-deterministic choice** of the form $C_1 \square C_2$, it can either result in C_1 ($C_1 \square C_2 \xrightarrow{\tau} C_1$, rule *alt$_1$*) or C_2 ($C_1 \square C_2 \xrightarrow{\tau} C_2$, rule *alt$_2$*). In both cases, no interaction is *executed*.

Lastly, if the term is a **parallel composition** of the form $C_1 \| C_2$ with $\exists (a_1, C_1') \in \{A \cup \tau\} \times \mathcal{E}$, $C_1 \xrightarrow{a_1} C_1'$ and $\exists (a_2, C_2') \in \{A \cup \tau\} \times \mathcal{E}$, $C_2 \xrightarrow{a_2} C_2'$, it can either result in $C_1' \| C_2$ ($C_1 \| C_2 \xrightarrow{a_1} C_1' \| C_2$, rule *par$_1$*) or $C_1 \| C_2'$ ($C_1 \| C_2 \xrightarrow{a_2} C_1 \| C_2'$, rule *par$_2$*) by executing the corresponding interaction. If $C_1 = \bot$ or $C_2 = \bot$, it results in the leftover term (rules *par$_3$* and *par$_4$*).

$$\frac{}{C? \xrightarrow{\tau} \bot \square C} \text{ [opt]} \qquad \frac{}{C* \xrightarrow{\tau} (C; C*)?} \text{ [star]}$$

$$\frac{}{C+ \xrightarrow{\tau} C; C*} \text{ [plus]} \qquad \frac{0 < i \leq j}{C\{i, j\} \xrightarrow{\tau} C; C\{i-1, j-1\}} \text{ [rep}_1\text{]}$$

$$\frac{i = 0 \wedge j > 0}{C\{i, j\} \xrightarrow{\tau} (C; C\{0, j-1\})?} \text{ [rep}_2\text{]} \qquad \frac{i = j = 0}{C\{i, j\} \xrightarrow{\tau} \bot} \text{ [rep}_3\text{]}$$

Replications. If the term is an **optional term** of the form $C?$, it is semantically equivalent to $\bot \square C$, meaning it can either result in $\bot$ or C ($C? \xrightarrow{\tau} \bot \square C$, rule *opt*).

If the term is an **unbounded replication** of the form $C*$, it is semantically equivalent to $(C; C*)?$ (recursive definition), meaning it results either in $\bot$ or $C; C*$ ($C* \xrightarrow{\tau} (C; C*)?$, rule *star*).

If the term is an **unbounded replication with at least one occurrence** of the form $C+$, it is semantically equivalent to $C; C*$ ($C+ \xrightarrow{\tau} C; C*$, rule plus).

The **bounded replication** $C\{i, j\}$ is defined by the rules *rep$_1$*, *rep$_2$* and *rep$_3$*. The first applies as long as $i > 0$, decrements both i and j and ensures at least i occurrences of C. The second applies for $i = 0 \wedge j > 0$, decrements j and ensures at most j occurrences of C. The last one applies for $i = j = 0$ and results in $\bot$ (termination).

$$\frac{0 < i \leq j \leq n \wedge \forall k, 1 \leq k \leq n}{\{i, j\} \text{ of } [C_1, ..., C_n] \xrightarrow{\tau} C_k; \{i-1, j-1\} \text{ of } [C_1, ..., C_{k-1}, C_{k+1}, ..., C_n]} \text{ [perm}_1\text{]}$$

$$\frac{0 = i < j \leq n \wedge \forall k, 1 \leq k \leq n}{\{i, j\} \text{ of } [C_1, ..., C_n] \xrightarrow{\tau} (C_k; \{0, j-1\} \text{ of } [C_1, ..., C_{k-1}, C_{k+1}, ..., C_n])?} \text{ [perm}_2\text{]}$$

$$\frac{0 = i = j}{\{i, j\} \text{ of } [C_1, ..., C_n] \xrightarrow{\tau} \bot} \text{ [perm}_3\text{]} \qquad \frac{}{\{i, j\} \text{ of } [] \xrightarrow{\tau} \bot} \text{ [perm}_4\text{]}$$

Permutations. The permutation operator, as defined by the above rules, represents the set of possible sequences made of at most one occurrence of each of the terms from the provided set $[C_1, ..., C_n]$ of size i to j (unless $n < i$ or $n < j$, as the size can not exceed n). The notation $[C_1, ..., C_{k-1}, C_{k+1}, ..., C_n]$ (as found in rule $perm_2$) stands for the set $[C_1, ..., C_n]$ minus the term C_k with $i \leq k \leq j$. Rules $perm_3$ and $perm_4$ ensure termination in cases where $j = 0$ and where the set of terms to choose from is empty, respectively.

Prefix Closed Semantics. Defined this way, xGDL syntax and semantics match those of regular expressions extended with parallelism and permutations. However, a xGDL specification defines the language of all possible sequences of interactions. All prefixes of a term accepted by a xGDL specification (including $\perp$) are also members of this language. Thus, unlike regular expressions, xGDL semantics is prefix closed.

3.3   xGDL Compilation

A xGDL specification defines a language over the set of possible interactions A. To ease subsequent manipulations (such as the composition with the closed system as defined Sect. 3.4), a xGDL specification is compiled to a practical verification guide, a deterministic finite automaton (DFA).

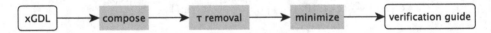

Fig. 1. The xGDL compilation flow.

The compilation flow, presented in Fig. 1, starts with a xGDL specification. By applying the semantic rules defined Sect. 3.2 the specification is straightforwardly converted to a non-deterministic finite automaton (NFA). The resulting NFA is then converted to a DFA. For this purpose, transitions carrying no interactions (τ) are considered as ϵ-transitions and are thus removed.

Lastly, this DFA is minimised. The result represents the compiled verification guide. The equivalence between the initial xGDL specification and the compiled verification guide follows directly from well known results in the automaton theory.

3.4   xGDL Guide and Closed System Composition

Given a closed transition system S, a set of interactions A, a labelling function L over $A \cup \{\tau\}$ and a xGDL verification guide G specified over A, the following defines the result their composition.

First, some additional notations are introduced:

- $G \times S$ denotes the resulting transition system;
- G_0, S_0 and $G_0 \times_0 S_0$ denote the initial states set of G, S and $G \times S$;
- (g, s) denotes a composite state;
- $s \xrightarrow{a} s'$ denotes the existence of a transition such that $L(s \rightarrow s') = a$.

Intuitively G and S are seen as transition systems labelled over $A \cup \{\tau\}$ (LTS). $G \times S$ is the result of their synchronous composition with stuttering steps and A as the vocabulary of synchronous behaviours.

The guide LTS G can be obtained through interpretation of a xGDL expression as described by the operational semantics (see Sect. 3.2). However, in the following, the DFA obtained after compilation (see Sect. 3.3) is considered instead. Both are equivalent for this section purpose, but the later being a minimal representation (least possible amount of states) it leads to better exploration results (smaller state space). It also ensures no τ-transitions in G, which eases our definitions.

The system LTS S is obtained by labelling each and every transition t_S from the system under study with $L(t_S) \in A \cup \{\tau\}$. A system transition labelled by $a \in A$ carries the execution of the corresponding interaction. A system transition labelled by τ denotes an *internal* step free of interactions.

The composition $G \times S$ is also a LTS and, as already stated, is obtained by a synchronous composition (over A) with stuttering steps (τ). The following rules define its initial states and transitions:
- Initial states: $\quad\quad\quad (g_0, s_0) \in G_0 \times_0 S_0 \quad \Leftrightarrow \quad g_0 \in G_0 \wedge s_0 \in S_0$;
- Stuttering steps: $\quad\quad (g, s) \xrightarrow{\tau} (g', s') \quad \Leftrightarrow \quad g = g' \ \wedge s \xrightarrow{\tau} s'$;
- Synchronisations: $a \neq \tau$, $(g, s) \xrightarrow{a} (g', s') \quad \Leftrightarrow \quad g \xrightarrow{a} g' \ \wedge s \xrightarrow{a} s'$.

Defined as such, G and S mutually constrain one another through their composition. The existence, in the resulting system, of a transition labelled by $a \neq \tau$ from a state (g, s) implies the existence of transitions labelled by a from both g and s.

However, most often in practical cases, all states from S are complete over A. Meaning, for all $a \in A$ and all s a system state, there is a transition from s and labelled by a (possibly modulo some stutters). This is due to A denoting possible interactions with the systems that can be expected at any time. In these cases, S does not constrain G in $G \times S$.

Neutral Guide. Given S, A and L, it is always possible to *build* a neutral guide 1 such that $S = 1 \times S$ (where = denotes a strong bi-simulation).

This can be proven by construction of 1 as the guide with one initial state $\{g_0\}$ and, for all $a \in A$, $g_0 \xrightarrow{a} g_0$. This particular guide follows directly from the xGDL expression $(a_0 \square a_1 \square \ ... \ \square a_{n-1})*$ with $A = \{a_0, a_1, \ ... \ , a_{n-1}\}$.

Subset of Interactions. It is important to note that, unless otherwise specified, the absence of references to an interaction within an xGDL specification *prohibits* that interaction from *happening*.

In cases where the xGDL specification is intended to be defined over a subset $A' \subset A$ of interactions, L (the labelling function) has to be filtered so that it doesn't label transitions by *ignored* interactions (in $A \setminus A'$).

Let L' be this filtered labelling function with $A' \cup \{\tau\}$ as its co-domain, for all t_S (transitions in S):

- $L(t_S) \in A' \cup \{\tau\}$ $\Rightarrow$ $L'(t_S) = L(t_S)$; (inside $A' \cup \{\tau\}$)
- $L(t_S) \in A \backslash A'$ $\Rightarrow$ $L'(t_S) = \tau$ (outside $A' \cup \{\tau\}$)

In other words, interaction labels in $A \backslash A'$ are interpreted as τ for the purpose of the composition and thus system transitions labelled by those are allowed to stutter (*to move independently from the guide*).

3.5   Partially Bounded Verification

Using a cyclic verification guide for closing the system is equivalent to the traditional model-checking process, in which the system is closed with an arbitrary environment. The context-aware verification approach showed that model-checking problems can be easily decomposed using acyclic verification guides to significantly improve the scalability of model checking. However, CaV is limited by the acylicity of the verification guides, which are difficult to extract and prove complete. Bounded model checking on the other hand, is more general and can be applied directly to model-checking problems. However in practice it is more often used as test procedure due to the difficulty of proving the completeness of the analysis. Based on the xGDL language, in this section, we propose a partially-bounded verification procedure.

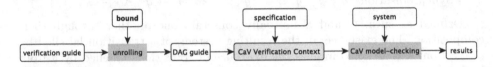

Fig. 2. Partially bounded verification flow

The approach, shown in Fig. 2, is similar to bounded model checking, with the particularity that only the verification guide is bounded. The compiled xGDL guide is unrolled to a predefined *bound*, through this unrolling a directed-acyclic graph (DAG) is obtained satisfying the CaV acylity requirement. This DAG guide is then associated to a specification to obtain a CaV verification context. The model-checking procedure then analyses this verification context in conjunction with the system (system in the figure). Since the DAG guide is acyclic, both the recursive state-space decomposition and the PastFree[ze] algorithms used by the Context-aware Verification approach, can be applied [26].

It should be noted that, in Fig. 2, the verification guide is unrolled prior to the verification step. This prior unrolling can be seen as the automatic extraction of an acyclic verification guide from an arbitrary environment. This extraction step, required by the CaV approach, was previously implicitly done by the designer during the manual specification of the acyclic verification guide.

Partially Bounded Verification and Completeness. This methodology is generally not complete, in the sense that the unrolling of a system along a bounded interaction scenario potentially implies that some states remain undiscovered (e.g. the states unravelled by a longer scenario). This imposes virtually the same limitation as the bounded model-checking procedures [10]. Namely, that the analysis should be accompanied by a completeness proof showing that the bound b_{guide} chosen for the interaction scenario enables the unrolling of its composition with the system to a depth at least equal to the **Completeness Threshold** $\mathbb{C}$. Moreover, given a cyclic environment and an arbitrary system, $\mathbb{C}$ is an upper bound on b_{guide}. Hence, if the Completeness Threshold of the composition is known it is sufficient, but not necessary, to unroll the cyclic environment model to that depth to achieve completeness.

For the verification of safety properties the completeness threshold is given by the reachability diameter r_d (the minimum number of steps required for reaching all reachable states) [19].

This partially bounded verification procedure effectively generalises the CaV approach to arbitrary systems. Based on this new approach, currently we investigate the possibility to automatically compute the minimal b_{guide} that guarantees that the composition of the interaction scenario with the system reaches the Completeness Threshold, which provides the necessary conditions for the completeness proof.

4   Case-Study: The Landing Gear System

This section showcases xGDL on a realistic case-study from the aerospace domain. In the process, we show that it is well suited for iterative state-space decomposition during model-checking.

The landing gear system (LGS) specification [6] includes three gears, each made of several physical parts. These are specified with (continuous) timed constraints, sensors and possible failures. Retraction and extension sequences can be initiated, interrupted and inverted at any time. This system raises a number of interesting issues during verification, some of which have already been subject to studies via model-checking [4, 15, 24, 26, 29].

The focus, here, is not to illustrate how the system can be translated into an executable model. Rather, given that the executable model is already provided, and that the analysis does not scale, this study shows why a language like xGDL is needed and how it can be used within a verification activity requiring several iterations.

Section 4.1 provides an overview of the LGS executable model. Section 4.2 illustrates the definition of the xGDL verification guide and how it can be decomposed, eventually bounded, to further push the limits of the verification.

4.1 LGS Executable Model

The LGS model is composed of the system-under-study along with the capabilities of its environment, both implemented using timed automatons in Fiacre language [3].

System-Under-Study. The LGS manages the extension and retraction of a the landing gears. The physical part includes three landing *boxes* to the front, the left, and the right of the plane. A landing box contains the gear itself as well as a door and hydraulic cylinders. The digital part is responsible of monitoring those physical components through sensors. If an anomaly is detected, this information is forwarded to the cockpit through visual indicators.

A more detailed description of this case study can be found in [6]. The Fiacre implementation of the physical and software parts matches the one proposed and studied via the CAV approach [24, 26].

Table 1. Possible failures and labels

Analog Switch		General Electro-Valve	
Opened	Closed	Opened	Closed
f_{1_1}	f_{1_2}	f_{2_1}	f_{2_2}

Door Electro-Valves				Gear Electro-Valves			
Extension		Retraction		Extension		Retraction	
Opened	Closed	Opened	Closed	Opened	Closed	Opened	Closed
f_{3_1}	f_{3_2}	f_{4_1}	f_{4_2}	f_{5_1}	f_{5_2}	f_{6_1}	f_{6_2}

Front	Left	Right	Front	Left	Right
Door			Gear		
f_7	f_8	f_9	f_{10}	f_{11}	f_{12}

Environment Capabilities and System Closure. The pilot can interact with the system through a handle. Switching its position induces *handle* events, which enable the retraction (or extension) sequence.

In addition, a failure may occur at any time. Table 1 lists the possible failures and labels them for future references. Couples (f_{n_1}, f_{n_2}) are exclusive, for example a door may not be blocked in two different positions.

The environment is modelled as one single state automaton in Fiacre. Each of its transitions models a capability, meaning one for the handling of the lever and one per possible failure. This automaton closes the system with its environment capabilities and is later referred as the *system closure automaton*.

Assumptions and Restrictions. The analysis is performed under the following assumptions: *(a)* the software modules are assumed failure-free. *(b)* the sensors, and the interconnect wires are assumed failure-free. *(c)* the failures are assumed permanent, such that if an equipment becomes blocked it remains blocked forever.

Scaling of the Analysis. The resulting state space is much too large[2] for explicit model-checking to scale as is. To address this issue, one can use the fact that at most three failures may happen in one *execution*. If the verification holds for all the valid subsets of three failures, then it holds for the initial problem as well [15]. Taking into account exclusive failures, there is a total of 720 valid subsets and, thus, that many verification tasks.

This can be achieved by various means. Each task can have its own model of the system with different, restricted closure automatons. Parameters can be added to the system and so on. However, these approaches raise new issues regarding the production, soundness, maintainability and further analysis of the various verification tasks. Next section, addresses these issues using the xGDL formalism for the specification of verification guides, which facilitates the decomposition of the state-space while providing the basis for proving its completeness. Moreover, when coupled with the partially-bounded verification procedure, the acyclicity requirement is met, enabling the use of the CAV-specific algorithms.

4.2   xGDL Verification Guides

Specifying the Verification Guide. To apply our approach, an interaction alphabet and a labelling function have to be defined over the executable model introduced in the previous section.

Interaction Alphabet. For this case study, the finite set of interactions considered are inferred from the environment capabilities as described Sect. 4.1. As such:

$$A = \{handle, \ f_{1_1}, \ f_{1_2}, \ ..., \ f_{6_1}, \ f_{6_2}, \ f_7, \ ..., \ f_{12}\}$$

Labelling Function. A transition from a system state to another involves zero or one Fiacre transition from the single state automaton modelling the environment capabilities. If present, the labelling function returns the corresponding label. If absent it returns τ, denoting the absence of environment interaction.

xGDL *Guide Expressions.* With the labelling function and its range being now defined, it is possible to write the xGDL expressions. The following introduces some useful examples:

	name		xGDL
- Handles:	G_{pilot}	$=$	$handle *$
- One exclusive failure: $1 \leq n \leq 6$,	F_n	$=$	$f_{n_1} \Box f_{n_2}$
- One non-exclusive failure: $7 \leq n \leq 12$,	F_n	$=$	f_n
- At most three failures:	F_{all}	$=$	$\{0, \ 3\} \ of \ [F_1, \ ..., \ F_{12}]$
- Considered scope:	G_{scope}	$=$	$G_{pilot} \ \| \ F_{all}$

---

[2] If the system is restricted to failure-free behaviours, it unfolds 3E+5 states. If restricted to one specific failure, 128Gb of memory is not enough [24,26] (potentially 1E+9 states). For the considered scope (three different failures), those figures hint for a state space several orders of magnitude higher than 1E+10.

G_{pilot} is a sequence of any number of *handle* interactions. The composition of this guide with the system, as defined in Sect. 3.4, induces an analysis restricted to the failure free behaviours (since the failures are not included).

F_n matches one failure injection. For $n \leq 6$, it references a couple of exclusive failures in an alternative so that only one or the other may happen.

F_{all} is a sequence of zero to three failures. The permutation operator is used to ensure uniqueness (a given failure cannot happen twice).

G_{scope} is the parallel composition of G_{pilot} and F_{all}. $G_{scope} \times S$ covers all the possible behaviours minus those outside the specification scope [6] (i.e. at most three unique failures and excludes impossible combinations). In other words, G_{scope} is not strictly neutral to the composition as it is limited to one of each failure and no more than three different ones. However, it precisely and exhaustively captures the system closure required by the specification.

Splitting the Analysis.　　With the xGDL expressions introduced above, $G_{scope} \times S$ defines the entire state space, target of the verification. As mentioned toward the end of Sect. 4.1, its size is prohibitive for the analysis and needs to be split into smaller, specialised verification tasks.

For this purpose, xGDL can be used to express those through specialised guides. Each of the 720 subsets of three different failures $\{f_i,\ f_j,\ f_k\}$ (with $f_i \neq f_j \neq f_k$) lead to specific xGDL guides:

$$handle * \ \| \ \{0,\ 3\} \ of \ [f_i,\ f_j,\ f_k]$$

Non Intrusive.　　Using this approach, **the system executable model (S) is an invariant of all the verification tasks**, including the initial one ($G_{scope} \times S$). This approach does not require custom environment closures nor the modification (parameterization) of the system model.

Thus, **one can focus on the languages recognised by the various xGDL expressions to provide a soundness proof** of these new verification tasks. To prove that the language of the initial guide is equal to the union of the languages of the guides generated after the splitting process is enough for safety requirements (reachability). For the LGS case study, this is expressed through the Theorem 1 and its proof.

Theorem 1. $language(G_{scope}) = \cup_{id=0}^{719} language(G_{id}^3)$
Where $G_{id}^3 = handle * \ \| \ \{0,\ 3\} \ of \ F_{id}^3$ with F_0^3 to F_{719}^3 the 720 valid subsets of three failures.

Proof. **By successive rewriting of the equality right hand size:**

0: $\cup_{id=0}^{719} language(G_{id}^3)$
1: $language(G_0^3 \ \square \ ... \ \square \ G_{719}^3)$
2: $language(\ (handle * \ \| \ \{0,\ 3\} \ of \ F_0^3) \ \square \ ... \ \square \ (handle * \ \| \ \{0,\ 3\} \ of \ F_7^3 19) \ )$
3: $language(\qquad handle * \ \| \ (\{0,\ 3\} \ of \ F_0^3 \ \square \ ... \ \square \ \{0,\ 3\} \ of \ F_{719}^3) \qquad)$
4: $language(\qquad\qquad handle * \ \| \ \{0,\ 3\} \ of \ F_{all} \qquad\qquad)$
5: $language(G_{scope})$

Step 0 to 1: the union of xGDL expressions languages is equal to the language of an alternative over those expressions. Step 1 to 2: unfolding of all the G_i^3. Step 2 to 3: the parallel operator is distributive over the alternative (i.e. $(A\|B)\square(A\|C) = A\|(B\square C)$) Step 3 to 4: the alternative over the length three permutations of F_{id}^3 subsets is equal to F_{all} (both strictly recognise all the valid, length three permutations). Step 4 to 5: per definition of G_{scope}. QED.

Further Refinements and Bounding the Verification. Model-checking of any of the 720 guides with three specific failures still did not scale. xGDL offers the possibility to further refine the verification guides and to partially bound the verification tasks in the guide specifications.

Table 2. Unrolling bounds required for completeness

Failure	f_{1_1}	f_{1_2}	f_{2_1}	f_{2_2}	f_{3_1}	f_{3_2}	f_{4_1}	f_{4_1}	f_{5_1}	f_{5_2}	f_{6_1}	f_{6_2}	f_7, f_8, f_9	f_{10}, f_{11}, f_{12}
Bound	16	16	18	17	20	20	18	20	20	X	18	X	20	20

Similarly to the guide with up to three failures, a guide including exactly one failure ($handle * \| \{1, 1\} \ of \ [F_1, ..., F_{12}]$) can be split into 18 guides:

$$G_i^1 = handle * \| f_i$$

Bounding those 18 verification tasks (as shown in Sect. 3.5) arbitrarily to 30 interactions allows the analysis to successfully terminate for 16 of these. To prove completeness, an option is to perform an analysis of the induced clusters of states, as discussed in [26]. In this case, a cyclic behaviour is detected after 16 to 20 interactions depending on the considered failure. Table 2 shows, for each failure, the bound required for completeness inferred from this post-mortem analysis.

For failures f_{5_2} and f_{6_2} (extension and retraction gear electro-valves blocked in closed position), further refinement is still needed. Since G_i^1 has exactly one interaction on the right hand side of the parallel operator, it is equivalent to the sequence:

$$G_i^1 = handle * \ ; \ f_i \ ; \ handle*$$

Additionally, for $handle*$, bounding the analysis and inferring the bound required for completeness shows 7 handles are enough to consider before the eventual failure. This can be captured as:

$$G_i^1 \Leftrightarrow handle\{0, 7\} \ ; \ f_i \ ; \ handle*$$

This last form can then be decomposed again in 16 different guides of the form $handle\{n, n\} \ ; \ f_i \ ; \ handle*$ with $0 \leq n \leq 7$ and $f_i \in \{f_{5_2}, f_{6_2}\}$. For both failures, the analysis bounded to 30 interactions scales for $0 \leq n \leq 4$ but would still require further refinement for $n > 4$.

The approach proposed in this study allows the use complementary analysis techniques on the same executable model and its properties. From this perspective, typically several directions are possible, such as: 1. further abstracting the model for symbolic model-checking; 2. exploit symmetry reduction or partial-order reduction.

Producing the various verification tasks is done without altering the formal specification of the initial challenge. Moreover, xGDL enables to dispatch the verification tasks to different, complementary tools.

5   Conclusion and Perspectives

This paper presented a guide description language along with a partially-bounded context-aware verification procedure. Through the xGDL specifications the acyclicity requirement imposed by the CaV methodology is lifted, which bridges the gap between the environment model and the verification guides. These cyclic verification guides are unrolled to a predefined depth before their composition with the system, which enables the use of the CaV state-space decomposition algorithms. The approach was illustrated on a landing gear system case study. The system/environment interactions where formally captured using one xGDL guide. Relying on this guide, the verification problem was decomposed in 720 sub-problems. This decomposition is accompanied by a coverage proof realised by rewriting of the guide structure. Most of the one-failure cases (16 out of 18) where discharged using the partially-bounded verification procedure, which used in conjunction with the PastFree algorithm of CaV provided the completeness proof, by bi-simulation on the clusters induced by the guide. The two failing guides, were further rewritten and decomposed (structurally), and the new form was partially-bounded (syntactically) using the completeness threshold of the failure free analysis. Currently, we are investigating an online verification procedure, which unrolls the guide during the verification while at the same time enabling the recursive state-space decomposition.

References

1. Barnat, J., Brim, L., Simecek, P.: Cluster-based I/O-efficient LTL model checking. In: Proceedings of the 2009 IEEE/ACM International Conference on Automated Software Engineering, pp. 635–639. ASE 2009. IEEE Computer Society, Washington (2009). https://doi.org/10.1109/ASE.2009.32
2. Bengtsson, J., Larsen, K., Larsson, F., Pettersson, P., Yi, W.: UPPAAL — a tool suite for automatic verification of real-time systems. In: Alur, R., Henzinger, T.A., Sontag, E.D. (eds.) HS 1995. LNCS, vol. 1066, pp. 232–243. Springer, Heidelberg (1996). https://doi.org/10.1007/BFb0020949
3. Berthomieu, B., et al.: Fiacre: an intermediate language for model verification in the topcased environment. In: European Congress on Embedded Real-Time Software (ERTS). SEE, Toulouse, France (Jan 2008). https://hal.inria.fr/inria-00262442

4. Berthomieu, B., Dal Zilio, S., Fronc, Ł.: Model-checking real-time properties of an aircraft landing gear system using fiacre. In: Boniol, F., Wiels, V., Ait Ameur, Y., Schewe, K.-D. (eds.) ABZ 2014. CCIS, vol. 433, pp. 110–125. Springer, Cham (2014). https://doi.org/10.1007/978-3-319-07512-9_8

5. Boniol, F., Dhaussy, P., Le Roux, L., Roger, J.C.: Model-based analysis. In: Embedded systems, Analysis and Modeling with SysML, UML and AADL, pp. 157–184. Wiley (May 2013). https://hal.archives-ouvertes.fr/hal-00843139

6. Boniol, F., Wiels, V.: The landing gear system case study. In: Boniol, F., Wiels, V., Ait Ameur, Y., Schewe, K.-D. (eds.) ABZ 2014. CCIS, vol. 433, pp. 1–18. Springer, Cham (2014). https://doi.org/10.1007/978-3-319-07512-9_1

7. Burch, J., Clarke, E., McMillan, K., Dill, D., Hwang, L.: Symbolic model checking: 10^{20} states and beyond. Inf. Comput. **98**(2), 142–170 (1992). https://doi.org/10.1016/0890-5401(92)90017-A

8. Clarke, E.M., Emerson, E.A., Sistla, A.P.: Automatic verification of finite-state concurrent systems using temporal logic specifications. ACM Trans. Program. Lang. Syst. **8**(2), 244–263 (1986). https://doi.org/10.1145/5397.5399

9. Clarke, E.M., Enders, R., Filkorn, T., Jha, S.: Exploiting symmetry in temporal logic model checking. Formal Methods Syst. Des. **9**(1), 77–104 (1996). https://doi.org/10.1007/BF00625969

10. Clarke, E., Biere, A., Raimi, R., Zhu, Y.: Bounded model checking using satisfiability solving. Formal Methods Syst. Des. **19**(1), 7–34 (2001). https://doi.org/10.1023/A:1011276507260

11. Clarke, E.M., Emerson, E.A.: Design and synthesis of synchronization skeletons using branching time temporal logic. In: Kozen, D. (ed.) Logic of Programs 1981. LNCS, vol. 131, pp. 52–71. Springer, Heidelberg (1982). https://doi.org/10.1007/BFb0025774

12. Dhaussy, P., Boniol, F., Landel, E.: Using context descriptions and property definition patterns for software formal verification. In: Proceedings of the 2008 IEEE International Conference on Software Testing Verification and Validation Workshop, pp. 89–96. ICSTW 2008. IEEE Computer Society, Washington (2008). https://doi.org/10.1109/ICSTW.2008.52

13. Dhaussy, P., Boniol, F., Roger, J.C., Le Roux, L.: Improving model checking with context modelling. In: Advances in Software Engineering 2012, ID 547157, 13 p (October 2012). https://doi.org/10.1155/2012/547157

14. Dhaussy, P., Pillain, P.-Y., Creff, S., Raji, A., Le Traon, Y., Baudry, B.: Evaluating context descriptions and property definition patterns for software formal validation. In: Schürr, A., Selic, B. (eds.) MODELS 2009. LNCS, vol. 5795, pp. 438–452. Springer, Heidelberg (2009). https://doi.org/10.1007/978-3-642-04425-0_34

15. Dhaussy, P., Teodorov, C.: Context-aware verification of a landing gear system. In: Boniol, F., Wiels, V., Ait Ameur, Y., Schewe, K.-D. (eds.) ABZ 2014. CCIS, vol. 433, pp. 52–65. Springer, Cham (2014). https://doi.org/10.1007/978-3-319-07512-9_4

16. Dumas, X., Dhaussy, P., Boniol, F., Bonnafous, E.: Application of partial-order methods for the verification of closed-loop SDL systems. In: Proceedings of the 2011 ACM Symposium on Applied Computing, pp. 1666–1673. SAC 2011. ACM, New York (2011). https://doi.org/10.1145/1982185.1982533

17. Godefroid, P.: The Ulg partial-order package for SPIN. In: SPIN Workshop. Montréal, Quebec (1995)

18. Holzmann, G.J.: The model checker SPIN. IEEE Trans. Softw. Eng. **23**(5), 279–295 (1997). https://doi.org/10.1109/32.588521

19. Kroening, D., Strichman, O.: Efficient computation of recurrence diameters. In: Zuck, L.D., Attie, P.C., Cortesi, A., Mukhopadhyay, S. (eds.) VMCAI 2003. LNCS, vol. 2575, pp. 298–309. Springer, Heidelberg (2003). https://doi.org/10.1007/3-540-36384-X_24

20. Parizek, P., Plasil, F.: Specification and generation of environment for model checking of software components. Electron. Notes Theor. Comput. Sci. **176**(2), 143–154 (2007). https://doi.org/10.1016/j.entcs.2006.02.036

21. Park, S., Kwon, G.: Avoidance of state explosion using dependency analysis in model checking control flow model. In: Gavrilova, M.L., et al. (eds.) ICCSA 2006. LNCS, vol. 3984, pp. 905–911. Springer, Heidelberg (2006). https://doi.org/10.1007/11751649_99

22. Peled, D.: Combining partial order reductions with on-the-fly model-checking. Formal Methods Syst. Des. **8**(1), 39–64 (1996). https://doi.org/10.1007/BF00121262

23. Queille, J.P., Sifakis, J.: Specification and verification of concurrent systems in CESAR. In: Dezani-Ciancaglini, M., Montanari, U. (eds.) Programming 1982. LNCS, vol. 137, pp. 337–351. Springer, Heidelberg (1982). https://doi.org/10.1007/3-540-11494-7_22

24. Teodorov, C., Dhaussy, P., Le Roux, L.: Environment-driven reachability for timed systems. Int. J. Softw. Tools Technol. Transfer **19**(2), 229–245 (2017). https://doi.org/10.1007/s10009-015-0401-2

25. Teodorov, C., Le Roux, L., Dhaussy, P.: Context-aware verification of a cruise-control system. In: Ait Ameur, Y., Bellatreche, L., Papadopoulos, G.A. (eds.) MEDI 2014. LNCS, vol. 8748, pp. 53–64. Springer, Cham (2014). https://doi.org/10.1007/978-3-319-11587-0_7

26. Teodorov, C., Le Roux, L., Drey, Z., Dhaussy, P.: Past-free[ze] reachability analysis: reaching further with DAG-directed exhaustive state-space analysis. Softw. Test. Verif. Reliab. **26**(7), 516–542 (2016). https://doi.org/10.1002/stvr.1611

27. Tkachuk, O., Dwyer, M.B.: Environment generation for validating event-driven software using model checking. IET Softw. **4**(3), 194–209 (2010). https://doi.org/10.1049/iet-sen.2009.0017

28. Valmari, A.: Stubborn sets for reduced state space generation. In: Rozenberg, G. (ed.) ICATPN 1989. LNCS, vol. 483, pp. 491–515. Springer, Heidelberg (1991). https://doi.org/10.1007/3-540-53863-1_36

29. Wiels, V., Ledinot, E., Belin, E., Dassault, M.: Experiences in using model checking to verify real time properties of a landing gear control system. In: Embedded Real-Time Systems (ERTS). Toulouse, France (Jan 2006)

30. Yatake, K., Aoki, T.: Automatic generation of model checking scripts based on environment modeling. In: Model Checking Software - 17th International SPIN Workshop, Enschede, The Netherlands, September 27–29, 2010. Proceedings, pp. 58–75 (2010). https://doi.org/10.1007/978-3-642-16164-3_5

31. Yu, Y., Manolios, P., Lamport, L.: Model checking TLA$^+$ specifications. In: Pierre, L., Kropf, T. (eds.) CHARME 1999. LNCS, vol. 1703, pp. 54–66. Springer, Heidelberg (1999). https://doi.org/10.1007/3-540-48153-2_6

Author Index

Printed in the United States
by Bookmasters

Printed in the United States
By Bookmasters